THE AMERICAN TREASURY
1455 - 1955

The American Treasury
1455-1955

SELECTED, ARRANGED, AND EDITED BY

CLIFTON FADIMAN

ASSISTED BY CHARLES VAN DOREN

Harper & Row, Publishers
New York, Evanston, and London

Grateful acknowledgment is made to the following for permission to reprint selections included in this book:

Abelard-Schumann, Inc. for quotations from *The Words of Justice Brandeis* by Solomon Goldman. Copyright 1953.

Miss Louise Andrews for poems from *The Burgess Nonsense Book* by Gelett Burgess. Copyright, 1901, by Frederick A. Stokes Co.

Miss Nellie Barnes for lines from "Ka-Ni-Ca Song," translated by James Powell, from *American Indian Love Lyrics and Other Verse* by Nellie Barnes. Copyright 1925, 1953 by Nellie Barnes.

Albert & Charles Boni, Inc. for lines from *The Bridge of San Luis Rey* by Thornton Wilder and quotations from *The Devil's Dictionary* by Ambrose Bierce.

Brandt & Brandt for lines from *Western Star*, Rinehart & Company, Copyright 1943 by Rosemary Carr Benét; *A Book of Americans*, Rinehart & Company, Copyright 1933 by Rosemary Carr Benét; *Selected Works of Stephen Vincent Benét*, Rinehart & Company, Copyright 1927, 1933, 1940 by Stephen Vincent Benét; "The Devil and Daniel Webster" in *Selected Works of Stephen Vincent Benét*, Rinehart & Company, Copyright 1936 by Stephen Vincent Benét; lines from *Poems 1923-1954*, Harcourt, Brace & Company, Copyright 1923, 1925, 1935, 1938, by E. E. Cummings, Copyright 1926 by Horace Liveright; lines from *Pencil in the Air* by Samuel Hoffenstein, Copyright 1947 by Samuel Hoffenstein; "I Like Americans"

from *Distressing Dialogues* by Nancy Boyd, Harper & Brothers, Copyright 1922, 1923 by Conde Nast Publications, Inc., Copyright 1924 by Edna St. Vincent Millay; "She Is Overheard Singing," "Thursday," "I would indeed that love were longer-lived," from "I Shall Forget You Presently, My Dear," "First Fig," "Second Fig," from *A Few Figs from Thistles*, Harper & Brothers, Copyright 1918, 1919, 1920 by Edna St. Vincent Millay; "God's World," from *Renascence and Other Poems*, Harper & Brothers, Copyright 1912 by Edna St. Vincent Millay; "Travel," "Passer Mortuus Est," from *Second April*, Harper & Brothers, Copyright 1921 by Edna St. Vincent Millay; "Euclid Alone Has Looked on Beauty Bare," "What Lips My Lips Have Kissed," from *The Harp Weaver and Other Poems*, Harper & Brothers, Copyright 1920 by Edna St. Vincent Millay; "Love Is Not All," from *Fatal Interview*, Harper & Brothers, Copyright 1931 by Edna St. Vincent Millay; "Down, down into the darkness of the grave" in "Dirge Without Music," from *The Buck in the Snow*, Harper & Brothers, Copyright 1928 by Edna St. Vincent Millay.

Paul Burlin for three songs from *The Indians' Book* by Natalie Curtis.

The Christian Science Publishing Society for lines from "Sea Town" by Frances Frost in *The Christian Science Monitor*, August 13, 1941.

Commentary for a quotation from an article by Morton Clurman.

Table of Contents

BOOK ONE:
WE LOOK AT OURSELVES AND OUR COUNTRY

BOOK TWO:

POETS AND VERSIFIERS

From Anne Bradstreet to Oscar Hammerstein

BOOK THREE:

VARIOUS AMERICANS ON THINGS IN GENERAL

How to Make Good and Pleasant Use of This Book

This is a book to read and a book to use.

We have arranged *The American Treasury* so that it may be read consecutively. This is especially true of Book One, which is deliberately organized to unfold as a picture of ourselves and our country. Of course the book may also be read by the dipping method.

If you like to read systematically, the Table of Contents will help you. If you refer to it, you will see that *The American Treasury* is made up of three Books. Book One deals with what we Americans (and some non-Americans, too) have said and written about ourselves and our country. Under each subhead the passages are arranged chronologically in order of publication or utterance. (There are a few minor exceptions to this general rule.) Book Two is a selection of American verse and song and doggerel. The passages within its first two divisions are arranged chronologically according to the birth date of the poet. Within the third division the songs are arranged roughly according to their publication dates. Book Three comprises something of what we Americans have said and written about a variety of matters exclusive of our own country. It contains seventeen divisions. Within each division the passages are arranged chronologically according to the birth date of the author.

If you want to use *The American Treasury* as a reference book, the key is of course the four-part index. The book is indexed by author, subject, title and familiar word and phrase.

We don't guarantee that in *The American Treasury* you'll find *any* and *every* American quotation you may have in mind. We do think, however, that you'll find most of those we should know and remember, plus a great many that will be novel to a fair number of us.

Certain personal enthusiasms and explanations of criteria will be found in my own General Preface, the separate introductions to each of the three Books, and the Envoi.

C. F.

Acknowledgments

All anthologists borrow from each other. They do not steal, for both borrower and lender are sourced in a common treasury; and the borrower is himself destined to be a lender to the next anthologist. Certain quotations are immortal because of this tradition of borrowing. They are here.

Sources of quotations are given in the vast majority of cases. Where the ascription is not given, the quotation has been taken from a secondary source (which *also* did not list the original one) and we were, up to press time, unable to trace the exact origin. In most of these cases the context would not have been particularly important anyway.

This book flows from the labors of two men, and it is they who must take the blame for the errors that have undoubtedly crept into a work of such large dimensions.

Help and counsel have been given us by the following, to whom we make grateful acknowledgment: Anne Whitmore; Professor Gail Kennedy of Amherst College; John Van Doren; Maxwell Fox and Shirley Robin of the Advertising Council, New York City; Major Vernon Pizer, Public Information Division, U.S. Army; Don M. Mankiewicz; the staffs of the New York Public and Columbia University Libraries; and almost the entire editorial staff of the publishers.

Certain parts of the section of the Editor's General Preface headed "A Note on the Practice of Quotation" are adapted from an essay that originally appeared in *Holiday* Magazine. The Editor is grateful to the Curtis Publishing Company, Philadelphia, for permission to reprint.

General Preface

1. THE AIMS AND SCOPE OF THIS BOOK

About three years ago the Editors began the organized reading and research of which the consequences are now in your hands. Our plan was wildly ambitious and fantastically simple. Between us we had been reading American history and literature for a total of over half a century. We proposed to retrace this old territory and to explore new domains as well. In other words, we were going to read and reread, in books, magazines and newspapers, as much American material as two fairly well-educated men could possibly plow through, working two or three years about six hours a day on the average. From this vast mass we would extract about 400,000 words of lively, interesting, well-phrased quotations, in prose and verse, excerpts or complete units, ranging in length from a word (see "How!" under Indians, page 35) to a 2,000-word complete sketch or story. We would then organize what we had into some meaningful design. Of this material only a part, though a large one, was to be narrowly literary. We intended, space permitting, to touch on the worlds of religion, journalism, politics, war, business, entertainment, sport, folk wisdom, song and balladry, law, education, and other fields.

But we had no exact notion of what we would finally come up with. We assumed that a large part would turn out to be familiar to many Americans—the familiar being frequently, though not invariably, the best. Beyond this we resolved to include nothing that did not interest the Editor, or that the Assistant Editor could not persuade the Editor to be interested in. Part of the material therefore was bound to prove, quite properly, canonical. But all of it, traditional or not, was in the final event to flow from the exercise of the Editor's personal choice.

The date of the earliest quotation we could find from an American source was *c.* 1455. It marks an important American statement, the Constitution of the Iroquois Confederacy. From 1455 the editors worked forward exactly half a millenium, collecting and arranging what Americans —and some non-Americans (see Book One, X)—have said, written, sung, thought, or laughed over, whether in the guise of that great folk artist Anon, or as philosophers or ad writers, presidents or baseball players, poets or financiers, generals or novelists, scientists or crackerbox sages.

Many excellent American anthologies in specialized fields are available. To our best knowledge, however, no such *omnium gatherum* as this has ever been attempted. Whether or not the attempt has been successful is for the reader to judge.

Though an unconventional one, this is still an anthology. On that point we lay a certain stress. The very *last* thing we did was to draw up the table of contents. The table of contents flowed from our reading and that reading was not guided by any preconceived ideas of "coverage" or "representation." The whole story of our country is not to be found here. It is not to be found in any single book or any series of books. Our modest claim is simply this: here is a collection of interesting, diverting, beautiful or inspiring statements made by 1,300 Americans. The statements are arranged in such a way as to tell us a great deal about ourselves in a reasonably systematic manner. We believe that from these pages, whether merely referred to, or read at random, or in sections, or clear through from cover to cover, some sense will emerge of who, where and why we are.

We do not know how many books we read or consulted. We could have continued to read for the rest of our lives. We stopped when we felt we *had* something. Not everything, but something.

What do we have?

We can put the answer in several ways.

Here is one way. We believe that this book comprises, as far as one book can, the *minimum* of American utterance that the intelligent citizen *ought* to be casually familiar with, in the degree that excerpts and short units can give him that familiarity. We are a mixed people, of varying backgrounds and cultures, busy specialists, practical, present-minded—in many respects good things to be. The danger exists, however, that these very qualities may make it difficult for us to share a more or less common field of reference, such as educated Frenchmen or Englishmen are presumed to have. This book hopes to supply a pilot model of such a field of reference, at any rate American reference. For while it is good for us to know different things, it is also good for us to know the same things. Such knowledge makes us feel more at home with one another. It unifies us in a way that force, even the force of law, can never do. It points to the only kind of conformity that can be adequately defended.

Let us put our aim in another way. We hope to convey, as far as these 6,000-odd passages can convey them, the slope and slant of the American people and their magnificent country; and to do this not by the exposition or interpretation furnished by one fallible mind, but through the very sound and pitch and timbre of the American voice itself.

Most of us, it is true, are inarticulate, or articulate only in action. It is also true that what is not articulated is often as pertinent as what is voiced. By its very nature voiceless America is incapable of being here represented. But one of the great advantages of a democratic state, as against a Communist one, is that in it those who *are* articulate, whether an Emerson or a Satchel Paige, are representative men, close to the country, speaking always for more than themselves, and of course for more than an imposed dogma. Bring enough of them together and they add up to a rough sum of ourselves.

Yet we must beware of parochialism, of judging home thoughts the only thoughts. All of us speak not merely as Americans, but as human beings. Remember Mark Twain's warning: "There is not a single characteristic which can be safely labeled as 'American.'" (He qualified this later by excepting our addiction to ice water.) In a more serious mood Woodrow Wilson, calling upon something very deep in the American spirit, cautioned us "always, also, to think first of humanity."

It was necessary therefore for the Editors to work out some pattern that would reveal Americans in as many moods as possible. We finally hit upon the arrangement shown in the table of contents. The material is divided into three Books. In Book One we overhear Americans talking about themselves, their land, their history and their daily lives. We hope that somehow these varied pages catch something of what Stephen Vincent Benét called "the pure elixir, the American thing." But this is not enough. The other two books attempt to provide a wider perspective. By his very nature the poet tends to the larger view, and it is he who supplies the content of Book Two. Finally, Book Three shows us talking and writing not about ourselves and our country, but about mankind and things in general, shoes and ships and sealing wax. Overlapping is unavoidable: Emerson appears in all three books.

The reader will note from the table of contents, from the contents themselves, from the length of many of the passages, that this is not a conventional book of quotations. Yet it is a book of quotations, for all that. In so far as it *is* such a book, capable of being used for *reference,* it has certain aims.

The first of these is conservative: to preserve the traditionally familiar.

The second is creative: to make the unfamiliar familiar, should it deserve the promotion.

The third is *re*-creative: to retrieve what was once familiar but has been allowed to lapse in our memories.

The fourth is experimental: to select, from the vast ocean of print of the last twenty-five years or so, the passages or utterances that will in our opinion become more and more frequently quoted during the next twenty-five years. One need hardly add that this is a risky procedure. We expect brickbats.

The fifth aim might be called "quoticidal." We believe the time has come to administer a gentle euthanasia to certain passages of American prose and poetry. *The American Treasury* is not "complete." It would be a duller book if it were. If this book has any indisputable merit, it is that you will not discover in it Senator Vest's tribute to the dog. Our omissions do not spring from snobbery, but from a conviction that as a people we have outgrown the kind of sentiment represented by certain authors. The time has come for us to lighten and so to purify the files.

Not that you will not meet in these pages plenty of platitudes. Platitudes are the daily bread of human discourse; we could not do without them. But for insincere or ill-phrased platitudes we have tried to substitute fresher or better-phrased ones. We have sought the lively, the engaging and the pointed, whether it be original or not. The familiar is not necessarily included on that score alone; one wants it also to be memorable. Much proverbial wisdom should be forgotten, not treasured. Everybody knows "Early to bed," but everybody also knows that it is nonsense.

As the compilers of a book of *reference,* then, we have kept in mind five objectives: preservation, creation, revival, experiment, destruction. But as the editors of a book to be used for *pleasure* as well as a deskside tool, our objective has been to provide for the whole family a large one-volume treasury of good reading, full of old favorites and odd surprises, wise or foolish, grave or gay, inspired or commonsensical, fit for the quiet of the library or for reading aloud at the fireside. We should like to think of this book as a kind of *American's Home Companion.*

There is at least one other reason for the existence of *The American Treasury.* It is discussed at some length in the second part of the General Preface, beginning on page xxvii.

So much for purposes. Now a word as to scope. The scope is, we think, wide. But it has its limits. For example, we have not tried to be "representative" of any single class or party or group. If Negroes are included, it is not because they are Negroes, but because some of them have said interesting things in an interesting way. We do not believe in pressure-group anthologies.

We wish that there were more women represented, as they form half of the American nation, and in certain respects the more interesting half. All we can say is that our reading did not seem to turn them up in great quantity, though a better balance is struck as we approach our own time.

We would like, too, to have discovered more examples of social or drawing-room wit. Our café wits find a place here, but they are not quite what we have in mind. We do not seem to have developed a solid tradition of drawing-room talkers, represented in England by a Disraeli, a Sydney Smith or a Labouchère.

We have not tried to re-animate corpses, however respected. There are whole ghost towns and worked-out mines of quotation (the elder Holmes, for example) that are here given only a token salute. Joel Chandler Harris is sparsely represented, not because he is a bad writer (he is a good writer) but because he is in every sense a dead writer. A major fault of many anthologies is ancestor worship. That one at least we hope to have avoided.

In the same spirit we have skirted the "official" and the pompous. The reader will not get much Henry Ward Beecher, and most of Andrew Carnegie has been allowed to rest quietly in the coffin of a ten-volume collected edition. Presidential utterances are included when they are lively or significant, and not when they are merely Presidential.

A man may be important and still be unquotable. John Dewey has influenced our lives radically, yet not by much we *remember* his having said. Nor is there much of him we can dig up that ever *will* become quotable. He's just not that kind of writer, and so, though Dewey is present, he is not present in proportion to his eminence.

The same is true of other figures. Five hundred years hence posterity may decide that the most important man ever born in the United States was the mathematical physicist Willard Gibbs. But formulas, however epochal, do not lend themselves to quotation, generally speaking.

In the same way, a book may be a fixed classic and still yield not a single phrase to our common tongue. *Two Years Before the Mast* is a fine book, yet nothing in it has crept, or will creep, into the language. The same is true of *Little Women*. But an absolute classic of the *highest* order (*Moby Dick*) gives us more and more quotations with every passing year. We have tried to draw our samples from those veins in which the blood runs hottest. Thus the "takes" are many and long from key books and writers—Emerson's *Essays, Walden,* William James, George Santayana.

Then there are those writers who, however interesting, simply do not lend themselves gladly to excerpts—Thomas Wolfe, for example, whose passion for endless statement makes him the anthologist's nightmare.

The careful reader will note that there are not many selections from contemporary political journalism. The reason is simple: in this case perspective is almost completely denied us. First we will have to make a little more history, if this battered world can stand any more.

Anecdotes, too, are for the most part excluded. To lower the bars here would have meant another book. Like all humanity, we are conditioned by time and space.

The reader will note that the Editors are firm believers in the idea that great writers say more and better things than do little writers. We do not apologize for the fact that our pages contain what amounts to virtual small anthologies of Mark Twain, Emerson, Thoreau, Whitman, Henry James, Santayana, Melville and a few others. Nothing can replace a thorough reading of these great men, but we do believe that anyone who wishes to familiarize himself with the most striking, characteristic, memorable things they have said—the things all of us should know, if we know no more than that—will find in these pages what he seeks.

To the Editor's mind the most interesting parts of any intellectual or historical process are the beginning and the end. As a people we Americans have far from reached the end. Yet we feel vaguely that we are at the end of *some*thing and at the beginning of something else. Accordingly we have weighted the book at both termini. There's a great deal from the Founders and a great deal from their descendants, the Flounderers.

It is commonly assumed that the "democratic" tradition which had its fountainhead in Jefferson produced our best writers or at least our more memorable ones. This is not entirely true, but it *is* true that they are better known. We find, on examining our selections, that we have, though not purposively, done something to redress the balance. The reader will find the conservative position, now being painstakingly rediscovered, reasonably well represented, from John Adams and Hamilton and Fisher Ames to H. L. Mencken, with way-stops at William Graham Sumner and the U.S. Army *Training Manual*. No one can complain of the representation given the most profound conservative philosopher our country has produced, George Santayana.

Speaking of Santayana, some may question the propriety of including him as an American. In his case, as in dozens of others where such a doubt legitimately exists, we have simply used horse sense. Though he passed most of his life beyond our borders, the world habitually thinks of Santayana as an American, though not a very American American. So, too, Henry James. At the end of his life he elected British citizenship, yet we cannot help feeling him as one of ours. The same is true of certain other expatriates, such as Ezra Pound.

On the other hand, expatriates such as Logan Pearsall Smith and James McNeill Whistler cut themselves off so completely from their roots that it would be improper to think of them as other than Englishmen. Proud as we may be of T. S. Eliot's American origin, it would be the merest chauvinism to deny that he is generally considered an Englishman and will certainly be so considered by posterity. He, like Smith and Whistler, is therefore not included in this book. Nor are W. H. Auden and Aldous Huxley, even though they dwell among us. Fifty years from now they may be considered Americans; at the moment, happy as we are to have them as fellow citizens, it is hard to think of them as other than English. But Agassiz (1807–1873), who passed most of his life in Europe and became a citizen only in 1861, takes his place in retrospect as part of our country, and so you will find him present. So is Charlie Chaplin, even though he never became a citizen, dwells abroad, and is certainly at the moment in conflict with our American beliefs. Einstein's is a marginal case. His roots were European but we had in the past few years become so accustomed to thinking of him as one of our own that the Editors have hesitantly included him. In general, decisions with respect to divided allegiances have been made not on any logical basis (there is none) but on the basis of feeling and ordinary common sense.

2. A Note on the Practice of Quotation

A work of this sort would not appear to contain any propaganda. Yet, in a vague way, we think of the whole book as propaganda. It is propaganda in a cause that to many may seem trivial. We do not believe it to be so.

In the course of one of his magnificent wartime broadcasts, Winston Churchill once introduced certain lines from "Say Not the Struggle Naught Availeth," by the English poet Arthur Hugh Clough. The reader may remember them. They ended

> But westward, look, the land is bright.

The speech was of momentous, the quotation of momentary, interest. Yet considerable attention was paid to the eight lines of quotation. What caught our fancy was the novelty of a practical twentieth-century statesman daring to embellish his argument by invoking the words of a dead minor poet. We had forgotten that among the public figures of an earlier day happy quotation was common practice. We were startled to see how effective it could still be in our own time.

But to get by with this sort of thing one must be a Churchill. In general we object to the man who quotes, as we object to the man who speaks perfect English, on the ground that he is being "superior." He who flashes a new Cadillac is enviable. He who flashes an old classical tag is pedantic. The job aspirant with good references is welcome as long as they are not from good authors.

Yet what are the young account executive's crewcut, his J. Press suit,

his button-down white shirt, his conservative diagonally-striped tie—
what are they but a series of neat quotations? Indeed the man himself
may be but a quotation, or a quotation of a quotation. But let this same
walking allusion to the Ivy League let fall a passing allusion to Henry
James—and how quickly are our suspicions aroused!

We prefer to think that the absence of inverted commas guarantees the
originality of a thought, whereas it may be merely that the utterer has
forgotten its source. "It is the little writer," says Havelock Ellis (and I
quote), "rather than the great writer who seems never to quote, and the
reason is that he is never really doing anything else."

But, to give the anti-quoter a fair shake, I submit an amusing attack on
the habit made about forty years ago by the superb American essayist
Frank Moore Colby. Here are a few sentences from his essay on "Quotation and Allusion":

> When young and helpless I once fell into a family that made it a daily duty
> to study up things to quote, and every Sunday morning at breakfast each would
> recite a passage memorized during the week. The steam from the coffee vanished
> into literary air, and the muffins, by the time we got to them, seemed to be
> bound in calf. . . . Large blocks of poetry would suddenly fall athwart the
> conversation, no one knew whence, while with bowed head the startled Philistine
> would wait for the seizure to pass. . . . One learns little more about a man
> from the feats of his literary memory than from the feats of his alimentary canal.

The kind of quoter Colby is talking about is practically nonexistent
these days. Even professors of literature, blushing to be thought either
professorial or literary, have stripped themselves of their allusions and use
a prose as single-gallused as that of any congressman up for re-election.
We live in a time in which men will take great pains to conceal their
knowledge. I know ambitious politicians who would give much to have
received a poor education.

We are nervous about quoting, not because we think the quotation may
fail of effect but because we fear its effect may be bad. A man is known
by the company he keeps and few can bear the accusation of consorting
with dead poets and sages. Why stand on the shoulders of titans when we
have two fine clay feet of our own?

One confusing thing about the quotation controversy is that certain
memorable statements on both sides have been made by the same man,
Emerson. In his *Journal* for May, 1845, he says sharply, "I hate quotations. Tell me what you know." In his essay "Quotation and Originality"
he notes warmly, "Next to the originator of a good sentence is the first
quoter of it."

In one sense we are quoting all the time. To whistle Tin Pan Alley's latest inanity is to quote. To repeat the opinions of our pet editorial writer is to quote. To transmit the tired gag of a television comic is to quote. To pass on the gossip columnist's modish anecdote is to quote. To agree with the boss is to repay him with automatic oral flattery—a kind of quote *pro quid*. Much of our conversation is but a series of dittos, often typed on fifth carbons.

This kind of quotation is socially acceptable, indeed in some circles mandatory. I do not quarrel with it. Long before we were human we were simian. We are all mimics.

I merely urge the claims of a different *kind* of quotation, drawn not from the trivial and the transitory but from the excellent and the traditional. I suggest that we raise our sights and our citations, that we stop feeling inferior because by chance we possess superior knowledge. The man who leans upon George Santayana is no more infirm than the man who leans upon Bob Hope.

"Only the past is immortal" (Delmore Schwartz). But its immortality is not unconditional. It cannot be kept alive solely by scholars and professional intellectuals. It must be kept alive by you and me. All mankind is but a carrier, and part of our precious burden consists of things that have been said perfectly. To repeat them appositely is to add to the general stock of knowledge and pleasure. Indeed it is a kind of good citizenship, for we are all citizens of History, a country whose ever-threatened borders we must be at any time prepared to defend. To still in ourselves the golden voices of the past is to regress toward the voiceless condition of the fishes.

Our American speech is not so rich that we can afford to quote only each other or the latest wisecrack. Current income cannot maintain our linguistic economy, at least not in the style to which it is accustomed. We must levy a tax upon the dead, a tax they will pay cheerfully for they have passed beyond the worries of the fiscal year.

Quotation—not the kind Colby was laughing at, but quotation used to make our talk gayer, our thought clearer—does not constrict or paralyze the language. On the contrary it enlarges it, gives it more scope and freedom. At the same time it surreptitiously infuses into our speech (now in peril of subsiding to a prairie flatness relieved only by the tumescences of current slang) a needed elegance, even splendor.

Our language, both written and spoken, seems to be undergoing an evolution akin to that of our architecture. Mies van der Rohe's functional box, stripped so as to remove all friction from living, risks also removing all living from living. Our picture windows open on a void or on another

picture window—a kind of architectural mirroring of clichés. Our industrial architecture is so clean-lined that it no longer arrests the eye, nor
rests it either. So with our language, even among our most admired stylists.
I plead for decoration; man is an ornamenting animal. I plead for a little
"unnecessary" mental furniture, transferred from the storehouses of great
or merely interesting writers and talkers. Quotation *is* embellishment and
rarely more than that. But embellishment has its value. Purely purposive
prose, oral or written, can become so dull as to fail of its purpose, which
is first of all to engage the attention.

If you quote, do not be too nice in your quotation, nor correct a man
if he misquotes slightly. It is not pedantry to speak of "fresh fields and
pastures new." It *is* pedantry to remind the speaker that Milton wrote
"fresh woods." Actually "fresh fields" is a slight improvement, at least for
mnemonic purposes. To quote with aptness and with pleasure is more
important than to quote with prissy correctness.

The nub of the problem has been touched by Fowler in his *Modern
English Usage*. He warns us:

> To each reader those quotations are agreeable that neither strike him as hack-
> neyed nor rebuke his ignorance by their complete novelty, but rouse dormant
> memories; quotation, then, should be adapted to the probable reader's degree
> of cultivation; which presents a very pretty problem to those who have a mixed
> audience to face; the less mixed the audience, the safer is it to quote for asso-
> ciation.

Our difficulty is that almost all our audiences *are* mixed. We no longer
possess what large segments of the citizenry of the nineteenth century
possessed—and what this book may help to re-endow us with—a common
body of knowledge, a common world of associations. No Senator today
would dare, as Gladstone as a matter of course did, to interlard his
speeches with long (and beautifully apt) passages from Lucretius or
Horace. He would not wish to infuriate his colleagues by presuming that
they knew Latin.

In these circumstances I think we must take the bull by the horns and,
making due allowances, quote whenever we feel that the allusion is interesting or helpful or amusing. If the audience is completely unfamiliar with
it, they will be less so after they have had it quoted to them. You must
run the risk of their thinking you snobbish. If the rest of what you say is
not "superior" or patronizing, they will revise their opinion. And if you
really are patronizing, refraining from quotation will not fool them.

Should your hearers happen to be familiar with your quotation, no
great harm is done, if it is not *too* hackneyed. The pleasure of recognition,

being rooted in self-esteem, is a solid one. Besides, a durable quotation is apt to be a good one, and therefore quite worthy of repetition. It will be a long time before constant usage blunts the edge of Thoreau's remark about circumstantial evidence and the trout in the milk.

What kinds of quotations *are* durable? Perhaps two main kinds.

The first is common currency. Once a saying or allusion has caught the fancy of the man in the street, the nonliterary citizen who uses it in all innocence of its origin, it is slated for a long life. Ben Franklin said many weighty things, a number of which you will find in these pages. But "snug as a bug in a rug" may outlast them all. (The phrase may very easily not be his anyway.)

That is one kind of quotation. The other kind is "literary" quotation. This is kept alive, not by the average man, but by the professional—the critic, the actor, the orator, the teacher, and, finally, the anthologist. These professionals are the connoisseurs of the memorable. It is they who actually *create* quotations. They snuff out what is good, print it, say it, repeat it—and lo! our literary treasury is enlarged. What was unknown becomes vaguely familiar; what was vaguely familiar at last becomes part of the language. But it is the professionals, with a specialized interest in words, who have contrived all this. A good example is the popularization during the last twenty-five years of Thoreau's remark about the mass of men leading lives of quiet desperation.

In the case of public figures, ability and quotability have no necessary relation. Mr. Hoover was a far abler President and in general a person of greater magnitude than Coolidge. But Coolidge was a "character," or at least made people think he was one, and so more of what he said than of what Mr. Hoover said will be remembered and quoted. A man who is both great *and* a character—Lincoln, Churchill—is, of course, sure of a long life as a quotee.

It is not unconditionally true that, as Max Eastman has said, "All vigorously imaginative minds can be quoted in sentences." The Scottish novelist George Douglas once wrote, "It's the danger of the aphorism that it states too much in trying to be small." Nevertheless it is a fact that the pithy is remembered when the profound is often neglected. In most general anthologies of quotations, Pope takes second place right after Shakespeare, not so much because he is wise as because he is neat. A few words, perfectly arranged, may well make a bid for immortality. This book is crowded with such happy examples of linguistic economy.

The American Treasury is designed as a volume in which things may be looked up. But it is also designed to set thousands of American words in motion on the lips of American citizens. We have said a great many things worth recalling or worth learning; and if this book, the product of considerable but always delightful labor, can aid in the renaissance of the art of quotation, it will have achieved one of its main purposes.

C. F.

BOOK ONE

* * * * * * * * * * *

WE LOOK AT OURSELVES AND OUR COUNTRY

* * * * * * * * * * *

* *INTRODUCTION* *

The book which follows comprises two-thirds of the entire volume. It is an effort to orchestrate almost a thousand American voices, ranging from shrill trebles to earth-shaking bassos. Each voice has something to say about ourselves and our country, whether it issue from Irvin Cobb defining "corn likker" or Thomas Jefferson defining our basic liberties. Because Americans seem to have reflected on as well as enjoyed liberty, liberty gets more space than liquor. We did not, however, plan it that way. Had a great many fascinating words been written or uttered about liquor, liberty might well have taken a back seat. In other words, just as Mr. Dooley once remarked that the Supreme Court followed the election returns, so our Table of Contents followed the quotations.

Despite our unscholarly methods—as they may seem to more orderly minds—the editors believe that out of this heterogeny something of ourselves emerges in a way barred to more systematic interpretation. We "cover" nothing—America is too vast to be put under any umbrella of words. But, at a hundred quick and no dead places, the reader touches the country's pulsing life, from its simple, glorious beginnings to the present bewildering day.

This whole volume is but a gigantic eavesdropping, and it is odd that so much of what we overhear should be about ourselves and our home. We seem to have sensed from the outset that we were something new, an ungrooved people fated to original adventure. Part of that adventure lay in the exultant discovery of a New World, overwhelming in its dimensions, dazzling in its variety. Part of it—the part that has really just begun— lay in the discovery, sometimes exultant, often rueful, often sorrowful, of what kind of men and women God had it in His mind to permit us to become. If we are self-fascinated, and I think we are, it is not the self-fascination of Narcissus, but the wonderment of the growing boy at his own half-apprehended powers and weaknesses. We are creatively obsessed by the American experiment and by us experimenters and experimentees. That is why the first Book is the largest and in certain respects the most interesting of the three.

We begin by asking the question, Who are we? Listen to the answers. They are many, varied, contradictory, often uncertain. There *is* a national character, but we are not yet sure what it is like, and even less sure that

2

it is formed or finished. We are a melting pot—but a nation too; a hell of a success, as Uncle Joe Cannon flatly announces in our first quotation—but in certain aspects a hell of a failure too.

But let us, an optimistic people, put our best foot forward and launch the book with Encomiums, with the great hopeful statements of our history. They are not complacent. They were not uttered by complacent people. Franklin and Jefferson, Henry Adams and Cardinal Spellman are not given to bragging. To hearken to them is not an exercise in self-satisfaction but a spur to our sense of responsibility.

There is the other side, however. Let us call it Sober Second Thoughts. We are a nation of self-critics, too. We are sharp with ourselves and with each other, though rarely in any spirit of self-repudiation. We assail each other, not out of dislike, but out of what may seem to the sophisticated a simple-minded idealism: that is, we want to improve each other. There is not a critic, from Emerson to Louis Kronenberger, who would for a moment entertain the fantastic idea that citizenship in any other country is preferable. Our expatriates are few, and most of them, wiser for their transient alienation, come home at last. Still, particularly since 1918, when we became a great power, we have been given to taking potshots at ourselves. As the Assistant Editor once put it, "Our position has become so unassailable that it has become more and more necessary to assail it."

After this brief exhibition of pro and con the reader is asked to listen to what we have said about some particular kinds of Americans: the Indians, the true and original early inhabitants, who have entered our cultural bloodstream more subtly than we know; the Negroes, the occasion for the only simon-pure tragic event in our career, the Civil War; the New Englanders, who, with the Virginians, furnished most of the basic ideas that have directed the national life; the Southerners, the most controversial element in our entire society, at once charming and frightening; and the Westerners, who are perhaps our future.

Section II represents an attempt to have Americans picture their own physical plant, which is not a country but a continent. We start with Hamilton's breathtakingly prescient "Learn to think continentally," a remark that in a way is the key signature of the whole American symphony. Then we hear Americans talking, rarely solemnly, about that part of the country they know best, whether it be O. Henry's furnished-room New York or Turner's frontier West. There are many odd surprises in this section, and there is a reason for each inclusion. We conclude with wonderful statements about our mountains, our plains, our rivers and r weather: the permanencies that have shaped and molded every m of us and will continue to do so forever.

Section III, What We Live By, digs deeper. In the long, long the history of a race is its intellectual history. It develops or d its basic ideas are viable or non-viable. The hordes of Tam

not for military reasons, but because Tamerlane had no ideas. If we succeed, it will be because our ideas please men, and not because of our steel
production index, useful and even inspiring as that may be. Section III
listens in on Americans talking about a few American ideas, or American
adaptations of Greek, Roman, French and English ideas. We live by religion (and certain of our creeds are preponderantly American, such as
Christian Science, Mormonism, Puritanism). We are not a literary people,
but one book, though decreasingly, is bone of our bone—the Bible. We
live by our democratic faith and we live also by attacking that faith (see
Some Views Askance) as if to test its strength. We live by a special conception of liberty, and lately we have begun to ask ourselves uneasily
whether security is not to be preferred to it. We live by a continuously
developing notion of justice and equality, expressed most clearly in dozens
of famous legal judgments. Finally we live by a strange patriotism, somewhat different from but not "better" than the patriotism of a non-Amer-
ican. Whatever our position in life, whether we are poor or rich or
uninterested in being either, we can all love our country and, in some
mysterious, wonderful way, feel that it loves us in return. (This fine
phrase is Mr. Van Doren's).

To this section, What We Live By, belong, of course, the great utterances of the Founding Fathers and Lincoln and John Marshall. You
would expect them, and you have them. But also there are dissenting
opinions by Mencken and Santayana and John Adams and William Graham Sumner, representing a strong anti-libertarian tradition which,
though it is rarely referred to in Fourth of July orations, is also a part,
and an essential part, of our pluralistic culture. The People are loved,
feared, sometimes even hated. But that very hatred bears witness to the
fact that They rule.

Thus in this section we have tried, while giving the classic utterances
their due, to escape from the conventional notion that Jeffersonian liberalism (which is not half so liberal as extremists would make it out to be)
dominates our political thought. If Elmer Davis is represented, so is Senator McCarthy, the most effective exponent of an American populism
which has its roots in the early nineteenth century and is completely unin-
fluenced by European thought of any kind. The Senator and Mr. Davis
are equally American. They differ violently in their ideas, but they speak
the same language and understand each other much better than either,
for example, would understand Sorel or Pareto. Frank Hague's "I am the
law" is not to be compared to Louis XIV's "L'état c'est moi." The New
Jersey accent marks it off as an expression, not of the complicated theological legalism of divine right, but as the perfect expression of that
element in the American character which *likes* bosses and distrusts lawyers. We will never understand ourselves unless we listen to all of us.

The following section, How We Live, tries to get down to cases. Here
tell each other not what we believe when we are making speeches, or

writing declarations, but what we believe when we are making a living, or playing, or teaching, or learning.

America has many businesses, one of them being the cultivation of her soul. But this is a long-term occupation, whose final result may never be witnessed. At the moment, and certainly since the first administration of Grant, our main business is and has been business itself, as Mr. Coolidge once reminded us.

But if we take work seriously, we also continually deride ourselves for taking work seriously. It is no mark of instability in us that Ford and Thoreau should both occupy places in our pantheon. We turn from one to the other, not because we are blind to the contradiction but because we are rich enough and varied enough in ourselves to be able to entertain that contradiction without schizophrenia. We even have a dim sense that we may be the only people in history to work out a means someday of reconciling Ford and Thoreau. If we cannot do it, nobody can.

Here then in this section we first overhear ourselves talking about our work, enthusiastically or critically, but always vividly, frequently humorously. We listen to leaders of labor and captains of capital and back of the harsh words know that all of us are both capitalists and laborers and that there are no permanent Haves or Have-Nots.

This book, I warn you, is like our country, full of gimmicks—verbal gimmicks. With affection and amusement the editors at this point made a collection of some of them. They are called advertising slogans, interesting in themselves, and more interesting in that we love to listen to them.

We play as hard as we work, sometimes harder. In the section At Play you will find a crazy-quilt assortment of the odd or bright or self-revealing things our entertainers have said; the most famous lines from our most famous plays, including many long quotations from the greatest play ever written in this country, Thornton Wilder's *Our Town*, quintessentially American and quietly universal; words from and about the movies, radio, television, the circus, swing, the comics. Here too are quotations about eating and drinking and smoking and travel and fashion and society. (There is little about love-making. Whether or not we make love well, we write dully about it.) But there is plenty about our real national passion, sports. After business itself, this is the activity most Americans are most fiercely concerned with. One of the longest quotations in the book— and one of the most fervid—is, quite properly, about baseball; and no one who knows the country will be surprised to observe that it was not written by a sports writer but by a learned professor of history.

We have listened to America at work and at play. Then follows a section entitled Information and Communication. Not only are we always talking about ourselves but we are always talking to each other. Here then are some of the best things we have said about the press. Jefferson preferred newspapers without a government to a government without newspapers, and many of us would make the same choice. Here too is a collection of remarks about education, which is a national enthusiasm, like baseball or carbonated drinks. Finally, there is a "highbrow" section called The Intellectual Climate. The odd thing is that we are a nation of non-intellectuals who keep complaining about our non-intellectualism. Mr. Van Doren points out to me that what is notable is that all these complaints got published. You will find them here.

We now come to Section V, Our Government and Politics. The content of this large and exciting division must be distinguished from the content of What We Live By. Here we are talking, not about theories of statecraft, but about the practice, sometimes even the trade, of government. All the shrewdest, sharpest things we have said about the art of American politics will be discovered here, together with hundreds of political phrases and slogans, so arranged as to tell a story.

The next section, How and Why We Fought, explains itself. It is one of the richest in the book. All our wars are represented and all our views on war. Studying the Civil War in terms of these brief, on-the-spot utterances, arranged in an illuminating order, is an experience more formal histories cannot give. Humor and heartbreak are here, and hatred, and reconciliation, and always courage, the kind of unself-conscious courage whose secret is known only to a non-military people. Over this whole section hangs a shadow. It is The Bomb. The editors have given it a special subsection all to itself, regretting that it deserves it.

We are nearing the end of our long, clamorous audition now. What next? A chapter about Heroes, Rogues and People. This is an odd one. We wanted somewhere to include a vast miscellany of stuff about American *individuals,* considered not as symbols or repositories of ideas, but as strange, colorful, or outsize human beings. Here then is Thoreau on John Brown, Davy Crockett on Davy Crockett, Dos Passos on Henry Ford, and Wilson Mizner settling the argument as to whether Grant or Lee was the greater general ("I don't know, gentlemen, but they paid off on Grant"). Here, too, to keep the balance fair, are the most famous or unforgettable insults Americans have ever offered other Americans. Here are the last words of the great and the notorious, together with a picturesque collection of epitaphs and inscriptions.

Three final sections deal with what we have said about the rest of the world; with our native proverbs; and finally—to my mind one of the most fascinating parts of the whole book—a rich assortment of quotations about us by *non*-Americans, from Leif Ericson to Sir Osbert Sitwell.

And there you have it—not the story of America, for that will never be told, but a thousand American voices, sly or eloquent, immortal or transient, arranged, it is hoped, so that something more than mere noise results. The editors believe that in them is something of the sound of America.

                                                                C. F.

I. Who We Are:
the Nature and Variety of Americans

IN GENERAL

•

ENCOMIUMS

America is a hell of a success.

JOSEPH GURNEY ("UNCLE JOE") CANNON

If there is a country in the world where concord, according to common calculation, would be least expected, it is America. Made up, as it is, of people from different nations, accustomed to different forms and habits of government, speaking different languages, and more different in their modes of worship, it would appear that the union of such a people was impracticable. But by the simple operation of constructing government on the principles of society and the rights of man, every difficulty retires, and the parts are brought into cordial unison.

THOMAS PAINE

I must soon quit the scene, but you may live to see our country flourish; as it will amazingly and rapidly after the war is over; like a field of young Indian corn, which long fair weather and sunshine had enfeebled and discolored, and which in that weak state, by a sudden gust of violent wind, hail, and rain, seemed to be threatened with absolute destruction; yet the storm being past, it recovers fresh verdure, shoots up with double vigor, and delights the eye not of its owner only, but of every observing traveler.

BENJAMIN FRANKLIN, letter to Washington, March 5, 1780

What then is the American, this new man? He is either an European, or the descendant of an European, hence that strange mixture of blood, which you will find in no other country. I could point out to you a family whose grandfather was an Englishman, whose wife was Dutch, whose son married a French woman, and whose present four sons now have four wives of different nations. *He* is an American, who, leaving behind him all his ancient prejudices and manners, receives new ones from the new mode of life he has embraced, the new government he obeys, and the new rank he holds. He became an American by being received in the broad lap of our great *Alma Mater*. Here individuals of all nations are melted

9

into a new race of men, whose labor and posterity will one day cause great changes in the world. Americans are the western pilgrims, who are carrying along with them that great mass of arts, sciences, vigor, and industry which began long since in the east; they will finish the great circle. The Americans were once scattered all over Europe; here they are incorporated into one of the finest systems of population which has ever appeared, and which will hereafter become distinct by the power of the different climates they inhabit. The American ought therefore to love his country much better than that wherein he or his forefathers were born. Here the rewards of his industry follow with equal steps the progress of his labor; his labor is founded on the basis of nature, *self-interest;* can it want a stronger allurement? Wives and children, who before in vain demanded of him a morsel of bread, now, fat and frolicsome, gladly help their father to clear those fields whence exuberant crops are to arise to feed and clothe them all; without any part being claimed, either by a despotic prince, a rich abbot, or a mighty lord. Here religion demands but little of him; a small voluntary salary to the minister, and gratitude to God; can he refuse these? The American is a new man, who acts upon new principles; he must therefore entertain new ideas, and form new opinions. From involuntary idleness, servile dependence, penury, and useless labor, he has passed to toils of a very different nature, rewarded by ample subsistence.

> MICHEL GUILLAUME JEAN DE CRÈVECOEUR, *Letters of an American Farmer,* 1782

. . . its soul, its climate, its equality, liberty, laws, people, and manners. My God! how little do my countrymen know what precious blessings they are in possession of, and which no other people on earth enjoy!

> THOMAS JEFFERSON, letter to Monroe, June 17, 1785

I have often and often in the course of the Session, and the vicissitudes of my hopes and fears as to its issue, looked at that behind the President without being able to tell whether it was rising or setting. But now at length I have the happiness to know that it is a rising and not a setting Sun.

> BENJAMIN FRANKLIN, Report of the Constitutional Convention, September 17, 1787. On the back of the President's chair a sunburst was painted, and Franklin made the remark as the last members signed the Constitution.

Our new federal government is very acceptable to a great majority of our citizens and will certainly be adopted immediately by *nine* and in the course of a year or 18 months by *all* the States. When this shall happen, *then* to be a citizen of the United States *with all its consequences* will be to be a citizen of the freest, purest, and happiest government upon the face of the earth.

> BENJAMIN RUSH, letter to John Coakley Lettsom, September 28, 1787

At the close of the eighteenth century nothing had occurred which warranted the belief that even the material difficulties of America could be removed. Radicals as extreme as Thomas Jefferson and Albert Gallatin were contented with avowing no higher aim than that America should reproduce the simpler forms of European republican society without European vices; and even this their opponents thought visionary. The United States had thus far made a single great step in advance of the Old World,—they had agreed to try the experiment of embracing half a continent in one republican system; but so little were they disposed to feel confidence in their success, that Jefferson himself did not look on this American idea as vital; he would not stake the future on so new an invention. "Whether we remain in one confederacy," he wrote in 1804, "or form into Atlantic and Mississippi confederations, I believe not very important to the happiness of either part." Even over his liberal mind history cast a spell so strong, that he thought the solitary American experiment in political confederation "not very important" beyond the Alleghenies.

The task of overcoming popular inertia in a democratic society was new, and seemed to offer peculiar difficulties. Without a scientific class to lead the way, and without a wealthy class to provide the means of experiment, the people of the United States were still required, by the nature of their problems, to become a speculating and scientific nation. They could do little without changing their old habit of mind, and without learning to love novelty for novelty's sake. Hitherto their timidity in using money had been proportioned to the scantiness of their means. Henceforward they were under every inducement to risk great stakes and frequent losses in order to win occasionally a thousand fold. In the colonial state they had naturally accepted old processes as the best, and European experience as final authority. As an independent people, with half a continent to civilize, they could not afford to waste time in following European examples, but must devise new processes of their own. A world which assumed that what had been must be, could not be scientific; yet in order to make the Americans a scientific people, they must be roused to feel the necessity of scientific training. Until they were satisfied that knowledge was money, they would not insist upon higher education; until they saw with their own eyes stones turned into gold, and vapor into cattle and corn, they would not learn the meaning of science.

HENRY ADAMS, *History of the United States*

A new episode in American history began in 1815. New subjects demanded new treatment, no longer dramatic but steadily tending to become scientific. The traits of American character were fixed; the rate of physical and economical growth was established; and history, certain that at a given distance of time the Union would contain so many millions of people, with wealth valued at so many millions of dollars, became thenceforward chiefly concerned to know what kind of people these millions were to be. They were intelligent, but what paths would their intelligence select? They were quick, but what solution of insoluble problems would quickness hurry? They were scientific, but what control would their science exercise over their destiny? They were mild, but what corruptions would their relaxations bring? They were peaceful, but by what machinery were their corruptions to be purged? What interests were to vivify a society so vast and uniform? What ideals were to ennoble it? What object, besides physical content, must a democratic continent aspire to attain? For the treatment of such questions, history required another century of experience.

HENRY ADAMS, *Ibid.*

The Era of Good Feelings.

> BENJAMIN RUSSELL, title of article in the Boston *Columbian Centinel,* of which Russell was editor, July 12, 1817. The phrase refers to the administration of James Monroe, which Russell considered a very quiet one.

If destruction be our lot we must ourselves be its author and finisher. As a nation of freemen we must live through all time, or die by suicide.

ABRAHAM LINCOLN, Lyceum address, 1838

There is something in the contemplation of the mode in which America has been settled that, in a noble breast, should forever extinguish the prejudices of national dislikes.

Settled by the people of all nations, all nations may claim her for their own. You can not spill a drop of American blood without spilling the blood of the whole world. Be he Englishman, German, Dane, or Scot: the European who scoffs at an American, calls his own brother *Raca,* and

stands in danger of the judgment. We are not a narrow tribe of men.
. . . No: our blood is as the flood of the Amazon, made up of a thousand
noble currents all pouring into one. We are not a nation, so much as
a world.

HERMAN MELVILLE, *Redburn*, 1849

Intrepid, unprincipled, reckless, predatory, with boundless ambition, civilized in externals but a savage at heart, America is, or may yet be, the
Paul Jones of nations.

HERMAN MELVILLE, *Israel Potter*, 1855

The Americans of all nations at any time upon the earth have probably
the fullest poetical nature. The United States themselves are essentially
the greatest poem. In the history of the earth hitherto the largest and
most stirring appear tame and orderly to their ample largeness and stir.
Here at last is something in the doings of man that corresponds with the
broadcast doings of the day and night. Here is not merely a nation but a
teeming nation of nations. Here is action untied from strings necessarily
blind to particulars and details magnificently moving in vast masses. Here
is the hospitality which forever indicates heroes. . . . Here are the
roughs and beards and space and ruggedness and nonchalance that the
soul loves. Here the performance, disdaining the trivial, unapproached in
the tremendous audacity of its crowds and groupings and the push of its
perspective spreads with crampless and flowing breadth and showers its
prolific and splendid extravagance. One sees it must indeed own the
riches of the summer and winter, and need never be bankrupt while corn
grows from the ground or the orchards drop apples or the bays contain
fish or men beget children upon women.

Other states indicate themselves in their deputies—but the genius of
the United States is not best or most in its executives or legislatures, nor
in its ambassadors or authors, or colleges or churches or parlors, nor even
in its newspapers or inventors—but always most in the common people,
south, north, west, east, in all its states, through all its mighty amplitude.
The largeness of Nature and of this nation were monstrous without a
corresponding largeness and generosity of the spirit of the citizen. Their
manners speech dress friendships—the freshness and candor of their
physiognomy—the picturesque looseness of their carriage . . . their
deathless attachment to freedom—their aversion to anything indecorous
or soft or mean—the practical acknowledgment of the citizens of one
state by the citizens of all other states—the fierceness of their roused resentment—their curiosity and welcome of novelty—their self-esteem and

wonderful sympathy—their susceptibility to a slight—the air they have of persons who never knew how it felt to stand in the presence of superiors —the fluency of their speech—their delight in music, the sure symptom of manly tenderness and native elegance of soul . . . their good temper and open-handedness—the terrible significance of their elections—the President's taking off his hat to them not they to him—these too are un-rhymed poetry. It awaits the gigantic and generous treatment worthy of it.

*   *   *

. . . go freely with powerful uneducated persons. . . .

*   *   *

The known universe has one complete lover and that is the greatest poet.

*   *   *

Men and women and the earth and all upon it are simply to be taken as they are, and the investigation of their past and present and future shall be unintermitted and shall be done with perfect candor.

*   *   *

A great poem is for ages and ages in common, and for all degrees and complexions, and all departments and sects, and for a woman as much as a man, and a man as much as a woman. A great poem is no finish to a man or woman but, rather a beginning.

WALT WHITMAN, *Leaves of Grass,* "Preface," 1855

The gentleman will please remember that when his half-civilized ancestors were hunting the wild boar in Silesia, mine were princes of the earth.

JUDAH P. BENJAMIN, in reply to an anti-Semitic remark by a Senator of German lineage, c. 1857

We are the Romans of the modern world—the great assimilating people.

OLIVER WENDELL HOLMES, *The Autocrat of the Breakfast Table,* 1858

The female woman is one of the greatest institooshuns of which this land can boast.

CHARLES FARRAR BROWNE ("ARTEMUS WARD"), *Artemus Ward: His Book,* "Woman's Rights," 1862

Our country has liberty without license and authority without despotism.

JAMES CARDINAL GIBBONS, 1887

Have you not learned that not stocks or bonds or stately homes, or products of mill or field are our country? It is the splendid thought that is in our minds.

BENJAMIN HARRISON

The mission of the United States is one of benevolent assimilation.

WILLIAM McKINLEY, letter, 1898

God has not been preparing the English-speaking and Teutonic peoples for a thousand years for nothing but vain and idle self-contemplation and self-admiration. No! He has made us master organizers of the world to establish system where chaos reigns. He has given us the spirit of progress to overwhelm the forces of reaction throughout the earth. He has made us adept in government that we may administer government among savage and senile peoples. Were it not for such a force as this the world would relapse into barbarism and night. And of all our race He has marked the American people as His chosen nation to finally lead in the regeneration of the world.

ALBERT J. BEVERIDGE, *Congressional Record,* Jan. 9, 1900

I was made by a Dago and presented to the American people on behalf of the French Government for the purpose of welcomin' Irish immigrants into the Dutch city of New York.

WILLIAM SIDNEY PORTER ("O. HENRY"), *Sixes and Sevens,* "The Lady Higher Up"

The general belief still is that Americans are not destined to renounce, but to enjoy.

HERBERT CROLY, *The Promise of American Life,* 1909

America is not a mere body of traders; it is a body of free men. Our greatness is built upon our freedom—is moral, not material. We have a great ardor for gain; but we have a deep passion for the rights of man.

WOODROW WILSON, speech, New York, December 6, 1911

Sometimes people call me an idealist. Well, that is the way I know I am an American. America is the only idealistic country in the world.

WOODROW WILSON, address, Sioux Falls, September 8, 1919

There is much forgetfulness [in the American], much callow disrespect
for what is past or alien; but there is a fund of vigor, goodness, and hope
such as no nation ever possessed before. In what sometimes looks like
American greediness and jostling for the front place, all is love of achievement, nothing is unkindness; it is a fearless people, and free from malice,
as you might see in their eyes and gestures, even if their conduct did not
prove it.

> GEORGE SANTAYANA, *Character and Opinion in the U. S.,*
> 1920

At the same time, the American is imaginative; for where life is intense,
imagination is intense also. Were he not imaginative he would not live so
much in the future. But his imagination is practical, and the future it
forecasts is immediate; it works with the clearest and least ambiguous
terms known to his experience, in terms of number, measure, contrivance,
economy, and speed. He is an idealist working on matter. Understanding
as he does the material potentialities of things, he is successful in invention, conservative in reform, and quick in emergencies. All his life he
jumps into the train after it has started and jumps out before it has
stopped; and he never once gets left behind, or breaks a leg. There is an
enthusiasm in his sympathetic handling of material forces which goes far
to cancel the illiberal character which it might otherwise assume. The
good workman hardly distinguishes his artistic intention from the potency
in himself and in things which is about to realize that intention. Accordingly his ideals fall into the form of premonitions and prophecies; and
his studious prophecies often come true. So do the happy workmanlike
ideals of the American. When a poor boy, perhaps, he dreams of an education, or at least a degree; he dreams of growing rich, and he grows rich
—only more slowly and modestly, perhaps, than he expected; he dreams
of marrying his Rebecca and, even if he marries a Leah instead, he ultimately finds in Leah his Rebecca after all. He dreams of helping to carry
on and to accelerate the movement of a vast, seething, progressive society,
and he actually does so. Ideals clinging so close to nature are almost sure
of fulfillment; the American beams with a certain self-confidence and
sense of mastery; he feels that God and nature are working with him.

> GEORGE SANTAYANA, *Ibid.*

The American is wonderfully alive; and his vitality, not having often
found a suitable outlet, makes him appear agitated on the surface; he is
always letting off an unnecessarily loud blast of incidental steam. He is

inquisitive, and ready with an answer to any question that he may put to himself of his own accord; but if you try to pour instruction into him, on matters that do not touch his own spontaneous life, he shows the most extraordinary powers of resistance and oblivescence; so that he often is remarkably expert in some directions and surprisingly obtuse in others. He seems to bear lightly the sorrowful burden of human knowledge. In a word, he is young.

GEORGE SANTAYANA, *Materialism and Idealism in the U. S.*

France was a land, England was a people, but America, having about it still the quality of the idea, was harder to utter—it was the graves at Shiloh, and the tired, drawn, nervous faces of its great men, and the country boys dying in the Argonne for a phrase that was empty before their bodies withered. It was a willingness of the heart.

F. SCOTT FITZGERALD

Our American keynote . . . a certain generosity; a certain carelessness, or looseness, if you will; a hatred of the sordid; an ability to forget the part for the sake of the whole; a desire for largeness; a willingness to stand exposed.

EZRA POUND, *Patria Mia*

The American Animal . . . is nothing but the big Honest Majority, that you might find in any country. He is not a politician, he is not a 100% American, he is not any organization, either uplift or downfall. . . . In fact, all I can find out about him is that he is just normal. . . . This normal breed is so far in the majority that there is no use to worry about the others. They are a lot of mavericks and strays.

WILL ROGERS

The Era of Wonderful Nonsense.

WESTBROOK PEGLER, of the era which ended in the Crash of 1929

Intellectually I know that America is no better than any other country; emotionally I know she is better than every other country.

SINCLAIR LEWIS, interview in Berlin, December 29, 1930

The American people never carry an umbrella. They prepare to walk in eternal sunshine.

ALFRED E. SMITH, 1931

Life Begins at Forty.

WALTER B. PITKIN, title of book, 1932

Two pervasive generalizations are possible about the United States. One is that, more than any other, it is a lucky country with an almost obsessive belief in the happy ending. . . . The other is that, more than any other country except England perhaps, it believes in compromise. . . . In these two considerations there lies great hope. An instinct for happiness often produces happiness; and nothing can be more valuable than reason, in an age shaken and made miserable by lack of faith, with a disintegration of so many values and with people pallid through fear and confusion and moral crisis.

JOHN GUNTHER, *Inside U.S.A.*

It is Europeans, for the most part, who have constructed these great ships, but without America they have no meaning. These ships are alive with the supreme ecstasy of the modern world, which is the voyage to America. There is no other experience that is remotely comparable to it, in its sense of joy, its exultancy, its drunken and magnificent hope which, against reason and knowledge, soars into a heaven of fabulous conviction, which believes in the miracle and sees it invariably achieved.

THOMAS WOLFE, *Of Time and the River,* 1935

The fabulous country—the place where miracles not only happen, but where they happen all the time.

THOMAS WOLFE, *Ibid.*

America—a place where the people have the right to complain about the lack of freedom.

LOUIS HIRSCH

America to me is not a territory and not a code, but a way of life. It is, in words that David Starr Jordan taught me, the land where hate dies away.

ALBERT GUÉRARD

It is men at work. It is the storm-tossed fishermen coming into Gloucester and Providence and Astoria. It is the farmer riding his great machine in the dust of harvest, the dairyman going to the barn before sunrise, the lineman mending the broken wire, the miner drilling for the blast. It is the servants of fire in the murky splendor of Pittsburgh, between the

Allegheny and the Monongahela, the trucks rumbling through the night, the locomotive engineer bringing the train in on time, the pilot in the clouds, the riveter running along the beam a hundred feet in air. It is the clerk in the office, the housewife doing the dishes and sending the children off to school. It is the teacher, doctor and parson tending and helping, body and soul, for small reward. . . .

It is a great number of people on pilgrimage, common and ordinary people, charged with the usual human failings, yet filled with such a hope as never caught the imaginations and the hearts of any nation on earth before. The hope of liberty. The hope of justice. The hope of a land in which a man can stand straight, without fear, without rancor.

The land and the people and the flag—the land a continent, the people of every race, the flag a symbol of what humanity may aspire to when the wars are over and the barriers are down; to these each generation must be dedicated and consecrated anew, to defend with life itself, if need be, but, above all, in friendliness, in hope, in courage, to live for.

> R. L. Duffus, editorial, *New York Times*, June 14, 1940

As I fell asleep, I thought to myself: "Well, now, I have lived one whole day in America and—just like they say—America is a country where anything, anything at all can happen."

And in twenty years—about this—I never changed my mind.

> George and Helen Papashvily, *Anything Can Happen*,
> "The First Day," 1943

I believe in America.
In her high destiny under God to stand before the people of the earth as a shining example of unselfish devotion to the ideals that have, under God, made us a great nation; the Christian ideal of liberty in harmonious unity; builded of respect for God's image in man and every man's right to life, liberty, and happiness.
I believe in America.
For the blood in the veins of America, our heart's blood comes from the wounds of many peoples, chaliced in humanity's name upon the altar of liberty.
I believe in America.
Not because of the tremendous resources of her fields and mountains, rivers and lakes, valleys and plains, but rather because America has been and must ever continue to be, under God, the Beacon of Liberty, the Hope of the Oppressed, the Refuge of the Weak, the Pledge and the Proof that humanity can live in mutual respect based on the law of God,

voiced through the conscience of man, and in mutual esteem, based on the responsibility of democratic life.

Lastly, I believe in America.

Because I believe in God and God's Providence that has been over us from the earliest days of our beginning. Believing in God, I am confident both of his merciful forgiveness of our national sins and His awareness of our national virtues. Believing in God's Providence, I am confident of our high resolve that this fair land, the visible setting of the vast, immaterial soul of the American nation, shall never lose its initial consecration to the common Fatherhood of God, so that we and our children's children shall live in peace and harmony among ourselves and with our neighbors. In this America, I believe; for this America, I live; for this America, I and millions of others would stand ready to die.

FRANCIS CARDINAL SPELLMAN, *American Credo,* 1943

America was largely populated by misrepresentation, and on the whole it has been a good thing for the newcomers. The average man is industrious but inert. If somebody on this side of the water had not gone to the trouble of luring people out of their Central European villages or their East European city slums they would have remained, by the million, in the ancient habitat, submerged and resigned. A cool statistical outline of what America had to offer, checked by a couple of actuaries and sworn to before a notary public, would never have filled the emigrant ships. A rainbow was needed—a land where the roads were paved with gold, where every man was as good as everybody else, where every man's native-born son had a fine chance to be elected President.

No colonization without misrepresentation. It is a rule that goes back very early in the building of America.

SIMEON STRUNSKY, *No Mean City,* 1944

America means far more than a continent bounded by two oceans. It is more than pride of military power, glory in war or in victory. It means more than vast expanses of farms, of great factories or mines, magnificent cities or millions of automobiles and radios. It is more even than the traditions of the great tide westward from Europe which pioneered the conquest of a continent. It is more than our literature, our music, our poetry. Other nations have these things also.

HERBERT HOOVER, *Woman's Home Companion,* 1947

Our mistakes, and we make many, are due in great part to our impatience.

We always want to see within a few years revolutionary results which take generations to come about. I am in favor of our foreign policy. We aim well. I'm opposed to excessive optimism. You see, we're good-hearted people, we're good people, accustomed to miracles in our own country, and we can't bear to see others suffer. Did you see what has become of California in the last ten years? You can't do the same abroad, apparently. We always want to do too much for too many people and too quickly.

SENATOR ALEXANDER WILEY, to Luigi Barzini, Jr.

The ordinary American who is now fifty or more has been somewhere and seen something. He has escaped the most deplorable of states—to be born, to subsist for many years, and then to die without having really lived. . . . He has taken the most terrific battering, by long odds, to which the nation was ever subjected, and he has survived.

GERALD W. JOHNSON, *Incredible Tale,* 1950

We would do better to . . . realize that our sobering position of leadership in the world is founded upon the fact that we have not stood still. The story of the changes in the contours of American life that we have hammered out in the first half of this twentieth century, is a triumphant story, however harsh may have been some of our experiences in the interim and however obscure may be the shape of the future. We would do well to think of our accomplishment this far as but the preface to what we may accomplish in the second half of the century if we can continue to invent, improve and change—and can keep a good heart. The courageous nation, like the courageous man, is not unhappy at the thought of dangers beside the road ahead, but welcomes them as challenges to be faced and overwhelmed along an adventurous course.

FREDERICK LEWIS ALLEN, *The Big Change,* 1952

My own guess is that this great development [the emergence of America to the leadership of the Western world] . . . will in some fashion be connected, by future interpreters, with the advent of an age of mass action, mass production, and mass psychology in American life. From being one of the most unorganized, the most invertebrate of nations in 1860, we have grown into the most powerfully and efficiently organized people on the globe. . . . Our thinking in 1864 was still individual thinking. Today it is largely mass thinking, shaped and colored by mass media of unparalleled and sometimes dismaying potency. . . . Our national outlook, once that of the individualistic pioneer, has become a social outlook. Without this pervasive internal change, our new position in the world would have been impossible.

The striking shift in our character and our world position in the last half-century, of course, has some direct results, already visible, in our interpretation of history. . . . The apologetic attitude of the years of the Great Depression is gone. We can henceforth be more confident and more energetic in asserting that our way of life, called decadent by our enemies, has proved itself historically to be freer, more flexible and more humane than any other. . . .

In the past, our historians were apologetic about our love of the dollar, our race to wealth, our interest in material objects. . . . Our writers in general—for our historians but followed the poets, the novelists and the dramatists—intimated that America had grown too fast, too coarsely, too muscularly. . . .

We can now assert that this historical attitude was erroneous. The nation grew none too fast. We can see today that all its wealth, all its strength, were needed to meet a succession of world crises—and we still dwell in a crisis era. Had we applied restrictions to keep our economy small, tame and pure, we would have lost the first World War. Had the United States not possessed the mightiest oil industry, the greatest steel industry, the largest automotive factories . . . and the most ingenious working force in the world, we would indubitably have lost the second World War. Were we significantly weaker today in technical skills, in great mills and factories and the scientific knowledge which gave us priority with the atomic bomb and hydrogen bomb, all Western Europe would be cowering—we ourselves would perhaps be cowering—before the knout held by the Kremlin. The architects of our material growth—the men like Whitney, McCormick, Westinghouse, Rockefeller, Carnegie, Hill and Ford—will yet stand forth in their true stature as builders of a strength which civilization found indispensable.

It will yet be realised that the industrial revolution in the United States came none too soon, and none too fast, and that the ensuing mass-production revolution, as yet so little understood by Americans, was not born a day too early.

ALLAN NEVINS, speech, Dearborn, September, 1953

There is in most Americans some spark of idealism, which can be fanned into a flame. It takes sometimes a divining rod to find what it is; but when found, and that means often, when disclosed to the owners, the results are often extraordinary.

Louis D. Brandeis, *The Words of Justice Brandeis,* 1953

America is a "happy-ending" nation.

Dore Schary, address to Harvard Club of Los Angeles

You cannot gauge the intelligence of an American by talking with him; you must work with him. The American polishes and refines his way of doing things—even the most commonplace—the way the French of the seventeenth century polished their maxims and aphorisms.

Eric Hoffer, *The Passionate State of Mind,* 1955

The books are full of familiar and affectionate talk about the little lands: the countries made out of islands in the sea, or river valleys, or a circle of mountains. "Map of Ireland!" they say of a young Gael, meaning you'd know him for Irish anywhere by the light in his eyes and the set of his jaw. Nobody says "Map of America!" of any of us—not even the slender girls with the long legs and the fine ankles who walk the streets of the world as other women never walked them. People know us well enough. . . . But nobody thinks "The map of America!" when we go by. You don't talk about continents that way. . . . The map of America goes on and on. The map of America is a map of endlessness, of opening out, of forever and ever. No man's face would make you think of it but his hope might, his courage might.

. . . America is big . . . in time, too. In the small countries the clocks strike all together—all one hour. With us it is still deep night at San Francisco, and dark still on the High Plains, and only barely gray on Lake Michigan, when the sun comes up at Marblehead. The same thing is true of the seasons. In the small countries the weather is all one weather more or less, but with us there are a thousand weathers and a choice of seasons. Beans will be out of the ground in Alabama when the snow is four feet deep in Minnesota and the garden around Charleston will be blooming when the oil burners at Kennebunkport are still blasting away. Some of us avoid the changes. . . . But most of us stay put: we wouldn't quit the American changes if we could. Change and diversity are the meaning of our world: the American dimension. It is because the season changes, the weather changes, the country changes that the map goes on and on. What can change will never have an ending.

America is a country of extremes. Those who think she should be all of a piece, all of a kind . . . every house like its neighbor and all minds alike, have never traveled on this continent. American wholeness, American singleness, American strength, is the wholeness, the singleness, the strength of many opposites made one. The Republic is a symbol of union because it is also a symbol of differences, and it will endure not because its deserts and seacoasts and forests and bayous and dead volcanoes are of one mind but because they are of several minds and are nevertheless together. . . .

If you could read a country the way you read the palm of a hand, the American lines of heart and head and life would be the three great branching rivers of the Mississippi Valley, but the American line of fortune would take a different course: it would follow the flow of steel and oil. It is the combination of steel and oil which has begotten American industry and it is American industry which has built the American cities. When a foreigner thinks of the United States he does not think of Frost and Faulkner, or of Harvard and Columbia and Yale, or of the Shenandoah and the Yellowstone; he thinks of New York and San Francisco and Chicago, and the steel that built them and the oil by which they live. It is the fabulous sky line [of New York City] which shapes itself in the imagination of the world when the name, America, is spoken. And the thought that goes with that sky line in the world's mind is the thought, "materialism." To our neighbors, East and West, the symbols of the Republic are enormous chimneys leaking their pink smoke into the clean, blue sky, or huge derricks wading into the sea itself for oil, or deserted mining towns where gold and silver were once dug. But we ourselves—what do we think of the world's talk? Consider that sky line. . . . Do steel and oil alone explain it? . . . Or have the minds of men imagined these tall towers?

Ours was a new continent. What have we done with it? What have we left behind us—as the sea leaves driftwood on the rocks? Much ugliness, much devastation—gullied fields, eroded prairies, burnt forests, filthy slums, imitative and pretentious buildings, litter, trash. Yes, all that: but like the driftwood, beauty too. Unintended beauty perhaps—unsuspected beauty: an enormous oil tank rounded by the shadow of its stair; a great bridge strung like a harp across sea water; the pure, remembering profiles of a country graveyard. And how did this beauty come here? By accident? By chance? Or did men make it? Are these perhaps the monuments of a particular temper of the human spirit—an American sensibility which expresses itself as well in the shuttered front of a city warehouse as in the trim competence of a valley farm or the weathered patience of a railroad station on a one-track line?

Because the movement of discoverers and conquerors and colonists was a movement from east to west across the Atlantic, and because the frontiersmen and the settlers moved across the continent from east to west, west has always been the direction of the future in American history. The American dream has been a dream of the west, of the world farther on. But now that the great journey across the ocean and the continent has come to . . . the coast of the Pacific, there are those who say we have come to the end of the dream also. We must look backward now, they say, not forward; we must fear, not hope; we must hate, not love; we must conform, not imagine. It is strange doctrine to hear from Americans. No man can come to the Pacific coast of this continent . . . and feel he has come to the *end* of anything. . . . California, it is quite true, has filled up with people: her valleys are richly farmed, her cities are among the greatest in the world, her industries are fabulous. But even so the American journey has not ended. America is never accomplished, America is always still to build; for men, as long as they are truly men, will dream of man's fulfillment. West is a country in the mind, and so eternal.

> ARCHIBALD MACLEISH, "Sweet Land of Liberty," *Collier's,*
> July 8, 1955

SOBER SECOND THOUGHTS

Nature will not have us fret and fume. She does not like our benevolence or our learning much better than she likes our frauds and wars. When we come out of the caucus, or the bank, or the Abolitionist-convention, or the Temperance-meeting, or the Transcendental club into the fields and woods, she says to us, "So hot? my little Sir."

> RALPH WALDO EMERSON, *Essays: First Series,* "Spiritual Laws"

America is formless, has no terrible and no beautiful condensation.

> RALPH WALDO EMERSON, *Journal*

Instead of being a mass of individuals, each one fearlessly blurting out his own convictions, as a nation, compared to other nations, we are a mass of cowards. More than all other people, we are afraid of each other.

> WENDELL PHILLIPS

The American is nomadic in religion, in ideas, in morals.

JAMES RUSSELL LOWELL, *Fireside Travels*, 1864

Nothing makes one so angry as when one is tired and comes home and must speak English.

Pennsylvania Dutch saying (*Nix mach's man so bös als wenn man müd ist und häm kemmt und mus' English schwetza.*)

It's a wretched business, this virtual quarrel of ours with our own country.

HENRY JAMES, *Roderick Hudson*, 1876

There is not a single human characteristic which can be safely labeled as "American."

SAMUEL L. CLEMENS ("MARK TWAIN")

The moral flabbiness born of the exclusive worship of the bitch-goddess SUCCESS. That—with the squalid cash interpretation put on the word success—is our national disease.

WILLIAM JAMES, letter to H. G. Wells, 1906

I indulge in no mere figure of speech when I say that our nation, the immortal spirit of our domain, lives in us—in our hearts and minds and consciences. There it must find its nutriment or die. This thought more than any other presents to our minds the impressiveness and responsibility of American citizenship. The land we live in seems to be strong and active. But how fares the land that lives in us?

GROVER CLEVELAND, address, February 22, 1907

The hyphenated American always hoists the American flag undermost.

THEODORE ROOSEVELT, *Fear God and Take Your Own Part*

There can be no fifty-fifty Americanism in this country. There is room here for only 100 percent Americanism, only for those who are American and nothing else.

THEODORE ROOSEVELT, speech, Saratoga

Every immigrant who comes here should be required within five years to learn English or leave the country.

THEODORE ROOSEVELT

To hell with Jews, Jesuits and steamships.

> PRESCOTT HALL, when President Taft vetoed a bill requir-
> ing literacy for immigrants, 1911

One of our defects as a nation is a tendency to use what have been called "weasel words." When a weasel sucks an egg, the meat is sucked out of the egg; and if you use a "weasel word" after another there is nothing left of the other.   THEODORE ROOSEVELT, speech in St. Louis, May, 1916

Superficially, the United States seems to suffer from an endless and astounding neophilism; actually all its thinking is done within the boundaries of a very small group of political, economic and religious ideas, most of them unsound. For example, there is the fundamental idea of democracy—the idea that all political power should remain in the hands of the populace, that its exercise by superior men is intrinsically immoral. Out of this idea spring innumerable notions and crazes that are no more, at bottom, than restatements of it in sentimental terms: rotation in office, direct elections, the initiative and referendum, the recall, the popular primary, and so on. Again, there is the primary doctrine that the possession of great wealth is a crime—a doctrine half a religious heritage and half the product of mere mob envy. Out of it have come free silver, trust-busting, government ownership, muck-raking, Populism, Bleaseism, Progressivism, the milder forms of Socialism, the whole gasconade of "reform" politics. Yet again, there is the ineradicable peasant suspicion of the man who is having a better time in the world—a suspicion grounded, like the foregoing, partly upon undisguised envy and partly upon archaic and barbaric religious taboos. Out of it have come all the glittering pearls of the uplift, from Abolition to Prohibition, and from the crusade against horseracing to the Mann Act. The whole political history of the United States is the history of these three ideas.

> H. L. MENCKEN, *Prejudices: First Series,* 1919

That all one has to do to gather a large crowd in New York is to stand on the curb a few moments and gaze intently at the sky.

That the postmasters in small towns read all the postcards.

That all theater box-office employes are very impolite and hate to sell a prospective patron a ticket.

That all newspaper reporters carry notebooks.

That, when shaving on a railway train, a man invariably cuts himself.

That the jokes in *Punch* are never funny.

That nicotine keeps the teeth in a sound condition.

That the wife of a rich man always wistfully looks back into the past and wishes she had married a poor man.

That the quality of the champagne may be judged by the amount of noise that the cork makes when it is popped.

That all French women are very passionate, and will sacrifice everything to love.

That beer is very fattening.

That the cloth used in suits made in England is so good that it never wears out.

That Philadelphia is a very sleepy town.

That if one swallows an ounce of olive oil before going to a banquet, one will not get drunk.

That the worst actress in the company is always the manager's wife.

> H. L. MENCKEN and GEORGE JEAN NATHAN, *American Credo*

The whole drift of our law is toward the absolute prohibition of all ideas that diverge in the slightest form from the accepted platitudes, and behind that drift of law there is a far more potent force of growing custom, and under that custom there is a national philosophy which erects conformity into the noblest of virtues and the free functioning of personality into a capital crime against society.

> H. L. MENCKEN

The first Rotarian was the first man to call John the Baptist Jack.

> H. L. MENCKEN

Q. If you find so much that is unworthy of reverence in the United States, then why do you live here?

A. Why do men go to zoos?

> H. L. MENCKEN, *Prejudices: Fifth Series,* 1926

You speak of how good your generation is, but I think they share with every generation since the Civil War in America the sense of being somehow about to inherit the earth. You've heard me say before that I think the faces of most American women over thirty are relief maps of petulant and bewildered unhappiness.

> F. SCOTT FITZGERALD, undated letter

America, my country, is almost a continent and hardly yet a nation.

Ezra Pound, *Patria Mia*

You are all a lost generation.

> Gertrude Stein, used by Ernest Hemingway as the motto
> of *The Sun Also Rises,* 1926. Hemingway states that the
> original was spoken to Mme. Stein by a garage owner in
> the *Midi,* who muttered that his young mechanics were
> *"une génération perdue."*

Suppose, I suggested to myself, that the giving of itself by an entire generation to mechanical things was really making all men impotent. There was a passion for size among all the men I had known. Almost every man I had known had a bigger house, a bigger factory, a faster automobile than his fellows.

Sherwood Anderson

"The trouble with this country is," observed Herndon, "that there are too many people going about saying, 'The trouble with this country is—.' "

Sinclair Lewis, *Dodsworth,* 1929

It takes no great perspicacity to detect and to complain of the standardization in American life. So many foreign and domestic commentators have pointed this feature out in exactly the same terms that the comment itself has become standardized and could be turned out by the thousands on little greeting cards, all from the same type-form: "American life has become too standardized."

Robert Benchley

Gertrude Stein always speaks of America as being now the oldest country in the world because by the methods of the Civil War and the commercial conceptions that followed it America created the twentieth century, and since all the other countries are now either living or commencing to be living a twentieth century life, America having begun the creation of the twentieth century in the sixties of the nineteenth century is now the oldest country in the world.

Gertrude Stein, *The Autobiography of Alice B. Toklas*

We hear about constitutional rights, free speech and the free press. Every time I hear those words I say to myself, "That man is a Red, that man is a Communist." You never heard a real American talk in that manner.

> FRANK HAGUE, speech before Jersey City Chamber of Commerce, January 12, 1938

We can put our children on wheels to see the world, but we cannot give them the kind of home that any town provided in the nineties, at any price.

> HENRY SEIDEL CANBY, *The Age of Confidence*

This age of power also is the age of steel. Age of rust would be a better designation. If it were not for our paints and protective coatings nothing would be left of this machine civilization a hundred years hence.

> WALDEMAR KAEMPFFERT, *Science Today and Tomorrow*

I believe that we are lost here in America, but I believe we shall be found. . . . I think that the true discovery of America is before us. I think the true fulfillment of our spirit, of our people, of our mighty and immortal land, is yet to come.

> THOMAS WOLFE, *You Can't Go Home Again,* 1940

I give you mom. I give you the destroying mother. . . . I give you the angel—and point to the sword in her hand. . . . Our society is too much an institution built to appease the rapacity of loving mothers.

> PHILIP WYLIE, *Generation of Vipers,* 1942

I am a man of medium height. I keep my records in a Weis Folder Reorder Number 8003. The unpaid balance of my estimated tax for the year 1945 is item 3 less the sum of items 4 and 5. My eyes are gray. My Selective Service order number is 10789. The serial number is T1654. I am in Class IV-A, and have been variously in Class 3-A, Class I-A (H), and Class 4-H. My social security number is 067-01-9841. I am married to U. S. Woman Number 067-01-9807. Her eyes are gray. This is not a joint declaration, nor is it made by an agent; therefore it need be signed only by me—and, as I said, I am a man of medium height.

I am the holder of a quit-claim deed recorded in Book 682, Page 501, in the county where I live. I hold Fire Insurance Policy Number 424747, continuing until the 23 day of October in the year nineteen hundred forty-five, at noon, and it is important that the written portions of all policies covering the same property read exactly alike. My cervical spine shows relatively good alignment with evidence of proliferative changes about the bodies consistent with early arthritis. (Essential clinical data: pain in neck radiating to mastoids and occipito-temporal region, not constant, moderately severe; patient in good general health and working.) My operator's licence is Number 16200. It expired December 31, 1943, more than a year ago, but I am still carrying it and it appears to be serving the purpose. I shall renew it when I get time. I have made, published, and declared my last will and testament, and it thereby revokes all other wills and codicils at any time heretofore made by me. I hold Basic A Mileage Ration 108950, O.P.A. Form R-525-C. The number of my car is 18-388. Tickets A-14 are valid through March 21st.

I was born in District Number 5903, New York State. My birth is registered in Volume 3/58 of the Department of Health. My father was a man of medium height. His telephone number was 484. My mother was a housewife. Her eyes were blue. Neither parent had a social security number and neither was secure socially. They drove to the depot behind an unnumbered horse.

I hold Individual Certificate Number 4320-209 with the Equitable Life Assurance Society, in which a corporation hereinafter called the employer has contracted to insure my life for the sum of two thousand dollars. My left front tire is Number 48KE8846, my right front tire is Number 63T6895. My rear tires are, from left to right, Number 6N4M5384 and Number A26E5806D. I brush my hair with Whiting-Adams Brush Number 010 and comb my hair with Pro-Phy-Lac-Tic Comb Number 1201. My shaving brush is sterilized. I take Pill Number 43934 after each meal and I can get more of them by calling ELdorado 5-6770. I spray my nose with De Vilbiss Atomizer Number 14. Sometimes I stop the pain with Squibb Pill, Control Number 3K49979 (aspirin). My wife (Number 067-01-9807) takes Pill Number 49345.

I hold War Ration Book 40289EW, from which have been torn Airplane Stamps Numbers 1, 2, and 3. I also hold Book 159378CD, from which have been torn Spare Number 2, Spare Number 37, and certain other coupons. My wife holds Book 40288EW and Book 159374CD. In accepting them, she recognized that they remained the property of the United States Government.

I have a black dog with cheeks of tan. Her number is 11032. It is an old number. I shall renew it when I get time. The analysis of her prepared food is guaranteed and is Case Number 1312. The ingredients are: Cereal Flaked feeds (from Corn, Rice, Bran, and Wheat), Meat Meal, Fish Liver and Glandular Meal, Soybean Oil Meal, Wheat Bran, Corn Germ Meal, 5% Kel-Centrate [containing Dried Skim Milk, Dehydrated

Cheese, Vitamin B_1 (Thiamin), Flavin Concentrate, Carotene, Yeast, Vitamin A and D Feeding Oil (containing 3,000 U.S.P. units Vitamin A and 400 U.S.P. units Vitamin D per gram), Diastase (Enzyme), Wheat Germ Meal, Rice Polish Extract], $1\frac{1}{2}\%$ Calcium Carbonate, $.00037\%$ Potassium Iodide, and $\frac{1}{4}\%$ Salt. She prefers offal.

When I finish what I am now writing it will be late in the day. It will be about half past five. I will then take up Purchase Order Number 245-9077-B-Final, which I received this morning from the Office of War Information and which covers the use of certain material they want to translate into a foreign language. Attached to the order are Standard Form Number 1034 (white) and three copies of Standard Form Number 1034a (yellow), also "Instructions for Preparation of Voucher by Vendor and Example of Prepared Voucher." The Appropriation Symbol of the Purchase Order is 1153700.001-501. The requisition number is B-827. The allotment is X5-207.1-R2-11. Voucher shall be prepared in ink, indelible pencil, or typewriter. For a while I will be vendor preparing voucher. Later on, when my head gets bad and the pain radiates, I will be voucher preparing vendor. I see that there is a list of twenty-one instructions which I will be following. Number One on the list is: "Name of payor agency as shown in the block 'appropriation symbol and title' in the upper left-hand corner of the Purchase Order." Number Five on the list is: "Vendor's personal account or invoice number," but whether that means Order Number 245-9077-B-Final, or Requisition B-827, or Allotment X5-207.1-R2-11, or Appropriation Symbol 1153700.001-501, I do not know, nor will I know later on in the evening after several hours of meditation, nor will I be able to find out by consulting Woman 067-01-9807, who is no better at filling out forms than I am, nor after taking Pill Number 43934, which tends merely to make me drowsy.

I owe a letter to Corporal 32413654, Hq and Hq Sq., VII AAF S.C., APO 953, c/o PM San Francisco, Calif., thanking him for the necktie he sent me at Christmas. In 1918 I was a private in the Army. My number was 4,345,016. I was a boy of medium height. I had light hair. I had no absences from duty under G.O. 31,1912, or G.O. 45,1914. The number of that war was Number One.

> E. B. WHITE, *The Second Tree from the Corner*, "About Myself"

"Uncle James" was cordial. That is the well-meant American substitute for being amiable; but it won't do. It is being amiable on principle and about nothing in particular; whereas true amiability presupposes discernment, tact, a sense for what other people really feel and want. To be cordial is like roughing a man's head to jolly him up, or kissing a child that doesn't want to be kissed. You are relieved when it's over.

GEORGE SANTAYANA, *Persons and Places,* 1943

An American will tinker with anything he can put his hands on. But how rarely can he be persuaded to tinker with an abstract idea.

LELAND STOWE, *They Shall Not Sleep,* 1944

I am ashamed to be an American. . . . The war has demonstrated one thing, that the Germans are superior to the Americans physically, intellectually, aesthetically, and morally.

CARL H. MOTE, *America Preferred,* quoted in New York *Post,* April 30, 1946

The people who settled in New England came here for religious freedom, but religious freedom to them meant freedom only for their kind of religion. They were not going to be any more liberal to others who differed with them in this new country, than others had been with them in countries from which they came. This attitude seems to be our attitude in many situations today.

ELEANOR ROOSEVELT

Without an external motive the average American would rather not do something he is not sure he can do well; he would rather see or hear an expert do it, even such a dubious expert as the ordinary radio singer.

ELMER DAVIS

I sometimes marvel at the extraordinary docility with which Americans submit to speeches.

ADLAI STEVENSON, speech, Chicago, 1950

The so-called expatriates of the nineteen twenties made a cult of "living," and they returned in the end to America because this cult is against the American grain. Living as an art was quite unnatural for them. Americans love the ability to do something, as they love power also, far more than they can ever love mere living. A pity, perhaps, but true.

VAN WYCK BROOKS, "A Winter's Notebook," *Nation,* November 14, 1953

I am sitting in the kitchen of the little house at Medfield. . . . I am writing a book. In it I am speaking to you. But I am also speaking to the world. To both I owe an accounting.

It is a terrible book. It is terrible in what it tells about men. If anything, it is more terrible in what it tells about the world in which you live. . . .

> WHITTAKER CHAMBERS, *Witness,* "Preface in the form of a letter to his children," 1953

If it weren't for Elmer Davis and a few more—but chiefly Elmer Davis—an observant traveler might conclude that the Americans were dying out. Like the moose in Newfoundland, which are reported to be perishing of some obscure psychological disorder—crashing half-blind into trees, mooning morosely around swamps, unable or unwilling even to rid themselves of their ticks.

A generation ago the Americans were fairly common in this country. You could hear them blundering about in the bush at all hours, sniffing at everything, snorting at what they didn't care for, elbowing their way through any kind of trouble, respecting themselves and intending to be respected by others, cautious maybe but hard to intimidate and impossible to stampede. One mark of an American was the way his neck would swell if you tried to tell him what to think or where to line up. Another was his courage, not always wise, and his humor, not always subtle, and the way he got round by himself.

American conservatives, back in those days, were men who believed in conserving America, including the American Constitution, including also the American Bill of Rights, regardless of the opposition—men like Charles Evans Hughes. American liberals were men who believed in the achievement of the American Revolution no matter who was against it. And neither side ran in packs. And neither side was herded by fear or by anything else. Where they have gone to now, and why, is the great American mystery. With the moose it is said to be the climate.

> ARCHIBALD MACLEISH, review of a book by Davis, *Nation,* March 6, 1954

Most Americans don't, in any vital sense, get together; they only do things together.

> LOUIS KRONENBERGER, *Company Manners,* 1954

In spite, or maybe because, of all that has been written on how to acquire friends, exude personality and dazzle dinner parties, America today boasts pathetically few interesting people. By interesting one means, of course, quite the reverse of "interesting"—quite the reverse of travelers who give memorably minute accounts of their trips to the interior of Kenya; or people who have the ear, or hold the hand, or scratch the back, of the great and celebrated. One means people—it seems sad to have to say what it means—who because of their brains, charm, liveliness, responsiveness, wit are a pleasure to be with. And a pleasure whether one chooses to talk sense or nonsense, since the test of interesting people is that subject matter doesn't matter.

Louis Kronenberger, Ibid.

At the moment, so far from having any leaning toward moderation, or even respect for it; we tend to look down on it as a form of mediocrity, a lack of adventurousness, an actual want of aspiration. . . . The American Way is so restlessly creative as to be essentially destructive; the American Way is to carry common sense almost to the point of madness.

Louis Kronenberger, Ibid.

IN PARTICULAR

•

INDIANS

How!

> Anon., incorrect version of Indian greeting *"A-Hau"*— "Peace be with you," or "All is well"

When your people come to me, they are permitted to use their own fashions, and I expect the same liberty when I come to you.

> Miantunnumoh, a sachem of the Narragansetts; said to Governor Dudley in 1640

I appeal to any white man if ever he entered Logan's cabin hungry, and he gave him not to eat; if ever he came cold and naked, and he clothed him not.

> Chief Logan, quoted by Irving, *Traits of Indian Character*

When I am dead, it will be noised through all the world, they will hear of it across the great waters, and say, Red Jacket the great orator is dead.

And white men will come and ask you for my body. They will wish to bury me. But do not let them take me. Clothe me in my simplest dress, put on my leggins and my moccasins, and hang the cross I have worn so long around my neck, and let it lie upon my bosom. Then bury me among my people. . . . I do not wish to rise among pale faces.

> RED JACKET, orator of the Senecas. He was buried among white people in the Old Mission Cemetery, East Buffalo, New York.

These lands are ours. No one has a right to remove us, because we were the first owners. The Great Spirit above has appointed this place for us, on which to light our fires, and here we will remain. As to boundaries, the Great Spirit knows no boundaries, nor will his red children acknowledge any.

> TECUMSEH, Chief of the Shawnees; to the messenger of the President of the United States in 1810

Father! You have got the arms and ammunition which our great father sent for his red children. If you have an idea of going away, give them to us, and you may go and welcome, for us. Our lives are in the hands of the Great Spirit. We are determined to defend our lands, and if it is His will, we wish to leave our bones upon them.

> TECUMSEH, to the English, before the War of 1812. He was right—the English deserted the Indians, and the Indian Confederacy was destroyed in November, 1811, by General Harrison at Tippecanoe.

Sell a country! Why not sell the air, the clouds and the great sea, as well as the earth? Did not the Great Spirit make them all for the use of his children?

> TECUMSEH

Am I a dog, that I should lie?

> METAKKSEGA, a chief of the western Ojibwa; said in 1826 when Governor Cass suggested that he should bind himself by an oath

Hear me, my warriors; my heart is sick and sad. Our chiefs are killed, the old men are all dead. It is cold, and we have no blankets; the little children are freezing to death. Hear me, my warriors; my heart is sick and sad. From where the sun now stands I will fight no more forever!

CHIEF JOSEPH, Nez Percé Tribe, late nineteenth century

The revolution that destroyed the neolithic world began with the voyage of John Cabot in 1498. No evidence has ever been found that before that date fishermen—Basque, Spanish, Portuguese, Breton, or English—visited the Grand Banks and went on the Canadian mainland. But many a historian has had to suppress the twitch of nerve that comes from certain inexplicable data, of which the most galling one is this: that as early as there are accounts of visits to these shores there are also Indians offering to trade furs for manufactured goods.

BERNARD DeVOTO, *The Course of Empire,* 1952

John Marshall has made his decision, now let him enforce it.

Attributed to ANDREW JACKSON by Horace Greeley, 1832. The Supreme Court had ruled that the national government had exclusive jurisdiction in the Cherokee Nation territory, in Georgia.

The life of the Iroquois, though void of those multiplying phases which vary the routine of civilized existence, was one of sharp excitement and sudden contrast. The chase, the war-path, the dance, the festival, the game of hazard, the race of political ambition, all had their votaries. When the assembled sachems had resolved on war against some foreign tribe, and when, from their great council-house of bark, in the Valley of Onondaga, their messengers had gone forth to invite the warriors to arms, then from east to west, through the farthest bounds of the confederacy, a thousand warlike hearts caught up the summons with glad alacrity. With fasting and praying, and consulting dreams and omens; with invoking the war-god, and dancing the frantic war-dance, the warriors sought to insure the triumph of their arms; and, these strange rites concluded, they began their stealthy progress full of confidence through the devious pathways of the forest. For days and weeks, in anxious expectation, the villagers await the result. And now, as evening closes, a shrill, wild cry, pealing from afar, over the darkening forest, proclaims the return of the victorious warriors. The village is alive with sudden commotion; and snatching sticks and stones, knives and hatchets, men, women, and children, yelling like fiends let loose, swarm out of the narrow portal, to visit upon the miserable captives a foretaste of the deadlier torments in store for them. And now,

the black arches of the forest glow with the fires of death; and with brandished torch and firebrand the frenzied multitude close around their victim. The pen shrinks to write, the heart sickens to conceive, the fierceness
of his agony; yet still, amid the din of his tormentors, rises his clear voice
of scorn and defiance. The work is done; the blackened trunk is flung to
the dogs, and, with clamorous shouts and hootings, the murderers seek to
drive away the spirit of their victim.

The Iroquois reckoned these barbarities among their most exquisite enjoyments; and yet they had other sources of pleasure, which made up in
frequency and innocence all that they lacked in intensity. Each passing
season had its feasts and dances, often mingling religion with social pas-
time. The young had their frolics and merry-makings; and the old had
their no less frequent councils, where conversation and laughter alter-
nated with grave deliberations for the public weal. There were also stated
periods marked by the recurrence of momentous ceremonies, in which the
whole community took part—the mystic sacrifice of the dogs, the wild
orgies of the dream feast, and the loathsome festival of the exhumation
of the dead. Yet in the intervals of war and hunting, these multiform
occupations would often fail; and, while the women were toiling in the
cornfields, the lazy warriors vainly sought relief from the scanty sources
of their own minds, and beguiled the hours with smoking or sleeping, with
gambling or gallantry.

If we seek for a single trait preeminently characteristic of the Iroquois,
we shall find it in that boundless pride which impelled them to style themselves, not inaptly as regards their own race, "the men surpassing all
others." "Must I," exclaimed one of their great warriors, as he fell
wounded among a crowd of Algonquins,—"must I, who have made the
whole earth tremble, now die by the hands of children?" Their power
kept pace with their pride. Their war-parties roamed over half America,
and their name was a terror from the Atlantic to the Mississippi; but,
when we ask the numerical strength of the dreaded confederacy, when we
discover that, in the days of their greatest triumphs, their united cantons
could not have numbered four thousand warriors, we stand amazed at the
folly and dissension which left so vast a region the prey of a handful of
bold marauders. Of the cities and villages now so thickly scattered over
the lost domain of the Iroquois, a single one might boast a more numerous
population than all the five united tribes.

FRANCIS PARKMAN, *The Conspiracy of Pontiac*

Of the Indian character much has been written foolishly, and credulously
believed. By the rhapsodies of poets, the cant of sentimentalists, and the

extravagance of some who should have known better, a counterfeit image has been tricked out, which might seek in vain for its likeness through every corner of the habitable earth; an image bearing no more resemblance to its original than the monarch of the tragedy and the hero of the epic poem bear to their living prototypes in the palace and the camp. The shadows of his wilderness home, and the darker mantle of his own inscrutable reserve, have made the Indian warrior a wonder and a mystery. Yet to the eye of rational observation there is nothing unintelligible in him. He is full, it is true, of contradiction. He deems himself the center of greatness and renown; his pride is proof against the fiercest torments of fire and steel; and yet the same man would beg for a dram of whisky, or pick up a crust of bread thrown to him like a dog, from the tent door of the traveler. At one moment, he is wary and cautious to the verge of cowardice; at the next, he abandons himself to a very insanity of recklessness; and the habitual self-restraint which throws an impenetrable veil over emotion is joined to the wild, impetuous passions of a beast or a madman.

Such inconsistencies, strange as they seem in our eyes, when viewed under a novel aspect, are but the ordinary incidents of humanity. The qualities of the mind are not uniform in their action through all the relations of life. With different men, and different races of men, pride, valor, prudence, have different forms of manifestation, and where in one instance they lie dormant, in another they are keenly awake. . . .

Nature has stamped the Indian with a hard and stern physiognomy. Ambition, revenge, envy, jealousy, are his ruling passions; and his cold temperament is little exposed to those effeminate vices which are the bane of milder races. With him revenge is an overpowering instinct; nay, more, it is a point of honor and a duty. His pride sets all language at defiance. He loathes the thought of coercion; and few of his race have ever stooped to perform a menial office. A wild love of liberty, an utter intolerance of control, lie at the basis of his character, and fire his whole existence. Yet, in spite of this haughty independence, he is a devout hero-worshiper; and high achievement in war or policy touches a chord to which his nature never fails to respond. He looks up with admiring reverence to the sages and heroes of his tribe; and it is this principle, joined to the respect for age, which springs from the patriarchal element in his social system, which, beyond all others, contributes union and harmony to the erratic members of an Indian community. With him the love of glory kindles into a burning passion; and to allay its cravings, he will dare cold and famine, fire, tempest, torture, and death itself.

These generous traits are overcast by much that is dark, cold, and sinister, by sleepless distrust, and rankling jealousy. Treacherous himself, he is always suspicious of treachery in others. Brave as he is—and few of mankind are braver—he will vent his passion by a secret stab rather than an open blow. His warfare is full of ambuscade and stratagem; and he never rushes into battle with that joyous self-abandonment, with which the warriors of the Gothic races flung themselves into the ranks of their enemies. In his feasts and his drinking-bouts we find none of that robust and full-toned mirth which reigned at the rude carousals of our barbaric ancestry. He is never joyful in his cups, and maudlin sorrow or maniacal rage is the sole result of his potations.

Over all emotion he throws the veil of an iron self-control, originating in a peculiar form of pride, and fostered by rigorous discipline from childhood upward. He is trained to conceal passion, and not to subdue it. The inscrutable warrior is aptly imaged by the hackneyed figure of a volcano covered with snow; and no man can say when or where the wild-fire will burst forth. This shallow self-mastery serves to give dignity to public deliberation, and harmony to social life. Wrangling and quarrel are strangers to an Indian dwelling; and while an assembly of the ancient Gauls was garrulous as a convocation of magpies, a Roman senate might have taken a lesson from the grave solemnity of an Indian council. In the midst of his family and friends, he hides affection, by nature none of the most tender, under a mask of icy coldness; and in the torturing fires of his enemy, the haughty sufferer maintains to the last his look of grim defiance.

His intellect is as peculiar as his moral organization. Among all savages, the powers of perception preponderate over those of reason and analysis; but this is more especially the case with the Indian. An acute judge of character, at least of such parts of it as his experience enables him to comprehend; keen to a proverb in all exercises of war and the chase, he seldom traces effects to their causes, or follows out actions to their remote results. Though a close observer of external nature, he no sooner attempts to account for her phenomena than he involves himself in the most ridiculous absurdities; and quite content with these puerilities, he has not the least desire to push his inquiries further. His curiosity, abundantly active within its own narrow circle, is dead to all things else; and to attempt to rouse it from its torpor is but a bootless task. He seldom takes cognizance of general or abstract ideas; and his language has scarcely the power to express them, except through the medium of figures drawn from the external world, and often highly picturesque and forcible. The absence of reflection makes him grossly improvident, and unfits him for pursuing any complicated scheme of war or policy.

Some races of men seem molded in wax, soft and melting, at once plastic and feeble. Some races, like some metals, combine the greatest flexibility with the greatest strength. But the Indian is hewn out of rock. You cannot change the form without destruction of the substance. Such, at least, has too often proved the case. Races of inferior energy have possessed a power of expansion and assimilation to which he is a stranger; and it is this fixed and rigid quality which has proved his ruin. He will not learn the arts of civilization, and he and his forest must perish together. The stern, unchanging features of his mind excite our admiration, from their very immutability; and we look with deep interest on the fate of this irreclaimable son of the wilderness, the child who will not be weaned from the breast of his rugged mother. And our interest increases when we discern in the unhappy wanderer, mingled among his vices, the germs of heroic virtues—a hand bountiful to bestow, as it is rapacious to receive, and, even in extreme famine, imparting its last morsel to a fellow-sufferer; a heart which, strong in friendship as in hate, thinks it not too much to lay down life for its chosen comrade; a soul true to its own idea of honor, and burning with an unquenchable thirst for greatness and renown.

FRANCIS PARKMAN, *Ibid.*

Indians is pizen wherever found.

CHARLES FARRAR BROWNE ("ARTEMUS WARD"), *Artemus Ward: His Book,* 1862

The only good Indian is a dead Indian.

PHILIP H. SHERIDAN, January, 1869

Another Redskin bit the dust!

ANON., "The Nick Carter Library"

My forefathers didn't come over on the *Mayflower,* but they met the boat.

WILL ROGERS, who was of Indian descent

NEGROES

That proclamation frees the slave but ignores the negro.

WENDELL PHILLIPS, of the Emancipation Proclamation

Thus now, as always, the evils which men fear they shall be called upon to encounter as a result of doing what is just and humane, are discovered,

when they are really encountered, not to be evils at all, but blessings pure
and simple.

> Report of the Committee for Securing Colored People in
> Philadelphia the Right to Street-Cars, 1866

Shortly before election, a colored political barbecue was held near Louisville and old Abram Jasper was asked to speak.

"Feller freemen," said he, "you all knows me. I is a Republican from
way back. When dar has been any work to do, I has done it. When dar's
been any votin to do, I has been in de thick of it. I is old line and tax-
paid. I has seed many changes, too. I has seed de Republicans up. I has
seed de Democrats up. But I is *yit* to see de nigger up.

"De other night I had a dream. Dremp I died and went to heaven.
When I got to de Pearly Gate, old Saint Peter he say:

" 'Who dar?' says he.

" 'Abram Jasper,' says I.

" 'Is you mounted or is you afoot?' says he.

" 'I is afoot,' says I.

" 'Well, you kain't git in here,' says he. 'Nobody lowed in here cept dem
as comes mounted,' says he.

" 'Dat's hard on me,' says I, 'atter comin all dat distance.' But he never
say nothin to me, an I starts back, an about halfway down de hill, who
does I meet but Charles Sumner an dat good old Horace Greeley!

" 'Whar you gwine, Mr. Greeley?' I says.

" 'I is gwine to heaven wid Mr. Sumner,' says he.

" 'Mr. Greeley,' says I, ''tain't no use. I is jes been up dar, an nobody's
lowed to git in cept dey comes mounted, an you is afoot.'

" 'Is dat a fack?'' says he.

"Mr. Greeley sorter scratch his head, an atter awhile he says, says he,
'Abram, I tell you what less do. Supposin you gits down on all fours an
Sumner an me will mount an ride you in, and in dat way we kin all git in.'

" 'Gentlemen,' says I, 'do you think you kin work it?'

" 'I *know* I kin,' says bof of dem.

"So down I gits on all fours, an Greeley an Sumner gits astraddle, and
we ambles up de hill agin, an prances up to de Gate, and old Saint Peter
say:

" 'Who dar?'

" 'We is, Charles Sumner an Horace Greeley,' says Mr. Greeley.

" 'Is you bof mounted or is you afoot?' says Peter.

" 'We is bof mounted,' says Mr. Greeley.

" 'All right,' says Peter. 'All right,' says he, 'jes hitch yo hoss outside, gentlemen, an come right in.' "

> Attributed to HENRY WATTERSON, 1880's

If one race be inferior to the other socially, the Constitution of the United States cannot put them on the same plane.

> Majority opinion of the Supreme Court in *Plessy* v. *Ferguson,* 1896

If evils will result from the commingling of the two races upon public highways established for the benefit of all, they will be infinitely less than those that will surely come from state legislation regulating the enjoyment of civil rights upon the basis of race. . . . The sure guaranty of the peace and security of each race is the clear, distinct, unconditional recognition by our governments, national and state, of every right that inheres in civic freedom, and of the equality before the law of all citizens of the United States without regard to race. . . . In the view of the Constitution, in the eyes of the law, there is in this country no superior, dominant, ruling class of citizens. There is no caste system here. The Constitution is color-blind, and neither knows nor tolerates classes among citizens.

> JOHN MARSHALL HARLAN, dissenting opinion in *Plessy* v. *Ferguson,* 1896

The white man cannot keep the Negro in the ditch without sitting down there with him.

> BOOKER T. WASHINGTON

Tell them that by way of the shop, the field, the skilled hand, habits of economy and thrift, by way of industrial school and college, we are coming. We are crawling up, working up, yea, bursting up. Often through oppression, unjust discrimination, and prejudice, but through them we are coming up, and with proper habits, intelligence, and property, there is no power on earth that can permanently stay our progress. . . .

While we are thus being tested, I beg of you to remember that wherever our life touches yours, we help or hinder. Wherever your life touches ours, you make us stronger or weaker. No member of your race in any part of our country can harm the meanest member of mine, without the proudest and bluest blood in Massachusetts being degraded. When Mississippi commits crime, New England commits crime, and in so much lowers the standard of your civilization. There is no escape—man drags man down, or man lifts man up.

BOOKER T. WASHINGTON, *The American Standard*

Not only as folk but as individual artists the Negro in America is a creator; and as such, he has exercised an influence greater than it is yet realized to be, and which is far in excess of what his numbers and status would seem to warrant.

There is one other contribution the Negro in America has made that will eventually influence national thought. I hesitate to stress it because it is so intangible. However, it is the contribution in spiritual values that he has made through the fortitude with which he has borne himself and steadily forced his way forward.

JAMES WELDON JOHNSON

It is a peculiar sensation, this double-consciousness, this sense of always looking at one's self through the eyes of others. . . . One feels his two-ness—an American, a Negro; two souls, two thoughts, two unreconciled strivings; two warring ideals in one dark body, whose dogged strength alone keeps it from being torn asunder.

W. E. B. DU BOIS, *The Souls of Black Folk*

The Constitution does not provide for first and second class citizens.

WENDELL L. WILLKIE, *An American Program*

By a peculiar logical inversion the Anglo-Saxon ruling class, its imitators, accomplices, and victims, have come to believe in a Negro problem. . . . While there is actually no Negro problem, there is definitely a Caucasian problem.

Continual reference to a Negro problem assumes that some profound difficulty has been or is being created for the human race by the so-called Negroes. This is typical ruling class arrogance, and . . . has no basis in fact. It has been centuries since any Negro nation has menaced the rest of humanity. The last of the Moors withdrew from Europe in 1492.

The so-called Negroes . . . have passed few if any Jim Crow laws . . . set up few white ghettos, carried on no discriminatory practices against whites, and have not devoted centuries of propaganda to prove the superiority of blacks over whites. . . .

While we may dismiss the concept of a Negro problem as a valuable dividend-paying fiction, it is clear that the Caucasian problem is painfully real and practically universal. Stated briefly, the problem confronting the colored peoples of the world is how to live in freedom, peace, and security without being invaded, subjugated, expropriated, exploited, persecuted, and humiliated by Caucasians justifying their actions by the myth of white racial superiority.

The term Negro itself is as fictitious as the theory of white racial superiority on which Anglo-Saxon civilization is based, but it is nevertheless one of the most effective smear devices developed since the Crusades. . . . Of course "white" and "Caucasian" are equally barren of scientific meaning. . . . There are actually no white people except albinos who are a very pale pink color. . . .

GEORGE S. SCHUYLER, What the Negro Wants, 1944

Paint him black and bring him over here.

> A young Negro girl when asked how she would punish Hitler. Quoted by Walter Winchell, March 26, 1945

Our fight for freedom begins when we get to San Francisco.

> A Negro soldier returning from Okinawa, 1945

Personally I would prefer to see my race and my civilization blotted out with the atomic bomb than to see it slowly but surely destroyed in the maelstrom of miscegenation, interbreeding, intermarriage, and mongrelization.

> SENATOR THEODORE BILBO, quoted by Duteil, *The Great Parade*

Negro blood is sure powerful—because just *one* drop of black blood makes a colored man. *One* drop—you are a Negro! Now, why is that? Why is Negro blood so much more powerful than any other kind of blood in the world? If a man has Irish blood in him, people will say, "He's *part* Irish." If he has a little Jewish blood, they'll say, "He's *half* Jewish." But if he has just a small bit of colored blood in him, BAM!—*"He's a Negro."* Not "He's *part* Negro." No, be it ever so little, if that blood is black, *"He's a Negro."* Now, that is what I do not understand—why our *one* drop is so powerful. Black is powerful. You can have 99 drops of white blood in your veins down South—but if that other *one* drop is black, shame on you. Even if you look white, you're black. That drop is really powerful. Explain it to me. You're colleged.

LANGSTON HUGHES, Simple Takes a Wife, 1953

A dark man shall see dark days. Bop comes out of them dark days. That's why real Bop is mad, wild, frantic, crazy—and not to be dug unless you've seen dark days, too. Folks who ain't suffered much cannot play Bop, neither appreciate it. They think Bop is nonsense—like you. They think it's just *crazy* crazy. They do not know Bop is also MAD crazy, SAD crazy, FRANTIC WILD CRAZY—beat out of somebody's head! That's what Bop is. Them young colored kids who started it, they know what Bop is.

LANGSTON HUGHES, Ibid.

NEW ENGLANDERS

Yankee, n. In Europe, an American. In the Northern States of our Union, a New Englander. In the Southern States the word is unknown. (See *Damyank.*)

AMBROSE BIERCE, The Devil's Dictionary

First Make thy Will.

> ANON., opening of "official" guide to voyagers to the New World in the late sixteenth century

& the wind shrinking upon them withall, they resolved to bear up againe for the Cape, and thought them selves hapy to gett out of those dangers before night overtooke them, as by Gods providence they did. And the next day they gott into the Cape-harbor wher they ridd in saftie.

WILLIAM BRADFORD, Journal, September 6, 1620

Thus out of small beginnings greater things have been produced by His hand that made all things of nothing, and gives being to all things that are; and as one small candle may light a thousand, so the light here kindled hath shone unto many; yea, in some sort, to our whole Nation.

WILLIAM BRADFORD, History of Plymouth Plantation

We had a long and troublesome passage, but the Lord made it safe and easy to us; and though we have met with many and great troubles, (as this bearer can certify thee,) yet he hath pleased to uphold us, and to give us hope of a happy issue.

> JOHN WINTHROP, letter to his wife, July 16, 1630, from Charleston in New England

The moral of the story of the Pilgrims is that if you work hard all your life and behave yourself every minute and take no time out for fun you will break practically even, if you can borrow enough money to pay your taxes.

> WILL CUPPY, *The Decline and Fall of Practically Every-body,* 1950

The most curious of all the facts in that welter we call Salem witchcraft is this: if you expunge from the record those documents that arise directly out of the affair, and those which treat it historically, like the *Magnalia* [of Cotton Mather] or Hale's and Calef's accounts, and a few twinges of memory such as appear in Sewall's *Diary,* the intellectual history of New England up to 1720 can be written as though no such thing ever happened. It had no effect on the ecclesiastical or political situation, it does not figure in the institutional or ideological development. Aside from a few oblique lamentations in election sermons (briefly noted among the catalogue of woes), for twenty-eight years this cataclysm hardly appears in the record.

> PERRY MILLER, *From Colony to Province,* 1953

A scooner let her be!

> ANDREW ROBINSON, Gloucester, Massachusetts, 1713. In this year Capt. Robinson, a fisherman, built a vessel entirely new in style. She had two masts with great fore-and-aft sails in place of the old square sails. Watching her slide down the ways, a spectator exclaimed, "Oh, how she scoons!"

I am as determined to preserve the independence of Vermont as Congress is that of the Union; and rather than fail I will retire with my hardy Green Mountain boys into the caverns of the mountains and make war on all mankind.

> ETHAN ALLEN. Vermont was independent, 1777 to 1791.

I felt the ground shake under my feet at my first contact with New England Town Meeting.

> THOMAS JEFFERSON

I shall enter on no encomium of Massachusetts; she needs none. There she is. Behold her, and judge for yourselves. There is her history; the world knows it by heart. The past, at least, is secure. There is Boston and

Concord and Lexington and Bunker Hill; and there they will remain forever.

> DANIEL WEBSTER, second speech on Foot's Resolution,
> January, 1830

The courage of New England is the courage of conscience.

> DANIEL WEBSTER

To get on, to get honour, to get honest.

> ROCKWOOD HOAR, "the three stages of the enterprising
> Yankee"

And who was the Gray Champion? Perhaps his name might be found in
the records of that stern Court of Justice, which passed a sentence, too
mighty for the age, but glorious in all after-times, for its humbling lesson
to the monarch and its high example to the subject. I have heard, that
whenever the descendants of the Puritans are to show the spirit of their
sires, the old man appears again. When eighty years had passed, he walked
once more in King Street. Five years later, in the twi-light of an April
morning, he stood on the green, beside the meeting-house, at Lexington,
where now the obelisk of granite, with a slab of slate inlaid, commemorates
the first fallen of the Revolution. And when our fathers were toiling at the
breastwork on Bunker's Hill, all through that night the old warrior walked
his rounds. Long, long may it be, ere he comes again! His hour is one of
darkness, and adversity, and peril. But should domestic tyranny oppress us,
or the invader's step pollute our soil, still may the Gray Champion come,
for he is the type of New England's hereditary spirit; and his shadowy
march, on the eve of danger, must ever be the pledge, that New England's
sons will vindicate their ancestry.

> NATHANIEL HAWTHORNE, *The Gray Champion*

And thus have these naked Nantucketers, these sea hermits, issuing from
their ant-hill in the sea, overrun and conquered the watery world like so
many Alexanders; parcelling out among them the Atlantic, Pacific, and
Indian Oceans, as the three pirate powers did Poland. Let America add
Mexico to Texas, and pile Cuba upon Canada; let the English overswarm
all India, and hang out their blazing banner from the sun; two thirds of
this terraqueous globe are the Nantucketer's. For the sea is his; he owns
it, as Emperors own empires; other seamen having but a right of way
through it. Merchant ships are but extension bridges; armed ones but

floating forts; even pirates and privateers, though following the sea as highwaymen the road, they but plunder other ships, other fragments of the land like themselves, without seeking to draw their living from the bottomless deep itself. The Nantucketer, he alone resides and riots on the sea; he alone, in Bible language, goes down to it in ships; to and fro ploughing it as his own special plantation. *There* is his home; *there* lies his business, which a Noah's flood would not interrupt, though it overwhelmed all the millions in China. He lives on the sea, as prairie cocks in the prairie; he hides among the waves, he climbs them as chamois hunters climb the Alps. For years he knows not the land; so that when he comes to it at last, it smells like another world, more strangely than the moon would to an Earthsman. With the landless gull, that at sunset folds her wings and is rocked to sleep between billows; so at nightfall, the Nantucketer, out of sight of land, furls his sails, and lays him to his rest, while under his very pillow rush herds of walruses and whales.

HERMAN MELVILLE, *Moby Dick,* xiv

The rock underlies all America: it only crops out here.

WENDELL PHILLIPS, speech, Plymouth, December 21, 1855

Unless one keeps in mind the social forces that found it convenient to array themselves in Puritan garb, the clear meaning of it all will be lost in the fogs of biblical disputation, and some of the ablest men the English race has ever bred will be reduced to crabbed theologians involved in tenuous subtleties and disputing endlessly over absurd dogmas. But tenacious disputants though they certainly were, pursuing their subtleties into the last refuge and cranny of logic, these Puritan dogmatists were very far from being vain practitioners of eccentricity. It is the manner and dress and not the matter of their arguments that is strange; and if we will resolutely translate the old phrases into modern equivalents, if we will put aside the theology and fasten attention on the politics and economics of the struggle, we shall have less difficulty in discovering that the new principle for which those old Puritans were groping was the later familiar doctrine of natural rights; and the final end and outcome of their concern for a more equitable relation of the individual to society, was the principle of a democratic commonwealth, established in the conception of political equalitarianism. Here are liberalisms in plenty to reward the search for the inner core of Puritanism.

VERNON PARRINGTON, *Main Currents in American Thought*

. . . Of all these familiar haunts the one that moved me most with a sense of personal identity with myself, was Coutances.

A great age it was, and a great people our Norman ancestors. Rather hard and grasping, and with no outward show of grace; little love for the exterior magnificences of Amiens, Chartres and Rouen; given to use the sword and plow rather than the chisel, and with apparently little or none of the brush, and with no sense of color comparable to that of other races, still our Norman grandpapas did great things in art, or at least in the narrow field of art that reflected their lives. I have rarely felt New England at its highest ideal power as it appeared to me, beautified and glorified, in the Cathedral of Coutances. Since then our ancestors have steadily declined and run out until we have reached pretty near the bottom. They have played their little part according to the schedule. They have lost their religion, their art and their military tastes. They cannot now comprehend the meaning of what they did at Mont St. Michel. They have kept only the qualities which were most useful, with a dull instinct recalling dead associations. So we get Boston.

> HENRY ADAMS, letter to Brooks Adams, September 8, 1895

I love Vermont because of her hills and valleys, her scenery and invigorating climate, but most of all because of her indomitable people. They are a race of pioneers who have almost beggared themselves to serve others. If the spirit of liberty should vanish in other parts of our Union and support of our institutions should languish, it could all be replenished from the generous store held by the people of this brave little State of Vermont.

> CALVIN COOLIDGE, from train platform; Bennington, 1928

I love the road. They don't expect so much from you. New York audiences just want to see how much you'll take off. . . . I love New England best of all. It's so easy to please. You don't have to do much in New England because they haven't had it.

> ANN CORIO, 1934

If two New Hampshiremen aren't a match for the devil, we might as well give the country back to the Indians.

> STEPHEN VINCENT BENÉT, *13 O'Clock,* "The Devil and Daniel Webster," 1936

The real New England Yankee is a person who takes the midnight train home from New York.

> LEVERETT SALTONSTALL, press conference, May 4, 1939

As time went on [in New England] the gristle of conscience, work, thrift, shrewdness, duty, became bone.

JAMES TRUSLOW ADAMS, Epic of America

New England is a finished place. Its destiny is that of Florence or Venice, not Milan, while the American empire careens onward toward its unpredicted end. . . . It is the first American section to be finished, to achieve stability in the conditions of its life. It is the first old civilization, the first permanent civilization in America.

BERNARD DEVOTO, New Engand: There She Stands

SOUTHERNERS

The Southern States are an aggregate, in fact, of communities, not of individuals. Every plantation is a little community, with the master at its head, who concentrates in himself the united interests of capital and labor, of which he is the common representative. These small communities aggregated make the State in all, whose action, labor, and capital is equally represented and perfectly harmonized. Hence the harmony, the union, the stability of that section. . . . [In the South labor and capital are] equally represented and harmonized. . . . [In the Union as a whole, the South is thus] the balance of the system; the great conservative power, which prevents other portions, less fortunately constituted, from rushing into conflict. In this tendency to conflict in the North, between labor and capital, which is constantly on the increase, the weight of the South has been and ever will be found on the conservative side; against the aggression of one or the other side, whichever may tend to disturb the equilibrium of our political system.

JOHN C. CALHOUN, speech in the Senate, January 9, 1838

There is and always has been in an advanced stage of wealth and civilization, a conflict between labor and capital. The condition of society in the South exempts us from the disorders and dangers resulting from this conflict; and which explains why it is that the political condition of the slaveholding states has been so much more stable and quiet than that of the North. . . . The experience of the next generation will fully test how vastly more favorable our condition of society is to that of other sections

for free and stable institutions, provided we are not disturbed by the interference of others, or shall . . . resist promptly and successfully such interference.

                                         JOHN C. CALHOUN, *Ibid.*

The Old South was one of the most remarkable societies which ever existed in the world. Was there ever another instance of a country in which
the relation of master and man arose, negligible exceptions aside, only
with reference to a special alien group—in which virtually the whole body
of the natives who had failed economically got off fully from the servitude
that, in one form or other, has almost universally been the penalty of such
failure—in which they were *parked,* as it were, and left to go to the devil
in the absolute enjoyment of their liberty?

                              W. J. CASH, *The Mind of the South,* 1946

Tall, largely built, handsome, genial, with liberal Virginia openness toward all he liked, he [Roony Lee, son of Robert E. Lee, at Harvard in
1854] had also the Virginia habit of command. . . . For a year, at least
. . . [he] was the most popular and prominent man in his class, but then
seemed slowly to drop into the background. The habit of command was
not enough, and the Virginian had little else. He was simple beyond analysis; so simple that even the simple New England student could not realize
him. No one knew enough to know how ignorant he was; how childlike;
how helpless before the relative complexity of a school. As an animal the
Southerner seemed to have every advantage, but even as an animal he
steadily lost ground.

    . . . Strictly, the Southerner had no mind; he had temperament. He
was not a scholar; he had no intellectual training; he could not analyze
an idea, and he could not even conceive of admitting two.

                         HENRY ADAMS, *The Education of Henry Adams*

To work industriously and steadily, especially under directions from another man, is, in the Southern tongue, to "work like a nigger;" and, from
childhood, the one thing in their condition which has made life valuable
to the mass of whites has been that the niggers are yet their inferiors. It is
this habit of considering themselves of a privileged class, and of disdaining something which they think beneath them, that is deemed to be the
chief blessing of slavery. It is termed "high tone," "high spirit," and is
supposed to give great military advantages to those who possess it. It

should give advantages of some sort, for its disadvantages are inexpressibly great.

FREDERICK LAW OLMSTED, *The Cotton Kingdom*, 1861

Perhaps you know that with us of the younger generation in the South, since the war pretty much of the whole of life has been merely not dying.

SIDNEY LANIER

Yesterday, about 4 P.M., the assembled wisdom of the State, whose achievements are illustrated on that theater, issued forth from the State House. About three-quarters of the crowd belonged to the African race. . . .

Here, then, is the outcome, the ripe, perfected fruit of the boasted civilization of the South, after two hundred years of experience. A white community, that had gradually risen from small beginnings, till it grew into wealth, culture, and refinement, and became accomplished in all the arts of civilization; that successfully asserted its resistance to a foreign tyranny by deeds of conspicuous valor, which achieved liberty and independence through the fire and tempest of civil war, and illustrated itself in the councils of the nation by orators and statesmen worthy of any age or nation—such a community is then reduced to this. It lies prostrate in the dust, ruled over by this strange conglomerate, gathered from the ranks of its own servile population. It is the spectacle of a society suddenly turned bottom-side up. The wealth, the intelligence, the culture, the wisdom of the State, have broken through the crust of that social volcano on which they were contentedly reposing, and have sunk out of sight, consumed by the subterranean fires they had with such temerity braved and defied.

In the place of this old aristocratic society stands the rude form of the most ignorant democracy that mankind ever saw, invested with the functions of government. It is the dregs of the population habilitated in the robes of their intelligent predecessors, and asserting over them the rule of ignorance and corruption, through the inexorable machinery of a majority of numbers. It is barbarism overwhelming civilization by physical force. It is the slave rioting in the halls of his master, and putting that master under his feet. And, though it is done without malice and without vengeance, it is nevertheless none the less completely and absolutely done. Let us approach nearer and take a closer view. We will enter the House of Representatives. Here sit one hundred and twenty-four members. Of these, twenty-three are white men, representing the remains of the old civilization. These are good-looking, substantial citizens. They are men of

weight and standing in the communities they represent. They are all from
the hill country. The frosts of sixty and seventy winters whiten the heads
of some of them. There they sit, grim and silent. They feel themselves to
be but loose stones, thrown in to partially obstruct a current they are
powerless to resist. They say little and do little as the days go by. They
simply watch the rising tide, and mark the progressive steps of the inun-
dation. They hold their places reluctantly. They feel themselves to be in
some sort martyrs, bound stoically to suffer in behalf of that still great
element in the State whose prostrate fortunes are becoming the sport of
an unpitying Fate. Grouped in a corner of the commodious and well-
furnished chamber, they stolidly survey the noisy riot that goes on in the
great black Left and Center, where the business and debates of the House
are conducted, and where sit the strange and extraordinary guides of the
fortunes of a once proud and haughty State. In this crucial trial of his
pride, his manhood, his prejudices, his spirit, it must be said of the Southern Bourbon of the Legislature that he comports himself with a dignity,
a reserve, and a decorum, that command admiration. He feels that the
iron hand of Destiny is upon him. He is gloomy, disconsolate, hopeless.
The gray heads of this generation openly profess that they look for no
relief. They see no way of escape. The recovery of influence, of position,
of control in the State, is felt by them to be impossible. They accept their
position with a stoicism that promises no reward here or hereafter. They
are the types of a conquered race. They staked all and lost all. Their
lives remain, their property and their children do not. War, emancipation,
and grinding taxation, have consumed them. Their struggle now is against
complete confiscation. They endure, and wait for the night.

JAMES S. PIKE, *The Prostrate State: South Carolina Under
Negro Government,* 1873

The New South is enamored of her new work. Her soul is stirred with the
breath of a new life. The light of a grander day is falling fair on her face.
She is thrilling with the consciousness of growing power and prosperity.
As she stands upright, full-statured and equal among the people of the
earth, breathing the keen air and looking out upon the expanding horizon,
she understands that her emancipation came because in the inscrutable
wisdom of God her honest purpose was crossed and her brave armies
beaten.

HENRY W. GRADY, "The New South," speech, 1886

Young feller, you will never appreciate the potentialities of the English language until you have heard a Southern mule driver search the soul of a mule.

OLIVER WENDELL HOLMES, JR.

The South is tired of the dark.

JONATHAN DANIELS

Too little is understood about social momentum as a force in human affairs; I really think we have it down here.

DAVID E. LILIENTHAL, when director of T.V.A.

A gentleman who would rather commit adultery than mention the word before a lady.

ELLEN GLASGOW, defining a Southern Colonel

That, without any fear of succeeding, the intrepid native Virginian will dauntlessly attempt to conceal his superiority to everybody else, remains a tribal virtue which has not escaped the comment of anthropologists.

JAMES BRANCH CABELL, Let Me Lie, "Is of Southern Ladies," 1947

These people are too lazy to entertain a hope.

ANON., said of the natives of the Mississippi bottoms

Mississippi will drink wet and vote dry—so long as any citizen can stagger to the polls.

WILL ROGERS

Change the name of Arkansaw? Hell, No! The man who would change the name of Arkansaw, by gosh, would use the meridian of longitude and the parallel of latitude for a seine and drag the Atlantic for whales. You may put your hand on the sun's face and make it night; bite a piece out of the moon and hurry the seasons; shake yourself and rumble the mountains; but, sir, you will never change the name of Arkansaw!

ANON. Sometimes attributed to Senator James Kimbrough Jones, during an argument in the Senate concerning the pronunciation of the last syllable of the state's name.

I just heard about a man in Oklahoma who went to a theatre where, for fifteen cents, he got two feature pictures, a Mickey Mouse, a newsreel, and two sets of dishes, and then demanded his money back because he didn't strike oil under his seat.

HOWARD DIETZ

Here in Texas maybe we got into the habit of confusing bigness with greatness.

EDNA FERBER, *Giant,* 1953

When in New York ah only dance at the Cotton Club. The only dance ah do is the Virginia reel. The only train ah ride is the Chattanooga Choo-Choo. When ah pass Grant's Tomb ah shut both eyes. Ah never go to the Yankee Stadium. Ah won't even go to the Polo Grounds unless a southpaw's pitchin'.

"SENATOR CLAGHORN," on Fred Allen's radio program, quoted in editorial in Richmond *Times-Dispatch*

WESTERNERS

You have no authority to throw the rights and properties of this people into the "hotch-potch" with the wild men on the Missouri, nor with the mixed, though more responsible race of Anglo-Hispano-Gallo-Americans who bask on the sands in the mouth of the Mississippi. . . . Do you suppose the people of the Northern and Atlantic States will, or ought to, look with patience and see Representatives and Senators from the Red River and Missouri pouring themselves upon this and the other floor, managing the concerns of a seaboard fifteen hundred miles, at least, from their residence?

JOSIAH QUINCY, speech in the House objecting to admitting Alabama into the Union, 1819

It is good for a man to be shifty in a new country.

SIMON SUGGS, c. 1846

Pike's Peak or Bust.

Slogan of gold seekers after discovery of gold near Pike's Peak, Colorado, 1858

The cowards never started and the weak ones died by the way.

Slogan of the Society of California

Bring Me Men to Match My Mountains.

Inscription in the State Library, Sacramento, California

To feel the importance of the Pacific Railroad, to measure the urgency of its early completion, to become impatient with government and contractor at every delay in the work, you must come across the Plains and Mountains to the Pacific Coast. Then you will see half a continent waiting for its vivifying influences. You will witness a boundless agriculture, fickle and hesitating for lack of the regular markets this would give. You will find mineral wealth, immeasurable, locked up, wastefully worked, or gambled away, until this shall open it to abundant labor, cheap capital, wood, water, science, ready oversight, steadiness of production. . . . You will find the world's commerce with India and China eagerly awaiting its opportunities. . . . It is touching to remember that between Plains and Pacific, in country and on coast, on the Columbia, on the Colorado, through all our long journey, the first question asked of us by every man and woman we have met,—whether rich or poor, high or humble,—has been, "When do you think the Pacific Railroad will be done?"

SAMUEL BOWLES, Across the Continent, 1865

The two trains pulled up facing each other, each crowded with workmen who sought advantageous positions to witness the ceremonies and literally covered the cars. The officers and invited guests formed on each side of the track, leaving it open to the south. . . . Prayer was offered; a number of spikes were driven in the two adjoining rails, each of the prominent persons present taking a hand, but very few hitting the spikes, to the great amusement of the crowd. . . . The engineers ran up their locomotives until they touched, the engineer upon each engine breaking a bottle of champagne upon the other one, and thus the two roads were wedded into one great trunk line from the Atlantic to the Pacific.

GRENVILLE M. DODGE, How We Built the Union Pacific.
The two lines met on May 10, 1869, at Promontory Point,
Utah.

In a little while all interest was taken up in stretching our necks and watching for the "pony rider"—the fleet messenger who sped across the continent from St. Joe to Sacramento, carrying letters nineteen hundred

miles in eight days! Think of that for perishable horse and human flesh
and blood to do! The pony-rider was usually a little bit of a man, brimful
of spirit and endurance. No matter what time of the day or night his
watch came, and no matter whether it was winter or summer, raining,
snowing, hailing, or sleeting, or whether his "beat" was a level straight
road or a crazy trail over mountain crags and precipices, or whether it
led through peaceful regions or regions that swarmed with hostile Indians,
he must be always ready to leap into the saddle and be off like the wind!
There was no idling-time for a pony-rider on duty. He rode fifty miles
without stopping, by daylight, moonlight, starlight, or through the blackness of darkness—just as it happened. He rode a splendid horse that was
born for a racer and fed and lodged like a gentleman; kept him at his
utmost speed for ten miles, and then, as he came crashing up to the station
where stood two men holding fast a fresh, impatient steed, the transfer of
rider and mailbag was made in the twinkling of an eye, and away flew
the eager pair and were out of sight before the spectator could get hardly
the ghost of a look. Both rider and horse went "flying light." The rider's
dress was thin, and fitted close; he wore a "roundabout," and a skull-cap,
and tucked his pantaloons into his boot-tops like a race-rider. He carried
no arms—he carried nothing that was not absolutely necessary, for even
the postage on his literary freight was worth *five dollars a letter*. He got
but little frivolous correspondence to carry—his bag had business letters
in it, mostly. His horse was stripped of all unnecessary weight, too. He
wore a little wafer of a racing saddle, and no visible blanket. He wore
light shoes, or none at all. The little flat mail-pockets strapped under the
rider's thighs would each hold about the bulk of a child's primer. They
held many and many an important business chapter and newspaper letter,
but these were written on paper as airy and thin as gold-leaf, nearly, and
thus bulk and weight were economized. The stage-coach traveled about a
hundred to a hundred and twenty-five miles a day (twenty-four hours),
the pony-rider about two hundred and fifty. There were about eighty
pony-riders in the saddle all the time, night and day, stretching in a long,
scattering procession from Missouri to California, forty flying eastward,
and forty toward the west, and among them making four hundred gallant
horses earn a stirring livelihood and see a deal of scenery every single day
in the year.

We had had a consuming desire, from the beginning, to see a pony-
rider, but somehow or other all that passed us and all that met us managed to streak by in the night, and so we heard only a whiz and a hail,
and the swift phantom of the desert was gone before we could get our
heads out of the windows. But now we were expecting one along every

moment and would see him in broad daylight. Presently the driver exclaims:

"Here he comes!"

Every neck is stretched farther and every eye strained wider. Away across the endless dead level of the prairie a black speck appears against the sky, and it is plain that it moves. Well, I should think so! In a second or two it becomes a horse and rider, rising and falling, rising and falling— sweeping toward us nearer and nearer—growing more and more distinct, more and more sharply defined—nearer and still nearer, and the flutter of the hoofs comes faintly to the ear—another instant a whoop and a hurrah from our upper deck, a wave of the rider's hand, but no reply, and man and horse burst past our excited faces and go swinging away like a belated fragment of a storm!

So sudden is it all and so like a flash of unreal fancy that, but for the flake of white foam left quivering and perishing on a mail sack after the vision had flashed by and disappeared, we might have doubted whether we had seen any actual horse and man at all, maybe.

SAMUEL L. CLEMENS ("MARK TWAIN"), *Roughing It*

The law west of the Pecos.

ROY BEAN, sign over saloon in West Texas, 1880's

Utah is the only place in the world where Jews are Gentiles.

Utah saying. Non-Mormons are called Gentiles.

East is East, and West is San Francisco. . . . Californians are a race of people; they are not merely inhabitants of a state.

WILLIAM SIDNEY PORTER ("O. HENRY")

The people [in Indiana] are gentle and easy spoken . . . all very sweet and kind Americans. But I can feel an *intolerance* in the air. We are *freer* in the East, and say what we think. In the West, I should be first mobbed with praise and then, if I differed, with rotten eggs. People are *freer from West to East.* In the West they are all terrible drinkers—they must be topers or temperance, just as they must be saints or sinners. People are *free* only as they are *rude* here.

WILLIAM DEAN HOWELLS, letter to his wife, 1899

I come from a State that raises corn and cotton and cockleburs and Democrats, and frothy eloquence neither convinces nor satisfies me. I am from Missouri. You have got to show me.

WILLARD D. VANDIVER, speech, 1899

Our shepherd is a queer character and hard to place in this wilderness. His bed is a hollow made in red dry-rot punky dust beside a log which forms a portion of the south wall of the corral. Here he lies with his wonderful everlasting clothing on, wrapped in a red blanket, breathing not only the dust of the decayed wood but also that of the corral, as if determined to take ammoniacal snuff all night after chewing tobacco all day. Following the sheep he carries a heavy six-shooter swung from his belt on one side and his luncheon on the other. The ancient cloth in which the meat, fresh from the frying-pan, is tied, serves as a filter through which the clear fat and gravy juices drip down on his right hip and leg in clustering stalactites. This oleaginous formation is soon broken up, however, and diffused and rubbed evenly into his scanty apparel, by sitting down, rolling over, crossing his legs while resting on logs, etc., making shirt and trousers watertight and shiny. His trousers, in particular, have become so adhesive with the mixed fat and resin that pine needles, thin flakes and fibers of bark, hair, mica scales, and minute grains of quartz, hornblende, etc., feathers, seed wings, moth and butterfly wings, legs and antennae of innumerable insects, or even whole insects such as the small beetles, moths, and mosquitoes, with flower petals, pollen dust, and indeed bits of all plants, animals, and minerals of the region adhere to them and are safely embedded, so that though far from being a naturalist he collects fragmentary specimens of everything and becomes richer than he knows. His specimens are kept passably fresh, too, by the purity of the air and the resiny bituminous beds into which they are pressed. Man is a microcosm, at least our shepherd is, or rather his trousers. These precious overalls are never taken off, and nobody knows how old they are, though one may guess by their thickness and concentric structure. Instead of wearing thin they wear thick, and in their stratification have no small geological significance.

JOHN MUIR, *My First Summer in the Sierra*, 1911

I insist that the Hoosier is different mentally and spiritually to the average American. He is softer, less sophisticated, more poetic. . . . He dreams a lot. He likes to play in simple ways. He is not as grasping as other Americans. . . . That may be due to the fact that he is not practical, being as

poetic and good natured as he is. . . . In a crude way, perhaps, he has
the temperament of the artist.

THEODORE DREISER, *A Hoosier Holiday*, 1916

The West, at bottom, is a form of society, rather than an area.

FREDERICK JACKSON TURNER, *The Frontier in American
History*, 1920

Other nations have been rich and powerful, but the United States has
believed that it has an original contribution to make to the history of
society by the production of a self-determining, self-restrained, intelligent
democracy. It is in the Middle West that society has formed on lines least
like Europe. It is here, if anywhere, that American democracy will make
its stand against the tendency to adjust to a European type.

FREDERICK JACKSON TURNER, *Ibid.*

I come from Indiana, the home of more first-rate second-class men than
any state in the Union.

THOMAS RILEY MARSHALL, *Recollections*

The western land, nervous under the beginning change. The Western
States, nervous as horses before a thunderstorm. The great owners, nervous, sensing a change, knowing nothing of the nature of the change. The
great owners, striking at the immediate thing, the widening government,
the growing labor unity; striking at new taxes, at plans; not knowing
these things are results, not causes. Results, not causes; results, not causes.
The causes lie deep and simply—the causes are a hunger in the stomach,
multiplied a million times; a hunger in a single soul, hunger for joy and
some security, multiplied a million times; muscles and mind aching to
grow, to work, to create, multiplied a million times. The last clear definite
function of man—muscles aching to work, minds aching to create beyond
the single need—this is man. To build a wall, to build a house, a dam,
and in the wall and house and dam to put something of Manself, and to
Manself take back something of the wall, the house, the dam; to take
hard muscles from the lifting, to take the clear lines and form from conceiving. For man, unlike any other thing organic or inorganic in the
universe, grows beyond his work, walks up the stairs of his concepts,
emerges ahead of his accomplishments. This you may say of man—when
theories change and crash, when schools, philosophies, when narrow dark
alleys of thought, national, religious, economic, grow and disintegrate,

man reaches, stumbles forward, painfully, mistakenly sometimes. Having stepped forward, he may slip back, but only half a step, never the full step back. This you may say and know it and know it. And this you can know —fear the time when Manself will not suffer and die for a concept, for this one quality is the foundation of Manself, and this one quality is man, distinctive in the universe.

JOHN STEINBECK, *The Grapes of Wrath,* 1939

"It wasn't Indians that were important, nor adventures, nor even getting out there. It was a whole bunch of people made into one big crawling beast. . . . It was westering and westering. Every man wanted something for himself, but the big beast that was all of them wanted only westering. . . . When we saw the mountains at last, we cried—all of us. But it wasn't getting here that mattered, it was movement and westering.

"We carried life out here and set it down the way those ants carry eggs. And I was the leader. The westering was as big as God, and the slow steps that made the movement piled up until the continent was crossed.

"Then we came down to the sea, and it was done."

"Maybe I could lead the people some day," Jody said.

The old man smiled. "There's no place to go. There's the ocean to stop you. There's a line of old men along the shore hating the ocean because it stopped them."

"In boats, I might, sir."

"No place to go, Jody. Every place is taken. But that's not the worst— no, not the worst. Westering has died out of the people. Westering isn't a hunger any more. It's all done."

JOHN STEINBECK, *The Red Pony,* "The Leader of the People"

This is the most fabulous place in the world. Anywhere else—*pouf,* I would not go. But this is different. Las Vegas is the only gay place left in the world. This is how Paris used to be before the war.

MARLENE DIETRICH, before taking three-week engagement in Las Vegas hotel at $30,000 a week

II. Where We Live: a Look at the Country

THINKING CONTINENTALLY

•

Not a place upon earth might be so happy as America. Her situation is remote from all the wrangling world, and she has nothing to do but to trade with them.

THOMAS PAINE, *The American Crisis*, 1776

Learn to think continentally.

ALEXANDER HAMILTON

Fifty-four Forty or Fight.

Attributed to WILLIAM ALLEN, 1844, re Canadian boundary of Oregon Territory

Our manifest destiny is to overspread the continent allotted by Providence for the free development of our yearly multiplying millions.

JOHN LOUIS O'SULLIVAN, 1845

In America the geography is sublime, but the men are not.

RALPH WALDO EMERSON, *Conduct of Life*, "Considerations by the Way"

A nation may be said to consist of its territory, its people, and its laws. The territory is the only part which is of certain durability. "One generation passeth away and another generation cometh, but the earth abideth forever." It is of the first importance to duly consider and estimate this ever-enduring part. That portion of the earth's surface which is owned and inhabited by the people of the United States is well adapted to be the home of one national family, and it is not well adapted for two or more. Its vast extent and its variety of climate and productions are of advantage in this age for one people, whatever they might have been in former ages. Steam, telegraphs, and intelligence have brought these to be an advantageous combination for one united people.

ABRAHAM LINCOLN, Annual Message to Congress, December 1, 1862

Seward's Folly.

> Phrase used in criticism of the government's purchase of
> Alaska, 1867

In the United States there is more space where nobody is than where
anybody is.

This is what makes America what it is.

GERTRUDE STEIN, *The Geographical History of America*

One of the facts which define the United States is that its national and
its imperial boundaries are the same. Another is that it is a political unit
which occupies a remarkably coherent geographical unit of continental
extent. The two facts are not discrete but inseparably related, and they
have affected all the other facts that go to define the United States. And
they cannot be separated from a feeling which, historically, the American
people have always had, a feeling that properly they must become what
they have become, a single society occupying the continental unit. That
feeling was a powerful force in the creation of the American nation and
the American empire. From the first coming of Europeans to North
America the continental reality, whether understood or misunderstood,
felt as the wilderness beyond the trading posts and settlements, helped to
shape the experience of men and societies.

BERNARD DEVOTO, *The Course of Empire,* 1952

The way to see America is from a lower berth about two in the morning.
You've just left a station—it was the jerk of pulling out that woke you—
and you raise the curtain a bit between thumb and forefinger to look out.
You are in the middle of Kansas or Arizona, in the middle of the space
where the freight cars spend the night and the men drink coffee out of
cans. Then comes the signal tower, some bushes, a few shacks and—
nothing. You see the last blue switch-light on the next track, and beyond
is America—dark and grassy, or sandy, or rocky—and no one there.
Nothing but the irrational universe with you in the center trying to reason
it out. It's only ten, fifteen minutes since you've left a thriving town but
life has already been swallowed up in that ocean of matter which is and
will remain as wild as it was made.

Come daylight, the fear vanishes but not the awe or the secret pleasure.

JACQUES BARZUN, *God's Country and Mine,* 1954

A CLOSER VIEW

•

THE EAST

The East is where trees come between you and the sky.

Western saying

There is a sumptuous variety about the New England weather that com-pels the stranger's admiration—and regret. The weather is always doing something there; always attending strictly to business; always getting up new designs and trying them on the people to see how they will go. But it gets through more business in spring than in any other season. In the spring I have counted one hundred and thirty-six different kinds of weather inside of four-and-twenty hours.

Samuel L. Clemens ("Mark Twain"), "The Weather," speech, New York, 1876

If you don't like the weather in New England, just wait a few minutes.

Samuel L. Clemens ("Mark Twain")

The most serious charge which can be brought against New England is not Puritanism but February.

Joseph Wood Krutch, The Twelve Seasons, 1949

Once, when Joe [the Indian guide] had called again, and we were listen-ing for moose, we heard, come faintly echoing, or creeping from afar, through the moss-clad aisles, a dull, dry, rushing sound with a solid core to it, yet as if half-smothered under the grasp of the luxuriant and fungus-like forest, like the shutting of a door in some distant entry of the damp and shaggy wilderness. If we had not been there, no mortal had heard it. When we asked Joe in a whisper what it was, he answered, "Tree fall."

Henry David Thoreau, The Maine Woods, "Chesuncook"

To my mind Maine is the most beautiful state we have in this country, but even more appealing is its homeliness.

Booth Tarkington

Men hang out their signs indicative of their respective trades: shoemakers hang out a gigantic shoe; jewelers, a monster watch; and the dentist hangs out a gold tooth; but up in the mountains of New Hampshire, God Almighty has hung out a sign to show that there He makes men.

DANIEL WEBSTER, "The Old Man of the Mountain"

Boston is a state of mind.

ANON., 1836

If you hear an owl hoot "To whom" instead of "To who," you can make up your mind he was born and educated in Boston.

ANON.

We say the cows laid out Boston. Well, there are worse surveyors.

RALPH WALDO EMERSON, *Conduct of Life,* "Wealth"

There are not ten men in Boston equal to Shakespeare.

Attributed to unnamed Bostonian by W. E. Gladstone

Only Bostonians can thoroughly understand Bostonians and thoroughly sympathize with the inconsequences of the Boston mind.

HENRY ADAMS, letter

The painful truth is that all of my New England generation, counting the half-century, 1820–1870, were in actual fact only one mind and nature; the individual was a facet of Boston. We knew each other to the last nervous center, and feared each other's knowledge. We looked through each other like microscopes. There was absolutely nothing in us that we did not understand merely by looking in the eye. There was hardly a difference even in depth, for Harvard College and Unitarianism kept us all shallow. We knew nothing—no! but really nothing! of the world. One cannot exaggerate the profundity of ignorance of Story in becoming a sculptor, or Sumner in becoming a statesman, or Emerson in becoming a philosopher. Story and Sumner and Emerson and Alcott, Lowell and Longfellow, Hillard, Winthrop, Motley, Prescott, and all the rest, were the same mind,—and so, poor worm!—was I!

HENRY ADAMS, letter to Henry James, 1903, on reading the latter's biography of William Wetmore Story

A Boston man is the east wind made flesh.

> Attributed to THOMAS GOLD APPLETON

Boston has opened and kept open more turnpikes that lead straight to free thought and free speech and free deeds than any other city of live or dead men.

> OLIVER WENDELL HOLMES

Boston State-House is the hub of the solar system. You couldn't pry that out of a Boston man if you had the tire of all creation straightened out for a crowbar.

> OLIVER WENDELL HOLMES, *The Autocrat of the Breakfast Table,* 1858

Marriage . . . is a damnably serious business, particularly around Boston.

> J. P. MARQUAND, *The Late George Apley,* 1937

Boston has carried the practice of hypocrisy to the nth degree of refinement, grace and failure.

> LINCOLN STEFFENS

[Newport] is, perhaps, the last place in the whole world which is known as standing for something.

> ROBERT R. YOUNG

I like to visit New York, but I wouldn't live there if you gave it to me.

> Popular saying

The Renowned and Ancient City of Gotham.

> WASHINGTON IRVING, chapter heading, *Salmagundi,* Wednesday, November 11, 1807. This is the earliest reference to New York City as Gotham. The proverb concerning the three wise men of Gotham probably refers to a village in Nottinghamshire.

Living in Brooklyn or New York city from this time forward my life, then, and still more the following years, was curiously identified with Fulton ferry, already becoming the greatest of its sort in the world for general importance, volume, variety, rapidity, and picturesqueness. Almost daily ('50 to '60) I cross'd on the boats, often up in the pilot-houses where I could get a full sweep, absorbing shows, accompaniments, surroundings. What oceanic currents, eddies, underneath—the great tides of humanity also, with ever-shifting movements! Indeed, I have always had a passion for ferries; to me they afford inimitable, streaming, never-failing, living poems. The river and bay scenery, all about New York island, any time of a fine day—the hurrying, splashing sea-tides—the changing panorama of steamers, all sizes, often a string of big ones outward bound to distant ports—the myriad of white-sail'd schooners, sloops, skiffs, and the marvellously beautiful yachts—the majestic Sound boats as they rounded the Battery and came along towards 5, afternoon, eastward bound—the prospect off toward Staten Island, or down the Narrows, or the other way up the Hudson—what refreshment of spirit such sights and experiences gave me years ago (and many a time since)!

> WALT WHITMAN, *Specimen Days,* "My Passion for Ferries"

There is more law at the end of a policeman's nightstick than in a decision of the Supreme Court.

> Of New York's slum districts after the Civil War

Carry out your own dead.

> WILSON MIZNER, sign in the Hotel Rand, New York, 1907, which he managed

In dress, habits, manners, provincialism, routine and narrowness, he acquired that charming insolence, that irritating completeness, that sophisticated crassness, that overbalanced poise that makes the Manhattan gentleman so delightfully small in his greatness.

> WILLIAM SIDNEY PORTER ("O. HENRY"), *Voice of the City,* "Defeat of the City"

Well, little old Noisyville-on-the-Subway is good enough for me.

> WILLIAM SIDNEY PORTER ("O. HENRY"), *The Four Million*

We must have a concrete idea of anything, even if it be an imaginary idea, before we can comprehend it. Now, I have a mental picture of John Doe that is as clear as a steel engraving. His eyes are weak blue; he wears a brown vest and a shiny black serge coat. He stands always in the sunshine chewing something; and he keeps half-shutting his pocket knife and opening it again with his thumb. And, if the Man Higher Up is ever found, take my assurance for it, he will be a large, pale man with blue wristlets

showing under his cuffs, and he will be sitting to have his shoes polished
within sound of a bowling alley, and there will be somewhere about him
turquoises.

> WILLIAM SIDNEY PORTER ("O. HENRY"), *Ibid.,* "Man
> About Town"

Restless, shifting, fugacious as time itself is a certain vast bulk of the population of the red brick district of the lower West Side. They flit from
furnished room to furnished room, transients forever—transients in abode,
transients in heart and mind. They sing "Home, Sweet Home" in ragtime; they carry their *lares et penates* in a bandbox; their vine is entwined
about a picture hat; a rubber plant is their fig tree.

   Hence the houses of this district, having had a thousand dwellers, should
have a thousand tales to tell, mostly dull ones no doubt; but it would be
strange if there could not be found a ghost or two in the wake of all those
vagrant guests.

> WILLIAM SIDNEY PORTER ("O. HENRY"), *Ibid.,* "The Fur-
> nished Room"

What else can you expect from a town that's shut off from the world by
the ocean on one side and New Jersey on the other?

> WILLIAM SIDNEY PORTER ("O. HENRY"), *The Gentle
> Grafter,* "A Tempered Wind"

Far below and around lay the city like a ragged purple dream, the wonderful, cruel, enchanting, bewildering, fatal, great city.

> WILLIAM SIDNEY PORTER ("O. HENRY")

Baghdad-on-the-Subway.

> WILLIAM SIDNEY PORTER ("O. HENRY")

The aspect the power wears then is indescribable; it is the power of the
most extravagant of cities, rejoicing, as with the voice of the morning, in
its might, its fortune, its unsurpassable conditions, and imparting to every
object and element, to the motion and expression of every floating, hurrying, panting thing, to the throb of ferries and tugs, to the plash of waves
and the play of winds and the glint of lights and the shrill of whistles and
the quality and authority of breeze-born cries—all, practically, a diffused,
wasted clamor of *detonations*—something of its sharp free accent and,
above all, of its sovereign sense of being "backed" and able to back. The

universal *applied* passion struck me as shining unprecedentedly out of the composition; in the bigness and bravery and insolence, especially, of everything that rushed and shrieked; in the air as of a great intricate frenzied dance, half merry, half desperate, or at least half defiant, performed on the huge watery floor. This appearance of the bold lacing-together, across the waters, of the scattered members of the monstrous organism—lacing as by the ceaseless play of an enormous system of steam-shuttles or electric bobbins (I scarce know what to call them), commensurate in form with their infinite work—does perhaps more than anything else to give the pitch of the vision of energy. One has the sense that the monster grows and grows, flinging abroad its loose limbs even as some unmannered young giant at his "larks," and that the binding stitches must forever fly further and faster and draw harder; the future complexity of the web, all under the sky and over the sea, becoming thus that of some colossal set of clockworks, some steel-souled machine-room of brandished arms and hammering fists and opening and closing jaws. The immeasurable bridges are but as the horizontal sheaths of pistons working at high pressure, day and night, and subject, one apprehends with perhaps inconsistent gloom, to certain, to fantastic, to merciless multiplication. In the light of this apprehension indeed the breezy brightness of the Bay puts on the semblance of the vast white page that awaits beyond any other perhaps the black overscoring of science.

HENRY JAMES, New York Harbor, from *The American Scene,* 1907

New York is not a civilization; it is a railroad station.

JOHN JAY CHAPMAN

The present in New York is so powerful that the past is lost. There is no past. Not a bookshelf, nor a cornice, nor a sign, nor a face, nor a type of mind endures for a generation, and a New York boy who goes away to boarding school returns to a new world at each vacation.

JOHN JAY CHAPMAN, letter, 1909

The dyed-in-the-wool New Yorker professes to hate the city of his adoption. Yet he would not live anywhere else. The furore of its high pressure living gets into the blood. The famous George M. Cohan, the actor, used to carol: "When you are away from old Broadway you are only camping out." That is the New Yorker's credo.

He knows that New York cannot be hurt by denouncing it. The people who love it most berate it the loudest.

O. O. McIntyre

There is this to be said for New York City; it is the one densely inhabited locality—with the possible exception of Hell—that has absolutely not a trace of local pride.

Irvin S. Cobb

New Yorkers are nice about giving you street directions; in fact, they seem quite proud of knowing where they are themselves.

Katharine Brush

In the midst of life we are in Brooklyn.

Oliver Herford

One hears the hoarse notes of the great ships in the river, and one remembers suddenly the princely girdle of proud, potent tides that bind the city, and suddenly New York blazes like a magnificent jewel in its fit setting of sea, and earth and stars.

Thomas Wolfe

. . . New York City, the incomparable, the brilliant star city of cities, the forty-ninth state, the Cyclopean paradox, the inferno with no out-of-bounds, the supreme expression of both the miseries and the splendors of contemporary civilization, the Macedonia of the United States. It meets the most severe test that may be applied to definition of a metropolis—it stays up all night. But also it becomes a small town when it rains.

John Gunther, Inside U.S.A.

The thing which in the subway is called congestion is highly esteemed in the night spots as intimacy.

Simeon Strunsky, No Mean City, 1944

I saw the skyline grow, and I saw the city grow, and sometimes I wonder if it was worth the price we paid. In those days we did not need interracial movements or good-will groups. Then a neighborhood meant so much.

Here in the most cosmopolitan community since the beginning of time, a city composed of sons and daughters of every one of the forty-eight states, and with men and women from every country in the civilized

world, we worked together. Here where there were and are more Irishmen than in Dublin, more Italians than in Rome, more Germans than in
any other city than Berlin, and more Jews than in Palestine—here we
lived together in peace, like one great family, and should so live today
and tomorrow.

We all went to school together, went to work together, and to the
theatre and to the fields of sport—with little rancor, no real hatred. We
lived like human beings, who asked only the opportunity to work out our
earthly existence and worship our God according to the dictates of our
conscience.

This I hold to be humanity. This is democracy. This was New York of
the yon days.

JAMES J. WALKER, speech, 1946

The most complicated and expensive thing ever built is Manhattan Island.
Under its asphalt skin are 12,100 miles of power cable, more than four
million miles of telephone wire, 27 miles of pneumatic tubes to speed
mail at thirty miles per hour, 54 miles of steam mains that heat a seventh
of the island's 67,601 structures, 1,200 miles of gas mains, 774 miles of
cavernous water mains (plus a water tunnel) to supply what the city
needs daily, and 560 miles of sewer to carry it off.

ANON., *Life*

When I was a boy, Fourteenth Street was where Twenty-third Street is
now, and Samuel J. Tilden and I used to play marbles on the lot where
the Grand Opera House still stood. Governor Lovelace brought the first
marble from England to this country on August 17, 1668, and gave it to
my Great-Aunt Amelia van Santvoort, of whom he was enamored. She
had several copies made, and Sam Tilden and I used to amuse ourselves
with them.

I remember the Sunday afternoons when Governor Lovelace would
com to tea at our house, although I could not have been much more
than a tad at the time. I can hear the rich clanking of the silver harness
as his magnificent equipage, with its twelve ebony outriders in cerise bom-
bazine, rolled up to our house at No. 239 East 174th Street. I was the
envy of all the kids on the block because I was allowed to sit in the carriage while the Governor went in to take tea with Great-Aunt Amelia.
I always chose Ada Rehan to sit beside me. She was a little golden-haired
thing at the time and none of us dreamed she would one day go out from
East 174th Street and shoot President Garfield.

Great-Aunt Amelia was a dowager of the old school. You don't see many of her kind around New York today, probably because the old school was torn down a good many years ago; its site is now occupied by Central Park. People used to say that the Queen, as they called Great-Aunt Amelia, looked more like my Aunt Theodosia than my Aunt Theodosia did.

But Aunt Caroline was really the great lady of our family. I can still see her descending the staircase, dressed for the opera in silk hat, satin-lined cape, immaculate shirt, white tie, and that magnificent, purple-black beard.

"Well, boy!" she would boom at me. "Well!"

"Well, Aunt Caroline!" I would say, doing my best to boom back at her.

She would chuckle and say, "Boy, I like your spirit! Tell Grimson I said to add an extra tot of brandy to your bedtime milk."

Oh, those lollipops at Preem's, just around the corner from the corner! Mm-m-m, I can still taste them! After school, we kids would rush home and shout, "Ma, gimme a penny for a lollipop at Preem's, willya, Ma? Hey, Ma, willya?" Then we would go tease Jake Astor, the second-hand-fur dealer around the corner. I shall never forget the day Minnie Maddern Fiske swiped the mink pelt from Jake's cart and stuffed it under Bishop Potter's cope.

Miss Hattie Pumplebutt was our teacher at P.S. 67. She was a demure wisp of a woman, with white hair parted in the middle, pince-nez that were forever dropping off her nose, always some lacy collar high around her throat, and paper cuffs. We adored her. Every once in a while she would climb up on her desk, flap her arms, shout "Whee-e-e! I'm a bobo-link!," and start crowing. Or she would take off suddenly and go skipping about the tops of our desks with a dexterity and sure-footedness truly marvellous in one of her age. When we grew old enough, we were told about Miss Pumplebutt. She took dope. Well, she made history and geography far more interesting than a lot of non-sniffing teachers I have known.

One day, Jim Fisk and I played hooky from school and went to the old Haymarket on Sixth Avenue, which was then between Fifth and Seventh. We had two beers apiece and thought we were quite men about town. I dared Jim to go over and shoot Stanford White, never dreaming the chump would do it. I didn't know he was loaded. I got Hail Columbia from Father for that escapade.

Father was very strict about the aristocratic old New York ritual of the

Saturday-night bath. Every Saturday night at eight sharp we would line up: Father, Mother, Diamond Jim Brady; Mrs. Dalrymple, the housekeeper; Absentweather, the butler; Aggie, the second girl; Aggie, the third girl; Aggie, the fourth girl; and twelve of us youngsters, each one equipped with soap and a towel. At a command from Father, we would leave our mansion on East Thirtieth Street and proceed solemnly up Fifth Avenue in single file to the old reservoir, keeping a sharp eye out for Indians. Then, at a signal from Papa, in we'd go. Everyone who was anyone in New York in those days had his Saturday-night bath in the reservoir, and it was there that I first saw and fell in love with the little girl whom I later made Duchess of Marlborough.

My Grandmamma Satterthwaite was a remarkable old lady. At the age of eighty-seven she could skip rope four hundred and twenty-two consecutive times without stopping, and every boy on the block was madly in love with her. Then her father failed in the crash of '87 and in no time she was out of pigtails, had her hair up, and was quite the young lady. I never did hear what became of her.

It rather amuses me to hear the youngsters of today enthusing about the croissants, etc., at Spodetti's and the other fashionable Fifth Avenue patisseries. Why, they aren't a patch on Horan's!

Mike Horan's place was at Minetta Lane and Washington Mews, and I clearly remember my father telling a somewhat startled Walt Whitman that old Mike Horan could bend a banana in two—with his bare hands! But I never saw him do it. We kids used to stand in front of his shop for hours after school waiting for Mike to bend a banana, but he never did. I can still hear the cheerful clang of his hammer on the anvil and the acrid smell of burning hoofs from the Loveland Dance Palace, across the way on Delancey Street, which was then Grand. Then the Civil War came and the property of the Loyalists was confiscated. I still have some old Loyalist property I confiscated on that occasion. I use it for a paperweight. Old Gammer Wilberforce was a Loyalist. We used to chase her down the street, shouting "Tory!" at her. Then she would chase us up the street, shouting:

"Blaine, Blaine, James G. Blaine!
Continental liar from the State of Maine!"

or:

"Ma! Ma! Where's my Pa?"
"Gone to the White House, ha, ha ha!"

Of course, very few white people ever went to Chinatown in those days. It was not until the Honorah Totweiler case that people became aware of Chinatown. I venture to say that few persons today would recall Honorah Totweiler, yet in 1832 the Honorah Totweiler case was the sensation of the country. In one day the circulation of the elder James Gordon Bennett jumped seventy-four thousand as a result of the Totweiler case.

One sunny afternoon in the autumn of September 23, 1832, a lovely and innocent girl, twelfth of eighteen daughters of Isaac Totweiler, a mercer, and Sapphira, his wife, set out from her home in Washington Mews to return a cup of sugar—but let the elder Bennett tell the story:

It is high time [Bennett wrote] that the people of these United States were awakened to the menace in which the old liberties for which our forefathers fought and bled, in buff and blue, by day and night, at Lexington and Concord, in '75 and '76, have been placed as a result of the waste, the orgy of spending, the deliberate falsifications, the betrayal of public trust, and the attempt to set up a bureaucratic and unconstitutional dictatorship, of the current Administration in Washington. Murphy must go, and Tammany with him!

After dinner on Sundays, my Grandpa Bemis would take a nap, with the *Times,* or something, thrown over his face to keep out the glare. If he was in a good humor when he awoke, he would take us youngsters up to Dick Canfield's to play games, but as he was never in a good humor when he awoke, we never went to Dick Canfield's to play games.

Sometimes, when we kids came home from school, Mrs. Rossiter, the housekeeper, would meet us in the hall and place a warning finger on her lips. We knew what that meant. We must be on our good behavior. The wealthy Mrs. Murgatroyd was calling on Mother. We would be ushered into the Presence, Mother would tell us to stop using our sleeves as a handkerchief, and then Mrs. Murgatroyd would laugh and say, "Oh, Annie, let the poor children alone. Sure, you're only young once." Then she would lift up her skirt to the knee, fish out a huge wallet from under her stocking, and give us each $2,000,000. We loved her. Not only did she have a pair of d———d shapely stems for an old lady her age, but she was reputed to be able to carry six schooners of beer in each hand.

I shall never forget the night of the fire. It was about three o'clock in the morning when it started, in an old distaff factory on West Twelfth Street. I was awakened by the crackling. I shivered, for my brother, as usual, had all the bedclothes, and there I was, with fully three inches of snow (one inch powder, two inches crust) on my bare back. The next morning there were seven feet of snow on West Twenty-seventh Street alone. You don't get that sort of winter nowadays. That was the winter

the elder John D. Rockefeller was frozen over solid from November to
May.

On Saturdays we used to go with Great-Aunt Tib to the Eden Musee
to see the wax figure of Lillian Russell. There was a woman! They don't
build girls like her nowadays. You can't get the material, and even if you
could, the contractors and the plumbers would gyp you and substitute
shoddy.

I was six when the riots occurred. No, I was *thirty*-six. I remember
because it was the year of the famous Horace Greeley hoax, and I used
to hear my parents laughing about it. It was commonly believed that
Mark Twain was the perpetrator of the hoax, although Charles A. Dana
insisted to his dying day that it was Lawrence Godkin. At any rate, the
hoax, or "sell," originated one night at the Union League Club when
Horace chanced to remark to Boss Tweed that his (Horace's) wife was
entertaining that night. The town was agog for days, no one having the
faintest notion that the story was not on the level. Greeley even threatened Berry Wall with a libel suit.

Well, that was New York, the old New York, the New York of gaslit
streets, and sparrows (and, of course, horses), and cobblestones. The
newsboy rolled the *Youth's Companion* into a missile and threw it on
your front stoop and the postmen wore uniforms of pink velvet and made
a point of bringing everybody a letter every day.

Eheu, fugaces!—

> FRANK SULLIVAN, "The Night the Old Nostalgia Burned
> Down," *The New Yorker*, May 25, 1946

On any person who desires such queer prizes, New York will bestow the
gift of loneliness and the gift of privacy. It is this largess that accounts for
the presence within the city's walls of a considerable section of the population; for the residents of Manhattan are to a large extent strangers who
have pulled up stakes somewhere and come to town, seeking sanctuary or
fulfillment or some greater or lesser grail. The capacity to make such
dubious gifts is a mysterious quality of New York. It can destroy an individual, or it can fulfill him, depending a good deal on luck. No one
should come to New York to live unless he is willing to be lucky.

> E. B. WHITE, *Here Is New York*

The terrain of New York is such that a resident sometimes travels farther,
in the end, than a commuter. Irving Berlin's journey from Cherry Street

in the lower East Side to an apartment uptown was through an alley and was only three or four miles in length; but it was like going three times around the world.

E. B. WHITE, *Ibid.*

New York, the capital of memoranda, in touch with Calcutta, in touch with Reykjavik, and always fooling with something.

E. B. WHITE, *Ibid.*

Commuters give the city its tidal restlessness; nature gives it solidity and continuity; but the settlers give it passion.

E. B. WHITE, *Ibid.*

The subtlest change in New York is something people don't speak much about but that is in everyone's mind. The city, for the first time in its long history, is destructible. A single flight of planes no bigger than a wedge of geese can quickly end this island fantasy, burn the towers, crumble the bridges, turn the underground passages into lethal chambers, cremate the millions. The intimation of mortality is part of New York now: in the sound of jets overhead, in the black headlines of the latest edition.

All dwellers in cities must live with the stubborn fact of annihilation; in New York the fact is somewhat more concentrated because of the concentration of the city itself, and because, of all targets, New York has a certain clear priority. In the mind of whatever perverted dreamer might loose the lightning, New York must hold a steady, irresistible charm.

It used to be that the Statue of Liberty was the signpost that proclaimed New York and translated it for all the world. Today Liberty shares the role with Death. Along the East River, from the razed slaughterhouses of Turtle Bay, as though in a race with the special flight of planes, men are carving out the permanent headquarters of the United Nations—the greatest housing project of them all. In its stride, New York takes on one more interior city, to shelter, this time, all governments, and to clear the slum called war. New York is not a capital city—it is not a national capital or a state capital. But it is by way of becoming the capital of the world. The buildings, as conceived by architects, will be cigar boxes set on end. Traffic will flow in a new tunnel under First Avenue. Forty-seventh Street will be widened (and if my guess is any good, trucks will appear late at night to plant tall trees surreptitiously, their roots to mingle with the intestines of the town). Once again the city will absorb, almost without showing any sign of it, a congress of visitors. It has already shown itself capable of stashing away the United Nations—a great many of the delegates have been around town during the past couple of years, and the citizenry has hardly caught a glimpse of their coattails or their black Homburgs.

This race—this race between the destroying planes and the struggling Parliament of Man—it sticks in all our heads. The city at last perfectly illustrates both the universal dilemma and the general solution, this riddle in steel and stone is at once the perfect target and the perfect demonstration of nonviolence, of racial brotherhood, this lofty target scraping the skies and meeting the destroying planes halfway, home of all people and all nations, capital of everything, housing the deliberations by which the planes are to be stayed and their errand forestalled.

A block or two west of the new City of Man in Turtle Bay there is an old willow tree that presides over an interior garden. It is a battered tree, long suffering and much climbed, held together by strands of wire but beloved of those who know it. In a way it symbolizes the city: life under difficulties, growth against odds, sap-rise in the midst of concrete, and the steady reaching for the sun. Whenever I look at it nowadays, and feel the cold shadow of the planes, I think: "This must be saved, this particular thing, this very tree." If it were to go, all would go—this city, this mischievous and marvelous monument which not to look upon would be like death.

E. B. WHITE, Ibid.

The lusts of the flesh can be gratified anywhere; it is not this sort of license that distinguishes New York. It is, rather, a lust of the total ego for recognition, even for eminence. More than elsewhere, everybody here wants to be Somebody.

SYDNEY J. HARRIS, Strictly Personal

Coney Island: where the surf is one third water and two thirds people.

JOHN STEINBECK

I have been the more particular in this description of my journey, and shall be so of my first journey into that city, that you may in your mind compare such unlikely beginnings with the figure I have since made there. I was in my working dress, my best clothes being to come round by sea. I was dirty from my journey; my pockets were stuffed out with shirts and stockings, and I knew no soul nor where to look for lodging. I was fatigued with traveling, rowing, and want of rest; I was very hungry; and my whole cash consisted of a Dutch dollar and about a shilling in copper. The latter I gave the people of the boat for my passage, who at first refused it, on account of my rowing; but I insisted on their taking it. A man being sometimes more generous when he has but a little money than when he has plenty, perhaps through fear of being thought to have but little.

Then I walked up the street, gazing about till near the market house I met a boy with bread. I had made many a meal on bread, and inquiring where he got it, I went immediately to the baker's he directed me to, in Second Street, and asked for biscuit, intending such as we had in Boston; but they, it seems, were not made in Philadelphia. Then I asked for a threepenny loaf, and was told they had none such. So not considering or knowing the difference of money, and the greater cheapness nor the names of his bread, I bade him give me threepenny worth of any sort. He gave me, accordingly, three great puffy rolls. I was surprised at the quantity, but took it, and having no room in my pockets, walked off with a roll under each arm, and eating the other. Thus I went up Market Street as far as Fourth Street, passing by the door of Mr. Read, my future wife's father; when she, standing at the door, saw me, and thought I made, as I certainly did, a most awkward, ridiculous appearance. Then I turned and went down Chestnut Street and part of Walnut Street, eating my roll all the way, and, coming round, found myself again at Market Street wharf, near the boat I came in, to which I went for a draught of the river water; and, being filled with one of my rolls, gave the other two to a woman and her child that came down the river in the boat with us, and were waiting to go farther.

Thus refreshed, I walked again up the street, which by this time had many clean-dressed people in it, who were all walking the same way. I joined them, and thereby was led into the great meeting house of the Quakers near the market. I sat down among them, and, after looking round awhile and hearing nothing said, being very drowsy through labor and want of rest the preceding night, I fell fast asleep, and continued so till the meeting broke up, when one was kind enough to rouse me. This was, therefore, the first house I was in, or slept in, in Philadelphia.

BENJAMIN FRANKLIN, *Autobiography*

Philadelphia then wasn't a place, but a state of consanguinity, which is an absolute final condition.

HENRY JAMES

They say that the lady from Philadelphia, who is staying in town, is very wise. Suppose I go and ask her what is best to be done?

LUCRETIA P. HALE, *The Peterkin Papers*

No matter what anybody says or thinks about Washington, it is us inescapably.

JOEL SAYRE, of the National Capital

THE SOUTH

We have lived long, gentlemen, but this [the Louisiana Purchase] is the noblest work of our lives.

ROBERT R. LIVINGSTON

Cotton farming, we used to say in the South, required three items of capital equipment: a strong back, a weak mind, and immunity to sunstroke. It involved . . . three operations: cotton was planted in the spring, mortgaged in the summer, and left to rot in the fall.

J. MITCHELL MORSE

> In profound appreciation
> Of the Boll Weevil and what he has done
> As the herald of prosperity
> This monument was erected
> By the citizens of
> Enterprise, Coffee County, Alabama.

Inscription, 1930's. The South was being bled white by the one-crop system, till the weevil forced the growing of other crops.

Harry Thaw shot the wrong architect.

WILSON MIZNER, observing with distaste a Palm Beach palace designed by Joseph Urban

Miami is the only city in the world where you can tell a lie at breakfast that will come true by evening.

WILLIAM JENNINGS BRYAN, of the Florida land boom

Georgia soil is so rich that when we throw corn to the chickens, they have to catch it on the fly or eat it off the stalk.

NUNNALLY JOHNSON to Louis Bromfield

The dark and bloody ground.

ANON.; the words are the translation of the Indian name, Kentucky

The multitudes of wild pigeons in our woods are astonishing. Indeed, after having viewed them so often, and under so many circumstances, I even now feel inclined to pause, and assure myself that what I am going to relate is a fact. Yet I have seen it all. . . .

Let us . . . inspect their place of nightly rendezvous. One of these curious roosting-places, on the banks of the Green River, in Kentucky, I repeatedly visited. It was, as is always the case, in a portion of the forest where the trees were of great magnitude, and where there was little underwood. I rode through it upwards of forty miles, and, crossing it in different parts, found its average breadth to be rather more than three miles. My first view of it was about a fortnight subsequent to the period when [the pigeons] had made choice of it, and I arrived there nearly two hours before sunset. Few pigeons were then to be seen, but a great number of persons, with horses and wagons, guns and ammunition, had already established encampments on the borders. Two farmers from the vicinity of Russelsville, distant more than a hundred miles, had driven upwards of three hundred hogs to be fattened on the pigeons which were to be slaughtered. Here and there the people employed in plucking and salting what had already been secured were seen sitting in the midst of large piles of these birds. The dung lay several inches deep, covering the whole extent of the roosting-place, like a bed of snow. Many trees two feet in diameter, I observed, were broken off at no great distance from the ground; and the branches of many of the largest and tallest had given way, as if the forest had been swept by a tornado. Everything proved to me that the number of birds resorting to this part of the forest must be immense beyond conception. As the period of their arrival approached, their foes anxiously prepared to receive them. Some were furnished with iron pots containing sulphur, others with torches of pine knots, many with poles, and the rest with guns. The sun was lost to our view, yet not a pigeon had arrived. Suddenly there burst forth a general cry of, "Here they come!" The noise which they made, though yet distant, reminded me of a hard gale at sea passing through the rigging of a close-reefed vessel. As the birds arrived and passed over me, I felt a current of air which surprised me. Thousands were soon knocked down by the pole-men. The birds continued to pour in. The fires were lighted, and a mag-nificent, as well as wonderful and almost terrifying, sight presented itself. The pigeons, arriving by thousands, alighted everywhere, one above an-other, until solid masses, as large as hogsheads, were formed on the branches all around. Here and there the perches gave way under the weight with a crash, and falling to the ground, destroyed hundreds of the birds beneath, forcing down the dense groups with which every stick was loaded. It was a scene of uproar and confusion. I found it quite useless to speak, or even to shout, to those persons who were nearest to me. Even the reports of the guns were seldom heard, and I was made aware of the firing only by seeing the shooters reloading.

No one dared venture within the line of devastation. The hogs had been penned up in due time, the picking up of the dead and wounded being left for the next morning's employment. The pigeons were constantly com-ing, and it was past midnight before I perceived a decrease in the number of those that arrived. The uproar continued the whole night; and as I was anxious to know to what distance the sound reached, I sent off a man, accustomed to perambulate the forest, who, returning two hours after-wards, informed me he had heard it distinctly when three miles from the spot. Towards the approach of day, the noise in some measure subsided, long before objects were distinguishable, the pigeons began to move off in a direction quite different from that in which they had arrived the night before, and at sunset all that were able to fly had disappeared. The howlings of the wolves now reached our ears, and the foxes, lynxes, cougars, bears, raccoons, opossums, and polecats were seen sneaking off, whilst eagles, and hawks of different species, accompanied by a crowd of vultures, came to supplant them, and enjoy their share of the spoil.

> JOHN JAMES AUDUBON, *Ornithological Biography,* Vol. I.
> The passenger pigeon is now, of course, extinct.

Why sir, on the north we are bounded by the Aurora Borealis, on the east we are bounded by the rising sun, on the south we are bounded by the precession of the Equinoxes, and on the west by the Day of Judge-ment.

> ANON., *The American Joe Miller,* a Kentuckian's reply to
> the question, "What are the boundaries of the United
> States?"

Heaven is a Kentucky of a place.

> ANON., *Kentucky,* "American Guide Series"

Take of London fog 30 parts; malaria 10 parts; gas leaks 20 parts; dew-drops gathered in a brick-yard at sunrise 25 parts; odor of honeysuckle 15 parts. Mix. The mixture will give you an approximate conception of a Nashville drizzle.

> WILLIAM SIDNEY PORTER ("O. HENRY"), *Strictly Business,* "A Municipal Report"

Arkansas chiggers are red-speckled. They are small, about the size of a common Fifth Avenue flea. Anatomically speaking they are composed of nine sets of sharp teeth, a drilling tool, and a brain trained to identify men from north of the Ohio River. Though strictly carnivorous, their habitat is tree foliage, short vegetation, and reclining Yankees.

> AVANTUS GREEN, *An Epitome of Arkansas*

Texas could exist without the United States, but the United States can-not, except at very great hazard, exist without Texas.

> SAM HOUSTON

If I owned Texas and Hell, I'd rent out Texas and live in Hell.

> PHILIP H. SHERIDAN

Texas occupies all the Continent of North America except the small part set aside for the United States, Mexico, and Canada . . . and is bounded on the north by 25 or 30 states, on the east by all the oceans in the world except the Pacific . . . and on the west by the Pacific Ocean, the Milky Way, and the Sidereal Universe.

Texas is so big that people in Brownsville call the Dallas people Yan-kees, and the citizens of El Paso sneer at the citizens of Texarkana as being snobs of the effete east.

It is 150 miles farther from El Paso to Texarkana than it is from Chi-cago to New York. Fort Worth is nearer St. Paul, Minnesota, than to Brownsville. . . . The United States with Texas off would look like a three-legged Boston terrier.

The chief occupation of the people of Texas is trying to keep from making all the money in the world. . . . Texans are so proud of Texas that they cannot sleep at night. . . .

> ANON., a supposed "speech" by a visitor to the state, printed in the Texas *Almanac*

[Houston] will be the New York of the late 20th century.

> J. RUSSELL SMITH

THE MIDDLE WEST

This is the country for a man to enjoy himself: Ohio, Indiana, and the Missouri Territory; where you may see prairie sixty miles long and ten broad, not a stick nor a stone in them, at two dollars an acre, that will produce from seventy to one hundred bushels of Indian corn per acre: too rich for wheat or any other kind of grain. I measured Indian corn in Ohio State last September more than fifteen feet high, and some of the ears had from four to seven hundred grains. I believe I saw more peaches and apples rotting on the ground than would sink the British fleet. I was at many plantations in Ohio where they no more knew the number of their hogs than myself. And they have such flocks of turkeys, geese, ducks, and hens as would surprise you; they live principally upon fowls and eggs, and in summer upon apple and peach pies. The poorest family has a cow or two and some sheep and in the fall can gather as many apples and peaches as serve the year round. Good rye whiskey; apple and peach brandy, at forty cents per gallon, which I think equal to rum. Excellent cider at three dollars per barrel of thirty-three gallons, barrel included.

There is enough to spare of everything a person can desire; have not heard either man or woman speak a word against the government or the price of provisions.

The poorest families adorn the table three times a day like a wedding dinner—tea, coffee, beef, fowls, pies, eggs, pickles, good bread; and their favorite beverage is whiskey or peach brandy. Say, is it so in England?

If you knew the difference between this country and England you would need no persuading to leave it and come hither. It abounds with game and deer; I often see ten or fifteen together; turkeys in abundance, weighing from eighteen to twenty-four pounds. The rivers abound with ducks and fish. There are some elk and bears. We have no hares, but swarms of rabbits: the woods are full of turtledoves, and eight or nine kinds of woodpeckers. Robin redbreast the size of your pigeon.

> SAMUEL CRABTREE, letter to his brother, 1818

Illinois is heaven for men and horses, but hell for women and oxen.

Popular saying in Illinois in the early nineteenth century

Honour to Pioneers That Broke Sod That Men to Come Might Live.

Inscription on State Capitol Building, Lincoln, Nebraska

The common fence in the eastern half of the United States was made of rails split from the tree trunks of the cleared fields. It was supplemented by the stone wall or rock fence in regions such as New England where there were as many rocks as there were trees. Of rails, the most familiar type was the Virginia worm or zigzag fence, remnants of which still exist in remote parts of the woodland states. This fence, along with the log cabin, made its way west until it came to the Great Plains which it could not enter or cross for the simple reason that there was no material for making it. Also, there were no rocks, especially in the eastern plains which the pioneers first entered. In short, fencing became economically impossible, and without fences there could be no farming because livestock and agricultural crops are mutually exclusive. For want of fencing the agricultural frontier was brought almost to a dead halt on the edge of the plains, and it was unable to move forward until a practical and economical substitute could be found. In the interval before a practical fence was invented, every device imaginable was tried, such as thorny hedges of bois d'arc, cactus, running roses; even mud fences were built to go along with sod houses. None of the substitutes were satisfactory and all were expensive. The fence problem may be said to have been acute from 1850 to 1875, leaving the Great Plains in the hands of the cattle kings of the open range. . . .

The solution in this case was neither borrowed from the Spaniards, as the method of handling range cattle on horseback had been, nor furnished by New England, as in the case of the Colt revolver. The solution, the invention of barbed wire, was the work of a group of farmers living in the open prairies of Illinois near the little town of DeKalb. Their names were Joseph Glidden, Jacob Haish, and perhaps a third, Isaac Ellwood. Joseph, Jacob, and Isaac did not make brick without straw, but they made fences requiring little timber. In 1873 the first two began making barbed wire, independently, and each obtained a patent. What they discovered was that a cheap and practical fence, one easy to construct and to maintain, could be made by twisting two wires with barbs spaced at regular intervals, and that three strands of this infernal contrivance stretched tight on posts would keep cattle and crops separated.

The success of Joseph, Jacob, and Isaac was phenomenal, and though they started as simple farmers they wound up as millionaires because they had the only fence that could be used in about half of the United States. Barbed wire was shipped into the plains by the trainload, and within twenty-five years nearly all the open range had become privately owned and was under fence. Ranching was converted from the open range into the big pasture type. With the possibility of fencing, the farmers, who had been stalled for a generation on the edge of the plains, resumed their march to the west.

WALTER PRESCOTT WEBB, *The Great Plains*

The Kansas spirit is the American spirit double-distilled. It is a new grafted product of American individualism, American idealism, American intolerance. Kansas is America in microcosm: as America conceives itself in respect to Europe, so Kansas conceives itself in respect to America. Within its borders Americanism, pure and undefiled, has a new lease of life. It is the mission of this self-selected people to see to it that it does not perish from off the earth. The light on the altar, however neglected elsewhere, must ever be replenished in Kansas. If this is provincialism, it is the provincialism of faith rather than of province. The devotion to the state is devotion to an ideal, not to a territory, and men can say "Dear old Kansas!" because the name symbolizes for them what the motto of the state so well expresses, *ad astra per aspera*.

CARL BECKER, *Kansas*, 1910

There is about [Indiana] a charm I shall not be able to express. . . . This is a region not unlike those which produce gold or fleet horses or oranges or adventurers.

THEODORE DREISER, *A Hoosier Holiday*, 1916

On a hill by the Mississippi where Chippewas had camped two generations ago, a girl stood in relief against the cornflower blue of Northern sky. She saw no Indians now; she saw flour-mills and the blinking windows of skyscrapers in Minneapolis and St. Paul. . . . A breeze which had crossed a thousand miles of wheatlands bellied her taffeta skirt in a line so graceful, so full of animation and moving beauty, that the heart of a chance watcher on the lower road tightened to wistfulness over her quality of suspended freedom. . . . The days of pioneering, of lassies in sunbonnets, and bears killed with axes in piney clearings, are deader now than Camelot; and a rebellious girl is the spirit of that bewildered empire called the American Middlewest.

SINCLAIR LEWIS, *Main Street,* 1920

Here—she meditated—is the newest empire of the world; the Northern Middlewest; a land of dairy herds and exquisite lakes, of new automobiles and tar-paper shanties and silos like red towers, of clumsy speech and a hope that is boundless. An empire which feeds a quarter of the world— yet its work is merely begun. They are pioneers, these sweaty wayfarers, for all their telephones and bank-accounts and automatic pianos and co-operative leagues. And for all its fat richness, theirs is a pioneer land. What is its future? she wondered. A future of cities and factory smut where now are loping empty fields? Homes universal and secure? Or placid chateaux ringed with sullen huts? Youth freed to find knowledge and laughter? Willingness to sift the sanctified lies? Or creamy-skinned fat women, smeared with grease and chalk, gorgeous in the skins of beasts and the bloody feathers of slain birds, playing bridge with puffy pink-nailed jeweled fingers, women who after much expenditure of labor and bad temper still grotesquely resemble their own flatulent lap-dogs? The ancient stale inequalities, or something different in history, unlike the tedious maturity of other empires? What future and what hope?

SINCLAIR LEWIS, *Ibid.*

[Village contentment is] the contentment of the quiet dead, who are scornful of the living for their restless walking. It is negation canonized as the one positive virtue. It is the prohibition of happiness. It is slavery self-sought and self-defended. It is dullness made God.

SINCLAIR LEWIS, *Ibid.*

Back in 1905, in America, it was almost universally known that though cities were evil and even in the farmland there were occasional men of wrath, our villages were approximately paradise. They were always made up of small white houses under large green trees; there was no poverty and no toil worth mentioning; every Sunday, sweet-tempered, silvery pastors poured forth comfort and learning; and while the banker might be a pretty doubtful dealer, he was inevitably worsted in the end by the honest yeomanry. But it was Neighborliness that was the glory of the small town. In the cities, nobody knew or cared; but back home, the Neighbors were one great happy family. They lent you money, without questioning . . . they soothed your brow in sickness . . . and when you had nevertheless passed beyond, they sat up with your corpse and your widow. Invariably they encouraged youth to go to bigger and nobler things.

And in 1905, I returned to my own Minnesota village for vacation after my Sophomore year at Yale, and after two months of it . . . I was converted to the faith that a good deal of this Neighborliness was a fake; that villages could be as inquisitorial as army barracks. So in the third month of vacation, fifteen years before it was published, I began to write *Main Street*.

SINCLAIR LEWIS, *Ibid.,* "Introduction," 1937

The Nation's Dust Bowl.

> Description of the Middle West during the great drought of the '30's

The Corn Belt is a gift of the gods—the rain god, the sun god, the ice god, and the gods of geology.

J. RUSSELL SMITH

. . . and the smell of woodsmoke in Ohio and the flaming maples, the nights of the frosty stars, the blazing moons that hang the same way in a thousand streets, slanting to silence on the steeple's slope; nights of the wheel, the rail, the bell, the wailing cry along the river's edge, and of the summer's ending, nights of the frost and silence and the barking of a dog, of people listening, and of words unspoken and the quiet heart, and nights of the old October that must come again, while we are waiting, waiting, waiting in the darkness for all of our friends and brothers who will not return.

THOMAS WOLFE, "One of the Girls in Our Party"

Chicago is stupefying . . . an Olympian freak, a fable, an allegory, an incomprehensible phenomenon . . . monstrous, multifarious, unnatural, indomitable, puissant, preposterous, transcendent . . . throw the diction-ary at it!

JULIAN STREET

Ohio is the farthest west of the east and the farthest north of the south.

LOUIS BROMFIELD

Many of the following items are to be encountered all over the United States; nevertheless I think of them as typically middle western. One could make a litany of forces, memories, institutions—for instance the ole swimmin' hole, the red brick schoolhouse, and the ritual of "working one's way" through college; or cartoons like that by John McCutcheon of the Chicago *Tribune* about Indian summer, football teams like the Green Bay Packers, and social phenomena like wrong-side-of-the-trackism in regard to where a person is born.

I could mention church suppers; county and state fairs, particularly on Governor's Day as in Iowa; the memory of portages and poems by Carl Sandburg; the tradition of paternalistic independent newspaper editors like Henry Justin Smith of the Chicago *Daily News;* small lakes in northern Indiana like saucepans full of limp bathing suits; the lawns, six inches deep with autumn leaves, before frame houses with big porches in middle-sized Wisconsin towns; and the rows of orange pumpkins outside Ohio filling stations.

Or I could talk of the great state universities, their athletics and their alumni; utterly nauseous conditions in the state insane asylums; bulletin boards in the local post offices, with their wide variety of reading matter —reports on migratory birds, advices on criminals by the FBI, and civil service jobs; about the use of the word "visit" as a synonym for the verb "see," and the fact that the most conservative vote is not, contrary to general opinion, that of the farmers but of businessmen in small towns; about the crushing social pressure exerted on youngsters by the corner drugstore, and place names like What Cheer, Iowa, and Peculiar, Missouri, about the middle western awe of a really good department store, like Marshall Field's in Chicago, and the ubiquitous night schools—especially their courses in law.

Then there are the motels and tourist camps which, what with Puritanism and the housing shortage, have become the chief haunts of the amorous; the fact that the United States is the country where most luxuries are cheap; a great instinct for horseplay in most Americans; the hired man who comes to work at 8:02 in the morning (or 7:59) instead of 8 sharp to demonstrate his independence and hatred of regimentation; the gap between the basic good will of citizens and their lack of concrete desire to put the good will into performance; and the nuggets of political conversation like "Don't know if he can vote his own wife, but he carries a lot of punch," "When we're in a war I'm for the president as long as it lasts," "There's a pretty high brand of government in this here state" (how many times did I hear that!), "He's the best rough-and-tumble swivel-chair lawyer in the county," and "The guy is so honest that there's nothing he'd steal but an election."

JOHN GUNTHER, *Inside U.S.A.*

THE WEST

I turn round and round irresolute sometimes for a quarter of an hour, until I decide, for the thousandth time, that I will walk into the southwest or west. Eastward I go only by force, but westward I go free. Thither no business leads me. It is hard for me to believe that I shall find fair landscapes or sufficient wildness and freedom behind the eastern horizon. I am not excited by the prospect of a walk thither; but I believe that the forest which I see in the western horizon stretches uninterruptedly toward the setting sun, and there are no towns or cities in it of enough consequence to disturb me. Let me live where I will, on this side is the city, on that the wilderness, and ever I am leaving the city more and more and withdrawing into the wilderness. I should not lay so much stress on this fact if I did not believe that something like this is the prevailing tendency of my countrymen. I must walk toward Oregon and not toward Europe.

HENRY DAVID THOREAU

Up to and including 1880 the country had a frontier of settlement, but at present the unsettled area has been so broken into by isolated bodies of settlement that there can hardly be said to be a frontier line. In the discussion of its extent, its westward movement, etc., it cannot, therefore, any longer have a place in the census reports.

Bulletin of the Superintendent of the Census, 1890

Stand at Cumberland Gap and watch the procession of civilization, marching single file—the buffalo following the trail to salt springs, the Indian, the fur trader and hunter, the cattle raiser, the pioneer farmer— and the frontier has passed by. Stand at South Pass in the Rockies a century later and see the same procession with wider intervals between.

FREDERICK JACKSON TURNER, *The Frontier in American History,* 1920

[The frontier is] the line of most rapid and effective Americanization.

FREDERICK JACKSON TURNER, *Ibid.*

From the conditions of frontier life came intellectual traits of profound importance. The works of travelers along each frontier from colonial days onward describe certain common traits, and these traits have, while softening down, still persisted as survivals in the place of their origin, even when a higher social organization succeeded. The result is that to the frontier the American intellect owes its striking characteristics. That coarseness and strength combined with acuteness and inquisitiveness; that practical, inventive turn of mind, quick to find expedients; that masterful grasp of material things, lacking in the artistic but powerful to effect great ends; that restless, nervous energy; that dominant individualism, working for good and for evil, and withal that buoyancy and exuberance which comes with freedom—these are traits of the frontier, or traits called out elsewhere because of the existence of the frontier. Since the days when the fleet of Columbus sailed into the waters of the New World, America has been another name for opportunity, and the people of the United States have taken their tone from the incessant expansion which has not only been open but has even been forced upon them. He would be a rash prophet who should assert that the expansive character of American life has now entirely ceased. Movement has been its dominant fact, and, unless this training has no effect upon a people, the American energy will continually demand a wider field for its exercise. But never again will such gifts of free land offer themselves. For a moment, at the frontier, the bonds of custom are broken and unrestraint is triumphant. There is not *tabula rasa*. The stubborn American environment is there with its imperious summons to accept its conditions; the inherited ways of doing things are also there; and yet, in spite of environment, and in spite of custom, each frontier did indeed furnish a new field of opportunity, a gate of escape from the bondage of the past; and freshness, and confidence, and scorn of older society, impatience of its restraints and its ideas, and indifference to its lessons, have accompanied the frontier. What the Mediterranean Sea was to the Greeks, breaking the bond of custom, offering new experience, calling out new institutions and activities, that, and more, the ever retreating frontier has been to the United States directly, and to the nations of Europe more remotely. And now, four centuries from the discovery of America, at the end of a hundred years of life under the Constitution, the frontier has gone, and with its going has closed the first period of American history.

FREDERICK JACKSON TURNER, *Ibid.*

American democracy was born of no theorist's dream; it was not carried in the *Susan Constant* to Virginia nor in the *Mayflower* to Plymouth. It came out of the American forest, and it gained strength each time it touched a new frontier.

FREDERICK JACKSON TURNER, *Ibid.*

The great open spaces of the American West ceased about 1890 to be a determining economic factor in the growth of the nation. They remain, and always must remain, an important psychological factor. The frontier of cultivation has merely reached its limits. It will be extended only as the Colorado and one or two other western rivers are impounded and used for irrigation. Some millions of acres will be brought under the plow, some hundreds of thousands of people settled upon them or nourished by them. But there will remain, between the Rocky Mountains and the Pacific Ocean, great areas never to be tamed. Travelers will cross them and roam about them in increasing numbers, cattle will graze upon the thin herbage along their borders, prospectors will explore them, often successfully, for petroleum and the precious and semi-precious metals. But that will be all. The mighty roar of civilization will be heard there, forever, as a thin, far-away clamor. The gods of the earth and the sky will rule to the end of time.

These are our perpetual open spaces, once of continental dimensions, now shrunk to the limits of a secondary European power. . . . They will remain forever, in their loneliness and silences, a dramatic contrast to our crowded and hurrying cities. And, so remaining, they will contribute an element to our national psychology which must not be overlooked by anyone who is trying to understand us. Every nation has a national myth, without which it would be not a nation but a mob. The open spaces in America are the symbol of our myth.

R. L. DUFFUS

To me the West is, as I look at my spurs now, a country where you can still ride a whole lot and can throw your rope without having it caught on a fence-post. The countries I mean, besides where the dude ranches are running, are countries where dudes would never go, with all my due compliments to them. There is countries where you can still ride one hundred miles without striking a fence or seeing a fence, and you'd be lucky if you found water in them countries. Them is the countries I know well.

WILL JAMES

The West begins where the average annual rainfall drops below twenty inches. When you reach the line that marks that drop—for convenience, the one hundredth meridian—you have reached the West.

BERNARD DEVOTO, *The Plundered Province*

A part of hell with the fires burnt out.

GENERAL GEORGE ARMSTRONG CUSTER, of the Bad Lands of South Dakota

We fertilize 'em with cornmeal, and irrigate with milk.

Idaho farmer, explaining why Idaho potatoes are so big

[In Nevada]: Sometimes we have the seasons in their regular order, and then again we have winter all the summer and summer all winter. Consequently, we have never yet come across an almanac that would just exactly fit this latitude. It is mighty regular about not raining, though. . . . It will start in here in November and rain about four, and sometimes as much as seven days on a stretch; after that, you may loan out your umbrella for twelve months, with the serene confidence which a Christian feels in four aces. Sometimes the winter begins in November and winds up in June, and sometimes there is a bare suspicion of winter in March and April, and summer all the balance of the year. But as a general thing . . . the climate is good, what there is of it.

SAMUEL L. CLEMENS ("MARK TWAIN"), *The Washoe Giant in San Francisco*

New Mexico has an austere and planetary look that daunts and challenges the soul.

ELIZABETH SHEPLEY SERGEANT

Snow falls so deep in New Mexico's mountains that it takes 40,000 automobile loads of Texas hot air each summer to melt it. . . .

New Mexico is game country too. If all the deer horns in the state were clustered together into one giant hat rack, it would make a good place for Texans to hang their hats when not talking through them. . . .

S. OMAR ("THE TENTMAKER") BARKER, of Tecolotenos, New Mexico, first published some years ago in the New York *Herald Tribune*

Nineteen suburbs in search of a metropolis.

Sobriquet for Los Angeles, 1940's

If you tilt the country sideways, Los Angeles is the place where everything loose will fall.

Attributed to FRANK LLOYD WRIGHT

Matthew Arnold once wrote that all people—whether or not they knew what the words meant—are divided into two basic types: the Platonists and the Aristotelians.

On much the same basis, I'd divide all Americans into two fundamental types—the people who like Los Angeles, and the people who like San Francisco. There are deep and irreconcilable differences between the two camps.

SYDNEY J. HARRIS, *Strictly Personal*

RIVER, MOUNTAIN AND PLAIN

The Father of Waters.

> The Mississippi. The name of the river is derived from the Algonquin *misi,* meaning great, and *sipi,* meaning river. Le Page du Pratz, *Histoire de la Louisiane,* 1758, translated the word erroneously as *le vieux père des rivières.*

The Big Drink.

> American phrase meaning any large body of water, such as the Mississippi (traced to 1846) or the Atlantic

There was little maize in the place, and the Governor moved to another town, half a league from the great river, where it was found in sufficiency. He went to look at the river, and saw that near it there was much timber of which piraguas might be made, and a good situation in which the camp might be placed. . . . The stream was swift and very deep; the water, always flowing turbidly, brought along from above many trees and much timber, driven onward by its force. There were many fish of several sorts, the greater part differing from those of the fresh waters of Spain.

> ANON., *Narrative of the Expedition of Hernando de Soto.*
> The river is the Mississippi; the time, the spring of 1542.

They [Cortes and his troops] had not advanced far, when, turning an angle of the sierra, they suddenly came on a view which more than compensated the toils of the preceding day. It was that of the Valley of Mexico, Tenochtitlan, as more commonly called by the natives; which, with its picturesque assemblage of water, woodland, and cultivated plains, its shining cities and shadowy hills, was spread out like some gay and gorgeous panorama before them. In the highly rarified atmosphere of these upper regions, even remote objects have a brilliancy of coloring and a distinctness of outline which seem to annihilate distance. Stretching far away at their feet were seen noble forests of oak, sycamore, and cedar, and beyond, yellow fields of maize and the towering maguey, intermingled with orchards and blooming gardens; for flowers, in such demand for their religious festivals, were even more abundant in this populous valley than in other parts of Anahuac. In the center of the great basin were beheld the lakes, occupying then a much larger portion of its surface than at present; their borders thickly studded with towns and hamlets, and, in the midst,—like some Indian empress with her coronal of pearls,—the fair city of Mexico, with her white towers and pyramidal temples, reposing, as it were, on the bosom of the waters,—the far-famed "Venice of the Aztecs." High over all rose the royal hill of Chapultepec, the residence of the Mexican monarchs, crowned with the same grove of gigantic cypresses which at this day fling their broad shadows over the land. In the distance beyond the blue waters of the lake, and nearly screened by intervening foliage, was seen a shining speck, the rival capital of Tezcuco, and, still further on, the dark belt of porphyry, girding the Valley around, like a rich setting which Nature had devised for the fairest of her jewels.

Such was the beautiful vision which broke on the eyes of the conquerors. And even now, when so sad a change has come over the scene; when the stately forests have been laid low, and the soil, unsheltered from the fierce radiance of a tropical sun, is in many places abandoned to sterility; when the waters have retired, leaving a broad and ghastly margin white with the incrustation of salts, while the cities and hamlets on their borders have moldered into ruins;—even now that desolation broods over the landscape, so indestructible are the lines of beauty which Nature has traced on its features, that no traveler, however cold, can gaze on them with any other emotions than those of astonishment and rapture.

What, then, must have been the emotions of the Spaniards, when, after working their toilsome way into the upper air, the cloudy tabernacle parted before their eyes, and they beheld these fair scenes in all their pristine magnificence and beauty! It was like the spectacle which greeted

the eyes of Moses from the summit of Pisgah, and, in the warm glow of
their feelings, they cried out, "It is the promised land!"

WILLIAM HICKLING PRESCOTT, *The Conquest of Mexico*

Late that afternoon, in the midst of a gloomy and barren prairie, we
came suddenly upon the great trail of the Pawnees, leading from their
villages on the Platte to their war and hunting grounds to the southward.
Here every summer passes the motley concourse: thousands of savages,
men, women, and children, horses and mules, laden with their weapons
and implements, and an innumerable multitude of unruly wolfish dogs,
who have not acquired the civilized accomplishment of barking, but howl
like their wild cousins of the prairie.

The permanent winter villages of the Pawnees stand on the lower
Platte, but throughout the summer the greater part of the inhabitants
are wandering over the plains,—a treacherous, cowardly banditti, who,
by a thousand acts of pillage and murder, have deserved chastisement at
the hands of government. . . .

A low, undulating line of sand-hills bounded the horizon before us.
That day we rode ten hours, and it was dusk before we entered the hollows and gorges of these gloomy little hills. At length we gained the summit, and the long-expected valley of the Platte lay before us. We all drew
rein, and sat joyfully looking down upon the prospect. It was right welcome; strange, too, and striking to the imagination, and yet it had not
one picturesque or beautiful feature; nor had it any of the features of
grandeur, other than its vast extent, its solitude, and its wildness. For
league after league, a plain as level as a lake was outspread beneath us;
here and there the Platte, divided into a dozen thread-like sluices, was
traversing it, and an occasional clump of wood, rising in the midst like a
shadowy island, relieved the monotony of the waste. No living thing was
moving throughout the vast landscape, except the lizards that darted over
the sand and through the rank grass and prickly pears at our feet.

We had passed the more tedious part of the journey; but four hundred
miles still intervened between us and Fort Laramie; and to reach that
point cost us the travel of three more weeks. During the whole of this
time we were passing up the middle of a long, narrow, sandy plain, reaching like an outstretched belt nearly to the Rocky Mountains. Two lines of
sandhills, broken often into the wildest and most fantastic forms, flanked
the valley at the distance of a mile or two on the right and left; while
beyond them lay a barren, trackless waste, extending for hundreds of
miles to the Arkansas on the one side, and the Missouri on the other. Before and behind us, the level monotony of the plain was unbroken as far

as the eye could reach. Sometimes it glared in the sun, an expanse of hot, bare sand; sometimes it was veiled by long coarse grass. Skulls and whitening bones of buffalo were scattered everywhere; the ground was tracked by myriads of them, and often covered with the circular indentations where the bulls had wallowed in the hot weather. From every gorge and ravine, opening from the hills, descended deep, well-worn paths, where the buffalo issue twice a day in regular procession to drink in the Platte. The river itself runs through the midst, a thin sheet of rapid, turbid water, half a mile wide, and scarcely two feet deep. Its low banks, for the most part without a bush or tree, are of loose sand, with which the stream is so charged that it grates on the teeth in drinking. The naked landscape is, of itself, dreary and monotonous enough; and yet the wild beasts and wild men that frequent the valley of the Platte make it a scene of interest and excitement to the traveller. Of those who have journeyed there, scarcely one, perhaps, fails to look back with fond regret to his horse and his rifle.

. . . Our New-England climate is mild and equable compared with that of the Platte. This very morning, for instance, was close and sultry, the sun rising with a faint oppressive heat; when suddenly darkness gathered in the west, and a furious blast of sleet and hail drove full in our faces, icy cold, and urged with such demoniac vehemence that it felt like a storm of needles. It was curious to see the horses; they faced about in extreme displeasure, holding their tails like whipped dogs, and shivering as the angry gusts, howling louder than a concert of wolves, swept over us. Wright's long chain of mules came sweeping round before the storm, like a flight of snow-birds driven by a winter tempest. Thus we all remained stationary for some minutes, crouching close to our horses' necks, much too surly to speak, though once the captain looked up from between the collars of his coat, his face blood-red, and the muscles of his mouth contracted by the cold into a most ludicrous grin of agony. He grumbled something that seemed like a curse, directed, as we believed, against the unhappy hour when he had first thought of leaving home. The thing was too good to last long; and the instant the puffs of wind subsided we pitched our tents, and remained in camp for the rest of a gloomy and lowering day. The emigrants also encamped near at hand. We being first on the ground, had appropriated all the wood within reach; so that our fire alone blazed cheerily. Around us soon gathered a group of uncouth figures, shivering in the drizzling rain. Conspicuous among them were two or three of the half-savage men who spend their reckless lives in trapping among the Rocky Mountains, or in trading for the Fur Company in the Indian villages. They were all of Canadian extraction; their hard, weather-beaten faces and bushy mustaches looked out from beneath the hoods of their white capotes with a bad and brutish expression, as if their owners might be the willing agents of any villainy. And such in fact is the character of many of these men.

FRANCIS PARKMAN, *The Oregon Trail*, 1847

August 13.—We are now ready to start on our way down the Great Unknown. . . . We are three quarters of a mile in the depths of the earth, and the great river shrinks into insignificance, as it dashes its angry waves against the walls and cliffs, that rise to the world above; they are but puny ripples, and we but pygmies, running up and down the sands, or lost among the boulders.

We have an unknown distance yet to run; an unknown river yet to explore. What falls there are, we know not; what rocks beset the channel, we know not; what walls rise over the river, we know not. Ah, well! we may conjecture many things. The men talk as cheerfully as ever; jests are bandied about freely this morning; but to me the cheer is somber and the jests are ghastly.

August 14.—. . . The walls, now, are more than a mile in height—a vertical distance difficult to appreciate. Stand on the south steps of the Treasury Building, in Washington, and look down Pennsylvania Avenue to Capitol Park, and measure this distance overhead, and imagine cliffs to extend to that altitude, and you will understand what I mean; or, stand at Canal Street, in New York, and look up Broadway to Grace Church, and you have about the distance; or, stand at Lake Street Bridge, in Chicago, and look down to the Central Depot, and you have it again.

A thousand feet of this is up through granite crags, then steep slopes and perpendicular cliffs rise, one above another, to the summit. The gorge is black and narrow below, red and gray and flaring above, with crags and angular projections on the walls, which, cut in many places by side canyons, seem to be a vast wilderness of rocks. Down in these grand, gloomy depths we glide, ever listening, for the mad waters keep up their roar; ever watching, ever peering ahead, for the narrow canyon is winding, and the river is closed in so that we can see but a few hundred yards, and what there may be below we know not; but we listen for falls, and watch for rocks, or stop now and then, in the bay of a recess, to admire the gigantic scenery. And ever, as we go, there is some new pinnacle or tower, some crag or peak, some distant view of the upper plateau, some strange shaped rock, or some deep, narrow side canyon. Then we come to another broken fall, which appears more difficult than the one we ran this morning.

September 10.—. . . The Indian name of the canyon is Pa-ru-nu-weap, or Roaring Water Canyon. . . .

> JOHN WESLEY POWELL, *Exploration of the Colorado River of the West: the Grand Canyon of the Colorado.* Powell was the first white man, perhaps the first man, to explore the canyon, around 1870.

When I had mastered the language of this water, and had come to know every trifling feature that bordered the great river as familiarly as I knew the letters of the alphabet, I had made a valuable acquisition. But I had lost something, too. I had lost something which could never be restored to me while I lived. All the grace, the beauty, the poetry, had gone out of the majestic river! I still kept in mind a certain wonderful sunset which I witnessed when steamboating was new to me. A broad expanse of the river was turned to blood; in the middle distance the red hue brightened into gold, through which a solitary log came floating, black and conspicuous; in one place a long, slanting mark lay sparkling upon the water; in another the surface was broken by boiling, tumbling rings, that were as many-tinted as an opal; where the ruddy flush was faintest, was a smooth spot that was covered with graceful circles and radiating lines, ever so delicately traced; the shore on our left was densely wooded, and the somber shadow that fell from this forest was broken in one place by a long, ruffled trail that shone like silver; and high above the forest wall a clean-stemmed dead tree waved a single leafy bough that glowed like flame in the unobstructed splendor that was flowing from the sun. There were graceful curves, reflected images, woody heights, soft distances; and over the whole scene, far and near, the dissolving lights drifted steadily, enriching it every passing moment with new marvels of coloring.

I stood like one bewitched. I drank it in, in a speechless rapture. The world was new to me, and I had never seen anything like this at home. But as I have said, a day came when I began to cease from noting the glories and the charms which the moon and the sun and the twilight wrought upon the river's face; another day came when I ceased altogether to note them. Then, if that sunset scene had been repeated, I should have looked upon it without rapture, and should have commented upon it, inwardly, after this fashion: "This sun means that we are going to have wind to-morrow; that floating log means that the river is rising, small thanks to it; that slanting mark on the water refers to a bluff reef which is going to kill somebody's steamboat one of these nights, if it keeps on stretching out like that; those tumbling 'boils' show a dissolving bar and a changing channel there; the lines and circles in the slick water over yonder are a warning that that troublesome place is shoaling up dangerously; that silver streak in the shadow of the forest is the 'break' from a new snag, and he has located himself in the very best place he could have found to fish for steamboats; that tall dead tree, with a single living branch, is not going to last long, and then how is a body ever going to get through this blind place at night without the friendly old landmark?"

No, the romance and the beauty were all gone from the river. All the value any feature of it had for me now was the amount of usefulness it could furnish toward compassing the safe piloting of a steamboat. Since those days, I have pitied doctors from my heart. What does the lovely flush in a beauty's cheek mean to a doctor but a "break" that ripples above some deadly disease? Are not all her visible charms sown thick with what are to him signs and symbols of hidden decay? Does he ever see her beauty at all, or doesn't he simply view her professionally, and comment upon her unwholesome condition all to himself? And doesn't he sometimes wonder whether he has gained most or lost most by learning his trade?

MARK TWAIN, *Life on the Mississippi,* 1875–1883

There seemed to be one small hope, however: if we could get through the intricate and dangerous Hat Island crossing before night, we could venture the rest for we would have plainer sailing and better water. But it would be insanity to attempt Hat Island at night. So there was a deal of looking at watches all the rest of the day, and a constant ciphering upon the speed we were making. Hat Island was the eternal subject; sometimes hope was high and sometimes we were delayed in a bad crossing, and down it went again. For hours all hands lay under the burden of this suppressed excitement; it was even communicated to me, and I got to feeling so solicitous about Hat Island, and under such an awful pressure of responsibility, that I wished I might have five minutes on shore to draw a good, full, relieving breath, and start over again. We were standing no regular watches. Each of our pilots ran such portions of the river as he had run when coming upstream, because of his greater familiarity with it; but both remained in the pilot-house constantly.

An hour before sunset Mr. Bixby took the wheel, and Mr. W. stepped aside. For the next thirty minutes every man held his watch in his hand and was restless, silent, and uneasy. At last somebody said, with a doomful sigh:

"Well, yonder's Hat Island—and we can't make it."

All the watches closed with a snap, everybody sighed and muttered something about its being "too bad, too bad—ah, if we could *only* have got there half an hour sooner!" and the place was thick with the atmosphere of disappointment. Some started to go out, but loitered, hearing no bell-tap to land. The sun dipped behind the horizon, the boat went on. Inquiring looks passed from one guest to another; and one who had his hand on the door-knob and had turned it, waited, then presently took away his hand and let the knob turn back again. We bore steadily down the bend. More looks were exchanged, and nods of surprised admiration —but no words. Insensibly the men drew together behind Mr. Bixby, as the sky darkened and one or two dim stars came out. The dead silence and the sense of waiting became oppressive. Mr. Bixby pulled the cord, and two deep, mellow notes from the big bell floated off on the night. Then a pause, and one more note was struck. The watchman's voice followed, from the hurricane-deck:

"Labboard lead, there! Stabboard lead!"

The cries of the leadsmen began to rise out of the distance, and were gruffly repeated by the word-passers on the hurricane-deck.

"M-a-r-k three! M-a-r-k three! Quarter-less-three! Half twain! Quarter twain! M-a-r-k twain! Quarter-less—"

Mr. Bixby pulled two bell-ropes, and was answered by faint jinglings far below in the engine-room, and the speed slackened. The steam began to whistle through the gauge-cocks. The cries of the leadsmen went on— and it is a weird sound, always, in the night. Every pilot in the lot was watching now, with fixed eyes, and talking under his breath. Nobody was calm and easy but Mr. Bixby. He would put his wheel down and stand on a spoke, and as the steamer swung into her (to me) utterly invisible marks—for we seemed to be in the midst of a wide and gloomy sea—he would meet and fasten her there. Out of the murmur of half-audible talk, one caught a coherent sentence now and then—such as:

"There; she's over the first reef all right!"

After a pause, another subdued voice:

"Her stern's coming down just *exactly* right, by *George!*"

"Now she's in the marks; over she goes!"

Somebody else muttered:

"Oh, it was done beautiful—*beautiful!*"

Now the engines were stopped altogether, and we drifted with the current. Not that I could see the boat drift, for I could not, the stars being all gone by this time. This drifting was the dismalest work; it held one's heart still. Presently I discovered a blacker gloom than that which surrounded us. It was the head of the island. We were closing right down upon it. We entered its deeper shadow, and so imminent seemed the peril that I was likely to suffocate; and I had the strongest impulse to do *something,* anything, to save the vessel. But still Mr. Bixby stood by his wheel, silent, intent as a cat, and all the pilots stood shoulder to shoulder at his back.

"She'll not make it!" somebody whispered.

The water grew shoaler and shoaler, by the leadsman's cries, till it was down to:

"Eight-and-a-half! E-i-g-h-t feet! E-i-g-h-t feet! Seven-and—"

Mr. Bixby said warningly through his speaking-tube to the engineer:

"Stand by, now!"

"Ay, ay, sir!"

"Seven-and-a-half! Seven feet! *Six*-and—"

We touched bottom! Mr. Bixby set a lot of bells ringing, shouted through the tube, *"Now,* let her have it—every ounce you've got!" then to his partner, "Put her hard down! snatch her! snatch her!" The boat rasped and ground her way through the sand, hung upon the apex of disaster a single tremendous instant, and then over she went! And such a shout as went up at Mr. Bixby's back never loosened the roof of a pilot-house before!

There was no more trouble after that. Mr. Bixby was a hero that night; and it was some little time, too, before his exploit ceased to be talked about by river-men.

Fully to realize the marvelous precision required in laying the great steamer in her marks in that murky waste of water, one should know that not only must she pick her intricate way through snags and blind reefs, and then shave the head of the island so closely as to brush the over-hanging foliage with her stern, but at one place she must pass almost within arm's reach of a sunken and invisible wreck that would snatch the hull timbers from under her if she should strike it, and destroy a quarter of a million dollars' worth of steamboat and cargo in five minutes, and maybe a hundred and fifty human lives into the bargain.

The last remark I heard that night was a compliment to Mr. Bixby, uttered in soliloquy and with unction by one of our guests. He said:

"By the Shadow of Death, but he's a lightning pilot!"

SAMUEL L. CLEMENS ("MARK TWAIN"), *Ibid.*

Two or three days and nights went by; I reckon I might say they swum by, they slid along so quiet and smooth and lovely. Here is the way we put in the time. It was a monstrous big river down there—sometimes a mile and a half wide; we run nights, and laid up and hid daytimes; soon as night was most gone we stopped navigating and tied up—nearly always in the dead water under a towhead; and then cut young cottonwoods and willows, and hid the raft with them. Then we set out the lines. Next we slid into the river and had a swim, so as to freshen up and cool off; then we set down on the sandy bottom where the water was about knee-deep, and watched the daylight come. Not a sound anywheres—perfectly still— just like the whole world was asleep, only sometimes the bullfrogs a-cluttering, maybe. The first thing to see, looking away over the water, was a kind of dull line—that was the woods on t'other side; you couldn't make nothing else out; then a pale place in the sky; then more paleness spreading around; then the river softened up away off, and warn't black any more, but gray; you could see little dark spots drifting along ever so far away—trading-scows, and such things; and long black streaks—rafts; sometimes you could hear a sweep screaking; or jumbled-up voices, it was so still, and sounds come so far; and by and by you could see a streak on the water which you know by the look of the streak that there's a snag there in a swift current which breaks on it and makes that streak look that way; and you see the mists curl up off the water, and the east reddens up, and the river, and you make out a log cabin in the edge of the woods, away on the bank on t'other side of the river, being a wood-yard, likely, and piled by them cheats so you can throw a dog through it anywheres; then the nice breeze springs up, and comes fanning you from over there, so cool and fresh and sweet to smell on account of the woods and the flowers; but sometimes not that way, because they've left dead fish lying around, gars and such, and they do get pretty rank; and next you've got the full day, and everything smiling in the sun, and the song-birds just going it!

A little smoke couldn't be noticed now, so we would take some fish off of the lines and cook up a hot breakfast. And afterwards we would watch the lonesomeness of the river, and kind of lazy along, and by and by lazy off to sleep. Wake up by and by, and look to see what done it, and maybe see a steamboat coughing along up-stream, so far off towards the other side you couldn't tell nothing about her only whether she was a stern-wheel or side-wheel; then for about an hour there wouldn't be nothing to hear nor nothing to see—just solid lonesomeness. Next you'd see a raft sliding by, away off yonder, and maybe a galoot on it chopping, because they're most always doing it on a raft; you'd see the ax flash and come down—you don't hear nothing; you see that ax go up again, and by the time it's above the man's head then you hear the *k'chunk!*—it had took all that time to come over the water. So we would put in the day, lazying around, listening to the stillness. Once there was a thick fog, and the rafts and things that went by was beating tin pans so the steamboats wouldn't run over them. A scow or a raft went by so close we could hear them talking and cussing and laughing—heard them plain; but we couldn't see no sign of them; it made you feel crawly; it was like spirits carrying on that way in the air. Jim said he believed it was spirits; but I says:

"No; spirits wouldn't say, 'Dern the dern fog.' "

> SAMUEL L. CLEMENS ("MARK TWAIN"), *The Adventures of Huckleberry Finn*

Well, when Tom and me got to the edge of the hill-top we looked away down into the village and could see three or four lights twinkling there, where there was sick folks, maybe; and the stars over us was sparkling ever so fine; and down by the village was the river, a whole mile broad, and awful still and grand.

> SAMUEL L. CLEMENS ("MARK TWAIN"), *Ibid.*

Looking westward from the summit of the Pacheco Pass one shining morning, a landscape was displayed that after all my wanderings still appears as the most beautiful that I have ever beheld. At my feet lay the Great Central Valley of California, level and flowery, like a lake of pure sunshine, forty or fifty miles wide, five hundred miles long, one rich furred garden of yellow compositae. And from the eastern boundary of this vast golden flowerbed rose the mighty Sierra, miles in height, and so gloriously colored and so radiant, it seemed not clothed with light, but wholly composed of it, like the wall of some celestial city. Along the top and extending a good way down, was a rich pearl-gray belt of snow; below it a belt of blue and dark purple, marking the extension of the forests; and stretching along the base of the range a broad belt of rose-purple; all these colors, from the blue sky to the yellow valley smoothly blending as they do in a rainbow, making a wall of light ineffably fine. Then it seemed to me that the Sierra should be called, not the Nevada or Snowy Range, but the Range of Light. And after ten years of wandering and wondering in the heart of it, rejoicing in its glorious floods of light, the white beams of the morning streaming through the passes, the noonday radiance on the crystal rocks, the flush of the alpenglow, and the irised spray of countless waterfalls, it still seems above all others the Range of Light. In general views no mark of man is visible upon it, nor anything to suggest the wonderful depth and grandeur of its sculpture. None of its magnificent forest-crowned ridges seems to rise much above the general level to publish its wealth. No great valley or river is seen, or group of well-marked features of any kind standing out as distinct pictures. Even the summit peaks, marshaled in glorious array so high in the sky, seem comparatively regular in form. Nevertheless the whole range five hundred miles long is furrowed with canyons two to five thousand feet deep, in which once flowed majestic glaciers, and in which now flow and sing the bright rejoicing rivers.

JOHN MUIR, *The Mountains of California,* 1894

The forests of America, however slighted by man, must have been a great delight to God; for they were the best He ever planted.

JOHN MUIR, *The American Forests*

Any fool can destroy trees. They cannot run away; and if they could, they would still be destroyed—chased and hunted down as long as fun or a dollar could be got out of their bark hides, branching horns, or magnificent bole backbones. Few that fell trees plant them; nor would planting avail much toward getting anything like the noble primeval forests. During a man's life only saplings can be grown, in the place of the old trees— tens of centuries old—that have been destroyed. It took more than three thousand years to make some of the trees in these Western woods—trees that still stand in perfect strength and beauty, waving and singing in the mighty forests of the Sierra. Through all the wonderful, eventful centuries since Christ's time—and long before that—God has cared for these trees, saved them from drought, disease, avalanches, and a thousand straining, leveling tempests and floods; but He cannot save them from fools—only Uncle Sam can do that.

JOHN MUIR, *Our National Parks,* 1901

Thence I drove them up the Drive, being so pretty a day, and E. [Edna Ferber] said, I could almost write a poem about the Hudson, I am so glad to be alive. Almost? I echoed, and forthwith fashioned this couplet:

It fills me full of joie de viver
To look across the Hudson River,

which I deemed as fine a poem as ever I wrote, but which occasioned no comment soever from the prosaic pair in the back seat [Miss Ferber and Alexander Woollcott].

FRANKLIN PIERCE ADAMS, *Diary of Our Own Samuel Pepys,*
March 22, 1924

On the afternoon of June 22, 1928, between three and four o'clock, I noticed an umbrella-shaped cloud in the west and southwest and from its appearance suspected there was a tornado in it. The air had that peculiar oppressiveness which nearly always precedes the coming of a tornado.

I saw at once my suspicions were correct. Hanging from the greenish black base of the cloud were three tornadoes. One was perilously near and apparently headed directly for my place. I lost no time hurrying with my family to our cyclone cellar.

The family had entered the cellar and I was in the doorway just about to enter and close the door when I decided I would take a last look at the approaching cloud. I have seen a number of these and did not lose my head, though the approaching tornado was an impressive sight.

The surrounding country is level and there was nothing to obscure the view. There was little or no rain falling from the cloud. Two of the tornadoes were some distance away and looked like great ropes dangling from the parent cloud, but the one nearest was shaped more like a funnel, with ragged clouds surrounding it. It appeared larger than the others and occupied the central position, with the great cumulus dome directly over it.

Steadily the cloud came on, the end gradually rising above the ground. I probably stood there only a few seconds, but was so impressed with the sight it seemed like a long time. At last the great shaggy end of the funnel hung directly overhead. Everything was still as death. There was a strong, gassy odor, and it seemed as though I could not breathe. There was a screaming, hissing sound coming directly from the end of the funnel. I looked up, and to my astonishment I saw right into the heart of the tornado. There was a circular opening in the center of the funnel, about fifty to one hundred feet in diameter and extending straight upward for a distance of at least half a mile, as best I could judge under the circumstances. The walls of this opening were rotating clouds and the whole was brilliantly lighted with constant flashes of lightning, which zig-zagged from side to side. Had it not been for the lightning, I could not have seen the opening, or any distance into it.

Around the rim of the great vortex small tornadoes were constantly forming and breaking away. These looked like tails as they writhed their way around the funnel. It was these that made the hissing sound. I noticed the rotation of the great whirl was anticlockwise, but some of the small twisters rotated clockwise. The opening was entirely hollow, except for something I could not exactly make out but suppose it was a detached wind cloud. This thing kept moving up and down. The tornado was not traveling at a great speed. I had plenty of time to get a good view of the whole thing, inside and out.

After it passed my place, it again dipped and demolished the house and barn of a farmer named Evans. The Evans family, like ourselves, had been out looking over their hailed-out wheat and saw the tornado coming. They lay down flat on the ground and caught hold of some plum bushes just before they felt themselves lifted by the wind. Evans later told me he could see the wreckage of his house, including the cook stove, going round and round over his head. The oldest daughter, seventeen, had all her clothes torn off, but none of the family was hurt.

> WILL KELLER, Kansas farmer, as told to Alonzo A. Justice of Dodge City weather bureau. This is a classic account of a tornado, a great American phenomenon.

Where can you match the mighty music of their names?—The Monongahela, the Colorado, the Rio Grande, the Columbia, the Tennessee, the Hudson (Sweet Thames!); the Kennebec, the Rappahannock, the Delaware, the Penobscot, the Wabash, the Chesapeake, the Swannanoa, the Indian River, the Niagara (Sweet Afton!); the Saint Lawrence, the Susquehanna, the Tombigbee, the Nantahala, the French Broad, the Chattahoochee, the Arizona, and the Potomac (Father Tiber!)—these are a few of their princely names, these are a few of their great, proud, glittering names, fit for the immense and lonely land that they inhabit.

Oh, Tiber! Father Tiber! You'd only be a suckling in that mighty land! And as for you, sweet Thames, flow gently till I end my song.

> THOMAS WOLFE, *Of Time and the River,* 1935

[The Missouri is] the hungriest river ever created . . . eating yellow clay banks and cornfields, eighty acres at a mouthful, winding up its banquet with a truck garden and picking its teeth with the timbers of a big red barn.

> STANLEY VESTAL, *The Missouri*

A river has no politics.

> DAVID E. LILIENTHAL, when director of T.V.A.

There is a grand circle in nature. The lines of those majestic swinging arcs are nowhere more clearly seen than by following the course of electric power in the Tennessee Valley's way of life. Water falls upon a mountain slope six thousand feet above the level of the river's mouth. It percolates through the roots and the subsurface channels, flows in a thousand tiny veins, until it comes together in one stream, then in another, and at last reaches a TVA lake where it is stored behind a dam. Down a huge steel tube it falls, turning a water wheel. Here the water's energy is transformed into electricity, and then, moving onward toward the sea, it continues on its course, through ten such lakes, over ten such water wheels. Each time, electric energy is created. That electricity, carried perhaps two hundred miles in a flash of time, heats to incredible temperatures a furnace that transforms inert phosphate ore into a chemical of great possibilities. That phosphatic chemical, put upon his land by a farmer, stirs new life in the land, induces the growth of pastures that capture the inexhaustible power of the sun. Those pastures, born of the energy of phosphate and electricity, feed the energies of animals and men, hold the soil, free the streams of silt, store up water in the soil. Slowly the water returns into the great man-made reservoirs, from which more electricity is generated as more water from the restored land flows on its endless course.

Such a cycle is restorative, not exhausting. It gives life as it sustains life. The principle of unity has been obeyed, the cycle has been closed. The yield is not the old sad tale of spoliation and poverty, but that of nature and science and man in the bounty of harmony.

DAVID E. LILIENTHAL, *TVA: Democracy on the March*

It doesn't matter what I think any more. You can't tear those dams down!

WENDELL L. WILLKIE, of T.V.A.

III. *What We Live By*

I believe in the United States of America as a government of the people, by the people, for the people; whose just powers are derived from the consent of the governed; a democracy in a republic; a sovereign state of many sovereign states; a perfect union, one and inseparable; established upon those principles of freedom, equality, justice and humanity for which American patriots sacrificed their lives and fortunes. I therefore believe it is my duty to my country to love it, to support its constitution, to obey its laws, to respect its flag, and to defend it against all enemies.

> WILLIAM TYLER PAGE, "The American's Creed," accepted by the House of Representatives on behalf of the American people, April 3, 1918

RELIGION

•

NATIVE RELIGIONS

INDIAN

I am Deganawidah and with the Five Nations' confederate lords I plant the Tree of the Great Peace. . . . Roots have spread out from the Tree of the Great Peace . . . and the name of these roots is the Great White Roots of Peace. If any man or any nation outside of the Five Nations shall show a desire to obey the laws of the Great Peace . . . they may trace the roots to their source . . . and they shall be welcomed to take shelter beneath the Tree. . . .

> Preamble to the Constitution of the United Nations (Iroquois), circa 1455.
>
> Franklin said of this Union: "It would be a strange thing if Six Nations of ignorant savages should be capable of forming a scheme for such a union, and be able to execute it in such a manner as that it has subsisted ages and appears indissoluble; and yet that a like union should be impracticable for ten or a dozen English colonies to whom it is more necessary and must be more advantageous, and who cannot be supposed to want an equal understanding of their interests." Quoted by Paul A. W. Wallace, *The White Roots of Peace*. The Iroquois incidentally had only one word for peace and for law. For them they were the same thing.
>
> Deganawidah was a more or less mythical character. A messenger came to the child's grandmother and said he would be born of a virgin mother. The name means Master of Things.

Many years ago we lived not here upon this earth but down under the ground. And there came a time when we had no fruit and there was nothing to eat. So we sent the humming-bird to see what he could find. Wherever he might find fruit or food of any kind, there the people would go. He flew up into the sky, and there he saw a grape-vine that had its roots in the under-world and grew up through a hole in the middle of the sky into the upper world. The humming-bird saw the hole in the sky and flew through it, and came to a land where mescal and fruits and

113

flowers of all kinds were growing. It was a good land. It was this world.

> "The Story of the First Woman Who Made the Son of
> God," from the Mohave-Apache legends

Once there were some mice under a crooked log and they believed they
were the only people in the whole world. One of them standing up and
stretching his little arms could just touch the under side of the log. He
thought that he was very tall and that he touched the sky. So he danced
and sang this song:

> Throughout the world
> Who is there like little me!
> Who is like me!
> I can touch the sky,
> I touch the sky indeed!

> CHASH-CHUNK-A (PETER SAMPSON WAVE), Winnebago
> Indians, *Wai-kun* (a fable)

There are birds of many colors—red, blue, green, yellow—yet it is all one
bird. There are horses of many colors—brown, black, yellow, white—yet
it is all one horse. So cattle, so all living things—animals, flowers, trees.
So men: in this land where once were only Indians are now men of every
color—white, black, yellow, red—yet all one people. That this should
come to pass was in the heart of the Great Mystery. It is right thus. And
everywhere there shall be peace.

> HIAMOVI (High Chief), Chief of Cheyennes and Dakotas,
> *The Indian's Book*

Brother, you say there is but one way to worship and serve the Great
Spirit. If there is but one religion, why do you white people differ so much
about it? Why are not all agreed, as you can all read the Book?

Brother, we do not understand these things. We are told that your
religion was given to your forefathers and has been handed down from
father to son. We also have a religion which was given to our forefathers
and has been handed down to us, their children. We worship in that way.
It teaches us to be thankful for all the favors we receive, to love each
other, and to be united. We never quarrel about religion.

Brother, the Great Spirit has made us all, but He has made a great
difference between His white and His red children. He has given us different complexions and different customs. To you He has given the arts.
To these, He has not opened our eyes. We know these things to be true.
Since He has made so great a difference between us in other things, why

may we not conclude that He has given us a different religion according to our understanding? The Great Spirit does right. He knows what is best for His children; we are satisfied.

Brother, we do not wish to destroy your religion or take it from you. We only want to enjoy our own.

RED JACKET, quoted by John Neihardt, *Black Elk Speaks*

Very early in life, the child began to realize that wisdom was all about and everywhere and that there were many things to know. There was no such thing as emptiness in the world. Even in the sky there were no vacant places. Everywhere there was life, visible and invisible, and every object possessed something that would be good for us to have also—even to the very stones. This gave a great interest to life. Even without human companionship one was never alone.

CHIEF STANDING BEAR, *Land of the Spotted Eagle*

My father? The sun is my father, and the earth is my mother; and on her bosom I will repose.

TECUMSEH, Chief of the Shawnees; said, indignantly, at Vincennes, in 1810, when told, "Your father requests you to take a chair"

Indian myths can seldom be dated but are likely to be less ancient than you think. It may have been the end of the eighteenth century when the priests added another chapter to the Mandan cosmology, in explanation of the beings who had come to their country, the center of the world. It was an addition to the story of creation. In the time of beginnings, this new story said, the first Mandans were preyed upon by fierce wolves, which seemed likely to destroy them. The culture hero and the friendliest god crossed the river to save the people. They killed all the old wolves. They taught the young ones not to attack men but to eat only the flesh of other animals. The rotting bodies of the old wolves remained. They threw these into the Missouri and as they floated downstream they turned into white men.

BERNARD DEVOTO, *The Course of Empire,* 1952

OTHERS

When we first set up Reformation in our Church way, did not this expose us to as greate an hazard as we could run both from abroad and at home?

Did not our friends in England many of them forewarne us of it ere we came away? Did not others send letters after us, to deterre us from it? Did not some among our selvs (and those no meane ones) inculcate our inevitable dangers at home from no smale Company left out of Church fellowship, and Civill Offices, and freedome hitherto? Yet we trusted in God (though there appeared no meanes of safety) and went on our way; and the Lord hath still preserved us, and frustrated all Councells and Attempts against us.

JOHN WINTHROP, Boston, 1643

If we will not be governed by God, we must be governed by tyrants.

WILLIAM PENN

God hath sifted a whole nation, that he might send choice grain into this wilderness.

WILLIAM STOUGHTON, 1695

I write the *Wonders* of the Christian Religion, flying from the depravations of *Europe,* to the *American Strand:* and, assisted by the Holy Author of that *Religion,* I do, with all conscience of *Truth,* required therein by Him, who is the *Truth* itself, report the *wonderful displays* of His infinite Power, Wisdom, Goodness, and Faithfulness, wherewith his Divine Providence hath *irradiated* an *Indian Wilderness.*

COTTON MATHER, *Magnalia Christi Americana,* 1702

Resolved, When I feel pain, to think of the pains of martyrdom, and of Hell.

JONATHAN EDWARDS, *Seventy Resolutions*

Resolved, never to do anything which I should be afraid to do if it were the last hour of my life.

JONATHAN EDWARDS, *Ibid.*

Resolved, That I will act so, in every respect, as I think I shall wish I had done, if I should at last be damned.

JONATHAN EDWARDS, *Ibid.,* July 8, 1723

From about that time, I began to have a new kind of apprehensions and ideas of Christ, and the work of redemption, and the glorious way of salvation by him. An inward, sweet sense of those things, at times, came into my heart; and my soul was led away in pleasant views and contemplations of them. And my mind was greatly engaged to spend my time in reading and meditating on Christ, on the beauty and excellency of his person, and the lovely way of salvation by free grace in him. I found no books so delightful to me, as those that treated of these subjects. Those words, Cant. ii: 1, used to be abundantly with me, *I am the Rose of Sharon, and the Lily of the valleys.* The words seemed to me, sweetly to represent the loveliness and beauty of Jesus Christ. The whole book of Canticles used to be pleasant to me, and I used to be much in reading it, about that time; and found, from time to time, an inward sweetness, that would carry me away, in my contemplations. This I know not how to express otherwise, than by a calm, sweet abstraction of soul from all the concerns of this world; and sometimes a kind of vision, or fixed ideas and imaginations, of being alone in the mountains, or some solitary wilderness, far from all mankind, sweetly conversing with Christ, and wrapt and swallowed up in God. The sense I had of divine things, would often of a sudden kindle up, as it were, a sweet burning in my heart; an ardor of soul, that I know not how to express.

Not long after I began to experience these things, I gave an account to my father of some things that had passed in my mind. I was pretty much affected by the discourse we had together; and when the discourse was ended, I walked abroad alone, in a solitary place in my father's pasture for contemplation. And as I was walking there and looking up on the sky and clouds, there came into my mind so sweet a sense of the glorious *majesty* and *grace* of God, that I know not how to express. I seemed to see them both in a sweet conjunction; majesty and meekness joined together; it was a gentle, and holy majesty; and also a majestic meekness; a high, great, and holy gentleness.

After this my sense of divine things gradually increased, and became more and more lively, and had more of that inward sweetness. The appearance of every thing was altered; there seemed to be, as it were, a calm, sweet cast, or appearance of divine glory, in almost every thing. God's excellency, his wisdom, his purity and love, seemed to appear in every thing; in the sun, moon, and stars; in the clouds, and blue sky; in the grass, flowers, trees; in the water, and all nature; which used greatly to fix my mind. I often used to sit and view the moon for continuance; and in the day, spent much time in viewing the clouds and sky, to behold the sweet glory of God in these things; in the mean time, singing forth, with a low voice, my contemplations of the Creator and Redeemer. And scarce anything, among all the works of nature, was so delightful to me as thunder and lightning; formerly, nothing had been so terrible to me.

Before, I used to be uncommonly terrified with thunder, and to be struck with terror when I saw a thunder storm rising; but now, on the contrary, it rejoiced me. I felt God, so to speak, at the first appearance of a thunder storm; and used to take the opportunity, at such times, to fix myself in order to view the clouds, and see the lightnings play, and hear the majestic and awful voice of God's thunder, which oftentimes was exceedingly entertaining, leading me to sweet contemplations of my great and glorious God. While thus engaged, it always seemed natural to me to sing, or chant for my meditations; or, to speak my thoughts in soliloquies with a singing voice.

JONATHAN EDWARDS, *A Personal Narrative,* 1739

The God that holds you over the pit of hell, much as one holds a spider, or some loathesome insect, over the fire, abhors you, and is dreadfully provoked; His wrath towards you burns like fire; He looks upon you as worthy of nothing else, but to be cast into the fire; He is of purer eyes than to bear to have you in His sight; you are ten thousand times so abominable in His eyes, as the most hateful and venemous serpent is in ours. You have offended Him infinitely more than ever a stubborn rebel did his prince: and yet it is nothing but His hand that holds you from falling into the fire every moment: it is ascribed to nothing else, that you did not go to hell the last night; that you was suffered to wake again in this world, after you closed your eyes to sleep; and there is no other reason to be given, why you have not dropped into hell since you arose in the morning, but that God's hand has held you up: there is no other reason to be given why you have not gone to hell, since you have sat here in the house of God, provoking His pure eyes by your sinful wicked manner of attending His solemn worship: yea, there is nothing else that is to be given as a reason why you do not this very minute drop down into hell.

> JONATHAN EDWARDS, the Enfield sermon, *Sinners in the Hands of an Angry God,* July 8, 1741. During the reading of this, Edwards' most famous sermon, there were moanings and cryings, until the shrieks became so awful that he had to pause. Of course he did not stop.

We can conceive but little of the matter: we cannot conceive what that sinking of the soul in such a case is. But to help your conception, imagine yourself to be cast into a fiery oven, all of a glowing heat, or into the midst of a glowing brick-kiln, or of a great furnace, where your pain would be as much greater than that occasioned by accidentally touching a coal of fire, as the heat is greater. Imagine also that your body were to lie there for a quarter of an hour, full of fire, as full within and without as a bright coal of fire, all the while full of quick sense; what horror would you feel at the entrance of such a furnace! And how long would that quarter of an hour seem to you! If it were to be measured by a glass, how long would the glass seem to be running! And after you had endured it for one minute, how overbearing would it be to you to think that you had it to endure the other fourteen!

But what would be the effect on your soul, if you knew you must lie there enduring that torment to the full for twenty-four hours! And how much greater would be the effect, if you knew you must endure it for a whole year; and how vastly greater still, if you knew you must endure it for a thousand years! O then, how would your heart sink, if you thought, if you knew, that you must bear it for ever and ever! That there would be no end! That after millions of millions of ages, your torment would be no nearer to an end, than ever it would; and that you never, never should be delivered!

JONATHAN EDWARDS, *Ibid.*

Hell is paved with the skulls of unbaptized children.

JONATHAN EDWARDS

[Damned infants are] young vipers and (to God) infinitely more hateful than vipers.

JONATHAN EDWARDS

To adopt the laws of God . . . until there is time to frame better.

First legislative measure passed by the State of Vermont

Puritanism, believing itself quick with the seed of religious liberty, laid, without knowing it, the egg of democracy.

JAMES RUSSELL LOWELL, *Among My Books*, "New England Two Centuries Ago"

Thank God I never was cheerful. I come from the happy stock of the Mathers, who, as you remember, passed sweet mornings reflecting on the goodness of God and the damnation of infants.

HENRY ADAMS

The objection to Puritans is not that they try to make us think as they do, but that they try to make us do as they think.

H. L. MENCKEN

As the colors of Autumn stream down the wind, scarlet in sumach and maple, spun gold in the birches, a splendor of smoldering fire in the oaks along the hill, and the last leaves flutter away, the dusk falls briefly about the worker bringing in from the field a late load of its fruit, and Arcturus is lost to sight and Orion swings upward that great sun upon his shoulder, we are stirred once more to ponder the Infinite Goodness that has set apart for us, in all this moving mystery of creation, a time of living and a home. In such a spirit I appoint Thursday, the twenty-fourth of November, a day of PUBLIC THANKSGIVING.

In such a spirit I call upon the people to acknowledge heartily, in friendly gathering and house of prayer, the increase of the season nearing now its close: the harvest of earth, the yield of patient mind and faithful hand, that have kept us fed and clothed and have made for us a shelter even against the storm.

It is right that we whose arc of sky has been darkened by no war hawk, who have been forced by no man to stand and speak when to speak was to choose between death and life, should give thanks also for the further mercies we have enjoyed, beyond desert or any estimation, of Justice, Freedom, Loving-kindness, Peace-resolving, as we prize them, to let no occasion go without some prompting or some effort worthy in a way however humble of these proudest among man's ideals which burn, though it may be like candles fitfully, in our gusty world with a light so clear we name its source divine.

WILBUR L. CROSS, Governor of Connecticut, *New York Times,* November 24, 1938

The first thanksgiving, held at Plymouth in 1621, has become enshrined in an American institution. In the seventeenth century, New England observed many days of rejoicing, but none in imitation of this original; all were ordered "pro temporibus et causis," according to the manner in which providence was dealing with the land. Accordingly, it observed mostly days of humiliation; over the years there were more chastisements than blessings. For the Puritan mind, to fix thanksgiving to a mechanical revolution of the calendar would be folly: who can say that in November there will be that for which thanks should be uttered rather than lamentation? By the time ceremonial gratitude can be channelized into an annual festival, calculated in advance, society is rewarding its own well-doing, not acknowledging divine favor. When this happens, Calvinism is dead; though the society doggedly persists in giving autumnal thanks, it no longer has a mechanism for confessing its shortcomings and seeking forgiveness for its trespasses.

> PERRY MILLER, *From Colony to Province,* 1953

16. That religion, or the duty which we owe to our Creator, and the manner of discharging it, can be directed only by reason and conviction, not by force or violence; and therefore all men are equally entitled to the free exercise of religion, according to the dictates of conscience; and that it is the mutual duty of all to practice Christian forbearance, love, and charity towards each other.

> PATRICK HENRY, Virginia Bill of Rights, "Article XVI," June 12, 1776

Friends [Quakers] believe in the fatherhood of God, the brotherhood of man and the neighborhood of Philadelphia.

> GILBERT WHITE, while President of Haverford College

Every force evolves a form.

> Shaker proverb

For I am God, and mine arm is not shortened and I will show miracles, signs and wonders, unto all those who believe on my name . . . and the time speedily cometh, that great things are to be shown forth unto the children of men. . . . Wherefore, I have called upon the weak things of the world, those who are unlearned and despised, to thresh the nations by the power of my Spirit; And their arm shall be mine arm, and I will be their shield and their buckler, and I will gird up their loins, and they shall fight manfully for me . . . and I will cause the heavens to shake for your good: and Satan shall tremble; and Zion shall rejoice upon the hills, and flourish. . . . Fear not, little flock, the kingdom is yours until I come, Behold I come quickly; even so: Amen.

> *The Book of Commandments* (the Mormon Scriptures), Ch. xxxvii, verses 9, 11, 14, 15, 26, 27, 30, 31

This, shipmates, this is that other lesson; and woe to that pilot of the living God who slights it. Woe to him whom this world charms from Gospel duty! Woe to him who seeks to pour oil upon the waters when

God has brewed them into a gale! Woe to him who seeks to please rather than to appal! Woe to him whose good name is more to him than goodness! Woe to him who, in this world, courts not dishonor! Woe to him who would not be true, even though to be false were salvation! Yea, woe to him who, as the great Pilot Paul has it, while preaching to others is himself a castaway! . . .

But oh! shipmates! on the starboard hand of every woe, there is a sure delight; and higher the top of that delight, than the bottom of the woe is deep. Is not the main-truck higher than the kelson is low? Delight is to him—a far, far upward, and inward delight—who against the proud gods and commodores of this earth, ever stands forth his own inexorable self. Delight is to him whose strong arms yet support him, when the ship of this base treacherous world has gone down beneath him. Delight is to him, who gives no quarter in the truth, and kills, burns, and destroys all sin though he pluck it out from under the robes of Senators and Judges. Delight,—top-gallant delight is to him, who acknowledges no law or lord, but the Lord his God, and is only a patriot to heaven. Delight is to him, whom all the waves of the billows of the seas of the boisterous mob can never shake from this sure Keel of the Ages. And eternal delight and deliciousness will be his, who coming to lay him down, can say with his final breath—O Father!—chiefly known to me by Thy rod—mortal or immortal, here I die. I have striven to be Thine, more than to be this world's, or mine own. Yet this is nothing: I leave eternity to Thee; for what is a man that he should live out the lifetime of his God?

> HERMAN MELVILLE, *Moby Dick*, "Father Mapple's Sermon," IX

We, on our side, are praying to Him to give us victory, because we believe we are right; but those on the other side pray to Him, look for victory, believing they are right. What must He think of us?

> ABRAHAM LINCOLN

When I hear a man preach, I like to see him act as if he were fighting bees.

> ABRAHAM LINCOLN

I cannot without mental reservations assent to long and complicated creeds and catechisms. If the church would ask simply for assent to the Saviour's statement of the substance of the law: "Thou shalt love the Lord thy God with all thy heart, and with all thy soul, and with all thy mind, and thy neighbour as thyself,"—that church would I gladly unite with.

> ABRAHAM LINCOLN, Rankin, *Personal Recollections of Lincoln*. Mr. Rankin's mother asked the President a question which he answered thus.

Health is not a condition of matter, but of Mind.

> MARY BAKER EDDY, *Science and Health with Key to the Scriptures*, 1875

Disease is an experience of so-called mortal mind. It is fear made manifest on the body.

> MARY BAKER EDDY, *Ibid.*

The prayer that reforms the sinner and heals the sick is an absolute faith that all things are possible to God,—a spiritual understanding of Him, an unselfed love.

> MARY BAKER EDDY, *Ibid.*

How would you define Christian Science?

   As the law of God, the law of good, interpreting and demonstrating the divine Principle and rule of universal harmony.

> MARY BAKER EDDY, *Rudimental Divine Science*

I, Mary Baker Eddy, ordain the *Bible,* and *Science and Health with Key to the Scriptures,* Pastor over The Mother Church—The First Church of Christ, Scientist, in Boston, Mass.—and they will continue to preach for this Church and the world.

> MARY BAKER EDDY, Article XIV, Section 1, Church By-Laws, 1895

There is no life, truth, intelligence, nor substance in matter. All is infinite Mind and its infinite manifestation, for God is All-in-all. Spirit is immortal Truth; matter is mortal error. Spirit is the real and eternal; matter is the unreal and temporal. Spirit is God, and man is His image and likeness. Therefore man is not material; he is spiritual.

> MARY BAKER EDDY, "The Scientific Statement of Being." The reading of this statement is the climax of every Christian Science service.

Brace up, my dear. Just pray to God. *She* will help you.

> MRS. OLIVER HAZARD PERRY BELMONT, advice to a disen-
> chanted suffragette

I am interested in the science of government, but I am more interested in religion. . . . I enjoy making a political speech . . . but I would rather speak on religion than on politics. I commenced speaking on the stump when I was only twenty, but I commenced speaking in the church six years earlier—and I shall be in the church even after I am out of politics.

> WILLIAM JENNINGS BRYAN, "The Prince of Peace," a lec-
> ture given in almost every corner of the world

Q. Do you claim that everything in the Bible should be literally interpreted?

A. I believe that everything in the Bible should be accepted as it is given there.

Q. But when you read that Jonah swallowed the whale—or that the whale swallowed Jonah—excuse me, please, how do you literally interpret it? . . . You believe that God made such a fish, and that it was big enough to swallow Jonah?

A. Yes, sir.

Q. Perfectly easy to believe that Jonah swallowed the whale?

A. If the Bible said so.

> WILLIAM JENNINGS BRYAN, cross examination by Clarence
> Darrow, at the Scopes Trial in Dayton, Tennessee, 1925

One miracle is just as easy to believe as another.

> WILLIAM JENNINGS BRYAN, *Ibid.*

If a minister believes and teaches evolution, he is a stinking skunk, a hypocrite, and a liar.

> WILLIAM A. ("BILLY") SUNDAY, interview, 1925

If there is no Hell, a good many preachers are obtaining money under false pretences.

> WILLIAM A. ("BILLY") SUNDAY

Many of you here tonight are like a plane in a fog which has lost contact with the airport. You are circling round and round in the monotony, confusion and drudgery of life. You can make contact with God tonight through Jesus Christ.

> WILLIAM ("BILLY") GRAHAM, sermon

Peace! It's wonderful!

> Saying of followers of Father Divine

Wishing you all success, and that as I AM, so might you be, this leaves ME well, healthy, joyful, peaceful, lively, loving, successful, prosperous, and Happy in Spirit, Body, and Mind, and in every organ, muscle, sinew, vein and bone and in every atom, fiber and cell of My Bodily Form.

> FATHER DIVINE, a typical salutation, quoted by George Sokolsky, *Atlantic Monthly*, June, 1938

For President Eliot, the enemies to his true faith were churches, creeds, priests, anything supernatural, any concern for a life after death, anything that professed to be sacramental. . . . His was to be a "simple and rational faith," and there was to be no place in it for "metaphysical complexities or magical rites. . . ." This is where President Eliot may have been wrong, at least wrong for our time, for it has now become frighteningly clear that if you try to ignore metaphysical considerations—I would say consideration of ultimate things—or cover them up in bursts of energy, they will rise up in perverted and distorted forms to mock one's thus too-circumscribed efforts. . . .

Personal religion, and understanding of and participation in the work of the Church, could apparently in many earlier generations be taken for granted. Latterly, they have tended to ebb away in the all but universal adoration of the state, and in almost idolatrous preoccupation with the secular order, the accumulation of knowledge, and with good works. There is not and cannot be a quarrel with any of these things in themselves, but only with the notion that they are independently sufficient goods.

And it is because these have been tried and the people are still not fed, that you especially are now presented with an immense new and most difficult responsibility. . . . It is leadership in religious knowledge and, even more, in religious experience—not increased industrial might, nor more research facilities, certainly not those things by themselves—of which we now have a most gaping need.

> NATHAN M. PUSEY, speech at Convocation of Harvard Divinity School, September, 1953

ON THE BIBLE

What you have told us is all very good. It is indeed bad to eat apples. It is better to make them all into cider.

> Reply of an Indian orator, after hearing a missionary's account of the Fall of Man, quoted by Franklin, *Remarks Concerning the Savages of North America*

Young man, my advice to you is that you cultivate an acquaintance with, and a firm belief in, the Holy Scriptures. This is your certain interest.

BENJAMIN FRANKLIN

That book, sir, is the rock on which our republic rests.

ANDREW JACKSON

It is remarkable that, notwithstanding the universal favor with which the New Testament is outwardly received . . . there is no hospitality shown to it, there is no appreciation of the order of truth with which it deals. I know of no book that has so few readers. There is none so truly strange, and heretical, and unpopular. . . . There are, indeed, severe things in it which no man should read aloud more than once. "Seek first the kingdom of heaven." "Lay not up for yourselves treasures on earth." "If thou wilt be perfect, go and sell that thou hast, and give to the poor, and thou shalt have treasure in heaven." "For what is a man profited, if he shall gain the whole world, and lose his own soul?" . . . Think of repeating these things to a New England audience! . . . Who, without cant, can read them aloud? Who, without cant, can hear them, and not go out of the meeting house? They never *were* read, they never *were* heard. Let but one of these sentences be rightly read, from any pulpit in the land, and there would not be left one stone of that meeting-house upon another.

> HENRY DAVID THOREAU, *A Week on the Concord and Merrimac Rivers*

In all my perplexities and distresses, the Bible has never failed to give me light and strength.

ROBERT E. LEE

The New Testament, and to a very large extent the Old, *is* the soul of man. You cannot criticize it. It criticizes you.

JOHN JAY CHAPMAN, letter, March 26, 1898

I have . . . been reading the Old Testament, a most bloodthirsty and perilous book for the young. Jehovah is beyond doubt the worst character in fiction.

E. A. ROBINSON, letter to Mrs. Henry Richards

The Bible is literature, not dogma.

GEORGE SANTAYANA

The foundations of our society and of our government rest so much on the teachings of the Bible, that it would be difficult to support them, if faith in these teachings should cease to be practically universal in our country.

CALVIN COOLIDGE

Unless we form the habit of going to the Bible in bright moments as well as in trouble, we cannot fully respond to its consolations, because we lack equilibrium between light and darkness.

HELEN KELLER

Jehovah has always seemed to me the most fascinating character in all fiction.

OLIVER HERFORD

The Bible is One Book for One World.

EDWARD VERNON ("EDDIE") RICKENBACKER

DEMOCRACY

•

WHAT IT IS

The foundation of authority is laid in the free consent of the people.

THOMAS HOOKER, *Fundamental Orders,* 1639, which served
as the basis for Connecticut's Constitution

There goes many a ship to sea, with many hundred souls in one ship, whose weal and woe is common, and is a true picture of a commonwealth,

or a human combination or society. It hath fallen out sometimes that both
papists and protestants, Jews and Turks, may be embarked in one ship;
upon which supposal I affirm, that all the liberty of conscience, that I
ever pleaded for, turns upon these two hinges—that none of the papists,
protestants, Jews, or Turks be forced to come to the ship's prayers or
worship, nor compelled from their own particular prayers or worship, if
they practice any. I further add, that I never denied, that notwithstanding this liberty, the commander of this ship ought to command the ship's
course, yea, and also command that justice, peace, and sobriety be kept
and practiced, both among the seamen and all the passengers.

If any of the seamen refuse to perform their services, or passengers to
pay their freight; if any refuse to help, in person or purse, toward the
common charges or defense; if any refuse to obey the common laws and
orders of the ship, concerning their common peace of preservation; if any
shall mutiny and rise up against their commanders and officers; if any
should preach or write that there ought to be no commanders or officers,
because all are equal in Christ, therefore no masters nor officers, no laws
nor orders, nor corrections nor punishments—I say, I never denied, but
in such cases, whatever is pretended, the commander or commanders may
judge, resist, compel, and punish such transgressors, according to their
deserts and merits.

> ROGER WILLIAMS, *Letter to the Townsmen of Providence,*
> January, 1655

Let the people think they govern, and they will be governed.

> WILLIAM PENN

Individuals themselves, each in his own personal and sovereign right, entered into a compact with each other to produce a government: and this
is the only mode in which governments have a right to arise, and the only
principle on which they have a right to exist.

> THOMAS PAINE

The two great points of difference between a democracy and a republic
are: first, the delegation of the government, in the latter, to a small number of citizens elected by the rest; secondly, the greater number of citizens,
and greater sphere of country, over which the latter may be extended.

The effect of the first difference is, on the one hand, to refine and enlarge the public views, by passing them through the medium of a chosen
body of citizens, whose wisdom may best discern the true interest of their

country, and whose patriotism and love of justice will be least likely to
sacrifice it to temporary or partial considerations. Under such a regulation, it may well happen that the public voice, pronounced by the representatives of the people, will be more consonant to the public good than
if pronounced by the people themselves, convened for the purpose.

JAMES MADISON, *The Federalist*, X, 1787

We have called by different names brethren of the same principle. We
are all Republicans, and we are all Federalists. If there be any among us
who would wish to dissolve this Union or to change its republican form,
let them stand undisturbed as monuments of the safety with which error
of opinion may be tolerated where reason is left free to combat it. I
know, indeed, that some honest men fear that a republican government
cannot be strong, that this government is not strong enough; but would
the honest patriot, in the full tide of successful experiment, abandon a
government which has so far kept us free and firm on the theoretic and
visionary fear that this government, the world's best hope, may by possibility want energy to preserve itself? I trust not. I believe this, on the
contrary, the strongest government on earth. I believe it is the only one
where every man, at the call of the laws, would fly to the standard of the
law, and would meet invasions of the public order as his own personal
concern. Sometimes it is said that man cannot be trusted with the government of himself. Can he, then, be trusted with the government of others?
Or have we found angels in the form of kings to govern him? Let history
answer this question.

THOMAS JEFFERSON, "First Inaugural," March 4, 1801

The will of the people is the only legitimate foundation of any government, and to protect its free expression should be our first object.

THOMAS JEFFERSON, *Ibid.*

The government of the Union, then, is emphatically and truly a government of the people. In form and in substance it emanates from them. Its
powers are granted by them, and are to be exercised directly on them and
for their benefit.

JOHN MARSHALL, *McCulloch* v. *Maryland,* 1819

I found . . . that the wisest and best of the species, or, what is much the
same thing, the most responsible, uniformly maintain that he who has the
largest stake in society is, in the nature of things, the most qualified to

administer its affairs. By a stake in society is meant, agreeable to universal convention, a multiplication of those interests which occupy us in our daily concerns—or what is vulgarly called property. This principle works by exciting us to do right through those heavy investments of our own which would inevitably suffer were we to do wrong. The proposition is now clear, nor can the premises readily be mistaken. Happiness is the aim of society; and property, or a vested interest in society, is the best pledge of our disinterestedness and justice, and the best qualification for its proper control. It follows as a legitimate corollary, that a multiplication of those interests will increase the stake, and render us more and more worthy of the trust by elevating us as near as may be to the pure and ethereal condition of the angels.

JAMES FENIMORE COOPER, *The Monikins,* a satire, 1835

I think lightly of what is called treason against a government. That may be your duty today, or mine. But treason against the people, against mankind, against God, is a great sin not lightly to be spoken of.

THEODORE PARKER, speech on the Mexican War, 1846

The progress from an absolute to a limited monarchy, from a limited monarchy to a democracy, is a progress toward a true respect for the individual. Even the Chinese philosopher was wise enough to regard the individual as the basis of the empire. Is a democracy, such as we know it, the last improvement possible in government? Is it not possible to take a step further towards recognizing and organizing the rights of man? There will never be a really free and enlightened State until the State comes to recognize the individual as a higher and independent power, from which all its own power and authority are derived, and treats him accordingly.

HENRY DAVID THOREAU, *Civil Disobedience*

"Blast them, Jack, what they call the public is a monster, like the idol we saw in Owyhee, with the head of a jackass, the body of a baboon, and the tail of a scorpion."

"I don't like that," said Jack; "when I'm ashore, I myself am part of the public."

"Your pardon, Jack; you are not. You are then a part of the people, just as you are aboard the frigate here. The public is one thing, Jack, and the people another."

"You are right," said Jack. . . . "The public and the people. Aye, aye, my lads, let us hate the one and cleave to the other."

HERMAN MELVILLE, *White-Jacket,* 1850

Men may seem detestable as joint-stock companies and nations; knaves, fools and murderers there may be; men may have mean and meagre faces; but man, in the ideal, is so noble and so sparkling, such a grand and glowing creature, that over any ignominious blemish in him all his fellows should run to throw their costliest robes. That immaculate manliness we feel in ourselves—so far within us that it remains intact though all the outer character seems gone—bleeds with keenest anguish at the spectacle of a valour-ruined man. Nor can piety itself, at such a shameful sight, completely stifle her upbraidings against the permitting stars. But this august dignity I speak of, it is not the dignity of kings and robes, but that abounding dignity which has no robed investiture. Thou shalt see it shining in the arm that wields a pick and drives a spike; that democratic dignity which, on all hands, radiates without end from God; Himself! The great God absolute! The centre and circumference of all democracy! His omnipresence, our divine equality!

HERMAN MELVILLE, Moby Dick, XXVI

If, then, to meanest mariners, and renegades and castaways, I shall hereafter ascribe high qualities, though dark; weave round them tragic glances; if even the most mournful, perchance the most abased, among them all, shall at times lift himself to the exalted mounts; if I shall touch that workman's arm with some ethereal light; if I shall spread a rainbow over his disastrous set of sun; then against all mortal critics bear me out in it, thou just Spirit of Equality, which hast spread one royal mantle of humanity over all my kind! Bear me out in it, thou great democratic God! who didst not refuse to the swart convict, Bunyan, the pale, poetic pearl; Thou who didst clothe with doubly hammered leaves of finest gold, the stumped and paupered arm of old Cervantes; Thou who didst pick up Andrew Jackson from the pebbles; who didst hurl him upon a war-horse; who didst thunder him higher than a throne! Thou who, in all Thy mighty, earthly marchings, ever cullest Thy selectest champions from the kingly commons; bear me out in it, O God!

HERMAN MELVILLE, Ibid.

No man is good enough to govern another man without that other's consent.

ABRAHAM LINCOLN, speech, Peoria, October 16, 1854

Democracy is direct self-government, over all the people, for all the people, by all the people.

THEODORE PARKER, sermon, July 4, 1858. The sentence was

later incorporated in a pamphlet, *On the Effect of Slavery on the American People,* and Lincoln is said (by his law partner, Herndon) to have marked it in his copy.

As I would not be a *slave,* so I would not be a *master.* Whatever differs from this, to the extent of the difference, is no democracy.

> ABRAHAM LINCOLN, "Fragment on Slavery," August 1, 1858 (date assigned by Hay and Nicolay)

While the people retain their virtue and vigilance, no administration, by any extreme of wickedness or folly, can very seriously injure the government in the short space of four years.

> ABRAHAM LINCOLN, "First Inaugural," March 4, 1861

Why should there not be a patient confidence in the ultimate justice of the people? Is there any better or equal hope in the world?

> ABRAHAM LINCOLN, *Ibid.*

This country, with its institutions, belongs to the people who inhabit it. Whenever they shall grow weary of the existing government, they can exercise their constitutional right of amending it, or their revolutionary right to dismember or overthrow it.

> ABRAHAM LINCOLN, *Ibid.*

Public opinion, though often formed upon a wrong basis, yet generally has a strong underlying sense of justice.

> ABRAHAM LINCOLN

Democracy is that form of society, no matter what its political classification, in which every man has a chance and knows that he has it.

> JAMES RUSSELL LOWELL

President Lincoln defined democracy to be "the government of the people, by the people, and for the people." This is a sufficiently compact statement of it as a political arrangement. Theodore Parker said that "Democracy meant not 'I'm as good as you are,' but 'You're as good as I am.'" And this is the ethical conception of it, necessary as a complement of the other.

> JAMES RUSSELL LOWELL

Democracy gives every man the right to be his own oppressor.

JAMES RUSSELL LOWELL

All free governments are managed by the combined wisdom and folly of the people.

JAMES A. GARFIELD

I grant [democracy] is an experiment, but it is the only direction society can take that is worth its taking. . . . Every other possible step is backward.

HENRY ADAMS, *Democracy,* 1880

I assert that the people of the United States . . . have sufficient patriotism and sufficient intelligence to sit in judgment on every question which has arisen or which will arise, no matter how long our government will endure. The great political questions are in their final analysis great moral questions, and it requires no extended experience in the handling of money to enable a man to tell right from wrong.

WILLIAM JENNINGS BRYAN

Men write many fine and plausible arguments in support of monarchy, but the fact remains that where every man in a state has a vote, brutal laws are impossible.

SAMUEL L. CLEMENS ("MARK TWAIN"), *A Connecticut Yankee in King Arthur's Court*

You cannot keep the people out of government and progress. If their intelligence does not rule, their ignorance will.

THOMAS B. REED

A government is not made representative or just by the mechanical expedient of electing its members by universal suffrage. It becomes representative only by embodying in its policy, whether by instinct or high intelligence, the people's conscious and unconscious interests.

GEORGE SANTAYANA, *The Life of Reason;* II, *Reason in Society*

Democracy is much broader than a special political form, a method of conducting government, of making laws and carrying on governmental administration by means of popular suffrage and elected officers. . . .

The political and governmental phase of democracy is a means, the best means so far found, for realizing ends that lie in the wide domain of human relationships and the development of human personality. It is . . . a way of life, social and individual.

JOHN DEWEY

Western democracy through the whole of its earlier period tended to the production of a society of which the most distinctive fact was the freedom of the individual to rise under conditions of social mobility, and whose ambition was the liberty and well-being of the masses. This conception has vitalized all American democracy, and has brought it into sharp contrasts with the democracies of history, and with those modern efforts of Europe to create an artificial democratic order by legislation. The problem of the United States is not to create democracy, but to conserve democratic institutions and ideals.

FREDERICK JACKSON TURNER, *The Frontier in American History*, 1920

The doctrine of Democracy, like any other of the living faiths of men, is so essentially mystical that it continually demands new formulation. To fail to recognise it in a new form, to call it hard names, to refuse to receive it, may mean to reject that which our fathers cherished and handed on as an inheritance not only to be preserved but also to be developed.

JANE ADDAMS, *The Spirit of Youth*

It would be folly to argue that the people cannot make political mistakes. They can and do make grave mistakes. They know it, they pay the penalty, but compared with the mistakes which have been made by every kind of autocracy they are unimportant.

CALVIN COOLIDGE

Democracy is based upon the conviction that there are extraordinary possibilities in ordinary people.

HARRY EMERSON FOSDICK, *Democracy*

Abuse [our system] as you will, at least it gives a bloodless measure of social forces—bloodless, have you thought of that?—a means of continuity, a principle of stability, a relief from the paralyzing terror of revolution. I have been where this was not true; in lands where one felt the pervasive foreboding of violence, of armed suppression, the inability of minorities to exert just those peaceful pressures, that seem to us so vicious; where government is conducted not by compromise, but by *coup d'état*. And I have looked back with contentment to my own country, distracted as she might be by a Babel of many voices, uncertain of her purposes and her path; where yet there can be revolution without machine guns, and men may quit a public office and retain a private life. Given an opportunity to oppose our will, a ground where we may test our mettle, we get the sense that there is some propriety in yielding to those who impose upon us. There has been an outlet, a place of reckoning, a means not of counting heads, but of matching wits and courage. If these are fairly measured, most of us acquiesce; we are conscious of a stronger power which it is idle to resist, until we in turn have organized in more formidable array and can impress ourselves in turn. And so I will not declaim against the evils of our time, the selfishness of class struggle, the disregard of the common good. Nor will I forsake the faith of our fathers in democracy, however I must transmute it, and make it unlovely to their eyes, were they here to see their strangely perverse disciple. If you will give me scales by which to weigh Tom and Dick and Harry as to their fitness to rule, and tell me how much each shall count, I will talk with you about some other kind of organisation. Plato jumped hurdles that are too high for my legs; maybe you can help me over, or lower them. But unless you do, I will stand in the place that I am accustomed to. I will say that there must be a trying-out of men, according to their qualities as God has made them; that it is a precious inheritance, which we must not abjure, that that chance exists; that we must write down our miscarriages to our own flaccid selves. Meanwhile we shall not bottle up the gases and prepare for the inevitable explosion.

> LEARNED HAND, address on ninety-first birthday of Justice
> O. W. Holmes, March 8, 1932

All the ills of democracy can be cured by more democracy.

> ALFRED E. SMITH, speech, 1933

Democracy is liberty plus economic security. We Americans want to pray, think as we please—and eat regular.

> MAURY MAVERICK

Democracy is a cause that is never won, but I believe it will never be lost.

> CHARLES A. BEARD

The case for democracy is that it accepts the rational and humane values as ends, and proposes as the means of realizing them the minimum of coercion and the maximum of voluntary assent.

CARL BECKER, *Yale Review,* June, 1940

The century on which we are entering can be and must be the century of the common man.

HENRY AGARD WALLACE, address, May 8, 1942

Proposition: The duty of a democracy is to know then what it knows now.

E. B. WHITE, *One Man's Meat,* "Compost"

We received a letter from the Writers' War Board the other day asking for a statement on "The Meaning of Democracy." It presumably is our duty to comply with such a request, and it is certainly our pleasure.

Surely the Board knows what democracy is. It is the line that forms on the right. It is the don't in Don't Shove. It is the hole in the stuffed shirt through which the sawdust slowly trickles; it is the dent in the high hat. Democracy is the recurrent suspicion that more than half of the people are right more than half of the time. It is the feeling of privacy in the voting booths, the feeling of communion in the libraries, the feeling of vitality everywhere. Democracy is the score at the beginning of the ninth. It is an idea which hasn't been disproved yet, a song the words of which have not gone bad. It's the mustard on the hot dog and the cream in the rationed coffee. Democracy is a request from a War Board, in the middle of a morning in the middle of a war, wanting to know what democracy is.

E. B. WHITE, "The Wild Flag," *New Yorker,* July 3, 1943

Democracy in general is what Americans do. Start out with this axiom and life becomes not only easier to understand but in the long run more fruitful. Start out with the opposite proposition, that democracy is something defined by Aristotle and amended by Thomas Jefferson and Karl Marx, and you will get far fewer results at the expenditure of a far greater volume of clamor and hard feelings.

. . . Democracy is what happens in New York City, on the final showing. New York's eight millions are by far the largest urban group in which democracy has ever operated. That is why people who want to understand democracy should spend less time in the library and more time . . . in the subway.

SIMEON STRUNSKY, *No Mean City,* 1944

Human rights rest on human dignity. The dignity of man is an ideal worth fighting for and worth dying for. It is not so, as William James would have said, because it satisfies our habits or emotions, but because it is true, and we can know it is true. Human dignity rests on evident propositions about the kind of animal man is. He is, though an animal, a rational and spiritual being. His minimum animal needs must be met if he is to live at all, but he cannot live a human life unless he has the chance to fulfill the immense want of his rational and spiritual nature. This is what Plato meant when he said, "We differ from most people in not regarding mere safety and existence as the most precious thing man can possess, but rather the gaining of all possible goodness and the keeping of it throughout life."

Men are essentially interdependent. It is clear enough that to sustain life they must live in society. It is just as clear that they must live in society to achieve the aspirations of their rational spiritual nature. Man is not inherently selfish, actuated alone by the principle of self-preservation and the desire for material security. Law and government answer to the needs of our common human nature and are established to help each of us in our own lives meet those needs. They are not imposed upon the individual wholly from without, with no sanction but that of force. They are necessary accompaniments of human coexistence.

Democracy is the best form of government because it is built upon these principles. It is the only form of government that is founded on the dignity of man, not the dignity of some men, of rich men, of educated men or of white men, but of all men. Its sanction is not the sanction of force, but the sanction of human nature. Equality and justice, the two great distinguishing characteristics of democracy, follow inevitably from the conception of men, all men, as rational and spiritual beings.

In this light freedom takes on meaning. It is not freedom to do as we please but freedom to achieve that autonomy which we approach in proportion as we develop our rational and spiritual nature. It is not mere freedom to live that concerns us most, but freedom to live human lives. Men must be free to exercise those powers which make them men.

ROBERT M. HUTCHINS, *Democracy and Human Nature*

Democracy is the most demanding of all forms of government in terms of the energy, imagination and public spirit required of the individual.

GEORGE C. MARSHALL

The story of the negro as a voter in the United States illustrates the essential character of democracy. Democracy is a process, not a static condition. It is becoming, rather than being. It can easily be lost, but never is fully won. Its essence is eternal struggle.

JUDGE WILLIAM H. HASTIE

This I *do* carry in my head, Senator.

I will do my best to make it clear. My convictions are not so much concerned with what I am against as what I am for; and that excludes a lot of things automatically.

Traditionally, democracy has been an affirmative doctrine rather than merely a negative one.

I believe—and I conceive the Constitution of the United States to rest, as does religion, upon the fundamental proposition of the integrity of the individual; and that all government and all private institutions must be designed to promote and protect and defend the integrity and the dignity of the individual; that that is the essential meaning of the Constitution and the Bill of Rights, as it is essentially the meaning of religion.

Any form of government, therefore, and any other institutions which make men means rather than ends, which exalt the state or any other institution above the importance of men, which place arbitrary power over men as a fundamental tenet of government are contrary to that conception, and, therefore, I am deeply opposed to them.

. . . It is very easy simply to say that one is not a Communist. And, of course, if despite my record it is necessary for me to state this very affirmatively, then it is a great disappointment to me.

It is very easy to talk about being against communism. It is equally important to believe those things which provide a satisfying and effective alternative. Democracy is that satisfying, affirmative alternative.

. . . This I deeply believe.

DAVID E. LILIENTHAL, before Joint Congressional Committee, February 4, 1947

Victory in the Mediterranean and European campaigns gave the lie to all who preached, or in our times shall preach, that the democracies are decadent, afraid to fight, unable to match the productivity of regimented economies, unwilling to sacrifice in a common cause.

DWIGHT D. EISENHOWER, *Crusade in Europe*

If we dedicate ourselves anew to making in America a demonstration of a free, just, and unafraid society at work, we can show all the world that

a government of the people and by the people can do more for the people
than any other kind of government on earth.

PAUL G. HOFFMAN, *American Freedom,* 1953

In spite of all this there has been a saving common sense about our democracy. The American story contains many pages describing the rise of
a dangerous demagoguery from the Know Nothings of the 1850's to the
Ku Klux Klan of our day, from Aaron Burr to Joe McCarthy. But the
end has always been victory for comparative reason and decency. The
struggle against demagoguery scarcely fits the St. George-against-the-
dragon myth so popular in folk lore. Our democratic St. George goes out
rather reluctantly with armor awry. The struggle is confused; our knight
wins by no clean thrust of lance or sword, but the dragon somehow poops
out and decent democracy is victor.

NORMAN THOMAS, speech on seventieth birthday, 1954

SOME VIEWS ASKANCE

If the people be governors who shall be governed?

JOHN COTTON

Monarchy is like a splendid ship, with all sails set; it moves majestically
on, then it hits a rock and sinks for ever. Democracy is like a raft. It never
sinks, but, damn it, your feet are always in the water.

FISHER AMES

There never was a democracy that did not commit suicide.

SAMUEL ADAMS

Our real disease is . . . democracy.

ALEXANDER HAMILTON

The mobs of great cities add just so much to the support of pure government as sores do to the strength of the human body.

THOMAS JEFFERSON

Any one of these talents that in fact commands or influences two votes in society gives to the man who possesses it, the character of an aristocrat, in my sense of the word. Pick up the first hundred men you meet and make a republic. Every man will have an equal vote, but when deliberations and discussions are opened, it will be found that twenty-five, by their talents, virtues being equal, will be able to carry fifty votes. Every one of these twenty-five is an aristocrat in my sense of the word; whether he obtains his one vote in addition to his own, by his birth, fortune, figure, eloquence, science, learning, craft, cunning, or even his character for good fellowship, and a *bon vivant.*

JOHN ADAMS, letter to Thomas Jefferson

The proposition that people are the best keepers of their own liberties is not true.

JOHN ADAMS

The publick is to be watched . . . in this country, as in other countries kings and aristocrats are to be watched.

JAMES FENIMORE COOPER, *The American Democrat,* 1838

Vox populi, vox humbug (The voice of the people is the voice of humbug).

WILLIAM T. SHERMAN, letter to his wife, June 2, 1863

Neither current events nor history show that the majority rules, or ever did rule.

JEFFERSON DAVIS, in conversation, July 17, 1864

It has long been a grave question whether any government, not too strong for the liberties of its people, can be strong enough to maintain its existence in great emergencies.

ABRAHAM LINCOLN, Response to a Serenade, Nov. 10, 1864

In modern times, movable capital has been immensely developed and even fixed capital has been made mobile by the joint-stock device. It has dissipated and largely defeated the social power of land property. . . . The effect of the creation of an immense stock of movable capital, of the opportunities in commerce and industry offered to men of talent, of the immense aid of science to industry, of the opening of new continents and the peopling of them by the poorest and worst in Europe, has been to produce modern mores. All our popular faiths, hopes, enjoyments, and powers are due to these great changes in the conditions of life. The new status makes us believe in all kinds of rosy doctrines about human welfare, and about the struggle for existence and the competition of life; it also gives us all our contempt for old-fashioned kings and nobles, creates democracies, and brings forth new social classes and gives them power. . . . When the earth is underpopulated and there is an economic demand for men, democracy is inevitable. That state of things cannot be permanent. Therefore democracy cannot last. It contains no absolute and "eternal" truth.

WILLIAM GRAHAM SUMNER, 1906

No American, no matter how sharp his critical sense, can ever get away from the notion that democracy is, in some subtle and mysterious way, more conducive to human progress and more pleasing to a just God than any of the systems of government which stand opposed to it. In the privacy of his study he may observe very clearly that it exalts the facile and specious man above the really competent man, and from this observation he may draw the conclusion that its abandonment would be desirable, but once he emerges from his academic seclusion and resumes the rubbing of noses with his fellow-men, he will begin to be tortured by a sneaking feeling that such ideas are heretical and unmanly, and the next time the band begins to play he will thrill with the best of them—or the worst.

H. L. MENCKEN, *Prejudices: First Series,* 1919

At no time, at no place, in solemn convention assembled, through no chosen agents, had the American people officially proclaimed the United States to be a democracy. The Constitution did not contain the word or any word lending countenance to it, except possibly the mention of "We, the people," in the preamble . . . when the Constitution was framed no respectable person called himself or herself a democrat.

CHARLES A. and MARY BEARD, *America in Midpassage*

Democracy. A government of the masses. Authority derived through mass meeting or any other forms of "direct" expression. Results in mobocracy. Attitude toward property is communistic—negating property rights. Attitude toward law is that the will of the majority shall regulate, whether it be based upon deliberation or governed by passion, prejudice, and impulse, without restraint or regard to consequences. Results in demagogism, license, agitation, discontent, anarchy.

ANON., United States Army *Training Manual,* No. 2000-25
(Government Printing Office, 1928), p. 91

LIBERTY

•

WHAT IT IS

It may be of some good use, to inform and rectify the judgments of some of the people, and may prevent such distempers as have arisen amongst us. The great questions that have troubled the country, are about the authority of the magistrates and the liberty of the people. It is yourselves who have called us to this office, and being called by you, we have our authority from God, in way of an ordinance, such as hath the image of God eminently stamped upon it, the contempt and violation whereof hath been vindicated with examples of divine vengeance. I entreat you to consider, that when you choose magistrates, you take them from among yourselves, men subject to like passions as you are. Therefore when you see infirmities in us, you should reflect upon your own, and that would make you bear the more with us, and not be severe censurers of the failings of your magistrates, when you have continual experience of the infirmities in yourselves and others. We account him a good servant, who breaks not his covenant. The covenant between you and us is the oath you have taken of us, which is to this purpose, that we shall govern you and judge your causes by the rules of God's laws and our own, according to our best skill. When you agree with a workman to build you a ship or houses, etc., he undertakes as well for his skill as for his faithfulness, for it is his profession, and you pay him for both. But when you call one to be a magistrate, he doth not profess nor undertake to have sufficient skill for that office, nor can you furnish him with gifts, etc., therefore you must run the hazard of his skill and ability. But if he fail in faithfulness, which by his oath he is bound to, that he must answer for. If it fall out that the case be clear to common apprehension, and the rule clear also, if he transgress here, the error is not in the skill, but in the evil of the will: it must be required of him. But if the case be doubtful, to men of such understanding and parts as your magistrates are, if your magistrates should err here, yourselves must bear it.

For the other point concerning liberty, I observe a great mistake in the country about that. There is a twofold liberty, natural (I mean as our nature is now corrupt) and civil or federal. The first is common to man with beasts and other creatures. By this, man, as he stands in relation to man simply, hath liberty to do what he lists; it is a liberty to evil as well as to good. This liberty is incompatible and inconsistent with authority, and cannot endure the least restraint of the most just authority. The exercize and maintaining of this liberty makes men grow more evil, and in time to be worse than brute beasts: *omnes sumus licentia deteriores*. This is that great enemy of truth and peace, that wild beast, which all the ordinances of God are bent against, to restrain and subdue it. The other kind of liberty I call civil or federal, it may also be termed moral, in reference to the covenant between God and man, in the moral law, and the politic covenants and constitutions, amongst men themselves. This liberty is the proper end and object of authority, and cannot subsist without it; and it is a liberty to that only which is good, just, and honest. This liberty you are to stand for, with the hazard (not only of your goods, but) of your lives, if need be. Whatsoever crosseth this, is not authority, but a distemper thereof. This liberty is maintained and exercised in a way of subjection to authority; it is of the same kind of liberty wherewith Christ hath made us free. The woman's own choice makes such a man her husband; yet being so chosen, he is her lord, and she is to be subject to him, yet in a way of liberty, not of bondage; and a true wife accounts her condition safe and free, but in her subjection to her husband's authority. Such is the liberty of the church under authority of Christ, her king and husband; his yoke is so easy and sweet to her as a bride's ornaments; and if through frowardness or wantonness, etc., she shake it off, at any time, she is at no rest in her spirit, until she take it up again; and whether her lord smiles upon her, and embraceth her in his arms, or whether he frowns, or rebukes, or smites her, she apprehends the sweetness of his love in all, and is refreshed, supported, and instructed by every such dispensation of his authority over her. On the other side, ye know who they are that complain of this yoke and say, let us break their bands, etc., we will not have this man to rule over us. Even so, brethren, it will be between you and your magistrates. If you stand for your natural corrupt liberties, and will do what is good in your own eyes, you will not endure the least weight of authority, but will murmur, and oppose, and be always striving to shake off that yoke; but if you will be satisfied to enjoy such civil and lawful liberties, such as Christ allows you, then you will quietly and cheerfully submit unto that authority which is set over you, in all the administrations of it, for your good. Wherein, if we fail at any time, we hope we shall be willing (by God's assistance) to hearken to good advice from any of you, or in any other way of God; so shall your liberties be preserved, in upholding the honor and power of authority amongst you.

> JOHN WINTHROP, speech at his trial for misdemeanor in office, upon which charge he was acquitted; from his *Journal*, May 4, 1645

No Cross, No Crown.

WILLIAM PENN, title of pamphlet, 1669

The question before the court and you, gentlemen of the jury, is not of
small nor private concern. It is not the cause of a poor printer, nor of
New York alone, which you are now trying. No! It may in its consequences affect every freeman that lives under a British government on the
main of America. It is the best cause. It is the cause of liberty; and I make
no doubt but your upright conduct this day will not only entitle you to
the love and esteem of your fellow-citizens; but every man who prefers
freedom to a life of slavery will bless and honor you, as men who have
baffled the attempt of tyranny; and by an impartial and uncorrupt verdict
have laid a noble foundation for securing to ourselves, our posterity, and
our neighbors that to which nature and the laws of our country have
given us a right—the liberty both of exposing and opposing arbitrary
power, in these parts of the world, at least, by speaking and writing truth.

> ANDREW HAMILTON, defense of John Peter Zenger, 1730.
> When Zenger was charged with seditious libel for exposing
> the corruption of the Crown-appointed Governor of New
> York, the first act of the judge was to disbar Zenger's two
> able lawyers because they dared attack his commission. The
> counsel appointed by the court, while conscientious, had no
> wish to become a martyr. He took it easy. Fortunately for
> Zenger and for the American people, he was also able to
> secure the services of Hamilton, whose appeal won an ac-
> quittal in the face of the judge's directed verdict of guilty.
> This case is often cited as the basis of American liberties in
> this sphere.

Where liberty dwells, there is my country.

BENJAMIN FRANKLIN, letter, 1785

God grant, that not only the love of liberty, but a thorough knowledge of
the Rights of Man, may pervade all the nations of the Earth, so that a
philosopher may set his foot anywhere on its surface, and say, "This is
my country."

BENJAMIN FRANKLIN

O! ye that love mankind! Ye that dare oppose not only the tyranny but
the tyrant, stand forth! Every spot of the old world is overrun with op-

pression. Freedom hath been hunted round the Globe. Asia and Africa have long expelled her. Europe regards her as a stranger and England hath given her warning to depart. O! receive the fugitive and prepare in time an asylum for mankind.

THOMAS PAINE

The God who gave us life, gave us liberty at the same time.

THOMAS JEFFERSON, *Summary View of the Rights of British America*, 1774

Liberty, when it begins to take root, is a plant of rapid growth.

GEORGE WASHINGTON

When in the Course of human events, it becomes necessary for one people to dissolve the political bands which have connected them with another, and to assume among the powers of the earth, the separate and equal station to which the Laws of Nature and of Nature's God entitle them, a decent respect to the opinions of mankind requires that they should declare the causes which impel them to the separation.

We hold these truths to be self-evident, that all men are created equal, that they are endowed by their Creator with certain unalienable Rights, that among these are Life, Liberty and the pursuit of Happiness. That to secure these rights, Governments are instituted among Men, deriving their just powers from the consent of the governed. That whenever any Form of Government becomes destructive of these ends, it is the Right of the People to alter or to abolish it, and to institute new Government, laying its foundation on such principles and organising its power in such form, as to them shall seem most likely to effect their Safety and Happiness. Prudence, indeed, will dictate that Governments long established should not be changed for light and transient causes; and accordingly all experience hath shewn, that mankind are more disposed to suffer, while evils are sufferable, than to right themselves by abolishing the forms to which they are accustomed. But when a long train of abuses and usurpations, pursuing invariably the same Object evinces a design to reduce them under absolute Despotism, it is their right, it is their duty, to throw off such Government, and to provide new Guards for their future security.— Such has been the patient suffrance of these Colonies; and such is now the necessity which constrains them to alter their former Systems of Government. The history of the present King of Great Britain is a history of repeated injuries and usurpations, all having in direct object the establishment of an absolute Tyranny over these States. To prove this, let Facts be submitted to a candid world. . . . [There follows a list of tyrannical and unlawful actions.]

Nor have We been wanting in attentions to our British brethren. We have warned them from time to time of attempts by their legislature to extend an unwarrantable jurisdiction over us. We have reminded them of the circumstances of our emigration and settlement here. We have appealed to their native justice and magnanimity, and we have conjured them by the ties of our common kindred to disavow these usurpations, which would inevitably interrupt our connections and correspondence. They too have been deaf to the voice of justice and of consanguinity. We must, therefore, acquiesce in the necessity, which denounces our Separation, and hold them, as we hold the rest of mankind, Enemies in War, in Peace Friends.

We, therefore, the Representatives of the United States of America, in General Congress, Assembled, appealing to the Supreme Judge of the world for the rectitude of our intentions, do, in the Name, and by authority of the good People of these Colonies, solemnly publish and declare, That these United Colonies are, and of Right ought to be, Free and Independent States; that they are Absolved from all Allegiance to the British Crown, and that all political connection between them and the State of Great Britain, is and ought to be totally dissolved; and that as Free and Independent States, they have full power to levy War, conclude Peace, contract Alliances, establish Commerce, and do all other Acts and Things which Independent States may of right do. And for the support of this Declaration, with a firm reliance on the protection of divine Providence, we mutually pledge to each other our Lives, our Fortunes and our Sacred Honor.

THOMAS JEFFERSON, The Declaration of Independence

Driven from every other corner of the earth, freedom of thought and the right of private judgment in matters of conscience direct their course to this happy country as their last resort.

SAMUEL ADAMS, speech, Philadelphia, 1776

A power over a man's subsistence amounts to a power over his will.

ALEXANDER HAMILTON, The Federalist

The Citizens of the United States of America have a right to applaud themselves for having given to mankind examples of an enlarged and liberal policy: a policy worthy of imitation. All possess alike liberty of conscience and immunities of citizenship. It is now no more that toleration is spoken of as if it was by the indulgence of one class of people that another enjoyed the exercise of their inherent natural rights. For happily the Government of the United States, which gives to bigotry no sanction, to persecution no assistance, requires only that they who live under its protection should demean themselves as good citizens in giving it on all occasions their effectual support.

> GEORGE WASHINGTON, letter to the Jewish Congregation of
> Newport, Rhode Island, 1790

Equal and exact justice to all men, . . . freedom of religion, freedom of the press, freedom of person under the protection of the habeas corpus; and trial by juries impartially selected,—these principles form the bright constellation which has gone before us.

> THOMAS JEFFERSON, "First Inaugural," March 4, 1801

Yet I will not believe our labors are lost. I shall not die without a hope that light and liberty are on steady advance. We have seen, indeed, once within the records of history, a complete eclipse of the human mind continuing for centuries. And this, too, by swarms of the same northern barbarians, conquering and taking possession of the countries and governments of the civilized world. Should this again be attempted, should the same northern hordes, allured again by the corn, wine, and oil of the south, be able again to settle their swarms in the countries of their growth, the art of printing alone, and the vast dissemination of books, will maintain the mind where it is, and raise the conquering ruffians to the level of the conquered, instead of degrading these to that of their conquerors. And even should the cloud of barbarism and despotism again obscure the science and libraries of Europe, this country remains to preserve and restore light and liberty to them. In short, the flames kindled on the 4th of July, 1776, have spread over too much of the globe to be extinguished by the feeble engines of despotism; on the contrary, they will consume these engines and all who work them.

> THOMAS JEFFERSON, letter to John Adams, Monticello,
> September 12, 1821

Nothing then is unchangeable but the inherent and unalienable rights of man.

> THOMAS JEFFERSON, 1824

With me, the liberty of the country is all in all. If this be preserved, every
thing will be preserved; but if lost, all will be lost.

JOHN C. CALHOUN, speech, 1848

No matter whose the lips that would speak, they must be free and un-
gagged. The community which dares not protect its humblest and most
hated member in the free utterances of his opinion, no matter how false
or hateful, is only a gang of slaves.

WENDELL PHILLIPS

I have never had a feeling politically that did not spring from the Declaration of Independence. . . . I have often inquired of myself what great
principle it was that kept this confederacy so long together. It was not the
mere matter of the separation of the colonies from the mother land, but
something in that declaration giving liberty, not alone to the people of
this country, but hope for the world for all future time. It was that which
gave promise that in due time the weights should be lifted from the
shoulders of all men, and that all should have an equal chance. This is
the sentiment embodied in the Declaration of Independence. . . . I
would rather be assassinated on the spot than surrender it.

ABRAHAM LINCOLN, address in Independence Hall, Philadelphia, February 22, 1861

Inalienable rights are those of which a man cannot divest himself by contract; which he may not, under any circumstances, lawfully demit; but he
may forfeit them by crime, and be wrongfully deprived of them by others.

MARK HOPKINS, lecture, Lowell Institute, Boston, 1862

The world has never had a good definition of the world liberty. And the
American people just now are much in need of one. We all declare for
liberty, but using the same word we do not mean the same thing. With
some, the word liberty may mean for each man to do as he pleases with
himself and the product of his labor; while with others the same word
may mean for some men to do as they please with other men and the
product of other men's labor. Here are two, not only different, but incompatible things, called by the same name, liberty. And it follows that each
of the things is by respective parties called by two different and incompatible names, liberty and tyranny.

   The shepherd drives the wolf from the sheep's throat, for which the sheep thanks the shepherd as his liberator, while the wolf denounces him for the same act. . . . Plainly the sheep and the wolf are not agreed upon a definition of liberty.

ABRAHAM LINCOLN, speech, Baltimore, April 18, 1864

Freedom is not caprice, but room to enlarge.

CYRUS A. BARTOL, *Radical Problems,* "Open Questions"

[Liberty] is always relative to actually felt oppression.

JOHN DEWEY, *Liberalism and Social Action*

The greatest aid that I know of that any man could give the world today would be a correct definition of "liberty." Everybody is running around in a circle announcing that somebody has pinched their "liberty." . . . So the question arises, "how much liberty can I get and get away with it?" Well, you can get no more than you give. That's my definition but you got perfect "liberty" to work out your own, so get in.

WILL ROGERS

Freedom means that if you are a professor, you don't have to alter science or history as a bureaucrat prescribes. If you own a newspaper, you don't limit your editorial opinions to what an official censor approves. . . . If you think taxes are too high, you can vote against those officials you think responsible. And there is no limitation upon your inherent American right to criticize anybody, anywhere, at any time.

WENDELL L. WILLKIE

Freedom is an indivisible word. If we want to enjoy it, we must be prepared to extend it to everyone.

WENDELL L. WILLKIE

Liberty is the only thing you cannot have unless you are willing to give it to others.

WILLIAM ALLEN WHITE, 1940

Liberty like charity must begin at home.

JAMES BRYANT CONANT, *Our Fighting Faith,* 1942

What then is the spirit of liberty? I cannot define it; I can only tell you my own faith. The spirit of liberty is the spirit which is not too sure that it is right. The spirit of liberty is the spirit which seeks to understand the minds of other men and women. The spirit of liberty is the spirit which weighs their interests alongside its own without bias. The spirit of liberty remembers that not even a sparrow falls to earth unheeded. The spirit of liberty is the spirit of Him who, near two thousand years ago, taught mankind that lesson it has never learned, but has never quite forgotten; that there may be a kingdom where the least shall be heard and considered side by side with the greatest.

LEARNED HAND, speech, I Am An American Day, 1944

To recognize ideas as dangerous—and to face the danger—is the mark of a free man and of a free society. The rest, in their degree, are all authoritarians.

CHARLES A. SIEPMANN, *Radio, Television and Society,* 1950

My definition of a free society is a society where it is safe to be unpopular.

ADLAI STEVENSON, speech, Detroit, October, 1952

Liberty . . . is something more than a political phenomenon, as tyrannical dictatorship contends; it is more than an economic phenomenon, as some disciples of free enterprise maintain. It is something more mature than that dream of rights without responsibilities which historic liberalism envisioned; it is certainly different from that terrorism of responsibilities without rights which Communism imposes. It is something wiser than free thought, and something freer than dictated thought. For freedom has its roots in man's spiritual nature. It does not rise out of any social organization, or any constitution, or any past, but out of the soul of man.

The Dignity of Man, statement issued at meeting of Catholic Bishops of the U.S., Washington, November, 1953

We have plenty of freedom in this country but not a great deal of independence.

JOHN W. RAPER, *What This World Needs,* 1954

I will not be a party to any treaty that makes anybody a slave; now that is all there is to it.

DWIGHT D. EISENHOWER, press conference, July 7, 1954

THE PRICE OF LIBERTY

He that would make his own liberty secure must guard even his enemy from oppression.

> THOMAS PAINE, *Dissertation on First Principle of Government*

Eternal Vigilance Is the Price of Liberty.

> Attributed to THOMAS JEFFERSON, inscription on National Archives Building, Washington. This phrase does not occur in Jefferson's writings. The closest quote is from John Philpot Curran, an Irish politician, in 1790: "The condition upon which God hath given liberty to man is eternal vigilance."

What signify a few lives lost in a century or two? The tree of liberty must be refreshed from time to time with the blood of patriots and tyrants. It is its natural manure.

> THOMAS JEFFERSON, letter to W. S. Smith, Nov. 13, 1787

A little rebellion now and then . . . is a medicine necessary for the sound health of the government.

> THOMAS JEFFERSON, letter to Madison

We have had so many years of prosperity, we have passed through so many difficulties and dangers without the loss of liberty—that we begin to think that we hold it by divine right from heaven itself. . . . It is harder to preserve than to obtain liberty. After years of prosperity, the tenure by which it is held is but too often forgotten; and I fear, Senators, that such is the case with us. There is no solicitude now about liberty. It was not so in the early days of the republic.

> JOHN C. CALHOUN, speech in the Senate, January, 1848

If by the mere force of numbers a majority should deprive a minority of any clearly written constitutional right, it might, in any moral point of view, justify revolution.

> ABRAHAM LINCOLN, "First Inaugural," March 4, 1861

Four score and seven years ago our fathers brought forth on this continent, a new nation, conceived in liberty, and dedicated to the proposition that all men are created equal.

Now we are engaged in a great civil war, testing whether that nation or any nation so conceived and so dedicated, can long endure. We are met on a great battlefield of that war. We have come to dedicate a portion of that field, as a final resting place for those who here gave their lives that that nation might live. It is altogether fitting and proper that we should do this.

But, in a larger sense, we can not dedicate—we can not consecrate—we can not hallow—this ground. The brave men, living and dead, who struggled here, have consecrated it, far above our poor power to add or detract. The world will little note, nor long remember what we say here, but it can never forget what they did here. It is for us the living, rather, to be dedicated here to the unfinished work which they who fought here have thus far so nobly advanced. It is rather for us to be here dedicated to the great task remaining before us—that from these honored dead we take increased devotion to that cause for which they gave the last full measure of devotion—that we here highly resolve that these dead shall not have died in vain—that this nation, under God, shall have a new birth of freedom—and that government of the people, by the people, for the people, shall not perish from the earth.

> ABRAHAM LINCOLN, address, Gettysburg, November 19, 1863. "The cheek of every American must tingle with shame as he reads the silly, flat and dishwatery utterances of the man who has to be pointed out to intelligent foreigners as the President of the United States." Editorial in Chicago *Times*, November 20.

When people are oppressed by their government it is a natural right they enjoy to relieve themselves of the oppression if they are strong enough, whether by withdrawing from it or by overthrowing it.

> ULYSSES S. GRANT

We Americans have boasted so much of Freedom that lately we almost expect it to make a living for us.

> EDGAR W. HOWE

We must keep in the forefront of our minds the fact that whenever we take away the liberties of those whom we hate, we are opening the way to loss of liberty for those we love.

WENDELL L. WILLKIE

The inescapable price of liberty is an ability to preserve it from destruction.

DOUGLAS MACARTHUR, to Pres. Quezon of the Philippines

The winning of freedom is not to be compared to the winning of a game —with the victory recorded forever in history. Freedom has its life in the hearts, the actions, the spirit of men and so it must be daily earned and refreshed—else like a flower cut from its life-giving roots, it will wither and die.

DWIGHT D. EISENHOWER, speech, English Speaking Union, London, 1944

We are reluctant to admit that we owe our liberties to men of a type that today we hate and fear—unruly men, disturbers of the peace, men who resent and denounce what Whitman called "the insolence of elected persons"—in a word, free men. It reminds us of the extent to which we have become prisoners of our doubts and fears, and we do not like such reminders. For freedom is always purchased at a great price, and even those who are willing to pay it have to admit that the price is great.

GERALD W. JOHNSON, *American Freedom and the Press*

LIBERTY AND/OR SECURITY

They that can give essential liberty to obtain a little temporary safety deserve neither liberty nor safety.

BENJAMIN FRANKLIN, *Historical Review of Pennsylvania*

I believe there are more instances of the abridgment of the freedom of the people by gradual and silent encroachments of those in power than by violent and sudden usurpations.

JAMES MADISON, Virginia Convention, June 16, 1788

In open violation of the Constitution, and of that well-established and wise maxim that all men are presumed to be innocent until proven guilty, according to the established rules of law, you request myself and the heads of departments to become our own accusers, and to furnish the evidence to convict ourselves. . . . For myself, I shall repel all such attempts as an invasion of the principles of justice, as well as of the Constitution; and I shall esteem it my sacred duty to the people of the United States to resist them as I would the establishment of a Spanish Inquisition.

> ANDREW JACKSON, reply to a Congressional Committee's demand for information, January 27, 1837

We have heard enough of liberty and the rights of man. It is high time to hear something of the duties of men and the rights of authority.

> ORESTES BROWNSON, *Essays and Reviews*, 1852

On principle, I dislike an oath which requires a man to swear he *has* not done wrong. It rejects the Christian principle of forgiveness on terms of repentance. I think it is enough if the man does no wrong *hereafter*.

> ABRAHAM LINCOLN, letter to Edwin M. Stanton, February 5, 1864, on the Loyalty Oath proposed by his cabinet

We better know there is fire whence we see much smoke rising than we could know it by one or two witnesses swearing to it. The witnesses may commit perjury, but the smoke cannot.

> ABRAHAM LINCOLN, unsent letter to J. R. Underwood and Henry Grider, October 26, 1864

It must be conceded that there are rights in every free government beyond the control of the state. A government which recognized no such rights, but held the lives, the liberty, and the property of its citizens subject at all times to the absolute disposition and unlimited control of even the most democratic depository of power is, after all, but a despotism of the many—of the majority, but none the less a despotism. The theory of our governments, state and national, is opposed to the deposit of unlimited power anywhere.

> SAMUEL FREEMAN MILLER, *Loan Assn.* v. *Topeka,* 1875

The only question at this point is: Which may we better trust, the play of free social forces or legislative and administrative interference? This question is as pertinent for those who expect to win by interference as for others, for whenever we try to get paternalized we only succeed in getting policed.

WILLIAM GRAHAM SUMNER, *State Interference,* 1887

The interests of liberty are peculiarly those of individuals, and hence of minorities, and freedom is in danger of being slain at her own altars if the passion for uniformity and control of opinion gathers head.

CHARLES EVANS HUGHES

The most stringent protection of free speech would not protect a man in falsely shouting fire in a theater and causing a panic.

OLIVER WENDELL HOLMES, JR., *Schenck* v. *U.S.,* 1919

Persecution of the expression of opinions seems to me perfectly logical. If you have no doubt of your premises or your power and want a certain result with all your heart you naturally express your wishes in law and sweep away all opposition. To allow opposition by speech seems to indicate that you think the speech impotent, as when a man says that he has squared the circle, or that you do not care whole-heartedly for the result, or that you doubt either your power or your premises. But when men have realized that time has upset many fighting faiths, they may come to believe even more than they believe the very foundations of their own conduct that the ultimate good desired is better reached by free trade in ideas— that the best test of truth is the power of the thought to get itself accepted in the competition of the market, and that truth is the only ground upon which their wishes safely can be carried out. That at any rate is the theory of our Constitution. It is an experiment, as all life is an experiment. Every year if not every day we have to wager our salvation upon some prophecy based upon imperfect knowledge. While that experiment is part of our system I think that we should be eternally vigilant against attempts to check the expression of opinions that we loathe and believe to be fraught with death, unless they so imminently threaten immediate interference with the lawful and pressing purposes of the country that an immediate check is required to save the country.

OLIVER WENDELL HOLMES, JR., dissenting opinion in *Abrams* v. *U.S.,* 1919

With effervescing opinions, as with the not yet forgotten champagne, the quickest way to let them get flat is to let them get exposed to the air.

OLIVER WENDELL HOLMES, JR., opinion, 1920

Like a prairie-fire, the blaze of revolution was sweeping over every American institution of law and order a year ago. It was eating its way into the homes of the American workman, its sharp tongues of revolutionary heat were licking the altars of the churches, leaping into the belfry of the school bell, crawling into the sacred corners of American homes, seeking to replace marriage vows with libertine laws, burning up the foundations of society.

A. MITCHELL PALMER, 1920

Mr. Justice Brandeis and I are of opinion that this judgment should be reversed. The general principle of free speech, it seems to me, must be taken to be included in the Fourteenth Amendment. . . . If I am right, then I think that the criterion sanctioned by the full court in *Schenck* vs. *United States,* 249, U.S. 47, 52, applies: "The question in every case is whether the words used are used in such circumstances and are of such a nature as to create a clear and present danger that they will bring about the substantive evils that [the state] has a right to prevent." . . . If what I think the correct test is applied, it is manifest that there was no present danger of an attempt to overthrow the government by force on the part of the admittedly small minority who shared the defendant's views. It is said that this Manifesto was more than a theory, that it was an incitement. Every idea is an incitement. It offers itself for belief, and, if believed, it is acted on unless some other belief outweighs it, or some failure of energy stifles the movement at its birth. The only difference between the expression of opinion and an incitement in the narrower sense is the speaker's enthusiasm for the result. Eloquence may set fire to reason. But whatever may be thought of the redundant discourse before us, it had no chance of starting a present conflagration. If, in the long run, the beliefs expressed in proletarian dictatorship are destined to be accepted by the dominant forces of the community, the only meaning of free speech is that they should be given their chance and have their way.

OLIVER WENDELL HOLMES, JR., dissenting opinion, *Gitlow* v. *People of New York,* 1925

You tell me that law is above freedom of utterance. And I reply that you can have no wise laws nor free enforcement of wise laws unless there is free expression of the wisdom of the people—and, alas, their folly with it. But if there is freedom, folly will die of its own poison, and the wisdom will survive. That is the history of the race. It is proof of man's kinship with God. You say that freedom of utterance is not for time of stress, and

I reply with the sad truth that only in time of stress is freedom of utterance in danger. No one questions it in calm days, because it is not needed. And the reverse is true also; only when free utterance is suppressed is it needed, and when it is needed, it is most vital to justice.

Peace is good. But if you are interested in peace through force and without free discussion—that is to say, free utterance decently and in order—your interest in justice is slight. And peace without justice is tyranny, no matter how you may sugar-coat it with expedience. This state today is in no more danger from suppression than from violence, because, in the end, suppression leads to violence. Violence, indeed, is the child of suppression. Whoever pleads for justice helps to keep the peace; and whoever tramples on the plea for justice temperately made in the name of peace only outrages peace and kills something fine in the heart of man which God put there when we got our manhood. When that is killed, brute meets brute on each side of the line.

So, dear friend, put fear out of your heart. This nation will survive, this state will prosper, the orderly business of life will go forward if only men can speak in whatever way given them to utter what their hearts hold— by voice, by posted card, by letter, or by press. Reason has never failed men. Only force and repression has made the wrecks in the world.

> WILLIAM ALLEN WHITE, "To an Anxious Friend," Emporia
> *Gazette,* July 27, 1922

Experience teaches us to be most on our guard to protect liberty when the government's purposes are beneficent.

> LOUIS D. BRANDEIS, dissent, *Olmstead* v. *U.S.,* 1928

The makers of our Constitution . . . sought to protect Americans in their beliefs, their thoughts, their emotions, and their sensations. They conferred, as against the government, the right to be left alone—the most comprehensive of rights and the right most valued by civilized men. To protect that right, every unjustifiable intrusion by the government upon the privacy of the individual, whatever the means employed, must be deemed a violation of the Fourth Amendment. And the use, as evidence in a criminal proceeding, of facts ascertained by such intrusion must be deemed a violation of the Fifth.

> LOUIS D. BRANDEIS, *Ibid.*

The American Association for the Advancement of Science feels grave concern over persistent and threatening inroads upon intellectual freedom which have been made in recent times in many parts of the world.

Our existing liberties have been won through ages of struggle and at enormous cost. If these are lost or seriously impaired there can be no hope of continued progress in science, of justice in government, of international or domestic peace; or even of lasting material well-being.

We regard the suppression of independent thought and of its free expression as a major crime against civilization itself. Yet oppression of this sort has been inflicted upon investigators, scholars, teachers, and professional men in many ways, whether by governmental action, administrative coercion, or extra-legal violence. We feel it our duty to denounce all such actions as intolerable forms of tyranny.

There can be no compromise on this issue, for even the commonwealth of learning cannot endure "half slave and half free."

By our life and training as scientists and by our heritage as Americans we must stand for freedom.

> Declaration, adopted 1933

It Can't Happen Here.

> SINCLAIR LEWIS, title of book, 1936, decrying American ignorance of the dangers of Fascism and Nazism

While Congress does not have power to deny to citizens the right to believe in, teach, or advocate communism, fascism, and nazism, it does have the right to focus the spotlight of publicity upon their activities.

> Report of the Dies Committee on Un-American Activities, May, 1938

The purpose of this committee is the task of protecting our constitutional democracy by . . . pitiless publicity.

> *Ibid.*

If there is any fixed star in our constitutional constellation, it is that no official, high or petty, can prescribe what should be called orthodox in politics, nationalism, religion or other matters of opinion, or force citizens to confess by words or act their faith therein.

> ROBERT H. JACKSON, majority opinion, *West Virginia State Board of Education* v. *Barnette.* The case concerned children of Jehovah's Witnesses who had refused to salute the flag.

A despot doesn't fear eloquent writers preaching freedom—he fears a drunken poet who may crack a joke that will take hold.

> E. B. White, *One Man's Meat*, "Salt Water Farm"

My thesis is that any organization of society which depresses free and spontaneous meddling is on the decline, however showy its immediate spoils; I maintain that in such a society Liberty is gone, little as its members may know it; that the Nirvana of the individual is too high a price to pay for a collective Paradise.

> Learned Hand

In any large scale activity involving the interplay of many people, standards tend to become debased to the level of the lowest. This is obviously what is happening in our society. The exceptional man prefers freedom to security; the mediocre man prefers security to freedom—security at the expense of freedom is what we are getting. The exceptional man finds his highest values in the satisfaction of the creative impulse, while the highest good of the mediocre is creature comfort—we are getting a society in which the supreme good, to which the government should bend all its efforts, is raising the standard of living. From this point of view, the advantages of a minimum government are obvious; the less the government controls, the fewer the things subject to this debasing action, whereas in a country in which the government controls everything, everything is debased.

> Percy Williams Bridgman, *Reflections of a Physicist*, 1950

Physically Americans were pioneers; in the realm of social and economic institutions, too, their tradition has been one of pioneering. . . . From the beginning Americans have known that there were new worlds to conquer, new truths to be discovered. Every effort to confine Americanism to a single pattern . . . is disloyalty to everything that is valid in Americanism.

> Henry Steele Commager, *Freedom, Loyalty and Dissent*

Let me assure you that those who shed crocodile tears for the families of traitors whom I expose, with no tears left over for the families of American boys who were betrayed by those traitors, are scaring no one. Let me assure you that regardless of how high-pitched becomes the squealing and screaming of those left-wing, bleeding-heart, phony liberals, this battle is going to go on.

> Joseph R. McCarthy, speech to Fifth Marine Division Conference, New York, 1951

The progress of science on furnishing the Government with means of espionage is not likely to stop with wire tapping. Ways may some day be developed by which the government, without removing papers from secret drawers, can reproduce them in court, and by which it will be enabled to expose to a jury the most intimate occurrences of the home. Advances in the psychic and related sciences may bring means of exploring unexpressed beliefs, thoughts, and emotions. "That places the liberty of every man in the hands of every petty officer" was said by James Otis of much lesser intrusions than these. To Lord Camden a far slighter intrusion seemed "subversive of all the comforts of society." Can it be that the Constitution affords no protection against such invasions of individual security?

LOUIS D. BRANDEIS, *The Works of Justice Brandeis,* 1953

Take my word for it, I don't enjoy this task. It is a dirty, disagreeable job, but a job which must be done. When I was a boy on the farm, my mother used to raise chickens. The greatest enemy the chickens had were skunks. In order to protect mother's chickens, my three brothers and I had to dig out and destroy these skunks. It was a dirty, foul, unpleasant, smelly job. And sometimes after it was done, people did not like to have us sit next to them in church.

JOSEPH R. MCCARTHY, speech

The problem with which the intellectuals of this country are confronted is very serious. The reactionary politicians have managed to instill suspision of all intellectual efforts into the public by dangling before their eyes a danger from without. Having succeeded so far they are now proceeding to suppress the freedom of teaching and to deprive of their positions all those who do not prove submissive, i.e., to starve them.

What ought the minority of intellectuals to do against this evil? Frankly, I can see only the revolutionary way of non-co-operation in the sense of Gandhi's. Every intellectual who is called before one of the committees ought to refuse to testify, i.e., he must be prepared for jail and economic ruin, in short, for the sacrifice of his personal welfare in the interest of the cultural welfare of this country.

This refusal to testify must be based on the assertion that it is shameful for a blameless citizen to submit to such an inquisition and that this kind of inquisition violates the spirit of the Constitution.

If enough people are ready to take this grave step they will be successful. If not, then the intellectuals of this country deserve nothing better than the slavery which is intended for them.

ALBERT EINSTEIN, letter to Mr. Frauenglass, June, 1953

In 1937, I began, like Lazarus, the impossible return. I begin to break away from Communism and to climb from deep within its underground, where for six years I had been buried, back into the world of free men.

WHITTAKER CHAMBERS, *Witness*, 1953

The informer is different, particularly the ex-Communist informer. He risks little. He sits in security and uses his special knowledge to destroy others. He has that special information to give because he knows these others' faces, voices, and lives, because he once lived within their confidence, in a shared faith. . . . If he had not done those things he would have no use as an informer. Because he has that use, the police protect him. When they whistle, he fetches a soiled bone of information. . . . He is no longer a man. He is free only to the degree in which he understands what he is doing and why he must do it. Let every ex-Communist look understandingly at that image. It is himself.

WHITTAKER CHAMBERS, *Ibid.*

God knows, there is risk in refusing to act till the facts are all in; but is there not greater risk in abandoning the conditions of all rational inquiry? I believe that that community is already in process of dissolution . . where orthodoxy chokes freedom of dissent . . where faith in the eventual supremacy of reason has become so timid that we dare not enter our convictions in the open list to win or lose . . The mutual confidence on which all else depends can be maintained only by an open mind and a brave reliance upon free discussion . . of this I am sure: . . we must not yield a foot upon demanding a fair field, and an honest race, to all ideas . . . by that wisdom alone shall we be saved.

LEARNED HAND

What weakness is it in us Americans that so often makes us embarrassed or afraid to indulge the gentle impulse, to seek the finer and rarer flavor, to admit frankly and without stammering apologies to an appreciation for the wonder of the poet's word and the miracle of the artist's brush, for all the beauty, in short, that has been recorded in the images of word and line created by the hands of men in past ages? What is it that makes us fear to acknowledge the greatness of other lands, or of other times, to shun the subtle and the unfamiliar?

What is it that causes us to huddle together, herdlike, in tastes and enthusiasms that represent only the common denominator of popular acquiescence, rather than to show ourselves receptive to the tremendous flights of creative imagination of which the individual mind has shown itself capable? Is it that we are forgetful of the true sources of our moral strength, afraid of ourselves, afraid to look into the chaos of our own breasts, afraid of the bright, penetrating light of the great teachers?

This fear of the untypical, this quest for security within the walls of secular uniformity—these are traits of our national character we would do well to beware of and to examine for their origins. They receive much encouragement these days, much automatic and unintended encouragement, by virtue of the growing standardization of the cultural and, in many respects, the educational influences to which our people are being subjected.

The immense impact of commercial advertising and the mass media on our lives is—let us make no mistake about it—an impact that tends to encourage passivity, to encourage acquiescence and uniformity, to place handicaps on individual contemplativeness and creativeness.

It may not seem to many of us too dangerous that we should all live, dress, eat, hear, and read substantially alike. But we forget how easily this uniformity of thought and habit can be exploited, when the will to exploit it is there. We forget how easily it can slip over into the domination of our spiritual and political lives by self-appointed custodians who contrive to set themselves at the head of popular emotional currents.

GEORGE F. KENNAN, speech at Notre Dame, May 15, 1953

We must be on guard against any and every activity which puts in jeopardy our rights as individuals to determine for ourselves what we should think, what we should discuss, and, with proper regard for the rights of others, what we should do. Freedom of thought is a basic human right, from which flow freedom of religion, freedom of the press, and freedom of assembly and association. But freedom of thought is a sterile and meaningless right, unless we are free to discuss, to criticize, and to debate. Criticism, discussion, and debate are the only means of peaceful progress. All history shows that without them a society must stagnate and die.

The thought control of dictatorships is imposed by force, but discussion, criticism, and debate can be stifled by fear as well as by force. Persecution by public opinion can be as powerful as purges and pogroms. Schoolteachers, government clerks and officials, and even businessmen can be frightened out of their rights under the First Amendment as effectively as if that amendment were repealed. Frightened men are, at best, irresponsible in their actions and, at worst, dangerous. Of all the forms of tyranny over the mind of man, none is more terrible than fear—to be afraid of being oneself among one's neighbors.

PAUL G. HOFFMAN, *American Freedom*, 1953

Security? What is that? Something negative, undead, suspicious and suspecting; an avarice and an avoidance; a self-surrendering and an innumerable cowardice. Who would be "secure"? Every and any slave. No free spirit ever dreamed of "security"—or, if he did, he laughed; and lived to shame his dream. No whole sinless sinful sleeping waking breathing human creature ever was (or could be) bought by, and sold for, "security." How monstrous and how feeble seems some unworld which would rather have its too than eat its cake.

E. E. CUMMINGS, *six nonlectures*, 1953

Freedom cannot be censored into existence. A democracy smugly disdainful of new ideas would be a sick democracy. A democracy chronically fearful of new ideas would be a dying democracy.

DWIGHT D. EISENHOWER, letter to American Library Association, June 24, 1953

This is no time for men who oppose Senator McCarthy's methods to keep silent. Or for those who approve. We can deny our heritage and our history—but we cannot escape responsibility for the result. There is no way for a citizen of the republic to abdicate his responsibilities. As a nation we have come into our full inheritance at an early age. We proclaim ourselves—as indeed we are—the defenders of the free world, what's left of it.

We cannot defend freedom abroad by deserting it at home. The actions of the junior Senator from Wisconsin have caused alarm and discomfort among our allies abroad and given comfort to our enemies. And whose fault is that? Not really his. He didn't create the situation of fear, merely exploited it, and skillfully. Cassius was right. "The fault, dear Brutus, is not in our stars but in ourselves."

EDWARD R. MURROW, *See It Now*, March 10, 1954

This nation was conceived in liberty and dedicated to the proposition that honest men may honestly disagree. . . . For almost four years we have been engaged in a cold civil war testing whether any nation so conceived and so dedicated can long endure. . . . This one thing is what makes us worth saving. If we go down it all goes down. And we shall go down, unless we recognize what we have to fight for and have the courage to fight for it. What makes Western civilization worth saving is the freedom of the mind, now under heavy attack from the primitives who have persisted among us. If we have not the courage to defend that faith, it won't matter much whether we are saved or not.

This republic was not established by cowards; and cowards will not preserve it.

> ELMER DAVIS, *But We Were Born Free,* 1954

Without commenting on the security system which has brought all this about, I do have a . . . word to say. Our country is fortunate in its scientists—in their high skill and their devotion. I know that they will work faithfully to preserve and strengthen this country. I hope that the fruit of their work will be used with humanity, with wisdom and with courage. I know that their counsel, when sought, will be given honestly and freely. I hope that it will be heard.

> J. ROBERT OPPENHEIMER, commenting on decision by Atomic Energy Commission that he was a security risk, June, 1954

When even one American—who has done nothing wrong—is forced by fear to shut his mind and close his mouth, then all Americans are in peril.

> HARRY S. TRUMAN

The snakes didn't like St. Patrick's methods, and the Communists don't like mine.

> JOSEPH R. MCCARTHY, at St. Patrick's Day dinner, 1954

It's no show just to protect the serious, the solemn, and the high-minded. We must protect the flippant, the zany, the heretical, and the downright queer. The Constitution gives every American the inalienable right to make a damnfool of himself.

> JOHN CIARDI, *Nation,* March 27, 1954

The right to be wrong is as important as the right to be admired.

> EDWARD R. MURROW, "Commencement Address," Hamilton College, June, 1954

The hard requirements of security, and the assertion of freedoms, thrust upon us a dilemma not easily resolved. In the present international situation our security measures exist, in the ultimate analysis, to protect our free institutions and traditions against repressive totalitarianism and its inevitable denial of human values. . . . We share the hope that some day we may return to happier times when our free institutions are not threatened and a peaceful and just world is not such a compelling principal preoccupation. Then security will cease to be a central issue . . . there will be no undue restraints upon freedom of mind and action, and loyalty and security as concepts will cease to have restrictive implications.

This state of affairs seems not to be a matter of early hope.

> GORDON GRAY and THOMAS ALFRED MORGAN, majority report of Security Board passing on Oppenheimer case, June, 1954

History shows that governments bent on a crusade or officials filled with ambitions have usually been inclined to take short cuts. The cause being a noble one (for it always is), the people being filled with alarm (for they usually are), the government being motivated by worthy aims (as it always professes), the demand for quick and easy justice mounts.

These short cuts are not as flagrant, perhaps, as a lynching. But the ends they produce are cumulative, and if they continue unabated they can silently rewrite even the fundamental law of the nation.

> WILLIAM O. DOUGLAS, quoted in the *Nation*, June 15, 1954

It isn't the layman that's ignorant. It's everybody that's ignorant. . . . The trouble with secrecy isn't that it inhibits science; it could, but in this country it's hardly been used that way. The trouble with secrecy is that it denies to the government itself the wisdom and the resources of the whole community, of the whole country. The only thing you can do is to let almost anyone say what he thinks, to try to give the best synopses, the best popularizations, and to let men deny what they think is false, argue [against] what they think is false, have a free and uncorrupted communication. . . . There aren't secrets about the world of nature. There are secrets about the thoughts and intentions of men.

> J. ROBERT OPPENHEIMER, interview with Edward R. Murrow, *See It Now*, January 7, 1955

I would do anything for a buck.

> HARVEY MATUSOW, *Diary*, August, 1953; quoted *The New York Times*, February 27, 1955

JUSTICE AND EQUALITY

•

Equal Justice Under Law.

> Inscription on Supreme Court Building, Washington

Justice in the Life and Conduct of the State Is Possible Only As It First Resides in the Hearts and Souls of the Citizens.

> Inscription on Department of Justice Building, Washington

The Place of Justice Is a Hallowed Place.

> Inscription over Pennsylvania Avenue entrance to Department of Justice Building, Washington.

Fidelity, Bravery, Integrity.

> Inscription on the seal of the F. B. I.

Any government is free to the people under it where the laws rule and the people are a party to the laws.

> WILLIAM PENN, *Frame of Government,* 1682

The law no passion can disturb. 'Tis void of desire and fear, lust and anger. . . . 'Tis deaf, inexorable, inflexible. On the one hand, it is inexorable to the cries and lamentations of the prisoner; on the other, it is deaf, deaf as an adder, to the clamors of the populace.

> JOHN ADAMS, defense of British soldiers on trial as murderers after the so-called Boston Massacre, 1770

The sober second thought of the people shall be law.

> FISHER AMES, speech in Congress, 1788

It is more dangerous that even a guilty person should be punished without the forms of law than that he should escape.

> THOMAS JEFFERSON, 1788

Justice is always the same, whether it be due from one man to a million, or from a million to one man.

> JOHN JAY

I told [John Marshall] it was law logic—an artificial system of reasoning, exclusively used in courts of justice, but good for nothing anywhere else.

JOHN QUINCY ADAMS

There are few Jews in the United States; in Maryland there are very few. But if there were only one—to that one, we ought to do justice.

> THOMAS KENNEDY, c. 1823. He was a leader of the fight to change a clause in the Maryland Constitution which required public office holders to make a "declaration of a belief in the Christian religion." In 1826 the clause was changed.

Justice, sir, is the great interest of man on earth.

DANIEL WEBSTER, *On Mr. Justice Story*, 1845

Under a government which imprisons any unjustly, the true place for a just man is also a prison.

HENRY DAVID THOREAU, *Civil Disobedience*

It is not to be forgotten, that while the law holds fast the thief and murderer, it lets itself go loose. When I have not paid the tax which the State demanded for that protection which I did not want, itself has robbed me; when I have asserted the liberty it presumed to declare, itself has imprisoned me. Poor creature! if it knows no better I will not blame it. If it cannot live but by those means, I can.

> HENRY DAVID THOREAU, *A Week on the Concord and Merrimac Rivers*

Our progress in degeneracy appears to me to be pretty rapid. As a nation, we began by declaring that *"all men are created equal."* We now practically read it "all men are created equal, *except negroes."* When the Know-Nothings get control, it will read "all men are created equal, except negroes, *and foreigners and Catholics."* When it comes to this I should prefer emigrating to some country where they make no pretense of loving liberty—to Russia, for instance, where despotism can be taken pure, and without the base alloy of hypocrisy.

ABRAHAM LINCOLN, letter to Speed, August 21, 1855

I know no method to secure the repeal of bad or obnoxious laws so effective as their stringent execution.

ULYSSES S. GRANT, "Inaugural Address," March 4, 1869

There is no calamity which a great nation can invite which equals that which follows a supine submission to wrong and injustice.

GROVER CLEVELAND, 1895

Anglo-Saxon civilization has taught the individual to protect his own rights; American civilization will teach him to respect the rights of others.

WILLIAM JENNINGS BRYAN, speech, Washington, 1899

We have a criminal jury system which is superior to any in the world; and its efficiency is only marred by the difficulty of finding twelve men every day who don't know anything and can't read.

SAMUEL L. CLEMENS ("MARK TWAIN"), *Sketches New and Old*

Inequality is as dear to the American heart as liberty itself.

WILLIAM DEAN HOWELLS, *Impressions and Experiences,* "New York Streets"

No man is above the law and no man is below it; nor do we ask any man's permission when we require him to obey it.

THEODORE ROOSEVELT, "Message to Congress," 1904

It is a disgrace to our civilization that men can be put to death by painful methods, which our laws have discarded as never suitable, and without the proofs of guilt which our laws call for in any case whatsoever. It would be a disgrace to us if amongst us men should burn a rattlesnake or a mad dog. The badness of the victim is not an element in the case at all. Torture and burning are forbidden, not because the victim is not bad enough, but because we are too good.

WILLIAM GRAHAM SUMNER, *Lynch-Law* (by James E. Cutler), "Foreword," 1905

The prophecies of what the courts will do in fact, and nothing more pretentious, are what I mean by the law.

OLIVER WENDELL HOLMES, JR.

[A dissent is] an appeal to the brooding spirit of the law, to the intelligence of a future day.

CHARLES EVANS HUGHES

Belief in equality is an element of the democratic credo. It is not, however, belief in equality of natural endowments. Those who proclaimed the idea of equality did not suppose they were enunciating a psychological doctrine, but a legal and political one. All individuals are entitled to equality of treatment by law and in its administration. Each one is affected equally in quality if not in quantity by the institutions under which he lives and has an equal right to express his judgment, although the weight of his judgment may not be equal in amount when it enters into the pooled result to that of others. In short, each one is equally an individual and entitled to equal opportunity of development of his own capacities, be they large or small in range. Moreover, each has needs of his own, as significant to him as those of others are to them. The very fact of natural and psychological inequality is all the more reason for establishment by law of equality of opportunity, since otherwise the former becomes a means of oppression of the less gifted.

JOHN DEWEY, *Equality*

One with the law is a majority.

CALVIN COOLIDGE, speech, 1920

The penalty for laughing in a courtroom is six months in jail; if it were not for this penalty, the jury would never hear the evidence.

H. L. MENCKEN

Justice, though due to the accused, is due to the accuser also. The concept of fairness must not be strained till it is narrowed to a filament. We are to keep the balance true.

BENJAMIN NATHAN CARDOZO, decision, *Snyder* v. *Commonwealth of Massachusetts,* January 8, 1934

I am the law.

FRANK HAGUE, statement at a legislative investigation, 1937

Let us, of the 75th Congress, declare that we would rather have an independent court, a fearless court, a court that will dare to announce its honest opinion in what it believes to be the defense of the liberties of the people, than a court that, out of fear or sense of obligation to the appointing power, or factional passion, approves any measure we may enact. We are not the judges of the judges. We are not above the Constitution. . . . Exhibiting this restraint, thus demonstrating our faith in the American system, we shall set an example that will protect the independent American judiciary from attack so long as this government stands. . . . We declare for the continuance and perpetuation of government and rule by law, as distinguished from government and rule by men, and in this we are but reasserting the principles basic to the Constitution of the United States. . . . We shall destroy the system when we reduce it to the imperfect standards of the men who operate it. We shall strengthen it and ourselves, we shall make justice and liberty for all men more certain when, by patience and self-restraint, we maintain it on the high plane on which it was conceived.

> Senate Judiciary Committee, 1937, reporting unfavorably President Roosevelt's "Court-Packing Bill"

It is not tolerance that one is entitled to in America. It is the right of every citizen in America to be treated by other citizens as an equal.

> WENDELL L. WILLKIE

We are a nation of many nationalities, many races, many religions—bound together by a single unity, the unity of freedom and equality. Whoever seeks to set one nationality against another, seeks to degrade all nationalities. Whoever seeks to set one race against another seeks to enslave all races. Whoever seeks to set one religion against another seeks to destroy all religion. I am fighting for a free America—for a country in which *all* men and women have equal rights to liberty and justice. I am fighting, as I always have fought, for the rights of the little man as well as the big man—for the weak as well as the strong, for those who are helpless as well as for those who can help themselves.

> FRANKLIN D. ROOSEVELT, 1940

Justice remains the greatest power on earth. To that tremendous power alone will we submit.

> HARRY S. TRUMAN, address at opening of Conference on United Nations Organization, San Francisco, 1945

We are not final because we are infallible, but we are infallible only because we are final.

> ROBERT H. JACKSON, of the Supreme Court, *Brown* v. *Allen,* 1953

LOVE OF COUNTRY

•

You will think me transported with enthusiasm, but I am not. I am well aware of the toil, and blood, and treasure, that it will cost us to maintain this declaration, and support and defend these States. Yet, through all the gloom, I can see the rays of ravishing light and glory. I can see that the end is more than worth all the means, and that posterity will triumph in that day's transaction, even although we should rue it, which I trust in God we shall not. . . . The second day of July, 1776, will be the most memorable epoch in the history of America. I am apt to believe that it will be celebrated by succeeding generations as the great anniversary festival. It ought to be commemorated as the day of deliverance, by solemn acts of devotion to God Almighty. It ought to be solemnized with pomp and parade, with shows, games, sports, guns, bells, bonfires, and illuminations, from one end of this continent to the other, from this time forward for evermore.

> JOHN ADAMS, letter to Mrs. Adams, July 3, 1776

I only regret that I have but one life to lose for my country.

> NATHAN HALE, last words before being hanged as a spy by the British, New York, September 22, 1776

That the flag of the thirteen United States be thirteen stripes, alternate red and blue; that the union be thirteen stars, white in a blue field, representing a new constellation.

> Resolution of Continental Congress, June 14, 1777

I wish the Bald Eagle had not been chosen as the Representative of our Country; he is a Bird of bad moral Character; like those among Men who live by Sharping and Robbing, he is generally poor, and often very lousy.

The Turkey is a much more respectable Bird, and withal a true original Native of America.

> BENJAMIN FRANKLIN, letter to Sarah Bache, Jan. 26, 1784

The name of American, which belongs to you in your national capacity, must always exalt the just pride of patriotism more than appellatives derived from local discriminations.

> GEORGE WASHINGTON, "Farewell Address," Sept. 17, 1796

Millions for defense but not a cent for tribute.

> ROBERT GOODLOE HARPER, toast, June 18, 1798

Protection and patriotism are reciprocal.

> JOHN C. CALHOUN, speech, House of Representatives, 1811

Our country! in her intercourse with foreign nations may she always be in the right; but our country, right or wrong!

> STEPHEN DECATUR, toast, April, 1816. G. K. Chesterton, *The Defendant,* opined that " 'My country, right or wrong,' is a thing no patriot would think of saying except in a desperate case. It is like saying, 'My mother, drunk or sober.' "

National honor is national property of the highest value.

> JAMES MONROE, "First Inaugural Address," March 4, 1817

May it [July 4] be to the world, what I believe it will be (to some parts sooner, to others later, but finally to all), the signal of arousing men to burst the chains under which monkish ignorance and superstition had persuaded them to bind themselves, and to assume the blessings and security of self-government. That form which we have substituted, restores the free right to the unbounded exercise of reason and freedom of opinion. All eyes are opened, or opening, to the rights of man. The general spread of the light of science has already laid open to every view the palpable truth, that the mass of mankind has not been born with saddles on their backs, nor a favored few, booted and spurred, ready to ride them legitimately, by the Grace of God. These are grounds of hope for others. For ourselves, let the annual return of this day forever refresh our recollections of these rights, and an undiminished devotion to them.

> THOMAS JEFFERSON, letter to Roger C. Weightman, June 24, 1826, refusing for reasons of health an invitation to be present at Independence Day celebration, Washington. This is Jefferson's last extant letter.

I have sometimes asked myself whether my country is the better for my having lived at all.

> THOMAS JEFFERSON

I name thee Old Glory!

> WILLIAM DRIVER, 1831, addressing the Stars and Stripes

Let it be borne on the flag under which we rally in every exigency, that we have one country, one constitution, one destiny.

DANIEL WEBSTER, 1837

Thank God! I—I also—am an American.

DANIEL WEBSTER, address on completion of Bunker Hill Monument, June 17, 1843

I was born an American; I live an American; I shall die an American.

DANIEL WEBSTER, speech, July 17, 1850

That which distinguishes this day [the Fourth of July] from all others is that then both orators and artillerymen shoot blank cartridges.

JOHN BURROUGHS, *Journal*, July 4, 1859

As we lay back in the stern sheets and the men gave way, he said to me: "Youngster, let that show you what it is to be without a family, without a home, and without a country. And if you are ever tempted to say a word or to do a thing that shall put a bar between you and your family, your home, and your country, pray God in his mercy to take you that instant home to his own heaven. Stick by your family, boy; forget you have a self, while you do everything for them. Think of your home, boy; write and send and talk about it. Let it be nearer and nearer to your thought the farther you have to travel from it; and rush back to it when you are free. . . . And for your country, boy," and the words rattled in his throat, "and for that flag," and he pointed to the ship, "never dream a dream but of serving her as she bids you, though the service carry you through a thousand hells. No matter what happens to you, no matter who flatters you or who abuses you, never look at another flag, never let a night pass but you pray God to bless that flag. Remember, boy, that behind all these men you have to do with, behind officers, and Government, and people even, there is the Country Herself, your Country, and that you belong to Her as you belong to your own mother. Stand by Her, boy, as you would stand by your mother, if those devils there had got hold of her to-day!"

EDWARD EVERETT HALE, "The Man Without a Country," *Atlantic Monthly*, 1863

I had no thought it was the end. I thought he was tired and would sleep. I knew he was happy and I wanted him to be alone.

But in an hour, when the doctor went in gently, he found Nolan had breathed his life away with a smile. He had something pressed to his lips. It was his father's badge of the Order of Cincinnati.

We looked in his Bible, and there was a slip of paper, at the place where he had marked the text: "They desire a country, even a heavenly: wherefore God is not ashamed to be called their God: for he hath prepared for them a city."

On this slip he had written: Bury me in the sea; it has been my home, and I love it. But will not someone set up a stone for my memory at Fort Adams or at Orleans, that my disgrace may not be more than I ought to bear? Say on it:

IN MEMORY OF

PHILIP NOLAN

LIEUTENANT IN THE ARMY OF THE UNITED STATES

He loved his country as no other man has loved her;
but no man deserved less at her hands.

EDWARD EVERETT HALE, *Ibid.*

Our country, right or wrong. When right to be kept right, when wrong to be put right.

CARL SCHURZ, speech in Congress, 1872

I pledge allegiance to the flag of the United States and to the republic for which it stands, one nation, under God, indivisible, with liberty and justice for all.

FRANCIS BELLAMY, the Pledge of Allegiance to the Flag, 1892; the phrase "under God" added by Congress, 1954

A safe and sane Fourth.

TOM MASSON, editorial in *Life,* 1896

It seems like the less a statesman amounts to, the more he loves the flag.

KIN HUBBARD

The man who loves other countries as much as his own stands on a level with the man who loves other women as much as he loves his own wife.

THEODORE ROOSEVELT, speech, 1918

The man who loves his country only that he may be free does not love his country. He loves only himself and his own ways and that is not self-government, but is the essence of despotism.

ELIHU ROOT

Patriotism:—A variety of hallucination which, if it seized a bacteriologist in his laboratory, would cause him to report the streptococcus purogenes to be as large as a Newfoundland dog, as intelligent as Socrates, as beautiful as Mont Blanc, and as respectable as a Yale professor.

H. L. MENCKEN

In the United States, doing good has come to be, like patriotism, a favorite device of persons with something to sell.

H. L. MENCKEN

Were I to have a vision of a full-fledged American it would be something like this: A man who, with sufficient knowledge of the past, would walk fairly constantly with the thought that he was blood-brother, if not by actual race then by the equally subtle method of mental vein transfusing into mental vein, of Washington and Lincoln; of Jefferson and Lee, and of all the men like them. Who would walk, because of this, carefully and proudly, and also humbly, lest he fail them. And, with a keen sense of the present and the future, would say to himself: "I am an American and therefore what I do, however small, is of importance."

Never in history have the times been more ripe for a sober discussion, a deep contemplation, of the kind of patriotism I imply. The American citizen is no longer a frontiersman; he can no longer make a million here and lose it there, and go on and make a million somewhere else, and meanwhile let his country take care of itself. The American is no longer a colonial, even in retrospect. Circumstances are forcing him into a deep, straight, independent form of thinking.

Pseudo-patriotism may be the last refuge of a scoundrel, but it is beginning to be apparent that before long, real patriotism, as so often before in history, will be not only the last, and only possible, refuge of the intelligent and far-visioned citizen, but also his sword, his rallying cry, and the emblem of his advance.

STRUTHERS BURT, *The Full-Fledged American*

If we go back across American history we find that as a nation among the other nations of the world this country has never kept silence as to what it stands for. For a hundred and fifty years and more we have told

the world that the American Republic stands for a certain way of life.
No matter what happened to the map of Europe, no matter what changes
of government and systems went on there, no matter what old thrones
and dynasties crashed to make way for something else, no matter what
new philosophies and orbits of influence were proclaimed, America never
kept silent.

> CARL SANDBURG, remarks to President Roosevelt, 1940,
> quoted by Robert E. Sherwood, *Roosevelt and Hopkins*

Ours is the only country deliberately founded on a good idea.

> JOHN GUNTHER, *Inside U.S.A.*

IV. How We Live

AT WORK

•

You must obey this, now, for a law—that "he that will not work shall not eat."

JOHN SMITH, *The Generall Historie of Virginia,* 1624

I do not believe a man can ever leave his business. He ought to think of it by day and dream of it by night. . . . Thinking men know that work is the salvation of the race, morally, physically, socially. Work does more than get us our living; it gets us our life.

HENRY FORD

THE BUSINESS OF AMERICA

In God We Trust.

ANON., the most extensively coined phrase in American life

The small landholders are the most precious part of a state.

THOMAS JEFFERSON, letter to Rev. James Madison, 1785

I think our governments will remain virtuous for many centuries; as long as they remain chiefly agricultural; and this will be as long as there shall be vacant lands in any part of America. When they get piled upon one another in large cities, as in Europe, they will become corrupt as in Europe, and go to eating one another as they do there.

THOMAS JEFFERSON, letter to Rev. James Madison, Paris, December 20, 1787

The almighty dollar, that great object of universal devotion throughout our land, seems to have no genuine devotees in these peculiar villages.

WASHINGTON IRVING, "The Creole Village," *Knickerbocker Magazine,* November, 1836

Business is the very soul of an American: he pursues it, not as a means of procuring for himself and his family the necessary comforts of life, but as the fountain of all human felicity. . . . It is as if all America were but one gigantic workshop, over the entrance of which there is the blazing inscription, "No admission here, except on business."

FRANCIS J. GRUND, 1836

We rail at trade, but the historian of the world will see that it was the principle of liberty; that it settled America, and destroyed feudalism, and made peace and keeps peace; that it will abolish slavery.

RALPH WALDO EMERSON, *Journal,* December 31, 1843

The best business you can go into you will find on your father's farm or in his workshop. If you have no family or friends to aid you, and no prospect open to you there, turn your face to the great West and there build up your home and fortune.

> HORACE GREELEY, *To Aspiring Young Men,* 1846. This is often quoted as "Go West, young man, and grow up with the country," a phrase which, though he may have spoken it, does not appear in Greeley's writings.

The greatest meliorator of the world is selfish, huckstering trade.

> RALPH WALDO EMERSON, *Society and Solitude,* "Works and Days"

I trust a good deal to common fame, as we all must. If a man has good corn, or woods, or boards, or pigs to sell, or can make better chairs or knives, crucibles or church organs than anybody else, you will find a broad, hard-beaten road to his house, though it be in the woods.

> RALPH WALDO EMERSON, *Journal,* 1855. This has been often quoted as "If you write a better book, or preach a better sermon, or build a better mousetrap than your neighbor, the world will make a beaten path to your door," but the words do not appear in any of Emerson's writings. It is quite possible that he used the "mousetrap image" in a lecture or in conversation; Mrs. Sarah S. B. Yule, *Borrowings,* 1889, states that she copied the words down in her notebook from the memory of a lecture heard many years before. Hers is the first known attribution of the phrase to Emerson.

From the time that his attention was first given to the subject, a strong and abiding impression was made upon his mind, that an object so desirable and important, and so necessary to man's comfort, as the making of gum elastic available to use, was most certainly placed within his reach. Having this presentiment, of which he could not divest himself under the most trying adversity, he was stimulated with the hope of ultimately attaining this object.

Beyond this he would refer the whole to the great Creator, who directs the operation of mind to the development of the properties of matter, in his own way, at the time when they are specially needed, influencing some mind for every work or calling. . . . Were he to refrain from expressing his views thus briefly, he would ever feel that he had done violence to his sentiments.

> CHARLES GOODYEAR, *Gum Elastic and Its Varieties*. This book, describing Goodyear's discovery of the vulcanization process, was printed on thin sheets of India rubber.

No! you dare not make war upon cotton; no power on earth dares to make war upon it. Cotton is king; until lately the Bank of England was king; but she tried to put her screws, as usual, the fall before the last, on the cotton crop, and was utterly vanquished. The last power has been conquered: who can doubt, that has looked at recent events, that cotton is supreme?

> JAMES H. HAMMOND, speech in the Senate, March 4, 1858

To such a pass our civilization and division of labor has come that A, a professional huckleberry-picker, has hired B's field and, we will suppose, is now gathering the crop, perhaps with the aid of a patented machine; C, a professed cook, is superintending the cooking of a pudding made of some of the berries; while Professor D, for whom the pudding is intended, sits in his library writing a book . . . a work on the Vacciniae, of course. And now the result of this downward course will be seen in that book, which should be the ultimate fruit of the huckleberry-field and account for the existence of the two professors who come between D and A. It will be worthless. There will be none of the spirit of the huckleberry in it. The reading of it will be a weariness to the flesh. To use a homely illustration, this is to save at the spile but waste at the bung. I believe in a different kind of division of labor, and that Professor D should divide himself between the library and the huckleberry-field.

> HENRY DAVID THOREAU, *Journal*

Most men would feel insulted, if it were proposed to employ them in throwing stones over a wall, and then in throwing them back, merely that they might earn their wages. But many are no more worthily employed now.

> HENRY DAVID THOREAU, "Life Without Principle," *Atlantic Monthly,* 1863

There were three waves of migration on this continent and the second was always the cattlemen. Ahead went the trappers and the Indian traders. . . . Behind the cattle came the farmers. . . . There were always cattle out ahead of the plows. And for a simplest reason. Beef and pork and mutton were the only crops in that land without roads which could take themselves to market. . . . Cattle made the first frontier where white men lived. And grass made cattle.

> ARCHIBALD MACLEISH, *Green River*

All is well since all grows better.

> ANDREW CARNEGIE, "Wealth," *North American Review,* June, 1889

Whether the law [of competition] be benign or not, we must say of it . . . it is here; we cannot evade it; no substitutes for it have been found; and while the law may sometimes be hard on the individual, it is best for the race, because it ensures the survival of the fittest in every department. We accept and welcome, therefore, as conditions to which we must accommodate ourselves, great inequality of environment; the concentration of business, industrial and commercial, in the hands of the few; and the law of competition between these, as being not only beneficial, but essential to the future progress of the race.

> ANDREW CARNEGIE, *Ibid.*

When you come before us and tell us that we are to disturb your business interests, we reply that you have disturbed our business interests by your course. We say to you that you have made the definition of a business man too limited in its application. The man who is employed for wages is as much a business man as his employer. The attorney in a country bank is as much a business man as the corporation counsel in a great metropolis; a merchant at the crossroads store is as much a business man as the merchant of New York; the farmer who goes forth in the morning and toils all day—who begins in the spring and toils all summer—and who by the application of brawn and muscle to the natural resources of the country, creates wealth, is as much a business man as the man who goes upon the Board of Trade and bets upon the price of grain.

> WILLIAM JENNINGS BRYAN, speech, Democratic National Convention, July, 1896

The fundamental principles which govern the handling of postage stamps and of millions of dollars are exactly the same. They are the common law of business, and the whole practice of commerce is founded on them. They are so simple that a fool can't learn them; so hard that a lazy man won't.

> PHILIP D. ARMOUR

All that the traffic will bear.

> Common saying about railroad freight rates, c. 1900

Men were mere nothings, mere animalculae, mere ephemerides that fluttered and fell and were forgotten between dawn and dusk. . . . Men were nought, death was nought, life was nought. Force only existed— Force that brought men into the world—Force that crowded them out to make way for the succeeding generation—Force that made the wheat grow—Force that garnered it from the soil to give place to the succeeding crop.

> FRANK NORRIS, *The Octopus*, 1901

I think people are going to buy quite a passel of these gasoline buggies and they need gasoline to make 'em go. It may be the thing has a future.

> FRANK PHILLIPS, founder of Phillips Oil Company, 1904

The Jungle.

> UPTON SINCLAIR, title of book, 1906. Sinclair remarked of the great success of this work, "I aimed at the public's heart and hit it in the stomach."

The ability to deal with people is as purchasable a commodity as sugar or coffee. And I pay more for that ability than for any other under the sun.

> JOHN D. ROCKEFELLER

I ascribe the success of the Standard Oil Company to its consistent policy of making the volume of its business large through the merit and cheapness of its products. It has spared no expense in utilizing the best and most efficient method of manufacture. It has sought for the best superintendents and paid the best wages. It has not hesitated to sacrifice old machinery and old plants for new and better ones. It has placed its manufactories at the points where they could supply markets at the least expense. It has not only sought markets for its principal products but for all possible by-products, sparing no expense in introducing them to the public in every nook and corner of the world. It has not hesitated to invest millions of dollars in methods for cheapening the gathering and distribution of oils by pipe lines, special cars, tank-steamers, and tank-wagons. It has erected tank stations at railroad centers in every part of the country to cheapen the storage and delivery of oil. It has had faith in American oil and has brought together vast sums of money for the purpose of making it what it is and for holding its market against the competition of Russia and all the countries which are producers of oil and competitors against American products.

> JOHN D. ROCKEFELLER, *Random Reminiscences,* 1908

We never deceived ourselves.

> JOHN D. ROCKEFELLER, to Henry George, explaining the
> success of the Standard Oil Company

The secret of success in my business is to buy old junk, fix it up a little and unload it upon other fellows.

> CHARLES T. YERKES

The gambling known as business looks with austere disfavor upon the business known as gambling.

> AMBROSE BIERCE

Three generations from shirt sleeves to shirt sleeves.

> Attributed to ANDREW CARNEGIE, 1908

What's it done f'r th' wurruld? says ye. It's done ivrything. It's give us fast ships an' an autymatic hist f'r th' hod, an' small flats an' a taste of solder in th' peaches. If annybody says th' wurruld ain't betther off thin it was, tell him that a masheen has been invinted that makes honey out iv pethrolyum. If he asts ye why they ain't anny Shakesperes today, say: "No, but we no longer make sausages be hand . . ."

I sometimes wondher whether pro-gress is anny more thin a kind iv shift. It's like a merry-go-round. We get up a speckled wooden horse an' th' mechanical pianny plays a chune an' away we go, hollerin'. We think we're thravellin' like th' divvle but th' man that doesn't care about merry-go-rounds knows that we will come back where we were. We get out dizzy an' sick an' lay on th' grass an' gasp: "Where am I? Is this th' meelin-yum?" An' he says: "No, 'tis Ar-rchey Road." Father Kelly says th' Agyptians done things we cudden't do an' th' Romans put up skyscrapers an' aven th' Chinks had tillyphones an' phonygrafts.

I've been up to th' top iv th' very highest buildin' in town, Hinnissy, an' I wasn't anny nearer Hivin thin if I was in th' sthreet. Th' stars was as far away as iver. An' down beneath is a lot iv us runnin' an' lapin' an' jumpin' about, pushin' each other over, haulin' little sthrips iv ir'n to pile up in little buildin's that ar-re called skyscrapers but not be th' sky; wurrukin' night an' day to make a masheen that'll carry us fr'm wan jack-rabbit colony to another an' yellin', "Pro-gress!" Pro-gress, oho! I can see th' stars winkin' at each other an' sayin': "Ain't they funny! Don't they think they're playin' hell!"

FINLEY PETER DUNNE ("MR. DOOLEY"), Machinery

"Th' American nation in th' Sixth Ward, is a fine people," he says. "They love th' eagle," he says, "on th' back iv a dollar."

FINLEY PETER DUNNE ("MR. DOOLEY"), Mr. Dooley in Peace and War

I will build a motorcar for the great multitudes.

HENRY FORD, launching the Model T in 1909

I shall refuse to answer; it is my trade secret.

GEORGE LYMAN KITTREDGE, when asked by efficiency experts at Harvard how much time he spent in preparing for his classes, 1912

Business underlies everything in our national life, including our spiritual life. Witness the fact that in the Lord's Prayer, the first petition is for daily bread. No one can worship God or love his neighbor on an empty stomach.

WOODROW WILSON, speech, New York, 1912

The truth is, we are all caught in a great economic system which is heartless.

WOODROW WILSON

All business sagacity reduces itself in the last analysis to a judicious use of sabotage.

THORSTEIN VEBLEN, *The Nature of Peace*, 1919

If you can forgive the magnificence and vanity of a successful politician, why are you unable to forgive a successful business man? Every time I strike a match, or turn an electric button, or use the telephone, I am indebted to a business man, but if in debt to any politician, I do not know it.

EDGAR W. HOWE

His name was George F. Babbitt and . . . he was nimble in the calling of selling houses for more than people could pay.

SINCLAIR LEWIS, *Babbitt*, 1922

"In my opinion, what the country needs, first and foremost, is a good, sound, business-like conduct of its affairs. What we need is—a business administration!" said Littlefield.

"I'm glad to hear you say that! [said Babbitt] I certainly am glad to hear you say that! I didn't know how you'd feel about it, with all your associations with colleges and so on, and I'm glad you feel that way. What this country needs—just at this present juncture—is neither a college president nor a lot of monkeying with foreign affairs, but a good—sound—economical—business—administration, that will give us a chance to have something like a decent turnover."

SINCLAIR LEWIS, *Ibid.*

My gasoline buggy was the first and for a long time the only automobile in Detroit. It was considered to be something of a nuisance, for it made a racket and it scared horses. Also it blocked traffic. For if I stopped my machine anywhere in town a crowd was around it before I could start up again. Finally, I had to carry a chain and chain it to a lamp post whenever I left it anywhere. And then there was trouble with the police. I do not know quite why, for my impression is that there were no speed limits in those days. Anyway, I had to get a special permit from the mayor and thus for a time enjoyed the distinction of being the only licensed chauffeur in America. I ran that machine about one thousand miles through 1895 and 1896 and then sold it to Charles Ainsley of Detroit for two hundred dollars. That was my first sale. I had built the car not to sell but only to experiment with. I wanted to start another car.

HENRY FORD, *My Life and Work*, 1922

It is considered good manufacturing practice, and not bad ethics, occasionally to change designs so that old models will become obsolete and new ones will have to be bought. . . . Our principle of business is precisely to the contrary. We cannot conceive how to serve the customer unless we make for him something that, as far as we can provide, will last forever. . . . We never make an improvement that renders any previous model obsolete. The parts of a specific model are not only interchangeable with all other cars of that model, but they are interchangeable with similar parts on all cars that we have turned out. You can take a car of ten years ago, and buying today's parts, make it with very little expense into a car of today.

> HENRY FORD, in 1923, quoted by Kouwenhoven, *Made in America*

The commodities that conduce to civilised living are thus far enjoyed by only a small fraction of the world's inhabitants. The experience of the Ford Motor Co. has been that mass production precedes mass consumption and makes it possible, by reducing costs. . . . If the production is increased 500%, costs may be cut 50%, and this decrease in cost, with its accompanying decrease in selling price, will probably multiply by 10 the number of people who can conveniently buy the product. This is a conservative illustration of production serving as the cause of demand instead of the effect.

> HENRY FORD, quoted by Burlingame, *Backgrounds of Power*

All Wrigley had was an idea. He was the first man to discover that American jaws must wag. So why not give them something to wag against?

> WILL ROGERS, *The Illiterate Digest*, 1924

He picked up twelve men from the bottom ranks of business and forged them into an organization that conquered the world.

> BRUCE BARTON, of Jesus Christ, *The Man Nobody Knows*

His father wants him to be a lawyer but I want him to go into a bank. It's always so nice and cool in a bank.

> HELEN HOKINSON, cartoon caption, 1920's

The business of America is business.

> CALVIN COOLIDGE, speech to Society of American Newspaper Editors, Washington, January 17, 1925. According to

I. Bernard Cohen, *Benjamin Franklin,* he added, "The chief ideal of the American people is idealism. I cannot repeat too often that America is a nation of idealists."

Prosperity is only an instrument to be used, not a deity to be worshipped.

CALVIN COOLIDGE

Civilization and profits go hand in hand.

CALVIN COOLIDGE

The work that religion, government, and war have failed in must be done by business. . . . That eternal job of administering this planet must be turned over to the despised business man.

EARNEST ELMO CALKINS, "Business the Civilizer," *Atlantic Monthly,* February, 1928

The American system of rugged individualism.

HERBERT HOOVER, speech, October 22, 1928

Marry the boss's daughter.

ROBERT EMMONS ROGERS, to the Class of 1929 at M.I.T.

The cold truth is that the individualist creed of everybody for himself and the devil take the hindmost is principally responsible for the distress in which Western civilization finds itself—with investment racketeering at one end and labor racketeering at the other. Whatever merits the creed may have had in days of primitive agriculture and industry, it is not applicable in an age of technology, science, and rationalized economy. Once useful, it has become a danger to society. Every thoughtful business man who is engaged in management as distinguished from stock speculation knows that stabilization, planning, orderly procedure, prudence, and the adjustment of production to demand are necessary to keep the economic machine running steadily and efficiently.

CHARLES A. *and* MARY BEARD, *The Myth of Rugged Individualism,* 1931

Clever chaps these disciples of Lenin and Stalin in the Government at Washington!

They are going to tax the country into prosperity.

They are going to make the country wealthy by stopping the spending of money.

They are going to improve business by decreasing business.

They are going to relieve unemployment by relieving those that are now employed of their jobs.

They are going to give all the money to the Government, so that the only people who will have any jobs will be Government employees.

WILLIAM RANDOLPH HEARST, editorial, March 26, 1932

The reason American cities are prosperous is that there is no place to sit down.

ALFRED J. TALLEY, on returning from Europe, 1935

Parable of the Isms:

Socialism: If you have two cows, you give one to your neighbor.

Communism: If you have two cows, you give them to the government and then the government gives you some milk.

Fascism: If you have two cows, you keep the cows and give the milk to the government; then the government sells you some milk.

New Dealism: If you have two cows, you shoot one and milk the other; then you pour the milk down the drain.

Nazism: If you have two cows, the government shoots you and keeps the cows.

Capitalism: If you have two cows, you sell one and buy a bull.

ANON.

I hear much that new opportunity for youth is gone. It occurs to me that for 150 years God-fearing people under the blessings of freedom built up quite a plant and equipment on this continent. It teems with millions of farms and homes and cattle and pigs, despite the AAA. There are railroads, highways, power plants and factories, stores and banks, and money-changers. There are towns and magnificent cities. There are newspapers, colleges, libraries, orchestras, bands, radios, and other noises. It is very sad, but did it ever occur to you that all the people who live in these houses, and all those who run this complicated machine are going to die? Just as sure as death the job is yours. And there are opportunities in every inch of it.

HERBERT HOOVER, address, Young Republican League, Colorado Springs, March 7, 1936

Commerce is the most important activity on the face of the earth. It is the foundation on which civilization is built. Religion, society, education— all have their roots in business, and would have to be reorganized in their material aspects should business fail.

JAMES R. ADAMS, *More Power to Advertising,* 1937

Our time is rich in inventive minds, the inventions of which could facilitate our lives considerably. We are crossing the seas by power and utilize power also in order to relieve humanity from all tiring muscular work. We have learned to fly and we are able to send messages and news without any difficulty over the entire world through electric waves.

However, the production and distribution of commodities is entirely unorganized so that everybody must live in fear of being eliminated from the economic cycle, in this way suffering for the want of everything. Furthermore, people living in different countries kill each other at irregular time intervals, so that also for this reason anyone who thinks about the future must live in fear and terror. This is due to the fact that the intelligence and character of the masses are incomparably lower than the intelligence and character of the few who produce something valuable for the community.

I trust that posterity will read these statements with a feeling of proud and justified superiority.

ALBERT EINSTEIN, message in the Time-Capsule, World's Fair, New York, 1939

I introduced a Constitutional amendment giving the federal government power at all times to regulate and control the production, conservation and distribution of food supplies. But it got no further than my bill providing the death penalty in time of war for corrupt contractors. Some day we will come to realize that the right to food, shelter and clothing at reasonable prices is as much an inalienable right as the right to life, liberty and the pursuit of happiness.

FIORELLO H. LA GUARDIA, *The Making of an Insurgent*

The man who builds a skyscraper to last for more than forty years is a traitor to the building trade.

Unidentified contractor quoted by Aldous Huxley, *Selected Snobberies*

Business is the lone God of our Congress. Let a man open a pie factory or begin to mold cement blocks and he becomes Privileged. His property is taxed as a sacred, eternal entity. His costs are deductible. Only the profit he pockets is thought of by our Congress as income; his every barrel of flour or bag of cement is capital. But let a man create books or serials in his head and Congress sees him as a social inferior, a mere wage earner.

The accumulation of intellectual property for a book may require three-quarters of a life. Its sale, for a year or two, may be considerable. After that one book—or after two or three—an author may return to pittances. What he has written may become the mental and emotional capital of his countrymen, or of the world, for generations. Yet Congress does not deem it equal to pies or bricks and sometimes skims away in a year the whole capital of the author—as if it were but annual income. America bounteously provides for the makers of bricks and pies; it shortchanges book-makers and the winners of Nobel Prizes. Indeed, such is the unconscious hostility of the mob toward the fruits of intelligence that, not long ago, a group of representatives, commercial he-whores and contumelious morons, endeavored to do away with copyright altogether on the grounds that what a man thought and wrote down, or what he felt and painted, belonged free of charge to the whole people: noneconomic, since it was Art. To such men as these, only junk fabricators, gadgeteers, tram operators, pop bottlers and the like are entitled to the best profit for their contribution to life. History will note the fact when history writes how American avarice held in open contempt all culture and all thought, decerebrated itself and so died headless.

PHILIP WYLIE, *Opus 21*, 1949

The average vice-president is a form of executive fungus that attaches itself to a desk. On a boat this growth would be called a barnacle.

FRED ALLEN

Business is my business.

HENRY KAISER

There are . . . other business societies—England, Holland, Belgium and France, for instance. But ours is the only culture now extant in which business so completely dominates the national scene that sports, sex, death, philanthropy and Easter Sunday are money-making propositions.

MARGARET HALSEY, *The Folks at Home*

It is a pleasure and a privilege to be here with you today. These great annual meetings are always an inspiration to me, and doubly so today.

After that glowing introduction by our toastmaster I must confess, however, that I'd like to turn the tables and tell a little story on Chuck. When I say it's about the nineteenth hole and a certain gentleman whose baritone was cracked, those of you who were at the Atlanta conference last year will know what I mean. But I won't tell it. Chuck Forbes is too good a friend of mine and, seriously, I know full well we all realize what a tower of strength his yeoman service has been to the association in these trying times.

Yes, gentleman, trying times. So you'll pardon me if I cast aside the glib reverberation of glittering generalities and the soothing syrup of sugar-coated platitudes and put it to you the only way I can: straight English.

We're losing the battle!

From every corner the people are being weaned from the Doctrines of the Founding Fathers. They are being detoured from the high-speed highways of progress by the utopian highwaymen.

Now, the man in the street is a pretty savvy fellow. Don't sell him short. Joe Doakes may be fooled for a while, but in the end he wants no part of the mumbo jumbo the global saboteurs are trying to sell him. After all, he is an American.

But he has to be told.

And we're not telling him!

Now let me say that I do not wish to turn the clock back. None of us do. All forward-looking businessmen see themselves as partners in a team in which the worker is a full-fledged member. I regard our employees as our greatest business asset, and I am sure, mindful as I am of the towering potentialities of purposeful energy in this group of clear-sighted leaders, that, in the final analysis, it is the rock foundation of your policies too.

But the team can't put the ball across for a first down just by wishing it. The guards and the tackles can't do their job if the quarterback doesn't let them in on the play. And we, the quarterbacks, are muffing the ball.

How are we to go over for a touchdown? My friends, this is the $64 question. I don't know the answers. I am just a plain-spoken businessman. I am not a soothsayer. I have no secret crystal ball. But I do know one thing: before we round the curve into the homestretch we have a job to do. It will not be easy. I offer no panaceas or nostrums. Instead, I would like to suggest that the real key to our problem lies in the application of the three E's.

What are the three E's?

ENTERPRISE! ENDEAVOR! EFFORT!

Each and every one of us must appoint himself a salesman—yes, a missionary, if you will—and get out and do some real grass-roots selling. And when we hit the dirt, let's not forget the customers—the greatest asset any business has.

Now, much has been done already. But let's not fool ourselves: the surface, as our chairman has so wisely said, has hardly been scratched. The program is still in its infancy. So let me give it to you straight from the shoulder. The full implementation, gentlemen, depends on *us*.

So, let's get on the beam! In cracker-barrel fashion, let's get down to earth. In good plain talk the man in the street can understand, let's remind Joe Doakes that the best helping hand he will ever find is the one at the end of his own shirt sleeve.

We have the know-how.

With sights set high, let's go over the top!

> WILLIAM H. WHYTE, JR., "The Language of Business," *Fortune,* November, 1950. Mr. Whyte insists this is not a parody. It is a loose compilation, based on a systematic count of the expressions and constructions most commonly used in current U.S. business speeches. Included are the sixty principal clichés of what *Fortune* calls *"reverse* gobble-degook or *shirt-sleeve* English, in which the less you have to say, the more emphatically you can say it."

Private property began the instant somebody had a mind of his own.

> E. E. CUMMINGS, "Jottings," Harvard *Wake,* 1951

Private property was the original source of freedom. It is still its main bulwark. Recent experience confirms this truth. Where men have yielded without serious resistance to the tyranny of new dictators, it is because they have lacked property. They dare not resist because resistance meant destitution. . . . There is no surer way to give men the courage to be free than to insure them a competence upon which they can rely. Men cannot be made free by laws unless they are in fact free because no man can buy and no man can coerce them. That is why the Englishman's belief that his home is his castle and that the king cannot enter it, like the American's conviction that he must be able to look any man in the eye and tell him to go to hell, are the very essence of the free man's way of life.

> WALTER LIPPMANN

It is told that such are the aerodynamics and wing-loading of the bumble-bee that, in principle, it cannot fly. It does, and the knowledge that it defies the august authority of Isaac Newton and Orville Wright must keep the bee in constant fear of crack-up. One can assume, in addition, that it is apprehensive of the matriarchy to which it is subject, for this is known to be an oppressive form of government. The bumblebee is a successful but an insecure insect.

If all this be true, and its standing in physics and entomology is perhaps not of the highest, life among the bumblebees must bear a remarkable resemblance to life in the United States in recent years. The present organization and management of the American economy are also in defiance of the rules—rules that derive their ultimate authority from men of such Newtonian stature as Bentham, Ricardo and Adam Smith. Nevertheless it works, and in the years since World War II quite brilliantly. The fact that it does so, in disregard of precept, has caused men to suppose that all must end in a terrible smash. And, as with the bee, there is deep concern over the intentions of those in authority. This also leads to apprehension and insecurity.

JOHN KENNETH GALBRAITH, *American Capitalism,* 1952

The world of free nations is looking to us—not just to our Government, but to us, the American people—for something more than our economic and military power. They are hoping to find in the American people the imagination, the courage and the moral and spiritual leadership which the world so desperately seeks. If the private leaders of American industry, labor and agriculture are able to work together well enough to do the tough but not impossible job which is staked out for us . . . . the whole free world will be immensely heartened.

HENRY FORD II, 1952

There was an old dream: the independent man in his own little shop or business. It *was* a good dream.

There is a new dream: a world of great machines, with man in control, devising and making use of these inanimate creatures to build a new kind of independence, a new awareness of beauty, a new spirit of brotherliness. . . .

Bigness can become an expression of the heroic size of man himself as he comes to a new-found greatness.

DAVID E. LILIENTHAL, *Big Business: A New Era,* 1952

What is good for the country is good for General Motors, and what's good for General Motors is good for the country.

CHARLES E. WILSON, to a Congressional Committee, 1952

If, as I happen to believe, the American people are displaying a readiness to turn back to the field of business for leadership, we businessmen must respond with a philosophy that merits confidence. . . . This means setting aside time out of our business lives to determine what are the essential values in the activities which fill our days, and then consciously relating our own efforts to their preservation. No two men will choose exactly the same scale of values . . . but that is the conservative strength of democracy. Our differences keep us in balance, and we move ahead when at last a common denominator appears in the thinking of all good citizens. To preserve the required balance, the businessman plays his part in the forming of opinion.

CLARENCE B. RANDALL, *Freedom's Faith,* 1953

I do not know of any group for whom the maintenance of freedom has more significance than businessmen. Totalitarian regimes have little or no place for them; in fact, there is no Russian word for a man of business.

PAUL G. HOFFMAN, *American Freedom,* 1953

You can't license a perfume salesman to handle a million-dollar-a-month casino, because he'd be in trouble by the end of the first day and then it would be the public would get the shaft as he tried to make up his losses. We've learned that the oldtime gambler will run a cleaner place, give the public the best breaks and have fewer hoodlums hanging around, than the amateur.

ROBBINS CAHILL, Executive Secretary, Tax Commission of Nevada, explaining why ex-racketeers and gamblers run Las Vegas gambling halls; *Time,* November 23, 1953

Familiarity has perhaps bred contempt in us Americans: until you have a washing machine, you cannot imagine how little difference it will make to you. It is still a European belief that money brings happiness, witness the bought journalist, the bought politician, the bought general, the venality of much of European literary life, inconceivable in this country of the dollar. It is true that America produces and consumes more cars, soap, and bathtubs than any other nation, but we live among these objects rather than by them. Americans build skyscrapers; Le Corbusier worships them. Ehrenburg, our Soviet critic, fell in love with the Check-O-Mat in American railway stations, writing home paragraphs of song to this gadget —while deploring American materialism. When an American heiress

wants to buy a man, she at once crosses the Atlantic. The only really ma-
terialistic people I have ever met have been Europeans.

MARY McCARTHY, *Perspective*, 1953

What has been done in Germany has been done in first instance by the
Germans themselves. Now, looking backward, many truths are obvious
that were unknown in the first days of German defeat. The dissolution of
an entire nation is a social impossibility; the wreckage of Germany that
so stupefied Germans and conquerors alike in 1945 was the wreckage of
buildings and stone. But it was impossible to destroy the skills in the fingers
of German workmen, the knowledge of German engineers, and the mana-
gerial know-how of German industrialists without the physical extermina-
tion of the German people, obviously a moral impossibility. The social
capital inherent in the accumulation of years of human experience is,
economically, a vaster asset than all installations of pits, turning wheels
and rails. If all American industry were leveled to the ground, America
would still be the greatest industrial nation on earth because of her social
capital.

THEODORE H. WHITE, *Fire in the Ashes*, 1953

Almost everywhere in America, our nation has done wonderfully in laying
out and hard-surfacing one lane of its inter-job highway. The sign on the
other, which leads from White-collar to Overalls, still reads, "Road
Closed. Proceed at Your Own Peril."

In Vermont we are proud to post the notice—and to try to live up to
it, "Open for Traffic in Both Directions."

DOROTHY CANFIELD FISHER, *Vermont Tradition*, 1953

The era is to be one of good feeling. It's being planned that way.

ANON., *U.S. News & World Report*, January, 1955, reporting that optimism "will dominate" 1955

CAPITAL AND LABOR

If we except the light and the air of heaven, no good thing has been or
can be enjoyed by us without having first cost labor. And inasmuch as
most good things are produced by labor, it follows that all such things of

right belong to those whose labor has produced them. But it has so happened, in all the ages of the world, that some have labored, and others have without labor enjoyed a large proportion of the fruits. This is wrong, and should not continue. To secure to each laborer the whole product of his labor, or as nearly as possible, is a worthy object of any good government.

> ABRAHAM LINCOLN, "Fragments of a Tariff Discussion,"
> December 1, 1847 (date assigned by Hay and Nicolay)

I hold that if the Almighty had ever made a set of men that should do all the eating and none of the work, He would have made them with mouths only and no hands; and if He had ever made another class that He intended should do all the work and no eating, He would have made them with hands only and no mouths.

> ABRAHAM LINCOLN, "Mud-Sill Theory of Labor"

. . . I am glad to see that a system of labor prevails in New England under which laborers can strike when they want to, where they are not obliged to work under all circumstances and are not tied down and obliged to labor whether you pay them or not! I like the system which lets a man quit when he wants to, and wish it might prevail everywhere. One of the reasons why I am opposed to slavery is just here. What is the true condition of the laborer? I take it that it is best for all to leave each man free to acquire property as fast as he can. Some will get wealthy. I don't approve of a law to prevent a man from getting rich; it would do more harm than good. So while we do not propose any war upon capital, we do wish to allow the humblest man an equal chance to get rich with everybody else. When one starts poor, as most do in the race of life, free society is such that he knows he can better his condition; he knows that there is no fixed condition of labor for his whole life. I am not ashamed to confess that twenty-five years ago I was a hired laborer, mauling rails, at work on a flatboat—just what might happen to any poor man's son. I want every man to have a chance—and I believe a black man is entitled to it—in which he can better his condition—when he may look forward and hope to be a hired laborer this year and the next, work for himself afterward, and finally to hire men to work for him. That is the true system. Up here in New England you have a soil that scarcely sprouts black-eyed beans, and yet where will you find wealthy men so wealthy, and poverty so rarely in extremity? There is not another such place on earth!

> ABRAHAM LINCOLN, speech, New Haven, March 6, 1860

An Injury to One Is the Concern of All.

> Slogan of the Knights of Labor, organized in the 1870's, Terence Powderly, leader

The equal right of all men to the use of the land is as clear as their equal right to breathe the air—it is a right proclaimed by the fact of their existence. For we cannot suppose that some men have a right to be in this world, and others no right.

> HENRY GEORGE, *Progress and Poverty*, 1879

For as labor cannot produce without the use of land, the denial of the equal right to use of land is necessarily the denial of the right of labor to its own produce.

> HENRY GEORGE, *Ibid.*

Take now . . . some hard-headed business man, who has no theories, but knows how to make money. Say to him: "Here is a little village; in ten years it will be a great city—in ten years the railroad will have taken the place of the stage coach, the electric light of the candle; it will abound with all the machinery and improvements that so enormously multiply the effective power of labor. Will, in ten years, interest be any higher?"

He will tell you, "No!"

"Will the wages of common labor be any higher . . .?"

He will tell you, "No, the wages of common labor will not be any higher. . . ."

"What, then, will be higher?"

"Rent, the value of land. Go, get yourself a piece of ground, and hold possession."

And if, under such circumstances, you take his advice, you need do nothing more. You may sit down and smoke your pipe; you may lie around like the lazzaroni of Naples or the lepers of Mexico; you may go up in a balloon or down a hole in the ground; and without doing one stroke of work, without adding one iota of wealth to the community, in ten years you will be rich! In the new city you may have a luxurious mansion, but among its public buildings will be an almshouse.

> HENRY GEORGE, *Ibid.*

We are peaceable.

> SAMUEL FIELDEN, teamster, to police in Haymarket Square, Chicago, May 4, 1886, who were moving in to break up a

crowd of union members protesting a police-firing on pickets at the McCormick plant the night before. At this moment somebody—no one has ever known who—threw the Haymarket bomb. Fielden had been speaking to the crowd, and his words were remembered. The bomb killed eight and wounded sixty-seven policemen, who regrouped and charged, firing their revolvers into the crowd and killing many workers. On November 11, 1887, four men were hanged for having thrown the bomb. As far as anyone knows, these four had nothing whatsoever to do with it.

The instinct of ownership is fundamental in man's nature.

WILLIAM JAMES

The trade unions are the legitimate outgrowth of modern societary and industrial conditions. . . . They were born of the necessity of workers to protect and defend themselves from incroachment, injustice and wrong. . . . To protect the workers in their inalienable rights to a higher and better life; to protect them, not only as equals before the law, but also in their rights to the product of their labor; to protect their lives, their limbs, their health, their homes, their firesides, their liberties as men, as workers, and as citizens; to overcome and conquer prejudice and antagonism; to secure to them the right to life, and the opportunity to maintain that life; the right to be full sharers in the abundance which is the result of their brain and brawn, and the civilization of which they are the founders and the mainstay; to this the workers are entitled. . . . The attainment of these is the glorious mission of the trade unions.

SAMUEL GOMPERS, speech, 1898

The rights and interests of the laboring man will be protected and cared for—not by the labor agitators, but by the Christian men to whom God in his infinite wisdom has given the control of the property interests of the country, and upon the successful management of which so much depends.

GEORGE F. BAER, on United Mine Workers' strike against the Reading Company, of which he was president, 1902

While there is a lower class, I am in it.
While there is a criminal element, I am of it.
While there is a soul in jail, I am not free.

EUGENE V. DEBS

I am not a labor leader. I don't want you to follow me or anyone else. If you are looking for a Moses to lead you out of the capitalist wilderness you will stay right where you are. I would not lead you into this promised land if I could, because if I could lead you in, someone else would lead you out.

EUGENE V. DEBS

It's too bad th' goolden days has passed. Capital still pats labor on th' back, but on'y with an axe. Labor rayfuses to be threated as a friend. It wants to be threated as an inimy. It thinks it gets more that way. They ar-re still a happy fam'ly, but it's more like an English fam'ly. They don't speak.

FINLEY PETER DUNNE ("MR. DOOLEY"), Labor and Cap-
ital

The working class and the employing class have nothing in common. Between the two a struggle must go on until the workers of the world organize as a class, take possession of the earth and the machinery of production, and abolish the wage system.

Preamble to the Constitution of the I.W.W., adopted at
Chicago, June, 1905

The corporation has come to stay, just as the trade union has come to stay. Each can do and has done great good. Each should be favored as long as it does good, but each should be sharply checked where it acts against law and justice.

THEODORE ROOSEVELT

We demand that big business give people a square deal; in return we must insist that when anyone engaged in big business honestly endeavors to do right, he shall himself be given a square deal.

THEODORE ROOSEVELT, Autobiography, 1913

We are bound, in any clear-sighted view of the larger exigencies of the relations of man with man, to fortify ourselves against such a perversion of the institutions of government as would adapt them to the nature of man as he ought to be, instead of the nature of man as he actually is, and would relax the rigour of law, in pity for the degree of injustice inherent in earthly life. . . . Looking at the larger good of society, we may say that the dollar is more than the man, and that *the rights of property are more important than the right to life.*

> PAUL ELMER MORE, *Shelburne Essays,* "Aristocracy and Justice"

If capital an' labor ever do git t'gether it's good night fer th' rest of us.

> KIN HUBBARD

Industry must manage to keep wages high and prices low. Otherwise it will limit the number of its customers. One's own employees should be one's best customers.

> HENRY FORD

There is no right to strike against the public peace by anybody, anywhere, any time.

> CALVIN COOLIDGE, reply to Samuel Gompers' request that the Boston Police Commissioner be removed by Coolidge, then Governor of Massachusetts, for requesting State Troops to break the Boston Police Strike, 1919

The fundamental idea of modern capitalism is not the right of the individual to possess and enjoy what he has earned, but the thesis that the exercise of this right redounds to the general good.

> RALPH BARTON PERRY, *Puritanism and Democracy*

Labor like Israel has many sorrows; its women weep for their fallen, and they lament for the future of the children of the race. It ill behooves one who has supped at labor's table, and who has been sheltered in labor's house, to curse with equal fervor and fine impartiality both labor and its adversaries when they become locked in deadly embrace.

> JOHN L. LEWIS, of President Roosevelt, after the latter had said to Lewis and the "Little Steel" negotiator in 1937, "A plague on both your houses"

Every day, I have a matutinal indisposition that emanates from the nauseous effluvia of that oppressive slave statute.

> JOHN L. LEWIS, of the Taft-Hartley Law, in 1953

SUCCESS AND FAILURE

THE HAVES

[The poor] have a more comfortable Life here, and far less danger as to the next Life. . . . A Rich Man has a *miserable* Life; for he is always full of Fear and Care. . . . Whereas a man that has but Food and Raiment with honest Labour, is free from these fears and Cares. . . . We need to *pity* and *love* Rich Men.

JOSEPH MORGAN, *The Nature of Riches,* 1732

A power has risen up in the government greater than the people themselves, consisting of many and various and powerful interests, combined into one mass, and held together by the cohesive power of the vast surplus in the banks.

JOHN C. CALHOUN, speech, May 27, 1836

A man who has a million dollars is as well off as if he were rich.

JOHN JACOB ASTOR, to Julia Ward Howe

The man who makes it the habit of his life to go to bed at nine o'clock, usually gets rich and is always reliable. . . . Rogues do their work at night. Honest men work by day. It's all a matter of habit, and good habits in America make any man rich. Wealth is largely a result of habit.

JOHN JACOB ASTOR

What do I care about the law? Hain't I got the power?

CORNELIUS VANDERBILT, in the 1860's

Gentlemen: You have undertaken to cheat me. I won't sue you, for the law is too slow. I'll ruin you.

CORNELIUS VANDERBILT

The reason why I defend the millions of the millionaire is . . . that I know no way in which to get the defense of society for my hundreds, except to give my help, as a member of society, to protect his millions.

WILLIAM GRAHAM SUMNER, *The Forgotten Man and Other Essays*

GLORIOUS OPPORTUNITY TO GET RICH—We are starting a cat ranch in Lacon with 100,000 cats. Each cat will average twelve kittens a year. The cat skins will sell for thirty cents each. One hundred men can skin 5,000 cats a day. We figure a daily profit of over $10,000. Now what shall we feed the cats? We will start a rat ranch next door with 1,000,000 rats. The rats will breed twelve times faster than the cats. So we will have four rats to feed each day to each cat. Now what shall we feed the rats? We will feed the rats the carcasses of the cats after they have been skinned. Now Get This! We feed the rats to the cats and the cats to the rats and get the skins for nothing.

> ANON., Prospectus of Lacon, Illinois, Cat-and-Rat Ranch.
> This hoax was carried by every newspaper in the U.S., 1875.

You can't keep such men down. They are very shrewd men. I don't believe that by any legislative enactment or anything else, through any of the States or all the States, you can keep such men down. You can't do it! They will be on top all the time. You see if they are not.

> WILLIAM H. VANDERBILT, 1879, of his generation of "Robber Barons"

To secure wealth is an honorable ambition, and is one great test of a person's usefulness to others. . . . I say, get rich, get rich!

> RUSSELL CONWELL, from his popular sermon, "Acres of Diamonds." This sermon was given by Conwell at least six thousand times, earning him $8,000,000.

Ninety-eight out of 100 of the rich men of America are honest. That is why they are rich.

> RUSSELL CONWELL, *Ibid.*

The man who dies rich dies disgraced.

> ANDREW CARNEGIE, "Wealth," *North American Review,* June, 1889

Surplus wealth is a sacred trust which its possessor is bound to administer in his lifetime for the good of the community.

> ANDREW CARNEGIE, *Ibid.*

This, then, is held to be the duty of the man of Wealth: First, to set an example of modest, unostentatious living, shunning display or extravagance; to provide moderately for the legitimate wants of those dependent upon him; and after doing so, to consider all surplus revenues which come to him simply as trust funds, which he is called upon to administer, and strictly bound as a matter of duty to administer in the manner which, in his judgment, is best calculated to produce the most beneficial results for the community—the man of wealth thus becoming the mere agent and trustee for his poorer brethren, bringing to their service his superior wisdom, experience, and ability to administer, doing for them better than they would or could do for themselves. . . . [In this principle] we have the true antidote for the temporary unequal distribution of wealth, the reconciliation of the rich and the poor—a reign of harmony, another ideal, differing, indeed, from that of the Communist in requiring only the further evolution of existing conditions, not the total overthrow of our civilization. . . . Thus is the problem of Rich and Poor to be solved. The laws of accumulation will be left free; the laws of distribution free. Individualism will continue, but the millionaire will be but a trustee for the poor. . . . Such, in my opinion, is the true Gospel concerning Wealth, obedience to which is destined some day to solve the problem of the Rich and the Poor and to bring "Peace on earth, among men good-will."

ANDREW CARNEGIE, *Ibid.*

The advantages of wealth are greatly exaggerated.

LELAND STANFORD

I am richer than [E. H.] Harriman. I have all the money I want and he hasn't.

JOHN MUIR, in conversation, 1899

The good Lord gave me my money, and how could I withhold it from the University of Chicago?

JOHN D. ROCKEFELLER, to first graduating class of the University

It is wrong to assume that men of immense wealth are always happy.

JOHN D. ROCKEFELLER, to his Sunday School Class

[John D. Rockefeller is] a kind iv society f'r th' prevention iv croolty to money. If he finds a man misusing his money he takes it away fr'm him an' adopts it.

PETER FINLEY DUNNE ("MR. DOOLEY")

When they speak they lie; when they are silent they are stealing.

> GEORGE GRAHAM VEST, of the Gilded Age millionaires

Whenever he doesn't like it, he can give it back to us.

> WILLIAM JENNINGS BRYAN, when J. P. Morgan announced that "America is good enough for me"

The savings of many in the hands of one.

> EUGENE V. DEBS, of wealth

Letters of a Self-Made Merchant to His Son.

> GEORGE HORACE LORIMER, title of series of articles in the *Saturday Evening Post,* 1902, a record of the sayings of Philip Armour, the meat-packer

Certain malefactors of great wealth.

> THEODORE ROOSEVELT, speech in Provincetown, August 20, 1907, referring to perpetrators of the Panic of 1907

The grim truth is that we as a class are condemned to death. We have outlived our time. . . . In fact, today we stand indicted before the court of civilization. We are charged openly with being parasites and the mass of evidence against us is so overwhelming that there is no doubt whatever about the verdict of history, if indeed it must come to a verdict.

> FREDERICK TOWNSEND MARTIN, *The Passing of the Idle Rich,* 1911

As I approach the end, I am more than a little puzzled to account for the instances I have seen of business success—money-getting. It comes from rather a low instinct. Certainly, as far as my observation goes, it is rarely met in combination with the finer or more interesting traits of character. I have known, and known tolerably well, a good many "successful" men —"big" financially—men famous during the last half-century; and a less interesting crowd I do not care to encounter. Not one that I have ever known would I care to meet again, either in this world or the next; nor is one of them associated in my mind with the idea of humour, thought or refinement. A set of mere money-getters and traders, they were essentially unattractive and uninteresting. The fact is that money-getting, like every- thing else, calls for a special aptitude and great concentration; and for it I did not have the first to any marked degree, and to it I never gave the

last. So, in now summing up, I may account myself fortunate in having
got out of my ventures as well as I did.

CHARLES FRANCIS ADAMS, *Autobiography*, 1916

America contained scores of men worth five million or upwards, whose
lives were no more worth living than those of their cooks.

HENRY ADAMS, *The Education of Henry Adams*

I must atone for my money.

OTTO KAHN

Do not be fooled into believing that because a man is rich he is necessarily smart. There is ample proof to the contrary.

JULIUS ROSENWALD

It must be great to be rich and let the other fellow keep up appearances.

KIN HUBBARD

The ideal income is a thousand dollars a day—and expenses.

PIERRE LORILLARD

No. They have more money.

ERNEST HEMINGWAY, to F. Scott Fitzgerald, the latter
having said that the rich "are not as we are"

As long as I live under the capitalist system, I expect to have my life
influenced by the demands of moneyed people. But I will be damned if
I propose to be at the beck and call of every itinerant scoundrel who has
two cents to invest in a postage stamp. This, sir, is my resignation.

WILLIAM FAULKNER, letter to the Postmaster General

In general, they were puritanical and pious. Only one of them, Fisk, was
given to free living, drinking, and flesh pots. . . . In private life they were
generally discreet, sober, well-controlled, their strongest lust being the
pecuniary appetite. The poverty which darkened the childhood of all of
them save Morgan, son of a banker, lent them sobriety, and the Protestant
teaching they received disciplined their will. . . . Not only did they have,
as Veblen has said, Old Testament traits of ferocity, jealousy, clannishness

and disingenuousness, but also the "economic virtues" which are associated with Christian sobriety.

MATTHEW JOSEPHSON, *The Robber Barons,* 1934

The royalists of the economic order have conceded that political freedom was the business of the government, but they have maintained that economic slavery was nobody's business. . . . These economic royalists complain that we seek to overthrow the institutions of America.

FRANKLIN D. ROOSEVELT, speech, 1936

Fortunes come. They are not made.

HENRY FORD, *New York Times,* 1938

I don't wanna be a millionaire. I just wanna live like one.

TOOTS SHOR

In all the world there is nothing more timorous than a million dollars, except ten millions. In revolutionary times the rich are always the people who are most afraid.

GERALD W. JOHNSON, *American Freedom and the Press*

To the child, the savage and the Wall Street operator everything seems possible—hence their credulity.

ERIC HOFFER, *The Passionate State of Mind,* 1955

THE HAVE-NOTS

Failure is more frequently from want of energy than from want of capital.

DANIEL WEBSTER

Gentlemen: I come to present the strong claims of suffering humanity. I come to place before the Legislature of Massachusetts the condition of the miserable, the desolate, the outcast. I come as the advocate of helpless, forgotten, insane, and idiotic men and women; of beings sunk to a condition from which the most unconcerned would start with real horror; of beings wretched in our prisons, and more wretched in our almshouses.

DOROTHEA LYNDE DIX, *Memorial* to Massachusetts Legislature, 1843. This paper gained public support and brought about the establishment of proper facilities at Worcester. It marked the beginning of her great crusade.

I read your letter in the vestibule of the Post Office, and it drew—what my troubles never have—the water to my eyes; so that I was glad of the sharply cold west wind that blew into them as I came homeward. . . . There was much that was very sweet—something too that was bitter—mingled with that same moisture. It is sweet to be remembered and cared for by one's friends. . . . It is bitter, nevertheless, to need their support. It is something else besides pride that teaches me that ill-success in life is really and justly a matter of shame. I am ashamed of it, and I ought to be. . . . Nobody has a right to live in the world, unless he be strong and able, and applies his ability to good purpose. . . . The only way in which a man can retain his self-respect, while availing himself of the generosity of his friends, is by making it an incitement to his utmost exertions, so that he may not need their help again. I shall look upon it so—nor will shun any drudgery that my hand shall find to do, if thereby I may win bread.

> NATHANIEL HAWTHORNE, letter to George Hilliard, January, 1850, in reply to a letter forwarding a sum of money from Hilliard and other friends. Two weeks after receipt of the money Hawthorne finished *The Scarlet Letter*.

We do not ride on the railroad; it rides upon us. Did you ever think what those sleepers are that underlie the railroad? Each one is a man, an Irishman, or a Yankee man. The rails are laid on them, and they are covered with sand, and the cars run smoothly over them. They are sound sleepers, I assure you. And every few years a new lot is laid down and run over; so that, if some have the pleasure of riding on a rail, others have the misfortune of being ridden upon.

> HENRY DAVID THOREAU, *Walden*

I won't give in but what I sympathize with the poor, but the number of poor who are to be sympathized with is very small. To sympathize with a man whom God has punished for his sins, thus to help him when God would still continue a just punishment, is to do wrong, no doubt about it.

> RUSSELL CONWELL, "Acres of Diamonds"

It seemed to me that what the nine hundred and ninety-four dupes needed was a new deal.

> SAMUEL L. CLEMENS ("MARK TWAIN"), *A Connecticut Yankee in King Arthur's Court*, remarking that in feudal society six men out of a thousand crack the whip over their fellows' necks

Only the poor are wasteful.

EDWARD H. HARRIMAN

Looking comprehensively at the matter . . . the general truth will stand, that no man in this land suffers from poverty unless it be more than his fault—unless it be his *sin.*

HENRY WARD BEECHER

It is said that a dollar a day is not enough for a wife and five or six children. No, not if the man smokes or drinks beer. It is not enough if they are to live as he would be glad to have them live. It is not enough to enable them to live as perhaps they would have a right to live in prosperous times. But is not a dollar a day enough to buy bread with? Water costs nothing; and a man who cannot live on bread is not fit to live. What is the use of a civilization that simply makes men incompetent to live under the conditions which exist?

> HENRY WARD BEECHER, in 1877, a year of depression and a particularly bloody strike of the railroad workers, whose pay had been cut an additional 10 per cent in July. The Reverend Mr. Beecher, who enjoyed an income of about $20,000 a year, was reported as saying the above in the *New York Times,* July 30, 1877.

So long as all the increased wealth which modern progress brings goes but to build up great fortunes, to increase luxury and make sharper the contrast between the House of Have and the House of Want, progress is not real and cannot be permanent.

HENRY GEORGE, *Progress and Poverty,* 1879

The public be damned! What does the public care for the railroads except to get as much out of them for as little consideration as possible!

> WILLIAM H. VANDERBILT, interview in a private railway car outside Chicago, October 2, 1882. Two reporters were questioning him. They asked about the new Nickel Plate Railroad—was it true it had been built only to blackmail Vanderbilt's New York Central system? "It's no good; poorly built," Vanderbilt growled. They asked about the new fast train he had just put on to cut the New York–Chicago running time—did it pay? "No, not a bit of it."

"But don't you run it for the public benefit?" one reporter insisted. Then the above.

This was published in every American newspaper the next day—except the Chicago *Tribune,* which altered the famous words to "Nonsense!" Everyone denounced Vanderbilt. In 1883 he retired from all his railroad presidencies, and ruled that henceforth Vanderbilts should serve as board chairmen only, not active railroad runners. In 1885 he died and was buried on Staten Island. Watchmen looked into his crypt every fifteen minutes to make sure the corpse was not stolen.

Who is the Forgotten Man? He is the clean, quiet, virtuous, domestic citizen, who pays his debts and his taxes and is never heard of out of his little circle.

WILLIAM GRAHAM SUMNER, *The Forgotten Man*

How the Other Half Lives.

JACOB AUGUST RIIS, title of book describing life in New York's tenements, 1890

Poverty is the strenuous life—without brass bands, or uniforms.

WILLIAM JAMES, *The Varieties of Religious Experience*

It is difficult to get a man to understand something when his salary depends upon his not understanding it.

UPTON SINCLAIR

One of the strangest things about life is that the poor, who need money the most, are the very ones that never have it.

FINLEY PETER DUNNE ("MR. DOOLEY")

The common stock of intellectual enjoyment should not be difficult of access because of the economic position of him who would approach it.

JANE ADDAMS, *Twenty Years at Hull House*

It's no disgrace to be poor, but it might as well be.

KIN HUBBARD

In theory, it is not respectable to be rich. In fact, poverty is a disgrace.

EDGAR W. HOWE

I found myself compelled to fight back from my eyes the tears, and quanch my heart trobling to my throat to not weep before him. But Sacco's name will live in the hearts of the people when your name, your laws, institutions, and your false god are but a dim rememoring of a cursed past in which man was wolf to the man.

BARTOLOMEO VANZETTI, "Last Speech to the Court"

I might have lived out my life, talking on street corners to scorning men. I might have died unmarked, unknown, a failure. Now we are not a failure. . . . Our words—our lives—our pains—nothing! The taking of our lives—lives of a good shoemaker and a poor fishpeddler—all! The last moment belongs to us—that agony is our triumph.

BARTOLOMEO VANZETTI, letter to his son, April, 1927

I would like you to . . . remember me as a comrade and friend to your father . . . and I assure you that neither have I been a criminal, that I have committed no robbery and no murder, but only fought modestly to abolish crimes from among mankind and for the liberty of all.

Remember Dante, each one who will say otherwise of your father and I, is a liar, insulting innocent dead men who have been brave in their life. Remember and know also, Dante, that if your father and I would have been cowards and hypocrits and rinnegetors of our faith, we would not have been put to death. They would not even have convicted a lebbrous dog; not even executed a deadly poisoned scorpion on such evidence as that they framed against us. They would have given a new trial to a matricide and habitual felon on the evidence we presented for a new trial.

Remember, Dante, remember always these things, we are not criminals; they convicted us on a frame-up; they denied us a new trial; and if we will be executed after seven years, four months and seventeen days of unspeakable torture and wrong, it is for what I have already told you; because we were for the poor and against the exploitation and oppression of the man by the man.

BARTOLOMEO VANZETTI, letter to Dante Sacco, August 21, 1927. Sacco and Vanzetti were executed on August 23.

I would steal before I would starve.

DANIEL WILLARD, speech, 1931

Most men and women are haunted by poverty, and all are helpless in the clutch of a relentless fate. . . . To prevent burglary the cause must be removed; it can never be done in any other way.

CLARENCE DARROW, *The Story of My Life,* 1932

I am a friend of the workingman, and I would rather be his friend than be one.

CLARENCE DARROW

The forgotten man at the bottom of the economic pyramid.

FRANKLIN D. ROOSEVELT, speech, April 7, 1932

A bad-looking mob animated by the spirit of revolution.

DOUGLAS MACARTHUR, of the Bonus Army on which he used force, July 29, 1932

The best behaved of any fifteen thousand hungry men assembled anywhere in the world. . . . Just think what fifteen thousand clubwomen would have done to Washington even if they wasn't hungry.

WILL ROGERS, of the Bonus Army

I see one-third of a nation ill-housed, ill-clad, ill-nourished.

FRANKLIN D. ROOSEVELT, "Second Inaugural Address," January 20, 1937

We who are liberal and progressive know that the poor are our equals in every sense except that of being equal to us.

LIONEL TRILLING, *The Liberal Imagination,* 1950

There are . . . dozens of ways of failing to make money. It is one thing to fail to make money because your single talent happens to be a flair amounting to genius for translating the plays of Aristophanes. It is quite another thing to fail to make money because you are a Negro. Or a child. Or a woman. Or because you want to run a small farm. Or because you want to be a nurse. Or because you have religious convictions against making money. Or because you went to West Point. Or because you do not enjoy the society of people who think too much about making and spending money. To say that a human being has failed to make money in the United States of America, is to say nothing about him at all. The description covers sexual degenerates, Abraham Lincoln and everything in between.

MARGARET HALSEY, *The Folks at Home*

Why would anybody be interested in some old man who was a failure?

GEORGE HUMPHREY, Secretary of the Treasury, comment on Hemingway's *The Old Man and the Sea,* 1953

CRISES AND PANICS

Bad times have a scientific value. These are occasions a good learner would not miss.

RALPH WALDO EMERSON, *Conduct of Life,* "Considerations by the Way"

Men have an indistinct notion that if they keep up this activity of joint stocks and spades long enough all will at length ride somewhere, in next to no time, and for nothing; but though a crowd rushes to the depot, and the conductor shouts "All aboard!" when the smoke is blown away and the vapor condensed, it will be perceived that a few are riding, but the rest are run over . . . and it will be called, and will be, "A melancholy accident."

HENRY DAVID THOREAU

Gone where the woodbine twineth.

JIM FISK, during Congressional Investigation of "Black Friday," September, 1869, referring to money he had lost trying to corner the market in gold. When asked what the phrase meant, he said, "Up the spout."

Nothing is lost save honor.

JIM FISK, after the Congressional Investigation following "Black Friday," 1869

There is scarcely an instance of a man who has made a fortune by speculation and kept it.

ANDREW CARNEGIE, *The Empire of Business*

Where are the c-c-customers' yachts?

> WILLIAM R. TRAVERS, on being shown a squadron of brokers' yachts in New York harbor

Remember, my son, that any man who is a bear on the future of this country will go broke.

> J. P. MORGAN, as reported by his son on December 10, 1908. Often quoted as: "Don't sell this country short."

Depressions may bring people closer to the church—but so do funerals.

> CLARENCE DARROW

The way to stop financial joy-riding is to arrest the chauffeur, not the automobile.

> WOODROW WILSON

Some people are suffering from lack of work, some from lack of water, many more from lack of wisdom.

> CALVIN COOLIDGE

When more and more people are thrown out of work, unemployment results.

> CALVIN COOLIDGE

We must deal with this question of unemployment, which I regard as the greatest economic blot on our capitalist system. There is no answer except that the managers of business have not yet learned how to make their system function so that men willing and able to work may do so. There is no limit to the consumption of the world. It is limited only in its individual compartments. We cannot eat more than so much bread or meat. We cannot wear more than so many clothes, and so we may have overproduction in individual lines. But there are innumerable wants of men yet unserved, and as long as culture grows, these wants will outrun our capacity to produce the things to satisfy them. The world does not owe men a living, but business, if it is to fulfill its ideal, owes men an opportunity to earn a living.

> OWEN D. YOUNG, "Dedication Address," Harvard Business School, 1927

A man with a million dollars used to be considered rich, but so many have

at least that much in these days . . . that a millionaire does not cause
any comment. . . . Ten thousand dollars invested ten years ago in the
common stock of General Motors would now be worth more than a million and a half dollars. . . . It may be said that this is a phenomenal
increase and that conditions are going to be different in the next ten/
years. That prophecy may be true, but it is not founded on experience.
. . . I think that we have scarcely started. . . . I am firm in my belief
that anyone not only can be rich but ought to be rich. . . . (But) no
one can become rich merely by saving. Mere saving is closely akin to the
socialist policy of dividing and likewise runs up against the same objection
that there is not enough around to save.

> JOHN J. RASKOB, interview, *Ladies' Home Journal*, August,
> 1929, two months before the Crash

It seems probable that stocks have been passing not so much from the
strong to the weak as from the smart to the dumb.

> LEONARD P. AYRES, of the Cleveland Trust Company, Oc-
> tober 15, 1929. The market broke on October 29.

. . . Bankers, brokers, clerks, messengers were almost at the end of their
strength; for days and nights they had been driving themselves to keep
pace with the most terrific volume of business that had ever descended
upon them. It did not seem as if they could stand it much longer. But the
worst was still ahead. It came the next day, Tuesday, October 29 [1929].

The big gong had hardly sounded in the great hall of the exchange at
ten o'clock Tuesday morning before the storm broke in full force. Huge
blocks of stock were thrown upon the market for what they would bring.
Five thousand shares, ten thousand shares appeared at a time on the
laboring ticker at fearful recessions in price. Not only were innumerable
small traders being sold out, but big ones, too, protagonists of the new
economic era who a few weeks before had counted themselves millionaires.
Again and again the specialist in a stock would find himself surrounded
by brokers fighting to sell—and nobody at all even thinking of buying. To
give one single example: during the bull market the common stock of the
White Sewing Machine Company had gone as high as 48; on Monday,
October 28, it had closed at 11⅛. In that black Tuesday, somebody—a
clever messenger boy for the exchange, it was rumored—had the bright
idea of putting in an order to buy at 1; and in the temporary complete
absence of other bids he actually got his stock for a dollar a share! The
scene on the floor was chaotic. Despite the jamming of the communication

system, orders to buy and sell—mostly to sell—came in faster than human beings could possibly handle them; it was on that day that an exhausted broker, at the close of the session, found a large wastebasket which he had stuffed with orders to be executed and had carefully set aside for safekeeping—and then had completely forgotten. Within half an hour of the opening the volume of trading had passed three million shares, by twelve o'clock it had passed eight million, by half-past one it had passed twelve million; and when the closing gong brought the day's madness to an end the gigantic record of 16,410,030 shares had been set. Toward the close there was a rally, but by that time the average price of fifty leading stocks, as compiled by the *New York Times,* had fallen nearly forty points. Meanwhile there was a near-panic in other markets—the foreign stock exchanges, the lesser American exchanges, the grain market.

FREDERICK LEWIS ALLEN, Only Yesterday, 1931

Wall Street Lays An Egg.

Headline, Variety, October, 1929

Believing that fundamental conditions of the country are sound . . . my son and I have for some days been purchasing sound common stocks.

> JOHN D. ROCKEFELLER, October 30, 1929. Rockefeller's announcement was an (unsuccessful) attempt to stop the panic.

For sleeping or jumping?

> Question (rumored) by hotel clerks of guests registering after the stock market crash, 1929

Conditions are fundamentally sound.

HERBERT HOOVER, speech, December, 1929

I not only "don't choose to run" but I don't want to leave a loophole in case I am drafted, so I won't "choose." I will say "won't run" no matter how bad the country will need a comedian by that time.

WILL ROGERS, syndicated article, June 28, 1931

This, apparently, is the only stable thing in my Administration.

> Attributed to HERBERT HOOVER, pointing to Washington Monument while dining in the South Portico of the White House, 1932

Prosperity is just around the corner.

> Repeated assurance of Republican Party, 1932

We'll hold the distinction of being the only nation in the history of the world that ever went to the poorhouse in an automobile.

> WILL ROGERS, 1932

I have known people to stop and buy an apple on the corner and then walk away as if they had solved the whole unemployment problem.

> HEYWOOD BROUN, *It Seems to Me,* 1933

The only thing we have to fear is fear itself.

> FRANKLIN D. ROOSEVELT, "First Inaugural Address," March 4, 1933. Thoreau, *Journal,* September 7, 1851: "Nothing is so much to be feared as fear. Atheism may comparatively be popular with God Himself."

Economic distress will teach men, if anything can, that realities are less dangerous than fancies, that factfinding is more effective than faultfinding.

> CARL BECKER, *Progress and Power,* 1935

An army or navy is a tool for the protection of misguided, inefficient, destructive Wall Street.

> HENRY FORD, quoted by Gunther, *Inside U.S.A.*

I define a recession as when your neighbor loses his job, but a depression is when you lose your own.

> DAVE BECK, 1954. Also attributed to a number of others.

ADVERTISING

VIEWPOINTS

Advertisements contain the only truth to be relied on in a newspaper.

> THOMAS JEFFERSON, letter to Nathaniel Macon

That "producer's economy," then beginning to prevail in America, which first creates articles and then attempts to create a demand for them; an economy that has flooded the country with breakfast foods, shaving soaps, poets, and professors of philosophy.

GEORGE SANTAYANA, *Persons and Places,* 1943

Business today consists of persuading crowds.

GERALD STANLEY LEE

The problem of improving the literary tastes of the people is the problem of the schools. The people who listen to our programs aren't intellectuals —they're ordinary people, good people, who win wars for us, produce our manufactured products and grow our food. They use a lot of soap.

NEIL HOSLER MCELROY, President of Procter and Gamble, on the soap operas sponsored by his company

When the Moscow radio recently agreed to countenance advertising, some instinct told me the Soviet broadcasters were headed for trouble. They were, too. Now, after only a few weeks of this notable experiment, complaints are pouring in from angry housewives. The Soviet laundry trust, one of the first to advertise on the air, is not—according to the housewives —living up to its promises. The laundry does not come back in five to seven days. The laundry does not take unlimited quantities of wash. And so on.

No, comrades, no! It's the wrong approach. The first law in advertising is to avoid the concrete promise—five days, indeed!—and cultivate the delightfully vague. "The Soviet laundry trust gets your clothes 22 per cent cleaner, 33 per cent whiter, 44 per cent dryer." It will be a long, long time before any Soviet housewife begins to wonder how anything can be 33 per cent whiter or what exactly are on the other end of those comparatives. We have had far more experience with these matters than you, comrades, and no American housewife has ever asked any such embarrassing questions.

JOHN CROSBY, New York *Herald Tribune,* August 18, 1947

SLOGANS

It Pays To Advertise. ANON.

When business is good it pays to advertise; when business is bad you've got to advertise. ANON., American saying

Ask Dad—He Knows. ANON., Sweet Caporal cigarettes

It's Toasted. ANON., Lucky Strike cigarettes

Mild As May. ANON., Marlboro cigarettes

Best In The Long Run. ANON., Goodrich tires

Built For Sleep. ANON., Simmons beds

The Candy Mint With A Hole. ANON., Life Savers

Chases Dirt. ANON., Old Dutch cleanser

A Clean Tooth Never Decays. ANON., Pro-Phy-Lac-Tic toothbrushes

Cleans As It Polishes. ANON., O'Cedar polish

Cocoa With That Chocolaty Taste. ANON., Runkel's Cocoa

Covers The Earth. ANON., Sherwin-Williams paint and varnish

Eventually—Why Not Now? ANON., Gold Medal flour

The Flavor Lasts. ANON., Wrigley's gum

From Contented Cows. ANON., Carnation milk

Hammer The Hammer. ANON., Iver Johnson arms

Like Old Friends They Wear Well. ANON., Meyers gloves

No Metal Can Touch You. ANON., Paris garters

The Skin You Love To Touch. ANON., Woodbury's facial soap

There's A Reason. ANON., Grape-Nuts

The Watch With The Purple Ribbon. ANON., South Bend watches

The Watch Of Railroad Accuracy. ANON., Hamilton watches

The Watch That Made The Dollar Famous.   ANON., Ingersoll watches

When It Rains—It Pours.   ANON., Morton's salt

Built Like A Skyscraper.   ANON., Shaw-Walker filing cabinets

Regular As Clockwork.   ANON., Nujol

Makes Every Meal An Event.   ANON., Premier salad dressing

America's Most Famous Dessert.   ANON., Jell-o

For Economical Transportation.   ANON., Chevrolet automobiles

Let The Kitchen Maid Be Your Kitchen Aid.
                                ANON., Kitchen Maid kitchen cabinets

His Master's Voice.   ANON., Victrola

No Springs—Honest Weight.   ANON., Toledo scales

It Beats—As It Sweeps—As It Cleans.   ANON., Hoover vacuum cleaners

Delicious And Refreshing.   ANON., Coca-Cola

The Pause That Refreshes.   ANON., Coca-Cola

Soft As Old Linen.   ANON., Scot tissue

You Just Know She Wears Them.   ANON., McCallum hosiery

The Coffee That Lets You Sleep.   ANON., Kaffee-Hag

Now You'll Like Bran.   ANON., Post Bran flakes

The Quality Is Remembered Long After The Price Is Forgotten.
                                           ANON., Simmons hardware

Concrete For Performance.   ANON., Portland Cement Association

Good To The Last Drop.   ANON., Maxwell House coffee

It Floats. ANON., Ivory soap

99$^{44}/_{100}$% Pure. ANON., Ivory soap

A Pillow For The Body. ANON., Sealy mattresses

Everywhere On Everything. ANON., Glidden paints and varnish

For The Gums. ANON., Forhan's tooth paste

Even Your Best Friends Won't Tell You. ANON., Listerine

Often A Bridesmaid, Never A Bride. ANON., Listerine

When Better Automobiles Are Built Buick Will Build Them. ANON.

A Block Of Ice Can't Get Out Of Order.
ANON., ice companies fighting new refrigerators, 1920's

Save The Surface And You Save All. ANON., the paint industry

In Any Event, You Need *Time*. ANON., *Time* magazine

Obey That Impulse. TOM MASSON, *Life* magazine, 1890's

Keep Posted! ANON., *Saturday Evening Post*

Banish Tattle-Tale Gray. ANON., Fels-Naptha soap

Hasn't Scratched Yet. ANON., Bon Ami

Reach For A Lucky Instead Of A Sweet.
GEORGE WASHINGTON HILL, 1928, Lucky Strike cigarettes

SPIT Is A Horrid Word. But It Is Much Worse At The End Of Your
Cigar. GEORGE WASHINGTON HILL, Lucky Strike cigarettes

Nature In The Raw Is Seldom Mild.
GEORGE WASHINGTON HILL, Lucky Strike cigarettes

If It Isn't An Eastman It Isn't A Kodak. ANON.

Kodak As You Go.   ANON.

You Push The Button And We Do The Rest.   ANON., Kodak

See America First.   ANON., 1914, when war cut off travel to Europe

From A Sandwich To A National Institution.

                          ANON., Reuben's, New York restaurant

Time To Re-Tire.   ANON., Fisk Tire Company

There's A Ford In Your Future.   ANON.

Ask The Man Who Owns One.   ANON., Packard automobiles

How Do You Know You Can't Write?

                          ANON., Newspaper Institute of America

Lydia Pinkham's Pink Pills For Pale People.   ANON.

Keep That Schoolgirl Complexion.   ANON., Palmolive soap

It's Smart To Be Thrifty.   ANON., Macy's

Children Cry For It.   ANON., Fletcher's Castoria

The More You Eat, The More You Want.   ANON., Cracker-Jack

Nobody But Nobody Undersells Gimbels.   ANON.

You Can Be Sure If It's Westinghouse.   ANON.

Say It With Flowers.   Attributed to P. F. O'KEEFE, Society of
                          American Florists, adopted 1917

The Instrument Of The Immortals.   ANON., Steinway pianos

Works While You Sleep.   GEORGE ADE, Cascarets

Stop; Look; Listen.   RALPH R. LIPTON

A Good Laugh Will Be Had By All When The Hoax Becomes Apparent.

> ANON., a sneezing powder

Did You Say Model? Yes, I Said Model. ANON.

Feels Good On The Back. ANON., Sloan's Liniment

If You Live On Earth, Own A Slice Of It.

> ANON., slogan of Martha's Vineyard real estate broker

Call for Philip Morris. ANON.

In Philadelphia Nearly Everybody Reads The Bulletin.

> ANON., Philadelphia *Evening Bulletin*

Think.　　THOMAS B. WATSON, slogan of International Business Machines Corporation, used since 1915. E. E. Cummings, "Jottings": "Think twice before you think."

Tell It To Sweeney—The Stuyvesants Don't Care—Much.

> LEO EDWARD McGIVENA, advertisement in the *News,* New York, 1932; the argument being that advertising must be directed to the middle class

If You Don't Know What You Want, We Have It.

> CHRISTOPHER MORLEY, slogan of antique shop

The Most Treasured Name In Perfume. ANON., Chanel No. 5

Wherever Particular People Congregate. ANON., Parliament cigarettes

They Satisfy. ANON., Chesterfield cigarettes

For A Treat Instead Of A Treatment. ANON., Old Gold cigarettes

Not A Cough In A Carload. ANON., Old Gold cigarettes

L—S—M—F—T—Lucky Strike Means Fine Tobacco. ANON.

The Breakfast Of Champions. ANON., Wheaties

The Beer That Made Milwaukee Famous.   ANON., Schlitz beer

Motorists Wise—Simoniz.   ANON.

Don't Envy Beauty—Use Pompeian.

ANON., Pompeian Complexion Cream

I'd Walk A Mile For A Camel.   ANON.

Absorbs The Shocks That Tire You Out.

ANON., O'Sullivan's heels, attributed to William Woodward

Uneeda Biscuit.   ANON., National Biscuit Company

They Laughed When I Sat Down At The Piano . . .

Slogan for a quick course in the piano; used also in other
versions for many products

AT PLAY

•

We may divide the whole struggle of the human race into two chapters:
first, the fight to get leisure; and then the second fight of civilization—
what shall we do with our leisure when we get it.

JAMES A. GARFIELD, during Presidential campaign, 1880

ENTERTAINMENT

THE THEATER

Please do not shoot the pianist. He is doing his best.

ANON., American saying

BLIZ BOFFS BUFF BIZ.

ANON., headline, *Variety*. A blizzard cut Buffalo theater
receipts.

L. Fields is my favorite comedian, and I would enjoy hearing him recite the alphabet.

> FRANKLIN PIERCE ADAMS, *Diary of Our Own Samuel Pepys,* April 9, 1917

I shewed him a letter from G. Ade, wherein he saith: "I have the low-born gift of remembering the unimportant and the trivial. I could not give you any important date in history, or name the Presidents in order; but I can still do all of the sticky sentimental songs that I heard at the Olympic about the time of the World's Fair." And so it is with me, too; nor does it fret me much, since all those dayes are in books, but the things I remember are mine alone.

> FRANKLIN PIERCE ADAMS, *Ibid.,* October 5, 1922

A parrot around Tallulah [Bankhead] must feel as frustrated as a klepto-maniac in a piano store.

> FRED ALLEN

A day away from Tallulah is like a month in the country.

> HOWARD DIETZ

One of my chief regrets during my years in the theater is that I couldn't sit in the audience and watch me.

> JOHN BARRYMORE

I always said that I'd like Barrymore's acting till the cows came home. Well, ladies and gentlemen, last night the cows came home.

> GEORGE JEAN NATHAN, review of *My Dear Children*

There's but one Hamlet to my mind: that's my brother Edwin. You see, between ourselves, he *is* Hamlet—melancholy and all!

> JOHN WILKES BOOTH

Bring on the gals!

> GENE BUCK, whenever, according to G. J. Nathan, things got "to be a bit droopy in the *Follies*"

Then there are no more actors.

> RUFUS CHOATE, when told of the death of Junius Brutus Booth, November 30, 1852

I am not a comedian and I can't get laughs. So I try for enthusiasm.

GEORGE M. COHAN

He was the kind of man who, coming in by the front door, seemed to be leaving by the rear.

BYRON DOBELL, of Groucho Marx

Last night Mr. Creston Clarke played *King Lear* at the Tabor Grand. All through the five acts of that Shakespearean tragedy he played the King as though under momentary apprehension that someone else was about to play the Ace.

> EUGENE FIELD, Denver *Tribune,* 1880 or 1881. This is the version given by Alexander Woollcott. Another version, attributed to a review in the Denver *Post:* "Last night a visiting actor, who shall be nameless, played King Lear. He played the King as though he expected someone to play the ace."

I do not *play* Lear. I *play* Hamlet, Richard, Shylock, Virginius, if you please, but by God, sir, I *am* Lear!

EDWIN FORREST, in his old age

I've done it before and I can do it again.

> OSCAR HAMMERSTEIN II, advertisement in *Variety,* 1944, listing previous flops

That big black giant.

> OSCAR HAMMERSTEIN II, *Me and Juliet,* 1953. The phrase refers to the audience, as seen from the stage.

Massey won't be satisfied until he's assassinated.

> GEORGE S. KAUFMAN, comment on Raymond Massey's performances as Abraham Lincoln

I am generally complimented with being truthful. What I am is merely honest. Who can truthfully say of any critic that he is truthful? I have capitalized honesty. It has been a profitable business. I have had little competition in the field of dramatic criticism, so the job has been an absurdly simple one. Some day, I shall write a chapter on the commercial value of mere critical honesty in America. Any one who practises it will either (1) get rich or (2) lose his job.

> GEORGE JEAN NATHAN, to Isaac Goldberg

The Great White Way.

> ALBERT BIGELOW PAINE, title of novel, 1901, later adopted as name for Broadway

Give me the truth. I'll exaggerate it and make it funny.

> WILL ROGERS, to his co-workers

I don't make jokes; I just watch the government and report the facts.

> WILL ROGERS

If you're there before it's over, you're on time.

> JAMES J. WALKER, of opera

I can't go to Shubert openings. So I wait three nights and go to their closings.

> WALTER WINCHELL

LINES FROM THE STAGE

ELIZA: Powers of mercy, protect me! How shall I escape these human bloodhounds? Ah! the window—the river of ice! That dark stream lies between me and liberty! Surely the ice will bear my trifling weight. It is my only chance of escape—better sink beneath the cold waters, with my child locked in my arms, than have him torn from me and sold into bondage. He sleeps upon my breast—Heaven, I put my trust in thee!

> GEORGE L. AIKEN, *Uncle Tom's Cabin,* 1852

TOM: Don't call me poor fellow. I *have* been poor fellow; but that's all past and gone now, I'm right in the door, going into glory! Oh, Mas'r George! *Heaven has come!* I've got the victory! the Lord has given it to me! Glory be to His name! [Dies].

> GEORGE L. AIKEN, *Ibid.,* Uncle Tom's last words

SCENE VII. Gorgeous clouds, tinted with sunlight. *Eva,* robed in white, is discovered on the back of a milk-white dove, with expanded wings, as if just soaring upwards. Her hands are extended over *St. Clare* and *Uncle Tom,* who are kneeling and gazing up to her. Impressive music. Slow curtain.

> GEORGE L. AIKEN, *Ibid.,* last scene

What Price Glory?

> MAXWELL ANDERSON and LAURENCE STALLINGS, title of play, 1924

> If two stand shoulder to shoulder against the gods,
> Happy together, the gods themselves are helpless
> Against them, while they stand so.

> MAXWELL ANDERSON, *Elizabeth the Queen,* Act II, 1930

When it rains, some spring on the planet Mercury, where the spring comes often, I'll meet you there, let's say.

> MAXWELL ANDERSON, *Winterset,* 1935, Mio to Miriamne

There's no such hell on earth as that of the man who knows himself doomed to mediocrity in the work he loves.

> PHILIP BARRY, *You and I*

That's all there is, there isn't any more.

> ETHEL BARRYMORE, last line added to *Sunday,* 1906

> Death to the Roman fiends, that make their mirth
> Out of the groans of bleeding misery!
> Ho, slaves, arise! it is your hour to kill!
> Kill and spare not—for wrath and liberty!
> Freedom for bondsmen—freedom and revenge!

> ROBERT MONTGOMERY BIRD, *The Gladiator,* 1831, a play written for Edwin Forrest. These lines were the climax of Act II, and invariably brought the audience to its feet cheering wildly.

The Song and Dance Man.

> GEORGE M. COHAN, title of play, 1923

What's all the shootin' for?

> GEORGE M. COHAN, *The Tavern*

GOD: I'll jest r'ar back an' pass a miracle.

> MARC CONNELLY, *The Green Pastures*, 1930

GABRIEL: How about cleanin' up de whole mess of 'em and sta'tin' all over ag'in wid some new kind of animal?
GOD: An' admit I'm licked?

> MARC CONNELLY, *Ibid.*

Even bein' Gawd ain't a bed of roses.

> MARC CONNELLY, *Ibid.*

Gangway for de Lawd God Jehovah!

> MARC CONNELLY, *Ibid.*

Oh, God!

> CLARENCE DAY, *Life with Father*. This, Father Day's favorite interjection, was changed to "Oh, fudge!" when the dramatization, by Howard Lindsay and Russel Crouse, was played in Boston in 1946. The play had been running for several weeks when the change was made.

Dere's a million good-lookin' guys, but I'm a novelty.

> JIMMY DURANTE

I got a million of 'em!

> JIMMY DURANTE

Dese are de conditions dat prevail.

> JIMMY DURANTE

Poor Little Rich Girl.

> ELEANOR GATES, title of play, 1913

GRANDPA VANDERHOF: Quiet, everybody! Quiet!
Well, Sir, we've been getting along pretty good for quite a while now, and we're certainly much obliged. Remember, all we ask is just to go along and be happy in our own sort of way. Of course we want to keep our health, but as far as anything else is concerned, we'll leave it to You. Thank You.

> MOSS HART and GEORGE S. KAUFMAN, *You Can't Take It With You*, 1936. He is saying grace.

Grace—take a law.

> Moss Hart and George S. Kaufman, *I'd Rather Be Right*, 1937. The line was spoken by the character of President Roosevelt, played by George M. Cohan, and the President was so pleased with it he often used it thereafter in dictation.

George Washington Slept Here.

> Moss Hart and George S. Kaufman, title of play, 1941

The son of a bitch stole my watch!

> Ben Hecht and Charles MacArthur, *The Front Page*, 1928, last line

The Jukes were an old family too.

> Lillian Hellman, *The Children's Hour*, 1934

Posterity? Why, posterity is just around the corner.

> George S. Kaufman, Morrie Ryskind and Ira Gershwin, *Of Thee I Sing*, 1931

I GASPIRI—"THE UPHOLSTERERS"

A Drama in Three Acts

Adapted from the Bukovinan of Casper Redmonda

CHARACTERS

Ian Obri, *A Blotter Salesman*
Johan Wasper, *his wife*
Greta, *their daughter*
Herbert Swope, *a nonentity*
Ffena, *their daughter, later their wife*
Egso, *a Pencil Guster*
Tono, *a Typical Wastebasket*

ACT I

(*A public street in a bathroom. A man named Tupper has evidently just taken a bath. A man named Brindle is now taking a bath. A man named Newburn comes out of the faucet which has been left running.*

He exits through the exhaust. Two strangers to each other meet on the bath mat.)

FIRST STRANGER: Where was you born?

SECOND STRANGER: Out of wedlock.

FIRST STRANGER: That's a mighty pretty country around there.

SECOND STRANGER: Are you married?

FIRST STRANGER: I don't know. There's a woman living with me, but I can't place her.

(Three outsiders named Klein go across the stage three times. They think they are in a public library. A woman's cough is heard off-stage left.)

A NEW CHARACTER: Who is that cough?

TWO MOORS: That is my cousin. She died a little while ago in a haphazard way.

A GREEK: And what a woman she was!

(The curtain is lowered for seven days to denote the lapse of a week.)

ACT III

(The Lincoln Highway. Two bearded glue lifters are seated at one side of the road.)

(TRANSLATOR'S NOTE: The principal industry in Phlace is hoarding hay. Peasants sit alongside of a road on which hay wagons are likely to pass. When a hay wagon does pass, the hay hoarders leap from their points of vantage and help themselves to a wisp of hay. On an average a hay hoarder accumulates a ton of hay every four years. This is called Mah Jong.)

FIRST GLUE LIFTER: Well, my man, how goes it?

SECOND GLUE LIFTER: *(Sings "My Man," to show how it goes.)*

(Eight realtors cross the stage in a friendly way. They are out of place.)

CURTAIN

RING LARDNER, *I Gaspiri*

Is everybody happy?

TED LEWIS

It's not what you do. . . . It's who you know and the smile on your face. It's contacts!

ARTHUR MILLER, *The Death of a Salesman*, 1949

The man who makes an appearance in the business world, the man who

creates personal interest, is the man who gets ahead. Be liked and you
will never want.

ARTHUR MILLER, Ibid.

He's not the finest character that ever lived. But he's a human being, and
a terrible thing is happening to him. So attention must be paid. He's not
to be allowed to fall into his grave like an old dog.

ARTHUR MILLER, Ibid.

CHARLEY: Nobody don't blame this man. You don't understand: Willy
was a salesman. And for a salesman, there is no rock bottom to the life.
He don't put a bolt to the nut, he don't tell you the law or give you
medicine. He's a man way out there in the blue, riding on a smile and a
shoestring. And when they start not smiling back—that's an earthquake.
And then you get yourself a couple of spots on your hat, and you're finished. Nobody dast blame this man. A salesman is got to dream, boy. It
comes with the territory.

ARTHUR MILLER, Ibid.

Waiting for Lefty.

> CLIFFORD ODETS, title of play, 1935. Lefty is a character
> who never appears but who is symbolic of the spirit of the
> Labor Movement.

Marriage is something special. I guess you have to deserve it.

CLIFFORD ODETS, Golden Boy, 1937

You can't insult me. I'm too ignorant.

CLIFFORD ODETS, Ibid.

For de little stealin' dey gits you in jail soon or late. For de big stealin'
dey makes you emperor and puts you in de Hall o' Fame when you croaks.
If dey's one thing I learns in ten years on de Pullman cars listenin' to de
white quality talk, it's dat same fact.

EUGENE O'NEILL, The Emperor Jones, 1920

The child was diseased at birth, stricken with a hereditary ill that only
the most vital men are able to shake off. I mean poverty—that most
deadly and prevalent of all diseases.

EUGENE O'NEILL, Ibid.

We're all poor nuts and things happen, and we yust get mixed in wrong, that's all.

Eugene O'Neill, *Anna Christie,* 1921

Dat ole davil, sea.

Eugene O'Neill, *Ibid.*

Yank: Sure! Lock me up! Put me in a cage! Dat's de on'y answer yuh know. G'wan, lock me up!
Policeman: What you been doin'?
Yank: Enough to gimme life for! I was born, see? Sure dat's de charge. Write it in de blotter. I was born, get me?

Eugene O'Neill, *The Hairy Ape,* 1922

Desire Under the Elms.

Eugene O'Neill, title of play, 1924

This is Daddy's bedtime secret for today: Man is born broken. He lives by mending. The grace of God is glue.

Eugene O'Neill, *The Great God Brown,* 1926

Strange interlude! Yes, our lives are merely strange dark interludes in the electrical display of God the Father!

Eugene O'Neill, *Strange Interlude,* 1928

Women are jealous of ships. They always suspect the sea. They know they're three of a kind when it comes to a man.

Eugene O'Neill, *Mourning Becomes Electra,* 1931

Ah, Wilderness!

Eugene O'Neill, title of play, 1933

The Iceman Cometh.

Eugene O'Neill, title of play, 1946

Vos you dere, Sharlie?

Jack Pearl

You can have too much champagne to drink but you can never have enough.

ELMER RICE, *The Winner,* 1954

In the time of your life—live!

WILLIAM SAROYAN, *The Time of Your Life*

If you give to a thief he cannot steal from you, and he is then no longer a thief.

WILLIAM SAROYAN, *The Human Comedy*

My father thanks you, my mother thanks you, my sister thanks you, and I thank you.

JULIUS TANNEN, vaudeville line used by George M. Cohan

I like a man that takes his time.

MAE WEST

Come up and see me some time.

MAE WEST

STAGE MANAGER: The morning star always gets wonderful bright the minute before it has to go.

THORNTON WILDER, *Our Town,* I, 1938

REBECCA: I never told you about that letter Jane Crofut got from her minister when she was sick. The minister of her church in the town she was in before she came here. He wrote Jane a letter and on the envelope the address was like this: It said: Jane Crofut, The Crofut Farm; Grover's Corners; Sutton County; New Hampshire; United States of America.
GEORGE: What's funny about that?
REBECCA: But listen, it's not finished: the United States of America; Continent of North America; Western Hemisphere; the Earth; the Solar System; the universe; the Mind of God—that's what it said on the envelope.
GEORGE: What do you know!
REBECCA: And the postman brought it just the same.
GEORGE: What do you know!

THORNTON WILDER, *Ibid.,* I

STAGE MANAGER: The Cartwright interests have just begun building a new bank in Grover's Corners—had to go to Vermont for the marble, sorry to say. And they've asked a friend of mine what they should put in the cornerstone for people to dig up a thousand years from now. Of course, they've put in a copy of the New York *Times* and a copy of Mr. Webb's *Sentinel*. We're kind of interested in this because some scientific fellas have found a way of painting all that reading matter with a kind of glue—silicate glue—that'll make it keep a thousand—two thousand years. We're putting in a Bible . . . and the Constitution of the United States and a copy of William Shakespeare's plays. What do you say, folks? What do you think? Y'know—Babylon once had two million people in it, and all we know about 'em is the names of the kings and some copies of wheat contracts and . . . the sales of slaves. Yet, every night all those families sat down to supper, and the father came home from his work, and the smoke went up the chimney,—same as here. And even in Greece and Rome, all we know about the real life of the people is what we can piece together out of the joking poems and the comedies they wrote for the theater back then. So I'm going to have a copy of this play put in the cornerstone and the people a thousand years from now'll know a few simple facts about us—more than the Treaty of Versailles and the Lindbergh flight. See what I mean? Well,—you people a thousand years from now,—in the provinces north of New York at the beginning of the Twentieth Century, people et three times a day: soon after sunrise; at noon; and at sunset. Every seventh day, by law and by religion, was a day of rest and all work come to a stop. The religion at that time was Christianity. I guess you have some other records about Christianity. The domestic set-up was marriage: a binding relation between a male and one female that lasted for life. Christianity strictly forbade killing, but you were allowed to kill animals, and you were allowed to kill human beings in war and government punishings. I guess we don't have to tell you about the government and business forms, because that's the kind of thing people seem to hand down first of all. Let me see now if there's anything else. Oh, yes,—at death people were buried in the ground just as they are. So, friends, this is the way we were in our growing up and in our marrying and in our doctoring and in our living and in our dying. Now we'll return to our day in Grover's Corners.

THORNTON WILDER, *Ibid.*, I

STAGE MANAGER: There are a lot of things to be said about a wedding; there are a lot of thoughts that go on during a wedding. We can't get them all into one wedding, naturally, and especially not into a wedding at Grover's Corners where they're awfully plain and short. In this wedding I play the minister. That gives me the right to say a few more things about it. For a while now, the play gets pretty serious. Y'see, some churches say that marriage is a sacrament. I don't quite know what that means, but I can guess. Like Mrs. Gibbs said a few minutes ago: People were made to live two-by-two. This is a good wedding, but people are so put together that even at a good wedding there's a lot of confusion way down deep in people's minds and we thought that that ought to be in our play, too. The real hero of this scene isn't on the stage at all, and you know who that is. It's like what one of those European fellas said: every child born into the world is Nature's attempt to make a perfect human being. Well, we've seen Nature pushing and contriving for some time now. We all know that nature's interested in quantity; but I think she's interested in quality, too,—that's why I'm in the ministry.—Maybe she's trying to make another good governor for New Hampshire. And don't forget the other witnesses at this wedding,—the ancestors. Millions of them. Most of them set out to live two-by-two, also. Millions of them. Well, that's all my sermon. 'Twan't very long, anyway.

THORNTON WILDER, *Ibid.*, II

STAGE MANAGER: This certainly is an important part of Grover's Corners. A lot of thoughts come up here, night and day, but there's no post office. Now I'm going to tell you some things you know already. You know'm as well as I do; but you don't take'm out and look at'm very often. I don't care what they say with their mouths—everybody knows that *something* is eternal. And it ain't houses and it ain't names, and it ain't earth, and it ain't even the stars . . . everybody knows in their bones that *something* is eternal, and that something has to do with human beings. All the greatest people ever lived have been telling us that for five thousand years and yet you'd be surprised how people are always losing hold of it. There's something way down deep that's eternal about every human being. (*Pause*) You know as well as I do that the dead don't stay interested in us living people for very long. Gradually, gradually, they let hold of the earth . . . and the ambitions they had . . . and the pleasures they had . . . and the things they suffered . . . and the people they loved. They get weaned away from earth—that's the way I put it,—weaned away. Yes, they stay here while the earth part of 'em burns away, burns out, and all that time they slowly get indifferent to what's goin' on in Grover's

Corners. They're waitin'. They're waitin' for something that they feel is comin'. Something important and great. Aren't they waitin' for the eternal part in them to come out clear?

THORNTON WILDER, Ibid., III

STAGE MANAGER: Most everybody's asleep in Grover's Corners. There are a few lights on: Shorty Hawkins, down at the depot, has just watched the Albany train go by. And at the livery stable somebody's sitting up late and talking.—Yes, it's clearing up. There are the stars—doing their old, old criss-cross journeys in the sky. Scholars haven't settled the matter yet, but they seem to think there are no living beings up there. They're just chalk . . . or fire. Only this one is straining away, straining away all the time to make something of itself. The strain's so bad that every sixteen hours everybody lies down and gets a rest. (*He winds his watch.*) Hm . . . Eleven o'clock in Grover's Corners.—You get a good rest, too. Good-night.

THORNTON WILDER, Ibid., last lines

Every good thing in the world stands on the razor-edge of danger.

THORNTON WILDER, The Skin of Our Teeth, 1942

Cheese it, the chops.

> ED WYNN, *Manhattan Mary,* playing a waiter, to the chef when a customer ordered lamb chops *au gratin*

THE MOVIES

Came the dawn.

> Common phrase in silent film titles, used, late 1920's, as a symbol of silly movie titles and pretentious films

Lights! Action! Camera!

> Movie makers' go-ahead signal, which came to be used at the start of any of the more mundane actions of life

THE TAMING OF THE SHREW

By William Shakespeare with additional dialogue by Sam Taylor.

Movie title, 1930's

STICKS NIX HIX PIX.

> Headline, *Variety,* 1935. Pictures about country people were found to be unpopular in the country.

Don't send me any more pictures where the hero signs his name with a feather.

> ANON., movie exhibitor to Hollywood studio

This is where we came in.

> Catch phrase arising from continuous showing of double-feature movies, 1940's

Movies are better than ever.

> Exhortative slogan with which the movie-makers attempted to lure their customers away from TV sets, 1950's

Hollywood is a great place if you're an orange.

> FRED ALLEN

Hollywood is a place where people from Iowa mistake each other for stars.

> FRED ALLEN

An associate producer is the only guy in Hollywood who will associate with a producer.

> FRED ALLEN

I don't give a damn about the [movie] industry. If they go broke, I don't give a damn. I don't hurt the industry. The industry hurts itself—as if General Motors deliberately put out a bad car.

> HUMPHREY BOGART, *Time,* June 7, 1954

Motion pictures are just a passing fancy and aren't worth comment in this newspaper.

> ARTHUR BRISBANE, Chicago *Record-Herald,* 1913

Comedy must be real and true to life. My comedy is actual life with the slightest twist or exaggeration. . . . I aimed exclusively at pleasing myself. For when I gave the subject thought, I became convinced it was the average man I tried to please. And was I not the average man?

> CHARLES CHAPLIN, quoted by Huff, *Charles Chaplin,* 1951

You Can't Cheat an Honest Man.

> W. C. FIELDS, title of moving picture

Why don't you go back to your reservation and milk your elk?

> W. C. FIELDS, to an Indian, in *My Little Chickadee*

The movies are the only court where the judge goes to the lawyer for advice.

> F. SCOTT FITZGERALD, *The Crackup,* 1945

Ay tank ay go home.

> GRETA GARBO

For messages I use Western Union. Pictures are for entertainment.

> HOWARD GOLDSTEIN, movie producer, 1953

God makes stars. It's up to the producers to find them.

> Attributed to SAM GOLDWYN

Wait a minute! Wait a minute! You ain't heard nothin' yet.

> AL JOLSON, *The Jazz Singer,* 1927. These words were to have been cut from the sound track of this, the first important "talking" picture, since they were addressed to the live audience of technicians and extras on the set, but a last minute decision left them in to become famous with Jolson.

These are the portals of imagination. Recover hope, all ye who enter here.

> SINCLAIR LEWIS, inscription for new movie theater in Sauk Center, Minnesota

The screen had just started to talk when Miss Bankhead interrupted in 1930.

> RICHARD MANEY

Frankly, my dear, I don't give a damn.

> MARGARET MITCHELL [Rhett Butler (Clark Gable) to
> Scarlett O'Hara (Vivian Leigh)], *Gone With the Wind*

It's a trip through a sewer in a glass-bottomed boat.

> WILSON MIZNER, comment on Hollywood, adapted by
> Jimmy Walker

Nothing will kill the movies except education.

> WILL ROGERS

Basically I think the screen is a great medium for writers. Eventually it will be possible to develop a story for the screen just as fully as you would wish to tell it on the stage or in the novel. That's the direction screen writing is taking, perhaps more slowly than many think is necessary, but the status of the screen writer has been very poor. It will take quite a long time to overcome the impression that screen writers are just pencil pushers.

> BUDD SCHULBERG, *The New York Times*, March 7, 1955

It is this unshakeable conviction which deadens Hollywood, which converts it from the Athens that it might be into the magnified Gopher Prairie that it is. Every writer or actor or artist of any kind who journeys there, however high his hopes or firm his integrity, is bound eventually to arrive at the point where he must utter the same unanswerable question: "What's the use?" And having done so, he must either depart at once, before the California climate dissolves the tissues of his conscience, or he must abandon his idealistic pretensions, settle down to a monotonous diet of the succulent fruits of the lotus, and live out his days, in sun-kissed contentment, accomplishing nothing of any enduring importance, taking the immediate cash and letting the eternal credit go.

> ROBERT E. SHERWOOD

Don't get me wrong—I love Hollywood.

> SIDNEY SKOLSKY

The only way to avoid Hollywood is to live there.

> IGOR STRAVINSKY

We must never forget that the cinema is an art. But it is an art so much more costly than the others . . . that the artist must tie himself to the

businessman. . . . In that lies all the drama—rather the comic opera—
of Hollywood: a group of fat businessmen—good fathers, not very funny,
who amuse themselves, big cigars in hand, discussing stock-market quotations, the percentage of returns on their stocks, world tendencies . . .
condemned to conjugal existence with this heap of drunkards, madmen,
divorcés, sloths, epileptics, morphinomaniacs and assorted bastards, who
are, in the considered opinion of the management, artists.

> PRESTON STURGES, *Arts* magazine, Paris, June, 1954

Beulah, peel me a grape.

> MAE WEST, to a servant, in *My Little Chickadee*

RADIO AND T.V.

What hath God wrought!

> First telegraph message, sent from Washington to Baltimore,
> May 24, 1844

We are in great haste to construct a magnetic telegraph from Maine to
Texas; but Maine and Texas, it may be, have nothing important to communicate. Either is in such a predicament as the man who was earnest to
be introduced to a distinguished deaf woman, but when he was presented,
and one end of her ear trumpet was put into his hand, had nothing to
say. As if the main object were to talk fast and not to talk sensibly. We
are eager to tunnel under the Atlantic and bring the Old World some
weeks nearer to the New; but perchance the first news that will leak
through into the broad, flapping American ear will be that the Princess
Adelaide has the whooping cough.

> HENRY DAVID THOREAU, *Walden*

That's the song they play on T.V. every Friday just before the fights.

> ANON., San Francisco first-grader, asked to identify "The
> Star Spangled Banner"

That's a joke, son.

> ANON., "Senator Claghorn" on the Fred Allen Show

Hi-yo Silver!

> ANON., the Lone Ranger

The sixty-four dollar question.

> ANON., phrase first used April 21, 1940, on C.B.S. program
> *Take It or Leave It*

Buy Christmas seals and help stamp out T.V.

> Saying, Hollywood, 1951

MRS. NUSSBAUM ON PSYCHIATRY

ALLEN: Mrs. Nussbaum, does your husband Pierre use much medicine?

MRS. N.: Medicine couldn't helping Pierre. He is confidentially—a mental.

ALLEN: Pierre is a mental case?

MRS. N.: All day he is sitting—on his head is tied a greasy string.

ALLEN: A greasy string?

MRS. N.: He is thinking he is a salami end. At night around his feet he is tying the greasy string.

ALLEN: Instead of his head, Pierre ties the greasy string around his feet?

MRS. N.: He thinks he is the other end of the salami.

ALLEN: Has he seen a doctor?

MRS. N.: A psychiatral.

ALLEN: A psychiatrist.

MRS. N.: Either way it is twenty dollars. He is saying to Pierre, "You are not a salami end. . . . You are not a salami end. . . ."

ALLEN: And?

MRS. N.: Pierre is saying, "All right, so I am not a salami end. I will be a pot roast."

ALLEN: Did Pierre go to the psychiatrist often?

MRS. N.: Every day. One day he is shaving off his head. He is a boiled potato. The next day he is standing in a long green bag. He is a pickle. Once he is coming home with three friends—they are cold cuts.

ALLEN: Tsk! Tsk! Tsk!

MRS. N.: Once, with caraway seeds in his hair, Pierre is a pumpernickel.

ALLEN: After Pierre kept going to the psychiatrist as a salami end, a pot roast, a boiled potato and cold cuts—what happened?

MRS. N.: The psychiatral is getting an idea.

ALLEN: An idea, eh?

MRS. N.: He is opening up a delicatessen.

ALLEN: And what became of Pierre?

MRS. N.: He is hanging in the window. . . . Dank you!

> FRED ALLEN, *Treadmill to Oblivion*, 1954; a sample from
> the Fred Allen Radio Show

Give-away programs are the buzzards of radio.

As buzzards swoop down on carrion so have give-away shows descended on the carcass of radio.

Like buzzarrds the give-away shows, if left to pursue their scavenging devices, will leave nothing but the picked bones of the last listener lying before his radio set.

Radio started as a medium of entertainment.

The give-away programs have reduced radio to a shoddy gambling device.

The networks that once vied with each other to present the nation's outstanding acting and musical talent are now infested with swarms of hustlers who are only concerned with the gimmick and a fast buck.

All the promoter of the give-away has to give to radio is the motley array of merchandise he has been able to wheedle out of dealers in return for brief mentions on his clambake.

The give-away program cannot help sales. Its sole appeal is to the greed of the listener. The person who regularly tunes in the give-away show has larceny in his heart. He has no interest in the sponsor's commercials or his products. The give-away fan is only concerned with his selfish incentive—to get something for nothing.

The give-away program cannot help the radio audience. Four or five people win prizes—millions of listeners win nothing. At the end of the program the losers are only thirty minutes older and mad at the sponsor, the master of ceremonies and themselves. The lucky (?) winners rarely receive cash. Their prizes are often useless. An old lady of seventy-five, who gets nosebleeds wearing high heels, wins an airplane. A man who becomes seasick at the sight of whitecaps on two Good Humor men wins a four-week cruise to South America. A housewife with no teeth wins a lifetime supply of dental floss. A small boy wins a six-room bungalow that has been erected on Fifth Avenue. How he is going to get the six-room bungalow from Fifth Avenue to where he lives is left to the small boy. If he brings the bungalow into the house his parents will probably kill him. If an occasional winner is unfortunate enough to win cash he is instantly surrounded by poor relatives, eager to borrow, real estate and insurance salesmen, anxious to help him invest, and the state and Federal tax collectors who cannot wait to inform him what he owes.

The give-away programs cannot help the radio networks.

The millions of listeners who seek entertainment will eventually flee the give-away programs and radio and turn to television, the theater and leapfrog. Radio City, instead of being a house of joy for the masses will become a Monte Carlo for morons.

What is the solution?

If I were king for one day, I would make every program in radio a give-away show; when the studios were filled with the people who encourage these atrocities I would lock the doors. With all of the morons in America trapped, the rest of the population could go about its business.

If the give-away programs prevail, radio's few remaining listeners will get into the spirit of the thing and give away their radios.

P.S. This was written in 1948. It has come to pass.

FRED ALLEN, *Ibid.*

A conference of radio executives is a meeting at which a group of men who, singly, can do nothing, agree collectively that nothing can be done.

FRED ALLEN

You wouldn't talk that way about me if I had my gag writers here!

JACK BENNY to Fred Allen

Radio brings you information at the speed of light, but it has not increased the speed of thought by a single m. p. h. In the wake of sensation, wisdom still plods in the dust far to the rear.

JOHN CROSBY, New York *Herald Tribune,* July 3, 1946

To put my problem to you frankly, Mr. Anthony, my husband threatens to leave me if I tune in your program once more.

RICHARD DECKER, cartoon caption, 1940's

Matrimony must be here to stay, it has survived the husband-and-wife programs on the air.

HERB GRAFFIS

Scientists of the University of Chicago have lately detected something that looks like moss growing on the planet Mars. Perhaps Mars was once inhabited by beings like ourselves, who had the misfortune, some millions of years ago, to invent television.

ROBERT M. HUTCHINS, *The Conflict in Education,* 1953

'Tain't funny, McGee.

FIBBER McGEE, gag line from radio show

When an instrumentality is taken over as a money-making device, those who live by it must seek a money-making formula. Radio has found its formula. Whereas the newspaper has found its vested interests in catastrophe, radio has found it in mediocrity.

> HARRY A. OVERSTREET, *The Mature Mind,* 1949

Radio has succumbed to its first enemy: it has become static.

> GILBERT SELDES, *The Great Audience,* 1951

A million sensitive people, capable of judgment, may tune out a demagogue, but if twenty million others listen to him, the minority will be swept away in whatever whirlwind of passion follows. *Not what one person can avoid hearing, but what everyone else does hear, is the heart of radio's power and the core of its responsibility.*

> GILBERT SELDES, *Ibid.*

Ladies and gentlemen, these things are *books.* They keep quiet. They do not suddenly dissolve into wavy lines or snowstorm effects. They do not pause to deliver a message from their sponsors. And every one of them is three-dimensional: they have length, breadth, and thickness for convenience in handling, and they live indefinitely in the fourth dimension of time.

> GEORGE STEVENS, advertisement, *Saturday Review,* 1953

An "orchestra" in radio circles is any ensemble comprising more than three players, while a "symphony" program is one that include Liszt's "Liebestraum."

> DEEMS TAYLOR, *Radio—A Brief for the Defense*

The ideal voice for radio may be defined as having no substance, no sex, no owner, and a message of importance to every housewife.

> HARRY V. WADE

We just want the facts, ma'am.

> JACK WEBB, catch line from *Dragnet*

My name's Friday. I'm a cop.

> JACK WEBB, introductory, *Dragnet*

Good evening, Mr. and Mrs. America and all the ships at sea!

> WALTER WINCHELL, radio catch phrase

In radio it is understood that whatever else happens, there must never be a silence. This hard condition is most noticeable in the aerial forums, in which the performers are expected to offer an immediate opinion on any subject, and do. Someone must always be speaking, either the ringmaster or one of the experts. The rule seems to be: make sense if you can, but if you can't make sense say something anyway. If you listen to one of these nervous exercises in intellectual rough-and-tumble, it is plain that a large part of the effort goes simply into preventing a lull in the conversation. The Quakers take a more sensible view of silence; they accord it equal recognition with sound. We doubt that radio will ever amount to a damn as long as it is haunted by the fear of nobody speaking.

E. B. White, *The Second Tree from the Corner,* "Sound"

MISCELLANEOUS

The theatre is a lottery. Making bad movies is no fun. Television is the same—everything's got to be perfect. Nightclubs are the only place to try out new ideas any more. They are the only place to be lousy in.

Eddie Albert, April, 1954

One of the principal features of my entertainment is that it contains so many things that don't have anything to do with it.

Charles Farrar Browne ("Artemus Ward"), *Artemus Ward: His Book,* 1862

It's jam, but arranged.

Mike Farley, 1936, when asked for a definition of "swing"

The Greatest Show On Earth.

Slogan, Ringling Brothers Barnum and Bailey Circus

From the time the "advance man" flung his highly colored posters over the fence till the coming of the glorious day we thought of little else. It was India and Arabia and the jungle to us. History and the magic and pomp of chivalry mingled in the parade of the morning, and the crowds, the clanging band, the haughty and alien beauty of the women, the gold embroidered housings, the stark majesty of the acrobats subdued us into silent worship. . . . To rob me of my memories of the circus would leave me as poor as those to whom life was a drab and hopeless round of toil.

It was our brief season of imaginative life. In one day—in a part of one day—we gained a thousand new conceptions of the world and of human nature. It was an embodiment of all that was skillful and beautiful in manly action. It was a compendium of biologic research but more important still, it brought to our ears the latest band pieces and taught us the most popular songs. It furnished us with jokes. It relieved our dullness. It gave us something to talk about.

We always went home wearied with excitement, and dusty and fretful —but content. We had seen it. . . . Next day as we resumed work in the field the memory of its splendors went with us like a golden cloud.

HAMLIN GARLAND, *A Son of the Middle Border*

The first one to catch a circus in a lie is a boy.

KIN HUBBARD

Hello, sucker!

TEXAS GUINAN, phrase used by her in greeting. Wilson Mizner claimed she borrowed it from him.

A Big Butter-and-Egg Man.

TEXAS GUINAN. She was introducing a customer who one night in 1924 paid everybody's cover charge at her night club and distributed fifty-dollar bills to the entertainers, and refused to tell his name but said he was in the dairy products business.

Fifty million Frenchmen can't be wrong.

TEXAS GUINAN

He is a one-stringed instrument made of candy.

JOHN H. O'BRIEN, "The Crooner," *Michigan Alumnus Quarterly,* October, 1934

Too bad there are so many people who care more about who writes their songs than their laws.

JOHN W. RAPER, *What This World Needs*

Jazz will endure just as long as people hear it through their feet instead of their brains.

JOHN PHILIP SOUSA

The marijuana of the nursery, the bane of the bassinet, the horror of the home, the curse of the kids, and a threat to the future.

> JOHN MASON BROWN, of comic books

When I recently conducted a symposium on the psychopathology of comic books I was blamed for not allotting more time to a representative of the comic-book business who was there. I am even more guilty than that: I once conducted a symposium on alcoholism and didn't invite a single distiller.

> FREDERIC WERTHAM, *Saturday Review,* May 29, 1948

EATING, DRINKING AND SMOKING

What one relishes, nourishes.

> BENJAMIN FRANKLIN, *Poor Richard's Almanac,* 1734

In general, mankind, since the improvement of cookery, eat twice as much as nature requires.

> BENJAMIN FRANKLIN

An American breakfast never failed to interest foreigners, on account of the variety and abundance of its dishes. On the main lines of travel, fresh meat and vegetables were invariably served at all meals; but Indian corn was the national crop, and Indian corn was eaten three times a day in another form as salt pork. The rich alone could afford fresh meat. Ice-chests were hardly known. In the country fresh meat could not regularly be got, except in the shape of poultry or game; but the hog cost nothing to keep, and very little to kill and preserve. Thus the ordinary rural American was brought up on salt pork and Indian corn, or rye; and the effect of this diet showed itself in dyspepsia.

> HENRY ADAMS, *History of the United States*

God made yeast, as well as dough, and loves fermentation just as dearly as he loves vegetation.

> RALPH WALDO EMERSON, *Essays: Second Series,* "New England Reformers"

The believing we do something when we do nothing is the first illusion of tobacco.

> RALPH WALDO EMERSON, *Journal*, October, 1861

A man of no conversation should smoke.

> RALPH WALDO EMERSON

I don't s'pose anybody on earth likes gingerbread better'n I do—and gets less'n I do.

> ABRAHAM LINCOLN, quoted by Sandburg, *Abraham Lincoln: The Prairie Years*

The way to a man's heart is through his stomach.

> SARA PAYSON WILLIS ("FANNY FERN"), *Willis Parton*

Temperance is moderation in the things that are good and total abstinence from the things that are bad.

> FRANCES E. WILLARD, definition of temperance. It was the accepted definition when the W.C.T.U. was organized as a total abstinence society in 1874, and handed down through its records.

Nothing helps scenery like ham and eggs.

> SAMUEL L. CLEMENS ("MARK TWAIN"), *Roughing It*

The true Southern watermelon is a boon apart, and not to be mentioned with commoner things. It is chief of this world's luxuries, king by the grace of God over all the fruits of the earth. When one has tasted it, he knows what angels eat. It was not a Southern watermelon that Eve took; we know it because she repented.

> SAMUEL L. CLEMENS ("MARK TWAIN"), *Pudd'nhead Wilson's Calendar*

Bacon would improve the flavor of an angel.

> SAMUEL L. CLEMENS ("MARK TWAIN")

More than one cigar at a time is excessive smoking.

> SAMUEL L. CLEMENS ("MARK TWAIN")

To cease smoking is the easiest thing I ever did; I ought to know because I've done it a thousand times.

SAMUEL L. CLEMENS ("MARK TWAIN")

My own childhood dates back only to sixty and seventy years ago . . . but such a treasure-packed cellar was very familiar to me. I was often sent down, with an old chisel and hammer, to chip off a week's supply of sweetenin' from the big barrel of dark crystallized maple sugar (white sugar was for company). Or with a basket to bring up potatoes from the bin, carrots from the box of sand, onions from the hanging shelves on which they were spread out, bushels and bushels of them, or—disagreeable sloppy task for a child—to fish out a slippery chunk of salt pork from the brine in a barrel. It was pleasanter to reach down from its hook a flitch of bacon, or a well-smoked shoulder of pork, to carve out a piece of cooking butter from the supply laid down under salt the summer before, to pick out from the water glass six or a dozen cooking eggs, and from the barrels pie-apples (with specks of decay) and eating apples, the sound, red-cheeked Northern Spies which later, polished to brilliance, would light up the side-table in the dining room. Their presence would go far beyond the dining room, and pervade the house with an aroma which, mingled with the smell (not disagreeable to a child) of creosote from the chimneys, became the characteristic odor of home, bringing back childhood with as actual a presence as Proust's famous little madeleine cake. From the pantry upstairs came dried peas for soup, dried beans to be baked for Saturday-night supper, and thick cream, sweet for baked potatoes and gravy, sour for biscuits, from the top of the milk in the great pans crowding the shelves.

It does no harm to celebrate the Horn of Plenty of those days, because the story of Vermont is often told as if it had always been meager, pinched and anxious. . . .

DOROTHY CANFIELD FISHER, *Vermont Tradition*, 1953

The sway of alcohol over mankind is unquestionably due to its power to stimulate the mystical faculties of human nature.

WILLIAM JAMES, *The Varieties of Religious Experience*

No opium-smoking in the elevators.

WILSON MIZNER, sign in Hotel Rand, which he managed, New York, 1907

Miss Tawney Apple has contracted neuritis from chilled cocktail shakers.

KIN HUBBARD, *Barbed Wire*

There's somebody at every dinner party who eats all the celery.

KIN HUBBARD

Ther ought t' be some way t' eat celery so it wouldn' sound like you wuz steppin' on a basket.

KIN HUBBARD

The oblong farinacious compound, faintly yet richly brown, stamped and smoking, not crisp nor brittle, but softly absorbent of the syrup dabbed upon it.

HENRY JAMES, of waffles

What this country needs is a good five-cent cigar.

THOMAS RILEY MARSHALL, during a boring debate, when a Senator began enumerating what the country needed. F.P.A. noted that "What this country needs is a good five-cent nickel," and Will Rogers added that "Our country has plenty of good five-cent cigars but the trouble is they charge fifteen cents for them."

If you will study the history of almost any criminal, you will find he is an inveterate cigarette smoker.

HENRY FORD, quoted by Gunther, *Inside U.S.A.*

There are two things that will be believed of any man whatsoever, and one of them is that he has taken to drink.

BOOTH TARKINGTON

I sometimes wish that people would put a little more emphasis upon the observance of the law than they do upon its enforcement.

CALVIN COOLIDGE, of Prohibition

Frenchmen drink wine just like we used to drink water before Prohibition.

RING LARDNER, *What of It?,* "The Other Side," 1925

My baby asked me would I write him a speech to read at his club and I says what subject and he says you can pick out your own provided it is a new subject which people ain't sick in tired of reading about it. So I thought a long wile and then I says how about Prohibition?

You are a wonder said the little one, slapping me on the back till it hurt.

So I set down and tore off a few 100 wds. in regards to different phrases of Prohibition but for the benefit of the majority of my readers who probably have not heard of same, I may as well exclaim the meaning of the verb Prohibition. Well the dictionary says it is the forbidding by law of the manufacture or sale of intoxicating liquors as beverages. Well they was a lot of people in the U. S. that was in flavor of such a forbidding and finely congress passed a law making the country dry and the law went into effect about the 20 of Jan. 1920 and the night before it went into effect everybody had a big party on acct. of it being the last chance to get boiled. As these wds. is written the party is just beginning to get good.

Now they's a little group of wilful men that keeps hollering that the law ain't no good and please modify it so as to give us light wines and beer but the gen. attitude in regards to this plea as revealed by a personal souse to souse canvas is who and the hell would drink them.

RING LARDNER, *What of It?*, "The Big Drought," 1925

If the penalty for selling honest old beer to minors was $100 fine why 2 to 14 years in a meat grinder would be mild for a guy that sells white pop on the theory that it is a drink.

RING LARDNER

One time during prohibition [Fields] heard that a friend on Long Island had just received two cases of contraband Irish whiskey. He and Grady drove out immediately. They and the friend spent the night making sure the government would be unable to recover part of the whiskey, at least, and Fields and Grady left for home around dawn. Owing to their host's generosity, they took five or six quarts along with them, externally. Both Fields and Grady later recalled that it was snowing when they left, and they settled down for an exhausting drive. En route they took frequent pulls at the whiskey and remarked at the surprising length of Long Island. Their heads were pretty fuzzy during the trip. They put in at filling stations now and then, gassed up, and sought information about the route. However, in response to a question like "How far's the Queensboro Bridge?" the attendants would only laugh, or stare stupidly. Also, as time wore on, the travelers got the cloudy impression that many people they talked to were essaying dialects, for some reason. "I don't recollect no place name of Manhasset," a man would tell them, and they would applaud, then careen on down the road, drinking his health. Their heads finally cleared, and Grady found himself looking out the window at a palm tree. They seemed to be in a hotel room. He dressed quickly and, while Fields slept on, exhausted by the Long Island roads, went down in search of a newspaper. The first intelligence he gleaned, when he got one, was that Ocala, Florida, was expecting no more than a moderate rainfall for that time of year, and that things looked good for a big citrus crop.

He went back to the hotel room and shook up Fields. "Paper here says we're in Ocala, Florida," he reported.

"I always said those Long Island roads were poorly marked," Fields replied.

They lingered on for a week and went on several picnics. They left after Fields had been fined two hundred and seven dollars for removing two hundred and seven dogwood blossoms from the municipal park.

> ROBERT LEWIS TAYLOR, *W. C. Fields: His Follies and Fortunes,* 1949

I do not favor the repeal of the Eighteenth Amendment. . . . Our country has deliberately undertaken a great social and economic experiment, noble in motive, far-reaching in purpose.

> HERBERT HOOVER, speech, August, 1928

The Schultz mob kidnapped Joe, and what they did to him was a warning to others. They took him into a dive and beat him so badly as to cripple him. They strung him up by the thumbs for that portion of the lesson. Then they placed a strip of gauze that had been smeared with some infectious matter over his eyes, and taped it securely. When they finally tossed him out into the street . . . he was on his way to blindness. . . . He quit the business.

> CRAIG THOMPSON and ALLEN RAYMOND, *Gang Rule in New York.* The business was beer.

And sweet corn. I shiver in the mistral as I think of what pleasure it would be to pluck ears of corn from their stalks and hurry them shrieking to the pot of boiling water destined for them. Not ears too young, of course. No silly rows of white grains. No protruding naked length of cob at the smaller end. Nothing immature, nothing unformed. The ears must be all at an even flush of growth, the rows close set, the grains full and well rooted. The color must be gold. Ten minutes in boiling water are enough, but not too much. Then butter and salt on three rows at a time— not two, which is childish; not four, which is gluttonous—and the three rows eaten steadily from left to right as one reads poetry. Have not the teeth, which can neither taste nor smell, their peculiar sensation when they are plunged into choice morsels? And is any sensation which they ever have more grateful than this, when they feel themselves measuring off the three rows, taking a preliminary hold of them, and then sinking to the cob, cleanly carrying away their booty? If there is a sensation more grateful it is only when the sweet corn has not been boiled, but has been roasted in its own husks in hot embers, so that it has the taste of smoke about it and here and there a part of the ear a little charred by the heat.

CARL VAN DOREN, New York *Herald Tribune*

There is no use talking about it one way or the other: what a man has eaten, that he remains.

CARL VAN DOREN, *Ibid*.

It smells like gangrene starting in a mildewed silo, it tastes like the wrath to come, and when you absorb a deep swig of it you have all the sensations of having swallowed a lighted kerosene lamp. A sudden, violent jolt of it has been known to stop the victim's watch, snap his suspenders and crack his glass eye right across.

IRVIN S. COBB, definition of "Corn Licker" given to Distillers' Code Authority, N.R.A.

You can always judge a man by what he eats and . . . therefore a country in which there is no free lunch is no longer a free country.

ARTHUR "BUGS" BAER

Somebody put pineapple juice in my pineapple juice!

W. C. FIELDS, outraged cry when he discovered that someone had tampered with his vacuum bottle of Martinis on the movie set; he always claimed that the bottle contained only pineapple juice

The Lost Weekend.

CHARLES JACKSON, title of novel, 1944

"It's broccoli, dear."

"I say it's spinach, and I say the hell with it."

> E. B. WHITE, caption of cartoon by Carl Rose, *New Yorker*

It's a naive domestic Burgundy without any breeding, but I think you'll be amused by its presumption.

> JAMES THURBER, cartoon caption, *New Yorker*

I must get out of these wet clothes and into a dry martini.

> ALEXANDER WOOLLCOTT

Of course. But no one ever has.

> ERWIN D. CANHAM, executive editor of the *Christian Science Monitor,* in its offices when John Gunther asked if he might smoke

A great deal of sentimental drivel has been drooled about the wonders of the oldtime farm kitchen, but the truth of it is that most of the cooking was frying—and not even in deep fat. The traditional American farmer . . . was scrawny-necked, flat-chested and pot-bellied from flatulent indigestion.

> CLYDE BRION DAVIS, *The Age of Indiscretion,* 1950

In the heroic age our forefathers invented self-government, the Constitution, and bourbon, and on the way to them they invented rye. . . . Our political institutions were shaped by our whiskeys, would be inconceivable without them, and share their nature. They are distilled not only from our native grains but from our native vigor, suavity, generosity, peacefulness, and love of accord. Whoever goes looking for us will find us there.

> BERNARD DEVOTO, *The Hour,* 1951

How fastidiously cold a second martini is to the palate but how warm to the heart, being drunk. What you seem to hear is not distant music but hope re-echoing in a now-lighted secrecy. These are good men, wise, considerate, indomitable. There is more richness than you remembered and you yourself have rediscovered the wit and sureness that the illusion hid. Observe the pinkness in Marjorie's cheeks, the eagerness in her eyes; she is shrewd and subtly formed; how sagacious the way she has done her hair, how pleasant her dress, how responsive her fingers.

The walls are breached. Are down. There were no walls.

Certainly I'll have another one. The water of life was given to us to make us see for a while that we are more nearly men and women, more nearly kind and gentle and generous, pleasanter and stronger, than without its vision there is any evidence we are. It is the healer, the weaver of forgiveness and reconciliation, the justifier of us to ourselves and one another. One more, and then with a spirit made whole again in a cleansed world, to dinner.

BERNARD DeVOTO, *Ibid.*

Who would marry Rita for her cooking?

DICK HAYMES, when asked at his wedding to her if Rita Hayworth had ever cooked anything for him

Nobody can be so revoltingly smug as the man who has just given up smoking.

SYDNEY J. HARRIS, *Strictly Personal*

Mix whiskey and water, and you spoil two good things.

American saying

Them doughnuts eats good. Try one—they don't go and digest on yuh.

Proprietor of a Martha's Vineyard lunchroom

FASHION AND SOCIETY

[Thomas Gold Appleton] was a good mixer of salads and of guests.

MAUD HOWE ELLIOTT

I know of no profession, art, or trade that women are working in today, as taxing on mental resource as being a leader of Society.

MRS. OLIVER HAZARD PERRY BELMONT, one of the queens of Newport

A lady's name should appear in the papers three times—when she is born, when she marries and when she dies.

MISS ALICE BRAYTON, of Newport

Why is "good society," or so much of it, insupportable, in spite of its charm of good manners, courage, and grace? Because it consists so largely of people who see life in terms of ceremonial and their own importance. They hear and they consider only what they wish to hear and what conduces to their comfort, thinking what they wish to think instead of what one *has* to think, however disconcerting the truth may be. They rationalize everything until it fits their pattern. But thinking what one has to think is thinking in terms of real values, and this alone is endurable to people with minds.

VAN WYCK BROOKS, *Nation,* November 14, 1953

No lady is ever a gentleman.

JAMES BRANCH CABELL, *Something About Eve,* 1927

Some civilised women would lose half their charm without dress, and some would lose all of it.

SAMUEL L. CLEMENS ("MARK TWAIN")

Clothes make the man. Naked people have little or no influence in society.

SAMUEL L. CLEMENS ("MARK TWAIN"), *More Maxims of Mark*

No civilized person ever goes to bed the same day he gets up.

RICHARD HARDING DAVIS, *Gallagher*

A great social success is a pretty girl who plays her cards as carefully as if she were plain.

F. SCOTT FITZGERALD, letter to his daughter

Making out an invitation list for a party brings out the worst in everyone. It is then that our most ruthless estimates of the people we know come into play.

SYDNEY J. HARRIS, *Strictly Personal*

Nobody can be as agreeable as an uninvited guest.

KIN HUBBARD

Th' weddin' last evenin' o' Miss Princess Bud an' Mr. Mingo Bain wuz th' most successful o' th' season, excellin' all former efforts by two pickle dishes.

KIN HUBBARD

A "lady" is a woman so incompetent as to have to take refuge in a secluded class, like kings and idiots, who have to be treated with special kindness because they can't take it.

> SINCLAIR LEWIS, debate, New York, November 19, 1941

I've had a wonderful evening—but this wasn't it.

> GROUCHO MARX, to a Hollywood hostess

Dancing is wonderful training for girls, it's the first way you learn to guess what a man is going to do before he does it.

> CHRISTOPHER MORLEY, *Kitty Foyle,* 1939

There are only about four hundred people in fashionable New York Society. If you go outside that number you strike people who are either not at ease in a ballroom or else make other people not at ease.

> WARD MCALLISTER, to Charles Crandall of the New York *Tribune,* 1888

A man may wear a red necktie, a green vest and tan shoes, and still be a gentleman.

> E. M. STATLER, *Statler Hotel Service Code,* 1921

I have a great deal of company in my house; especially in the morning, when nobody calls.

> HENRY DAVID THOREAU, *Walden*

Society is commonly too cheap. We meet at very short intervals, not having had time to acquire any new value for each other.

> HENRY DAVID THOREAU, *Ibid.*

It would be better if there were but one inhabitant to a square mile, as where I live. The value of a man is not in his skin, that we should touch him.

> HENRY DAVID THOREAU, *Ibid.*

Conspicuous consumption of valuable goods is a means of reputability to the gentleman of leisure. As wealth accumulates on his hands, his own unaided effort will not avail to sufficiently put his opulence in evidence by this method. The aid of friends and competitors is therefore brought in by resorting to the giving of valuable presents and expensive feasts and entertainments. Presents and feasts had probably another origin than that of naive ostentation, but they acquired their utility for this purpose very early, and they have retained their character to the present; so that their utility in this respect has now long been the substantial ground on which these usages rest. Costly entertainments, such as the potlatch or the ball, are peculiarly adapted to serve this end. The competitor with whom the entertainer wishes to institute a comparison is, by this method, made to serve as a means to the end. He consumes vicariously for his host at the same time that he is a witness to the consumption of that excess of good things which his host is unable to dispose of single-handed, and he is also made to witness his host's facility in etiquette.

THORSTEIN VEBLEN, *The Theory of the Leisure Class*, 1899

Woman's apparel not only goes beyond that of the modern man in the degree in which it argues exemption from labor; it also adds a peculiar and highly characteristic feature which differs in kind from anything habitually practised by the men. This feature is the class of contrivances of which the corset is the typical example. The corset is, in economic theory, substantially a mutilation, undergone for the purpose of lowering the subject's vitality and rendering her permanently and obviously unfit for work. It is true, the corset impairs the personal attractions of the wearer, but the loss suffered on that score is offset by the gain in reputability which comes of her visibly increased expensiveness and infirmity. It may broadly be set down that the womanliness of woman's apparel resolves itself, in point of substantial fact, into the more effective hindrance to useful exertion offered by the garments peculiar to women.

THORSTEIN VEBLEN, *Ibid.*

TRAVEL

In America there are two classes of travel—first class, and with children.

ROBERT BENCHLEY

A Cent and a Half a Mile, a Mile and a Half an Hour.

ANON., slogan (though not entirely complimentary) of the Erie Canal, opened 1825. It took about five days to get from New York to Buffalo. It is worth noting that the new Thru-

way charges a toll of one and a quarter cents a mile, and
no doubt a man in an average American car could make the
trip in something under seven hours if he pressed.

Nothing has spread socialistic feeling in this country more than the automobile. . . . They are a picture of the arrogance of wealth with all its
independence and carelessness.

WOODROW WILSON in 1906

Everywhere you see families touring by motor, and the patriotic American, regarding most of them, can only console himself with the thought
that this is a necessary stage in the education of the masses. The American
travels, a French observer has remarked, not to see, but to come back
home and say that he has seen; the quantity of what he has seen is apt
to be impressive, but the quality usually makes little difference, to him or
to those who hear his story. He visits town after town, most of them like
his own home town; and those that are not like it subtly begin to undergo
a change under his influence, so that wherever he goes he may feel at
home.

It would be better for his legs, doubtless, if he walked, and it might also
give some of his nerve centers a needed rest; but he can get nowhere, as a
rule, by walking, even if there were any roads he could safely walk on. It
would be better, infinitely better, for him and for his country, if he valued
the vanishing differences in the places he visits, rather than their increasing similarities. Year by year, of course, he does; more families acquire
from their travels a sense of the value of diversity, an appreciation of local
color; but the destruction of local color, the spread of standardization,
goes on at an even faster rate.

Yet probably the automobile, in this as in other directions, is worth
what it costs, high as the price may be.

ELMER DAVIS

Drive carefully; the life you save may be your own.

Common highway sign, U.S.

Mom, please drive carefully. The life you save may be my replacement.

PRIVATE PAUL FELKNOR, JR., in a letter from Korea

It's hard to find a surviving accident victim who can bear to talk. After
you come to, the gnawing, searing pain throughout your body is accounted
for by learning that you have both collarbones smashed, both shoulder

blades splintered, your right arm broken in three places and three ribs cracked, with every chance of bad internal ruptures. But the pain can't distract you, as the shock begins to wear off, from realising that you are probably on your way out. You can't forget that, not even when they shift you from the ground to the stretcher and your broken ribs bite into your lungs and the sharp ends of your collarbones slide over to stab deep into each side of your screaming throat. When you've stopped screaming, it all comes back—you're dying and you hate yourself for it. That isn't fiction either. It's what it actually feels like to be one of that 36,000.

And every time you pass on a blind curve, every time you hit it up on a slippery road, every time you step on it harder than your reflexes will safely take, every time you drive with your reactions slowed down by a drink or two, every time you follow the man ahead too closely, you're gambling a few seconds against this kind of blood and agony and sudden death.

Take a look at yourself as the man in the white jacket shakes his head over you, tells the boys with the stretcher not to bother and turns away to somebody else who isn't quite dead yet. And then take it easy.

> J. C. Furnas, *Sudden Death and How to Avoid It* (with Ernest A. Smith)

Mrs. Tipton Bud's uncle met with a serious auto accident t'day, owin' t' a near-sighted windshield.

> Kin Hubbard

Only 20% of automobile accidents are caused by women. But that 20% hospitalizes 80% of the men.

> Sam Levenson

A motorist is a man who, after seeing a serious wreck, drives carefully for several blocks.

> Jane Pickens

The ultimate goal of automobile designers is to produce a car into whose driving seat the operator will sink without a trace.

> E. B. White, *One Man's Meat*, "Motor Cars"

Have all the traffic lights on the streets turn red—and keep them that way.

> George S. Kaufman, solution for the New York traffic problem

SPORTS

BASEBALL

How 'bout that!

MEL ALLEN

The $100,000 Infield.

Sobriquet of Philadelphia Athletics infield, c. 1910

Whoever wants to know the heart and mind of America had better learn baseball, the rules and realities of the game—and do it by watching first some high school or small-town teams. The big league games are too fast for the beginner and the newspapers don't help. To read them with profit you have to know a language that comes easy only after philosophy has taught you to judge practice. Here is scholarship that takes effort on the part of the outsider, but it is so bred into the native that it never becomes a dreary round of technicalities. The wonderful purging of the passions that we all experienced in the fall of '51, the despair groaned out over the fate of the Dodgers, from whom the league pennant was snatched at the last minute, gives us some idea of what Greek tragedy was like. Baseball *is* Greek in being national, heroic, and broken up in the rivalries of city-states. How sad that Europe knows nothing like it! Its Olympics generate anger, not unity, and its interstate politics follow no rules that a people can grasp. At least Americans understand baseball, the true realm of clear ideas.

That baseball fitly expresses the powers of the nation's mind and body is a merit separate from the glory of being the most active, agile, articulate and brainy of all group games. It is of and for our century. Tennis belongs to the individualistic past—a hero, or at most a pair of friends or lovers, against the world. The idea of baseball is a team, an outfit, a section, a gang, a union, a cell, a commando squad—in short, a twentieth-century setup of opposite numbers.

Baseball takes its mystic nine and scatters them wide. A kind of individualism thereby returns, but it is limited—eternal vigilance is the price of victory. Just because they're far apart, the outfield can't dream or play she-loves-me-not with daisies. The infield is like a steel net held in the

hands of the catcher. He is the psychologist and historian for the staff—
or else his signals will give the opposition hits. The value of his headpiece
is shown by the ironmongery worn to protect it. The pitcher, on the other
hand, is the wayward man of genius, whom others will direct. They will
expect nothing from him but virtuosity. He is surrounded no doubt by
mere talent, unless one excepts that transplanted acrobat, the shortstop.
What a brilliant invention is his role despite its exposure to ludicrous
lapses! One man to each base, and then the free lance, the trouble shooter,
the movable feast for the eyes, whose motion animates the whole fore-
ground.

The rules keep pace with this imaginative creation so rich in allusions
to real life. How excellent, for instance, that a foul tip muffed by the
catcher gives the batter another chance. It is the recognition of Chance
that knows no argument. But on the other hand, how wise and just that
the third strike must not be dropped. This points to the fact that near the
end of any struggle life asks for more than is needful in order to clinch
success. A victory has to be won, not snatched. We find also our American
innocence in calling "World Series" the annual games between the winners in each big league. The world doesn't know or care and couldn't
compete if it wanted to, but since it's us children having fun, why, the
world is our stage. I said Baseball was Greek. Is there not a poetic symbol
in the new meaning—our meaning—of "Ruth hits Homer?"

Once the crack of the bat has sent the ball skimmiting left of second
between the infielder's legs, six men converge or distend their defense to
keep the runner from advancing along the prescribed path. The ball is not
the center of interest as in those vulgar predatory games like football,
basketball, and polo. Man running is the force to be contained. His getting to first or second base starts a capitalization dreadful to think of:
every hit pushes him on. Bases full and a homer make four runs, while
the defenders, helpless without the magic power of the ball lying over the
fence, cry out their anguish and dig up the sod with their spikes.

But fate is controlled by the rules. Opportunity swings from one side to
the other because innings alternate quickly, keep up spirit in the players,
interest in the beholders. So does the profusion of different acts to be
performed—pitching, throwing, catching, batting, running, stealing, sliding, signaling. Blows are similarly varied. Flies, Texas Leaguers, grounders,
baseline fouls—praise God the human neck is a universal joint! And there
is no set pace. Under the hot sun, the minutes creep as a deliberate pitcher
tries his feints and curves for three strikes called, or conversely walks a
threatening batter. But the batter is not invariably a tailor's dummy. In a
hundredth of a second there may be a hissing rocket down right field, a

cloud of dust over first base—the bleachers all a-yell—a double play, and the other side up to bat.

Accuracy and speed, the practiced eye and hefty arm, the mind to take in and readjust to the unexpected, the possession of more than one talent and the willingness to work in harness without special orders—these are the American virtues that shine in baseball. There has never been a good player who was dumb. Beef and bulk and mere endurance count for little, judgment and daring for much. Baseball is among group games played with a ball what fencing is to games of combat. But being spread out, baseball has something sociable and friendly about it that I especially love. The ball is not shuttling in a confined space, as in tennis. Nor does baseball go to the other extreme of solitary whanging and counting stopped on the brink of pointlessness, like golf. Baseball is a kind of collective chess with arms and legs in full play under sunlight.

How adaptable, too! Three kids in a back yard are enough to create the same quality of drama. All of us in our tennis days have pounded balls with a racket against a wall, for practice. But that is nothing compared with batting in an empty lot, or catching at twilight, with a fellow who'll let you use his mitt when your palms get too raw. Every part of baseball equipment is inherently attractive and of a most enchanting functionalism. A man cannot have too much leather about him; and a catcher's mitt is just the right amount for one hand. It's too bad the chest protector and shinpads are so hot and at a distance so like corrugated cardboard. Otherwise, the team is elegance itself in its striped knee breeches and loose shirts, colored stockings and peaked caps. Except for brief moments of sliding, you can see them all in one eyeful, unlike the muddy hecatombs of football. To watch a football game is to be in prolonged neurotic doubt as to what you're seeing. It's more like an emergency happening at a distance than a game. I don't wonder the spectators take to drink. Who has ever seen a baseball fan drinking within the meaning of the act? He wants all his senses sharp and clear, his eyesight above all. He gulps down soda pop, which is a harmless way of replenishing his energy by the ingestion of sugar diluted in water and colored pink.

Happy the man in the bleachers. He is enjoying the spectacle that the gods on Olympus contrived only with difficulty when they sent Helen to Troy and picked their teams. And the gods missed the fun of doing this by catching a bat near the narrow end and measuring hand over hand for first pick. In Troy, New York, the game scheduled for 2 P.M. will break no bones, yet it will be a real fight between Southpaw Dick and Red Larsen. For those whom civilized play doesn't fully satisfy, there will be provided a scapegoat in a blue suit—the umpire, yell-proof and even-handed

as justice, which he demonstrates with outstretched arms when calling
"Safe!"

And the next day in the paper: learned comment, statistical summaries,
and the verbal imagery of meta-euphoric experts. In the face of so much
joy, one can only ask, Were you there when Dodger Joe parked the pellet
beyond the pale?

> Jacques Barzun, *God's Country and Mine,* 1954

The Gas-House Gang.

> Sobriquet of the St. Louis Cardinals in the 1930's

The Peerless Leader.

> Sobriquet of Frank Chance, from which Red Smith de-
> rived his "The Practically Peerless Leader" (Leo Durocher)

The Georgia Peach.

> Sobriquet of Ty Cobb

Me and Paul'll win two games apiece.

> Dizzy Dean, when asked how the St. Louis Cardinal pitch-
> ing staff could expect to defeat Detroit in the World Series
> of 1934. Dizzy and Paul Dean won the first, second, sixth
> and seventh games of the Series, thus won by the Cardinals,
> four games to three.

Shucks, if I'd known Paul was gonna pitch a no-hitter, I'd a pitched one
too.

> Dizzy Dean, after a double-header in the first game of
> which he had pitched a one-hitter, only to have his brother,
> Paul, pitch a no-hitter in the night-cap

The Yankee Clipper.

> Mel Allen, sobriquet of Joe DiMaggio

The Bums.

> Sobriquet of the Brooklyn Dodgers

Wait till next year!

> Perennial slogan of Brooklyn Dodger fans

Sittin' in the cat bird seat.

> American saying, popularized by Red Barber to mean the
> Dodgers were in an advantageous position, such as with two
> men on base and Dixie Walker up

The Giants is dead.

> CHUCK DRESSEN, 1951, when in midsummer the Giants
> appeared hopelessly behind his league-leading Dodgers. The
> Giants won the pennant from the Dodgers in the ninth in-
> ning of the third game of a three-game playoff series.

Bonehead.

> CHARLES DRYDEN, reviving an old word, applied it to Fred
> Merkle, New York Giant first baseman, who forgot to touch
> second base in a decisive game with the Chicago Cubs, thus
> letting them win the game. A riot ensued at the park, and
> the Cubs won the pennant by the margin of this game,
> played September 23, 1908. Merkle retired soon after, una-
> ble to bear the obloquy of being continuously referred to as
> "Bonehead" Merkle.

Nice guys finish last.

> LEO DUROCHER, when his character was criticized

The Iron Horse.

> Sobriquet of Lou Gehrig

On this day I consider myself the luckiest man on the face of the earth.
I might have been given a bad break—but I've got an awful lot to live
for.

> LOU GEHRIG, speech, Yankee Stadium, 1939. He died
> shortly thereafter, having known at the time that he suf-
> fered from an incurable disease.

Knowin' all about baseball is just about as profitable as bein' a good
whittler.

> KIN HUBBARD

The Old Meal Ticket.

> Sobriquet of Carl Hubbell

So, for an afternoon, I sit in pleasant surroundings, including the sun, and enjoy myself and my associates in the fraternity of fandom. As the game goes on I not only like it for what it is but I get to thinking of other games and other players, and I like that, too. Bobby Doerr goes back of second to rob Charlie Keller of a single to center, and I remember other great keystone sackers I have seen, Eddie Collins and Gehringer and Hornsby, and so on around the diamond and through the day. I like the sudden, sharp yell of the crowd when a batter catches hold of one with the tying run at first, and the electric tension that goes through a park when a runner and an outfielder's throw are staging a race for the plate. I like the peanut butcher's yapping chant up and down the aisles. I like being for a brief while in a good-natured place that is a self-sufficient little world of its own. This can probably be called escapism. All right, then, it is escapism.

If memory serves, seeing a ball game was not always so pastoral. In the stands, as on the field, things are more orderly than I seem to remember they were at that old West Side park in Chicago. And that is all right with me, now. I do not find Mr. Williams, of Boston, a villain when he busts one into the right-field stand. I find him a great ball player, and I suspect I enjoy the sight the more for the detachment with which I view it.

I suspect also, however, that no one ever recovers absolutely from the kind of early conditioning I had. Picking up the sports page in the morning, I can still feel something like a pang if the Cubs or the White Sox lost a ball game the day before. And if they both lost, I can even feel slightly depressed until about 10 A.M.

JOHN K. HUTCHENS, *New York Times,* July 14, 1946

Say it ain't so, Joe.

> A little boy who accosted Shoeless Joe Jackson on the street after the airing of the "Black Sox" scandal of 1920, and begged him to say that he and other White Sox players had not received money to "throw" the World Series of 1919

I should of stood in bed.

> JOE JACOBS, after leaving a sickbed to go to the 1935 World Series between Detroit and Chicago. He bet on Chicago; Detroit won; he made this comment on his return to New York.

Games played with the ball, and others of that nature, are too violent for the body, and stamp no character on the mind.

THOMAS JEFFERSON, letter to Peter Carr, August 19, 1785

The Big Train.

Sobriquet of Walter Johnson

You can't hit what you can't see.

Of Walter Johnson's fast ball

Hit 'em where they ain't.

WILLIE KEELER

Son, when you pitch a strike Mr. Hornsby will let you know it.

BILL KLEM, to a rookie pitcher who complained that the pitches Rogers Hornsby did not swing at were always called balls by Umpire Klem

Well, in New York's part o' the innin' Doyle cracked one and Ike run back a mile and a half and caught it with one hand. We was all sayin' what a whale of a play it was, but he had to apologize just the same as for gettin' struck out.

"That stand's so high," he says, "that a man don't never see a ball till it's right on top o' you."

"Didn't you see that one?" ast Cap.

"Not at first," says Ike; "not till it raised up above the roof o' the stand."

"Then why did you start back as soon as the ball was hit?" says Cap.

"I knowed by the sound that he'd got a good hold of it," says Ike.

"Yes," says Cap, "but how'd you know what direction to run in?"

"Doyle usually hits 'em that way, the way I run," says Ike.

"Why don't you play blindfolded?" says Carey.

"Might as well, with that big high stand to bother a man," says Ike. "If I could of saw the ball all the time I'd of got it in my hip pocket."

RING LARDNER, Alibi Ike

Carey went on to tell me what Ike had been pullin' out there. He'd dropped the first fly ball that was hit to him and told Carey his glove wasn't broke in good yet, and Carey says the glove could easy of been Kid Gleason's gran'father. He made a whale of a catch out o' the next one and Carey says "Nice work!" or somethin' like that, but Ike says he could have caught the ball with his back turned only he slipped when he started after it and, besides that, the air currents fooled him.

"I thought you done well to get to the ball," says Carey.

"I ought to been settin' under it," says Ike.

"What did you hit last year?" Carey ast him.

"I had malaria most of the season," says Ike. "I wound up with .356."

"Where would I have to go to get malaria?" says Carey, but Ike didn't wise up.

. . . "He's got the world beat," says Carey to Jack and I. "I've knew lots o' guys that had an alibi for every mistake they made; I've heard pitchers say that the ball slipped when somebody cracked one off'n 'em; I've heard infielders complain of a sore arm after heavin' one into the stand, and I've saw outfielders tooken sick with a dizzy spell when they've misjudged a fly ball. But this baby can't even go to bed without apologizin', and I bet he excuses himself to the razor when he gets ready to shave."

"And at that," says Jack, "he's goin' to make us a good man."

"Yes," says Carey, "unless rheumatism keeps his battin' average down to .400."

Ring Lardner, Ibid.

I'm not boastin' about my first experience with [Walter] Johnson, though. They can't never tell me he throws them balls with his arm. He's got a gun concealed about his person and he shoots 'em up there. I was leadin' off in Murphy's place and the game was a little delayed in startin', because I'd watched the big guy warm up and wasn't in no hurry to get to that plate. Before I left the bench Connie says:

"Don't try to take no healthy swing. Just meet 'em and you'll get along better."

So I tried to just meet the first one he throwed; but when I stuck out my bat Henry was throwin' the pill back to Johnson. Then I thought: Maybe if I start swingin' now at the second one I'll hit the third one. So I let the second one come over and the umps guessed it was another strike, though I'll bet a thousand bucks he couldn't see it no more'n I could.

While Johnson was still windin' up to pitch again I started to swing— and the big cuss crosses me with a slow one. I lunged at it twice and missed it both times, and the force o' my wallop throwed me clean back to the bench. The Ath-a-letics was all laughin' at me and I laughed too, because I was glad that much of it was over.

RING LARDNER, *Horeshoes*, 1926

Although he is a bad fielder he is also a very poor hitter.

RING LARDNER

A sensational event was changing from the brown suit to the gray the contents of his pockets. He was earnest about these objects. They were of eternal importance, like baseball or the Republican Party.

SINCLAIR LEWIS, *Babbitt*, 1922

Good field no hit.

ADOLPH LUQUE, telegram, reporting on a rookie prospect

Most males who don't care about big-league baseball conceal their indifference as carefully as they would conceal a laughable physical deficiency.

RUSSELL MALONEY

The Wild Hoss of the Osage.

Sobriquet of Pepper Martin

Big Six.

Sobriquet of Christy Mathewson

Say, hey!

WILLIE MAYS

All this comin' and goin'. Rookies flyin' up the road and old-timers flyin' down, and nobody in between but me an' old John Mize, standin' pat, watchin' 'em go by.

And I ain't even sure about ol' John. Maybe he's flyin' on, too. If he is, I can always watch 'em go by myself. Time ain't gonna mess with me!

LEROY "SATCHEL" PAIGE, *Collier's*, June 13, 1953

At the beginning of the World Series of 1947, I experienced a completely new emotion, when the National Anthem was played. This time, I thought, it is being played for me, as much as for anyone else. This is organized major league baseball, and I am standing here with all the others; and everything that takes place includes me.

JACKIE ROBINSON, *This I Believe*

The Sultan of Swat.

> Sobriquet of Babe Ruth

All I can tell 'em is I pick a good one and sock it. I get back to the dug-out and they ask me what it was I hit and I tell 'em I don't know except it looked good.

> GEORGE HERMAN ("BABE") RUTH

Are the Dodgers still in the league?

> BILL TERRY, 1934

The House That Ruth Built.

> Sobriquet of Yankee Stadium

The Bronx Bombers.

> Sobriquet of the New York Yankees

Murderers Row.

> Sobriquet of the 1927 New York Yankees batting order

BOXING

I'll bet th' hardest thing about prize fightin' is pickin' up yer teeth with a boxin' glove on.

> KIN HUBBARD

I fought once too often. But I'm glad that it was an American who beat me and that the championship stays in this country. Very truly yours, John L. Sullivan.

> JOHN L. SULLIVAN, spoken from the ring after the loss of his title to "Gentleman Jim" Corbett, September 7, 1892

Sharkey kept coming in like the surf.

> ANON., of the Jeffries-Sharkey fight, Coney Island, 1899

The bigger they are, the harder they fall.

> Attributed to ROBERT FITZSIMMONS, before his fight with Jeffries, a much larger man, San Francisco, July 25, 1902

He said he'd bring home the bacon, and the honey boy has gone and done it.

> "TINY" JOHNSON, mother of Jack Johnson, when he defeated Jeffries, July 4, 1910

Tell 'em to start counting ten over him, and he'll get up.

> WILSON MIZNER, on hearing that Stanley Ketchel, the great middleweight fighter, had been shot and killed

The Manassa Mauler.

> Sobriquet of Jack Dempsey

We wuz robbed!

> JOE JACOBS, after the fight between Max Schmeling and Jack Sharkey, June 21, 1932, when Sharkey had been awarded the decision and the heavyweight title. Jacobs, Schmeling's manager, shouted this protest into the radio microphone so that it was heard from coast to coast.

The Brown Bomber.

> Sobriquet of Joe Louis

He can run but he can't hide.

> JOE LOUIS, interview before second Louis-Conn fight referring to the reports that Conn was not going to stand up and be hit but attempt to fight at long range and thus gain a decision. It is said that Conn was terrified when he heard the phrase and was almost paralyzed with fear when he stepped into the ring. If Joe Louis said it, it would frighten anybody.

The story in Sunday's *News* was read by thousands of lovers of the manly art. It was well written and full of human interest. Its slight inaccuracies went unchallenged, though three readers, besides Wallie Adams and Midge Kelly, saw and recognized them. The three were Grace, Tommy Haley and Jerome Harris and the comments they made were not for publication.

Neither the Mrs. Kelly in Chicago nor the Mrs. Kelly in Milwaukee knew that there was such a paper as the New York *News*. And even if they had known of it and that it contained two columns of reading matter about Midge, neither mother nor wife could have bought it. For the *News* on Sunday is a nickel a copy.

Joe Morgan could have written more accurately, no doubt, if instead of Wallie Adams, he had interviewed Ellen Kelly and Connie Kelly and Emma Kelly and Grace and Jerome Harris and Tommy Haley and Hap Collins and two or three Milwaukee bartenders.

But a story built on their evidence would never have passed the sporting editor.

"Suppose you can prove it," that gentleman would have said. "It wouldn't get us anything but abuse to print it. The people don't want to see him knocked. He's champion."

RING LARDNER, Champion, closing lines

FOOTBALL

I do not see the relationship of these highly industrialized affairs on Saturday afternoons to higher learning in America.

ROBERT M. HUTCHINS, on football

Football season is the only time of year when girls whistle at men in sweaters.

ROBERT Q. LEWIS

The only people who are doing anything to "sell" education are the football players. They are doing noble work, especially when we consider how few samples they carry.

B. K. SANDWELL, New York Times, October 4, 1953

The football critic pretends to hate bad play, but he loves it. What he really hates is good play, for good play makes his services unnecessary. His long suit is disgust, and vulgar abuse is always trumps.

JOHN D. SHERIDAN

Outlined against a blue-gray October sky, the Four Horsemen rode again. In dramatic lore they are known as Famine, Pestilence, Destruction and Death. . . . Their real names are Stuhldreher, Miller, Crowley and Layden.

GRANTLAND RICE, report of Notre-Dame–Army football
game, 1924. The "Four Horsemen" made up the Notre-
Dame backfield.

The Galloping Ghost.

                                                    Sobriquet of Red Grange

The Seven Blocks of Granite.

                                    Sobriquet of the Fordham line, 1937–38

Mr. Inside and Mr. Outside.

              Sobriquets of Glenn Davis and Felix ("Doc") Blanchard,
              Army, 1942–44

                              OTHERS

Had it not been called sport it might have seemed like work.

                        HARRY LEON WILSON, *Ruggles of Red Gap*

Luther Motts, founder an' president o' the "Fit-at-Fifty Club," dropped
dead with his skates on.

                          KIN HUBBARD, *Abe Martin's Broadcast*

Nature-Fakers.

              THEODORE ROOSEVELT, *Everybody's Magazine*, Sept., 1907

Fishing is a delusion entirely surrounded by liars in old clothes.

                                                    DON MARQUIS

There are only two occasions when Americans respect privacy, especially
in Presidents. Those are prayer and fishing. So that some have taken to
fishing.

                  HERBERT HOOVER, "Let's Go Fishin'," *Collier's*, 1944

In the exclusive set (no diphtheria cases allowed) in which I travel, I am
known as a heel in the matter of parlor games. I will drink with them,
wrassle with them and, now and again, leer at the ladies, but when they
bring out the bundles of pencils and the pads of paper and start putting
down all the things they can think of beginning with "W," or enumerating
each other's bad qualities on a scale of 100 (no hard-feeling results, mind
you—just life-long enmity), I tiptoe noisily out of the room and say: "The
hell with you."

    For this reason, I am not usually included in any little games that may be planned in advance. If they foresee an evening of "Consequences" coming over them, they whisper "Get Benchley out of the house. Get him a horse to ride, or some beads to string—anything to get him out of the way." For, I forgot to tell you, not only am I a non-participant in parlor games, but I am a militant non-participant. I heckle from the sidelines. I throw stones and spit at the players. Hence the nickname: "Sweet Old Bob," or sometimes just the initials.

ROBERT BENCHLEY, *After 1903 What?*, "Ladies Wild"

There are few things that are so unpardonably neglected in our country as poker. The upper class knows very little about it. Now and then you find ambassadors who have a sort of general knowledge of the game, but the ignorance of the people is fearful. Why, I have known clergymen, good men, kind-hearted, liberal, sincere, and all that, who did not know the meaning of a "flush." It is enough to make one ashamed of one's species.

SAMUEL L. CLEMENS ("MARK TWAIN"), quoted by Johnson, *A Bibliography of Mark Twain*

Put up or shut up.

Popular saying believed to have originated from the game of poker

Handbook: a book maker whose operation bears the distinguishing feature that he makes his own line of prices. Now extinct.

Hard play, soft play: intelligent play, stupid play. Most gambling houses will operate on a low percentage against hard players, figuring soft players, under the same rules, to provide the profits.

Raking off the top of the pile: stealing, by an employee or manager of a gambling house, from the owners by keeping the books in such a way as to conceal the true profits. The phrase is now employed by Nevada operators to describe the process whereby the State's tax (which is levied only against profits) is minimized.

Mechanic: strictly, one who cheats at cards; now used loosely to describe any cheater.

Pigeon: a forged parimutuel ticket.

Pencil artist: one who creates pigeons.

If money: money wagered on an event on the condition that a previous bet must win. Thus one may bet $5 on a horse running in a race, with $10 to be invested on another animal *if* the first wins.

Morning (or overnight) line: in happier days a line of odds at which horses could be backed before the day's racing began; now, merely the "probable odds" at which the tote opens.

Daily trouble: the daily double.

Evener: one who plays "to stay even." The usual illustration is of the man who says: "I hope I break even today. My wife needs an operation."

Gilooly (or Gilhooley) bird: an arbitrarily chosen poker hand that beats everything. The classic story is of a stranger who wandered into a poker game, held four aces, had them beaten by an opponent who laid down the four of clubs, the six of diamonds, the eight of hearts, the ten of spades, and the jack of hearts, and claimed a "Gilooly bird." A sign on the wall behind the stranger was then pointed out reading "Gilooly bird beats anything." Later, when the stranger held the same hand and tried to play it for a winner, he was shown another sign reading: "Only One Gilooly Bird Per Evening."

Eagle bird: a winner on whom the book has taken no bets whatsoever, hence a "good" winner for the book.

Dutch book: a line of prices which, through carelessness on the book-maker's part, offers the player an opportunity to bet various sums on all contestants with a certainty of winning something; also called "minus book"; also "to dutch a book": the bet against such a line.

To make nine the hard way: to be caught cheating at dice. From a story, perhaps apocryphal, of a "mechanic" who, in switching dice, allowed three of them to fall to the table, making "nine" with three threes.

To bicycle: in quiniela betting, to make all possible combinations involving three contestants: as 1&2, 1&3, 2&3.

Bicyle, the: in low-ball, the lowest possible hand, usually 5-4-3-2-A, sometimes 6-4-3-2-A, by local rules.

DON M. MANKIEWICZ, *some gambling terms*

The sun don't always shine on the same little dog's tail.

> SAM SNEAD, after winning Master's Tournament, referring to Ben Hogan (whom Snead beat in a playoff in this tournament), 1954

When you have shot one bird flying you have shot all birds flying. They are all different and they fly in different ways but the sensation is the same and the last one is as good as the first.

> ERNEST HEMINGWAY, *Fathers and Sons*

Mr. Longtail.

> Sobriquet of Whirlaway

The Gray Champion.

> Sobriquet of Native Dancer

Big Red.

> Sobriquet of Man o' War

Old Bones.

> Sobriquet of Exterminator

1. Avoid fried meats which angry up the blood.
2. If your stomach disputes you, lie down and pacify it with cool thoughts.
3. Keep the juices flowing by jangling around gently as you move.
4. Go very light on the vices, such as carrying on in society. The social ramble ain't restful.
5. Avoid running at all times.
6. Don't look back. Something might be gaining on you.

> LEROY "SATCHEL" PAIGE, "How to Keep Young," *Collier's,* June 13, 1953

Skidoodle is a game I invented some years ago to exercise without doin' myself permanent harm. I throw the ball on one bounce to another man, he bounces it back at me. We jangle around. Nobody falls down exhausted.

> LEROY "SATCHEL" PAIGE, *Ibid.*

Any man who has to ask about the annual upkeep of a yacht can't afford one.

> J. P. MORGAN

You can do business with anyone, but you can only sail a boat with a gentleman.

> J. P. MORGAN, at Bar Harbor

To possibly the world's worst yacht builder, but absolutely the world's most cheerful loser.

> WILL ROGERS, suggested inscription for a cup to be bought
> by American citizens and presented to Sir Thomas Lipton
> as compensation for his five unsuccessful attempts to take
> the America's cup

INFORMATION AND COMMUNICATION

•

THE PRESS

The basis of our governments being the opinion of the people, the very first object should be to keep that right; and were it left to me to decide whether we should have a government without newspapers, or newspapers without a government, I should not hesitate a moment to prefer the latter. But I should mean that every man should receive those papers, and be capable of reading them.

> THOMAS JEFFERSON, letter to Colonel Edward Carrington,
> Paris, January 16, 1787

Blame is safer than praise. I hate to be defended in a newspaper.

> RALPH WALDO EMERSON, *Essays: First Series,* "Compensation"

We live under a government of men and morning newspapers.

> WENDELL PHILLIPS

It is a newspaper's duty to print the news, and raise hell.

> WILBUR F. STOREY, Statement of Aims of the Chicago
> *Times,* which Storey edited, 1861

Read not the Times. Read the Eternities.

> HENRY DAVID THOREAU, "Life Without Principle," *Atlantic
> Monthly,* 1863

Blessed are they who never read a newspaper, for they shall see Nature, and, through her, God.

HENRY DAVID THOREAU, *Essays and Other Writings*

If words were invented to conceal thought, newspapers are a great improvement on a bad invention.

HENRY DAVID THOREAU

When the world gets to be so intelligent that no man shall be more intelligent than any other man, and no man shall be swayed by his passions and interests, then there will be no need of editorial expressions of opinion, and editorial arguments and appeals will lose their power.

EDWIN LAWRENCE GODKIN, *Nation,* 1868

The pressure of public opinion is like the pressure of the atmosphere; you can't see it—but, all the same, it is sixteen pounds to the square inch.

JAMES RUSSELL LOWELL, interview with Julian Hawthorne

Remember, son, many a good story has been ruined by over-verification.

JAMES GORDON BENNETT

A convention of colored editors have gravely resolved never to mention in their papers the name of the aspiring youth who shot President Garfield. Things have come to a pretty pass when a man can't keep his name out of the newspapers without shooting the chief magistrate of his beloved country.

AMROSE BIERCE

Writing good editorials is chiefly telling the people what they think, not what you think.

ARTHUR BRISBANE

Now as to sensationalism, the people must have it—just as the Chinese take opium, the ignorant man takes whiskey, and the higher class person takes a philosophical discussion.

ARTHUR BRISBANE

What the good Lord lets happen I am not ashamed to print in my paper.

CHARLES A. DANA, of the New York *Sun*

When a dog bites a man that is not news, but when a man bites a dog that is news.

CHARLES A. DANA, What Is News?

If you say a true and important thing once, in the most striking way, people read it, and say to themselves, "That is very likely so," and forget it. If you keep on saying it, over and over again, even with less felicity of expression, you'll hammer it into their heads so firmly that they'll say, "It *is* so"; and they'll remember forever it is so.

CHARLES A. DANA, often in the eighties and nineties

Journalism consists in buying white paper at two cents a pound and selling it at ten cents a pound.

CHARLES A. DANA

The Yellow Kid.

> R. F. OUTCAULT, a colored "comic" drawn for the New York *World* and taken over by the New York *Journal*, c. 1892. The title gave rise to the term "yellow journalism."

The Chief suggests . . .

> WILLIAM RANDOLPH HEARST. His memos always started with these words.

An editor—a person employed on a newspaper, whose business it is to separate the wheat from the chaff, and to see that the chaff is printed.

ELBERT HUBBARD

I know that my retirement will make no difference in its cardinal principles; that it will always fight for progress and reform, never tolerate injustice or corruption, always fight demagogues of all parties, never belong to any party, always oppose privileged classes and public plunderers, never lack sympathy with the poor, always remain devoted to the public welfare; never be satisfied with merely printing news; always be drastically independent; never be afraid to attack wrong, whether by predatory plutocracy or predatory poverty.

> JOSEPH PULITZER, statement on his retirement from the editorship of the St. Louis *Post-Dispatch*, October 16, 1890. Every day since, these words have appeared on the newspaper's masthead.

Always tell the truth, always take the humane and moral side, always remember that right feeling is the vital spark of strong writing, and that publicity, *publicity*, PUBLICITY is the greatest moral factor and force in our public life.

> JOSEPH PULITZER, advice to his editors on the New York *World*, December 29, 1895

It will be my earnest aim that the *New York Times* give the news, all the news, in concise and attractive form, in language that is permissible in good society, and give it early, if not earlier, than it can be learned through any other medium. To give the news impartially, without fear or favor, regardless of party, sect, or interest involved; to make the columns of the *New York Times* a forum for the consideration of all public questions of public importance, and, to that end, to invite intelligent discussion from all shades of opinion.

> ADOLPH S. OCHS, salutatory on assuming control of the *New York Times,* August 18, 1896

If a tabloid prints that sort of thing, it's smut; but when the *New York Times* prints it, it's a sociological study.

> ADOLPH S. OCHS, when asked by Lester Markel how the *Times* could have covered a lovers' lane murder so completely

Always ask yourself, is it Posty?

> GEORGE HORACE LORIMER, editor of the *Saturday Evening Post;* advice to his writers. He read every line of every issue to make sure.

The *faculty of attention* has utterly vanished from the general anglo-saxon mind, extinguished at its source by the big blatant *Bayadère* of Journalism, of the newspaper and the *picture* (above all) magazine; who keeps screaming "Look at *me, I* am the thing, and I only, the thing that will keep you in relation with me *all the time* without your having to attend *one minute* of the time."

> HENRY JAMES, letter to W. D. Howells, 1902

The public be informed.

> IVY LEDBETTER LEE, 1906

There are only two forces that can carry light to all corners of the globe
—the sun in the heavens and the Associated Press.

> SAMUEL L. CLEMENS ("MARK TWAIN"), speech, New
> York, September 19, 1906

Newspapers are read at the breakfast and dinner tables. God's great gift
to man is appetite. Put nothing in the paper that will destroy it.

> WILLIAM ROCKHILL NELSON, of the Kansas City *Star*

All I know is what I see in the papers.

> WILL ROGERS

The editor who hollers for more population without regard to the kind of
population is a fool who doesn't know his own business.

> WILLIAM ALLEN WHITE, Emporia *Gazette,* Dec. 4, 1924

The tendency in journalism is to write from the top of your mind. You
have to write so much that you come, after a while, absolutely to dread
being seized by a deep and genuine emotion which will use up all your
energies and leave you limp as a wet dishrag before it is through with you.

> DON MARQUIS, *Yale Review,* 1926

The press is overstepping in every direction the obvious bounds of propriety and decency. Gossip is no longer the resource of the idle and of the
vicious, but has become a trade, which is pursued with industry as well as
effrontery. To satisfy a prurient taste the details of sexual relations are
spread broadcast in the columns of the daily papers. To occupy the indolent, column upon column is filled with idle gossip, which can only be
procured by intrusion upon the domestic circle. The intensity and complexity of life, attendant upon advancing civilization, have rendered necessary some retreat from the world, and man, under the refining influence
of culture, has become more sensitive to publicity, so that solitude and
privacy have become more essential to the individual; but modern invention and enterprise have, through invasions upon his privacy, subjected
him to mental pain and distress, far greater than could be inflicted by
mere bodily injury. Nor is the harm wrought by such invasions confined
to the suffering of those who may be made the subjects of journalistic or
other enterprises. Each crop of unseemly gossip, thus harvested, becomes
the seed of more, and in direct proportion to its circulation, results in a
lowering of social standards and of morality. Even gossip apparently

harmless, when widely and persistently circulated, is potent for evil. It both belittles and perverts. It belittles by inverting the relative importance of things, thus dwarfing the thoughts and aspirations of a people. When personal gossip attains the dignity of print, and crowds the space available for matters of real interest to the community, what wonder that the ignorant and thoughtless mistake its relative importance. Easy of comprehension, appealing to that weaker side of human nature which is never wholly cast down by the misfortunes and frailties of our neighbors, no one can be surprised that it usurps the place of interest in brains capable of other things. Triviality destroys at once robustness of thought and delicacy of feeling. No enthusiasm can flourish, no generous impulse can survive under its blighting influence.

LOUIS D. BRANDEIS, *Words of Justice Brandeis,* 1953

The day has clearly gone forever of societies small enough for their members to have personal acquaintance with one another, and to find their station through the appraisal of those who have any first-hand knowledge of them. Publicity is an evil substitute, and the art of publicity is a black art; but it has come to stay, every year adds to its potency and to the finality of its judgments. The hand that rules the press, the radio, the screen, and the far-spread magazine rules the country; whether we like it or not, we must learn to accept it. And yet it is the power of reiterated suggestion and consecrated platitude that at this moment has brought our entire civilization to imminent peril of destruction. The individual is as helpless against it as the child is helpless against the formulas with which he is indoctrinated. Not only is it possible by these means to shape his tastes, his feelings, his desires, and his hopes; but it is possible to convert him into a fanatical zealot, ready to torture and destroy and to suffer mutilation and death for an obscene faith, baseless in fact, and morally monstrous. This, the vastest conflict with which mankind has ever been faced, whose outcome still remains undecided, in the end turns upon whether the individual can survive; upon whether the ultimate value shall be this wistful, cloudy, errant You or I, or that Great Beast, Leviathan, that phantom conjured up as an *ignis fatuus* in our darkness and a scapegoat for our futility.

LEARNED HAND

The relation of American freedom and the press is singular. The word is precisely applicable, for this relation is unique, curious, and somewhat enigmatic, all of which are elements of singularity. It is unique because it has not been established in any other great nation. It is curious because it was established here informally, not to say inadvertently. It is enigmatic because it has defied exact definition for more than two hundred years.

GERALD W. JOHNSON, *American Freedom and the Press*

It is a common assertion that suppression of a free press is the first act of every modern dictator, but the assertion is inaccurate. Gagging the press is merely a reflection of the first act of a dictator, which is to abolish the freedom of the people, with or without their consent.

So it is a dubious assertion when one calls freedom of the press the bulwark of our liberty. It is closer to truth to say that freedom of the press is the measure of our liberty. If "the general spirit of the people" is low, nothing can save freedom of the press; but when the spirit is high, no politician can lay hands upon it.

GERALD W. JOHNSON, *Ibid.*

I once had a professor who, in reaction to the old saw that a photograph never lies, said that a photograph always lies. I did not at the time understand what he meant, rather uncharitably dismissing the remark as that of a pedant trying to impress his class with some brand of iconoclasm. What he may have had in mind is now clear to me. Every phenomenon and experience in life has a nearly infinite number of aspects. A man becomes aware of these to the extent that the native acuity and breadth of his senses and perceptual faculties will permit. The camera has but two senses, those of line and light; only these can be recorded in any picture, which, accordingly, must be incomplete and, to this degree, inaccurate.

In this connection one might despair the trend in modern life to depict nearly everything photographically, as in the illustrated newspapers, the mammoth picture weeklies and monthlies, even in the home snapshot album. By getting so much of their information from photographs these days, men have come to lean on a few oversimplified and easily comprehended dimensions for their day-to-day enlightenment. Pictures, whether on neolithic cave walls, in the Louvre, on a movie or television screen or in the pages of a magazine or book, have always been attractive because of their ease of comprehension and the amount of precise information apparently there. But even when sound and movement are added, any picture constitutes only a few-dimensional aspect of a multi-dimensional phenomenon. In recent years the printing press and the various visual-projection techniques have made pictures a dominant institution for mass communication and learning. One wonders if this tendency to feed on something that "always lies" may not be one of the sins of our times.

PAUL VAHL, *Coro-Coro,* 1954

A man from the *Post,* a man from the *Globe,* and a gentleman from the *Boston Evening Transcript.*

> Attributed to a Beacon Street butler announcing several newspaper reporters

To Injure No Man But to Bless All Mankind.

> Motto of *Christian Science Monitor,* Boston

Independent in All Things, Neutral in Nothing.

> Motto of San Francisco *Chronicle*

We are against people who push other people around just for the fun of it.

> RALPH INGERSOLL, interview, April, 1940; motto of *PM*

Editor . . . The People; Associate Editor . . . Eugene Talmadge.

> Masthead of Hopeville (Georgia) *Statesman*

Light For All.

> Motto of the Baltimore *Sun,* May 17, 1837

All the News That's Fit to Print.

> ADOLPH S. OCHS, motto of *The New York Times,* 1896

Not for the Old Lady in Dubuque.

> Motto of *New Yorker* magazine, 1920's

EDUCATION

The greatest glory of a freeborn people is to transmit that freedom to their children.

> WILLIAM HARVARD

It is . . . a small college, and yet there are those who love it.

> DANIEL WEBSTER, Dartmouth College case, 1819

If this boy passes the examinations he will be admitted; and if the white students choose to withdraw, all the income of the college will be devoted to his education.

> EDWARD EVERETT, while President of Harvard; reply to a protest against the admittance of a Negro student, 1848

And, as for me, if, by any possibility, there be any as yet undiscovered prime thing in me; if I shall ever deserve any real repute in that small but high hushed world which I might not be unreasonably ambitious of; if hereafter I shall do anything that, upon the whole, a man might rather have done than to have left undone; if, at my death, my executors, or more properly my creditors, find any precious MSS. in my desk, then here I prospectively ascribe all the honor and the glory to whaling; for a whale-ship was my Yale College and my Harvard.

> HERMAN MELVILLE, *Moby Dick*, XXIV

Schoolhouses are the republican line of fortifications.

> HORACE MANN

I am not willing that this discussion should close without mention of the value of a true teacher. Give me a log hut, with only a simple bench, Mark Hopkins on one end and I on the other, and you may have all the buildings, apparatus and libraries without him.

> JAMES A. GARFIELD, address to Williams College Alumni, New York, December 28, 1871; quoted by Hinsdale, *President Garfield and Education,* 1882

The best claim that a college education can possibly make on your respect, the best thing it can aspire to accomplish for you, is this: that it should *help you to know a good man when you see him.*

> WILLIAM JAMES, *Memories and Studies,* "The Social Value of the College-Bred," 1911

Education was free. That subject my father had written about repeatedly, as comprising his chief hope for us children, the essence of American opportunity, the treasure that no thief could touch, not even misfortune or poverty. It was the one thing that he was able to promise us when he sent for us; surer, safer than bread or shelter. On our second day I was thrilled with the realization of what this freedom of education meant. A little girl from across the alley came and offered to conduct us to school. My father was out, but we five between us had a few words of English by this time.

We knew the word school. We understood. This child, who had never seen us till yesterday, who could not pronounce our names, who was not much better dressed than we, was able to offer us the freedom of the schools of Boston! No application made, no questions asked, no examinations, rulings, exclusions; no machinations, no fees. The doors stood open for every one of us. The smallest child could show us the way.

This incident impressed me more than anything I had heard in advance of the freedom of education in America. It was a concrete proof—almost the thing itself. One had to experience it to understand it.

MARY ANTIN, *The Promised Land,* 1912

I never got a mark higher than 75 per cent in my life; and I have a strong prejudice against any boy who can get such marks. It means low ambitions. An endeavor to please the elders is at the bottom of high marks and of mediocre careers.

JOHN J. CHAPMAN, letter to S. S. Drury, May 18, 1914

The use of a university is to make young gentlemen as unlike their fathers as possible.

WOODROW WILSON, 1914

Getting education is like getting measles; you have to go where measles is.

ABRAHAM FLEXNER, to Albert Jay Nock

Nations . . . borrow billions for war; no nation has ever borrowed largely for education. Probably no nation is rich enough to pay for both war and civilization. We must make our choice; we cannot have both.

ABRAHAM FLEXNER, *Universities*

The Common School Is the Greatest Discovery Ever Made by Man.

ABRAHAM FLEXNER, inscription in Hall of Fame

The old Fifth Reader of 1844 we never used in our school. My brother's copy was a wonderful mine for me. The front cover was gone, and a part of the Rhetorician's Guide, which told us when to let our voices fall, when they should rise, and when the circumflex was required. I never regretted the loss. But the text consisted of some hundreds of pages of closely printed selections made by Alexander McGuffey with all the family judgment and taste. There was Pope with "Hector's Attack on the Grecian Walls." . . . There was "How the Water Comes Down at Lodore."

There was oratory—Pitt, Burke, Fox, Barré, Otis. Adams, Webster, Hayne. I had the volume all to myself. There were months when it was my only resource in my favorite dissipation of reading.

A small ration, these McGuffey Readers, for an omnivorous mind, but by no means a negligible one. I did not use them with any intelligence. I simply enjoyed them. I found a tune to which I could sing Browning's "How They Brought the Good News from Ghent to Aix" and sang it at the top of my voice as I followed my cows or the plow or harrow. I shouted "Ivry" to the vastnesses of the prairie. I deepened my boyish voice to orotund on "Now godlike Hector and his troops descend" and "They tug, they sweat, but neither gain nor yield, One foot, one inch, of the contested field!"

And somehow I was inoculated with a little of the virus of good literature. I gained no knowledge that it was anything of the sort. I got not the slightest glimpse into the world of letters as a world. Nobody ever said a word to me about that. I read nothing about it for years and years afterward. But when I did come to read the English classics, I felt as one who meets in after years a charming person with whom he has had a chance encounter on the train. I had already met the gentleman.

HERBERT QUICK, *One Man's Life, An Autobiography*, 1925

Some few years ago I was looking about the school supply stores in the city, trying to find desks and chairs which seemed thoroughly suitable . . . to the needs of the children. . . . Finally one dealer . . . made this remark: "I am afraid we have not what you want. You want something at which the children may work; these are all for listening."

That tells the story of traditional education. It is all made "for listening."

JOHN DEWEY, *School and Society*

The aim of education should be to teach the child to think, not what to think.

JOHN DEWEY

We learn to do by doing.

JOHN DEWEY

You can always tell a Harvard man, but you can't tell him much.

Attributed to JAMES BARNES

The worst calamity that ever befell American education was Eliot's refusal of the presidency of a textile manufacturing company.

> ALBERT JAY NOCK, of Charles W. Eliot, President of Harvard and champion of the elective system in education, *A Journal of These Days,* 1934

Don't sell your books and keep your diplomas. Sell your diplomas, if you can get anyone to buy them, and keep your books.

> WALTER B. PITKIN, "Commencement Day Address"

The heart of the problem of a general education is the continuance of the liberal and humane tradition. Neither the mere acquisition of information nor the development of special skills and talents can give the broad basis of understanding which is essential if our civilization is to be preserved.

> JAMES BRYANT CONANT, *General Education in a Free Society,* "Introduction"

The primary concern of American education today is not the development of the appreciation of the "good life" in young gentlemen born to the purple. Our purpose is to cultivate in the largest number of our future citizens an appreciation both of the responsibilities and the benefits which come to them because they are American and free.

> JAMES BRYANT CONANT, *Ibid.*

The problem we face in education is how to produce informed individuals capable of leadership; how to produce people who can think independently, and whose thinking is based on sound knowledge. Students cannot be regarded as mere receptacles for information.

> ROBERT M. HUTCHINS

Part of the American myth is that people who are handed the skin of a dead sheep at graduation time think that it will keep their minds alive forever.

> JOHN MASON BROWN

Many years ago, like you, I sat in the halls of Harvard and brought out of them whatever I did bring out. One man carries away one thing; another, another; some, perhaps, nothing. For myself I learned and took away . . . a creed which has endured and whose conviction has grown upon me as the years have passed. You were not taught it in words; you gathered it unwittingly from uncorrupted and incorruptible masters. It was in the air; you did not affirm or proclaim it; you would have felt ashamed to demonstrate the obvious. You came to know that you could hold no certain title to beliefs that you had not won; and indeed you did not win many. But that did not so much matter, for you had come into possession of a touchstone; you had learned how to judge a good title; and, although tomorrow might turn up a flaw in it, you believed that you could detect the flaw. And chiefly and best of all, you were in the company of those who thought that the noblest of man's works was the pursuit of truth; who valued the goal so highly that they were never quite convinced that the goal they had reached was the goal they were after; who believed that man's highest courage was to bet his all on what was no more than the best guess he could make; who asked no warranties and distrusted all such; who faced the puzzle of life without any kit of ready-made answers, yet trusting that, if they persevered long enough, they would find—in the words of John Dewey—that they might safely "lean back on things."

LEARNED HAND, at Harvard Club Annual Dinner, 1952

Don't join the book burners. Don't think you're going to conceal faults by concealing evidence that they ever existed. Don't be afraid to go in your library and read every book, as long as any document does not offend our own ideas of decency. That should be the only censorship.

How will we defeat communism unless we know what it is, what it teaches, and why does it have such an appeal for men, why are so many people swearing allegiance to it? It's almost a religion, albeit one of the nether religions.

And we have got to fight it with something better, not try to conceal the thinking of our own people. They are part of America. And even if they think ideas that are contrary to ours, their right to say them, their right to record them, and their right to have them at places where they're accessible to others is unquestioned, or it's not America.

DWIGHT D. EISENHOWER, remarks, Dartmouth College Commencement, June 14, 1953

Our task is to keep American life reasonable. This is more than any two institutions—or, sometimes I think, all of us together—can do. We shall need all the encouragement we can get.

NATHAN M. PUSEY, speech at Yale, November 21, 1953

We come then to the question presented: Does segregation of children in

public schools solely on the basis of race, even though the physical facilities and other "tangible" factors may be equal, deprive the children of the
minority group of equal educational opportunities? We believe that it
does.

> Unanimous decision of the Supreme Court banning racial
> segregation in public schools, May 17, 1954

We conclude that in the field of public education the doctrine of "separate
but equal" has no place. Separate educational facilities are inherently unequal.

> *Ibid.*

Man's right to knowledge and the free use thereof.

> Motto of Columbia University's Bicentennial, 1954

Do you need a liberal education? I say that it is unpatriotic not to read
great books. . . . The democratic enterprise is emperiled if any one of
us says, "I do not have to try to think for myself, or make the most of
myself, or become a citizen of the world republic of learning." The death
of democracy is not likely to be an assassination from ambush. It will be
a slow extinction from apathy, indifference, and undernourishment.

> ROBERT M. HUTCHINS, *Great Books,* 1954

I must reiterate that you can set no store by your education in childhood
and youth, no matter how good it was. Childhood and youth are no time
to get an education. They are the time to get ready to get an education.
The most that we can hope for from these uninteresting and chaotic periods of life is that during them we shall be set on the right path, the path
of realizing our human possibilities through intellectual effort and aesthetic appreciation. The great issues, now issues of life and death for civilization, call for mature minds.

> ROBERT M. HUTCHINS, *Ibid.*

Don't let your studies interfere with your college education.

> Unofficial motto of American college students

It is a tradition here not to walk on the grass. This tradition goes into
effect at noon today.

> Sign reported on a Midwestern college campus

THE INTELLECTUAL CLIMATE

Numerous local causes, such as a new country, new associations of people, new combinations of ideas in arts and sciences, and some intercourse with tribes wholly unknown in Europe, will introduce new words into the American tongue. These causes will produce, in a course of time, a language in North America as different from the future language of England as the modern Dutch, Danish and Swedish are from the German, or from one another.

NOAH WEBSTER, *Dissertations on the English Language*

In democracies writers will be more afraid of the people than for them.

FISHER AMES, *Essay on American Literature,* 1804–06

The new circumstances under which we are placed call for new words, new phrases, and for the transfer of old words to new objects. An American dialect will therefore be formed.

THOMAS JEFFERSON, letter to John Waldo, 1813

There are no annals for the historian; no follies (beyond the most vulgar and commonplace) for the satirist; no manners for the dramatist; no obscure fictions for the writer of romance; no gross and hardy offences against decorum for the moralist; nor any of the rich artificial auxiliaries of poetry. . . . I have never seen a nation so much alike in my life, as the people of the United States, and what is more, they are not only like each other, but they are remarkably like that which common sense tells them they ought to resemble. No doubt, traits of character that are a little peculiar, without, however, being either very poetical, or very rich, are to be found in remote districts; but they are rare, and not always happy exceptions. . . . There is no costume for the peasant, (there is scarcely a peasant at all,) no wig for the judge, no baton for the general, no diadem for the chief magistrate.

JAMES FENIMORE COOPER, *Notions of the Americans, Picked Up by a Traveling Bachelor,* 1828

It does not follow because many books are written by persons born in America that there exists an American literature. Books which imitate or represent the thoughts and life of Europe do not constitute an American literature. Before such can exist, an original idea must animate this nation and fresh currents of life must call into life fresh thoughts along its shores.

MARGARET FULLER, New York *Tribune*, 1833

Is it not the chief disgrace in the world, not to be an unit; not to be reckoned one character; not to yield that peculiar fruit which each man was created to bear, but to be reckoned in the gross, in the hundred, or the thousand, of the party, the section, to which we belong; and our opinion predicted geographically, as the north, or the south? Not so, brothers and friends—please God, ours shall not be so. We will walk on our own feet; we will work with our own hands; we will speak our own minds. The study of letters shall be no longer a name for pity, for doubt, and for sensual indulgence. The dread of man and the love of man shall be a wall of defence and a wreath of joy around all. A nation of men will for the first time exist, because each believes himself inspired by the Divine Soul which also inspires all men.

RALPH WALDO EMERSON, *The American Scholar*. This, the Phi Beta Kappa address at Harvard, 1837, was termed by O. W. Holmes "the declaration of American intellectual independence."

I ask not for the great, the remote, the romantic; what is doing in Italy or Arabia. I embrace the common. . . . The meal in the firkin; the milk in the pan; the ballad in the street; the news of the boat; the form and the gait of the body . . .

RALPH WALDO EMERSON, *Ibid.*

The common faults of American language are an ambition of effect, a want of simplicity, and a turgid abuse of terms.

JAMES FENIMORE COOPER, *The American Democrat*, 1838

In order more effectually to promote the great purposes of human culture; to establish the external relations of life on a basis of wisdom and purity; to apply the principles of justice and love to our social organization in accordance with the laws of Divine Providence; to substitute a system of brotherly coöperation for one of selfish competition; to secure to our children and those who may be entrusted to our care, the benefits of the highest physical, intellectual and moral education, which in the progress of knowledge the resources at our command will permit; to institute an attractive, efficient, and productive system of industry; to prevent the exercise of worldly anxiety, by the competent supply of our necessary wants; to diminish the desire of excessive accumulation, by making the acquisition of individual property subservient to upright and disinterested uses; to guarantee to each other forever the means of physical support, and of spiritual progress; and thus to impart a greater freedom, simplicity, truthfulness, refinement, and moral dignity, to our mode of life;—we the undersigned do unite in a voluntary Association . . .

> CHARLES A. DANA, NATHANIEL HAWTHORNE, *et al.*, Constitution of Brook Farm Association, 1841

No author, without a trial, can conceive of the difficulty of writing a romance about a country where there is no shadow, no antiquity, no mystery, no picturesque and gloomy wrong, nor anything but a commonplace prosperity, in broad and simple daylight, as is happily the case with my dear land. It will be very long, I trust, before romance-writers may find congenial and easily handled themes, either in the annals of our stalwart republic, or in any characteristic and probable events of our individual lives.

> NATHANIEL HAWTHORNE, *The Marble Faun,* "Preface"

Oh, that we could have ivy in America! What is there to beautify us, when our time of ruin comes?

> NATHANIEL HAWTHORNE, *Notebook,* March, 1854 (while in England)

The American bards shall be mark'd for generosity and affection, and for encouraging competitors. They shall be Kosmos, without monopoly or secrecy, glad to pass anything to anyone—hungry for equals night and day. They shall not be careful of riches and privilege—they shall be riches and privilege—they shall perceive who the most affluent man is. The most affluent man is he that confronts all the shows he sees by equivalents out of the stronger wealth of himself. The American bard shall delineate no class of persons, nor one or two out of the strata of interests, nor love most nor truth most, nor the soul most, nor the body most—and not be for the Eastern states more than the Western, or the Northern states more than the Southern.

> WALT WHITMAN, *Leaves of Grass,* "Preface" to first edition

I hail with joy the oceanic, variegated, intense practical energy, the demand for facts, even the business materialism of the current age, our

States. But wo to the age or land in which these things, movements, stopping at themselves, do not tend to ideas. As fuel to flame, and flame to the heavens, so must wealth, science, materialism—even this democracy of which we make so much—unerringly feed the highest mind, the soul. Infinitude the flight: fathomless the mystery. Man, so diminutive, dilates beyond the sensible universe, competes with, outcopes space and time, meditating even one great idea. Thus, and thus only, does a human being, his spirit, ascend above, and justify, objective Nature, which, probably nothing in itself, is incredibly and divinely serviceable, indispensable, real, here. And as the purport of objective Nature is doubtless folded, hidden, somewhere here—as somewhere here is what this globe and its manifold forms, and the light of day, and night's darkness, and life itself, with all its experiences, are for—it is here the great literature, especially verse, must get its inspiration and throbbing blood. Then may we attain to a poetry worthy the immortal soul of man, and which, while absorbing materials, and, in their own sense, the shows of Nature, will, above all, have, both directly and indirectly, a freeing, fluidizing, expanding, religious character, exulting with science, fructifying the moral elements, and stimulating aspirations, and meditations on the unknown.

WALT WHITMAN, *Democratic Vistas*

We are Americans born—*il faut en prendre son parti*. I look upon it as a great blessing; and I think that to be an American is an excellent preparation for culture. We have exquisite qualities as a race, and it seems to me that we are ahead of the European races in the fact that more than either of them we can deal freely with forms of civilization not our own, can pick and choose and assimilate and in short . . . claim our property wherever we find it.

HENRY JAMES, letter to Perry, 1867

One of those damn literary fellers.

SIMON CAMERON, speech in the Senate, March 7, 1876, referring to Richard Henry Dana, who had been nominated by Grant as Ambassador to Great Britain. Cameron succeeded in defeating the nomination.

But our author must accept the awkward as well as the graceful side of his fame; for he has the advantage of pointing a valuable moral. This moral is that the flower of art blooms only where the soil is deep, that it takes a great deal of history to produce a little literature, that it needs a complex social machinery to set a writer in motion.

HENRY JAMES, Hawthorne, 1879

The negative side of the spectacle on which Hawthorne looked out, in his contemplative saunterings and reveries, might, indeed, with a little ingenuity, be made almost ludicrous; one might enumerate the items of high civilization, as it exists in other countries, which are absent from the texture of American life, until it should become a wonder to know what was left. No State, in the European sense of the word, and indeed barely a specific national name. No sovereign, no court, no personal loyalty, no aristocracy, no church, no clergy, no army, no diplomatic service, no country gentlemen, no palaces, no castles, nor manors, nor old country houses, nor parsonages, nor thatched cottages, nor ivied ruins; no cathedrals, nor abbeys, nor little Norman churches; no great universities nor public schools—no Oxford, nor Eton, nor Harrow; no literature, no novels, no museums, no pictures, no political society, no sporting class— no Epsom nor Ascot! Some such list as that might be drawn up of the absent things in American life. . . . The natural remark, in the almost lurid light of such an indictment, would be that if these things are left out, everything is left out. The American knows that a good deal remains; what it is that remains—that is his secret, his joke, as one may say. . . .

HENRY JAMES, Ibid.

If American life is on the whole, as I make no doubt whatever, more innocent than that of any other country, nowhere is the fact more patent than in Mr. Howells' novels, which exhibit so constant a study of the actual and so small a perception of evil.

HENRY JAMES, William Dean Howells

The Englishmen I have met not only kill, but bury in unfathomable depths, the Americans I have met. A set of people less framed to provoke national self-complacency than the latter it would be hard to imagine. There is but one word to use in regard to them—vulgar, vulgar, vulgar. Their ignorance—their stingy, defiant, grudging attitude towards everything European—their perpetual reference of all things to some American standard or precedent which exists only in their own unscrupulous windbags—and then our unhappy poverty of voice, of speech, and of physiognomy—these things glare at you hideously. . . . On the other hand, we seem a people of character, we seem to have energy, capacity and intellectual stuff in ample measure. What I have pointed at as our vices are the elements of modern man with *culture* quite left out. It's the absolute and incredible lack of *culture* that strikes you in common travelling Americans.

> HENRY JAMES, letter to William James

Concluding with two items for the imaginative genius of the West, when it worthily rises—First, what Herder taught the young Goethe, that really great poetry is always (like the Homeric or Biblical canticles) the result of a national spirit, and not the privilege of a polish'd and select few; Second, that the strongest and sweetest songs yet remain to be sung.

> WALT WHITMAN, "A Backward Glance O'er Travel'd Roads." These were the last words of his last edition of *Leaves of Grass,* 1892.

I guess the English hav more wit, and the Amerikans more humour. We havn't had time yet to bile down our humour and get the wit out ov it.

> HENRY WHEELER SHAW ("JOSH BILLINGS")

When people see a banker taking a glass of beer in a cafe, they say, "There is Smith." When they behold a writer taking a glass of beer, they say, "Send for the police!"

> STEPHEN CRANE, 1896

This will never be a civilized country until we expend more money for books than we do for chewing-gum.

> ELBERT HUBBARD, *The Philistine*

The humorous story is American, the comic story is English, the witty story is French. The humorous story depends for its effect upon the *manner* of telling; the comic story and the witty story upon the matter. The humorous story is told gravely; the teller does his best to conceal the fact that he even dimly suspects that there is anything funny about it. The humorous story is strictly a work of art, high and delicate art, and only an artist can tell it; but no art is necessary in telling the comic and witty story, anybody can do it.

> SAMUEL L. CLEMENS ("MARK TWAIN"), *How to Tell a Story*

To string incongruities and absurdities together in a wandering and sometimes purposeless way, and seem innocently unaware that they are absurdities, is the basis of American art.

> SAMUEL L. CLEMENS ("MARK TWAIN"), *Ibid.*

Nobody has heard of Davis; you may ask all around and you will see. You never see his name mentioned in print; these things are of no use to Davis, not any more than they are to the wind and the sea. You never see one of Davis's books floating on top of the United States, but put on your diving armor and get yourself lowered away down and down and down till you strike the dense region, the sunless region of eternal drudgery and starvation wages—there you will find them by the million. The man that gets that market, his fortune is made, his bread and butter are safe, for those people will never go back on him. An author may have a reputation which is confined to the surface, and lose it and become pitied, then despised, then forgotten, entirely forgotten—the frequent steps in a surface reputation. A surface reputation, however great, is always mortal, and always killable if you go at it right—with pins and needles, and quiet slow poison, not with the club and the tomahawk. But it is a different matter with the submerged reputation—down in the deep water; once a favorite there, always a favorite; once beloved, always beloved; once respected, always respected, honored, and believed in. For what the reviewer says never finds its way down into those placid deeps, nor the newspaper sneers, nor any breath of the winds of slander blowing above. Down there they never hear of these things. Their idol may be painted clay, up there at the surface, and fade and waste and crumple and blow away, there being much weather there; but down below he is gold and adamant and indestructible.

> SAMUEL L. CLEMENS ("MARK TWAIN"), a paragraph dictated to Albert Bigelow Paine, while the latter was writing his *Biography* (c.1905)—pretending it was what "an Albany bookseller had said to Robert Louis Stevenson about a hack named Davis"

There are only three cities in America that are "story cities": New York, of course, and New Orleans, and, best of the lot, San Francisco.

> WILLIAM SIDNEY PORTER ("O. HENRY")

Any agonizing that tends to hurry what I believe in the end to be inevitable, our American Risorgimento, is dear to me. That awakening will make the Italian Renaissance look like a tempest in a teapot! The force we

have, and the impulse, but the guiding sense, the discrimination in applying the force we must wait and strive for.

EZRA POUND, letter to Harriet Monroe, 1912

At the time when he was trying to release humanity from the cross of
gold on which, as he said, it was crucified, the Apostle of Free Silver—in
this matter, at least, representing the old American frame of mind—announced that the opinion of all the professors in the United States would
not affect his opinions in the least. Now this, plainly, was a very formidable dilemma. For on the one hand stood a body of supposed experts in
economic theory, on the other a man whose profession it was to change
and reform economic practice,—the one knowing, the other doing; and
not only was there no compatibility between them but an openly avowed
and cynical contempt of theory on the part of practice was a principal
element in the popularity of a popular hero. Was Mr. Bryan, however,
to blame for it? To know anything of the economic theory which is taught
in American universities—in many cases compulsorily taught—is to confess that blame is not the right word. For this economic theory is at least
equally cynical. It revolves round and round in its tree-top dream of the
economic man; and no matter how much the wind blows political economy never comes down. Incompatibility, mutual contempt between theory
and practice, is in the very nature of things.

One might extend the illustration to literature, merely substituting one
professor for another and putting any typical best-selling novelist in the
place of Mr. Bryan. . . .

These two attitudes of mind have been phrased once for all in our ver-
nacular as "Highbrow and Lowbrow." I have proposed these terms to a
Russian, an Englishman, and a German, asking each in turn whether in
his country there was anything to correspond with the conceptions implied
in them. In each case they have been returned to me as quite American,
authentically our very own, and, I should add, highly suggestive.

What side of American life is not touched by this antithesis? What explanation of American life is more central or more illuminating? In everything one finds this frank acceptance of twin values which are not
expected to have anything in common: on the one hand a quite unclouded, quite unhypocritical assumption of transcendent theory ("high
ideals"); on the other a simultaneous acceptance of catchpenny realities.
Between university ethics and business ethics, between American culture
and American humor, between Good Government and Tammany, between academic pedantry and pavement slang, there is no community, no
genial middle ground.

The very accent of the words "Highbrow" and "Lowbrow" implies an instinctive perception that this is a very unsatisfactory state of affairs. For both are used in a derogatory sense. The "Highbrow" is the superior person whose virtue is admitted but felt to be an inept unpalatable virtue; while the "Lowbrow" is a good fellow one readily takes to, but with a certain scorn for him and all his works. And what is true of them as personal types is true of what they stand for. They are equally undesirable, and they are incompatible; but they divide American life between them.

Van Wyck Brooks, *America's Coming of Age,* 1915

There are just three of my contemporaries living on this shore, but we have all lost our minds or our senses and no one thinks it worth while to tell us so. No books come out. I am not aware that there are any writers left, certainly none in my branch, which was extinct five and twenty years ago and more. No one even remembers the name of Lord Macaulay. I once wrote some books myself, but no one has even mentioned the fact to me for more than a generation. I have a vague recollection that once some young person *did* mention an anecdote to me that came from one of my books and that he attributed it to some one else.

Henry Adams, letter to Charles Milnes Gaskell, 1917

There is a great library of books; every man of reasonable intelligence will look into it, to see what it contains that may be of value to him. And its value is not anywhere near as great as has been intimated; probably seven-tenths of it is rubbish, although much rubbish is curious and interesting. Select the wisest and best man in your community, and he knows more than Adam Smith; with his years he will have acquired a practical philosophy better fitted to your needs than the philosophy of Marcus Aurelius. There are a number of things you do not know. Who knows it better? Those who have lived longer, had more experience, and have greater and clearer brain power. And there are plenty of such men in your community willing to talk, if you will listen, and get rid of the disposition to tell what *you* think.

Edgar W. Howe, *Ventures in Common Sense,* 1919

The very significance—the note of ridicule and slight contempt—which attaches to the word "culture" in America, would be quite unintelligible to the French of any class. It is inconceivable to them that anyone should consider it superfluous, and even slightly comic, to know a great deal, to know the best in every line, to know, in fact, as much as possible.

There are ignorant and vulgar-minded people in France, as in other countries; but instead of dragging the popular standard of culture down to their own level, and ridiculing knowledge as the affectation of a self-conscious clique, they are obliged to esteem it, to pretend to have it, and to try and talk its language—which is not a bad way of beginning to acquire it.

The odd Anglo-Saxon view that a love of beauty and an interest in ideas imply effeminacy is quite unintelligible to the French; as unintelligible as, for instance, the other notion that athletics make men manly.

The French would say that athletics make men muscular, that education makes them efficient, and that what makes them manly is their general view of life, or, in other words, the completeness of their intellectual honesty.

EDITH WHARTON, *French Ways and Their Meaning*, 1919

Mr. Howells, I feel sure, will forgive me if I quote here a comment I once heard him make on theatrical taste in America. We had been talking of that strange exigency of the American public which compels the dramatist (if he wishes to be played) to wind up his play, whatever its point of departure, with the "happy-ever-after" of the fairy-tales; and I had remarked that this did not imply a preference for comedy, but that, on the contrary, our audiences want to be harrowed (and even slightly shocked) from eight till ten-thirty, and then consoled and reassured before eleven.

"Yes," said Mr. Howells; "what the American public wants is *a tragedy with a happy ending.*"

What Mr. Howells said of the American theatre is true of the whole American attitude toward life.

"A tragedy with a happy ending" is exactly what the child wants before he goes to sleep: the reassurance that "all's well with the world" as he lies in his cosy nursery. It is a good thing that the child should receive this reassurance; but as long as he needs it he remains a child, and the world he lives in is a nursery-world. Things are not always and everywhere well with the world, and each man has to find it out as he grows up. It is the finding out that makes him grow, and until he has faced the fact and digested the lesson he is not grown up—he is still in the nursery.

EDITH WHARTON, *Ibid.*

The truth is, as everyone knows, that the great artists of the world are never Puritans, and seldom ever ordinarily respectable. No virtuous man

—that is, virtuous in the Y. M. C. A. sense—has ever painted a picture worth looking at, or written a symphony worth hearing, or a book worth reading, and it is highly improbable that the thing has ever been done by a virtuous woman. The actual effect of repression, lamentable though it may be, is to destroy idealism altogether.

H. L. MENCKEN

A new movement usually is not a stampede to some new object but a stampede away from some old person. When a young American writer seems mad it is usually because an old one drives him almost crazy.

FRANK MOORE COLBY, *The Colby Essays*

Our most anxious social class is that known by courtesy as the intellectuals. Indeed public anxiety is often the only mark by which you can tell that a person belongs to it; and in many of our higher intellectual circles the fear of a peril to civilization from at least one quarter is a necessary qualification for membership.

FRANK MOORE COLBY, *Ibid.,* "A Potted Flower"

The official language of the State of Illinois shall be known hereafter as the American language, and not as the English language.

Acts of the Legislature of Illinois, ch. 127, sec. 178, 1923

Publishing a volume of verse is like dropping a rose-petal down the Grand Canyon and waiting for the echo.

DON MARQUIS

The female reader is the Iron Madonna who strangles in her fond embrace the American novelist.

H. H. BOYESEN

To a true-blue professor of literature in an American university, literature is not something that a plain human being, living today, painfully sits down to produce. No; it is something dead; it is something magically produced by superhuman beings who must, if they are to be regarded as artists at all, have died at least one hundred years before the diabolical invention of the typewriter.

SINCLAIR LEWIS, "The American Fear of Literature," address given at Stockholm on receiving the Nobel Prize, December 12, 1930

Our American professors like their literature clear, cold, pure, and very dead.

SINCLAIR LEWIS, Ibid.

The attitudes of the decade that followed the war, before the depression set in, already seem a long way off.

The attitude of the Menckenian gentleman, ironic, beer-loving and "civilized," living principally on the satisfaction of feeling superior to the broker and enjoying the debauchment of American life as a burlesque show or three-ring circus; the attitude of old-American-stock smugness, with its drawing aloof from the rabble in the name of old Uncle Gilead Pilcher who was Governor of Connecticut or Grandfather Timothy Merrymount who was killed in the Civil War—though the parvenus kept crashing the gate so fast, while the prosperity boom was on, that it was becoming harder and harder to get one's aloofness properly recognized; the liberal attitude that American capitalism was going to show a new wonder to the world by gradually and comfortably socializing itself and that we should just have to respect it in the meantime, taking a great interest in Dwight D. Morrow and Owen D. Young; the attitude of trying to get a kick out of the sheer size and energy of American enterprises, irrespective of what they were aiming at; the attitude of proudly withdrawing and cultivating a refined sensibility or of losing oneself completely in abstruse intellectual pursuits—scholastic philosophy, symbolic logic or metaphysical physics; the attitude of letting oneself be carried along by the mad hilarity and heartbreak of jazz, living only for the excitement of the evening; the attitude of keeping one's mind and morals impregnably disinfected with the feeble fascism-classicism of humanism.

. . . Today they all look rather queer: they are no use in our present predicament, and we can see how superficial they were. We can see now that they all represented attempts on the part of the more thoughtful Americans to reconcile themselves to a world dominated by salesmen and brokers—and that they all involved compromises with the salesman and the broker. Mencken and Nathan laughed at the broker, but they justified the system which produced him and they got along with him very well, provided he enjoyed George Moore and had pretensions to a taste in liquor; the jazz-age romantics spent the broker's money as speedily and wildly as possible and tried to laugh off the office and the factory with boyish and girlish jokes; the old-American-stockers sniffed at him, but though they salved their consciences thus, they were usually glad to get in on any of his good things that were going; the liberals, who had been vaguely unhappy, later became vaguely resigned and could never bring themselves to the point of serious quarreling with him; the poets and philosophers hid from him—and the physicists grew more and more mystical in the laboratories subsidized mainly by the profits from industrial investments; the humanists, in volume after volume, endeavoured by sheer hollow thunder to induce people to find in the stock exchange the harmony and dignity of the Parthenon.

EDMUND WILSON, *New Republic*, March 23, 1932

I couldn't write the things they publish now, with no beginning and no end, and a little incest in the middle.

IRVIN S. COBB

You can find all the exaggerations you want in Baron Munchausen, but you cannot find a phrase to match those in any writer of English before Mark Twain. Even Lord Byron's wit was not lighted with these exploits of poetic humor. In Charles Dickens you could search all day for a phrase to print on the page with them. "Mark Twain can be quoted in single sentences," says Stephen Leacock, "Dickens mostly in pages." But all vigorously imaginative minds can be quoted in sentences—all of the tribe of Shakespeare. And American humorists, casual and unsustained as their flights are, belong to the tribe of Shakespeare. It is as though the revival of an Elizabethan gleam and range of vision which we call the romantic movement, and which occurred in poetry in England at the beginning of the nineteenth century, occurred a half century later in the United States and in humor instead of poetry.

MAX EASTMAN, *The Enjoyment of Laughter*, 1936

All mythical heroes have been exaggerations, but they have been serious ones. America came too late for that. Her demigods were born in laughter; they are consciously preposterous; they are cockalorum demigods. That is the natively American thing—not that her primitive humor is exaggerative, but that her primitive exaggerations were humorous.

MAX EASTMAN, *Ibid.*

I am not prepared to say that there are absolutely no national characteristics in the music of great composers; but I do believe that they are not nearly so clear-cut or important as we have deluded ourselves into thinking they are. In general, a great composer is national only when he is at his second best. At the height of his powers, when he has ceased being decorative or merely exciting, and becomes eloquent and moving, he is likely to sound merely like himself. The great American music of the future will be a music to which America will listen and respond. But it will not be the music of Sitting Bull or Booker T. Washington—or even George. It will belong to us, because one of us made it; but it will, like all great music, belong to the world. And the world will not be curious regarding the name and address of the composer.

DEEMS TAYLOR, *Of Men and Music*, 1937

I write about myself, my home, my street and my city, and not about "America," the word that is the chief enemy of modern poetry.

KARL SHAPIRO, letter written from an army camp

Living as I have done physically if not spiritually on the Continent most of my life, I have become aware, as home-staying Anglo-Saxons find no occasion to be, of the fragility of both liberty and culture. We Americans were too apt to dwell on the seamy side of both, taking their invulnerability and their permanence for granted. We forget that even at home neither liberty nor culture is so secure that it can dispense with being fought for.

. . . Art is not actual life, it is true, but it is ideated life and perhaps as important. What distinguishes us from the other higher mammalia is precisely the capacity for this ideated life. This capacity leads higher and higher, and the longed-for goal is far away. But the goal of totalitarianism is not distant, and if it wins through it will shape man into a completely mechanized brute, guaranteed to remain a brute till he becomes a domestic animal.

Every individual who feels the need of a human society must learn to understand his responsibility towards art almost as towards life. He must avoid encouraging the undesirable let alone the bestializing forms, not only of life but of art as well. This he can do only if he takes the trouble to educate himself for the ideated as he does for the actual world. For art can offer the surest escape from the tedium of threatening totalitarianism. This art must not be reckless, freakish, fantastic (as permitted in ages of freedom), but must console and ennoble and transport us from the workaday world to realms of ideated happiness.

BERNARD BERENSON, *Aesthetics and History*, 1948

There is no country other than the United States in which, in so permanent a work as an encyclopedia, it is desirable to treat the writing of fiction with the following surly remarks.

In a democracy like this, while we stimulate a young man with belief that he may some day be president—at least of a motor agency—we also fail to inform him that in his competition with other equally fortunate freemen it will be well for him to have more talent and industry than the others. This is especially the case with writing fiction. Thanks to sentimental schoolteachers and the advertisements of firms which are not without guile in screaming that they can teach you to write, there is a general belief that anybody, man or woman, who has failed at plumbing, farming or housewifery, has only to take a couple of easy lessons—dealing with such trade secrets as: should you write with a pen or typewriter; and are blonde airplane stewardesses or red-haired girls from Iceland the snappier heroines just now—to be able to compose a novel which will win the Pulitzer Prize and be sold to the movies for a million dollars. . . . If I knew a novice who really wanted to write, I would urge him to spend ten years (1) in looking at and listening to everything about him and asking himself, "What is this really like, not what have I always heard about it?" and (2) in reading such novelists as Tolstoy, Dostoevsky, Chekhov, Hawthorne, Herman Melville, Hemingway, Cather, Thomas Wolfe, Dos Passos, Henry James, Mark Twain, Wharton, Faulkner, Richard Wright, Maritta Wolff, Caldwell, Farrell, Steinbeck, Dickens, Hardy, Thackeray, Evelyn Waugh, Scott, the Brontë sisters, Samuel Butler, H. G. Wells, Arnold Bennett, E. M. Forster, Kipling, Maugham, George Moore, Balzac, and Proust.

I would not guarantee that at the end of this probation he would be able to write one good paragraph, but certainly he would be less likely to write a bad one, and he would have had a golden decade. And if he did write at all then, *and if he had talent,* his work might faintly belong with that of the masters, and not be standardized junk turned out on an assembly line—ill made and selling cheap.

SINCLAIR LEWIS, American People's Encyclopedia, 1948

America is the only country in the world, where a man who uses a word that isn't understood by another man, is made to feel inferior to that other man.

SAMUEL GRAFTON

We are still haunted by a kind of political fear of the intellect which Tocqueville observed in us more than a century ago.

LIONEL TRILLING, The Liberal Imagination

What is common to . . . all other-directed people is that their contempo-

raries are the source of direction for the individual—either those known
to him or those with whom he is indirectly acquainted, through friends
and through the mass media. This source is of course "internalized" in the
sense that dependence on it for guidance in life is implanted early. The
goals toward which the other-directed person strives shift with that guidance: it is only the process of striving itself and the process of paying close
attention to the signals from others that remain unaltered throughout
life. This mode of keeping in touch with others permits a close behavioral
conformity, not through drill in behavior itself, as in the tradition-directed
character, but rather through an exceptional sensitivity to the actions and
wishes of others.

Of course, it matters very much who these "others" are: whether they
are the individual's immediate circle or a "higher" circle or the anonymous voices of the mass media; whether the individual fears the hostility
of chance acquaintances or only of those who "count." But his need for
approval and direction from others—and contemporary others rather than
ancestors—goes beyond the reasons that lead most people in any era to
care very much what others think of them. While all people want and
need to be liked by some of the people some of the time, it is only the
modern other-directed types who make this their chief source of direction
and chief area of sensitivity.

It is perhaps the insatiable force of this psychological need for approval
that differentiates people of the metropolitan, American upper middle
class, whom we regard as other-directed, from very similar types that have
appeared in capital cities and among other classes in previous historical
periods, whether in Imperial Canton, in eighteenth- and nineteenth-century Europe, or in ancient Athens, Alexandria, or Rome. In all these
groups fashion not only ruled as a substitute for morals and customs, but
it was a rapidly changing fashion that held sway. It could do so because,
although the mass media were in their infancy, the group corresponding to
the American upper middle class was comparably small and the elite
structure was extremely reverberant. . . .

[And, too,] we must differentiate the nineteenth-century American,
gregarious and subservient to public opinion though he was found to be
by Tocqueville, Bryce, and others, from the other-directed American as
he emerges today, an American who in his character is more capable of
and more interested in maintaining responsive contact with others both
at work and at play. This point needs to be emphasized, since the distinction is easily misunderstood. The inner-directed person, though he often
sought and sometimes achieved a relative independence of public opinion
and of what the neighbors thought of him, was in most cases very much

concerned with his good repute and, at least in America, with "keeping up with the Joneses." These conformities, however, were primarily external, typified in such details as clothes, curtains, and bank credit. For, indeed, the conformities were to a standard, evidence of which was provided by the "best people" in one's milieu. In contrast with this pattern, the other-directed person, though he has his eye very much on the Joneses, aims to keep up with them not so much in external details as in the quality of his inner experience. That is, his great sensitivity keeps him in touch with others on many more levels than the externals of appearance and propriety. Nor does any ideal of independence or of reliance on God alone modify his desire to look to the others—and the "good guys" as well as the best people—for guidance in what experiences to seek and in how to interpret them.

DAVID RIESMAN, NATHAN GLAZER and REUEL DENNEY,
The Lonely Crowd, 1950

A. I like Superman better than the others because they can't do everything Superman can do. Batman can't fly and that is very important.

Q. Would you like to be able to fly?

A. I would like to be able to fly if everybody else did, but otherwise it would be kind of conspicuous.

A twelve-year-old girl, interview quoted by Riesman *et. al.,*
from *Communications Research* by Lazarsfeld and Stanton

Eggheads of the world, unite. You have nothing to lose but your yolks.

ADLAI STEVENSON

What the American people have to learn is that architecture is the great mother-art, the art behind which all the others are definitely, distinctly and inevitably related. Until the time comes that when we speak of Art we immediately think of buildings, we will have no culture of our own.

FRANK LLOYD WRIGHT, *New York Times* "Magazine,"
October 4, 1953

Wherever it may be found and in whatever form the new illiteracy is nourished by several simple articles of faith. The essence of them is this: First, the individual exists only as a member of a group. He fulfils himself only as he works with others; of himself he is nothing. His tensions, his frustrations—these are penalties for his failure at adjustment, and they should, at all costs, be exorcised. Ideally there should be no conflict between man and society, and the good world that we must strive for is one in which all are harmonious with one another and in which the measure of man's activity is how well he contributes to that harmony. Above all else he must *get along*.

> WILLIAM H. WHYTE, JR., "The New Illiteracy," *Saturday Review*, November 21, 1953

The compelling fact about art in America is that it is not organic. It has almost no share in shaping our life; it offers, rather, compensation for the shapelessness. And just because we prescribe a certain amount of art for ourselves as a kind of corrective—being "deficient" in art as we might be in calcium or iron—we regard it less as ordinary nourishment than as a tonic, something we gulp rather than sip, regard with esteem and yet suspicion, and either require to be made up with a pleasant taste or exult in because it tastes unpleasant.

> LOUIS KRONENBERGER, *Company Manners*, 1954

V. Our Government and Politics

OUR THEORY OF GOVERNMENT

•

GENERAL THEORY

E Pluribus Unum.

> ANON., used on title page of *Gentleman's Journal*, January,
> 1692. Motto for seal of U.S. proposed originally on August
> 10, 1776, by a committee composed of Franklin, Adams and
> Jefferson; adopted June 20, 1782; the motto added to cer-
> tain coins, 1796. The actual selection of the motto for the
> seal is sometimes credited to Pierre Eugène du Simitière,
> who submitted a design for the seal which was not accepted,
> but which is said to have contained the words.

By a faction, I understand a number of citizens, whether amounting to a
majority or a minority of the whole, who are united and actuated by
some common impulse of passion, or of interest, adverse to the rights of
other citizens, or to the permanent and aggregate interests of the community.

JAMES MADISON, *The Federalist*, X, 1787

The latent causes of faction are . . . sown in the nature of man; and we
see them everywhere brought into different degrees of activity, according
to the different circumstances of civil society. A zeal for different opinions
concerning religion, concerning government, and many other points, as
well of speculation as of practice; an attachment to different leaders am-
bitiously contending for pre-eminence and power; or two persons of other
descriptions whose fortunes have been interesting to the human passions,
have, in turn, divided mankind into parties, inflamed them with mutual
animosity, and rendered them much more disposed to vex and oppress
each other than to co-operate for their common good. So strong is this
propensity of mankind to fall into mutual animosities, that where no substantial occasion presents itself, the most frivolous and fanciful distinctions
have been sufficient to kindle their unfriendly passions and excite their
most violent conflicts. But the most common and durable source of factions has been the various and unequal distribution of property. Those
who hold and those who are without property have ever formed distinct
interests in society. Those who are creditors, and those who are debtors,
fall under a like discrimination. A landed interest, a manufacturing inter-

313

est, a mercantile interest, a moneyed interest, with many lesser interests, grow up of necessity in civilized nations, and divide them into different classes, actuated by different sentiments and views. The regulation of these various and interfering interests forms the principal task of modern legislation, and involves the spirit of party and faction in the necessary and ordinary operations of the government.

JAMES MADISON, *Ibid.*

Ambition must be made to counteract ambition. . . . It may be a reflection on human nature that such devices should be necessary to control the abuses of government. But what is government itself, but the greatest of all reflections on human nature? If men were angels, no government would be necessary. . . . In framing a government which is to be administered by men over men, the great difficulty lies in this: you must first enable the government to control the governed; and in the next place oblige it to control itself.

JAMES MADISON, *Ibid.*

It is of great importance in a republic not only to guard against the oppression of its rulers, but to guard one part of the society against the injustice of the other part.

ALEXANDER HAMILTON, *The Federalist*

It seems to have been reserved to the people of this country, by their conduct and example, to decide the important question, whether societies of men are really capable or not of establishing good government from reflection and choice, or whether they are forever destined to depend for their political constitutions on accident and force.

ALEXANDER HAMILTON, *Ibid.*

[The Federalist Papers is] in my opinion, the best commentary on the principles of government, which ever was written.

THOMAS JEFFERSON, letter to Madison, Nov. 18, 1788

Men will pursue their interests. It is as easy to change human nature as to oppose the strong current of selfish passions. A wise legislator will gently divert the channel, and direct it, if possible, to the public good.

ALEXANDER HAMILTON, speech to Constitutional Convention, New York, July, 1788

The preservation of the sacred fire of liberty, and the destiny of the republican model of government, are justly considered as deeply, perhaps as finally staked, on the experiment entrusted to the hands of the American people.

GEORGE WASHINGTON, "First Inaugural," April 30, 1789

A national debt, if it is not excessive, will be to us a national blessing.

ALEXANDER HAMILTON

The principle of spending money to be paid by posterity, under the name of funding, is but swindling futurity on a large scale.

THOMAS JEFFERSON

It may well be doubted whether the nature of society and of the government does not prescribe some limits to the legislative power; and if any be prescribed, where are they to be found, if the property of an individual, fairly and honestly acquired, may be seized without compensation?

JOHN MARSHALL, *Fletcher* v. *Peck,* 1810. This is the first case in which the Supreme Court held a state law void under the Constitution.

As long as our Government is administered for the good of the people, and is regulated by their will; as long as it secures to us the rights of persons and of property, liberty of conscience and of the press, it will be worth defending.

ANDREW JACKSON, "First Inaugural," March 4, 1829

There are no necessary evils in government. Its evils exist only in its abuses. If it would confine itself to equal protection, and, as Heaven does its rain, shower its favors alike on the high and on the low, the rich and the poor, it would be an unqualified blessing.

ANDREW JACKSON

I have paid no poll-tax for six years. I was put into a jail once on this account, for one night; and, as I stood considering the walls of solid stone, two or three feet thick, the door of wood and iron, a foot thick, and the iron grating which strained the light, I could not help being struck with the foolishness of that institution which treated me as if I were mere flesh and blood and bones, to be locked up. I wondered that it should have concluded at length that this was the best use it could put me to, and had never thought to avail itself of my services in some way. I saw that, if there was a wall of stone between me and my townsmen, there was a still more difficult one to climb or break through before they could get to be as free as I was. I did not for a moment feel confined, and the walls seemed a great waste of stone and mortar. I felt as if I alone of all my townsmen had paid my tax. They plainly did not know how to treat me, but behaved like persons who are underbred. In every threat and in every compliment there was a blunder; for they thought that my chief desire was to stand the other side of that stone wall. I could not but smile to see how industriously they locked the door on my meditations, which followed them out again without let or hindrance, and *they* were really all that was dangerous. As they could not reach me, they had resolved to punish my body; just as boys, if they cannot come at some person against whom they have a spite, will abuse his dog. I saw that the State was half-witted, that it was timid as a lone woman with her silver spoons, and that it did not know its friends from its foes, and I lost all my remaining respect for it, and pitied it.

HENRY DAVID THOREAU, *Civil Disobedience*

This government never of itself furthered any enterprise, but by the alacrity with which it got out of its way. *It* does not keep the country free. *It* does not settle the West. It does not educate. The character inherent in the American people has done all that has been accomplished; and it would have done somewhat more, if the government had not sometimes got in its way.

HENRY DAVID THOREAU, *Ibid.*

I went to the store the other day to buy a bolt for our front door, for as I told the storekeeper, the Governor was coming here. "Aye," said he, "and the Legislature too." "Then I will take two bolts," said I. He said that there had been a steady demand for bolts and locks of late, for our protectors were coming.

HENRY DAVID THOREAU, *Journal,* September 8, 1859

The office of government is not to confer happiness, but to give men opportunity to work out happiness for themselves.

WILLIAM ELLERY CHANNING, *Life . . . of Bonaparte*

The legitimate object of government is to do for a community of people whatever they need to have done, but cannot do at all, or cannot so well do, for themselves, in their separate and individual capacities. In all the people can individually do as well for themselves, government ought not to interfere. The desirable things which the individuals of a people cannot do, or cannot well do, for themselves, fall into two classes: those which have relations to wrongs, and those which have not. Each of these branch off into an infinite variety of subdivisions.

The first—that in relation to wrongs—embraces all crimes, misdemeanours, and non-performance of contracts. The other embraces all which, in its nature, and without wrong, requires combined action, as public roads and highways, public schools, charities, pauperism, orphanage, estates of the deceased, and the machinery of government itself.

From this it appears that if all men were just, there still would be some, though not so much, need of government.

> ABRAHAM LINCOLN, "Fragment on Government," July 1, 1854 (date assigned by Hay and Nicolay)

Though the President is commander-in-chief, Congress is his commander; and, God willing, he shall obey. He and his minions shall learn that this is not a government of kings and satraps, but a government of the people, and that Congress is the people.

> THADDEUS STEVENS, Speech in the House of Representatives, January 3, 1867

The best system is to have one party govern and the other party watch.

> THOMAS B. REED, speech in the House, April 22, 1880

If you live in a town run by a committee—be on the committee.

> WILLIAM GRAHAM SUMNER, 1883

Though the people support the government the government should not support the people.

> GROVER CLEVELAND

In a republic like ours, where all men are equal, this attempt to array the rich against the poor or the poor against the rich is socialism, communism, devilism.

> SENATOR JOHN SHERMAN, of the Income Tax, which, in the '90's, was being suggested as a means of shifting some of the burden of taxation from the poor to the rich

Accountancy—that is government.

> LOUIS D. BRANDEIS, before House Committee on Interstate
> and Foreign Commerce, January 30, 1914

Government is not an exact science.

> LOUIS D. BRANDEIS, opinion in *Truax* v. *Corrigan,* 1921

Government after all is a very simple thing.

> WARREN G. HARDING

The cost of government will continue to increase, I care not what party
is in power.

> REED SMOOT, speech in the Senate, 1925

The government is mainly an expensive organization to regulate evildoers,
and tax those who behave; government does little for fairly respectable
people except annoy them.

> EDGAR W. HOWE, *Notes for My Biographer,* 1926

The politician says: "I will give you what you want." The statesman says:
"What you think you want is this. What it is possible for you to get is that.
What you really want, therefore, is the following."

> WALTER LIPPMANN, *A Preface to Morals,* 1929

In a democracy, the opposition is not only tolerated as constitutional, but
must be maintained because it is indispensable.

> WALTER LIPPMANN

What is the State? It is the duly constituted representative of an organized
society of human beings, created by them for their mutual protection and
well-being. "The State" or "The Government" is but the machinery
through which such mutual aid and protection are achieved. The cave
man fought for existence unaided or even opposed by his fellow men, but
today the humblest citizen of our State stands protected by all the power
and strength of his Government. Our Government is not the master but
the creature of the people. The duty of the State toward the citizens is
the duty of the servant to its master. The people have created it; the
people, by common consent, permit its continual existence.

One of these duties of the State is that of caring for those of its citizens
who find themselves the victims of such adverse circumstance as make
them unable to obtain even the necessities for mere existence without the

aid of others. That responsibility is recognized by every civilized Nation. . . .

To these unfortunate citizens aid must be extended by Government, not as a matter of charity, but as a matter of social duty.

> FRANKLIN D. ROOSEVELT, speech to New York State Legislature, August 28, 1931

To stay experimentation in things social and economic is a grave responsibility. Denial of the right to experiment may be fraught with serious consequences to the nation. It is one of the happy incidents of the federal system that a single courageous state may, if its citizens choose, serve as a laboratory, and try novel social economic experiments without risk to the rest of the country. This Court has the power to prevent an experiment. We may strike down the statute which embodies it on the ground that, in our opinion, the measure is arbitrary, capricious, or unreasonable. We have power to do this, because the due process clause has been held by the Court applicable to matters of substantive law as well as to matters of procedure. But, in the exercise of this high power, we must be ever on our guard, lest we erect our prejudices into legal principles. If we would guide by the light of reason, we must let our minds be bold.

> LOUIS D. BRANDEIS, dissenting opinion, *New State Ice Co.* v. *Liebmann,* 285 U.S. 262, 1932

Government is itself an art, one of the subtlest of the arts. It is neither business, nor technology, nor applied science. It is the art of making men live together in peace and with reasonable happiness. Among the instruments for governing are organization, technological skill, and scientific methods. But they are all instruments, not ends. And that is why the art of governing has been achieved best by men to whom governing is itself a profession. One of the shallowest disdains is the sneer against the professional politician. The invidious implication of the phrase is, of course, against those who pursue self-interest through politics. But too prevalently the baby is thrown out with the bath. We forget that the most successful statesmen have been professionals.

> FELIX FRANKFURTER, *The Public and Its Government*

One of the best solutions of the problem of a bureaucracy is less bureaucracy.

> JOHN W. BRICKER

I am against government by crony.

HAROLD L. ICKES, resigning as Sec. of the Interior, 1946

I cannot agree that it should be the declared public policy of Illinois that a cat visiting a neighbor's yard or crossing the highway is a public nuisance. It is in the nature of cats to do a certain amount of unescorted roaming. . . . Also consider the owner's dilemma: To escort a cat abroad on a leash is against the nature of the cat, and to permit it to venture forth for exercise unattended into a night of new dangers is against the nature of the owner. Moreover, cats perform useful service, particularly in rural areas, in combatting rodents—work they necessarily perform alone and without regard for property lines. . . . The problem of cat versus bird is old as time. If we attempt to resolve it by legislation, who knows but what we may be called upon to take sides as well in the age-old problem of dog versus cat, bird versus bird, or even bird versus worm. In my opinion, the State of Illinois and its local governing bodies already have enough to do without trying to control feline delinquency.

For these reasons, and not because I love birds less or cats the more, I veto and withhold my approval of Senate Bill No. 93.

ADLAI STEVENSON, veto of "Cat Bill," April 23, 1949

Well, Mr. Commissioner, ain't it a damn good thing we don't git all the Government we pay for?

A rich Texas farmer (oil) who came to Washington to see how his tax money was spent, and was told that the U.S. collects $70 billion a year in taxes

If we abolish the 16th [income tax] Amendment, some people will say, "How are we going to pay the expenses of the Government?" To hell with that! I want to know how I am going to pay my own expenses.

CHARLES COBURN, before Hinsdale (Ill.) Chamber of Commerce, 1954

THE CONSTITUTION

The Style of this confederacy shall be "The United States of America."

Opening words of the Articles of Confederation, 1781

We the People of the United States, in Order to form a more perfect Union, establish Justice, insure domestic Tranquillity, provide for the common defense, promote the general Welfare, and secure the Blessings of Liberty to ourselves and our Posterity, do ordain and establish this Constitution for the United States of America.

> The Preamble to the Constitution

I do solemnly swear that I will faithfully execute the office of President of the United States, and will, to the best of my ability, preserve, protect and defend the Constitution of the United States.

> Oath prescribed by the Constitution for the President

Congress shall make no law respecting an establishment of religion, or prohibiting the free exercise thereof; or abridging the freedom of speech, or of the press; or the right of the people peaceably to assemble, and to petition the Government for a redress of grievances.

> The First Amendment to the Constitution

No person shall be held to answer for a capital, or otherwise infamous crime, unless on a presentment or indictment of a Grand Jury, except in cases arising in the land or naval forces, or in the Militia, when in actual service in time of War or public danger; nor shall any person be subject for the same offense to be twice put in jeopardy of life or limb, nor shall be compelled in any criminal case to be a witness against himself, nor be deprived of life, liberty, or property, without due process of law; nor shall private property be taken for public use, without just compensation.

> The Fifth Amendment to the Constitution

Neither slavery nor involuntary servitude, except as a punishment for crime whereof the party shall have been duly convicted, shall exist within the United States, or any place subject to their jurisdiction.

> The Thirteenth Amendment to the Constitution. Proposed by Congress on January 31, 1865; declared ratified on December 18, 1865.

All persons born or naturalized in the United States, and subject to the jurisdiction thereof, are citizens of the United States and of the State wherein they reside. No State shall make or enforce any law which shall abridge the privileges or immunities of citizens of the United States; nor shall any State deprive any person of life, liberty, or property, without due process of law; nor deny to any person within its jurisdiction the equal protection of the laws.

> The Fourteenth Amendment to the Constitution. This amendment was proposed by Congress on June 13, 1866; declared ratified on July 28, 1868.

The right of citizens of the United States to vote shall not be denied or abridged by the United States or by any State on account of race, color, or previous condition of servitude.

> The Fifteenth Amendment to the Constitution. Proposed by Congress on February 26, 1869; declared ratified March 30, 1870.

The Congress shall have power to lay and collect taxes on incomes, from whatever source derived, without apportionment among the several States, and without regard to any census or enumeration.

> The Sixteenth Amendment to the Constitution. Proposed by Congress on July 12, 1909; declared ratified February 25, 1913.

After one year from the ratification of this article the manufacture, sale, or transportation of intoxicating liquors within, the importation thereof into, or the exportation thereof from the United States and all territory subject to the jurisdiction thereof for beverage purposes is hereby prohibited.

> The Eighteenth Amendment to the Constitution. Proposed by Congress on December 18, 1917; declared ratified January 29, 1919.

The right of citizens of the United States to vote shall not be abridged by the United States or by any State on account of sex.

> The Nineteenth Amendment to the Constitution. Proposed by Congress June 4, 1919; declared ratified August 26, 1920.

The eighteenth article of amendment to the Constitution of the United States is hereby repealed.

> The Twenty-first Amendment to the Constitution. Proposed by Congress February 20, 1933; declared ratified December 5, 1933.

When we are planning for posterity, we ought to remember that virtue is not hereditary.

THOMAS PAINE, *Common Sense*

It is not merely patriotic pride that compels one to assert that never in the history of assemblies has there been a convention of men richer in political experience and in practical knowledge, or endowed with a profounder insight into the springs of human action and the intimate essence of government. It is indeed an astounding fact that at one time so many men skilled in statecraft could be found on the very frontiers of civilization among a population numbering about four million whites. It is no less a cause for admiration that their instrument of government should have survived the trials and crises of a century that saw the wreck of more than a score of paper constitutions.

CHARLES A. BEARD, of the Federal Convention, Philadelphia, 1787, *The Supreme Court and the Constitution*

It is too probable that no plan we propose will be adopted. Perhaps another dreadful conflict is to be sustained. If to please the people, we offer what we ourselves disapprove, how can we afterwards defend our work? Let us raise a standard to which the wise and honest can repair. The event is in the hand of God.

GEORGE WASHINGTON, speech at the Federal Convention, 1787, as quoted by Gouverneur Morris in his funeral oration, December 31, 1799

I cannot help expressing a wish that every member . . . doubt a little of his own infallibility.

BENJAMIN FRANKLIN, speech to Constitutional Convention, September 17, 1787

The warmest friends and the best supporters the Constitution has, do not contend that it is free from imperfections; but they found them unavoidable and are sensible, if evil is likely to arise therefrom, the remedy must come hereafter; for in the present moment, it is not to be obtained; and, as there is a Constitutional door open for it, I think the people (for it is with them to Judge) can as they will have the advantage of experience on their Side, decide with as much propriety on the alterations and amendments which are necessary as ourselves. I do not think we are more

inspired, have more wisdom, or possess more virtue than those who will
come after us.

> GEORGE WASHINGTON, letter to Bushrod Washington, No-
> vember 10, 1787

You will permit me to say, that a greater Drama is now acting on this
Theatre than has heretofore been brought on the American stage, or any
other in the World. We exhibit at present the Novel and astonishing
Spectacle of a whole People deliberating calmly on what form of government will be most conducive to their happiness; and deciding with an
unexpected degree of unanimity in favour of a System which they conceive calculated to answer the purpose.

> GEORGE WASHINGTON, letter to Sir Edward Newenham,
> August 29, 1788

There is no position which depends on clearer principles, than that every
act of a delegated authority, contrary to the tenor of the commission under
which it is exercised, is void. No legislative act, therefore, contrary to the
Constitution, can be valid. To deny this, would be to affirm, that the
deputy is greater than his principle; that the servant is above his master;
that the representatives of the people are superior to the people themselves; that men acting by virtue of powers, may do not only what their
powers do not authorize, but what they forbid.

> ALEXANDER HAMILTON, *The Federalist*, XIII

Constitutions should consist only of general provisions; the reason is that
they must necessarily be permanent, and that they cannot calculate for
the possible change of things.

> ALEXANDER HAMILTON, speech in the Senate, 1788

The basis of our political system is the right of the people to make and
alter their constitutions of government. But the constitution which at any
time exists, 'till changed by an explicit and authentic act of the whole
people, is sacredly obligatory upon all. The very idea of the power and
the right of the people to establish government presupposes the duty of
every individual to obey the established government.

> GEORGE WASHINGTON, "Farewell Address," Sept. 19, 1796

Some men look at Constitutions with sanctimonious reverence, and deem
them like the ark of the covenant, too sacred to be touched. They ascribe

to the men of the preceding age a wisdom more than human, and suppose what they did to be beyond amendment. . . . Laws and institutions must go hand in hand with the progress of the human mind. . . . We might as well require a man to wear the coat that fitted him as a boy, as civilized society to remain ever under the regime of their ancestors.

THOMAS JEFFERSON

The Constitution of the United States was made not merely for the generation that then existed, but for posterity—unlimited, undefined, endless, perpetual posterity.

HENRY CLAY, speech in the Senate, 1850

What's the Constitution between friends?

Attributed to TIMOTHY CAMPBELL, New York Congressman

My boy, about seventy-five years ago I learned I was not God. And so, when the people of the various States want to do something and I can't find anything in the Constitution expressly forbidding them to do it, I say, whether I like it or not: "Damn it, let 'em do it!"

OLIVER WENDELL HOLMES, JR.

We are under a Constitution, but the Constitution is what the judges say it is.

CHARLES EVANS HUGHES, speech

The theory that the Constitution is a written document is a legal fiction. The idea that it can be understood by a study of its language and the history of its past development is equally mythical. It is what the Government and the people who count in public affairs recognize and respect as such, what they think it is. More than this. It is not merely what it has been, or what it is today. It is always becoming something else, and those who criticize it and the acts done under it, as well as those who praise, help us to make it what it will be tomorrow.

CHARLES A. and MARY BEARD, *The American Leviathan*

PUBLIC SERVANTS

•

THE PRESIDENT

My movements to the chair of government will be accompanied by feelings not unlike those of a culprit who is going to the place of his execution.

GEORGE WASHINGTON, letter, 1789

The friends of Crawford lacked but one of being half of the New York delegation so that the diversion of a single vote from Mr. Adams would produce a tie. General Van Rensselaer was, through his first wife, a brother-in-law to General Hamilton and had at an early age imbibed his dislike of the Adamses. He at no time entertained the idea of voting for Mr. Adams and communicated his views to me at an early period and without reserve. On the morning of the election he came to my room and told me he had some thought of voting for General Jackson and asked me whether it would make any difference in the general result, adding that as he had uniformly told me that he intended to vote for Crawford he did not think it proper to change his determination without letting me know it. I told him that as his vote could not benefit Mr. Crawford, it was of no importance to us whether it was given to him or to General Jackson, but submitted whether, as his intention was known to others as well as myself, there was an adequate motive for subjecting himself to the imputation of fickleness of purpose by a change which would produce no beneficial result to any one. He reflected a moment and then said I was right and that he would adhere to Crawford.

As I entered the Chamber, Mr. Cuthbert met me and said that it was not necessary that I should do anything in the matter, as Mr. Van Rensselaer had at that moment assured him that he certainly would not vote for Mr. Adams on the first ballot. I remained to see the voting, which took place presently afterward, and was pained to witness Mr. Van Rensselaer's obvious agitation and distress. When the votes of the New York delegation were counted, it was found that Mr. Adams had a majority of *one*. The vote of the state was of course given to him, and he was elected. Mr. Van Rensselaer at once admitted that he had voted for Mr. Adams and thus changed the anticipated result.

I had asked no explanation of the General nor did I intend to do so, as I was satisfied that he could not give any that it would be agreeable to him to make. But an evening or two after the election, whilst on our way to visit Mrs. Decatur, he volunteered an explanation which he did not make confidential but of which I did not speak until a long time afterward, and, to the best of my recollections, for the first time to Mr. Clay. He said that after what had passed between us, he felt it to be due to me that he should explain the change in his vote which I had so little reason to expect. He then proceeded to inform me that when he arrived at the Capitol, Mr. Clay invited him to the Speaker's room, where he found Mr. Webster; that they took the ground that the question of election or no election would depend upon his vote; that they portrayed to him the consequences that would in all probability result from a disorganization of the government and referred in very impressive terms to the great stake he had in the preservation of order from his large estate and kindred considerations. He said that his mind was much disturbed by these views, which he had not before regarded in so serious a light, but that he returned to the Chamber determined not to vote for Mr. Adams on the first ballot, whatever he might be induced to do ultimately if their anticipations of a failure to make an election should prove to be well founded. He took his seat fully resolved to vote for Mr. Crawford, but before the box reached him, he dropped his head upon the edge of the desk and made a brief appeal to his Maker for His guidance in the matter —a practice he frequently observed on great emergencies—and when he removed his hand from his eyes he saw on the floor directly below him a ticket bearing the name of John Quincy Adams. This occurrence, at a moment of great excitement and anxiety, he was led to regard as an answer to his appeal; and taking up the ticket, he put it in the box. In this way it was that Mr. Adams was made President.

> MARTIN VAN BUREN, *Autobiography*. The election of 1824 was curiously indecisive. Andrew Jackson received 99 electoral votes; Adams 84; Crawford (William H.) 41; and Clay 37. The contest was thrown into the House of Representatives, where each of the twenty states had one vote. The decision was still close, and New York proved to be the pivotal state.

I pray Heaven to bestow the best of blessings on this House and all that shall hereafter inhabit it. May none but honest and wise men ever rule under this roof.

> JOHN ADAMS, first tenant of the White House; words inscribed by Franklin D. Roosevelt above fireplace in State Dining Room

The example of four Presidents voluntarily retiring at the end of their eighth year, and the progress of public opinion, that the principle is salutary, have given it in practice the force of precedent and usage; insomuch, that, should a President consent to be a candidate for a third election, I trust he would be rejected, on this demonstration of ambitious views.

> THOMAS JEFFERSON, *Autobiography*

I would rather be right than be President.

> HENRY CLAY, speech, 1850. John C. Calhoun, who had
> been Vice-President in 1824, added, "I guess it's all right
> to be half right—and Vice President."

Nobody has ever expected me to be president. In my poor, lean, lank face nobody has ever seen that any cabbages were sprouting.

> ABRAHAM LINCOLN, "Second Campaign Speech" against
> Douglas, July 17, 1858

Seriously, I do not think I am fit for the Presidency.

> ABRAHAM LINCOLN, letter to T. J. Pickett, March 5, 1859

My friends, no one, not in my situation, can appreciate my feeling of sadness at this parting. To this place, and the kindness of these people I owe everything. Here I have lived a quarter of a century, and have passed from a young to an old man. Here my children have been born, and one is buried. I now leave, not knowing when, or whether ever, I may return, with a task before me greater than that which rested upon Washington. Without the assistance of that Divine Being who ever attended him, I cannot succeed. With that assistance I cannot fail. Trusting in Him who can go along with me, and remain with you and be everywhere for good, let us confidently hope that all will yet be well. To His care commending you, as I hope in your prayers you will commend me, I bid you an affectionate farewell.

> ABRAHAM LINCOLN, address on leaving Springfield, February 11, 1861

If you are as happy, my dear sir, on entering this house as I am in leaving it and returning home, you are the happiest man in this country.

> JAMES BUCHANAN, to A. Lincoln, at the White House,
> March 4, 1861

If I were to try to read, much less answer, all the attacks made on me, this shop might as well be closed for any other business. I do the very best I know how—the very best I can; and I mean to keep doing so until the end. If the end brings me out all right, what is said against me won't amount to anything. If the end brings me out wrong, ten angels swearing I was right would make no difference.

> ABRAHAM LINCOLN, conversation at the White House, reported by Frank Carpenter

I desire so to conduct the affairs of this administration that if at the end, when I come to lay down the reins of power, I have lost every other friend on earth, I shall at least have one friend left, and that friend shall be down inside of me.

> ABRAHAM LINCOLN, reply to Missouri Committee of Seventy, 1864

I would rather that the people should wonder why I wasn't President than why I am.

> SALMON P. CHASE, to the editor of the Indianapolis *Independent,* July, 1864

If nominated, I will not accept. If elected, I will not serve.

> WILLIAM TECUMSEH SHERMAN, answer to telegram from the Republican Convention asking him to be the Presidential candidate in 1884

If forced to choose between the penitentiary and the White House for four years, I would say the penitentiary, thank you.

> WILLIAM TECUMSEH SHERMAN

I can retire to private life with the consciousness that I shall receive from posterity the credit of having been elected to the highest position in the gift of the people, without any of the cares and responsibilities of the office.

> SAMUEL TILDEN, when informed that though he had won the popular vote over Hayes he would not be President, 1877. The votes of the Electoral College were in favor of Hayes, and no one wished to fight another Civil War over the question.

Franklin, I hope you never become President.

> GROVER CLEVELAND, to the boy Franklin D. Roosevelt

If the American people want me for this high office, I shall be only too willing to serve them. . . . Since studying this subject I am convinced that the office of President is not such a very difficult one to fill.

> ADMIRAL GEORGE DEWEY, announcing his candidacy, 1900

A presidential campaign may easily degenerate into a mere personal contest, and so lose its real dignity. There is no indispensable man.

> WOODROW WILSON, speech accepting Democratic nomination, August 7, 1912

A great nation is not led by a man who simply repeats the talk of the street-corners or the opinions of the newspapers. A nation is led by a man who hears more than those things; or who, rather, hearing those things, understands them better, unites them, puts them into a common meaning; speaks, not the rumours of the street, but a new principle for a new age; a man [to whom] the voices of the nation . . . unite in a single meaning and reveal to him a single vision, so that he can speak what no man else knows, the common meaning of the common voice. Such is the man who leads a great, free, democratic nation.

> WOODROW WILSON

When I was a boy I was told that anyone could become President; I'm beginning to believe it.

> CLARENCE DARROW

My God, this is a hell of a job! I have no trouble with my enemies. I can take care of my enemies all right. But my damn friends, my God-damn friends, White, they're the ones that keep me walking the floor nights!

> WARREN G. HARDING, quoted by William Allen White, *Autobiography*

I had some nice talks with Herbert Hoover before he went West for Christmas. He is certainly a wonder, and I wish we could make him President of the U. S. There could not be a better one.

> FRANKLIN D. ROOSEVELT, letter to Hugh Gibson, 1920

On the night of August 2, 1923, I was awakened by my father coming up the stairs, calling my name. I noticed that his voice trembled. As the only times I had ever observed that before were when death had visited our family, I knew that something of the gravest nature had occurred.

His emotion was partly due to the knowledge that a man whom he had met and liked was gone, partly to the feeling that must possess all of our citizens when the life of their President is taken from them.

But he must have been moved also by the thought of the many sacrifices he had made to place me where I was, the twenty-five mile drives in storms and zero weather over our mountain roads to carry me to the academy, and all the tenderness and care he had lavished upon me in the thirty-eight years since the death of my mother, in the hope that I might sometime rise to a position of importance, which he now saw realized.

He [was now] the first to address me as President of the United States. It was the culmination of the lifelong desire of a father for the success of his son.

He placed in my hands an official report and told me that President Harding had just passed away. . . .

CALVIN COOLIDGE, Autobiography, 1929

I thought I could swing it.

> CALVIN COOLIDGE, when asked by the painter Charles Hopkinson, who was painting the President's portrait and was disappointed by the lack of animation in his subject's face, what was the first thought that came into his mind when he heard of the death of President Harding. Coolidge's expression did not change.

I do not choose to run for President in 1928.

CALVIN COOLIDGE, August 2, 1927

[Landon] is just the solid, common type of man we need in the White House.

> ELEANOR MEDILL ("CISSIE") PATTERSON, 1936. Harold L. Ickes quipped, "Landon is the poor man's Hoover."

At 3:35 PM I was presiding over Senate. Senate adjourned about five o'clock and Sam Rayburn called me up and asked me if I could stop off at his office—some legislative matters about which he wanted to talk. I arrived at Rayburn's office about 5:05 and there was a call from Steve Early, asking me to come to the White House as quickly as possible. I told Sam Rayburn and some Congressman, who were present, to say nothing about it; I would probably be back in a few minutes, expecting probably I was going to see the President because Bishop Atwood was to be buried that day; and I thought maybe the President was in town for the funeral and wanted to go over some matter with me before returning to Warm Springs.

Before going I went to my office, got my hat. Tom Harty drove me up to the White House. Arrived there about 5:25 PM and was ushered into Mrs. Roosevelt's study on second floor.

Mrs. Roosevelt and Steve Early and Colonel and Mrs. Boettiger were there. Mrs. Roosevelt put her arm around my shoulder and said, "The President is dead." That was the first inkling I had of the seriousness of the situation.

I then asked them what I could do, and she said, "What can we do for you?" Before I had a chance to say anything, Secretary of State Stettinius came in. He evidently had received the news, because he was in tears. . . .

. . . I was very much shocked. I am not easily shocked but was certainly shocked when I was told of the President's death and the weight of the government had fallen on my shoulders. I did not know what reaction the country would have to the death of a man whom they all practically worshipped. . . . I was not familiar with any of these things, and it was really something to think about but I decided the best thing to do was to go home and get as much rest as possible and face the music.

My wife and daughter and mother-in-law were at the apartment of our next door neighbor. . . . They had had a turkey dinner and they gave us something to eat. I had not had anything to eat since noon. Went to bed, went to sleep, and did not worry any more that day.

HARRY S. TRUMAN, Diary, April 12, 1945

The finest prison in the world.

HARRY S. TRUMAN, of the White House

Had dinner by myself tonight. Worked in the Lee House office until dinner time. A butler came in very formally and said "Mr. President, dinner is served." I walk into the dining room in the Blair House. Barnett in tails and white tie pulls out my chair, pushes me up to the table. John in tails and white tie brings me a fruit cup, Barnett takes away the empty cup. John brings me a plate, Barnett brings me a tenderloin, John brings me asparagus, Barnett brings me carrots and beets. I have to eat alone and in silence in candle-lit room. I ring. Barnett takes the plate and butter plates. John comes in with a napkin and silver tray—there are no crumbs but John has to brush them off the table anyway. Barnett brings me a plate with a finger bowl and doily on it. I remove the finger bowl and doily and John puts a glass saucer and a little bowl on the plate. Barnett brings me some chocolate custard. John brings me a demitasse (at home a little cup of coffee—about two good gulps) and my dinner is over. I take a hand bath in the finger bowl and go back to work. What a life!

HARRY S. TRUMAN, *Diary*, November 1, 1949

OTHERS

I shall never *ask*, never *refuse*, nor ever *resign* an office.

BENJAMIN FRANKLIN, *Autobiography*

When a man assumes a public trust, he should consider himself as public property.

THOMAS JEFFERSON

If a due participation of office is a matter of right, how are vacancies to be obtained? Those by death are few: by resignation, none.

THOMAS JEFFERSON, letter to committee of New Haven merchants, 1801

The very essence of a free government consists in considering offices as public trusts.

JOHN C. CALHOUN. Cleveland's administration later took its motto from this statement: "A public office is a public trust."

To ask for an office is to pay too high a price for it.

CARL SCHURZ, 1860

The Millionaires' Club.

Sobriquet of the Senate, 1890's

Public office is the last refuge of the incompetent.

Attributed to BOIES PENROSE

Reader, suppose you were an idiot. And suppose you were a member of Congress. But I repeat myself.

> SAMUEL L. CLEMENS ("MARK TWAIN"), quoted by Paine,
> *Mark Twain: A Biography*

Every man who takes office in Washington either grows or swells.

> WOODROW WILSON

Now and then an innocent man is sent to the legislature.

> KIN HUBBARD

Once there were two brothers. One ran away to sea, the other was elected Vice-President, and nothing was ever heard of either of them again.

> THOMAS RILEY MARSHALL, *Recollections*

[The Vice-President is like a man in] a cataleptic fit. He is conscious of all that goes on, but has no part in it.

> THOMAS RILEY MARSHALL, *Ibid.*

The U.S. Senate may not be the most refined and deliberative body in existence but they got the most unique rules. Any member can call any-body in the world anything he can think of and they can't answer him, sue him, or fight him. Our constitution protects aliens, drunks and U.S. Senators. There ought to be one day (just one) when there is open season on senators.

> WILL ROGERS, 1935

You can't make a Senator do anything.

> KARL E. MUNDT, when asked about Vice-President Nixon's
> plan for limiting Senator McCarthy's cross-examinations,
> Army-McCarthy Hearings, April–May, 1954

Well, I wouldn't call it a vote of confidence.

> JOSEPH R. McCARTHY, when his censure was voted by the
> Senate, December, 1954, and he was asked what it meant

LIBERALS AND CONSERVATIVES

•

I argue this way—if a man is right, he can't be too radical. If he is wrong, he can't be too conservative.

HENRY WHEELER SHAW ("JOSH BILLINGS")

The days of liberalism are numbered. First the horrors of competition discredited it, and now the trial of war, which it foolishly thought it could elude. The vogue of culture, too, has declined. We see that the man whose success is merely personal—the actor, the sophist, the millionaire, the aesthete—is incurably vulgar. The rightness of liberalism is exactly proportional to the diversity of human nature, to its vague hold on its ideals. Where this vagueness and play of variation stop, and they stop not far below the surface, the sphere of public organization should begin. It is in the subsoil of uniformity, of tradition, of dire necessity that human welfare is rooted, together with wisdom and unaffected art, and the flowers of culture that do not draw their sap from that soil are only paper flowers.

GEORGE SANTAYANA, *Soliloquies in England,* 1923

To have standards means practically to select and reject: and this again means that one must discipline one's feelings or affections, to use the older word, to some ethical center. If the discipline is to be effective, so that a man will like and dislike the right things, it is as a rule necessary that it should become a habit, and that almost from infancy. One cannot wait until the child has reached the so-called age of reason, until, in short, he is in a position to do his own selecting, for in the meanwhile he may have become the victim of bad habits. This is the true prison house that is in danger of closing on the growing boy. Habit must, as Aristotle says, precede reason. . . .

If a community is to transmit certain habits to its young, it must normally come to some kind of agreement as to what habits are desirable; it must in the liberal meaning of that word achieve a convention. Here is a chief difference between the true and the false liberal. It has been said of our modernists that they have only one convention and that is that there shall be no more conventions. An individualism that is thus purely temperamental is incompatible with the survival of civilization. What is civilized in most people is precisely that part of them which is conventional.

It is, to be sure, difficult to have a convention without falling into mere conventionalism, two things that the modernist confounds; but then, everything that is worth while is difficult.

IRVING BABBITT, *Democracy and Leadership*, 1924

Let us admit the case of the conservative: if we once start thinking no one can guarantee where we shall come out, except that many objects, ends and institutions are doomed. Every thinker puts some portion of an apparently stable world in peril and no one can wholly predict what will emerge in its place.

JOHN DEWEY

A liberal is a man who is willing to spend somebody else's money.

CARTER GLASS, 1938

A Radical is a man with both feet firmly planted in the air.

FRANKLIN D. ROOSEVELT, radio speech, October 26, 1939

A Conservative is a man with two perfectly good legs who, however, has never learned to walk.

FRANKLIN D. ROOSEVELT, *Ibid.*

A Reactionary is a somnambulist walking backward.

FRANKLIN D. ROOSEVELT, *Ibid.*

What is a liberal? He may be an earnest soul, unimpeachable in his fidelity to the roots and anchors of the American system, who wants the maximum measure of life, liberty and happiness for our total people. In that sense I want my party to be "liberal."

On the other hand, he may seek the substitution of socialism for free enterprise, and paternalism for individual responsibility. In that sense I do not want my party to be "liberal." I am not interested in equality of servitude.

ARTHUR H. VANDENBERG, speech, 1949

The liberal tradition does not need defending. It needs liberals.

MARGARET HALSEY

No man can be a conservative until he has something to lose.

JAMES P. WARBURG

I have been much interested in the continued debate raging in the news-papers as to whether I am headed left, center or right. I think it would be more relevant to ask: Is the man moving forward or backward, or is he grounded?

ADLAI STEVENSON, speech, New York, 1952

Conservatism is the worship of dead Revolutionaries.

CLINTON ROSSITER, *Seedtime of the Republic*, 1953

Conservative and Radical are usually opposed as antitheses. But not so: radical literally means "to the roots"; the conservative who knows the real basis of his conserving is the true radical.

JAMES A. PIKE, *The Art of Being Conservative*, 1954

POLITICS

•

I am not a federalist, because I never submitted the whole system of my opinions to the creed of any party of men whatever, in religion, in philoso-phy, in politics or in anything else, where I was capable of thinking for myself. Such an addiction, is the last degradation of a free and moral agent. If I could not go to heaven but with a party, I would not go there at all.

THOMAS JEFFERSON, letter to Francis Hopkinson, Paris, March 13, 1789

Indignantly [frown] upon the first dawning of every attempt to alienate any portion of our country from the rest or to enfeeble the sacred ties which now link together the various parts. . . . Let me now . . . warn you in the most solemn manner against the baneful effects of the spirit of party generally. . . . It serves always to distract the public councils and enfeebles the public administration. It agitates the community with ill-founded jealousies and false alarms; kindles the animosity of one part against another; foments occasionally riot and insurrection. It opens the door to foreign influence and corruption, which find a facilitated access to the government itself through the channels of party passion. . . .

There is an opinion that parties in free countries are useful checks upon the administration of the government, and serve to keep alive the spirit of liberty. This within certain limits is probably true; and in governments of a monarchical cast patriotism may look with indulgence, if not with favor, upon the spirit of party. But in those of the popular character, in governments purely elective, it is a spirit not to be encouraged. . . .

> GEORGE WASHINGTON, "Farewell Address," Sept. 19, 1796

I know, sir, that it is the habit of some gentlemen to speak with censure or reproach of the politics of New York. . . . It may be, sir, that the politicians of New York are not as fastidious as some gentlemen are as to disclosing the principles on which they act. They boldly preach what they practice. When they are not contending for victory, they avow their intention of enjoying the fruits of it. . . . They see nothing wrong in the rule that to the victor belong the spoils of the enemy.

> WILLIAM L. MARCY, Senator from New York, speech during a debate in 1832, defending Martin Van Buren's nomination as Minister to England from the attacks of Henry Clay

I presume you-all know who I am. I am humble Abe Lincoln. I have been solicited by many friends to become a candidate for the legislature. My politics are short and sweet like the old woman's dance. I am in favor of a national bank. I am in favor of the internal improvements system, and a high protective tariff. These are my sentiments and political principles. If elected I shall be thankful. If not it will be the same.

> ABRAHAM LINCOLN, his first speech, delivered while running for the (Illinois) state legislature, 1832

Thirty years ago, when Mr. Webster at the bar or in the Senate filled the eyes and minds of young men, you might hear often cited as Mr. Webster's three rules: first, never to do today what he could defer till to-morrow; secondly, never to do himself what he could make another do for him; and, thirdly, never to pay any debt today.

> RALPH WALDO EMERSON, Letters and Social Aims. "A strong conviction that something must be done is the parent of many bad measures."—Daniel Webster

When, in the course of human events, it becomes necessary for one portion of the family of man to assume among the people of the earth a position different from that which they have hitherto occupied, but one to which the laws of nature and of nature's God entitle them, a decent respect to the opinions of mankind requires that they should declare the causes that impel them to such a course.

We hold these truths to be self-evident: that all men and women are created equal.

> ANON., Seneca Falls Declaration of Sentiments, 1848

You scratch my back and I'll scratch yours.

> Attributed to SIMON CAMERON, c. 1850

An honest politician is one who when he is bought will stay bought.

> SIMON CAMERON

The ballot is stronger than the bullet.

> ABRAHAM LINCOLN, speech, Bloomington, May 29, 1856

Parties are not built by deportment, or by ladies' magazines, or gush.

> ROSCOE CONKLING

You can always get the truth from an American statesman after he has turned seventy, or given up all hope of the Presidency.

> WENDELL PHILLIPS

I never said all Democrats were saloonkeepers; what I said was all saloonkeepers were Democrats.

> HORACE GREELEY

Politics makes strange bedfellows.

> CHARLES DUDLEY WARNER, *My Summer in a Garden,* 1870

If you shoot a Republican out of season, the fine will be ten dollars and costs.

> Saying in Jackson, Mississippi

Politician:—An animal who can sit on a fence and yet keep both ears to the ground.

> ANON.

If you can't lick 'em, join 'em.

> American Political Saying

As long as I count the votes, what are you going to do about it?

> WILLIAM MARCY TWEED

Figures won't lie, but liars will figure.

> CHARLES HENRY GROSVENOR, whose predictions of elec-
> tions were remarkably accurate, and who admitted, in the
> above phrase, that his figures could be misinterpreted

I placed it where it would do the most good.

> OAKES AMES, letter to Henry S. McComb, referring to
> *Crédit Mobilier* stock distributed to Congressmen, 1872

Let no guilty man escape.

> ULYSSES S. GRANT, when it was discovered that his per-
> sonal secretary and other friends were involved in the
> Whisky Ring scandal, 1875

That party never had but two objects—grand and petty larceny.

> ROBERT G. INGERSOLL, of the Democratic party, speech, In-
> dianapolis, 1876

When I want to buy up any politicians I always find the anti-monopolists
the most purchasable. They don't come so high.

> WILLIAM H. VANDERBILT, interview aboard his special train
> approaching Chicago, October 8, 1882

I work for the men the people work for.

> Attributed to MATTHEW STANLEY QUAY, political boss of
> Pennsylvania, when asked, after having elevated himself to
> the United States Senate in 1887, why he did not work for
> the people

The Democratic party is like a mule—without pride of ancestry or hope
of posterity.

> EMORY STORRS, speech during campaign of 1888; also at-
> tributed to William C. Linton, Ignatius Donnelly and Judge
> Gay Gordon

We have exchanged the Washingtonian dignity for the Jeffersonian simplicity, which in due time came to be only another name for the Jackso-
nian vulgarity.

> HENRY CODMAN POTTER, address, 1889

The purification of politics is an iridescent dream. Government is force.
. . . The Decalogue and the Golden Rule have no place in a political
campaign. The commander who lost the battle through the activity of
his moral nature would be the derision and jest of history.

> JOHN JAMES INGALLS, New York *World,* 1890

There are two ideas of government. There are those who believe that if
you legislate to make the well-to-do prosperous, this prosperity will leak
through on those below. The Democratic idea has been that if you legislate to make the masses prosperous their prosperity will find its way up
and through every class and rest upon them.

> WILLIAM JENNINGS BRYAN, speech, Democratic National
> Convention, July, 1896

Man an' boy I've seen the Dimmycratic party hangin' to th' ropes a score
iv times. I've seen it dead an' burrid an' th' Raypublicans kindly buildin'
a monymint f'r it an' preparin' to spind their declinin' days in th' custom
house. I've gone to sleep nights wonderin' where I'd throw away me vote
afther this an' whin I woke up there was that crazy-headed, ol' loon iv a
party with its hair sthreamin' in its eyes, an' an axe in its hand, chasin'
Raypublicans into th' tall grass. 'Tis niver so good as whin 'tis broke, whin
rayspectable people speak iv it in whispers, an' whin it has no leaders an'
only wan principel, to go in an' take it away fr'm th' other fellows. Something will turn up, ye bet, Hinnessey. Th' Raypublican party may die iv
overfeedin' or all th' leaders pump out so much ile they won't feel like
leadin'. An' annyhow they'se always wan ray iv light ahead. We're sure
to have hard times. . . .

> FINLEY PETER DUNNE ("MR. DOOLEY"), *Mr. Dooley Dis-
> cusses Party Politics*

No matter whether th' Constitution follows th' flag or not, th' Supreme
Court follows th' illiction returns.

> FINLEY PETER DUNNE ("MR. DOOLEY"), of a series of de-
> cisions by the Supreme Court validating the proceedings of
> the Congress and the administration, 1900–1904, which in
> effect denied to the Philippines "equal rights under the
> Constitution"

Arena, n. In politics, an imaginary rat-pit in which the statesman wrestles
with his record.

> AMBROSE BIERCE, *The Devil's Dictionary*

We bought the s.o.b. but he didn't stay bought.

> Attributed to HENRY C. FRICK, of Theodore Roosevelt,
> after a group of Wall Street operators had helped to elect
> Roosevelt in 1904

When I say I believe in a square deal I do not mean, and nobody who speaks the truth can mean, that he believes it possible to give every man the best hand. If the cards do not come to any man, or if they do come, and he has not got the power to play them, that is his affair. All I mean is that there shall not be any crookedness in the dealing.

> THEODORE ROOSEVELT, speech in Dallas, April 5, 1905

Men with the muck-rake are often indispensable to the well-being of society, but only if they know when to stop raking the muck.

> THEODORE ROOSEVELT, Washington, April 14, 1906

A straw vote only shows which way the hot air blows.

> WILLIAM SIDNEY PORTER ("O. HENRY"), *Rolling Stones,*
> "A Ruler of Men"

Taft is an amiable island, entirely surrounded by men who know exactly what they want.

> JONATHAN PRENTISS DOLLIVER, of President Taft, 1909

Reform must come from within, not from without. You cannot legislate for virtue.

> JAMES CARDINAL GIBBONS, address, Baltimore, September
> 13, 1909

In uplifting, get underneath.

> GEORGE ADE, *Fables in Slang,* "The Good Fairy"

Curious thing about reformers: They don't seem to get a lot of pleasure out of their labours unless the ones they reform resist and suffer, and show a proper sense of their degradation. I bet a lot of reformers would quit to-morrow if they knew their work wasn't going to bother people any.

> HARRY LEON WILSON, *Ma Pettingill*

When Dr. Johnson defined patriotism as the last refuge of a scoundrel, he was unconscious of the then undeveloped capabilities of the word reform.

ROSCOE CONKLING

I took the Isthmus, started the Canal, and then left Congress—not to debate the Canal, but to debate me.

THEODORE ROOSEVELT, New York Times, March 24, 1911

My hat is in the ring. The fight is on and I am stripped to the buff.

> THEODORE ROOSEVELT, announcing informally to reporters that he would attempt to be Republican candidate for the Presidency, February, 1912

It takes more than bullets to kill a Bull Moose.

> THEODORE ROOSEVELT, interpolated remark in speech at Milwaukee, October 14, 1912, after being shot and lightly wounded by an assailant

The lunatic fringe in all reform movements.

THEODORE ROOSEVELT, Autobiography, 1913

You can't beat somebody with nobody.

ANON., usually attributed to "Uncle Joe" Cannon

Can you let me know what positions you have at your disposal with which to reward deserving Democrats?

> WILLIAM JENNINGS BRYAN, letter to W. W. Vick, Receiver General of Customs in Santo Domingo, August, 1913

Modern politics is a struggle not of men but of forces. The men become every year more and more creatures of force, massed about central powerhouses.

HENRY ADAMS, The Education of Henry Adams

Practical politics consists in ignoring facts.

HENRY ADAMS, Ibid.

All dressed up, with nowhere to go.

> WILLIAM ALLEN WHITE, of the Progressive party in 1916, after Theodore Roosevelt retired from Presidential competition

The people are always worsted in an election.

> EDGAR W. HOWE, *Ventures in Common Sense,* 1919

The convention will be deadlocked, and after the other candidates have gone their limit, some twelve or fifteen men, worn out and bleary-eyed for lack of sleep, will sit down, about two o'clock in the morning, around a table in a smoke-filled room in some hotel, and decide the nomination. When that time comes, Harding will be selected.

> HARRY M. DAUGHERTY, campaign manager for Harding, 1920. The prediction was uncannily accurate. The room was in the Blackstone Hotel, Chicago, and it was about two o'clock on the morning of Saturday, June 12, 1920, that a small group of party elders got together and chose Harding. See *New York Times,* June 13, 1920. It was after this that Harding said, to a group of reporters who rushed to him when the news broke, "We drew to a pair of deuces and filled."

Senator Lodge, I have no further communication to make.

> WOODROW WILSON, last words of Woodrow Wilson as President, March 4, 1920, to the man who had been his bitterest political enemy

There are a great many things that I believe that I know are not so; for instance, I believe that the Democratic party is always right.

> THOMAS RILEY MARSHALL, *Recollections*

Alabama casts 24 votes for Oscar W. Underwood.

> Catch phrase of 1924 Democratic National Convention, uttered on each of the 103 ballots by the spokesman for the first delegation on the list of states. John W. Davis was nominated on the 103rd ballot.

Bad officials are elected by good citizens who do not vote.

> GEORGE JEAN NATHAN

Wouldn' th' way things are goin' these days make a fine argyment in favor of woman suffrage if we didn't already have it?

> KIN HUBBARD

Congressional investigations are for the benefit of photographers.

WILL ROGERS

Politicians act as though they thought the will of the people is a document bequeathing them something.

JOHN W. RAPER, *What This World Needs*

Any party which takes credit for the rain must not be surprised if its opponents blame it for the drought.

DWIGHT MORROW

The grass will grow in the streets of a hundred cities.

HERBERT HOOVER, speech, October 31, 1932, on the necessity of keeping a high protective tariff

[It is] dangerous to change parties in mid-Depression.

DAVID LAWRENCE, advising the readers of his column to vote for Hoover, 1932

It is common sense to take a method and try it. If it fails, admit it frankly and try another. But above all, try something.

FRANKLIN D. ROOSEVELT, speech during campaign, 1932

You can't adopt politics as a profession and remain honest.

LOUIS MCHENRY HOWE, address to Columbia School of Journalism, January 17, 1933

Never vote for a tax bill nor against an appropriation bill.

American political maxim

[Politicians] are the semi-failures in business and the professions, men of mediocre mentality, dubious morals, and magnificent commonplaceness.

WALTER B. PITKIN, *The Twilight of the American Mind*

Of course, we must draw some sort of distinction between wishing to overthrow the government and not liking the present administration.

HELEN E. HOKINSON, cartoon caption, *New Yorker*, 1930's

Statistics are like alienists—they will testify for either side.

FIORELLO H. LA GUARDIA, "The Banking Investigations," *Liberty*, May 13, 1933

It will be red fire at first and dead cats afterwards. This is just like mounting the guillotine on the infinitesimal gamble that the ax won't work.

> HUGH S. JOHNSON, to friends who congratulated him on
> his (rumored, later actual) appointment as head of N.R.A.,
> June, 1933

Politics is the art by which politicians obtain campaign contributions from the rich and votes from the poor on the pretext of protecting each from the other.

> OSCAR AMERINGER, *If You Don't Weaken,* 1940

I say this in dead earnest—if, because of some fine speeches about humanity, you return this Administration to office, you will be serving under an American totalitarian government before the long third term is finished.

> WENDELL L. WILLKIE, speech during campaign, 1940

I've had a glorious day here in New England.

> FRANKLIN D. ROOSEVELT, speech in Boston during 1940
> campaign after riding many hours in an open car in a
> heavy rain

I consider it a public duty to answer falsifications with facts. I will not pretend that I find this an unpleasant duty. I am an old campaigner, and I love a good fight.

> FRANKLIN D. ROOSEVELT, Philadelphia, October 23, 1940

In moments of oratory in campaigns we all expand a little.

> WENDELL L. WILLKIE, in Senate Committee Investigation
> of Lend-Lease, which Willkie had attacked during cam-
> paign a few months before. It was this sentence which gave
> rise to the phrase "campaign oratory."

Bricker is an honest Harding.

> ALICE ROOSEVELT LONGWORTH, 1944

For eleven long years we have been in the middle of the stream. We are not amphibious. We want to get across. We want to feel dry and solid ground under our feet again.

> EARL WARREN, "Keynote Address," Republican National
> Convention, June, 1944

These Republican leaders have not been content with attacks upon me, or on my wife, or on my sons—no, not content with that, they now include my little dog Fala. Unlike the members of my family, he resents this. Being a scottie, as soon as he learned that the Republican fiction writers had concocted a story that I had left him behind on an Aleutian island and had sent a destroyer back to find him—at a cost to the taxpayers of two, or three, or eight, or twenty million dollars—his Scotch soul was furious. He has not been the same dog since.

> Franklin D. Roosevelt, speech to Teamsters Union, September 23, 1944

Politics is the science of how who gets what, when and why.

> Sidney Hillman, *Political Primer for All Americans*, 1944

The politicians were talking themselves red, white, and blue in the face.

> Clare Boothe Luce

When you speak of better times, Hubert, do you mean when the war is over or when the Democrats are over?

> Gardner Rea, cartoon caption, *New Yorker*, 1940's

In politics, it is remarkable what you can do with a hundred dollars if you spend it yourself. It is also sad to think of how little you can do in politics with a hundred dollars if you let someone else spend it.

> William Allen White, *Autobiography*

The maneuvers in a battle are like the maneuvers in politics. In the military they have what they call a five paragraph order.

In the first paragraph you make an estimate of the enemy, his condition and what he can do.

In the second paragraph, you make an estimate of your condition and what *you* can do.

In the third paragraph you decide what you are *going* to do.

In the fourth paragraph—you set up your logistics and supply sources to *carry out* what you are going to do.

And in the fifth paragraph, you tell *where* you are going to be so that everybody can reach you.

That is all there is to politics.

> Harry S. Truman

I have just made some additions to my Kitchen Cabinet, which I will pass on to my successor in case the Cow should fall down when she goes over the moon.

I appointed a Secretary for Inflation. I have given him the worry of convincing the people that no matter how high the prices go, nor how low wages become, there just is not any danger to things temporal or eternal. I am of the opinion that he will take a real load off my mind—if Congress does not.

Then I have appointed a Secretary of Reaction. I want him to abolish flying machines and tell me how to restore oxcarts, oar boats and sailing ships. What a load he can take off my mind if he will put the atom back together so it cannot be broken up. What a worry that will abolish for both me and Vishinsky.

I have appointed a Secretary for Columnists. His duties are to listen to all radio commentators, read all columnists in the newspapers from ivory tower to lowest gossip, coordinate them and give me the result so I can run the United States and the World as it should be. I have several able men in reserve besides the present holder of the job, because I think in a week or two the present Secretary for Columnists will need the services of a psychiatrist and will in all probability end up in St. Elizabeth's.

I have appointed a Secretary of Semantics—a most important post. He is to furnish me with 40 to 50 dollar words. Tell me how to say yes and no in the same sentence without a contradiction. He is to tell me the combination of words that will put me against inflation in San Francisco and for it in New York. He is to show me how to keep silent—and say everything. You can very well see how he can save me an immense amount of worry.

HARRY S. TRUMAN, memorandum written December, 1947

I look upon the future with considerable optimism, as there seems to be only one direction for the future of Harvard football and the Republican Party to go.

ROSWELL BURCHARD PERKINS, Assistant Secretary of Health, Education and Welfare, when graduating from Harvard in 1947

A politician is one who pretends that he is subject to the universal hunger for esteem; but he cannot successfully pretend thus unless he is free of it. This is the basic hypocrisy of politics and the final triumph of the leader comes with the awe that is aroused in men when they suspect, but never know for certain, that their leader is indifferent to their approval, indifferent and a hypocrite. What?—they say to themselves—: what? can it be that there is absent from this man that serpent's nest which is lodged within us all and which is at once our torture and our delight—the thirst for praise, the necessity of self-justification, the assertion of one's self, cruelty, and envy?

> THORNTON WILDER, *The Ides of March,* 1948

DEWEY DEFEATS TRUMAN: PUTS G. O. P. BACK IN WHITE HOUSE.

> ANON., headline in first edition of Chicago *Tribune,* November 3, 1948. Mr. Truman keeps a copy of this paper as a precious souvenir.

My father was a Democrat; my mother was a Republican; I am an Episcopalian.

> GEORGE C. MARSHALL, in 1952. He refused actively to support either Stevenson or Eisenhower for the Presidency; both of them had, at various times, worked under him.

Let's talk sense to the American people. Let's tell them the truth, that there are no gains without pains, that we are now on the eve of great decisions, not easy decisions, like resistance when you're attacked, but a long, patient, costly struggle which alone can assure triumph over the great enemies of man—war, poverty and tyranny—and the assaults upon human dignity which are the most grievous consequences of each.

> ADLAI STEVENSON, "Acceptance Speech," Chicago, July, 1952

If the Republicans stop telling lies about us, we will stop telling the truth about them.

> ADLAI STEVENSON, 1952

It is often easier to fight for principles than to live up to them.

> ADLAI STEVENSON, speech to American Legion, New York, August, 1952

Consider the groups who seek to identify their special interests with the general welfare. I find it sobering to think that their pressures might one day be focused on me. I have resisted them before and I hope the Almighty will give me the strength to do so again and again. And I should tell you now, as I would tell other organized groups, that I stand to resist pressure from veterans, too, if I think their demands are excessive or in conflict with the public interest, which must always be the paramount interest.

Let me suggest, incidentally, that we are rapidly becoming a nation of veterans. If we were all to claim a special reward for our service, beyond that to which specific disability or sacrifice has created a just claim, who would be left to pay? After all, we are Americans first and veterans second.

ADLAI STEVENSON, *Ibid.*

Someone asked me, as I came in, down on the street, how I felt, and I was reminded of a story that a fellow-townsman of ours used to tell—Abraham Lincoln. They asked him how he felt once after an unsuccessful election. He said he felt like a little boy who has stubbed his toe in the dark. He said that he was too old to cry, but it hurt too much to laugh.

ADLAI STEVENSON, speech, November 5, 1952 (Election Night), when the Republican victory was apparent

It is not too much to say, that the future of the world lies less in the struggle within the Kremlin than in the struggle within the American Congress.

THEODORE H. WHITE, *Fire in the Ashes,* 1953

Politics is the only profession in which a man improves with age. This is not because he grows wiser but because a man with one foot in the grave has the ideal political attitude of "to hell with tomorrow."

The crowd has a giddy faith in the aged politico. It knows that a dying man is least worried about disasters and will, therefore, shy less at them. But it is not only insensitivity that makes the venerable beloved. Power is the only immorality possible to old men. History-making is the only spree on which the doddering may embark. And history is the great diversion of the crowd.

BEN HECHT, *A Child of the Century,* 1954

Just as a man of muscle may be attracted to pugilism, so a man without character is drawn into politics. It is a calling that turns his flaws into assets. It demands of him that he wear his passions like detachable cuffs, that he be spurious and pompous, and that he make himself heard—like a firecracker under a tin can. His chief intellectual achievement is a weather vane sewed to the back of his collar. And he must be as fearless as a pyromaniac. He must also share with the crowd its mysterious faith in calamity—as if calamity alone would solve the confusions of economics, religion and philosophy.

BEN HECHT, Ibid.

The Democratic label is now the property of men and women who have been unwilling to recognise evil or who bent to whispered pleas from the lips of traitors . . . men and women who wear the political label stitched with the idiocy of a Truman, rotted by the deceit of an Acheson, corrupted by the Red slime of a White.

JOSEPH R. McCARTHY, speech, Madison, 1954

[McCarthy] replied that he followed a maxim taught to him by an Indian named "Charlie" with whom he had worked on a farm. Charlie, according to Senator McCarthy, urged the rule of conduct that if one was ever approached by another person in a not completely friendly fashion, one should start kicking at the other person as fast as possible below the belt until the other person was rendered helpless. Senator McCarthy stated that he followed that principle in this case.

H. STRUVE HENSEL, affidavit filed with Chairman Mundt anent charges in Army-McCarthy Hearings, June, 1954

Half our politicians wouldn't be where they are except for opposing crime, and the other half wouldn't be where they are except for supporting it.

BERGEN EVANS, The Spoor of Spooks, 1954

POLITICAL SLOGANS AND PHRASES

•

Those Who Own the Country Ought to Govern It.

JOHN JAY, slogan of the Federal party

No ill luck stirring but what lights upon Uncle Sam's shoulders.

ANON., editorial, Troy (New York) Post, September 7, 1813. The earliest known use of the phrase "Uncle Sam." There is a legend that the original Uncle Sam was Samuel Wilson, of Troy, an army contractor, b. 1766, d. 1854.

Talking for Buncombe.

> FELIX WALKER, speech on the Missouri Bill, House of Rep-
> resentatives, February 25, 1820. Walker was representative
> from North Carolina, and Buncombe County was part of
> his district. Toward the close of the debate, Walker rose to
> speak, and was asked not to so the vote could be taken, but
> he refused, saying he was bound to make "a speech for
> Buncombe."

The Man in the Street.

> RALPH WALDO EMERSON, Conduct of Life, "Worship"

Two Dollars a Day and Roast Beef.

> Slogan of Harrison-Tyler campaign, 1840

Tippecanoe and Tyler Too.

> Harrison-Tyler campaign slogan, 1840

No More Slave States; No Slave Territories.

> SALMON PORTLAND CHASE, platform of Free-Soil National
> Convention, 1848

We inscribe on our banner Free Soil, Free Speech, Free Labor, and Free
Men.

> Motto of the Free-Soil party, insurgent Democrats who
> nominated Van Buren in 1848

We join ourselves to no party that does not carry the American flag, and
keep step to the music of the Union.

> RUFUS CHOATE, letter to Whig Convention, Oct. 1, 1855

Free Soil, Free Men, Free Speech, Fré-mont.

> Campaign slogan of John C. Frémont, 1856, first nominee
> of the Republican party

The Crime Against Kansas.

> CHARLES SUMNER, title of speech in Senate, 1856. In this
> speech Sumner spoke too harshly of Senator Butler of North
> Carolina, whereupon Butler's young kinsman, Preston
> Brooks, assaulted Sumner on the Senate floor and inflicted
> an injury from which he never fully recovered.

I have not permitted myself, gentlemen, to conclude that I am the best man in the country; but I am reminded, in this connection, of a story of an old Dutch farmer, who remarked to a companion that "it was not best to swap horses when crossing streams."

> ABRAHAM LINCOLN, reply to National Union League's congratulations on his renomination, June 9, 1864

I have come home to look after my fences.

> JOHN SHERMAN, speech to his neighbors in Mansfield, Ohio, referring to the fences around his farm. Said to be the origin of the political phrase.

Swinging round the circle.

> ANDREW JOHNSON, of his trip to Chicago, which he made into a campaign tour, 1866

Let us have peace.

> ULYSSES S. GRANT, "Acceptance Speech," May 29, 1868

Now is the time for all good men to come to the aid of the party.

> CHARLES E. WELLER, sentence used to test the first typewriter, constructed at Milwaukee by Christopher L. Sholes, 1867. The sentence was also used as a slogan in U. S. Grant's first Presidential campaign, 1868

No king, no clown
To rule this town!

> WILLIAM O. BARTLETT, New York *Sun* editorial writer. A phrase (often attributed to Charles A. Dana) much used in the *Sun's* fight against Tammany Hall, 1870's and '80's

Turn the Rascals Out!

> CHARLES A. DANA, slogan of Horace Greeley's Liberal Republican party, 1872

Waving the Bloody Shirt.

> OLIVER PERRY MORTON, of the use of the Civil War as a campaign issue

The Solid South.

> Attributed to JOHN SINGLETON MOSBY, in a letter, 1876; used widely in the campaign of 1878

Hew to the line, let the chips fall where they may.

> ROSCOE CONKLING, speech putting Grant's name in nomi-
> nation at Republican National Convention, June, 1880

I stand today to voice the sentiment of the young men of my state when
I speak for Grover Cleveland. His name is upon their lips. His name is in
their hearts. They love him, gentlemen, and respect him, and they love
him and respect him not only for himself, for his character, for his integrity, for his iron will, but they love him most for the enemies he has made.

> EDWARD STUYVESANT BRAGG, speech at Democratic Na-
> tional Convention, 1884

We are Republicans, and don't propose to leave our party and identify
ourselves with the party whose antecedents have been Rum, Romanism,
and Rebellion.

> SAMUEL DICKINSON BURCHARD, speaking for a group of
> clergymen calling on Republican Presidential Candidate
> James G. Blaine, New York, October 29, 1884. Unfortu-
> nately for the Republicans, who lost the election because
> of this widely publicized remark, the shorthand clerk at the
> conference was a Democrat, who happily reported the in-
> cident to the newspapers.

A Public Office Is a Public Trust.

> Slogan of Cleveland's 1884 campaign. The use of this
> phrase as a slogan was thought up by a Democratic press
> agent. It is an old phrase. Charles Sumner, in a speech in
> the Senate, May, 1872, could say: "The phrase, 'public
> office is a public trust,' has of late become common prop-
> erty." See also Calhoun, page 333.

Mugwump.

> An Algonquin Indian word, meaning "Big Chief," used in
> Eliot's translation of the Bible, 1661. Said to have been first
> used in political sense in 1872 by the Indianapolis *Sentinel.*

A mugwump is a fellow with his mug on one side of the fence and his
wump on the other.

> ANON., campaign slogan, 1884; the liberal Independents
> who split from the Republican party to support Cleveland
> instead of Blaine were called mugwumps.

After an existence of nearly twenty years of almost innocuous desuetude these laws are brought forth.

> GROVER CLEVELAND, message, March 1, 1886, referring to Tenure of Office Act

Our progress toward a wise conclusion will not be improved by dwelling upon the theories of protection and free trade. . . .

It is a condition that confronts us—not a theory.

> GROVER CLEVELAND, "Message to Congress," Dec., 1887

As Maine goes, so goes the country.

> Political maxim after election of Harrison, 1888

You shall not press down upon the brow of labor this crown of thorns— you shall not crucify mankind upon a cross of gold.

> WILLIAM JENNINGS BRYAN, speech, Democratic National Convention, July, 1896. On December 22, 1894, eighteen months before, in a speech before the House of Representatives, Bryan, who knew a good thing when he said it, spoke as follows: "I shall not help crucify mankind upon a cross of gold. I shall not aid in pressing down upon the bleeding brow of labor this crown of thorns."

I wish to preach, not the doctrine of ignoble ease, but the doctrine of the strenuous life.

> THEODORE ROOSEVELT, speech, Chicago, April, 1899

The Full Dinner Pail.

> Campaign slogan, 1900, McKinley being the Republican candidate

A man who is good enough to shed his blood for the country is good enough to be given a square deal afterward. More than that no man is entitled to, and less than that no man shall have.

> THEODORE ROOSEVELT, Springfield, Illinois, July 4, 1903

I feel as fit as a bull moose.

> THEODORE ROOSEVELT, reply to reporter on the eve of the Progressive Party Convention, August 7, 1912

We stand at Armageddon, and we battle for the Lord.

> THEODORE ROOSEVELT, speech on eve of Republican Convention, June, 1912

The Ananias Club.

> A fictitious club thus named by newspapermen, the members of which were men who Theodore Roosevelt announced were misquoting or misrepresenting him

He Kept Us Out of War.

> ANON., campaign slogan for Wilson, 1916. According to William Allen White a speech by Congressman Martin W. Littleton in 1916 started the famous phrase.

America's present need is . . . not nostrums but normalcy.

> WARREN G. HARDING, speech, Boston, May 10, 1920

Keep Cool With Coolidge.

> Campaign slogan, 1924

We offer one who has the will to win—who not only deserves success but commands it. Victory is his habit—the happy warrior, Alfred Smith.

> FRANKLIN D. ROOSEVELT, nominating speech, Democratic National Convention, 1928. The phrase occurs in Wordsworth's "The Character of the Happy Warrior."

Let's look at the record.

> ALFRED E. SMITH. "He could make statistics sit up, beg, roll over and bark."—Robert Moses

Nothing doing. That's just baloney. Everybody knows I can't lay bricks.

> ALFRED E. SMITH, at the laying of the cornerstone of the New York State Office Building, when asked to permit a moving picture of him laying the brick

A Chicken in Every Pot, a Car in Every Garage.

> Republican National Committee advertisement, 1928

Sons of the Wild Jackass.

> GEORGE HIGGINS MOSES, phrase applied to Western and

> Southern "radical" Republicans, after the election of Herbert Hoover, 1928

Don't Swap Barrels Going Over Niagara.

> Slogan ascribed ironically to the Republicans during Roosevelt-Hoover campaign, 1932. It refers, of course, to the time-honored Republican slogan, "Don't Switch Horses in Midstream" (Lincoln first to use it).

I pledge you, I pledge myself, to a new deal for the American people. Let us all here assembled constitute ourselves prophets of a new order of competence and courage. This is more than a political campaign; it is a call to arms.

> FRANKLIN D. ROOSEVELT, speech accepting Democratic nomination, 1932

The brains trust.

> JAMES M. KIERAN, in a conversation with Franklin D. Roosevelt, August, 1932, referring to the professors and such who were flocking to the Roosevelt campaign banner. The newspapers converted the phrase, which has been attributed to others, to "brain trust," and it there remains.

Soak the Rich.

> Denunciation of Franklin D. Roosevelt's tax program, 1935

Share the Wealth.

> HUEY LONG, political slogan, 1930's

Every Man a King.

> HUEY LONG, political slogan, 1930's

That Man in the White House.

> Uncomplimentary remark applied often to F.D.R. after 1935

This generation of Americans has a rendezvous with destiny.

> FRANKLIN D. ROOSEVELT, speech, 1936

As Maine goes, so goes Vermont.

> JAMES A. FARLEY, after Roosevelt's landslide victory over

Landon in 1936, in which Landon won only Maine and Vermont

We will spend and spend, tax and tax, elect and elect.

> ANON., of the W.P.A. and other New Deal measures; often ascribed to (and vehemently denied by) Harry Hopkins

I still remember: he is one of that great historic trio which has voted consistently against every measure for the relief of agriculture: Martin, Barton and Fish.

> FRANKLIN D. ROOSEVELT, speech in Boston, 1940 campaign

Safe on 3rd.

> ANON., inscription on placard carried by people of Hyde Park, New York, coming to congratulate Franklin D. Roosevelt on his election victory, November, 1940. This was the only election in which he carried Hyde Park.

Clear everything with Sidney.

> Attributed to FRANKLIN D. ROOSEVELT by Robert Hannegan during Democratic National Convention, Chicago, 1944. Sidney Hillman was head of the C.I.O. and his support in the choice of a Vice-President was desirable, but no Democrat ever admitted that Roosevelt used the phrase.

Tom Dewey has thrown his diapers into the ring.

> HAROLD L. ICKES, during the Presidential campaign, 1944

It's Time for a Change.

> Slogan of the Republican party, 1952

Twenty Years of Treason.

> Slogan of small minority of the Republican party, 1952; they refer to the Democrats. Often attributed to Senator McCarthy.

I've always liked bird dogs better than kennel-fed dogs myself. You know, one who'll get out and hunt for food rather than sit on his fanny and yell.

> CHARLES E. WILSON, press conference, Detroit, Oct. 12, 1954

VI. How and Why We Fought

WAR: VIEWPOINTS

•

The surest way to prevent war is not to fear it.

JOHN RANDOLPH, speech in the House, 1806

Few men exhibit greater diversity, or, if we may so express it, greater antithesis of character than the native warrior of North America. In war, he is daring, boastful, cunning, ruthless, self-denying, and self-devoted; in peace, just, generous, hospitable, revengeful, superstitious, modest, and commonly chaste.

JAMES FENIMORE COOPER, *The Last of the Mohicans*

The discipline which makes the soldiers of a free country reliable in battle is not to be gained by harsh or tyrannical treatment. On the contrary, such treatment is far more likely to destroy than to make an army. It is possible to give commands in such manner as to inspire an intense desire to obey; while the opposite manner cannot fail to excite strong resentment and a desire to disobey. The one mode or the other springs from a corresponding spirit in the breast of the commander. He who feels the respect which is due to others cannot fail to inspire in them regard for himself; while he who feels disrespect toward others . . . cannot fail to inspire hatred against himself.

MAJOR GENERAL JOHN M. SCHOFIELD, address, West Point, August, 1887; later cast on bronze tablet at entrance to old South Barracks. Every plebe must memorize the words.

Much is required of those to whom much is given. So viewed, the ability speedily to put forth the nation's power . . . is one of the clear duties involved in the Christian word "watchfulness"—readiness for the call that may come, whether unexpectedly or not.

ADMIRAL ALFRED THAYER MAHAN, 1899

There is a homely adage which runs, "Speak softly and carry a big stick; you will go far." If the American nation will speak softly and yet build and keep at a pitch of the highest training a thoroughly efficient navy, the Monroe Doctrine will go far.

THEODORE ROOSEVELT, address at Minnesota State Fair, September 2, 1901

361

It is only the warlike power of a civilized people that can give peace to the world.

> THEODORE ROOSEVELT, speech during 1900 campaign

The people that do not expand leave, and can leave, nothing behind them. . . . Nations that expand and nations that do not expand may both ultimately go down, but the one leaves heirs and a glorious memory, and the other leaves neither.

> THEODORE ROOSEVELT, *The Strenuous Life,* 1900

We must bear in mind that the great end in view is righteousness, justice as between man and man, nation and nation, the chance to lead our lives on a somewhat higher level, with a broader spirit of brotherly love for one another. Peace is generally good in itself, but it is never the highest good unless it comes as the handmaid of righteousness; and it becomes a very evil thing if it serves merely as a mask for cowardice and sloth, or as an instrument to further the ends of despotism or anarchy.

> THEODORE ROOSEVELT, "Nobel Peace Prize Speech," Christiana, Norway, 1910

There is no nation on earth so dangerous as a nation fully armed, and bankrupt at home.

> HENRY CABOT LODGE, speech before the National Security League, Washington, January 22, 1916

The order to engage the enemy may come from lips belonging to a man familiarly describable in terms of human failings, possibly of vulgarities; but these defects are hidden and made non-tainting behind the limits and barriers within which the man has been isolated and consecrated. If happily this man, in his person, is valiant, kindly, glamourous, then the order enjoys all the added benefit of this personal setting, much as the jewel is more advantageously displayed in a beautiful case. Yet it merely is *through* the man, through his years of training and testing, his consecration, that the order to steam into death roars out to his crew, roars straight up out of the living depths beneath a hundred million people fighting for a richer and more significant life, depths where a band of lonely Pilgrims still make the first covenant to "submit to such government and such governors as they should by common consent agree to make and choose" . . . where gentlemen still rear the spacious and graceful mansions on the fragrant margins of tidewater . . . where a frozen Army, dying and forlorn on icebound Pennsylvania hills, still bleeds out a gleaming pattern within the loom of its dreaming, iron leader's will . . . where women, like rare, embattled flowers, fighting back to back with their men in a fantastic ordeal of isolation and raddled death, earn for themselves an unparalleled freedom . . . where the dream of schools free and open to all of whatever creed and aim is passionately realized even through famine and corruption . . . where Poe and Bierce sing of desire and hope lost in the ferocity of a lovely and monumental wilderness . . . where Willard Gibbs still launches the theorems that gave to the modern world the chemistry of its very life . . . where prairie schooners still breast the mystery of vaster landscapes than men with women and children ever had dared before . . . where two brothers still conquer first the yearning desert of the sky . . . where a lesser, seven hour a day slavery to the machine is substituted for the bestializing, dawn to dusk slavery to the land . . . where Melville, with his pale monster, still chants in mephitic, beguiling frightfulness his rebuttal to Dante's *Comedy* . . . the cogent summons from these depths it is, in times of clear right or inescapable wrong, crystallized, reposed within the essentially irrelevant person of the Captain, together there with the covenant pledging the decision of their efforts to Death or Victory, this it is before which the men of Delilah's world stand, salute and obey.

MARCUS GOODRICH, *Delilah*

Men, the stuff you hear about Americans wanting to stay out of this war is a lot of bull. Americans love to fight, traditionally. All real Americans love the sting of battle.

When you were kids, you all admired the champion marble player, the fastest runner, the big league ballplayer, the toughest boxer. The Americans love a winner. . . . [They] play to win; all the time. I wouldn't give a hoot for a man who lost and laughed. That's why Americans have never lost, and will never lose, a war. The very thought of losing is hateful to an American.

GENERAL GEORGE S. PATTON, JR., speech to troops of Third Army before leaving England for France, July, 1944

If man does find the solution for world peace it will be the most revolutionary reversal of his record we have ever known.

GEORGE C. MARSHALL, *Report of Chief of Staff*, 1945

A "brass hat" is an officer of at least one rank higher than you whom you don't like and who doesn't like you.

> KENNETH CLAIBORNE ROYALL, speech, Chamber of Commerce, Wilson, North Carolina, February 15, 1946

In planning any operation, it is vital to remember, and constantly repeat to oneself, two things: "In war nothing is impossible, provided you use audacity," and "Do not take counsel of your fears." If these two principles are adhered to, with American troops victory is certain.

> GENERAL GEORGE S. PATTON, JR., *War As I Knew It,* 1947

In my experience all very successful commanders are prima donnas, and must be so treated.

> GENERAL GEORGE S. PATTON, JR., *Ibid.*

It is sad to remember that, when anyone has fairly mastered the art of command, the necessity for that art usually expires—either through the termination of the war or through the advanced age of the commander.

> GENERAL GEORGE S. PATTON, JR., *Ibid.*

There are those who contend that the best strategist is the commander most distantly removed from his troops. For where units exist merely as symbols on a map the strategist can perform in a vacuum and his judgment cannot be infected by compassion for his troops. If war were fought with push-button devices, one might make a science of command. But because war is as much a conflict of passion as it is of force, no commander can become a strategist until first he knows his men. Far from being a handicap to command, compassion is the measure of it. For unless one values the lives of his soldiers and is tormented by their ordeals, he is unfit to command. He is unfit to appraise the cost of an objective in terms of human life.

. . . Eisenhower found as I did that the well-springs of humility lie in the field. For however arduous the task of a commander, he cannot face the men who shall live or die by his orders without sensing how much easier is his task than the one he has set them to perform.

> GENERAL OMAR N. BRADLEY, *A Soldier's Story*

I hate war as only a soldier who has lived it can, only as one who has seen its brutality, its futility, its *stupidity.*

> DWIGHT D. EISENHOWER, quoted by Gunther, *Eisenhower*

In war there is no substitute for victory.

> Douglas MacArthur, address before a joint meeting of
> Congress, April 19, 1951

I know war as few other men now living know it, and nothing to me is more revolting. I have long advocated its complete abolition, as its very destructiveness on both friend and foe has rendered it useless as a means of settling international disputes.

> Douglas MacArthur, *Ibid.*

There are only two kinds of wars—Indian wars and coalition wars. All wars of the future are coalition wars and we have to learn how to fight them.

> General Alfred Gruenther, of N.A.T.O., 1953

I have spoken to people in four continents. I know how much it means to them to be told that in the United States there are people who are governed by conscience; that Americans believe in the natural goodness of man; that they know that citizenship in the human community does not cancel out citizenship in the national community; that many Americans are working for a world which can at last free itself of anarchy; that some day soon it will be possible for peoples everywhere to release their vast energies for revitalizing the good earth in the making of a better world, a better life.

War is an invention of the human mind. The human mind can invent peace.

> Norman Cousins, *Who Speaks for Man?*, 1953

THE WARS

•

THE REVOLUTION

Proclaim liberty throughout the land unto all the inhabitants thereof.

> Leviticus, 25:10; inscription on the Liberty Bell. The bell
> was ordered with these words by the Pennsylvania Provin-
> cial Assembly on November 1, 1751. Twenty-five years later
> it tolled while the Declaration of Independence was signed.

Taxation without representation is tyranny.

> James Otis, 1765

Caesar had his Brutus, Charles the First had his Cromwell, and George the Third ["Treason!" cried the Speaker]—may profit by their example. If this be treason, make the most of it.

> PATRICK HENRY, speech in the House of Burgesses, Richmond, Virginia, May 29, 1765

Let us contemplate our forefathers, and posterity, and resolve to maintain the rights bequeathed to us from the former, for the sake of the latter. The necessity of the times, more than ever, calls for our utmost circumspection, deliberation, fortitude and perseverance. Let us remember that "if we suffer tamely a lawless attack upon our liberty, we encourage it, and involve others in our doom." It is a very serious consideration . . . that millions yet unborn may be the miserable sharers in the event.

> SAMUEL ADAMS, speech, 1771

This is the most magnificent movement of all.

> JOHN ADAMS, of the Boston Tea Party, 1773

Blandishments will not fascinate us, nor will threats of a "halter" intimidate. For, under God, we are determined that wheresoever, whensoever, or howsoever we shall be called to make our exit, we will die free men.

> JOSIAH QUINCY, *Observations on the Boston Port Bill,* 1774

The die was now cast; I had passed the Rubicon. Swim or sink, live or die, survive or perish with my country was my unalterable determination.

> JOHN ADAMS, *Works,* IV, 1774. Daniel Webster, in his *Eulogy of Adams and Jefferson* (1826), paraphrased the words thus: "Sink or swim, live or die, survive or perish, I give my hand and my heart to this vote."

What a glorious morning is this!

> SAMUEL ADAMS, hearing firing in Boston, April 19, 1775

Stand your ground. Don't fire unless fired upon, but if they mean to have a war let it begin here.

> CAPTAIN JOHN PARKER, to his Minute Men on Lexington Green, April 19, 1775. The Revolutionary War therewith began.

As to pay, Sir, I beg leave to assure the Congress, that, as no pecuniary consideration could have tempted me to accept this arduous employment, at the expense of my domestic ease and happiness, I do not wish to make any profit from it. I will keep an exact account of my expenses. Those, I doubt not, they will discharge; and that is all I desire.

> GEORGE WASHINGTON, answer to Congress on his appointment as Commander-in-Chief, June 16, 1775

Men, you are all marksmen—don't one of you fire until you see the whites of their eyes.

> ISRAEL PUTNAM, Battle of Bunker Hill, June 17, 1775

There is a time to pray and a time to fight. This is the time to fight.

> JOHN PETER GABRIEL MUHLENBERG, sermon, 1775

You are a Member of Parliament, and one of that Majority which has doomed my Country to Destruction. You have begun to burn our Towns, and murder our People,—Look upon your Hands!—They are stained with the Blood of your relations!—You and I were long Friends:—you are now my Enemy,—and I am, Yours, B. Franklin.

> BENJAMIN FRANKLIN, letter to William Strahan, July 5, 1775. This letter, to an old friend, was never sent.

MR. PRESIDENT: It is natural for man to indulge in the illusions of hope. We are apt to shut our eyes against a painful truth, and listen to the song of that siren till she transforms us into beasts. Is this the part of wise men, engaged in a great and arduous struggle for liberty? Are we disposed to be of the number of those who, having eyes, see not, and having ears, hear not, the things which so nearly concern their temporal salvation? For my part, whatever anguish of spirit it may cost, I am willing to know the whole truth; to know the worst, and to provide for it.

. . . If we wish to be free; if we mean to preserve inviolate those inestimable privileges for which we have been so long contending; if we mean not basely to abandon the noble struggle in which we have been so long engaged, and which we have pledged ourselves never to abandon until the glorious object of our contest shall be obtained—we must fight! I repeat it, sir, we must fight! An appeal to arms, and to the God of hosts, is all that is left us.

. . . It is vain, sir, to extenuate the matter. The gentlemen may cry, Peace, peace! but there is no peace. The war has actually begun! The next gale that sweeps from the north will bring to our ears the clash of resounding arms! Our brethren are already in the field! Why stand we

here idle? What is it that the gentlemen wish? What would they have?
Is life so dear or peace so sweet as to be purchased at the price of chains
and slavery? Forbid it, Almighty God. I know not what course others
may take, but as for me, give me liberty or give me death!

> PATRICK HENRY, speech in the Virginia Revolutionary
> Council, Richmond, 1775. The speech was not written down
> at the time, and the above form of it we owe to William
> Wirt, Henry's biographer.

In the new code of laws which I suppose it will be necessary for you to
make I desire you would remember the ladies and be more generous and
favorable to them than your ancestors.

> ABIGAIL ADAMS, letter to John Adams, March 31, 1776

These are the times that try men's souls. The summer soldier and the
sunshine patriot will, in this crisis, shrink from the service of their country; but he that stands it *now*, deserves the love and thanks of man and
woman. Tyranny, like hell, is not easily conquered; yet we have this consolation with us, that the harder the conflict, the more glorious the triumph. . . . It is the object only of war that makes it honorable. And if
there was ever a just war since the world began, it is this in which America is now engaged. . . . We fight not to enslave, but to set a country
free, and to make room upon the earth for honest men to live in.

> THOMAS PAINE, *The American Crisis*, 1776

All right, just give me some wedges and a mallet, and half a dozen men
of my own choosing, and I'll soon take it for you.

> ISRAEL PUTNAM, speech before capture in 1776 of Fort Os-
> wegatchie (now Ogdensburg), New York

Don't give up the ship! You will beat them off!

> JAMES MUGFORD, last words, as he lay dying in his schooner,
> the *Franklin*, during a British attack in Boston Harbor, May
> 19, 1776

Sir, I know the uncertainty of human affairs, but I see, I see clearly,
through this day's business. You and I, indeed, may rue it. We may not
live to the time when this Declaration shall be made good. We may die;
die colonists; die slaves; die, it may be, ignominiously and on the scaffold.
Be it so.

Be it so. If it be the pleasure of Heaven that my country shall require the poor offering of my life, the victim shall be ready, at the appointed hour of sacrifice, come when that hour may. But while I do live, let me have a country, and that a free country. . . .

Sir, before God, I believe the hour is come. My judgment approves this measure, and my whole heart is in it. All I have, and all that I am, and all that I hope, in this life, I am now ready to stake upon it; and I leave off as I began, that live or die, survive or perish, I am for the Declaration.

JOHN ADAMS, speech, 1776

There, I guess King George will be able to read that.

JOHN HANCOCK, affixing a bold signature to the Declaration of Independence, July 4, 1776

We must indeed all hang together, or most assuredly we will all hang separately.

BENJAMIN FRANKLIN, at signing of Declaration of Independence; but his biographer, Carl Van Doren, was never able to find proof that Franklin actually said this

The time is now near at hand which must probably determine whether Americans are to be freemen or slaves; whether they are to have any property they can call their own; whether their houses and farms are to be pillaged and destroyed, and themselves consigned to a state of wretchedness from which no human efforts will deliver them. The fate of unborn millions will now depend, under God, on the courage and conduct of this army. Our cruel and unrelenting enemy leaves us only the choice of a brave resistance, or the most abject submission. We have, therefore, to resolve to conquer or to die.

GEORGE WASHINGTON, address to American troops before the Battle of Long Island, July, 1776

Don't Tread on Me.

Motto of first flag of the Revolution, raised on John Paul Jones's ship, the *Alfred*, 1776

The spirit of '76.

THOMAS JEFFERSON, letter to Monroe; title of painting by Archibald M. Willard (1836–1918)

Put none but Americans on guard tonight.

> GEORGE WASHINGTON, based on his "Circular Letter" to
> regimental commanders regarding recruits for his body-
> guard: "You will therefore send me none but natives,"
> April 30, 1777

My men, yonder are the Hessians. They were bought for seven pounds
and ten pence a man. Are you worth more? Prove it. Tonight, the American flag floats from yonder hill or Molly Stark sleeps a widow!

> GENERAL JOHN STARK, before the Battle of Bennington,
> August 16, 1777

On our way to England the frigate lost part of her crew with the scurvy,
but as for us the General, as well as the Captain and his officers, were
astonished on the score of our being all brave and hearty. The former
even expressed himself in this manner: "What, are none of them d——d
Yankees sick!" Somebody made answer, "Not one." "D——n them," says
he, "there is nothing but fire and lightning will kill them."

> NATHANIEL FANNING, *Memoirs,* of his captivity in 1778

I have not yet begun to fight!

> JOHN PAUL JONES, in the Battle off Flamborough Head,
> England, on September 23, 1779, between the British ship
> *Serapis* and the American vessel *Bonhomme Richard.* The
> battle had been in progress for nearly an hour, and the crisis
> of the bloody conflict seemed to be at hand. Several of
> Jones's men, thinking him killed, asked the British for quar-
> ter. Captain Pearson of the *Serapis* demanded to know if
> the *Bonhomme Richard* had struck. Jones's reply is ordinar-
> ily assumed to have been the above.
>
> Actually there is no evidence that he said this. Contem-
> porary accounts differ, and those that approximate most
> closely to this phrase are not to be trusted. Jones himself
> never wrote the phrase in describing the battle. Rather, in
> a discussion of it some years later, he said that he had said,
> "I do not dream of surrendering, but I am determined to
> make you strike." It is unlikely that Jones would have de-
> nied the colorful phrase if he had actually used it.

Ever since I arrived at the state of manhood, and acquainted myself with
the general history of mankind, I have felt a sincere passion for liberty.

The history of nations, doomed to perpetual slavery in consequence of yielding up to tyrants their natural-born liberties, I read with a sort of philosophical horror; so that the first systematical and bloody attempt, at Lexington, to enslave America thoroughly electrified my mind, and fully determined me to take part with my country.

ETHAN ALLEN, narrative of his captivity, 1779

The garrison being asleep, except the sentries, we gave three huzzas which greatly surprised them. One of the sentries made a pass at one of my officers with a charged bayonet, and slightly wounded him. My first thought was to kill him with my sword; but, in an instant, I altered the design and fury of the blow to a slight cut on the side of the head; upon which he dropped his gun and asked quarter, which I readily granted him, and demanded of him the place where the commanding officer kept. He showed me a pair of stairs in the front of the barrack, on the west part of the garrison, which led up to a second story in said barrack, to which I immediately repaired, and ordered the commander, Captain De la Place, to come forth instantly, or I would sacrifice the whole garrison; at which the Captain came immediately to the door, with his breeches in his hand, when I ordered him to deliver me the fort instantly.

He asked me by what authority I demanded it.

I answered him, "In the name of the great Jehovah, and the Continental Congress."

The authority of the Congress being very little known at that time, he began to speak again. But I interrupted him and, with my drawn sword over his head, again demanded an immediate surrender of the garrison; with which he then complied, and ordered his men to be forthwith paraded without arms, as he had given up the garrison. . . . This surprise was carried into execution in the gray of the morning of the tenth day of May, 1775. The sun seemed to rise that morning with a superior luster, and Ticonderoga and its dependencies smiled on its conquerors, who tossed about the flowing bowl, and wished success to Congress and the liberty and freedom of America.

ETHAN ALLEN, Ibid.

May we never see another war! For in my opinion there never was a good war or a bad peace.

BENJAMIN FRANKLIN, letter to Josiah Quincy, Sept., 1783

Having now finished the work assigned me, I retire from the great theatre of action; and, bidding an affectionate farewell to this august body, under

whose orders I have so long acted, I here offer my commission, and take
my leave of all the employments of public life.

> GEORGE WASHINGTON, resignation from the Army, Decem-
> ber 23, 1783

It appears that there is still an option left to the United States of America. . . . This is the moment when the eyes of the whole world are turned
upon them, this is the moment to establish or ruin their national character forever.

> GEORGE WASHINGTON, "Circular Letter," written after re-
> tirement from command of the Army

There is nothing more common, than to confound the terms of the American revolution with those of the late American war. The American war
is over: but this is far from being the case with the American revolution.
On the contrary, nothing but the first act of the great drama is closed.
It remains yet to establish and perfect our new forms of government; and
to prepare the principles, morals, and manners of our citizens, for these
forms of government, after they are established and brought to perfection.

> BENJAMIN RUSH, "Address to the People of the United
> States," 1787

I must study politics and war, that my sons may have liberty to study
mathematics and philosophy, geography, natural history and naval architecture, navigation, commerce, and agriculture, in order to give their
children a right to study painting, poetry, music, architecture, statuary,
tapestry, and porcelain.

> JOHN ADAMS

"My histories tell me that you men of the Revolution took up arms
against intolerable oppressions."

"What were they? Oppressions? I didn't feel them."

"What, were you not oppressed by the *Stamp Act?*"

"I never saw one of those stamps. . . . I am certain I never paid a
penny for one of them."

"Well, what then about the tea-tax?"

"Tea-tax! I never drank a drop of the stuff; the boys threw it all over-
board."

"Then I suppose you had been reading Harrington or Sidney and
Locke about the eternal principles of liberty."

"Never heard of 'em. We read only the *Bible,* the *Catechism,* Watts's *Psalms and Hymns,* and the *Almanack.*"

"Well, then, what was the matter? And what did you mean in going to the fight?"

"Young man, what we meant in going for those red-coats was this: we always had governed ourselves, and we always meant to. They didn't mean we should."

> Mellen Chamberlin, account of conversation with veteran of Revolutionary War, 1842; from *John Adams,* 1890

THE CIVIL WAR

SLAVERY

This is to the monthly meeting held at Richard Worrell's:

These are the reasons why we are against the traffic of menbody, as followeth: Is there any that would be done or handled at this manner? viz., to be sold or made a slave for all the time of his life? How fearful and faint-hearted are many at sea, when they see a strange vessel, being afraid it should be a Turk, and they should be taken, and sold for slaves into Turkey. Now, what is *this* better done, than Turks do? Yea, rather it is worse for them, which say they are Christians; for we hear that the most part of such negers are brought hither against their will and consent, and that many of them are stolen. Now, though they are black, we cannot conceive there is more liberty to have them slaves, as it is to have other white ones. There is a saying, that we should do to all men like as we will be done ourselves; making no difference of what generation, descent, or colour they are. And those who steal and rob men, and those who buy or purchase them, are they not all alike? Here is liberty of conscience, which is right and reasonable; here ought to be likewise liberty of the body, except of evil-doers, which is another case. But to bring men hither, or to rob and sell them against their will, we stand against.

> *Resolutions* of Germantown Mennonites, February 18, 1688. This is the earliest protest against slavery in the American colonies.

I never mean, unless some particular circumstance should compel me to it, to possess another slave by purchase, it being among my first wishes to see some plan adopted by which slavery in this country may be abolished by law.

> GEORGE WASHINGTON, letter to J. F. Mercer, Sept. 9, 1786

Indeed I tremble for my country when I reflect that God is just; that His justice cannot sleep forever; that considering numbers, nature and natural means only, a revolution of the wheel of fortune, an exchange of situation is among possible events; that it may become probable by supernatural interference!

> THOMAS JEFFERSON, *Notes on Virginia,* Query XVIII. The subject is slavery; the exchange of situation is the possible reversal of white and black.

I am in earnest. I will not equivocate; I will not excuse; I will not retreat a single inch; and I will be heard!

> WILLIAM LLOYD GARRISON, "Salutatory" of the *Liberator,* January 1, 1831

I will be as harsh as truth and as uncompromising as justice.

> WILLIAM LLOYD GARRISON, *Liberator,* 1831

I warn the abolitionists, ignorant and infatuated barbarians as they are, that if chance shall throw any of them into our hands, they may expect a felon's death!

> JAMES HENRY HAMMOND of South Carolina, 1836

But I take higher ground. I hold that in the present state of civilization, where two races of different origin, and distinguished by color and other physical differences, as well as intellectual, are brought together, the relation now existing in the slaveholding states between the two is, instead of an evil, a good—a positive good. I feel myself called upon to speak freely upon the subject, when the honor and interests of those I represent are involved. I hold, then, that there never has yet existed a wealthy and civilized society in which one portion of the community did not, in point of fact, live on the labor of the other. Broad and general as is this assertion, it is fully born out by history.

> JOHN C. CALHOUN, speech in the Senate, 1837

Our country is the world; our countrymen are all mankind.

> WILLIAM LLOYD GARRISON, "Prospectus" of the *Liberator,* December 15, 1837

Many in the South once believed that it [slavery] was a moral and political evil. That folly and delusion are gone. We see it now in its true light, and regard it as the most safe and stable basis for free institutions in the world.

> JOHN C. CALHOUN, speech, 1838

If you put a chain around the neck of a slave, the other end fastens itself around your own.

> RALPH WALDO EMERSON, *Essays: First Series,* "Compensation"

The compact which exists between the North and the South is a covenant with death and an agreement with hell.

> WILLIAM LLOYD GARRISON, "Resolution" adopted by the Anti-Slavery Society, January 27, 1843

Abolitionism is not a hobby, got up for political or associated aggrandisements; it is not a political ruse; it is not a spasm of sympathy, which lasts but for a moment, leaving the system weak and worn; it is not a fever of enthusiasm; it is not the fruit of fanaticism; it is not a spirit of faction. It is of heaven, not of men. It lies in the heart as a vital principle. It is an essential part of Christianity, and aside from it there can be no humanity. Its scope is not confined to the slave population of the United States, but embraces mankind. Opposition cannot weary it, force cannot put it down, fire cannot consume it.

> WILLIAM LLOYD GARRISON

You are numerically more powerful than the slave states, and greatness and magnanimity should ever be allied.

> HENRY CLAY, speech in the Senate, January 29, 1850; an attempt to effect a compromise on the slave question, which was successful for ten years

The parties in this conflict are not merely abolitionists and slaveholders—they are atheists, socialists, communists, red republicans, jacobins on the one side, and the friends of order and regulated freedom on the other. In one word, the world is the battleground—Christianity and atheism the combatants; and the progress of humanity the stake.

> REV. J. H. THORNWELL, President of University of South Carolina, 1850

Sold down the river.

>Of slaves sold to plantations in the Deep South, c. 1850

Uncle Tom's Cabin.

>HARRIET BEECHER STOWE, title of book published serially
>in *The National Era,* 1851–52. The book had a great effect
>on anti-slavery feeling; when President Lincoln met Mrs.
>Stowe in 1863 he peered at her and smilingly said: "So
>you're the little woman who made the great book" (Sand-
>burg, *Abraham Lincoln: The War Years*). When she was
>an old lady a man complimented her on having written it.
>"I did not write it," she replied. "God wrote it. I merely did
>His dictation."

Slavery is a wisely devised institution of heaven devised for the benefit,
improvement, and safety, morally, socially, and physically, of a barbarous
and inferior race, who would otherwise perish by famine or by filth, by
the sword, by disease, by waste, and destinies forever gnawing, consuming,
and finally destroying.

>WILLIAM GILMORE SIMMS, North Carolina writer, 1852

The malignant abuse lavished on the slaveholders of America by writers
in this country and England can be accounted for but in one way consistently with any degree of charitable consideration for the slanderers. They
have no knowledge of the thing abused. They substitute an ideal of their
own contriving for the reality. They regard slavery as a system of chains,
whips, and tortures. They consider its abuses as its necessary conditions,
and a cruel master its fair representative. . . . With these people the
cruelty of slavery is an affair of tropes and figures. But they have dealt so
long in metaphorical fetters and prisons, that they have brought themselves to believe that the Negroes work in chains and live in dungeons.

To prove the evils of slavery, they collect, from all quarters, its abuses,
and show the same regard for fairness and common sense as would do to
gather all the atrocities of their own country committed by husbands and
wives, parents and children, masters and servants, priest and people, and
denounce these several relations in life in consequence of their abuses.

The laborer suffers wrong and cruelty in England, but they say it is
against the law, against public opinion; he may apply to the courts for
redress; these are open to him. Cruelty to the slaves is equally against the
law. It is equally condemned by public opinion; and as to the courts of

law being open to the pauper hireling, we may remember the reply of Sheridan to a similar remark, Yes, and so are the London hotels. . . .

Slavery is that system of labor which exchanges subsistence for work, which secures a life-maintenance from the master to the slave, and gives a life-labor from the slave to the master. The slave is an apprentice for life, and owes his labor to his master; the master owes support, during life, to the slave. Slavery is the Negro system of labor. He is lazy and improvident. Slavery makes all work, and it insures homes, food, and clothing for all. It permits no idleness, and it provides for sickness, infancy, and old age. It allows no tramping or skulking, and it knows no pauperism.

This is the whole system substantially. . . .

If slavery is subject to abuses, it has its advantages also. It establishes more permanent, and, therefore, kinder relations between capital and labor. It removes what Stuart Mill calls "the widening and imbittering feud between the class of labor and the class of capital." . . . There is no such thing with slavery as a laborer for whom nobody cares or provides. The most wretched feature in hireling labor is the isolated, miserable creature who has no home, no work, no food, and in whom no one is particularly interested. *This is seen among hirelings only.*

. . . The quarrel is with the master, and the design is to calumniate him and injure him. And why this attack on the master? Who, among its pretended friends, will dare to say that they have done for the African race what the slaveholders of North America have done and are doing? What Abolitionist has bestowed on the Negro the same enduring patience, the same useful education, the same care and attendance? . . . [The Abolitionists] use the slave for the purposes of self-glorification only, indifferent about his present or future condition. They are ambitious to bring about a great social revolution—what its effects may be they do not care to enquire.

WILLIAM J. GRAYSON, *The Hireling and the Slave,* 1854

I could travel from Boston to Chicago by the light of my own effigies.

STEPHEN A. DOUGLAS, after the passage in 1854 of the Kansas-Nebraska Bill which he had supported

A peculiar institution.

Phrase describing slavery in the South, the origin of which is mysterious. One of the earliest known uses is in an article in the New York *Tribune,* October 19, 1854.

In this enlightened age there are few, I believe, but what will acknowledge that slavery as an institution is a moral and political evil in any country. It is useless to expatiate on its disadvantages. I think it, however, a greater evil to the white than to the black race, and while my feelings are strongly enlisted in behalf of the latter, my sympathies are more strong for the former.

ROBERT E. LEE, letter to his wife, December 27, 1856

They [the blacks] had no right which the white man was bound to respect.

ROGER B. TANEY, opinion, *Dred Scott* v. *Sanford,* 1857

The right of property in a slave is distinctly and expressly affirmed in the Constitution. No word can be found in the Constitution which gives Congress a greater power over slave property or which entitles property of that kind to less protection than property of any other description.

ROGER B. TANEY, *Ibid.*

And upon a full and careful consideration of the subject, the court is of the opinion that, upon the facts stated in the plea in abatement, Dred Scott was not a citizen of Missouri within the meaning of the Constitution of the United States, and not entitled as such to sue in its courts; and, consequently, that the Circuit Court had no jurisdiction of the case, and that the judgment on the plea in abatement is erroneous. . . .

ROGER B. TANEY, *Ibid.*

Slaves, if you please, are not property like other property in this: that you can easily rob us of them; but as to the *right* in them, that man has to overthrow the whole history of the world, he has to overthrow every treatise on jurisprudence, he has to ignore the common sentiment of mankind . . . ere he can reach the conclusion that the person who owns a slave . . . has no other property in that slave than the mere title which is given by the statute law of the land where it is found.

JUDAH P. BENJAMIN, speech in the Senate, March 11, 1858

If we could first know where we are, and whither we are tending, we could better judge what to do, and how to do it. We are now far into the fifth year since a policy was initiated with the avowed object and confident promise of putting an end to slavery agitation. Under the operation of that policy, that agitation has not only not ceased but has constantly augmented. In my opinion, it will not cease until a crisis shall have been reached and passed. "A house divided against itself cannot stand." I believe this government cannot endure permanently half slave and half free. I do not expect the Union to be dissolved—I do not expect the house to fall—but I do expect it will cease to be divided. It will become all one thing, or all the other. Either the opponents of slavery will arrest the further spread of it, and place it where the public mind shall rest in the belief that it is in the course of ultimate extinction; or its advocates will push it forward till it shall become alike lawful in all the States, old as well as new, North as well as South.

Have we no tendency to the latter condition?

> ABRAHAM LINCOLN, speech at Republican State Convention, Springfield, June 16, 1858

Let us discard all this quibbling about this man and the other man, this race and that race and the other race being inferior, and therefore they must be placed in an inferior position. Let us discard all these things, and unite as one people throughout this land, until we shall once more stand up declaring that all men are created equal.

> ABRAHAM LINCOLN, speech, Chicago, July 10, 1858

In the right to eat the bread . . . which his own hand earns, he [the Negro] *is my equal and the equal of Judge Douglas, and the equal of every living man.*

> ABRAHAM LINCOLN, Lincoln-Douglas Debates, August, 1858

I will say, then, that I am not, nor ever have been, in favor of bringing about in any way the social and political equality of the white and black races: that I am not, nor ever have been, in favor of making voters or jurors of negroes, nor of qualifying them to hold office, nor to intermarry with white people. . . .

And inasmuch as they cannot so live, while they do remain together there must be the position of superior and inferior, and I as much as any other man am in favor of having the superior position assigned to the white man.

> ABRAHAM LINCOLN, speech, Charleston, September 18, 1858. Cf. speech in Chicago, July 10, 1858.

I may be very insane; and I am so, if insane at all. But if that be so, insanity is like a very pleasant dream to me. I am not in the least degree conscious of my ravings, of my fears, or of any terrible visions whatever;

but fancy myself entirely composed, and that my sleep, in particular, is as sweet as that of a healthy, joyous little infant. I pray God that He will grant me a continuance of the same calm but delightful dream, until I come to know of those realities which eyes have not seen and which ears have not heard. I have scarce realized that I am in prison or in irons at all. I certainly think I was never more cheerful in my life.

> JOHN BROWN, to the Hon. D. R. Tilden, November 28, 1859. Brown was hanged on December 2. The talk of insanity is important; his mother and maternal grandmother died insane, and a number of other members of his immediate family, including his first wife, were insane.

I think, my friend, you are guilty of a great wrong against God and humanity—I say it without wishing to be offensive—and it would be perfectly right for any one to interfere with you so far as to free those you wilfully and wickedly hold in bondage. I do not say this insultingly. . . . I pity the poor in bondage that have none to help them; that is why I am here; not to gratify any personal animosity, revenge or vindictive spirit. It is my sympathy with the oppressed and the wronged, that are as good as you and as precious in the sight of God. . . . *I wish to say, furthermore, that you had better—all you people at the South—prepare yourselves for a settlement of that question that must come up for settlement sooner than you are prepared for it*. The sooner you are prepared the better. You may dispose of me very easily. I am nearly disposed of now; but this question is still to be settled—this negro question I mean; the end of that is not yet.

> JOHN BROWN, before his death, to his inquisitors

I am yet too young to understand that God is any respecter of persons. I believe that to have interfered as I have done—as I have always freely admitted I have done—in behalf of His despised poor, was not wrong but right. Now if it is deemed necessary that I should forfeit my life for the furtherance of the ends of justice and mingle my blood further with the blood of my children and with the blood of millions in this slave country whose rights are disregarded by wicked, cruel, and unjust enactments—I submit; so let it be done!

> JOHN BROWN, speech to the court at Harpers Ferry

[The Confederate Government] is founded upon exactly the opposite ideas; its foundations are laid, its cornerstone rests, upon the great truth that the Negro is not equal to the white man; subordination to the superior race is his natural and moral condition.

ALEXANDER STEPHENS, Savannah, March 21, 1861

"Mister Ward, don't yur blud bile at the thawt that three million and a half of your culled brethren air a clanking their chains in the South?" Sez I, "not a bile! Let 'em clank!"

CHARLES FARRAR BROWNE ("ARTEMUS WARD"), *Artemus Ward: His Book,* "Oberlin," 1862

The subject [the Emancipation Proclamation] is one upon which I have thought much for weeks past, and I may even say for months. I am approached with the most opposite opinions and advice, and that by religious men who are equally certain that they represent the divine will. I am sure that either the one or the other class is mistaken in that belief, and perhaps in some respects both. I hope it will not be irreverent for me to say that if it is probable that God would reveal His will to others on a point so connected with my duty, it might be supposed He would reveal it directly to me; for, unless I am more deceived in myself than I often am, it is my earnest desire to know the will of Providence in this matter. And if I can learn what it is, I will do it.

These are not, however, the days of miracles, and I suppose it will be granted that I am not to expect a direct revelation. I must study the plain physical facts of the case, ascertain what is possible, and learn what appears to be wise and right.

The subject is difficult, and good men do not agree.

ABRAHAM LINCOLN, reply to a Committee of Religious Denominations, September 13, 1862

The dogmas of the quiet past are inadequate to the stormy present. The occasion is piled high with difficulty, and we must rise—with the occasion. As our case is new, so we must think anew, and act anew. We must disenthrall ourselves, and then we shall save our country.

Fellow-citizens, *we* cannot escape history. We of this Congress and this administration, will be remembered in spite of ourselves. No personal significance, or insignificance, can spare one or another of us. The fiery trial through which we pass, will light us down, in honor or dishonor, to the latest generation. We *say* we are for the Union. The world will not forget that we say this. We know how to save the Union. The world knows we do know how to save it. We—*even we here*—hold the power, and bear the responsibility. In *giving freedom* to the *slave,* we *assure* freedom to the *free*—honorable alike in what we give, and what we preserve. We shall nobly save, or meanly lose, the last best hope of earth. Other means may succeed; this could not fail. The way is plain, peaceful, generous, just— a way which, if followed, the world will forever applaud, and God must forever bless.

> ABRAHAM LINCOLN, "Annual Message to Congress," December 1, 1862

If he [the Negro] knows enough to be hanged, he knows enough to vote.

> FREDERICK DOUGLASS, speech to the American Anti-Slavery Society, Philadelphia, December, 1863

Allez preech agin the Nigger. Preech agin amalgamashun at least 4 Sundays per month. Lern to spell and pronownce "Missenegenegenashun." It's a good word.

> PETROLEUM VESUVIUS NASBY, during campaign of 1864

I never knew a man who wished himself to be a slave. Consider if you know any *good* thing that no man desires for himself.

> ABRAHAM LINCOLN, written in an album at a Sanitary Commission Fair, 1864

Whenever I hear any one arguing for slavery, I feel a strong impulse to see it tried on him personally.

> ABRAHAM LINCOLN, address to an Indiana Regiment, March 17, 1865

The day you make soldiers of them is the beginning of the end of the revolution. If slaves will make good soldiers our whole theory of slavery is wrong.

> Unidentified Southerner, when in 1865 the use of Negroes as soldiers was authorized; quoted by Cole, *The Irrepressible Conflict*

Looking upon African slavery from the same standpoint held by the noble framers of our Constitution, I have ever considered it one of the greatest blessings (both for themselves and us) that God ever bestowed upon a favorite nation.

> JOHN WILKES BOOTH, letter left with his sister Asia before his assassination of Lincoln, April 14, 1865

Forty Acres and a Mule.

> Derisive remark to freed slaves, 1866, re extravagant hopes
> as to the government's generosity

No doubt the Confederates, victorious, would have abolished slavery by
the middle 80's. They were headed that way before the war, and the more
sagacious of them were all in favor of it. But they were in favor of it on
sound economic grounds, and not on the brummagem moral grounds
which persuaded the North. The difference here is immense. In human
history a moral victory is always a disaster, for it debauches and degrades
both the victor and the vanquished. The triumph of sin in 1865 would
have stimulated and helped to civilize both sides.

> H. L. Mencken, "The Calamity of Appomattox," *Amer-
> ican Mercury,* September, 1930

THE UNION AND THE CONFEDERACY

If this bill [for the admission of Orleans Territory as a State] passes, it is
my deliberate opinion that it is virtually a dissolution of the Union; that
it will free the States from their moral obligation; and, as it will be the
right of all, so it will be the duty of some, definitely to prepare for separation,—amicably if they can, violently if they must.

> Josiah Quincy, Jr., speech in the House of Representa-
> tives, January 14, 1811

The advice nearest my heart and deepest in my convictions is, that the
Union of the states be cherished and perpetuated. Let the open enemy of
it be regarded as a Pandora with her box opened, and the disguised one
as the serpent creeping with his deadly wiles into paradise.

> James Madison, "Advice to My Country, Conclusion,"
> found among his papers after his death

I had for a long time ceased to read the newspapers, or pay any attention
to public affairs, confident that they were in good hands, and content to
be a passenger in our bark to the shore from which I am not distant. But
this momentous question [the Missouri Compromise], like a firebell in
the night, awakened and filled me with terror. I considered it at once as
the knell of the Union. It is hushed, indeed, for the moment. But this is
a reprieve only, not a final sentence. A geographical line, coinciding with
a marked principle, once conceived and held up to the angry passions of

men, will never be obliterated; and every new irritation will make it deeper and deeper.

> THOMAS JEFFERSON, letter to John Holmes, April 22, 1820

Liberty and Union, now and forever, one and inseparable!

> DANIEL WEBSTER, speech on Foot's Resolution, January 26, 1830

Our Federal Union! It must and shall be preserved!

> ANDREW JACKSON, toast, Jefferson Birthday banquet, 1830. John C. Calhoun rose after this toast and, his hand shaking so that the wine ran down the side of his glass, proposed: "The Union, *next to our liberty,* most dear! May we all remember that it can only be preserved by respecting the rights of the States and by distributing equally the benefits and burdens of the Union." Jackson's is the one that was remembered, which proves that the shorter the toast the longer the life.

I have heard something said about allegiance to the South. I know no South, no North, no East, no West, to which I owe any allegiance. . . . The gentleman speaks of Virginia being my country. The Union, sir, is my country.

> HENRY CLAY, speech in the Senate, 1848

I hear with distress and anguish the word "secession," especially when it falls from the lips of those who are patriotic, and known to the country, and known all over the world, for their political services. Secession! Peaceable secession! Sir, your eyes and mine are never destined to see that miracle. The dismemberment of this vast country without convulsion! The breaking up of the fountains of the great deep without ruffling the surface! Who is so foolish, I beg every body's pardon, as to expect to see any such thing? Sir, he who sees these States, now revolving in harmony around a common centre, and expects to see them quit their places and fly off without convulsion, may look the next hour to see the heavenly bodies rush from their spheres, and jostle against each other in the realms of space, without causing the wreck of the universe. There can be no such thing as a peaceable secession. Peaceable secession is an utter impossibility. Is the great Constitution under which we live, covering this whole country, is it to be thawed and melted away by secession, as the snows on the mountain melt under the influence of a vernal sun, disappear almost unobserved, and run off? No, Sir! No, Sir! I will not state what might produce the disruption of the Union; but, Sir, I see as plainly as I see the sun in heaven what that disruption itself must produce; I see that it must produce war, and such a war as I will not describe, *in its twofold character.*

Peaceable secession! Peaceable secession! The concurrent agreement of all the members of this great republic to separate! A voluntary separation, with alimony on one side and on the other. Why, what would be the result? Where is the line to be drawn? What States are to secede? What is to remain American? What am I to be? An American no longer? Am I to become a sectional man, a local man, a separatist, with no country in common with the gentlemen who sit around me here, or who fill the other house of Congress? Heaven forbid! Where is the flag of the republic to remain? Where is the eagle still to tower? or is he to cower, and shrink, and fall to the ground? Why, Sir, our ancestors, our fathers and our grandfathers, those of them that are yet living amongst us with prolonged lives, would rebuke and reproach us; and our children and our grandchildren would cry out shame upon us, if we of this generation should dishonor these ensigns of the power of the government and the harmony of that Union which is every day felt among us with so much joy and gratitude. What is to become of the army? What is to become of the navy? What is to become of the public lands? How is each of the thirty States to defend itself? I know, although the idea has not been stated distinctly, there is to be, or it is supposed possible there will be, a Southern Confederacy. I do not mean, when I allude to this statement, that any one seriously contemplates such a state of things. I do not mean to say that it is true, but I have heard it suggested elsewhere, that the idea has been entertained, that, after the dissolution of this Union, a Southern Confederacy might be formed. I am sorry, Sir, that it has ever been thought of, talked of, or dreamed of, in the wildest flights of human imagination. But the idea, so far as it exists, must be of a separation, assigning the slave States to one side and the free States to the other. Sir, I may express myself too strongly perhaps, but there are impossibilities in the natural as well as in the physical world, and I hold the idea of the separation of these States, those that are free to form one government, and those that are slave-holding to form another, as such an impossibility. We could not separate the States by any such line, if we were to draw it. We could not sit down here to-day and draw a line of separation that would satisfy any five men in the country. There are natural causes that would keep and tie us together, and there are social and domestic relations which we could not break if we would, and which we should not if we could.

. . . Sir, I am ashamed to pursue this line of remark. I dislike it, I have an utter disgust for it. I would rather hear of natural blasts and mildews, war, pestilence, and famine, than to hear gentlemen talk of secession. To break up this great government! to dismember this glorious country! to astonish Europe with an act of folly such as Europe for two centuries has never beheld in any government or any people! No, Sir, no, Sir! There will be no secession! Gentlemen are not serious when they talk of secession.

> DANIEL WEBSTER, speech on the Constitution and the Union, Senate, March 7, 1850. This speech was largely responsible for the Compromise of 1850, but it lost Webster much of his Northern following.

The Constitution in all its provisions looks to an indestructible Union composed of indestructible States.

> SALMON P. CHASE

An Ordinance to Dissolve the Union between the State of South Carolina and other States with her under the compact entitled the United States of America:

We, the people of the State of South Carolina, in Convention assembled, do declare and ordain, and it is hereby declared and ordained, that the ordinance adopted by us in Convention, on the 23d day of May, in the year of our Lord 1788, whereby the Constitution of the United States of America was ratified, and also all Acts and parts of Acts of the General Assembly of this State ratifying the amendments of the said Constitution, are hereby repealed, and that the union now subsisting between South Carolina and other States under the name of the United States of America is hereby dissolved.

> South Carolina Ordinance of Secession, December 20, 1860. When Lincoln was elected, the legislature of South Carolina called a convention to meet December 17, 1860, to consider secession. On December 20 secession was unanimously voted —the first state to so do.

We, the People of the Confederate States, each State acting in its sovereign and independent character, in order to form a permanent Federal

Government, establish justice, insure domestic tranquillity, and secure the blessings of liberty to ourselves and our posterity—invoking the favor and guidance of Almighty God—do ordain and establish this Constitution for the Confederate States of America.

Preamble to the Constitution of the Confederate States

Say to the seceded States, "Wayward sisters, depart in peace."

GENERAL WINFIELD SCOTT, letter to William H. Seward, March 3, 1861

No government proper ever had a provision in its organic law for its own termination.

ABRAHAM LINCOLN, "First Inaugural," March 4, 1861

1. RESOLVED, That any vote of secession or other act by which any State may undertake to put an end to the supremacy of the Constitution within its territory is inoperative and void against the Constitution, and when sustained by force it becomes a practical *abdication* by the State of all rights under the Constitution, while the treason which it involves still further works an instant *forfeiture* of all those functions and powers essential to the continued existence of the State as a body politic, so that from that time forward the territory falls under the exclusive jurisdiction of Congress as other territory, and the State being, according to the language of the law, *felo-de-se*, ceases to exist.

CHARLES SUMNER, *Resolution on the Theory of Secession and Reconstruction*, February 11, 1862, the so-called "state suicide" theory

My paramount object in this struggle is to save the Union, and it is not either to save or to destroy slavery. If I could save the Union without freeing any slave, I would do it; and if I could save it by freeing all the slaves, I would do it; and if I could save it by freeing some and leaving others alone, I would also do that. What I do about slavery and the colored race, I do because I believe it helps to save the Union; and what I forbear, I forbear because I do not believe it would help to save the Union. I shall do less whenever I shall believe what I am doing hurts the cause, and I shall do more whenever I shall believe doing more will help the cause. I shall try to correct errors when shown to be errors, and I shall adopt new views so fast as they shall appear to be true views.

I have here stated my purpose according to my view of official duty; and I intend no modification of my oft-expressed personal wish that all men everywhere could be free.

> ABRAHAM LINCOLN, letter to Horace Greeley, August 22, 1862

We all agree that the seceded States, so called, are out of their proper practical relation with the Union; and that the sole object of the government, civil and military, in regard to those States is to again get them into that proper practical relation. I believe it is not only possible, but in fact, easier, to do this, without deciding, or even considering, whether these States have even been out of the Union, than with it. Finding themselves safely at home, it would be utterly immaterial whether they had ever been abroad. Let us all join in doing the acts necessary to restoring the proper practical relations between these States and the Union; and each forever after, innocently indulge his own opinion whether, in doing the acts, he brought the States from without, into the Union, or only gave them proper assistance, they never having been out of it.

> ABRAHAM LINCOLN, last public address, April 11, 1865

The consolidation of the states into one vast republic, sure to be aggressive abroad and despotic at home, will be the certain precursor of that ruin which has overwhelmed all those that have preceded it.

> ROBERT E. LEE, letter to Lord Acton, December 15, 1866

THE WAR ITSELF

An irrepressible conflict between opposing and enduring forces.

> WILLIAM H. SEWARD, speech on Dred Scott Decision, October, 1858

Neither let us be slandered from our duty by false accusations against us, nor frightened from it by menaces of destruction to the government, nor of dungeons to ourselves. Let us have faith that right makes might, and in that faith let us to the end dare to do our duty as we understand it.

> ABRAHAM LINCOLN, address at Cooper Union, Feb. 27, 1860

You aggress upon our rights and homes, and under the will of God, we will defend them.

> JEFFERSON DAVIS, to Northern (Republican) Senators, January 10, 1861, after discussion of President Lincoln's message concerning the secession of South Carolina

All we ask is to be left alone.

> JEFFERSON DAVIS, "Inaugural Address," February 18, 1861

In your hands, my dissatisfied fellow-countrymen, and not in mine, is the momentous issue of civil war. The government will not assail you. You can have no conflict without being yourselves the aggressors. You have no oath registered in heaven to destroy the government, while I shall have the most solemn one to "preserve, protect, and defend it."

I am loathe to close. We are not enemies, but friends. We must not be enemies. Though passion may have strained, it must not break our bonds of affection. The mystic chords of memory, stretching from every battle-field and patriot grave to every living heart and hearthstone all over this broad land, will yet swell the chorus of the Union when again touched, as surely they will be, by the better angels of our nature.

> ABRAHAM LINCOLN, "First Inaugural Address," March 4, 1861. The last paragraph was written by W. H. Seward and given to Lincoln with the suggestion that the speech should contain some "rhetoric." Lincoln rewrote the paragraph and read it unwillingly.

Having defended Fort Sumter for thirty-four hours, until the quarters were entirely burned, the main gates destroyed by fire, the gorge walls seriously impaired, the magazine surrounded by flames and its door closed from the effects of the heat, four barrels and three cartridges of powder only being available and no provisions remaining but pork, I accepted terms of evacuation offered by General Beauregard (being the same offered by him on the 11th instant, prior to the commencement of hostilities) and marched out of the fort on Sunday afternoon, being the 14th instant, with colors flying and drums beating, bringing away company and private property, and saluting my flag with fifty guns.

> ROBERT ANDERSON, Major, First Artillery, dispatch from the steamer *Baltic,* off Sandy Hook, to Simon Cameron, Lincoln's first Secretary of War, April 18, 1861

I have been unable to make up my mind to raise my hand against my native state, my relatives, my children, and my home.

> ROBERT E. LEE, resigning his commission in the United States Army when Virginia seceded from the Union, April, 1861. "If a man loves his own State and is content to be ruined with her, let us shoot him if we can, but allow him an honorable burial in the soil he fights for."—Nathaniel Hawthorne, referring to Lee's statement

Yell like furies when you charge!

> GENERAL THOMAS JONATHAN ("STONEWALL") JACKSON, at the Battle of Bull Run, July, 1861. The battle was a great Confederate victory, Jackson holding his troops back until the Union Armies were upon them, when the Rebels jumped up from the underbrush, fired one crashing point-blank volley, and charged with fixed bayonets. The Union soldiers ran all the way to Washington. This was the first time the ear-piercing rebel yell was heard on a battlefield.

Let us determine to die here, and we will conquer. There is Jackson standing like a stone wall. Rally behind the Virginians!

> GENERAL BERNARD ELLIOTT BEE, at the first Battle of Bull Run. General Jackson was ever afterward "Stonewall" Jackson.

I always make it a rule to get there first with the most men.

> GENERAL NATHAN BEDFORD FORREST

Boys, things look tough. But remember, the eyes of Dixieland are on you. The beauty and chivalry of the South know our desperate plight and thank God for it, as only in extremities like this are heroes made. The hated Yankees are preparing to charge—let them come! Don't shoot until you see the whites of their eyes and feel their fetid breath on your cheeks. A volley at such close range should wreak havoc. Then, my brave fellows, take to the bayonet and fight it out hand to hand, until the case is hopeless. Then you can retreat—but, seeing I'm lame, I'll start now.

> Unknown Confederate general, as told by Wilson Mizner

All quiet along the Potomac.

> GENERAL GEORGE BRINTON McCLELLAN, *Report* (often repeated) from his Union headquarters during 1861

No terms except an unconditional and immediate surrender can be accepted. I propose to move immediately upon your works.

> GENERAL ULYSSES S. GRANT, reply to proposal for armistice made by General Simon B. Buckner, Fort Donelson, February 16, 1862

The cheese box on a raft.

> Description of ironclad *Monitor,* 1862

Sending men to that army is like shoveling fleas across a barnyard—they don't get there.

> ABRAHAM LINCOLN, of McClellan's Army

My dear McClellan: If you don't want to use the Army I should like to borrow it for a while. Yours respectfully, A. Lincoln.

> ABRAHAM LINCOLN, unsent letter protesting against McClellan's "waiting campaign" of 1862

In great contests each party claims to act in accordance with the will of God. Both may be, and one must be, wrong. God cannot be for and against the same thing at the same time. In the present civil war it is quite possible that God's purpose is something different from the purpose of either party; and yet the human instrumentalities, working just as they do, are of the best adaptation to effect his purpose. I am almost ready to say that this is probably true; that God wills this contest, and wills that it shall not end yet. By his mere great power on the minds of the now contestants, he could have either saved or destroyed the Union without a human contest. Yet the contest began. And, having begun, he could give the final victory to either side any day. Yet the contest proceeds.

> ABRAHAM LINCOLN, "Meditation on the Divine Will," September 2, 1862 (date assgned by Hay and Nicolay)

If General Lee had Grant's resources he would soon end the war; but Old Jack can do it without resources.

> GENERAL GEORGE E. PICKETT, letter to his fiancée, October 11, 1862, of "Stonewall" Jackson

In times like the present, men should utter nothing for which they would not willingly be responsible through time and in eternity.

> ABRAHAM LINCOLN, "Annual Message to Congress," December 1, 1862

It is well that war is so terrible—we would grow too fond of it.

> GENERAL ROBERT E. LEE to General Longstreet, as they
> watched the Federals dying at Fredericksburg, Dec., 1862

I have placed you at the head of the Army of the Potomac. Of course I
have done this upon what appears to me to be sufficient reasons, and yet
I think it best for you to know that there are some things in regard to
which I am not quite satisfied with you. I believe you to be a brave and
skillful soldier, which of course I like. I also believe you do not mix politics with your profession, in which you are right. You have confidence in
yourself, which is a valuable if not indispensable quality. You are ambitious, which, within reasonable bounds, does good rather than harm; but
I think that during General Burnside's command of the army you have
taken counsel of your ambition and thwarted him as much as you could,
in which you did a great wrong to the country and to a meritorious and
honorable brother officer. I have heard, in such a way as to believe it, of
your recently saying that both the Army and the Government needed a
dictator. Of course it was not for this, but in spite of it, that I have given
you the command. Only those generals who gain successes can set up dictators. What I now ask of you is military success, and I will risk the
dictatorship. The Government will support you to the utmost of its ability,
which is neither more nor less than it has done and will do for all commanders. I much fear that the spirit which you have aided to infuse into
the army, of criticizing their commander and withholding confidence from
him, will now turn upon you. I shall assist you as far as I can to put it
down. Neither you nor Napoleon, if he were alive again, could get any
good out of an army while such spirit prevails in it. And now beware of
rashness. Beware of rashness, but with energy and sleepless vigilance go
forward and give us victories.

> ABRAHAM LINCOLN, letter to Major General Joseph Hooker,
> January 26, 1863

I would be very happy to oblige you, if my passes were respected. But the
fact is, sir, I have, within the last two years, given passes to two hundred
and fifty thousand men to go to Richmond, and not one has got there yet.

> ABRAHAM LINCOLN, reply to a man who asked for a "safe
> conduct" to Richmond, 1863

Let your military measures be strong enough to repel the invader and
keep the peace, and not so strong as to unnecessarily harass and persecute
the people. It is a difficult role, and so much greater will be the honor if

you perform it well. If both factions, or neither, shall abuse you, you will probably be right. Beware of being assailed by one and praised by the other.

> ABRAHAM LINCOLN, letter to General John M. Schofield, May 27, 1863

Put the Vermonters in front and keep the ranks closed up.

> Order to a detachment of troops at Gettysburg

General Pickett, finding the battle broken while the enemy was still reinforcing, called the troops off. There was no indication of panic. The broken files marched back in steady step. The effort was nobly made and failed from blows that could not be fended.

> GENERAL JAMES LONGSTREET, *From Manassas to Appomattox,* the end of Pickett's famous charge during the Battle of Gettysburg, July 3, 1863

That bloody old man has murdered all my soldiers.

> Attributed to GENERAL GEORGE E. PICKETT, of General Lee, after the unsuccessful charge at Gettysburg, July 3, 1863. Lee had ordered the charge, counting on support which never came.

All this has been my fault. It is I that have lost this fight.

> GENERAL ROBERT E. LEE, as he rode out alone to meet the survivors of Pickett's charge

On the Fourth—far from a glorious Fourth to us or to any with love for his fellow-men—I wrote you just a line of heartbreak. The sacrifice of life on that blood-soaked field on that fatal third was too awful for the heralding of victory, even for the victorious foe, who, I think, believe as we do, that it decided the fate of our cause. No words can picture the anguish of that roll call—the breathless waits between responses. The "Here" of those who, by God's mercy, had miraculously escaped the awful rain of shot and shell was a sob—a gasp—a knell—for the unanswered name of his comrade. There was no tone of thankfulness for having been spared to answer to their names, but rather a toll, and an unanswered wish that they, too, had been among the missing. Even now I can hear them cheering as I gave the order, "Forward!" I can feel the thrill of their joyous voices as they called out all along the line, "We'll follow you, Marse

George. We'll follow you—we'll follow you." Oh, how faithfully they kept their word—following me on—on—to their death, and I believing in the promised support, led them on—on—on—Oh God! I can't write you a love letter today, my Sally, for . . . the overpowering thought of those whose lives were sacrificed—of the broken-hearted widows and mothers and orphans.

> GENERAL GEORGE E. PICKETT, letter to his wife, Gettysburg, July 6, 1863

For every Southern boy fourteen years old, not once but whenever he wants it, there is the instant when it's still not two o'clock on that July afternoon in 1863, the brigades are in position behind the rail fence, the guns are laid and ready in the woods and the furled flags are already loosened to break out and Pickett himself with his long oiled ringlets and his hat in one hand probably and his sword in the other looking up the hill waiting for Longstreet to give the word and it's all in the balance, it hasn't happened yet. . . .

> WILLIAM FAULKNER

Allow what you will for *esprit de corps,* for this or for that, the thing that sent [the Southerner] swinging up the slope at Gettysburg on that celebrated, gallant afternoon was before all else nothing more or less than the thing which elsewhere accounted for his violence—was nothing more or less than his conviction, the conviction of every farmer among what was essentially only a band of farmers, that nothing living could cross him and get away with it.

> W. J. CASH, *The Mind of the South,* 1946

The Father of Waters again goes unvexed to the sea.

> ABRAHAM LINCOLN, letter to James C. Conkling, August 26, 1863. The fall of Vicksburg, July 4, 1863, put the entire length of the Mississippi in Union hands.

A Rich Man's War and a Poor Man's Fight.

> Slogan of the draft rioters in New York, July, 1863. The draft exempted anyone able to pay $300 for a substitute.

I claim not to have controlled events, but confess plainly that events have controlled me.

> ABRAHAM LINCOLN, letter to A. G. Hodges, April 4, 1864

I propose to fight it out on this line if it takes all summer.

> GENERAL ULYSSES S. GRANT, dispatch to Washington, Spotsylvania Court House, May 11, 1864

Get down, you damn fool, before you get shot!

> CAPTAIN OLIVER WENDELL HOLMES, JR., to President Lincoln, during attack on Fort Stevens, July 11, 1864, the latter wishing to see the action and young Captain Holmes not recognizing him

Damn the torpedoes! Captain Drayton, go ahead! Jouett, full speed!

> ADMIRAL DAVID GLASGOW FARRAGUT, at the Battle of Mobile Bay, August 5, 1864. A number of alternate versions exist, among which the best known is simply "Damn the torpedoes! Go ahead!"

I almost always feel inclined, when I happen to say anything to soldiers, to impress upon them, in a few brief remarks, the importance of success in this contest. It is not merely for today, but for all time to come, that we should perpetuate for our children's children that great and free government which we have enjoyed all our lives. I beg you to remember this, not merely for my sake, but for yours. I happen, temporarily, to occupy this White House. I am a living witness that any one of your children may look to come here as my father's child has. It is in order that each of you may have, through this free government which we have enjoyed, an open field and a fair chance for your industry, enterprise and intelligence; that you all may have equal privileges in the race of life, with all its desirable human aspirations. It is for this the struggle should be maintained, that we may not lose our birthright. . . . The nation is worth fighting for, to secure such an inestimable jewel.

> ABRAHAM LINCOLN, speech to 164th Ohio Regiment, August 18, 1864

Hold the fort! I am coming.

> GENERAL WILLIAM TECUMSEH SHERMAN, message to General John M. Corse, holding a pass near Allatoona, Georgia, October 5, 1864

If the people [of Georgia] raise a howl against my barbarity and cruelty, I will answer that war is war, and not popularity-seeking.

> GENERAL WILLIAM TECUMSEH SHERMAN, during his march to the sea

About 7 A.M. of November 16th we rode out of Atlanta by the Decatur road, filled by the marching troops and wagons of the Fourteenth Corps; and reaching the hill, just outside of the old rebel works, we naturally paused to look back upon the scenes of our past battles. We stood upon the very ground whereon was fought the bloody battle of July 22nd, and could see the copse of wood where McPherson fell. Behind us lay Atlanta, smouldering and in ruins, the black smoke rising high in air, and hanging like a pall over the ruined city. Away off in the distance, on the McDonough road, was the rear of Howard's column, the gun-barrels glistening in the sun, the white-topped wagons stretching away to the south; and right before us the Fourteenth Corps, marching steadily and rapidly, with a cheery look and swinging pace, that made light of the thousand miles that lay between us and Richmond. Some band, by accident, struck up the anthem of "John Brown's soul goes marching on"; the men caught up the strain, and never before or since have I heard the chorus of "Glory, glory, hallelujah!" done with more spirit, or in better harmony of time and place.

Then we turned our horses' heads to the east; Atlanta was soon lost behind the screen of trees, and became a thing of the past. Around it clings many a thought of desperate battle, of hope and fear, that now seem like the memory of a dream; and I have never seen the place since. The day was extremely beautiful, clear sunlight, with bracing air, and an unusual feeling of exhilaration seemed to pervade all minds—a feeling of something to come, vague and undefined, still full of venture and intense interest. Even the common soldiers caught the inspiration, and many a group called out to me as I worked my way past them, "Uncle Billy, I guess Grant is waiting for us at Richmond!" Indeed, the general sentiment was that we were marching for Richmond, and that there we should end the war, but how and when they seemed to care not; nor did they measure the distance, or count the cost in life, or bother their brains about the great rivers to be crossed, and the food required for man and beast, that had to be gathered by the way. There was a "devil-may-care" feeling pervading officers and men, that made me feel the full load of responsibility, for success would be accepted as a matter of course, whereas, should we fail, this "march" would be adjudged the wild adventure of a crazy fool.

GENERAL WILLIAM TECUMSEH SHERMAN, *Memoirs*, 1875

I have been shown in the files of the War Department a statement of the Adjutant General of Massachusetts that you are the mother of five sons who died gloriously on the field of battle. I feel how weak and fruitless must be any word of mine which should attempt to beguile you from the grief of a loss so overwhelming. But I cannot refrain from tendering to you the consolation that may be found in the thanks of the republic they died to save. I pray that our heavenly Father may assuage the anguish of your bereavement, and leave you only the cherished memory of the loved and lost, and the solemn pride that must be yours to have laid so costly a sacrifice upon the altar of freedom.

> ABRAHAM LINCOLN, letter to Mrs. Bixby, November 21, 1864. The President had been misinformed: one of Mrs. Bixby's sons deserted and one was honorably discharged, though two were killed. But there is considerable doubt that Lincoln actually wrote such a letter.

The crow that flies over the Valley of Virginia must henceforth carry his rations with him.

> GENERAL PHILIP H. SHERIDAN, after having scorched the earth of Virginia, 1865

Face the other way, boys; we're going back!

> GENERAL PHILIP H. SHERIDAN

On the occasion corresponding to this four years ago, all thoughts were anxiously directed to an impending civil war. All dreaded it—all sought to avert it. While the inaugural address was being delivered from this place, devoted altogether to saving the Union without war, insurgent agents were in the city seeking to destroy it without war—seeking to dissolve the Union, and divide effects, by negotiation. Both parties deprecated war; but one of them would make war rather than let the nation survive; and the other would accept war rather than let it perish. And the war came.

One-eighth of the whole population were colored slaves, not distributed generally over the Union, but localized in the Southern part of it. These slaves constituted a peculiar and powerful interest. All knew that this interest was, somehow, the cause of the war. To strengthen, perpetuate, and extend this interest was the object for which the insurgents would rend the Union, even by war; while the government claimed no right to do more than to restrict the territorial enlargement of it.

Neither party expected for the war the magnitude or the duration which it has already attained. Neither anticipated that the cause of the conflict might cease with, or even before, the conflict itself should cease. Each looked for an easier triumph, and a result less fundamental and astounding. Both read the same Bible, and pray to the same God; and each invoked His aid against the other. It may seem strange that any men should ask a just God's assistance in wringing their bread from the sweat of other men's faces; but let us judge not, that we be not judged. The prayers of both could not be answered—that of neither has been answered fully.

The Almighty has His own purposes. "Woe unto the world because of offenses! for it must needs be that offenses come; but woe to that man by whom the offense cometh." If we shall suppose that American slavery is one of those offenses which, in the providence of God, must needs come, but which, having continued through His appointed time, He now wills to remove, and that He gives to both North and South this terrible war, as the woe due to those by whom the offense came, shall we discern therein any departure from those divine attributes which the believers in a living God always ascribe to Him? Fondly do we hope—fervently do we pray—that this mighty scourge of war may speedily pass away. Yet, if God wills that it continue until all the wealth piled by the bondsman's two hundred and fifty years of unrequited toil shall be sunk, and until every drop of blood drawn with the lash shall be paid by another drawn with the sword, as was said three thousand years ago, so still it must be said, "The judgments of the Lord are true and righteous altogether."

With malice toward none; with charity for all; with firmness in the right, as God gives us to see the right, let us strive on to finish the work we are in; to bind up the nation's wounds; to care for him who shall have borne the battle, and for his widow, and his orphan—to do all which may achieve and cherish a just and lasting peace among ourselves, and with all nations.

ABRAHAM LINCOLN, "Second Inaugural," March 4, 1865

Billy, I fear that I shall meet with some terrible end.

ABRAHAM LINCOLN, prediction to William Herndon, often repeated

I had known General Lee in the old army, and had served with him in the Mexican War; but did not suppose, owing to the difference in our age and rank, that he would remember me; while I would more naturally remember him distinctly, because he was the chief of staff of General Scott in the Mexican War.

When I left camp that morning I had not expected so soon the result that was then taking place, and consequently was in rough garb. I was without a sword, as I usually was when on horseback on the field, and wore a soldier's blouse for a coat, with the shoulder straps of my rank to indicate to the army who I was. When I went into the house I found General Lee. We greeted each other, and after shaking hands took our seats. I had my staff with me, a good portion of whom were in the room during the whole of the interview.

What General Lee's feelings were I do not know. As he was a man of much dignity, with an impassible face, it was impossible to say whether he felt inwardly glad that the end had finally come, or felt sad over the result, and was too manly to show it. Whatever his feelings, they were entirely concealed from my observation; but my own feelings, which had been quite jubilant on the receipt of his letter, were sad and depressed. I felt like anything rather than rejoicing at the downfall of a foe who had fought so long and so valiantly.

> GENERAL ULYSSES S. GRANT, *Memoirs*, 1885–86, of the meeting at Appomattox

The war is over—the rebels are our countrymen again.

> GENERAL ULYSSES S. GRANT, stopping his men from cheering after Lee surrendered at Appomattox Court House, April 9, 1865

After four years of arduous service marked by unsurpassed courage and fortitude the Army of Northern Virginia has been compelled to yield to overwhelming numbers and resources.

I need not tell the survivors of so many hard-fought battles, who have remained steadfast to the last, that I have consented to this result from no distrust of them.

But, feeling that valour and devotion could accomplish nothing that could compensate for the loss that must have attended the continuance of the contest I determined to avoid the useless sacrifice of those whose past services have endeared them to their countrymen.

By the terms of the agreement, officers and men can return to their homes and remain until exchanged. You will take with you the satisfaction that proceeds from the consciousness of duty faithfully performed, and I earnestly pray that a merciful God will extend to you His blessing and protection.

With an unceasing admiration of your constancy and devotion to your country, and a grateful remembrance of your kind and generous consideration for myself, I bid you all an affectionate farewell.

> GENERAL ROBERT E. LEE, *General Order Number Nine*

(farewell to his army), Appomattox Court House, April 10, 1865

Sic semper tyrannis! The South is avenged!

> JOHN WILKES BOOTH, spoken as he jumped onto the stage after having shot Lincoln at Ford's Theatre, April 14, 1865. The first three words are the motto of the Commonwealth of Virginia: "Thus always to tyrants."

My aim was to whip the rebels, to humble their pride, to follow them to their inmost recesses, and make them fear and dread us. Fear is the beginning of wisdom.

> GENERAL WILLIAM TECUMSEH SHERMAN, after the war

The war being at an end, the Southern states having laid down their arms, and the questions at issue between them and the Northern states having been decided, I believe it to be the duty of everyone to unite in the restoration of the country and the re-establishment of peace and harmony.

> GENERAL ROBERT E. LEE, 1865

It is only necessary, in my opinion, that truth should be known for the rights of every one to be secured. I know of no surer way of eliciting the truth than by burying contention with the war.

> GENERAL ROBERT E. LEE, letter to J. William Jones

The principle [State's Rights] for which we contended is bound to reassert itself, though it may be at another time and in another form.

> JEFFERSON DAVIS, after the Civil War

I am sick and tired of war. Its glory is all moonshine. It is only those who have never fired a shot nor heard the shrieks and groans of the wounded who cry aloud for blood, more vengeance, more desolation. War is hell.

> GENERAL WILLIAM TECUMSEH SHERMAN

I have never desired bloody punishments to any great extent, but there are punishments quite as appalling and longer remembered than death. They are more advisable, because they would reach a greater number. Strip a proud nobility of their bloated estates; reduce them to a level with plain republicans, send them forth to labor and teach their children to enter the workshops or handle a plow, and you will thus humiliate the proud traitors.

THADDEUS STEVENS, after the Civil War

The Four Years' War is over—and in the peaceful, strong, exciting, fresh occasions of today, and of the future, that strange, sad war is hurrying even now to be forgotten. The camp, the drill, the lines of sentries, the prisons, the hospitals—(ah! the hospitals!)—all have passed away—all seem now like a dream. A new race, a young and lusty generation, already sweeps in with oceanic currents, obliterating the war, and all its scars, its mounded graves, and all its reminiscences of hatred, conflict, death. So let it be obliterated. I say the life of the present and the future makes undeniable demands upon us each and all, south, north, east, west. To help put the United States (even if only in imagination) hand in hand, in one unbroken circle in a chant—to rouse them to the unprecedented grandeur of the part they are to play, and are even now playing—to the thought of their great future, and the attitude conform'd to it—especially their great esthetic, moral, scientific future (of which their vulgar material and political present is but as the preparatory tuning of instruments by an orchestra), these, as hitherto, are still, for me, among my hopes, ambitions.

WALT WHITMAN, *Thou Mother with Thy Equal Brood*

The years of the war tried our devotion to the Union; the time of peace may test the sincerity of our faith in democracy.

HERMAN MELVILLE, *Battle-Pieces*, "Prose Supplement"

A few immortal sentences, breathing the omnipotence of divine justice, have been potent to break despotic fetters and abolish the whipping-post and slave market; but oppression neither went down in blood nor did the breath of freedom come from the cannon's mouth. Love is the liberator.

MARY BAKER EDDY, of the Civil War

In our youth our hearts were touched with fire. It was given us to learn at the outset that life is a profound and passionate thing.

OLIVER WENDELL HOLMES, JR., of his generation of Civil War soldiers

If you have advanced in line, and have seen ahead of you the spot which you must pass where the rifle bullets are striking; if you have ridden by night at a walk toward the line of fire at the dead angle of Spotsylvania, where for twenty-four hours the soldiers were fighting on the two sides

of an earthwork, and in the morning the dead and dying lay piled in a
row six feet deep, and as you rode had heard the bullets splashing in the
mud and earth about you; if you have been on the picket line at night in
a black and unknown wood, and have heard the spat of bullets upon the
trees, and as you moved have felt your foot slip upon a dead man's body;
if you have had a blind fierce gallop against the enemy, with your blood
up and a pace that left no time for fear—if, in short . . . you have
known the vicissitudes of terror and of triumph in war, you know that
there is such a thing as the faith I spoke of. You know your own weakness and are modest; but you know that man has in him that unspeakable
somewhat which makes him capable of miracle, able to lift himself by the
might of his own soul, unaided, able to face annihilation for a blind
belief.

> OLIVER WENDELL HOLMES, JR., quoted by Smith, *Creative
> Skeptics*, 1934

Democracy is still upon its trial. The civic genius of our people is its only
bulwark, and neither laws nor monuments, neither battleships nor public
libraries, nor great newspapers nor bombing sticks; neither mechanical
invention nor political adroitness, nor churches nor universities nor civil
service examinations can save us from degeneration if the inner mystery
be lost. That mystery, at once the secret and the glory of our English-
speaking race, consists in nothing but two common habits, two inveterate
habits carried into public life—habits so homely that they lend themselves
to no rhetorical expression, yet habits more precious, perhaps, than any
that the human race has gained. They can never be too often pointed out
or praised. One of them is the habit of trained and disciplined good temper towards the opposite party when it fairly wins its innings. It was by
breaking away from this habit that the Slave States nearly wrecked our
Nation. The other is that of fierce and merciless resentment toward every
man or set of men who break the public peace. By holding to this habit
the free States saved her life.

> WILLIAM JAMES, *Memories and Studies*, "Robert Gould
> Shaw," 1911

[The Civil War] created in this country what had never existed before
—a national consciousness. It was not the salvation of the Union; it was
the rebirth of the Union.

> WOODROW WILSON, "Memorial Day Address," 1915

The war left the South prostrate; Reconstruction left it maddened.

> JAMES TRUSLOW ADAMS, *Epic of America*

For those men believed in something. They counted life a light thing to lay down in the faith they bore. They were terrible in battle. They were generous in victory. They rose up from defeat to fight again, and while they lived they were formidable. There were not enough of them; that is all.

> JOHN W. THOMASON, JR., *Lone Star Preacher,* "Introduction," 1940; of the Confederate Army

The Civil War was our great national trauma. A savage fraternal conflict, it released deep sentiments of guilt and remorse—sentiments which have reverberated through our history and our literature ever since. Literature in the end came to terms with these sentiments by yielding to the South in fantasy the victory it had been denied in fact; this tendency culminated on the popular level in *Gone with the Wind* and on the highbrow level in the Nashville cult of agrarianism. But history, a less malleable medium, was constricted by the intractable fact that the war had taken place, and by the related assumption that it was, in William H. Seward's phrase, an "irrepressible conflict," and hence a justified one.

> ARTHUR SCHLESINGER, JR., "The Causes of the Civil War," *Partisan Review,* 1949

WORLD WAR I

Never, from the day of barbarism down to our own time, has every man in a society been a soldier until now; and the armaments of today are immensely more costly than ever before. There is only one limit possible to the war preparations of a modern European state; that is, the last man and the last dollar it can control. What will come of the mixture of sentimental social philosophy and warlike policy? There is only one thing rationally to be expected, and that is a frightful effusion of blood in revolution and war during the century now opening.

> WILLIAM GRAHAM SUMNER, 1900; *Selected Essays,* 1924

Our whole duty, for the present, at any rate, is summed up in the motto, "America first." Let us think of America before we think of Europe, in order that America may be fit to be Europe's friend when the day of tested friendship comes. The test of friendship is not now sympathy with the one side or the other, but getting ready to help both sides when the struggle is over.

> WOODROW WILSON, speech, April 20, 1915

There is such a thing as a man being too proud to fight.

> WOODROW WILSON, speech at Philadelphia, May 10, 1915. The phrase caused widespread criticism among pro-Allied Americans. In *Fighting Years,* 1939, Oswald Garrison Villard says he was the author of the phrase.

Out of the Trenches and Back to Their Homes by Christmas.

> HENRY FORD, slogan of Peace Delegation sent to Europe to stop the war, December, 1915

There may at any moment come a time when I cannot preserve both the honor and the peace of the United States. Do not exact of me an impossible and contradictory thing.

> WOODROW WILSON, speech, Milwaukee, January 21, 1916

America can not be an ostrich with its head in the sand.

> WOODROW WILSON, speech, Des Moines, February 1, 1916

A little group of wilful men.

> WOODROW WILSON, statement, March 3, 1916, referring to a group of eleven senators who, by filibustering tactics, had prevented the passage of a bill authorizing Wilson to arm American merchantmen

Wake up, America.

> AUGUSTUS P. GARDINER, speech, October 16, 1916

Peace without victory.

> WOODROW WILSON, report to Congress, January 22, 1917, on replies from belligerent European nations as to basis for armistice

Victory would mean peace forced upon the loser, a victor's terms imposed upon the vanquished. It would be accepted in humiliation, under duress, at an intolerable sacrifice, and would leave a sting, a resentment, a bitter memory upon which terms of peace would rest, not permanently, but only as upon quicksand. Only a peace between equals can last.

> WOODROW WILSON, address to the Senate, Jan. 22, 1917

The world must be made safe for democracy.

> WOODROW WILSON, address to Congress, April 2, 1917, asking a declaration of war against Germany

It is a distressing and oppressive duty, gentlemen of Congress, which I have performed in thus addressing you. There are, it may be, many months of fiery trial and sacrifice ahead of us. It is a fearful thing to lead this great and peaceful people into war, into the most terrible and disastrous of all wars. Civilization itself seems to be in the balance, but right is more precious than peace, and we shall fight for the things which we have always carried nearest our hearts, for democracy, for the right of those who submit to authority to have a voice in their own government, for the rights and liberties of small nations, for the universal dominion of right by such a concert of free peoples as will bring peace and safety to all nations, and make the world itself at last free. To such a task we can dedicate our lives, our fortunes, everything we are, everything we have, with the pride of those who know the day has come when America is privileged to spend her blood and might for the principles that gave her birth, and the happiness and peace which she has treasured. God helping her, she can do no other.

> WOODROW WILSON, *Ibid.*

America has joined forces with the Allied Powers, and what we have of blood and treasure are yours. Therefore it is that with loving pride we drape the colors in tribute of respect to this citizen of your great republic. And here and now in the presence of the illustrious dead we pledge our hearts and our honor in carrying this war to a successful issue. Lafayette, we are here.

> CHARLES E. STANTON, address at the tomb of Lafayette, Picpus Cemetery, Paris, July 4, 1917. Stanton was chief disbursing officer of the A.E.F. in France, and had been deputed by General Pershing to speak on this occasion.

The red hand of the waiter pouring the Chartreuse, green like a stormy sunset, into small glasses before them broke into the vivid imaginings that had been unfolding in their talk through dinner. No, they had been saying, it could not go on; some day amid the rending crash of shells and the whine of shrapnel fragments, people everywhere, in all uniforms, in trenches, packed in camions, in stretchers, in hospitals, crowded behind guns, involved in telephone apparatus, generals at their dinner-tables, colonels sipping liqueurs, majors developing photographs, would jump to their feet and burst out laughing at the solemn inanity, at the stupid vicious pomposity of what they were doing. Laughter would untune the sky. It would be a new progress of Bacchus. Drunk with laughter at the sudden vision of the silliness of the world, officers and soldiers, prisoners working on the roads, deserters being driven towards the trenches would throw down their guns and their spades and their heavy packs, and start marching, or driving in artillery wagons or in camions, staff cars, private trains, towards their capitals, where they would laugh the deputies, the senators, the congressmen, the M. P.'s out of their chairs, laugh the presidents and the prime ministers, and kaisers and dictators out of their plush-carpeted offices; the sun would wear a broad grin and would whisper the joke to the moon, who would giggle and ripple with it all night long.

JOHN DOS PASSOS, *One Man's Initiation,* 1917

Bonds or Bondage.

FRANK HUMMERT, slogan

Food Will Win the War.

Slogan, 1917–1918

Force, force to the utmost.

WOODROW WILSON, address, April 6, 1918

Hell, Heaven or Hoboken by Christmas.

Attributed to GENERAL JOHN JOSEPH PERSHING, 1918

Come on, you sons of bitches! Do you want to live forever?

GUNNERY SERGEANT DANIEL DALY, U.S. Marine Corps, at Lucy-le-Bocage, on the fringe of Belleau Wood, June 4, 1918. Also variously attributed.

1. Open covenants of peace, openly arrived at, after which there shall be no private international understandings of any kind . . .

2. Absolute freedom of navigation upon the seas . . .

3. The removal . . . of all economic barriers and the establishment of an equality of trade conditions among all the nations consenting to the peace . . .

4. Adequate guarantees . . . that national armaments will be reduced.

5. A free, open-minded, and absolutely impartial adjustment of all colonial claims . . .

6. The evacuation of all Russian territory, and such a settlement of all questions affecting Russia as will secure . . . for her . . . the independent determination of her own political development and national policy . . .

7. Belgium . . . must be evacuated and restored . . .

8. All French territory should be freed . . . and the wrong done to France by Prussia in 1871 in the matter of Alsace-Lorraine . . . should be righted . . .

9. A readjustment of the frontiers of Italy . . . along clearly recognizable lines of nationality.

10. The peoples of Austria-Hungary . . . should be accorded the freest oportunity of autonomous development.

11. Rumania, Serbia, and Montenegro should be evacuated . . . [and] Serbia accorded free . . . access to the sea . . .

12. The Turkish portions of the present Ottoman Empire should be assured a secure sovereignty, but the other nationalities which are now under Turkish rule should be assured . . . autonomous development, and the Dardanelles should be permanently opened . . . to . . . all nations . . .

13. An independent Polish state should be erected . . . which should be assured a free and secure access to the sea . . .

14. A general association of nations must be formed . . . for the purpose of affording mutual guarantees of political independence and territorial integrity to great and small states alike.

> Woodrow Wilson, the Fourteen Points: the basis for the
> Versailles Peace Treaty, 1919

January 18, 1919, in the midst of serried uniforms, cocked hats and gold braid, decorations, epaulettes, orders of merit and knighthood, the High Contracting Parties, the allied and associated powers met in the Salon de l'Horloge at the quai d'Orsay to dictate the peace,

but the grand assembly of the peace conference was too public a place to make peace in

so the High Contracting Parties

formed the Council of Ten, went into the Gobelin Room and, surrounded by Rubens's History of Marie de Medici,

began to dictate the peace.

But the Council of Ten was too public a place to make peace in
so they formed the Council of Four.
Orlando went home in a huff
and then there were three:
Clemenceau,
Lloyd George,
Woodrow Wilson.
Three old men shuffling the pack,
dealing out the cards:
the Rhineland, Danzig, the Polish corridor, the Ruhr, self determination of small nations, the Saar, League of Nations, mandates, the
Mespot, Freedom of the Seas, Transjordania, Shantung, Fiume and the
Island of Yap:
machine gun fire and arson
starvation, lice, cholera, typhus;
oil was trumps.

JOHN DOS PASSOS, *U.S.A.*

Why deceive ourselves. We are making no Peace here in Paris. What is
there to make it out of?

GENERAL TASKER BLISS, Peace Commissioner in Paris, 1919

The peace that passeth understanding.

WILLIAM ALLEN WHITE, *Autobiography,* of the Versailles
Treaty

I can predict with absolute certainty that within another generation there
will be another world war [if America does not join the League of Na-
tions]. . . . What the Germans used [in this war] were toys as compared
with what would be used in the next war.

WOODROW WILSON, speech, September 3, 1919

Hell'n Maria, we did the job, didn't we?

CHARLES GATES DAWES, when the Graham Committee
attempted to draw him into political criticism of the conduct of the First World War

I was always embarrassed by the words sacred, glorious and sacrifice and the expression in vain. We had heard them, standing in the rain almost out of earshot, so that only the shouted words came through, and had read them, on proclamations that were slapped up by billposters over other proclamations, now for a long time, and I had seen nothing sacred, and the things that were glorious had no glory and the sacrifices were like the stockyards at Chicago if nothing was done with the meat except to bury it.

ERNEST HEMINGWAY, *A Farewell to Arms,* 1929

WORLD WAR II

We are the only Nation in the world that waits until we get into a war before we start getting ready for it. Pacifists say, "If you are ready for war, you will have one." I bet there has not been a man insulted Jack Dempsey since he has been champion.

WILL ROGERS, 1924

The fighting plane and the bomber, ever on the alert and in scattered formation when resting on their bases, furnish the only hope of defense at Pearl Harbour. If our warships there were to be found bottled up in a surprise attack from the air and our airplanes destroyed on the ground, nothing but a miracle would help us hold our Far East possessions. It would break our backs. The same prediction applies to the Philippines, which would be at the mercy of squadrons of bombers, our warships paralyzed or scuttling for cover.

GENERAL WILLIAM ("BILLY") MITCHELL, in 1924

Too little and too late.

ALLAN NEVINS, *Current History,* 1935. The phrase came later to refer to the unpreparedness of the Allied Powers, 1939–42.

The Flying Fortress.

ANON., newspaper reporter, when he saw the B-17 for the first time, late 1930's

Be neutral. Be American.

> WILLIAM RANDOLPH HEARST, instructions to his editors
> after war began in Europe, 1939

We must be the great arsenal of democracy.

> FRANKLIN D. ROOSEVELT, "Fireside Talk," Dec. 29, 1940

When I finished skimming the pages, I turned to Nomura and put my eye on him.

"I must say," I said, "that in all my conversations with you during the last nine months I have never uttered one word of untrtuh. This is borne out absolutely by the record. In all my fifty years of public service I have never seen a document that was more crowded with infamous falsehoods and distortions—infamous falsehoods and distortions on a scale so huge that I never imagined until today that any Government on this planet was capable of uttering them."

Nomura seemed about to say something. His face was impassive, but I felt he was under great emotional strain. I stopped him with a motion of my hand. I nodded toward the door. The Ambassadors turned without a word and walked out, their heads down.

I have seen it stated that I "cussed out" the Japanese envoys in rich Tennessee mountain language, but the fact is I told them exactly what I said above. No "cussing out" could have made it any stronger.

> CORDELL HULL, *Memoirs,* 1948

Yesterday, December 7, 1941—a date which will live in infamy—the United States of America was suddenly and deliberately attacked by naval and air forces of the Empire of Japan.

> FRANKLIN D. ROOSEVELT, speech to Congress requesting a
> declaration of war against the Axis Powers, Dec. 8, 1941

Praise the Lord and pass the ammunition.

> HOWELL MAURICE FORGY, on board the cruiser *New Or-*
> *leans,* Pearl Harbor, December 7, 1941

The difficult we do immediately. The impossible takes a little longer.

> Slogan of the U.S. Army Corps of Engineers

Hurry up and wait,

> Army saying, World War II

Look out for the hook!

> Army saying, World War II. It refers to the inoculations that recruits receive.

If it moves, salute it.
If it doesn't move, pick it up.
If you can't pick it up, paint it.

> "The Sad Sack's Catechism," World War II

Kilroy was here.

> Army saying, World War II

Don't you know there's a war on?

> Popular saying, 1942–1943

Sighted sub. Sank same.

> DAVID FRANCIS MASON, report to base of naval pilot, March, 1942

I shall return.

> GENERAL DOUGLAS MACARTHUR, upon leaving the Philippines, March 11, 1942

Bataan has fallen, but the spirit that made it stand—a beacon to all the liberty-loving people of the world—cannot fall!

> LIEUTENANT NORMAN REYES, radio report from a tunnel in the rock fortress of Corregidor, April 9, 1942

There are no atheists in the foxholes.

> Attributed to WILLIAM THOMAS CUMMINGS, field sermon on Bataan, 1942

Send us more Japs!

> Message from the defenders of Wake Island, answering a Navy request to report if anything was needed. The position of the defenders was hopeless.

Suppose you're a sergeant machine-gunner, and your army is retreating and the enemy advancing. The captain takes you to a machine gun covering the road. "You're to stay here and hold this position," he tells you.

"For how long?" you ask. "Never mind," he answers, "just hold it." Then you know you're expendable. In a way anything can be expendable— money or gasoline or equipment or most usually men. They are expending you and that machine gun to get time.

WILLIAM L. WHITE, *They Were Expendable*

We all know that books burn—yet we have the greater knowledge that books cannot be killed by fire. People die, but books never die. No man and no force can abolish memory. In this war, we know, books are weapons.

FRANKLIN D. ROOSEVELT, message to the American Book-sellers Association, April 23, 1942

The object of this war is to make sure that everybody in the world has the privilege of drinking a quart of milk a day.

HENRY AGARD WALLACE, address, May 8, 1942

I claim we got a hell of a beating. We got run out of Burma, and it is humiliating as hell. I think we should find out what caused it and go back and retake it.

GENERAL JOSEPH WARREN STILWELL, May, 1942

God of the free, we pledge our hearts and lives today to the cause of all free mankind. . . . Grant us a common faith that man shall know bread and peace, that he shall know justice and righteousness, freedom and se-curity, an equal chance to do his best, not only in our own lands, but throughout the world. And in that faith let us march toward the clean world our hands can make. Amen.

STEPHEN VINCENT BENÉT, *We Stand United and Other Radio Scripts,* 1942; read by President Roosevelt during U.N. Day ceremonies, White House, June 15, 1942

Strike repeat strike.

ADMIRAL WILLIAM FREDERICK HALSEY, JR., reply to division commanders in Pacific when asked for his instructions, October 24, 1942

Go to Hell, Babe Ruth—American, you die.

Japanese war cry, Pacific, 1942

We shall attack and attack until we are exhausted, and then we shall attack again.

GENERAL GEORGE S. PATTON, JR., slogan given to his troops before sailing for North Africa, November 15, 1942

Individually the Marines in that outfit were as brave as any fighters in any army in the world, I am positive; but when fear began to be epidemic in that closed-in place, no one was immune. No one could resist it.

The first sign of flight among those men was in their eyes. At first they watched what was going on as calmly as an audience at some play. Then suddenly they were looking around for the nearest exit. They would look at Captain Rigaud's face, looking for some sign that he would order them to retire; or their eyes would dart along the trail back, as they wished they could.

I myself kept looking at Captain Rigaud, to see what he would do with us. His expression had not changed. It had the same look of desperate vigilance that it had worn all along the trail.

The next sign of the growing fear was the way the men started moving around. When a mortar shell would go off near by, they would scramble away from the vicinity to new cover, as if the thing could explode a second time.

The men began to think that it was time to get away from that whole place.

Any men who were men would have taken flight from that impossible place. Some Japanese might not have, if they had had specific orders to stay there; but they would no longer have been much use to the Emperor. I think even most Japanese would have fled. Certainly Germans would have: they are good fighters: they have the sense to live and fight more advantageously another day. I think it is safe to say that Italians would have fled.

The Marines had been deeply enough indoctrinated so that even flight did not wipe out the formulas, and soon the word came whispering back along the line:

"Withdraw."

"Withdraw."

"Withdraw . . ."

Then they started moving back, slowly at first, then running wildly, scrambling from place of cover to momentary cover.

This was a distressing sight, and though I myself was more than eager to be away from that spot, I had a helpless desire to do something to stop the flight. It seemed wrong. One had heard so much about how the Ma-

rines kill ten Japs for every man they lose (which is true), of the callous-
ness of the Marines (true in a way), and of our endless successes against
the Japs (true in sum total). Captain Rigaud had told me that this
would probably be an easy job. It sounded so. And yet here were our men
running away.

I couldn't do anything about it because I was caught up in the general
feeling. It is curious how this feeling communicated itself. Except for the
hard knot which is inside some men, courage is largely the desire to show
other men that you have it. And so, in a large group, when a majority
have somehow signalled to each other a willingness to quit acting, it is
very hard indeed not to quit. The only way to avoid it is to be put to
shame by a small group of men to whom this acting is life itself, and who
refuse to quit; or by a naturally courageous man doing a brave deed.

It was at this moment that Charles Alfred Rigaud, the boy with tired
circles under his eyes, showed himself to be a good officer and a grown
man.

Despite snipers all around us, despite the machine guns and the mortar
fire, he stood right up on his feet and shouted out: "Who in Christ's name
gave that order?"

This was enough to freeze the men in their tracks. They threw themselves on the ground, in attitudes of defense; they took cover behind trees
from both the enemy and the anger of their captain.

Next, by a combination of blistering sarcasm, orders and cajolery, he
not only got the men back into positions: he got them into a mood to
fight again.

"Where do you guys think you're going?" he shouted. And: "Get back
in there. . . . Take cover, you. . . . What do you guys do, just invent
orders? . . . Listen, it's going to get dark and we got a job to do. . . .
You guys make me ashamed. . . ."

But the most telling thing he said was: "Gosh, and they call you Marines."

JOHN HERSEY, *Into the Valley,* 1943

We Shall Come Again and Kill Out Separately Yanki-Joker.

> Panel found by incoming American soldiers in Kiska Har-
> bour, the Aleutians, 1943

On the long man-killing climb above the end of the mule trail they used
anywhere from twenty to three hundred men a night. They rang in cooks,
truck drivers, clerks, and anybody else they could lay their hands on. A
lot of stuff was packed up by the fighting soldiers themselves. On a big

night, when they were building up supplies for an attack, another battalion which was in reserve sent three hundred first-line combat troops to do the packing. The mule packs would leave the olive groves in bunches of twenty, starting just after dark. American soldiers were posted within shouting distance of each other all along the trail, to keep the Italians from getting lost in the dark.

Those guides—everybody who thought he was having a tough time in this war should know about them. They were men who had fought all through a long and bitter battle at the top of the mountain. For more than a week they had been up there, perched behind rocks in the rain and cold, eating cold K rations, sleeping without blankets, scourged constantly with artillery and mortar shells, fighting and ducking and growing more and more weary, seeing their comrades wounded one by one and taken down the mountain.

Finally sickness and exhaustion overtook many of those who were left, so they were sent back down the mountain under their own power to report to the medics there and then go to a rest camp. It took most of them the better part of a day to get two thirds of the way down, so sore were their feet and so weary their muscles.

And then—when actually in sight of their haven of rest and peace—they were stopped and pressed into guide service, because there just wasn't anybody else to do it. So there they stayed on the mountainside, for at last three additional days and nights that I know of, just lying miserably along the trail, shouting in the darkness to guide the mules.

They had no blankets to keep them warm, no beds but the rocks. And they did it without complaining. The human spirit is an astounding thing.

ERNIE PYLE, *Brave Men*

Hell, we haven't started to fight. Our artillery hasn't been overrun yet.

GENERAL TERRY ALLEN, invasion of Sicily, July, 1943

I want you to get that man out of bed right away. Get him back to the front. I won't have these men who really are wounded see that man babied so.

GENERAL GEORGE S. PATTON, JR., to colonel commanding hospital at Sant' Agata, Sicily, August, 1943. This accompanied the famous slapping incident, not known by the public until Drew Pearson's radio broadcast of Nov. 21, 1943.

If we take the generally accepted definition of bravery as a quality which knows not fear, I have never seen a brave man. All men are frightened.

The more intelligent they are, the more they are frightened. The courageous man is the man who forces himself, in spite of his fear, to carry on.
Discipline, pride, self-respect, self-confidence, and the love of glory are
attributes which will make a man courageous even when he is afraid.

The greatest weapon against the so-called "battle fatigue" is ridicule.
If soldiers would realize that a large proportion of men allegedly suffering
from battle fatigue are really using an easy way out, they would be less
sympathetic. Any man who says he has battle fatigue is avoiding danger
and forcing on those who have more hardihood than himself the obligation of meeting it. If the soldiers would make fun of those who begin to
show battle fatigue, they would prevent its spread and also save the man
who allows himself to malinger by this means from an after-life of humiliation and regret.

> GENERAL GEORGE S. PATTON, JR., *War As I Knew It,* 1947

If you go long enough without a bath even the fleas will let you alone.

> ERNIE PYLE, *Here Is Your War*

One Down, Two to Go.

> Newspaper headline in most U.S. papers, when Italy sur-
> rendered, September 8, 1943

The Seabees are always happy to welcome the Marines.

> LIEUTENANT BOB RYAN, greeting Marines as they landed at
> Segi, New Georgia, September, 1943. Supposed to land with
> or just after the Marines, the Seabees had somehow man-
> aged to land before them on Segi.

Back the Attack!

> Slogan of Fifth War Loan drive, June, 1944

People of Western Europe: A landing was made this morning on the
coast of France by troops of the Allied Expeditionary Force. This landing
is part of the concerted United Nations plan for the liberation of Europe,
made in conjunction with our great Russian allies. . . . I call upon all
who love freedom to stand with us now. Together we shall achieve victory.

> GENERAL DWIGHT D. EISENHOWER, broadcast, June 6,
> 1944 (D-Day)

Then darkness enveloped the whole American armada. Not a pinpoint of
light showed from those hundreds of ships as they surged on through the

night toward their destiny, carrying across the ageless and indifferent sea tens of thousands of young men, fighting for . . . for . . . well, at least for each other.

> ERNIE PYLE, *Brave Men,* Normandy landing, June 6, 1944

I'm a rabid one-man movement bent on tracking down and stamping out everybody in the world who doesn't fully appreciate the common front-line soldier.

> ERNIE PYLE, *Ibid.*

I do not pretend that my feeling is the spirit of our armies. If it were, we probably would not have had the power to win. Most men are stronger. Our soldiers still can hate, or glorify, or be glad, with true emotion. For them, death has a pang and victory a sweet scent. But for me war has become a flat, black depression without highlights, a revulsion of the mind and an exhaustion of the spirit.

> ERNIE PYLE, *Ibid.*

He's right, Joe, when we ain't fightin' we should ack like sojers.

> BILL MAULDIN, cartoon caption, *Up Front,* 1944

I feel like a fugitive from th' law of averages.

> BILL MAULDIN, *Ibid.*

Look at an infantryman's eyes and you can tell how much war he has seen.

> BILL MAULDIN, *Ibid.*

Keep 'Em Flying.

> HAROLD N. GILBERT, slogan of Air Forces, World War II

Sure, we all want to get home. We want to get this thing over with. But the quickest way to get it over with is to go get the bastards. The quicker they're whipped, the quicker we go home. The shortest way home is through Berlin.

And there's one thing you'll be able to say when you do go home. When you're sitting around your fireside, with your brat on your knee, and he asks you what you did in the great World War II, you won't have to say you shovelled . . . in Louisiana.

> GENERAL GEORGE S. PATTON, JR., speech to troops of Third Army, before invasion of France, July, 1944

Americans, with arms in their hands, are fools as well as cowards to surrender.

> GENERAL GEORGE S. PATTON, JR., letters of instruction to his Third Army

Move forward out of fire.

> GEORGE S. PATTON, JR., *Ibid.*

Any commander who fails to obtain his objective, and who is not dead or severely wounded, has not done his full duty.

> GEORGE S. PATTON, JR., *Ibid.*

We sure liberated the hell out of this place.

> ANON., an American soldier in the ruins of a French village, 1944, quoted by Miller, *The Far Shore*

We didn't have a damn thing to do with the taking of Paris. We just came in a couple of days later when somebody got the bright idea of having the parade and we just happened to be there and that's all there is to it. What can you do, though—that's just the way it goes. And after all, we did a helluva lot of things that we didn't get credit for.

As long as I live I don't guess I'll ever see a parade like that. Most of us slept in pup tents in the Bois de Boulogne the night before, and it rained like hell and we were pretty dirty, so they picked out the cleanest guys to stand up in front and on the outside. I had a bright new shiny patch, so they put me on the outside. It was a good place to be, too, because every guy marching on the outside had at least one girl on his arm kissing him and hugging him.

We were marching 24 abreast down the Champs Elysees and we had a helluva time trying to march, because the whole street was jammed with people laughing and yelling and crying and singing. They were throwing flowers at us and bringing us big bottles of wine.

The first regiment never did get through. They just broke in and grabbed the guys and lifted some of them on their shoulders and carried them into cafes and bars and their homes and wouldn't let them go. I hear it was a helluva job trying to round them all up later.

> PRIVATE FIRST CLASS VERNER ODEGARD, as reported by Ralph Martin, in *Yank*

DEAR IKE: Today I spat in the Seine.

> GENERAL GEORGE S. PATTON, JR., penned postscript to for-

mal military report to Eisenhower, August 26, 1944, when
one of Patton's units crossed the Seine at Melun, thus out-
flanking Paris

Our ships have been salvaged and are retiring at high speed toward the
Japanese fleet.

> ADMIRAL WILLIAM FREDERICK HALSEY, JR., radio message,
> October, 1944, after Japanese claims that most of the
> American Third Fleet had been sunk or was retiring

Send them our latitude and longitude.

> ADMIRAL WILLIAM FREDERICK HALSEY, JR., suggested reply
> to Japanese question: "Where is the American fleet?" Oc-
> tober, 1944

Nuts!

> GENERAL ANTHONY CLEMENT MCAULIFFE, reply to Ger-
> man summons to surrender, Bastogne, Belgium, December
> 22, 1944

Sure, there were lots of bodies we never identified. You know what a direct hit by a shell does to a guy. Or a mine, or a solid hit with a grenade,
even. Sometimes all we have is a leg or a hunk of arm.

The ones that stink the worst are the guys who got internal wounds and
are dead about three weeks with the blood staying inside and rotting, and
when you move the body the blood comes out of the nose and mouth.
Then some of them bloat up in the sun, they bloat up so big that they
bust the buttons and then they get blue and the skin peels. They don't all
get blue, some of them get black.

But they all stink. There's only one stink and that's it. You never get
used to it, either. As long as you live, you never get used to it. And after
a while, the stink gets in your clothes and you can taste it in your mouth.

You know what I think? I think maybe if every civilian in the world
could smell that stink, then maybe we wouldn't have any more wars.

> TECHNICAL SERGEANT DONALD HAGUALL, of Forty-eighth
> Quartermaster Graves Registration; as reported by Ralph
> Martin in *Yank*

They are not wrapped as gifts (there was no time to wrap them), but
you will find them under the lighted tree with the other presents. They

are the extra gifts, the ones with the hard names. Certain towns and villages. Certain docks and installations. Atolls in a sea. Assorted airstrips, beachheads, supply dumps, rail junctions. Here is a gift to hold in your hand—Hill 660. Vital from a strategic standpoint. "From the Marines," the card says. Here is a small strip of the Italian coast. Merry Christmas from the members of the American Fifth (who waded ashore). This is Kwajalein, Maloelap, Wotje. This is Eniwetok. Place them with your other atolls, over by the knitted scarf from Aunt Lucy. Here is Gea. If the size isn't right, remember it was selected at night, in darkness. Roi, Mellu, Boggerlapp, Ennugarret, Ennumennet, Ennubirr. Amphibious forces send season's greetings. How pretty! A little reef-fringed islet in a coral sea. Kwajalein! A remembrance at Christmas from the Seventh Division. Los Negros Island. Put it with the others of the Admiralty Group. Elements of the First Cavalry Division (dismounted) have sent Momote airfield, a very useful present. Manus, largest of the Admiralties. Lorengau, taken from the Japanese garrison in the underground bunkers. Talasea airdrome. Wotho Atoll (a gift from the Twenty-Second Marine Regiment). Emirau Island, and ten more atolls in the Marshalls to make your Christmas bright in 1944: Ujae, Lae, Lib, Namu, Ailinglapalap (never mind the names), together with a hundred-and-fifty-mile strip of the northern New Guinea coast, Tanahmera Bay and Humboldt Bay, together with Hollandia. "From some American troops covered with red mud."

Here is a novel gift—a monastery on a hill. It seems to have been damaged. A bridge on Highway 6. A mountain stronghold, Castelforte (Little Cassino, they used to call it). And over here the roads—Via Casilina and the Appian Way. Valleys, plains, hills, roads, and the towns and villages. Santa Maria Infante, San Pietro, Monte Cerri, and Monte Bracchi. One reads the names on the cards with affection. Best wishes from the Fifth. Gaeta, Cisterna, Terracina, the heights behind Velletri, the Alban Hills, Mount Peschio, and the fortress of Lazio. Velletri and Valmontone. Best wishes from the Fifth. The suburbs of Rome, and Rome. The Eternal City! Holiday greetings from the American Fifth.

Who wouldn't love the Norman coast for Christmas? Who hasn't hoped for the Atlantic Wall, the impregnable? Here is the whole thing under the lighted tree. First the beaches (greetings from the Navy and the Coast Guard), then the cliffs, the fields behind the cliffs, the inland villages and towns, the key places, the hedgerows, the lanes, the houses, and the barns. Ste. Mère Eglise (with greetings from Omar Bradley and foot soldiers). This Norman cliff (best from the Rangers). St. Jacques de Nehou (from the Eighty-Second Airborne Division, with its best). Cherbourg—street by street, and house by house. St. Remy des Landes, La Broquière, Baudreville, Neufmesnil, La Poterie, the railroad station at La Haye du Puits.

And then St. Lô, and the whole vista of France. When have we received such presents? Saipan in the Marianas—only they forgot to take the price tag off. Saipan cost 9752 in dead, wounded, and missing, but that includes a mountain called Tapotchau. Guam. "Merry Christmas from Conolly, Geiger, and the boys." Tinian, across the way. Avranches, Gavray, Torigny-sur-Vire, a German army in full retreat under your tree. A bridge at Pontorson, a bridge at Ducey, with regards from those who take bridges. Rennes, capital of Brittany (our columns fan out). Merry Christmas, all! Brest, Nantes, St. Malo, a strategic fortress defended for two weeks by a madman. Toulon, Nice, St. Tropez, Cannes (it is very gay, the Riviera, very fashionable). And now (but you must close your eyes for this one) . . . Paris.

Still the gifts come. You haven't even noticed the gift of the rivers Marne and Aisne. Château-Thierry, Soissons (this is where you came in). Verdun, Sedan (greetings from the American First Army, greetings from the sons of the fathers). Here is a most unusual gift, a bit of German soil. Priceless. A German village, Roetgen. A forest south of Aachen. Liége, the Belfort Gap, Geilenkirchen, Crucifix Hill, Urbach. Morotai Island in the Halmaheras. An airport on Peleliu. Angaur (from the Wildcats). Nijmegen Bridge, across the Rhine. Cecina, Monteverdi, more towns, more villages on the Tyrrhenian coast. Leghorn. And, as a special remembrance, sixty-two ships of the Japanese Navy, all yours. Tacloban, Dulag, San Pablo . . . Ormoc. Valleys and villages in the Burmese jungle. Gifts in incredible profusion and all unwrapped, from old and new friends: gifts with a made-in-China label, gifts from Russians, Poles, Brittish, French, gifts from Eisenhower, de Gaulle, Montgomery, Malinovsky, an umbrella from the Air Forces, gifts from engineers, rear gunners, privates first class . . . there isn't time to look at them all. It will take years. This is a Christmas you will never forget, people have been so generous.

E. B. WHITE, "The Wild Flag," *New Yorker*, Dec. 23, 1944

Austin White—Chicago, Ill.—1918
Austin White—Chicago, Ill.—1945
This is the last time I want to write my name here.

AUSTIN WHITE, inscription discovered by a *Yank* reporter on a wall of the fortress of Verdun

The mission of this Allied Force was fulfilled at 3 A.M., local time, May 7, 1945. Eisenhower.

GENERAL DWIGHT D. EISENHOWER, telegram to the Combined Chiefs of Staff, at the end of World War II, Europe

We call Japanese soldiers fanatics when they die rather than surrender, whereas American soldiers who do the same thing are heroes.

> ROBERT M. HUTCHINS, "Convocation Address," June, 1945

Let us pray that peace be now restored to the world, and that God will preserve it always.

These proceedings are closed.

> GENERAL DOUGLAS MACARTHUR, speech after the surrender of the Japanese aboard the battleship *Missouri*, September 2, 1945

Sam's discovery was basically simple, natural, reasonable. He had discovered that nurses lived in the long, yellow house. He had discovered two large windows in the middle of the second-story front, and that these windows had none but shade curtains, retracted. He had discovered (the telescope is a powerful glass and the room was well illumined by sunlight) that the windows belonged to the bathroom. It is, of course, redundant to say that he had also discovered a nurse in the shower stall in the far left-hand corner of the room. All of this would seem to be a model of logic, of sweet reasonableness: what could possibly be more logical than that there be a hospital at this base, that there be nurses attached to this hospital, that these nurses live in a house, that this house have a bathroom, that this bathroom have windows, that these nurses bathe? Nothing, you would think. And yet to these signalmen and quartermasters (who had last seen a white woman, probably fat, certainly fully clothed, perhaps fourteen months ago) this vision was literally that, a vision, and a miracle, and not a very small miracle, either. Like Sam, they were stricken with reverence in its presence, and like Sam, their remarks were reverent; those who could speak at all. "Holy Christ!" a few of them managed to breathe, and "Son-of-a-bitch!" That was all. Those are the only legitimate things a man can say when suddenly confronted with the imponderable.

> THOMAS HEGGEN, *Mr. Roberts*, 1946

I'm coming to Old Yellowstain. Coming to him. See, while I was studying law 'n' old Keefer here was writing his play for the Theatre Guild, and Willie here was on the playing fields of Prinshton, all that time these birds we call regulars—these stuffy, stupid Prussians, in the Navy and the Army—were manning guns. Course they weren't doing it to save my Mom from Hitler, they were doing it for dough, like everybody else does what they do. Question is, in the last analysis—last analysis—*what* do they do for dough? Old Yellowstain, for dough, was standing guard on this fat dumb and happy country of ours. Meantime me, I was advancing my little free non-Prussian life for dough. Of course, we figured in those days, only fools go into armed service. Bad pay, no millionaire future, and you can't call your mind or body your own. Not for sensitive intellectuals. So when all hell broke loose and the Germans started running out of soap and figured, well it's time to come over and melt down old Mrs. Greenwald—who's gonna stop them? Not her boy Barney. Can't stop a Nazi with a lawbook. So I dropped the lawbooks and ran to learn how to fly. Stout fellow. Meantime, and it took a year and a half before I was any good, who was keeping Mama out of the soap dish? Captain Queeg.

> HERMAN WOUK, *The Caine Mutiny;* Barney Greenwald is speaking

OTHER WARS

Be Always Sure You're Right—Then Go Ahead.

> DAVY CROCKETT, his motto; became motto of War of 1812

Strike wherever we can reach the enemy, at sea and on land. But if we fail, let us fail like men, lash ourselves to our gallant tars, and expire together in one common struggle, fighting for FREE TRADE AND SEAMEN'S RIGHTS.

> HENRY CLAY, during War of 1812

Don't give up the ship!

> CAPTAIN JAMES LAWRENCE, command given as he lay dying aboard his frigate, the *Chesapeake,* June 1, 1813. The ship was taken by the British after a bloody fight. Another version of this famous quote: "Tell the men to fire faster and not to give up the ship; fight her till she sinks."

Wednesday, August 19th, 1812, 6:30 P.M., the Birth of a World Power.

> CHARLES FRANCIS ADAMS, title of essay in *American Historical Review,* 1880's. The date is that of the defeat of the *Guerrière* by the *Constitution.*

We have met the enemy and they are ours—two ships, two brigs, one schooner and one sloop.

> COMMANDER OLIVER HAZARD PERRY, dispatch to General William Henry Harrison, announcing his victory at the Battle of Lake Erie, September 10, 1813

Old Fuss and Feathers.

> Sobriquet bestowed on General Winfield Scott by his troops during the Black Hawk War

This is no war of defense, but one of unnecessary and of offensive aggression. It is Mexico that is defending her firesides, her castles and altars, not we.

> HENRY CLAY, 1844

Uncle Joshua always says, in nine cases out of ten it costs more to rob an orchard than it would to buy the apples.

> SEBA SMITH ("MAJOR JACK DOWNING"), to General Pierce, of the Mexican War

All wars, to be just, must have some distinct and legitimate objects to be accomplished. . . . One of the strangest . . . circumstances attending this war is, that though it has lasted upwards of eight months, at a cost of many millions of dollars, and the sacrifice of many valuable lives, both in battle and by the diseases of the camp, no man can tell for what object it is prosecuted. And it is to be doubted whether any man, save the President and his Cabinet, knows the real and secret designs that provoked its existence. To suppress inquiry, and silence all opposition to conduct so monstrous, an executive ukase has been sent forth, strongly intimating, if not clearly threatening, the charge of treason, against all who may dare to call in question the wisdom or propriety of his measures.

It is to be seen whether the free people of this country have so soon forgotten the principles of their ancestors as to be so easily awed by the arrogance of power. For a very little further interference with the freedom of discussion, Charles X, of France, lost his throne; and for a very little greater stretch of royal prerogative, Charles I, of England, lost his head. There are some things more to be dreaded than the loss of a throne, or even the loss of a head—amongst which may be named the anathema of a nation's curse, and the infamy that usually follows it.

> ALEXANDER STEPHENS, speech in the House on the Mexican War

Commandancy of the Alamo, Bexar, February 24, 1836.—To the people
of Texas and all Americans in the world. Fellow citizens and compatriots:
I am besieged by a thousand or more of the Mexicans under Santa Anna.
I have sustained a continual bombardment and cannonade for twenty-
four hours and have not lost a man. The enemy has demanded a surrender at discretion; otherwise the garrison are to be put to the sword if the
fort is taken. I have answered the demand with a cannon shot, and our
flag still waves proudly from the walls. *I shall never surrender or retreat.*
Then I call on you in the name of liberty, of patriotism, and everything
dear to the American character, to come to our aid with all dispatch. The
enemy is receiving reinforcements daily and will no doubt increase to
three or four thousand in four or five days. If this call is neglected, I am
determined to sustain myself as long as possible and die like a soldier who
never forgets what is due to his own honor and that of our country. VIC-
TORY OR DEATH.

> LIEUTENANT COLONEL WILLIAM BARRET TRAVIS, the last
> message from the Alamo

Thermopylae had its messenger of defeat. The Alamo had none.

> Message found written on the walls of the Alamo (in blood
> or candle smoke) when U.S. troops recaptured it from
> Santa Anna, after the massacre of March 6, 1836

Remember the Alamo.

> Battle cry of Sam Houston's troops at San Jacinto, April,
> 1836, where the Texans defeated the Mexicans and took
> General Santa Anna prisoner; on March 6 Santa Anna had
> taken Fort Alamo, in San Antonio, and massacred its gar-
> rison of 180 men, among them Davy Crockett and James
> Bowie. The phrase is sometimes attributed to Colonel Sid-
> ney Sherman.

If I were a Mexican I would tell you, "Have you not room enough in
your own country to bury your dead?"

> THOWAS CORWIN, speech in Congress, denouncing the
> Mexican War, February 11, 1847

General Taylor never surrenders.

> THOMAS L. CRITTENDEN, reply, on behalf of General Zach-
> ary Taylor, at the Battle of Buena Vista, February 22, 1847,

when summoned to surrender by General Santa Anna. The
phrase became the slogan of the presidential campaign of
1848, when Taylor was elected.

Since the far beginning, too, it has been these towers, consecrated to Victory or Death, that have been man's antidote for his own inevitable passion to ravage and destroy the very things he has so hardly wrested from
chaos. It was just such towers that held back the barbarians from destroying the incipient clusters of civilization long enough for the barbarians
themselves to become infected by the germ; and it was behind such towers
and the unrecreant corpses of their defenders that Aristotle founded
Science, Giotto painted, Dante sang, Christ was permitted his sacrifice
within significant organization, and Pericles' Athens marked the period
to man's emotional and mental attitude towards life.

MARCUS GOODRICH, *Delilah,* of the Alamo

The marines have landed, and the situation is well in hand.

RICHARD HARDING DAVIS, cablegram from Panama, 1885

Remember the Maine!

Slogan of the Spanish-American War. On February 15,
1898, the American battleship *Maine* was destroyed by a
mine in the harbor of Havana, Cuba.

Please remain. You furnish the pictures and I'll furnish the war.

WILLIAM RANDOLPH HEARST, telegram to Frederic Rem-
ington, when the latter wished to return home from Cuba,
March, 1898

You may fire when you are ready, Gridley.

ADMIRAL GEORGE DEWEY, to the captain of his flagship, at
the Battle of Manila, May 1, 1898

There's glory enough for all.

WINFIELD SCOTT SCHLEY, comment following controversy
as to whether Commander Schley or Commander William
T. Sampson should be credited with the naval victory at
Santiago, July 3, 1898

Don't cheer, boys; the poor devils are dying.

CAPTAIN JOHN WOODWARD PHILIP, of the battleship *Texas,*

as his ship swept past the burning Spanish ship *Viscaya,*
Battle of Santiago, July 3, 1898

We shall not, I believe, be obliged to alter our policy of watchful waiting.
WOODROW WILSON, "Message to Congress," December 2,
1913. The reference is to Mexico.

We are in the midst of a cold war which is getting warmer.
BERNARD BARUCH, spoken before Senate Committee, 1948.
Mr. Baruch coined the phrase in 1947.

The emphasis often placed solely on the military aspects of world affairs
does a disservice to the cause of peace. The more that present differences
are talked about and treated exclusively as a military problem the more
they tend to become so.
GEORGE C. MARSHALL

Retreat, Hell! We're just fighting in another direction.
GENERAL O. P. SMITH, U.S.M.C., at Changjin Reservoir,
in northern Korea, fall, 1950

So we won't have to fight in Wichita.
CAPTAIN JAMES JABARA, of Wichita, when asked why we
were fighting in Korea; quoted by Adlai Stevenson in a
speech, 1952

That's the way the ball bounces.
Army saying, Korean War

BUGOUT—A rapidly executed retrograde movement; to leave an area in
great haste
PANIC BUTTON—That mythical button which, when pushed, arouses or
inspires panic. To "push the panic button" is to become unduly
alarmed, or to spread alarming tales.
No SWEAT—No trouble
BRAIN WASH—To corner someone and talk him down with exposition of
your position or stand on a subject
CLOBBER—To tear up badly; originally an Air Force term (World War
II) now adopted by all services
HAVA-NO—I do not have it

HAVA-YES—I do have it

SUKOSHI—Just a small one; used in reference to anything: a drink, a woman, a man, time left

MOOSIE-MAID—A mistress; permanent-type girl friend as opposed to the short-term type

MOOSE—Contraction of Moosie-maid

MOOSE MAN—A man who has a Moose. (Moose is an American derivation of a Japanese word *"muse-mai"* which actually means "small daughter.")

CHOTTO-MOTTE—Just a minute (Japanese)

TAKU-SAN (TAKSAN)—An abundance, plenty (as opposed to *sukoshi*)

ICHI-BAN—Fine, good, everything is in good shape

NUMBER ONE—First rate. This term originated in Korea. Like "hava-yes" and "hava-no" it started with the Korean's basic attempts to make himself understood in his small grasp of English. As time went on it became standard that the best of anything—food, the tactical situation, a man's reputation, anything—was number one. Opposing this is "number ten," the worst.

BALI-BALI—Hurry up

CHANGEE-CHANGEE—To alter or to exchange

SLICKY-SLICKY—To pull a "slick" deal; to steal by stealth, or to "borrow" something without the owner's knowledge

CHIGEE—A Korean laborer belonging to a man-power transport outfit

CHOGI—Hurry up, bring, or carry; derived from a bastardization of the Korean name of the carrying frame used throughout Korea

A-FRAME—Soldier's name for the chogi-frame; so named because the frame looks like an open-topped "A"

CHOP CHOP—Food

THE BIG R—Rotation home

LITTLE R, R & R—Rest and Recuperation leave in Japan

IDIWAH (*eedeewah*)—Come here. This has a rather insulting connotation when used to adults, since it is normally said in Korean only to children.

I'LL CLUE YOU—I'll let you in on the real facts; I'll steer you straight

NEVER HOTCHEE—It will never happen; don't you believe it

WHATS-A-MATTER-YOU, GI?—Frequently used expression growing out of Korean's early use of English

YOU SPEAK HOW MUCH—Tell me how much it is; or tell me how much you will offer. A bartering term.

WHIRLEY-BIRD; CHOPPER; EGG BEATER—Helicopter

GOOK—The Asiatic enemy. This term finally became used primarily in reference to the North Koreans.

JOE CHINK—The Chinese enemy. I believe this term was originated by
the Negro soldiers in the Korean fighting.

>   MAJOR VERNON PIZER, Army phrases, Korean War

I know the Lord had to be with my body, for my feet couldn't have taken
me over some of the roads I walked on.

>   PRIVATE FIRST CLASS FLOYD PHILPOTT, after his release
>   from a Korean prisoner-of-war camp, April, 1953

Anybody's who's dumb enough to get captured shouldn't be called a hero.

>   GENERAL WILLIAM F. DEAN, revisiting his boyhood town,
>   November, 1953

Local defense will always be important. But there is no local defense which
alone will contain the mighty land power of the Communist world. Local
defense must be reinforced by the further deterrent of massive retaliatory
power. [The Administration has made a basic decision] to depend primarily upon a great capacity to retaliate instantly by means and at places
of our choosing.

>   JOHN FOSTER DULLES, to the Council on Foreign Relations,
>   New York, January 12, 1954

THE BOMB

•

At the rate of progress since 1800, every American who lived into the year
2000 would know how to control unlimited power. . . . To him the nineteenth century would stand on the same plane as the fourth—equally
childlike—and he would only wonder how both of them, knowing so little,
and so weak in force, should have done so much.

>   HENRY ADAMS, *The Education of Henry Adams*

Some recent work by E. Fermi and L. Szilard, which has been communicated to me in manuscript, leads me to expect that the element uranium
may be turned into a new and important source of energy in the immediate future.

>   ALBERT EINSTEIN, letter to Pres. Roosevelt, August 2, 1939

The Italian navigator has landed; the natives are friendly.

> ANON., code message, telegraphed to scientists on December 2, 1942, to indicate that the first self-sustaining nuclear chain reaction had been made to work by Enrico Fermi and a group of researchers

> On December 2, 1942
> Man Achieved Here
> The First Self-Sustaining Chain Reaction
> And Thereby Initiated the
> Controlled Release of Nuclear Energy

> ANON., inscription on plaque on wall at University of Chicago. The wall is only a façade, concealing the west stands of a football stadium that is no longer used—it was under this stadium that Enrico Fermi and others started the whole business.

Back at the right waist window, Sgt. Bob Shumard, the assistant flight engineer, turned his polaroids to full intensity and prepared to take advantage of the fact that he had the best seat for the show. When the bomb went off it looked blue through his polaroids, but he noted that the interior of the plane lighted up as though flash bulbs had been set off inside the cabin. He adjusted his polaroids to mild intensity and looked down at Hiroshima. A large white cloud was spreading rapidly over the whole area, obscuring everything and rising very rapidly. Shumard shouted into the intercom: "There it goes, and it's coming right back at us!"

Looking way down again, he noted that outside the smoke circle and racing ahead of it were three large concentric circles. These appeared to Shumard to be heat rings, since they looked like the transparent wavy vapor seen coming off hot objects. He craned to see what happened to them, but the lieutenant who had been asleep was now awake and was climbing all over Shumard's neck.

He lost the rings during this interval and could not find them again.

The engineer noted that his instruments were still functioning normally, and then he looked out his little hatch. He said nothing.

When Stiborik got no instrument reaction to the blast, he looked too.

"Jesus Christ," said Lt. Jeppson. "If people knew what we were doing we could have sold tickets for $100,000."

Ferebee, the bombardier, felt only one reaction: He was damn glad to be rid of the bomb. Then he set to work filling out the strike-report form which was to be radioed in.

Back in the tail Caron noted the turbulence and called to the pilot: "Colonel, it's coming toward us fast." He got no reply, but the plane changed its course and outdistanced the cloud.

They looked after it as long as they could see it, a great ringed cumulus-type shaft rising higher and higher through the clouds. Then they flew on and it was gone. The tail-gunner called to the pilot: "Colonel, that was worth the 25¢ ride on the Cyclone at Coney Island."

The colonel called back, "I'll collect the two bits when we land."

"You'll have to wait till pay day," said the tail gunner.

Maj. Ferebee filled out the strike report and gave it to Capt. Parsons, who had been in charge of the bomb.

"This report," said the captain, "is going directly to the President."

The Navy captain wondered aloud: "How can you destroy so much and sacrifice so little? We didn't even damage the plane."

ROBERT SCHWARTZ, *Yank,* August, 1945

Sixteen hours ago an American airplane dropped one bomb on Hiroshima. . . . It is a harnessing of the basic power of the universe. The force from which the sun draws its powers has been loosed against those who brought war to the Far East.

HARRY S. TRUMAN, announcement of the first atomic bomb, August 6, 1945

We have spent two billion dollars on the greatest scientific gamble in history—and won.

HARRY S. TRUMAN, *Ibid.*

We flew southward down the channel and at 11:33 crossed the coastline and headed straight for Nagasaki about 100 miles to the west. Here again we circled until we found an opening in the clouds. It was 12:01 and the goal of our mission had been reached.

We heard the prearranged signal on our radio, put on our arc-welder's glasses and watched tensely the maneuverings of the strike ship about half a mile in front of us.

"There she goes!" someone said.

Out of the belly of *The Great Artiste* what looked like a black object went downward.

Captain Bock swung around to get out of range; but even though we were turning away in the opposite direction, and despite the fact that it was broad daylight in our cabin, all of us became aware of a giant flash that broke through the dark barrier of our arc-welder's lenses and flooded our cabin with intense light.

We removed our glasses after the first flash, but the light still lingered on, a bluish-green that illuminated the entire sky all around. A tremendous blast wave struck our ship and made it tremble from nose to tail. This was followed by four more blasts in rapid succession, each resounding like the boom of cannon fire hitting our plane from all directions.

Observers in the tail of our ship saw a giant ball of fire rise as though from the bowels of the earth, belching forth enormous white smoke rings. Next they saw a gigantic pillar of purple fire, 10,000 feet high, shooting skyward with enormous speed.

By the time our ship had made another turn in the direction of the atomic explosion, the pillar of purple fire had reached the level of our altitude. Only about forty-five seconds had passed. Awestruck, we watched it shoot upward like a meteor coming from the earth instead of from outer space, becoming ever more alive as it climbed skyward through the white clouds. It was no longer smoke, or dust, or even a cloud of fire. It was a living thing, a new species of being born before our incredulous eyes.

At one stage of its evolution, covering millions of years in terms of seconds, the entity assumed the form of a giant square totem pole, with its base about three miles long, tapering off to about a mile at the top. Its bottom was brown, its center was amber, its top white. But it was a living totem pole, carved with many grotesque masks grimacing at the earth.

Then, just when it appeared as if the thing had settled down in a state of permanence, there came shooting out of the top a giant mushroom that increased the height of the pillar to a total of 45,000 feet. The mushroom top was even more alive than the pillar, seething and boiling in a white fury of creamy foam, sizzling upward and then descending earthward, a thousand Old Faithful geysers rolled into one.

It kept struggling in an elemental fury, like a creature in the act of breaking the bonds that held it down. In a few seconds it had freed itself from its gigantic stem and floated upward with tremendous speed, its momentum carrying it into the stratosphere to a height of about 60,000 feet.

But no sooner did this happen than another mushroom, smaller in size than the first, began emerging out of the pillar. It was as though the decapitated monster was growing a new head.

As the first mushroom floated off into the blue, it changed its shape into a flower-like form, its giant petal curving downward, creamy white outside, rose-colored inside. It still retained that shape when we last gazed at it from a distance of about 200 miles.

WILLIAM L. LAURENCE, *New York Times,* Sept. 19, 1945

Walking into Hiroshima in broad daylight, wearing an American uniform and knowing that you were one of the first Americans the people in the utterly ruined city have laid eyes on since the bombing, was not a comfortable feeling. I couldn't help wondering what would have happened if I'd been a Jap entering Brooklyn after Japan had dropped an atomic bomb, or, for that matter, any kind of bomb, on Flatbush. I was accompanied by the crew of a B-17 who were wearing Air Forces insignia all over themselves the way an Irishman wears green on St. Patrick's Day, and that didn't help matters. But the Hiroshima Japs—men, women, and children, gave us exactly the same treatment we got in Yokohama, Tokyo, Kuri, and all the other Jap towns we have visited—the same prolonged, unabashed, curious stares unmixed with any expression either of hatred or welcome.

All through Hiroshima we've passed close to men and women pointing at ashes that evidently used to be homes of relatives or friends. We've seen them at the wrecked police station trying to locate missing people and walking toward their shrines to pray. I noticed one woman leaning over a water faucet, the only thing left of her home, filling a pan to wash some clothes. There was no wreckage around her, no broken walls or glassless windows—just the water pipe, with the faucet on the end of it, sticking up out of the ashes. "It's tough on them, sure," said a GI with me, "but it saved a lot of guys' lives."

One of the Jap Navy officers acting as our interpreters was born in Sacramento, California. We asked him if the people in this part of Japan accepted the atomic bomb as one of the misfortunes of war and held no particular resentment against us for it. Or, we asked, do they hate us?

The officer studied his boots and then peered quizzically through his tortoise-rimmed glasses.

"They hate you," he said.

SERGEANT JOE MCCARTHY, *Yank*

Up to last Monday I must confess that I did not have much hope for a world state. I have believed that no moral basis for it existed and that we had no world conscience and no sense of world community sufficient to keep a world state together. But the alternatives now seem clear. One is world suicide; another is agreement among sovereign states to abstain from using the bomb. This will not be effective. The only hope, therefore, of abolishing war is through the monopoly of atomic force by a world organization.

R. M. Hutchins, *Chicago Round Table,* August 12, 1945

There are two principles that have been cornerstones of the structure of modern science. The first—that matter can be neither created nor destroyed but only altered in form—was enunciated in the nineteenth century and is familiar to every student of chemistry; it has led to the principle known as the law of conservation of mass. The second—that energy can be neither created nor destroyed but only altered in form— emerged in the nineteenth century and has ever since been the plague of inventors of perpetual-motion machines; it is known as the law of conservation of energy.

These two principles have constantly guided and disciplined the development and application of science. For all practical purposes they were unaltered and separate until some five years ago. For most practical purposes they still are so, but it is known that they are, in fact, two phases of a single principle for we have discovered that energy may sometimes be converted into matter and matter into energy. Specifically, such a conversion is observed in the phenomenon of nuclear fission of uranium, a process in which atomic nuclei split into fragments with the release of an enormous amount of energy.

Henry D. Smyth, *Atomic Energy for Military Purposes,* the "Smyth Report," 1945

Since I do not foresee that atomic energy is to be a great boon for a long time, I have to say that for the present it is a menace. Perhaps it is well that it should be. It may intimidate the human race into bringing order into its international affairs, which, without the pressure of fear, it would not do.

Albert Einstein, *Atlantic Monthly,* November, 1945

It has been announced that the critical concentration of uranium is one pound. (Half-pound packages of it are harmless.) What the critical concentration of lethargy is is still anybody's guess. . . . It seems that one of the characteristics of atomic energy is that it frightens most those who possess it. The United States, being in the saddle but having not the slightest desire to ride, is far more nervous about the bomb than are the countries that do not yet know the trick and are merely engaged in finding it out. These unatomic countries have something to occupy their hands and their minds, some logical goal. We in America have reached

the goal, and nobody knows which way you turn after you have learned
how to destroy the world in a single night.

E. B. WHITE, *The Wild Flag*, November 3, 1945

I do not believe that civilization will be wiped out in a war fought with
the atomic bomb. Perhaps two-thirds of the people of the earth might be
killed, but enough men capable of thinking, and enough books, would be
left to start again, and civilization could be restored.

ALBERT EINSTEIN, *Atlantic Monthly*, November, 1945

What takes place can be illustrated with the help of our rich man. The
atom M is a rich miser who, during his life, gives away no money (*energy*). But in his will he bequeaths his fortune to his sons M' and M'', on
condition that they give to the community a small amount, less than one-
thousandth of the whole estate (*energy or mass*). The sons together have
somewhat less than the father had (*the mass sum $M' + M''$ is somewhat
smaller than the mass M of the radioactive atom*). But the part given to
the community is still so enormously large (*considered as kinetic energy*)
that it brings with it a great threat of evil. Averting that threat has become the most urgent problem of our time.

ALBERT EINSTEIN, *Science Illustrated,* 1946

The only way to make a man trustworthy is to trust him; and the surest
way to make him untrustworthy is to distrust him and show him your
distrust.

HENRY L. STIMSON, "The Bomb and the Opportunity,"
Harper's Magazine, March, 1946

This was the first chance [Miss Sasaki] had had to look at the ruins of
Hiroshima; the last time she had been carried through the city's streets,
she had been hovering on the edge of unconsciousness. Even though the
wreckage had been described to her, and though she was still in pain, the
sight horrified and amazed her, and there was something she noticed
about it that particularly gave her the creeps. Over everything—up
through the wreckage of the city, in gutters, along the riverbanks, tangled
among tiles and tin roofing, climbing on charred tree trunks—was a
blanket of fresh, vivid, lush, optimistic green; the verdancy rose even from
the foundations of ruined houses. Weeds already hid the ashes, and wild
flowers were in bloom among the city's bones. The bomb had not only
left the underground organs of plants intact; it had stimulated them.
Everywhere were bluets and Spanish bayonets, goosefoot, morning glories

and day lilies, the hairy-fruited bean, purslane and clotbur and sesame and panic grass and feverfew. Especially in a circle at the center, sickle-senna grew in extraordinary regeneration, not only standing among the charred remnants of the same plant but pushing up in new places, among bricks and through cracks in the asphalt. It actually seemed as if a load of sickle-senna seed had been dropped along with the bomb.

JOHN HERSEY, *Hiroshima, The New Yorker,* 1946

We are here to make a choice between the quick and the dead.

BERNARD BARUCH, prefaced remarks to speech before U.N. Atomic Energy Commission, June 14, 1946

They say that when the bombs explode over Bikini, the heat will equal the interior heat of stars. This is of the utmost interest to scientists, every one of whom owes his existence to the earth's having cooled off.

E. B. WHITE, *The Wild Flag,* May 4, 1946

. . . The bomb has been made more effective. . . . Unless another war is prevented it is likely to bring destruction on a scale never before held possible and even now hardly conceived, and . . . little civilization would survive it.

ALBERT EINSTEIN, *Atlantic Monthly,* November, 1947

The armament race between the U.S.A. and the U.S.S.R., originally supposed to be a preventive measure, assumes hysterical character. On both sides, the means to mass destruction are perfected with feverish haste—behind the respective walls of secrecy. The H-bomb appears on the public horizon as a probably attainable goal. Its accelerated development has been solemnly proclaimed by the President.

If successful, radioactive poisoning of the atmosphere and hence annihilation of any life on earth has been brought within the range of technical possibilities. The ghostlike character of this development lies in its apparently compulsory trend. Every step appears as the unavoidable consequence of the preceding one. In the end, there beckons more and more clearly general annihilation.

ALBERT EINSTEIN, speech, Princeton, February, 1950

Some people seem to think that talking with your antagonist is appeasement. It is not. Talking with your antagonist to avoid strife is a moral duty. Appeasement comes when, in order to avoid strife and to achieve a supposed security, you sacrifice a principle which you know to be sacredly right. The international inspection of all atomic-energy activities is such a principle. We cannot surrender it.

> BRIAN McMAHON, "A Program for Atomic Peace," *Reader's Digest,* 1950

It is hard to understand why our town must be destroyed to make a bomb that will destroy someone else's town that they love as much as we love ours.

> ANON., sign on the outskirts of Ellenton, South Carolina, when the Atomic Energy Commission decided to make its first H-Bomb plant on the Savannah River near the town, which had of course to be evacuated

The cloud itself was kind of rough, yet it looked smooth—something like a cauliflower.

> ANON., an American sailor, observing the first H-bomb explosion, November 1, 1952

Recently in the thermonuclear tests at Eniwetok, we have entered another stage in the world-shaking development of atomic energy. From now on man moves into a new era of destructive power, capable of creating explosions of a new order of magnitude, dwarfing the mushroom clouds of Hiroshima and Nagasaki.

> HARRY S. TRUMAN, "Message to Congress," January 7, 1953

Whereas the end of the world is approaching . . .

This characteristic phrase, which opened the royal proclamations during the tenth century, might have been written today. At present, there is a general and universal physical fear, with only one question: "When will I be blown up?"

The idea of the end of the world had recurred again and again in the past, and yet the earth has not ceased to exist. However, prophecies in the near and distant past were based upon revelations in the Bible, the superstitions of astrology, or bad scientific theory. Today the warnings come from absolute and irrefutable scientific fact: the basic power of the universe has been released, and man is rapidly attaining the position where he can end the earth as an inhabited world.

> KENNETH HEUER, *The End of the World,* 1953

A REPORTER: Many people in Congress, I think many elsewhere, have been reaching out and grasping for some information as to what happens when the H-bomb goes off. . . .

STRAUSS: Well, the nature of an H-bomb is that, in effect, it can be made as large as the military requirement demands, that is to say, an H-bomb can be made as—large enough to take out a city.

REPORTERS: What?

STRAUSS: To take out a city, to destroy a city.

A REPORTER: How big a city?

STRAUSS: Any city.

A REPORTER: Any city? New York?

STRAUSS: The metropolitan area, yes [i.e., the heart of Manhattan, as he later elaborated].

LEWIS L. STRAUSS, press conference, March 30, 1954

In the name of sanity let our Government now pause and seek the counsel of sane men: men who have not participated in the errors we have made and are not committed, out of pride, to defending them. Let us cease all further experiments with even more horrifying weapons of destruction, lest our own self-induced fears further upset our mental balance.

Let us all, as responsible citizens, not the cowed subjects of an all-wise state, weigh the alternatives and canvass new lines of approach to the problems of power and peace.

If as a nation we have become mad it is time for the world to take note of that madness. If we are still humane and sane, then it is time for the powerful voice of sanity to be heard once more in our land.

LEWIS MUMFORD, letter to the New York Times, March 27, 1954. The subject was the announcement of the hydrogen bomb explosions.

VII. Heroes, Rogues and People

HEROES

•

He did not go to the college called Harvard, good old Alma Mater as
she is. He was not fed on the pap that is there furnished. As he phrased
it, "I know no more of grammar than one of your calves." But he went to
the great university of the West, where he sedulously pursued the study
of Liberty, for which he had early betrayed a fondness, and having taken
many degrees, he finally commenced the public practice of Humanity in
Kansas, as you all know. Such were *his humanities,* and not any study of
grammar. He would have left a Greek accent slanting the wrong way,
and righted up a falling man.

HENRY DAVID THOREAU, *A Plea for Captain John Brown*

He stands out of the darkness of time—alone, racked, deadly pale. He
wears a long white smock, with big pompoms down its front. His head is
crowned with a high, pointed, white clown's cap. He is Canio. Hundreds
and hundreds, sitting in long, silent rows, breathless, chained by enchant-
ment, watch and listen. From the lives of those hundreds reality vanishes.
I sit among them, stunned and shaken by the Voice of Gold. Did he who
had it deserve his unique fame? Yes, yes, a thousand times yes.

THOMAS R. YBARRA, *Caruso,* 1953

[Charlie Chaplin] was destined by his genius to be the one universal man
of modern times.

GILBERT SELDES, quoted by Huff, *Charles Chaplin,* 1951

Almost every body that knows the forest, understands parfectly well that
Davy Crockett never loses powder and ball, havin' ben brought up to
believe it a sin to throw away ammunition, and that is the benefit of a
vartuous eddikation. I war out in the forest one arternoon, and had jist
got to a place called the Great Gap, when I seed a rackkoon setting all
alone upon a tree. I clapped the breech of Brown Betty to my shoulder,
and war jist going to put a piece of lead between his shoulders, when he
lifted one paw, and sez he, "Is your name Crockett?"

Sez I, "You are rite for wonst, my name is Davy Crockett."

"Then," sez he, "you needn't take no further trouble, for I may as well
come down without another word." And the cretur walked rite down
from the tree, for he considered himself shot.

441

I stoops now and pats him on the head, and sez I, "I hope I may be shot myself before I hurt a hair of your head, for I never had sich a compliment in my life."

"Seeing as how you say that," sez he, "I'll jist walk off for the present, not doubting your word a bit, d'ye see, but lest you should kinder happen to change your mind."

The Sensible Varmint, from a *Crockett Almanac,* 1841

The one citizen of the New World fit to have his name uttered in the same breath with that of Plato.

JOHN DEWEY, of Emerson

He stops still, listens to his heart, and writes as he listens.

EGON FRIEDELL, *A Cultural History,* of Emerson

I was simmering, simmering, simmering; Emerson brought me to a boil.

WALT WHITMAN, as reported by John Taylor Trowbridge

No Emersonian exists now or ever did. One cannot be both a self-reliant man and a follower.

RALPH L. RUSK, *Times* "Book Review," May 24, 1953

Not a word, but I like to go and see him stand up there and look as though he thought everyone was as good as he.

A scrubwoman who always attended Emerson's lectures in Concord, when asked (by Mrs. Hoar) if she "understood Mr. Emerson"

Henry Ford as an old man
is a passionate antiquarian,
(lives besieged on his father's farm embedded in an estate of thousands of millionaire acres, protected by an army of servicemen, secretaries, secret agents, dicks under orders of an English exprizefighter,
always afraid of the feet in broken shoes on the roads, afraid the gangs will kidnap his grandchildren,
that a crank will shoot him,
that Change and the idle hands out of work will break through the gates and the high fences;
protected by a private army against

the new America of starved children and hollow bellies and cracked
shoes stamping on souplines,

that has swallowed up the old thrifty farmlands
of Wayne County, Michigan,
as if they had never been).
Henry Ford as an old man
is a passionate antiquarian.

He rebuilt his father's farmhouse and put it back exactly in the state
he remembered it in as a boy. He built a village of museums for buggies,
sleighs, coaches, old plows, waterwheels, obsolete models of motorcars.
He scoured the country for fiddlers to play old-fashioned square-dances.

Even old taverns he bought and put back into their original shape, as
well as Thomas Edison's early laboratories.

When he bought the Wayside Inn near Sudbury, Massachusetts, he
had the new highway where the newmodel cars roared and slithered and
hissed oilily past (*the new noise of the automobile*),

moved away from the door,
put back the old bad road,
so that everything might be
the way it used to be,
in the days of horses and buggies.

JOHN DOS PASSOS, *U.S.A.*, 1937

She'll never run! She'll never run!

> Kibitzers' cry as Robert Fulton attempted to start the en-
> gines of the *Clermont,* September 4, 1807. As soon as the
> steamboat started to move upriver, the crowd on the bank
> began to shout, "She'll never stop! She'll never stop!" To
> his uneasy passengers, Fulton announced: "Gentlemen, you
> need not be uneasy; you shall be in Albany before twelve
> o'clock tomorrow." They were.

If to be venerated for benevolence: if to be admired for talents: if to be
esteemed for patriotism: if to be beloved for philanthropy, can gratify the
human mind, you must have the pleasing consolation that you have not
lived in vain.

GEORGE WASHINGTON, letter to Benjamin Franklin, 1789

I succeed Dr. Franklin. No man can replace him.

THOMAS JEFFERSON, at the Court of France when a noble-

man asked him if he replaced Franklin as American Ambassador, 1785

I can't spare this man; he fights.

> ABRAHAM LINCOLN, of General Grant, 1862

If I knew what brand of whiskey he drinks, I would send a barrel or so
to some other generals.

> ABRAHAM LINCOLN, to critics of General Grant who
> claimed that he drank too much. That Lincoln actually
> said this is doubtful.

When Grant once gets possession of a place, he holds on to it as if he had
inherited it.

> ABRAHAM LINCOLN, to Benjamin F. Butler, June 22, 1864

I don't know, gentlemen, but they paid off on Grant.

> WILSON MIZNER, ending argument about whether Grant or
> Lee was the greater general

[Grant's] story is a strange allegory of America itself, of the way failure
follows success, of the incomprehensible manner in which the endowment
that wins a noble victory is never the endowment that can use the victory
after it has been won. There is a will-o'-the-wisp strain flickering through
American history, an unending effort to lay hands on a great prize clearly
seen, fairly won and then strangely elusive.

> BRUCE CATTON, *U. S. Grant and the American Military
> Tradition*, 1954

[Talleyrand] said that he had known, during his life, many of the more
marked men of his time, but that he had never, on the whole, known one
equal to Hamilton. I was much surprised, as well as gratified, by the remark; but still feeling that, as an American, I was, in some sort, a party
concerned by patriotism in the compliment, I answered,—with a little
reserve, perhaps with a little modesty,—that the great military commanders and the great statesmen of Europe had dealt with much larger masses
of men, and much wider interests than Hamilton ever had. *"Mais, mon-
sieur,"* the Prince instantly replied, *"Hamilton avait déviné l'Europe."*
("But, sir, Hamilton anticipated Europe.")

> GEORGE TICKNOR, *Journal,* 1818

Hawthorne isn't a handsome man, nor an engaging one personally. He
has the look all the time, to one who doesn't know him, of a rogue who
suddenly finds himself in a company of detectives. But in spite of his
rusticity, I felt a sympathy with him amounting to anguish, and couldn't
take my eyes off him all the dinner. . . . The idea I got was, and it was
very powerfully impressed on me, that we are all monstrously corrupt,
hopelessly bereft of human consciousness, and that it is the intention of
the Divine Providence to overrun us and obliterate us in a new Gothic
and Vandalic invasion. . . . The old world is breaking up on all hands
—the glimpse of the everlasting granite I caught in Hawthorne shows that
there is stock enough for fifty better.

> HENRY JAMES, SR., letter to Emerson after seeing Haw-
> thorne at a meeting in Boston, about 1862

Hawthorne was out of touch with his time, and he will be out of touch
with any time. He thought man was immortal: a mistake made only by
the greatest writers.

> MARK VAN DOREN, *Hawthorne,* 1949

Lord of San Simeon.

> ANON., sobriquet of William Randolph Hearst, derived
> from his holdings of 200,000 acres between the California
> Coast and the Santa Lucia Mountains.

I wish it had been possible for Raphael to paint General Jackson!

> NATHANIEL HAWTHORNE, *Notebooks,* 1858 (in Florence)

He was the most American of Americans—an embodied Declaration of
Independence—the Fourth of July incarnate.

> JAMES PARTON, *Life of Andrew Jackson,* 1859

You are better off than I am, for while you have lost your *left,* I have
lost my *right* arm.

> ROBERT E. LEE, letter to "Stonewall" Jackson, May 4, 1863.
> Jackson was wounded at Chancellorsville, May 2, and his
> arm was amputated on May 3. Lee lost his "right arm" for
> good when Jackson died a week later.

You enquire why so young a man as Mr. Jefferson was placed at the head
of the committee for preparing a Declaration of Independence? I answer: It was the Frankfort advice, to place Virginia at the head of

everything. Mr. Richard Henry Lee might be gone to Virginia, to his sick family, for aught I know, but that was not the reason of Mr. Jefferson's appointment. There were three committees appointed at the same time, one for the Declaration of Independence, another for preparing articles of confederation, and another for preparing a treaty to be proposed to France. Mr. Lee was chosen for the Committee of Confederation, and it was not thought convenient that the same person should be upon both. Mr. Jefferson came into Congress in June, 1775, and brought with him a reputation for literature, science, and a happy talent of composition. Writings of his were handed about, remarkable for the peculiar felicity of expression. Though a silent member in Congress, he was so prompt, frank, explicit, and decisive upon committees and in conversation—not even Samuel Adams was more so—that he soon seized upon my heart; and upon this occasion I gave him my vote, and did all in my power to procure the votes of others. I think he had one more vote than any other, and that placed him at the head of the committee. I had the next highest number, and that placed me second. The committee met, discussed the subject, and then appointed Mr. Jefferson and me to make the draft, I suppose because we were the two first on the list.

The subcommittee met. Jefferson proposed to me to make the draft. I said, "I will not. You should do it." "Oh! no." "Why will you not? You ought to do it." "I will not." "Reasons enough." "What can be your reasons?" "Reason first, you are a Virginian, and a Virginian ought to appear at the head of this business. Reason second, I am obnoxious, suspected, and unpopular. You are very much otherwise. Reason third, you can write ten times better than I can." "Well," said Jefferson, "if you are decided, I will do as well as I can." "Very well. When you have drawn it up, we will have a meeting."

A meeting we accordingly had, and conned the paper over. I was delighted with its high tone and the flights of oratory with which it abounded. . . . I consented to report it, and do not now remember that I made or suggested a single alteration.

We reported it to the committee of five. It was read, and I do not remember that Franklin or Sherman criticized anything. We were all in haste. Congress was impatient, and the instrument was reported, as I believe, in Jefferson's handwriting, as he first drew it. Congress cut off about a quarter of it, as I expected they would. . . .

JOHN ADAMS, letter to Timothy Pickering, August 6, 1822

[Jefferson was] a gentleman of thirty-two who could calculate an eclipse, survey an estate, tie an artery, plan an edifice, try a cause, break a horse, dance a minuet and play the violin.

JAMES PARTON, *Life of Jefferson*

The contradictions in Jefferson's character have always rendered it a fascinating study. Excepting his rival, Alexander Hamilton, no American has been the object of estimates so widely differing and so difficult to reconcile. Almost every other American statesman might be described in a parenthesis. A few broad strokes of the brush would paint the portraits of all the early Presidents with this exception, and a few more strokes would answer for any member of their cabinets; but Jefferson could be painted only touch by touch, with a fine pencil, and the perfection of the likeness depended upon the shifting and uncertain flicker of its semi-transparent shadows.

HENRY ADAMS, *History of the United States*

Thomas Jefferson, Benjamin Franklin and Count Rumford are the three greatest minds that America has produced.

FRANKLIN D. ROOSEVELT, while President

I must mention that beautiful creature, Helen Keller, whom I have known for these many years. I am filled with the wonder of her knowledge, acquired because shut out from all distractions. If I could have been deaf, dumb, and blind I also might have arrived at something.

SAMUEL L. CLEMENS, ("MARK TWAIN"), speech

He was a Caesar without his ambition, a Frederick without his tyranny, a Napoleon without his selfishness, and a Washington without his reward.

BENJAMIN HARVEY HILL, of General Robert E. Lee

Yes, he is a great favorite everywhere. He is to be President of the United States some day; if I had not thought so I never would have married him, for you can see he is not pretty. But look at him! Doesn't he look as if he would make a magnificent President?

MARY TODD LINCOLN, c. 1845

As you justly remark, each and every one has had a little romance in their early days—but as my husband was *truth itself,* and as he always assured me, he had cared for no one but myself . . . I shall assuredly remain firm in my conviction that *Ann Rutledge* is a myth—for in all his confidential communications such a romantic name was never breathed.

MARY TODD LINCOLN, letter to Judge Davis

Blackguard and buffoon as [Lincoln] is, he has pursued his end with an energy as untiring as an Indian, and a singleness of purpose that might almost be called patriotic.

ANON., in the Charleston *Mercury,* January 10, 1865

I see the President almost every day, as I happen to live where he passes to and from his lodgings out of town. . . . We have got so that we exchange bows, and very cordial ones.

WALT WHITMAN, *Specimen Days,* "Abraham Lincoln" (August 12, 1863)

By and by there was a little stir on the staircase and in the passageway, and in lounged a tall, loose-jointed figure, of an exaggerated Yankee port and demeanor, whom (as being about the homeliest man I ever saw, yet by no means repulsive or disagreeable) it was impossible not to recognize as Uncle Abe.

Unquestionably, Western man though he be and Kentuckian by birth, President Lincoln is the essential representative of all Yankees and the veritable specimen, physically, of what the world seems determined to regard as our characteristic qualities. It is the strangest and yet the fittest thing in the jumble of human vicissitudes that he, out of so many millions, unlooked for, unselected by any intelligible process that could be based upon his genuine qualities, unknown to those who chose him, and unsuspected of what endowments may adapt him for his tremendous responsibility, should have found the way open for him to fling his lank personality into the chair of state—where, I presume, it was his first impulse to throw his legs on the council table and tell the cabinet ministers a story. There is no describing his lengthy awkwardness nor the uncouthness of his movement, and yet it seemed as if I had been in the habit of seeing him daily and had shaken hands with him a thousand times in some village street; so true was he to the aspect of the pattern American, though with a certain extravagance which, possibly, I exaggerated still further by the delighted eagerness with which I took it in. If put to guess his calling and livelihood, I should have taken him for a country schoolmaster as soon as anything else. He was dressed in a rusty black frock coat and pantaloons, unbrushed, and worn so faithfully that the suit had adapted itself to the curves and angularities of his figure and had grown to be an outer skin of the man. He had shabby slippers on his feet. His hair was black, still unmixed with gray, stiff, somewhat bushy, and had apparently been acquainted with neither brush nor comb that morning, after the disarrangement of the pillow; and as to a night-cap, Uncle Abe probably knows nothing of such effeminacies. His complexion is dark and sallow, betokening, I fear, an insalubrious atmosphere around the White House; he has thick black eyebrows and an impending brow; his nose is large, and the lines about his mouth are very strongly defined.

The whole physiognomy is as coarse a one as you would meet anywhere in the length and breadth of the states, but withal it is redeemed, illuminated, softened, and brightened by a kindly though serious look out of the eyes and an expression of homely sagacity that seems weighted with rich results of village experience. A great deal of native sense; no bookish cultivation, no refinement; honest at heart, and thoroughly so, and yet, in some sort, sly—at least, endowed with a sort of tact and wisdom that are akin to craft, and would impel him, I think, to take an antagonist in flank, rather than to make a bull run at him right in front. But, on the whole, I like this sallow, queer, sagacious visage, with the homely human sympathies that warmed it and, for my small share in the matter, would as lief have Uncle Abe for a ruler as any man whom it would have been practicable to put in his place.

NATHANIEL HAWTHORNE, *Tales, Sketches and Other Papers*

I will make a prophecy that may now sound peculiar. In fifty years Lincoln's name will be inscribed close to Washington's on this Republic's roll of honor.

CARL SCHURZ, letter to Theodore Petrasch, Oct. 12, 1864

What think you of the inaugural? That rail-splitting lawyer is one of the wonders of the day. Once at Gettysburg and now again on a greater occasion he has shown a capacity for rising to the demands of the hour. . . . This inaugural strikes me in its grand simplicity and directness as being for all time the historical keynote of this war.

CHARLES FRANCIS ADAMS, letter to his father, Charles Francis Adams (1807–1886), shortly after Lincoln's "Second Inaugural Address," March 4, 1865

God reigns and the Government at Washington still lives.

JAMES A. GARFIELD, reassuring crowd in Wall Street, New York, on the news of the assassination of Lincoln, April 15, 1865. Garfield was himself assassinated sixteen years later.

Of all the days of the war, there are two especially I can never forget. Those were the days following the news, in New York and Brooklyn, of that first Bull Run defeat, and the day of Abraham Lincoln's death. I was home in Brooklyn on both occasions. The day of the murder we heard the news very early in the morning. Mother prepared breakfast—and other meals afterward—as usual; but not a mouthful was eaten all day by either of us. We each drank half a cup of coffee; that was all. Little was said. We got every newspaper morning and evening, and the frequent extras of that period, and passed them silently to each other.

> WALT WHITMAN, *Specimen Days,* "The Stupor Passes—
> Something Else Begins"

No lurking illusion or other error, false in itself, and clad for the moment in robes of splendor, ever passed undetected or unchallenged over the threshold of his mind—that point which divides vision from the realm and home of thought. Names to him were nothing, and titles naught— assumption always standing back abashed at his cold, intellectual glare. Neither his perceptions nor intellectual visions were perverted, distorted, or diseased. He saw all things through a perfect, mental lens. There was no diffraction or refraction there. He was not impulsive, fanciful, or imaginative, but cold, calm, and precise.

> WILLIAM HERNDON, speech after the death of Lincoln

He was thoroughly American, had never crossed the sea, had never been spoiled by English insularity or French dissipation; a quiet, native, aboriginal man, as an acorn from the oak; no aping of foreigners, no frivolous accomplishments, Kentuckian born, working on a farm, a flatboatman, a captain in the Black Hawk War, a country lawyer, a representative in the rural legislature of Illinois;—on such modest foundations the broad structure of his frame was laid.

> RALPH WALDO EMERSON, "Memorial Speech," Concord,
> April, 1865

It is absurd to call him a modest man. No great man is ever modest. It was his intellectual arrogance and unconscious assumption of superiority that men like Chase and Sumner could never forgive.

> JOHN HAY, of Lincoln

Lincoln was a supreme politician. He understood politics because he understood human nature. . . . There was no flabby philanthropy about

Abraham Lincoln. He was all solid, hard, keen intelligence combined with goodness.

CHARLES A. DANA

Alone among American Presidents, it is possible to imagine Lincoln, grown up in a different milieu, becoming a distinguished writer. But actually the poetry of Lincoln has not all been put into his writings. It was acted out in his life. With nothing of the deliberate histrionics of the Roosevelts or of the evangelical mask of Wilson, he created himself as a poetic figure, and he thus imposed himself on the nation. For the molding of American opinion by Lincoln was a matter of style and imagination as well as of moral authority, or compelling argument and obstinate will. When we put ourselves back into the period, we realize that it was not at all inevitable to think of it as Lincoln thought, and we come to see that Lincoln's conception of the progress and meaning of the Civil War was indeed an interpretation that he partly took over from others but that he partly made others accept.

EDMUND WILSON, *The Union as Religious Mysticism*

In the poem that Lincoln lived, Booth had been prepared for, too, and the tragic conclusion was necessary to justify all the rest. It was dramatically and morally inevitable that this prophet who had overruled opposition and sent thousands of men to their deaths should finally attest his good faith by laying down his own life with theirs.

EDMUND WILSON, *Ibid.*

In the spring of '27, something bright and alien flashed across the sky. A young Minnesotan who seemed to have had nothing to do with his generation did a heroic thing, and for a moment people set down their glasses in country clubs and speakeasies and thought of their old best dreams.

F. SCOTT FITZGERALD, of Lindbergh

Charles Lindbergh, New York is yours. I don't give it to you. You won it. And one other thing. Before you go, you will have to provide us with a new street-cleaning department to clean up the mess.

JAMES J. WALKER, welcoming Lindbergh, after the ticker-tape parade up Broadway, 1927

The average American loves his family. If he has any love left over for some other person, he generally selects Mark Twain.

THOMAS ALVA EDISON

Emerson, Longfellow, Lowell, Holmes—I knew them all and all the rest of the sages, poets, seers, critics, humorists; they were like one another and like other literary men; but Clemens was sole, incomparable, the Lincoln of our literature.

WILLIAM DEAN HOWELLS, *My Mark Twain*

The difference between papa and mama is, that mama loves morals and papa loves cats.

SUSIE CLEMENS, daughter of Mark Twain

[On Wednesday Melville and I] took a pretty long walk together, and sat down in a hollow among the sand hills (sheltering ourselves from the high, cool wind) and smoked a cigar. Melville, as he always does, began to reason of Providence and futurity, and of everything that lies beyond human ken, and informed me that he had "pretty much made up his mind to be annihilated;" but still he does not seem to rest in that anticipation; and, I think, will never rest until he does get hold of a definite belief. It is strange how he persists—and has persisted ever since I knew him, and probably long before—in wandering to and fro over these deserts, as dismal and monotonous as the sand hills amid which we were sitting. He can neither believe, nor be comfortable in his unbelief; and he is too honest and courageous not to try to do one or the other. If he were a religious man, he would be one of the most truly religious and reverential; he has a very high and noble nature, and better worth immortality than most of us.

NATHANIEL HAWTHORNE, *Notebooks,* November, 1856 (in Liverpool)

Mrs. Hawthorne used to tell of one evening when [Melville] came in, and presently began to relate the story of a fight which he had seen on an island in the Pacific, between some savages, and of the prodigies of valor one of them performed with a heavy club. The narrative was extremely graphic; and when Melville had gone, and Mr. and Mrs. Hawthorne were talking over his visit, the latter said, "Where is that club with which Mr. Melville was laying about him so?" Mr. Hawthorne thought he must have taken it with him; Mrs. Hawthorne thought he had put it in the corner; but it was not to be found. The next time Melville came, they asked him about it; whereupon it appeared that the club was still in the Pacific island, if it were anywhere.

JULIAN HAWTHORNE, *Nathaniel Hawthorne and His Wife*

The maritime history of Massachusetts, then, as distinct from that of America, ends with the passing of the clipper. 'T was a glorious ending! Never, in these United States, has the brain of man conceived, or the hand of man fashioned, so perfect a thing as the clipper ship. In her, the long-suppressed artistic impulse of a practical, hard-worked race burst into flower. The *Flying Cloud* was our Rheims, the *Sovereign of the Seas* our Parthenon, the *Lightning* our Amiens; but they were monuments carved from snow. For a brief moment of time they flashed their splendor around the world, then disappeared with the sudden completeness of the wild pigeon. One by one they sailed out of Boston, to return no more. A tragic or mysterious end was the final privilege of many, favored by the gods. Others, with lofty rig cut down to cautious dimensions, with glistening decks and topsides scarred and neglected, limped about the seas under foreign flags, like faded beauties forced upon the street.

The master builders, reluctant to raise barnyard fowls where once they had reared eagles, dropped off one by one. Donald McKay, dying almost in poverty after a career that should have brought him wealth and honor, sleeps at Newburyport among the comrades of his young manhood. The commonwealth, so generous in laurel to second-rate politicians and third-rate soldiers, contains no memorial line to this man who helped to make her name immortal. But in the elm branches over his grave the brave west winds that he loved so well, murmur soft versions of the tunes they once played on the shrouds of his glorious ships.

> SAMUEL ELIOT MORISON, *The Maritime History of Massachusetts,* 1921

Biting nails—good, hard, bitter Republican nails—we are compelled to admit that Franklin Roosevelt is the most unaccountable President that this United States has ever seen. He has added a vast impudent courage to a vivid but constructive imagination, and he has displayed his capacity for statesmanship in the large and simple billboard language that the common people can understand; moreover, that the people admire, even when it is their deadly poison. We have got to hand it to him.

Well, darn your smiling old picture, here it is! Here, reluctantly, amid seething and snorting, it is. We, who hate your gaudy guts, salute you.

> WILLIAM ALLEN WHITE, Emporia *Gazette,* March, 1945

I told William McKinley it was a mistake to nominate that wild man at Philadelphia. . . . Now look, that damned cowboy is President of the United States!

> MARK HANNA, on the funeral train carrying McKinley

from Buffalo to Washington. The "cowboy" is of course
Theodore Roosevelt.

At last they brought him to Werowocomoco, where was Powhatan, their
emperor. Here more than two hundred of those grim courtiers stood wondering at him, as he had been a monster; till Powhatan and his train had
put themselves in their greatest braveries. Before a fire upon a seat like a
bedstead, he sat covered with a great robe, made of raccoon skins, and
all the tails hanging by. On either hand did sit a young wench of sixteen
or eighteen years, and along on each side the house, two rows of men,
and behind them as many women, with all their heads and shoulders
painted red, many of their heads bedecked with the white down of birds,
but every one with something, and a great chain of white beads about
their necks. At his entrance before the king, all the people gave a great
shout. The queen of Appamatuck was appointed to bring him water to
wash his hands, and another brought him a bunch of feathers, instead of
a towel to dry them. Having feasted him after their best barbarous manner they could, a long consultation was held, but the conclusion was, two
great stones were brought before Powhatan: then as many as could lay
hands upon him, dragged him to them, and thereon laid his head, and
being ready with their clubs to beat out his brains, Pocahontas, the king's
dearest daughter, when no entreaty could prevail, got his head in her
arms, and laid her own upon his to save his from death: whereat the emperor was contented he should live to make him hatchets, and her bells,
beads, and copper; for they thought him as well of all occupations as
themselves.

JOHN SMITH, *The Generall Historie of Virginia,* 1624

He thought everything a discovery of his own, from moonlight to the
planting of acorns and nuts by squirrels. This is a defect in his character,
but one of his chief charms as a writer.

JAMES RUSSELL LOWELL, "Thoreau," *North American
Review,* October, 1865

"Walden" is the only book I own, although there are some others un-
claimed on my shelves. Every man, I think, reads one book in his life,
and this one is mine. It is not the best book I ever encountered, perhaps,
but it is for me the handiest, and I keep it about me in much the same
way one carries a handkerchief—for relief in moments of defluxion or
despair.

E. B. WHITE, *The Second Tree from the Corner*

George Washington—the Joshua, who commanded the sun and the moon
to stand still, and they obeyed him.

> BENJAMIN FRANKLIN, at an official dinner. The British
> Ambassador proposed as a toast: "England—the sun—
> whose bright beams enlighten and fructify the remotest cor-
> ners of the earth." The French Ambassador proposed:
> "France—the moon—whose mild, steady, and cheering rays
> are the delight of all nations, consoling them in darkness."
> Franklin then proposed the above toast.

To the memory of the Man, first in war, first in peace, and first in the
hearts of his countrymen.

> HENRY ("LIGHT-HORSE HARRY") LEE, eulogy on George
> Washington adopted by the Congress December 26, 1799

"George," said his father, "do you know who killed that beautiful little
cherry tree yonder in the garden?" This was a *tough question;* and George
staggered under it for a moment; but quickly recovered himself: and
looking at his father with the inexpressible charm of all-conquering truth,
he bravely cried out, "I can't tell a lie, Pa; you know I can't tell a lie. I
did cut it with my hatchet."—"Run to my arms, you dearest boy," cried
his father in transports, "run to my arms; glad am I, George, that you
killed my tree; for you have payed me for it a thousand fold. Such an act
of heroism in my son is more worth than a thousand trees, though blossomed with silver, and their fruits of purest gold."

> MASON LOCKE WEEMS, *The Life of George Washington.*
> The story appeared for the first time in the fifth edition of
> the work.

His mind was great and powerful, without being of the very first order;
his penetration strong, though not so acute as that of a Newton, Bacon
or Locke; and as far as he saw, no judgment was ever sounder. It was
slow in operation, being little aided by invention or imagination, but sure
in conclusion. . . . Hearing all suggestions, he selected whatever was
best; and certainly no General ever planned his battles more judiciously.
But if deranged during the course of the action . . . he was slow in readjustment. . . . He was incapable of fear, meeting personal dangers with
the calmest unconcern.

Perhaps the strongest feature in his character was prudence, never acting until every circumstance, every consideration was maturely weighed.
. . . His integrity was most pure, his justice the most inflexible I have

ever known, no motives of interest or consanguinity, of friendship or hatred, being able to bias his decision. He was, indeed, in every sense of the words, a wise, a good, and a great man. His temper was naturally irritable and high toned; but reflection and resolution had obtained a firm and habitual ascendancy over it. If ever, however, it broke its bonds, he was most tremendous in his wrath.

In his expenses he was honorable, but exact; liberal in contributions to whatever promised utility; but frowning and unyielding on all visionary projects and all unworthy calls on his charity. His heart was not warm in its affections; but he exactly calculated every man's value, and gave him a solid esteem proportioned to it.

His person, you know, was fine, his stature exactly what one would wish, his deportment easy, erect and noble; the best horseman of his age, and the most graceful figure that could be seen on horseback.

Although in the circle of his friends, where he might be unreserved with safety, he took a free share in conversation, his colloquial talents were not above mediocrity, possessing neither copiousness of ideas, nor fluency of words. In public, when called on for a sudden opinion, he was unready, short and embarrassed. Yet he wrote readily, rather diffusely, in an easy and correct style. This he had acquired by conversation with the world, for his education was merely reading, writing and common arithmetic, to which he added surveying at a later day. His time was employed in action chiefly, reading little, and that only in agriculture and English history. . . . His agricultural proceedings occupied most of his leisure hours within doors.

On the whole, his character was, in its mass, perfect, in nothing bad, in few points indifferent; and it may truly be said, that never did nature and fortune combine more perfectly to make a man great, and to place him . . . in an everlasting remembrance.

THOMAS JEFFERSON, of Washington

Washington is in the clear upper sky.

DANIEL WEBSTER, *Eulogy of Adams and Jefferson,* 1826

The prevailin' weakness of most public men is to Slop over. G. Washington never slopt over.

CHARLES FARRAR BROWNE ("ARTEMUS WARD"), *Fourth of July Oration*

Three or four times I thought my temples would burst with the gush of blood. . . . When I came out I was almost afraid to come near him.

It seemed to me as if he was like the mount that might not be touched and that burned with fire. I was beside myself, and am so still.

> GEORGE TICKNOR, *Journal,* after hearing a speech by Daniel Webster

Do men now mourn for him, the great man eloquent? I put on sackcloth long ago.

> THEODORE PARKER, sermon, October 31, 1852, on Daniel Webster

It's a story they tell in the border country, where Massachusetts joins Vermont and New Hampshire.

Yes, Dan'l Webster's dead—or, at least, they buried him. But every time there's a thunderstorm around Marshfield, they say you can hear his rolling voice in the hollows of the sky. And they say that if you go to his grave and speak loud and clear, "Dan'l Webster—Dan'l Webster!" the ground'll begin to shiver and the trees begin to shake. And after a while you'll hear a deep voice saying, "Neighbor, how stands the Union?" Then you better answer the Union stands as she should, rock bottomed and copper sheathed, one and indivisible, or he's liable to rear right out of the ground. At least, that's what I was told when I was a youngster.

You see, for a while, he was the biggest man in the country. He never got to be President, but he was the biggest man. There were thousands that trusted in him right next to God Almighty, and they told stories about him and all the things that belonged to him that were like the stories of patriarchs and such. They said, when he stood up to speak, stars and stripes came right out in the sky, and once he spoke against a river and made it sink into the ground. They said, when he walked the woods with his fishing rod, Killall, the trout would jump out of the streams right into his pockets, for they knew it was no use putting up a fight against him; and, when he argued a case, he could turn on the harps of the blessed and the shaking of the earth underground. That was the kind of man he was, and his big farm up at Marshfield was suitable to him. The chickens he raised were all white meat down through the drumstick, the cows were tended like children, and the big ram he called Goliath had horns with a curl like a morning-glory vine and could butt through an iron door. But Dan'l wasn't one of your gentleman farmers; he knew all the ways of the land, and he'd be up by candlelight to see that the chores got done. A man with a mouth like a mastiff, a brow like a mountain and eyes like burning anthracite—that was Dan'l Webster in his prime. And the big-

gest case he argued never got written down in the books, for he argued
it against the devil, nip and tuck and no holds barred.

> STEPHEN VINCENT BENÉT, *13 O'clock,* "The Devil and
> Daniel Webster," 1936

Well, he looks like a man.

> ABRAHAM LINCOLN, on having Whitman pointed out to
> him walking past the White House

I greet you at the beginning of a great career.

> RALPH WALDO EMERSON, letter to Whitman on being
> shown the first edition of *Leaves of Grass*

The Good Gray Poet.

> WILLIAM DOUGLAS O'CONNOR, title of book about Walt
> Whitman, 1866

Success four flights Thursday morning all against twenty-one mile wind
started from level with engine power alone average speed through air
thirty-one miles longest 59 seconds inform press home Christmas.

> ORVILLE and WILBUR WRIGHT, telegram to their father,
> Kitty Hawk, North Carolina, December 17, 1903

By original scientific research the Wright Brothers discovered the principles of human flight. As inventors, builders and fliers they further developed the aeroplane, taught man to fly, and opened the era of aviation.

> Label on the Kitty Hawk Plane at the Smithsonian Insti-
> tution

In the rush of new names: Farman, Blériot, Curtiss, Ferber, Esnault-
Peltrie, Delagrange;
in the snorting impact of bombs and the whine and rattle of shrapnel
and the sudden stutter of machineguns after the motor's been shut off
overhead,
and we flatten into the mud
and make ourselves small cowering in the corners of ruined walls,
the Wright brothers passed out of the headlines but not even the headlines or the bitter smear of newsprint or the choke of smokescreen and
gas or chatter of brokers on the stockmarket or barking of phantom millions or oratory of brasshats laying wreaths on new monuments
can blur the memory

of the chilly December day
two shivering bicycle mechanics from Dayton, Ohio,
first felt their homemade contraption
whittled out of hickory sticks,
gummed together with Arnstein's bicycle cement,
stretched with muslin they'd sewn on their sister's sewingmachine in
their own backyard on Hawthorn Street in Dayton, Ohio,
soar into the air
above the dunes and the wide beach
at Kitty Hawk.

JOHN DOS PASSOS, *U.S.A.*, 1937

ROGUES AND INSULTS

•

The Pilgrim Fathers landed . . . and fell upon their knees. Then they
fell upon the aborigines.

ANON.

This day the Continental Congress declared the United Colonies free and
independent States.

ANON., notice, quoted in its entirety, on the last page of the
Pennsylvania *Evening Post*, July 2, 1776

He has peculiar powers as an assailant, and almost always, even when
attacked, gets himself into that attitude by making war upon his accuser;
and he has, withal, an instinct for the jugular and the carotid artery, as
unerring as that of any carnivorous animal.

RUFUS CHOATE, of John Quincy Adams

I could readily see in Emerson, notwithstanding his merit, a gaping flaw.
It was, the insinuation, that had he lived in those days when the world
was made, he might have offered some valuable suggestions.

HERMAN MELVILLE, letter to Evert Duyckinck, 1849

There are the thieves, but where is Christ?

ANON., a New York stockbroker, observing side-by-side portraits of Jim Fisk and Jay Gould

There goes Jim Fisk with his hands in his own pockets for a change.

> ANON., contemporary saying

[John Nance Garner is a] labor-baiting, poker-playing, whisky-drinking, evil old man.

> JOHN L. LEWIS, 1939

Judge Gary never saw a blast furnace until after his death.

> BENJAMIN STOLBERG, *The Story of the C.I.O.*, 1938

Stuffed shirt.

> Attributed to FAY TEMPLETON, about 1899. She applied the
> words, so it is said, to a certain John Gates.

Let us summon from the shades the immortal soul of James Harlan, born in 1820, entered into rest in 1899. In the year 1865 this Harlan resigned from the United States Senate to enter the Cabinet of Abraham Lincoln as Secretary of the Interior. One of the clerks in that department, at $600 a year, was Walt Whitman, lately emerged from three years of service as an army nurse during the Civil War. One day, discovering that Whitman was the author of a book called "Leaves of Grass," Harlan ordered him incontinently kicked out, and it was done forthwith. Let us remember this event and this man; he is too precious to die. Let us repair, once a year, to our accustomed houses of worship and there give thanks to God that one day in 1865 brought together the greatest poet that America has ever produced and the damndest ass.

> H. L. MENCKEN, first printed in the *Smart Set*, June, 1919,
> and thereafter every year; *American Mercury*, April, 1924

I always thought Henry James' drooling on the social relations of important Americans in the Old World a trifle underbred.

> OLIVER WENDELL HOLMES, JR., *Holmes-Laski Letters*

To be really cosmopolitan, a man must be at home even in his own country.

> THOMAS WENTWORTH HIGGINSON, *Short Studies of American Authors*, "Henry James," 1879

There's nothing wrong with Oscar Levant—nothing that a miracle couldn't cure.

> ALEXANDER WOOLLCOTT

God damn your god damned old hellfired god damned soul to hell god
damn you and goddam your god damned family's god damned hellfired
god damned soul to hell and good damnation god damn them and god
damn your god damn friends to hell.

> PETE MUGGINS, letter to Abraham Lincoln, Fillmore, Lou-
> isiana, November 25, 1860

He is a man of splendid abilities, but utterly corrupt. He shines and stinks
like rotten mackerel by moonlight.

> JOHN RANDOLPH, of Edward Livingston

Frank Munsey, the great publisher, is dead. Frank Munsey contributed to
the journalism of his day the great talent of a meat packer, the morals of
a money changer and the manners of an undertaker. He and his kind
have about succeeded in transforming a once noble profession into an
eight per-cent security. May he rest in trust!

> WILLIAM ALLEN WHITE, obituary in the Emporia *Gazette*,
> December 23, 1925

That dirty little atheist.

> THEODORE ROOSEVELT, of Tom Paine. Roosevelt had never
> read *The Age of Reason*.

[You look like] a dishonest Abe Lincoln.

> ALEXANDER WOOLLCOTT to Harold Ross

'Tis th' Biography iv a Hero be Wan who Knows! . . . But if I was him
I'd call th' book *Alone in Cubia*.

> FINLEY PETER DUNNE ("MR. DOOLEY"), review of Theo-
> dore Roosevelt's *Accounts of the Rough Riders*

Theodore Roosevelt was president of the society of the first man up San
Juan Hill.

> FINLEY PETER DUNNE ("MR. DOOLEY")

Theodore, if there is one thing more than another for which I admire
you, it is your original discovery of the ten commandments.

> THOMAS B. REED to Theodore Roosevelt

There is a fake giant among real pygmies.

> ARTHUR RYDER, observing a pretentious colleague sur-
> rounded by admirers

The gentleman need not worry. He will never be either.

> THOMAS B. REED, retort to Congressman Springer, when
> the latter quoted Clay's "I would rather be right than
> President"

Henry Thoreau is like the wood-god who solicits the wandering poet and draws him into antres vast and deserts idle, and bereaves him of his memory, and leaves him naked, plaiting vines and with twigs in his hand. . . . As for taking Thoreau's arm, I should as soon take the arm of an elm tree.

> RALPH WALDO EMERSON, *Journal,* August, 1848

The character which Mr. Washington has attempted to act in this world is so nearly allied to hypocrisy, that it slides into it. It is laughable to hear him talk of his sympathetic feelings, when he has always been known among his friends for not having any.

> THOMAS PAINE, open letter to George Washington, 1796

There but for the grace of God goes God.

> ANON., saying, of, among others, Orson Welles while he
> was making *Citizen Kane*

Walt sends me all his books. But tell Walt I am not satisfied—not satisfied. I expect him to make the songs of the Nation—but he seems to be contented to make the inventories.

> RALPH WALDO EMERSON, to Marvin, of Walt Whitman

The Barefoot Boy from Wall Street.

> HAROLD L. ICKES, description of Wendell Willkie, Presidential campaign, 1940

This New Jersey Nero who mistakes his pinafore for a toga.

> EDNA FERBER, of Alexander Woollcott

Just a big dreamer with a sense of double entry.

> HARPO MARX, of Alexander Woollcott

LAST WORDS

•

The last days of most men, even of most great men, are interesting only because convention and a certain inveterate morbidity in the reading public make them so. But the last days of a rebel have a real significance. They furnish a test, unfairly severe, but a test nevertheless. In the old days a priest offered the dying heretic a crucifix. The waiting spectators took the news to the world, and the world usually hoped that the message would be: "He is saved and he is cancelled out. You need let his paradoxes trouble you no more and you may cease to look for the answers you could not find. It was all merely pride and bravado. We were right and he admits it. He did not mean what he said." Some scene of which this is the simplified symbol must be acted out when any rebel comes to the end of his days and the question is always, "Did he or did he not persist to the end?"

JOSEPH WOOD KRUTCH, *Thoreau*, 1948

A distinguished man should be as particular about his last words as he is about his last breath. . . . There is hardly a case on record where a man came to his last moment unprepared and said a good thing—hardly a case where a man trusted to that last moment and did not make a solemn botch of it and go out of the world feeling absurd.

SAMUEL L. CLEMENS ("MARK TWAIN"), *Last Words of Great Men*

This will surely be a lesson to me.

A Tennessee Negro on the gallows, speech recorded by Irvin S. Cobb, c. 1915

Thomas Jefferson still lives.

JOHN ADAMS. Jefferson had died a few hours earlier on the same day, July 4, 1826.

This is the last of earth! I am content.

JOHN QUINCY ADAMS, "The Old Man Eloquent," February 21, 1848

Now comes the mystery.

HENRY WARD BEECHER, March 8, 1887

Tell mother—tell mother—I died for my country.

> JOHN WILKES BOOTH, April 26, 1865, *Dictionary of American Biography*

Useless, useless.

> JOHN WILKES BOOTH, the traditional version. On April 26, 1865, Federal troops trapped the assassin in a Virginia barn. A soldier fired through the door and Booth was dragged out with a wound through his neck. He lay conscious all night on a farmhouse porch, bleeding to death and sucking noisily on a rag soaked in brandy. Toward morning he asked to see his hands—he could no longer feel or move them. A soldier lifted them up and Booth muttered the above.

This *is* a beautiful country.

> JOHN BROWN, December 2, 1859, riding to the gallows seated on his coffin

How far are we from home?

> JOHN BURROUGHS, March 29, 1921, homeward bound on a train from California

The South, the poor South!

> JOHN C. CALHOUN, March 31, 1850

I have tried so hard to do the right.

> GROVER CLEVELAND, June 24, 1908

Support the Constitution and obey the law.

> STEPHEN A. DOUGLAS, June 3, 1861

I petition to Your Honors not for my own life, for I know I must die, and my appointed time is set; but the Lord he knows it is that, if it be possible, no more innocent blood may be shed, which undoubtedly cannot be avoided in the way and course you go in. I question not but Your Honors do to the utmost of your powers in the discovery and detecting of witchcraft and witches, and would not be guilty of innocent blood for the world. But, by my own innocency, I know you are in the wrong way.

> MARY EASTY, before her execution, Salem, 1692

A dying man can do nothing easy.

> BENJAMIN FRANKLIN, to his daughter who advised him to

> change his position in bed so he could breathe more easily,
> April 17, 1790

Why fear death? It is the most beautiful adventure of life.

> CHARLES FROHMAN, before going down with the *Lusitania*,
> May 7, 1915

But I have got to die. How can I die better than serving humanity? Besides, so dying will do more for the cause than anything I am likely to be able to do in the rest of my life.

> HENRY GEORGE, when told by his doctors that to run for
> Mayor of New York against Tammany in 1897 would
> probably kill him. Five days before the election he suffered
> (October 29) a fatal stroke of apoplexy. A hundred thousand mourners filed past his bier in Grand Central Palace
> and an equal number failed to gain admittance.

I must arrange my pillows for another weary night.

> WASHINGTON IRVING, November 28, 1859

I hope and trust to meet you all in Heaven, both white and black—both white and black.

> ANDREW JACKSON, to his assembled household which included his slaves, June 8, 1845

Let us cross over the river, and rest under the shade of the trees.

> THOMAS JONATHAN ("STONEWALL") JACKSON, May 10,
> 1863. General Jackson was shot by his own troops by mistake at the battle of Chancellorsville and died of pneumonia a week later.

So here it is at last, the distinguished thing!

> HENRY JAMES, a sentence "heard" by him, as he put it,
> when he suffered his first stroke, December 2, 1915. He
> died three months later.

Nurse, take away the candle and spare my blushes.

> HENRY JAMES, after the departure of Sir Edmund Gosse,
> to whom James had paid no attention while being told he
> had received the Order of Merit. He died Feb. 28, 1916

Let the tent be struck.

ROBERT E. LEE, October 12, 1870

I always talk better lying down.

JAMES MADISON, June 28, 1836

Why should I talk to you? I've just been talking to your boss.

WILSON MIZNER, to a priest, on his deathbed, 1933

It's not the drop that's going to worry me; it's the sudden stop.

KENNETH NEU, remark to the executioner before being
hanged at New Orleans, January 2, 1935

My best friend would be the man who would blow my brains out with
a pistol.

EDGAR ALLAN POE, to his doctor, October 7, 1849

Turn up the lights. I don't want to go home in the dark.

WILLIAM SIDNEY PORTER ("O. HENRY"), June 5, 1910. He
referred, smiling, to a popular song of the day, "I'm Afraid
to Go Home in the Dark."

Today we are faced with the pre-eminent fact that, if civilization is to
survive, we must cultivate the science of human relationships—the ability
of all peoples, of all kinds, to live together and work together in the same
world, at peace.

FRANKLIN D. ROOSEVELT, address written for Jefferson Day
Dinners broadcast, April 13, 1945. The President died suddenly at Warm Springs, Georgia, on April 12; his last
spoken words were: "I've got a terrible headache."

Put out the light.

THEODORE ROOSEVELT, January 6, 1919

I have always been deeply impressed by an old Jewish proverb which says,
"What you give for the cause of charity in health is gold; what you give
in sickness is silver; what you give after death is lead."

NATHAN STRAUS, Will, first paragraph. He died January
11, 1931.

Moose . . . Indians . . .

HENRY DAVID THOREAU, May 6, 1862

It is well. I die hard, but I am not afraid to go.

GEORGE WASHINGTON, December 14, 1799

I still live.

DANIEL WEBSTER. On his last afternoon, October 24, 1852, he heard the doctor say, "Give him a spoonful of brandy in fifteen minutes, another in half an hour, and another in three quarters of an hour, if he still lives." These directions were followed until the time came for the third spoonful, when the attendants could not decide whether he was alive. While they deliberated Webster suddenly raised his head and feebly spoke the above words. The brandy was given him, and he sank into sleep, from which he did not awake.

Bury me where the birds will sing over my grave.

ALEXANDER WILSON, ornithologist, August 23, 1813

The people of Germany are just as responsible for Hitler as the people of Chicago are for the Chicago *Tribune*.

ALEXANDER WOOLLCOTT, before collapsing at the microphone, January 23, 1943, where he was taking part in a program on the subject "Is Germany incurable?" He died a few hours later.

EPITAPHS AND INSCRIPTIONS

•

Who is most dead—a hero by whose monument you stand, or his descendants of whom you have never heard?

HENRY DAVID THOREAU, *A Week on the Concord and Merrimack Rivers*

Here Rests in
Honored Glory
An American
Soldier
Known But to God
Inscription on Tomb of Unknown Soldier, Arlington

Here lies a soldier of
The Revolution whose identity
Is known but to God.
His was an idealism
That recognized a Supreme
Being, that planted
Religious liberty on our
Shores, that overthrew
Despotism, that established
A people's government,
That wrote a Constitution
Setting metes and bounds
Of delegated authority,
That fixed a standard of
Value upon men above
Gold and lifted high the
Torch of civil liberty
Along the pathway of
Mankind.
In ourselves his soul
Exists as part of ours,
His memory's mansion.

WILLIAM TYLER PAGE, tribute for the Tomb of the Unknown Revolutionary Soldier in Presbyterian Meeting House churchyard, Alexandria, Virginia

On the Fourth of July, 1776,
He Pledged His Life, Fortune and Sacred Honour
To the Independence of His Country.
On the Third of September, 1783,
He Affixed His Seal to the Definitive Treaty with Great Britain
Which Acknowledges That Independence
And Consummated the Redemption of That Pledge.
On the Fourth of July, 1826,
He Was Summoned
To the Independence of Immortality
And to the Judgment of His God.

Tablet erected to John Adams in the First Parish Church, Quincy, Massachusetts

Sherwood Anderson, Former Elyria Manufacturer, Dies.

> Headline in Elyria (Ohio) *Chronicle-Telegram*. Anderson died on March 6, 1941.

Here lies Vera Bemish—
For twenty years she preserved her virginity—
A very good record for this here vicinity.

> Epitaph said to have been found (by Fulton Oursler) on a grave in Virginia

I see the marks of God in the heavens and the earth; but how much more in a liberal intellect, in magnanimity, in a philanthropy which forgives every wrong, and which never despairs of the cause of Christ and human virtue: I do and I must reverence human nature. I bless it for its kind affections. I honor it for its achievements in science and art, and still more for its examples of heroic and saintly virtue. These are marks of a divine origin and the pledges of a celestial inheritance; and I thank God that my own lot is bound up with that of the human race.

> WILLIAM ELLERY CHANNING, inscription on Channing Memorial, Public Garden, Boston

I found Mr. Paine's telegram when I came in late last night; and suddenly your father was set apart from all other men in a strange majesty. Death had touched his familiar image into historic grandeur.

You have lost a father. Shall I dare to tell you of the desolation of an old man who has lost a friend, and finds himself alone in the great world which has now wholly perished around?

> WILLIAM DEAN HOWELLS, letter to Clara Clemens, April 22, 1910

Thar's a great rejoicin' among the bears of Kaintuck, and the alligators of the Massissippi rolls up thar shiny ribs to the sun, and has grown so fat and lazy that they will hardly move out of the way for a steamboat. The rattlesnakes come up out of thar holes and frolic within ten foot of the clearings, and the foxes goes to sleep in the goose-pens. It is bekase the rifle of Crockett is silent forever, and the print of his moccasins is found no more in our woods. His old fox-skin cap hangs up in the cabin, and every hunter, whether he are a Puke, a Wolverine, or a Sucker, never looks at it without turnin' away his head and droppin' a salt tear.

. . . He are dead now, and if you want to see old Kaintuck's tears, go thar, and speak o her gallant Kurnill, and thar's not a human but what

will turn away and go behind some tree and dry up thar tears. He are
dead now, and may he rest forever and a day arter.

>   ANON., "The Death of Davy Crockett," *Crockett Almanac*

The body of Benjamin Franklin, printer, (like the cover of an old book,
its contents torn out and stript of its lettering and gilding), lies here, food
for worms; but the work shall not be lost, for it will (as he believed)
appear once more in a new and more elegant edition, revised and corrected by the Author.

>   BENJAMIN FRANKLIN, epitaph written for himself sixty-two
>   years before his death

On the whole, I'd rather be in Philadelphia.

>   W. C. FIELDS, epitaph suggested by himself

Yesterday, May 23, we buried Hawthorne in Sleepy Hollow, in a pomp
of sunshine and verdure and gentle winds. . . . I thought there was a
tragic element in the event—in the painful solitude of the man, which, I
suppose, could not longer be endured, and he died of it.

>   RALPH WALDO EMERSON, *Journal,* May 24, 1864

Here lies the body of Harry Hershfield.
If not notify Ginsberg and Co., Undertakers, at once.

>   HARRY HERSHFIELD, epitaph suggested by himself

Isn't the highest deepest note of the whole thing the never-to-be-lost
memory of that evening hour at Mount Auburn—at the Cambridge Cemetery when I took my way alone—after much waiting for the favoring
hour—to that unspeakable group of graves. It was late, in November;
the trees all bare, the dusk to fall early, the air all still (at Cambridge, in
general, *so* still), with the western sky more and more turning to that
terrible, deadly, pure polar pink that shows behind American winter
woods. But I can't go over this—I can only, oh, so gently, so tenderly,
brush it and breathe upon it—breathe upon it and brush it. It was the
emotion; it was the hour; it was the blessed flood of emotion that broke
out at the touch of one's sudden *vision* and carried me away. I seemed
then to know why I had done this; I seemed then to know why I had
come—and to feel how not to have come would have been miserably,
horribly to miss it. It made everything right—it made everything priceless. The moon was there, early, white and young, and seemed reflected
in the white face of the great empty Stadium, forming one of the bound-

aries of Soldiers' Field, that looked over at me, stared over at me, through the clear twilight, from across the Charles. Everything was there, everything *came;* the recognition, stillness, the strangeness, the pity and the sanctity and the terror, the breath-catching passion and the divine relief of tears. William's inspired transcript, on the exquisite little Florentine urn of Alice's ashes, William's divine gift to us, and to her, of the Dantean lines—

> *Dopo lungo exilio e martiro*
> *Viene a questa pace—*

took me so at the throat by its penetrating *rightness,* that it was as if one sank down on one's knees in a kind of anguish of gratitude before something for which one had waited with a long, deep *ache.* But why do I write of the all unutterable and the all abysmal? Why does my pen not drop from my hand on approaching the infinite pity and tragedy of all the past? It dies, poor helpless pen, with what it meets of the ineffable, what it meets of the cold Medusa-face of life, of all the life *lived,* on every side. *Basta, basta!*

HENRY JAMES, Notebook, 1904

In Loving Memory of My Beloved Son
Jesse W. James
Died April 3, 1882
Aged 34 Years, 6 Months, 28 Days
Murdered by a Traitor and Coward Whose
Name Is Not Worthy to Appear Here

Inscription on grave near Kearney, Missouri

I sit heavily stricken and in darkness—for from far back in dimmest childhood he had been my ideal Elder Brother, and I still, through all the years, saw in him, even as a small timorous boy yet, my protector, my backer, my authority and my pride. His extinction changes the face of life for me—besides the mere missing of his inexhaustible company and personality, originality, the whole unspeakably vivid and beautiful presence of him. And his noble intellectual vitality was still but at its climax —he had still two or three ardent purposes and plans. He had cast them away, however, at the end—I mean that, dreadfully suffering, he wanted only to die.

HENRY JAMES, letter to T. S. Perry. William James died
August 26, 1910.

. . . On the faces of the obelisk the following inscription, and not a word more

"Here was buried

Thomas Jefferson

Author of the Declaration of American Independence

of the Statute of Virginia for religious freedom

And Father of the University of Virginia."

because by these, as testimonials that I have lived, I wish most to be remembered.

> Thomas Jefferson, directions for his tomb, found after his death in his own handwriting

I have sworn upon the altar of God eternal hostility against every form of tyranny over the mind of man.

> Thomas Jefferson, inscribed in Jefferson Memorial, Washington

John Luther

Jones

1864–1900

To the Memory of the Locomo-

tive Engineer, Whose Name as

"Casey Jones" Became a Part of

Folklore and the American

Language. "For I'm going to run her

till she leaves the rail—or make it on

time with the southbound mail."

Inscription on monument in Calvary Cemetery, Jackson, Tennessee. Jones was an engineer in the service of the Illinois Central and was particularly honored among his fellows for his skill in handling his train and for his exceptional use of the train whistle. He was killed in a train wreck at Vaughan, Mississippi, in 1900. In death his hand clutched the whistle of the Cannonball Express. A Negro friend, Wallace Saunders of Canton, Mississippi, a cinder pit man, is credited with writing the first stanza of the famous ballad.

Duty then is the sublimest word in our language. Do your duty in all things. You cannot do more. You should never wish to do less.

> Robert E. Lee, inscribed beneath his bust in Hall of Fame

I had retired to bed about half past ten on the evening of the 14th of April and was just getting asleep when Mrs. Welles, my wife, said some one was at our door. Sitting up in bed, I heard a voice twice call to John, my son, whose sleeping room was on the second floor directly over the front entrance. I arose at once and raised a window, when my messenger, James Smith, called to me that Mr. Lincoln, the President, had been shot, and said Secretary Seward and his son, Assistant Secretary Frederick Seward, were assassinated. James was much alarmed and excited. I told him his story was very incoherent and improbable, that he was associating men who were not together and liable to attack at the same time. "Where," I inquired, "was the President when shot?" James said he was at Ford's Theater on Tenth Street. "Well," said I, "Secretary Seward is an invalid in bed in his house yonder on Fifteenth Street." James said he had been there, stopped in at the house to make inquiry before alarming me.

I immediately dressed myself and, against the earnest remonstrance and appeals of my wife, went directly to Mr. Seward's, whose residence was on the east side of the square, mine being on the north. . . .

The President had been carried across the street from the theater to the house of a Mr. Peterson. We entered by ascending a flight of steps above the basement and passing through a long hall to the rear, where the President lay extended on a bed, breathing heavily. Several surgeons were present, at least six, I should think more. Among them I was glad to observe Doctor Hall, who, however, soon left. I inquired of Doctor Hall, as I entered, the true condition of the President. He replied the President was dead to all intents, although he might live three hours or perhaps longer.

The giant sufferer lay extended diagonally across the bed, which was not long enough for him. He had been stripped of his clothes. His large arms, which were occasionally exposed, were of a size which one would scarce have expected from his spare appearance. His slow, full respiration lifted the clothes with each breath that he took. His features were calm and striking. I had never seen them appear to better advantage than for the first hour, perhaps, that I was there. After that his right eye began to swell and that part of his face became discolored. . . .

A little before seven I went into the room where the dying President was rapidly drawing near the closing moments. His wife soon after made her last visit to him. The death struggle had begun. Robert, his son, stood with several others at the head of the bed. He bore himself well but on two occasions gave way to overpowering grief and sobbed aloud, turning his head and leaning on the shoulder of Senator Sumner. The respiration of the President became suspended at intervals and at last entirely ceased at twenty-two minutes past seven.

. . . I went after breakfast to the Executive Mansion. There was a cheerless, cold rain, and everything seemed gloomy. On the Avenue in front of the White House were several hundred colored people, mostly women and children, weeping and wailing their loss. This crowd did not appear to diminish through the whole of that cold, wet day; they seemed not to know what was to be their fate since their great benefactor was dead, and their hopeless grief affected me more than almost anything else, though strong and brave men wept when I met them.

GIDEON WELLES, *Diary*, April 15, 1865

Now he belongs to the ages.

EDWIN MCMASTERS STANTON, spoken after the death of Abraham Lincoln, April 15, 1865

In this temple as in the hearts of the people for whom he saved the Union the memory of Abraham Lincoln is enshrined forever.

ANON. (Daniel Chester French, sculptor?), inscription in Lincoln Memorial, Washington

Who Is There to Mourn for Logan?

Inscription on an obelisk erected to the memory of Tah-gah-jute, or Logan, Chief of the Cayugas, in Fort Hill Cemetery, Auburn, New York. The monument of the chief, whose entire family was murdered by white men, surmounts a mound which is said to be an ancient Indian altar.

Matty Was Master of Them All.

Inscription on bust of Christy Matthewson, Cooperstown, New York

DEAR FANNY: It is with deep regret that I learn of the death of your kind and brave Father; and, especially, that it is affecting your young heart beyond what is common in such cases. In this sad world of ours sorrow comes to all; and, to the young, it comes with bitterest agony, because it takes them unawares. The older have learned ever to expect it. I am anxious to afford some alleviation of your present distress. Perfect relief is not possible, except with time. You can not now realize that you will ever feel better. Is not this so? And yet it is a mistake. You are sure to be happy again. To know this, which is certainly true, will make you some less miserable now. I have had experience enough to know what I say, and you need only to believe it, to feel better at once. The memory of your dear Father, instead of an agony, will yet be a sad sweet feeling in your heart, of a purer, and holier sort than you have known before.

> ABRAHAM LINCOLN, letter to Fanny McCullough, December 23, 1862

If, after I depart this vale, you ever remember me and have thought to please my ghost, forgive some sinner and wink your eye at some homely girl.

> H. L. MENCKEN, epitaph, from *Smart Set*, December, 1921

Excuse my dust.

> DOROTHY PARKER, epitaph suggested by herself

Major John Pitcairn
Fatally Wounded
While Rallying the Royal Marines
At the Battle of Bunker Hill
Was carried from the Field to the Boats
On the Back of His Son
Who Kissed Him and Returned to Duty.
He died June 17, 1775 and His Body
Was Interred Beneath This Church

> Inscription on tablet in Christ Church, Boston

At This Spot
The
77th Infantry Division
Lost a Buddy
Ernie Pyle
18 April 1945

> Inscription on Pyle's grave, Ie Shima (near Iwo Jima) in the Pacific

Live Your Life So That Whenever You Lose You Are Ahead.

> WILLIAM PENN ADAIR ("WILL") ROGERS, memorial inscription at Claremore, Oklahoma

The drums are wrapped in crepe and are muffled, as you can hear, and the pace of the musicians is so slow. And behind them, these are Navy boys—and now, just, just coming, past the Treasury, I can see the horses drawing the caisson, and most generally folks are having as tough a time as I am, trying to see it. And behind it, behind it, is the car bearing the man on whose shoulders now fall the terrific burdens and responsibilities that were handled so well by the man to whose body we're paying our last respects now. God bless him, President Truman! We return you to the studios.

> ARTHUR GODFREY, radio broadcast of funeral of Franklin D. Roosevelt, April, 1945

By the simple fact of dying, he has again attacked in strength.

He now personifies all the American dead . . . as though he had chosen the great legacy of light that Death leaves to the great.

> ANON., obituary in the *New Yorker*, April 21, 1945, of Franklin D. Roosevelt

His dream was a simple dream; it was pure and had no frills; he wanted the magazine to be good, to be funny, and to be fair.

> Obituary of Harold Ross, editor of the *New Yorker* 1925–1951, in the *New Yorker*

Al Shean
Beloved Father
Born May 12, 1868
I Could Have Lived Longer
But Now It's Too Late
Absolutely Mr. Gallagher—Positively Mr. Shean
August 12, 1949

> Inscription on grave of member of famous vaudeville team, in Mount Pleasant Cemetery, Pleasantville, New York

To the Memory of Leland Stanford, Jr., and the Glory of God.

> Original dedication motto of Stanford University

To the Glory of God and the Memory of Leland Stanford, Jr.

> Rededication motto after the San Francisco earthquake had destroyed the chapel

I Repose in This Quiet and Secluded Spot
Not from Any Natural Preference for Solitude,

But Finding Other Cemeteries Limited as to Race,
By Charter Rules,
I Have Chosen This That I Might Illustrate
In My Death
The Principles Which I Advocated
Through a Long Life:
Equality of Man Before His Creator

> THADDEUS STEVENS, epitaph on his grave at Schreiners Cemetery, Lancaster, Pennsylvania

Here lies the bird who was heard by millions of people who were waiting to hear Amos 'n' Andy.

> LOWELL THOMAS, epitaph suggested by himself

When we assumed the soldier, we did not lay aside the citizen.

> GEORGE WASHINGTON, address to the provincial Congress of New York, June 26, 1775; inscribed in the Memorial Amphitheater, Arlington Cemetery

Washington, the brave, the wise, the good,
Supreme in war, in council, and in peace.
Valiant without ambition, discreet without fear, confident without presumption.
In disaster, calm; in success, moderate; in all, himself.
The hero, the patriot, the Christian.
The father of nations, the friend of mankind,
Who, when he had won all, renounced all, and sought in the bosom of his family and of nature, retirement, and in the hope of religion, immortality.

> Inscription at Mount Vernon

In all our history no name shines with a purer light.

> Inscription on memorial to Roger Williams in the Capitol, Washington

I believe in America because in it we are free—
free to choose our government, to speak our minds,
to observe our different religions.
Because we are generous with our freedom, we share
our rights with those who disagree with us.
Because we hate no people and covet no people's lands.

Because we are blessed with a natural and varied abundance.
Because we have great dreams and because we have the
opportunity to make those dreams come true.

> WENDELL L. WILLKIE, his creed, inscribed on a marker
> near his grave in East Hill Cemetery, Rushville, Indiana

God gave him a great vision.
The Devil gave him an imperious heart.
The proud heart is still.
The vision lives.

> WILLIAM ALLEN WHITE, epitaph of Woodrow Wilson

Tom
Son of
W. O. and Julia E.
Wolfe
A Beloved American Author
Oct. 3, 1900—Sept. 15, 1938
The Last Voyage, the Longest, the Best.
Look Homeward, Angel.
Death Bent to Touch His Chosen Son with
Mercy, Love, and Pity, and Put the Seal
of Honor on Him When He Died.
The Web and the Rock

Inscription on grave of Thomas Wolfe, Asheville, North
Carolina

When he died
Nobody laughed, nobody cried.
Where he went, how he fares,
Nobody knows, nobody cares.

> Epitaph from a grave in Martha's Vineyard

Brigham Young. Born on this spot in 1801. A man of much courage and
superb equipment.

> Inscription on stone tablet near Whitingham, Vermont

VIII. We Look at the World

ONE WORLD

•

An American's country does not end with the Statue of Liberty or the Twelve Mile Limit.

SAMUEL PUTNAM, *Expatriate,* 1931

Peace, commerce, and honest friendship with all nations,—entangling alliances with none.

THOMAS JEFFERSON, "First Inaugural," March 4, 1801

I believe that our Great Maker is preparing the world, in His own good time, to become one nation, speaking one language.

GROVER CLEVELAND, "Inaugural Address," 1893

Whether they will or no, Americans must begin to look outward.

ALFRED THAYER MAHAN, *The Interest of America in Sea Power,* 1897

Dollar Diplomacy.

Slogan referring to efforts on the part of Philander C. Knox, Secretary of State under Taft, to promote the employment of American capital abroad, 1909

We are provincials no longer. The tragical events of the thirty months of vital turmoil through which we have just passed have made us citizens of the world. There can be no turning back. Our own fortunes as a nation are involved, whether we would have it so or not.

And yet we are not the less Americans on that account. We shall be the more American if we but remain true to the principles in which we have been bred. They are not the principles of a province or of a single continent. We have known and boasted all along that they were the principles of a liberated mankind.

WOODROW WILSON, "Second Inaugural," March 4, 1917

I had rather have everybody on my side than to be armed to the teeth.

WOODROW WILSON, address at Columbus, Ohio, September 4, 1919

I hope we shall never forget that we created this nation, not to serve ourselves, but to serve mankind.

> WOODROW WILSON

Nationalism is an infantile disease. It is the measles of mankind.

> ALBERT EINSTEIN, to George Sylvester Viereck, 1921

American diplomacy is easy on the brain but hell on the feet.

> CHARLES GATES DAWES, while Ambassador to Great Brittain. Henry Prather Fletcher, ex-Ambassador to Italy, commented, "It depends on which you use."

I haven't been abroad in so long that I almost speak English without an accent.

> ROBERT BENCHLEY, *The Old Sea Rover Speaks*

Why is it, whenever a group of internationalists get together, they always decide that Uncle Sam must be the goat?

> BERTRAND H. SNELL, interview, May 7, 1931

In the field of world policy I would dedicate this nation to the policy of the good neighbor.

> FRANKLIN D. ROOSEVELT, "First Inaugural Address," March 4, 1933

World Peace Through World Trade.

> THOMAS B. WATSON, slogan of International Business Machines

But we build and defend not for our generation alone. We defend the foundations laid by our fathers. We build a life for generations yet unborn. We defend and we build a way of life, not for America alone, but for all mankind.

> FRANKLIN D. ROOSEVELT, "Fireside Chat," 1940

In the future days, which we seek to make secure, we look forward to a world founded upon four essential human freedoms.

The first is freedom of speech and expression—everywhere in the world.

The second is freedom of every person to worship God in his own way —everywhere in the world.

The third is freedom from want—which, translated into world terms, means economic understandings which will secure to every nation a healthy peaceful life for its inhabitants—everywhere in the world.

The fourth is freedom from fear—which, translated into world terms, means a worldwide reduction of armaments to such a point and in such a thorough fashion that no nation will be in a position to commit an act of aggression against any neighbor—anywhere in the world.

> FRANKLIN D. ROOSEVELT, the Four Freedoms, "Message to Congress," January 6, 1941

Sovereignty is to be used, not hoarded.

> WENDELL L. WILLKIE, 1941

We cannot think about the future of America without considering the future of the world.

> THOMAS E. DEWEY, speech, 1942

Much of what Mr. Wallace calls his global thinking is, no matter how you slice it, still Globaloney.

> CLARE BOOTHE LUCE, speech, House of Representatives, February 9, 1943, referring to Vice-Pres. Henry Wallace

One World.

> WENDELL L. WILLKIE, title of book, 1943

Clubs, fraternities, nations—these are the beloved barriers in the way of a workable world; these will have to surrender some of their rights and some of their ribs. A "fraternity" is the antithesis of *fraternity*. The first (that is, the order of organization) is predicated on the idea of exclusion; the second (that is, the abstract thing) is based on a feeling of total equality. Anyone who remembers back to his fraternity days at college recalls the enthusiasts in his group, the rabid members, both old and young, who were obsessed with the mythical charm of membership in their particular order. They were usually men who were incapable of genuine brotherhood or at least unaware of its implications. Fraternity begins when the exclusion formula is found to be distasteful. The effect of any organization of a social and brotherly nature is to strengthen rather than to diminish the lines which divide people into classes; the effect of states and nations is the same, and eventually these lines will have to be softened; these powers will have to be generalized. It is written on the wall that this is so. I'm not inventing it, I'm just copying it off the wall.

> E. B. WHITE, *One Man's Meat,* "Intimations"

The people of the earth having agreed
    that the advancement of man
in spiritual excellence and physical welfare
is the common goal of mankind;
    that universal peace is the prerequisite
for the pursuit of that goal;
    that justice in turn is the prerequisite of peace,
and peace and justice stand or fall together;
    that iniquity and war inseparably spring
from the competitive anarchy of the national state;
    that therefore the age of nations must end,
and the era of humanity begin;

the governments of the nations have decided
    to order their separate sovereignties
in one government of justice,
to which they surrender their arms;
    and to establish, as they do establish,
this Constitution
as the covenant and fundamental law
of the Federal Republic of the World.

•

The universal government of justice as covenanted and pledged in this Constitution is founded on the Rights of Man.

The principles underlying the Rights of Man are and shall be permanently stated in the Duty

of everyone everywhere, whether a citizen sharing in the responsibilities and privileges of World Government or a ward and pupil of the World Commonwealth:

to serve with word and deed, and with productive labor according to his ability, the spiritual and physical advancement of the living and of those to come, as the common cause of all generations of men;

to do unto others as he would like others to do unto him;

to abstain from violence,

except for the repulse of violence as commanded or granted under law.

•   •   •   •   •

The four elements of life—earth, water, air, energy—are the common property of the human race. The management and use of such portions thereof as are vested in or assigned to particular ownership, private or corporate or national or regional, of definite or indefinite tenure, of individualist or collectivist economy, shall be subordinated in each and all cases to the interest of the common good.

> The Preamble and extracts from Declaration of Duties and Rights, *Preliminary Draft of a World Constitution,* as proposed and signed by: Robert M. Hutchins, G. A. Borgese, Mortimer J. Adler, Stringfellow Barr, Albert Guérard, Harold A. Innis, Erich Kahler, Wilber G. Katz, Charles H. McIlwain, Robert Redfield, Rexford G. Tugwell.
>
> It is interesting that the first systematic attempt to work out a theoretical world constitution for the Atomic Age should have been made by a group of American scholars. The *Preliminary Draft* was published in 1948.

I hope that you will pardon me for an unusual posture of sitting down, during the presentation of what I want to say, but I know that you will realize that it makes it a lot easier for me, in not having to carry about ten pounds of steel around on the bottom of my legs, and also because of the fact that I have just completed a 14,000 mile trip. Speaking in all frankness, the question of whether it is entirely fruitful lies to a great extent in your hands.

> FRANKLIN D. ROOSEVELT, report to Congress on Yalta Conference, March 1, 1945

When Kansas and Colorado have a quarrel over the water in the Arkansas River they don't call out the National Guard in each State and go to war over it. They bring a suit in the Supreme Court of the United States and abide by the decision. There isn't a reason in the world why we cannot do that internationally.

> HARRY S. TRUMAN, speech, Kansas City, April, 1945

Abilene, Kansas, and Denison, Texas, would together add in size to possibly one-five-hundredth part of Greater London. Yet kinship among nations is not determined in such measurements as proximity, size, and age. Rather we should turn to those inner things, call them what you will—I mean those intangibles that are the real treasures free men possess.

> DWIGHT D. EISENHOWER, Guildhall address, London, 1945

Mr. President, I should like to make a brief statement in connection with the resolution. I dislike very much to interrupt consideration of the tax bill. On the other hand, it may be a welcome respite for Senators to hear of something besides taxes for a few moments.

Mr. President, this is a rather momentous occasion in my experience in the Senate. This is the first resolution I have ever introduced. Furthermore, it is a resolution which may be rather startling to some, and, to say the least, controversial.

My proposal in the resolution is that the Senate go on record as favoring the creation of a world republic.

GLENN H. TAYLOR, in the Senate, October 24, 1945

Make an original and four copies, Miss Eberhard, one for each delegate. A delegate, on his way to assembly, carries two sets of instructions: one dictated by his own conscience (but not read) and one handed him by his constituents. Herewith we hand to each delegate to the first assembly of the United Nations Organization his instructions:

When you sit down, sit down as an American if it makes you feel comfortable, but when you rise to speak, get up like a man anywhere.

Do not bring home any bacon; it will have turned rancid on the journey. Bring home instead a silken thread, by which you may find your way back.

Bear in mind always that foreign policy is domestic policy with its hat on. The purpose of the meeting, although not so stated anywhere, is to replace policy with law, and to make common cause.

Make common cause.

Think not to represent us by safeguarding our interests. Represent us by perceiving that our interests are other people's, and theirs ours.

When you think with longing of the place where you were born, remember that the sun leaves it daily to go somewhere else. When you think with love of America, think of the impurity of its blood-lines and of how no American ever won a prize in a dog show.

Carry good men with you in your portfolio, along with the order of the day. Read the men with the short first names: Walt Whitman, John Donne, Manny Kant, Abe Lincoln, Tom Paine, Al Einstein. Read them and weep. Then read them again, without tears.

If you would speak up for us, do not speak up for America, speak up for people, for the free man. We are not dispatching you to build national greatness. Unless you understand this, and believe it, you might better be at the race track, where you can have a good time simply by guessing wrong.

Never forget that the nature of peace is commonly misstated. Peace is not to be had by preventing aggression, for it is always too late for that. Peace is to be had when people's antagonisms and antipathies are subject to the discipline of law and the decency of government.

Do not try to save the world by loving thy neighbor; it will only make him nervous. Save the world by respecting thy neighbor's rights under law and insisting that he respect yours (under the same law). In short, save the world. . . .

Do not be confused by the noise of the atomic bomb. The bomb is the pea shooter come home to roost. But when you dream, dream of essential matters, of mass-energy relationships, of man-man relationships. The scientists have out-dreamed you, little delegate, so dream well.

> E. B. WHITE, *The Wild Flag, New Yorker,* Jan. 12, 1946

The world state is inherent in the United Nations as an oak tree is in an acorn.

> WALTER LIPPMANN, *One World or None,* 1946

Yes I do, but it is better for aged diplomats to be bored than for young men to die.

> WARREN AUSTIN, on being asked whether during the long U.N. debates he did not become tired

What is the aim of our propaganda? Friendship? To many Americans this is the end-all. And nothing has done us more grievous harm—for we are offended terribly when love is not forthcoming from others. It is quite impossible anyway. We have only to look at India; since their departure, the British, who never gave a damn whether anybody liked them or not, have become increasingly popular, while we, who did our best to expedite that departure, are becoming increasingly unpopular.

> ANON., *U.S.A., The Permanent Revolution,* by the editors of *Fortune*

Biologically it has always been One World.

> GUSTAV ECKSTEIN, 1948

The United States will be secure in an absolute sense only if the institution of war itself is abolished under a regime of law. . . . We will not be rid of war until the nations arrive at the agreement to live together in peace and to this end give to the United Nations the legal and physical powers under a regime of law to keep the peace.

> *Report to the President,* U.S. Air Policy Commission, 1948

We shall have to learn to think, not just as Americans, but as members of the human race—as peculiarly and uniquely fortunate members of the human race, endowed with an enormous potential for creative action. We shall have to learn to think, not in terms of charity or in terms of enlightened self-defense, but in terms of pioneers opening up new horizons, clearing new fields of progress and conquering the desert areas. We shall have to shake off the corroding fear of losing what we possess and recapture the spirit of adventure, along with the affinity for all men everywhere seeking change for the better, which once made our nation a symbol of hope throughout the world.

> JAMES P. WARBURG

To me it is enough to know that the continuation of the existence of human beings is in serious doubt if no supra-national solution can be achieved.

> ALBERT EINSTEIN, letter, February, 1952

Whatever America hopes to bring to pass in this world must first come to pass in the heart of America.

> DWIGHT D. EISENHOWER, "Inaugural Address," 1953

OUR NEIGHBORS

•

EUROPE

What would you think of a proposition if I should make it, of a family compact between England, France, and America? America would be as happy as the Sabine girls, if she could be the means of uniting in perpetual peace her father and her husband.

> BENJAMIN FRANKLIN, letter to David Hartley, Oct. 16, 1783

I send you enclos'd the propos'd new Federal Constitution for these States. I was engag'd 4 Months of the last Summer in the Convention that form'd it. It is now sent by Congress to the several States for their Confirmation. If it succeeds, I do not see why you might not in Europe carry the Project of good Henry the 4th into Execution, by forming a Federal Union and One Grand Republick of all its different States and Kingdoms, by means of a like Convention, for we had many Interests to reconcile.

Benjamin Franklin, letter to Grand, October 22, 1787

Let Americans disdain to be the instruments of European greatness! Let the thirteen States, bound together in a strict and indissoluble Union, concur in erecting one great American system, superior to the control of all transatlantic force or influence, and able to dictate the terms of the connection between the old and the new world!

Alexander Hamilton, *Federalist*, XI, 1787

There is not a crowned head in Europe whose talents or merits would entitle him to be elected a vestryman by the people of any parish in America.

Thomas Jefferson

The American continents . . . are henceforth not to be considered as subjects for future colonization by any European powers. . . .

We owe it, therefore, to candor, and to the amicable relations existing between the United States and those powers to declare that we should consider any attempt on their part to extend their system to any portion of this hemisphere as dangerous to our peace and safety. With the existing colonies or dependencies of any European power . . . we shall not interfere. But with the governments . . . whose independence we have . . . acknowledged, we could not view any interposition for the purpose of oppressing them, or controlling, in any other manner, their destiny, by any European power, in any other light than as a manifestation of an unfriendly disposition towards the United States.

James Monroe, "First Inaugural Address," March 4, 1817
—"The Monroe Doctrine"

For some reason or other, the European has rarely been able to see America except in caricature. . . . We do not ask to be sprinkled with rose-water, but may perhaps fairly protest against being drenched with the rinsings of an unclean imagination.

> JAMES RUSSELL LOWELL, *On a Certain Condescension in Foreigners*

It's a complex fate, being an American, and one of the responsibilities it entails is fighting against a superstitious valuation of Europe.

> HENRY JAMES, letter, 1872

They hired the money, didn't they?

> CALVIN COOLIDGE, of French and British difficulty in paying war debts

These wars in Europe are not wars in which our civilization is defending itself against some Asiatic intruder. There is no Genghis Khan or Xerxes marching against our Western nations. This is simply one more of those age-old struggles within our own family of nations.

> CHARLES A. LINDBERGH, speech, America First rally, 1940

The Wave of the Future.

> ANNE MORROW LINDBERGH, title of book, 1940. The book advocated domestic reforms in keeping with those of certain European countries.

When I was in Mexico, two years ago, my sleep was constantly disturbed by the barking of wild dogs which, besides their discordant howling, constitute a great danger of epidemics in the American influence zone. Thus I had the idea to have these animals exported to Europe to feed the hungry inhabitants.

> COLONEL ROBERT R. McCORMICK, in the Chicago *Tribune,* during national debate concerning the sending of food to Europe, 1946

If only we could shake off Europe! Fussy and censorious mother, spendthrift sibling, run-down neighbor, complaining grandparent, shameless sponge and smuggest critic, she is surely the most infuriating of our burdens. If we could cast that weight into the mill pond, would we not then be as free as a cloud . . .?

The thirteen-year old does not understand that the concealed object of his impatience is neither parent, friend nor cousin but himself, and that it is himself from whom he hopelessly seeks to flee. Is it so with us and our image of Europe?

> JAMES BURNHAM, *What Europe Thinks of America,* "Introduction," 1953

We Americans have always thought either too much or too little of ourselves, as we have thought either too much or too little of Europe. As in the nineteenth century we thought too much of Europe, so we are in danger of thinking too little of it now.

> VAN WYCK BROOKS, "A Writer's Notebook," *Nation,* November 14. 1953

GREAT BRITAIN

We must marry ourselves to the British fleet and nation.

> THOMAS JEFFERSON, 1802

The feudal system survives in the steep inequality of property and privilege, in the limited franchise, in the social barriers which confine patronage and promotion to a caste, and still more in the submissive ideas pervading these people. The fagging of the schools is repeated in the social classes. An Englishman shows no mercy to those below him in the social scale, as he looks for none from those above him: any forbearance from his superiors surprizes him, and they suffer in his good opinion. But the feudal system can be seen with less pain on large historical grounds. It was pleaded in mitigation of the rotten borough, that it worked well, that substantial justice was done. Fox, Burke, Pitt, Erskine, Wilberforce, Sheridan, Romilly, or whatever national man, were by this means sent to Parliament, when their return by large constituencies would have been doubtful. So now we say, that the right measures of England are the men it bred; that it has yielded more able men in five hundred years than any other nation; and, though we must not play Providence, and balance the chances of producing ten great men against the comfort of ten thousand mean men, yet retrospectively we may strike a balance, and prefer one Alfred, one Shakespeare, one Milton, one Sidney, one Raleigh, one Wellington, to a million foolish democrats.

The American system is more democratic, more humane; yet the American people do not yield better or more able men, or more inventions or books or benefits, than the English. Congress is not wiser or better than Parliament.

RALPH WALDO EMERSON, *English Traits*

I saw everywhere in the country proofs of sense and spirit, and success of every sort: I like the people; they are as good as they are handsome; they have everything and can do everything; but meantime, I surely know that as soon as I return to Massachusetts I shall lapse at once into the feeling, which the geography of America inevitably inspires, that we play the game with immense advantage; that there and not here is the seat and centre of the British race; and that no skill or activity can long compete with the prodigious natural advantages of that country, in the hands of the same race; and that England, an old and exhausted island, must one day be contented, like other parents, to be strong only in her children.

RALPH WALDO EMERSON, *Ibid.*

Steam is almost an Englishman. I do not know but they will send him to Parliament next, to make laws.

RALPH WALDO EMERSON, *Ibid.*

It is difficult to speak adequately or justly of London. It is not a pleasant place; it is not agreeable, or cheerful, or easy, or exempt from reproach. It is only magnificent. You can draw up a tremendous list of reasons why it should be insupportable. The fogs, the smoke, the dirt, the darkness, the wet, the distances, the ugliness, the brutal size of the place, the horrible numerosity of society, the manner in which this senseless bigness is fatal to amenity, to convenience, to conversation, to good manners—all this and much more you may expiate upon. You may call it dreary, heavy, stupid, dull, inhuman, vulgar at heart and tiresome in form. I have said all these things at times so strongly that I have said, "Ah, London, you too are impossible?" But these are occasional moods; and for one who takes it as I take it, London as a whole is the most possible form of life. I take it as an artist and a bachelor; as one who has the passion of observation and whose business is the study of human life. It is the biggest aggregation of human life—the most complete compendium of the world.

HENRY JAMES, 1876

The English are the only people who can do great things without being clever.

HENRY JAMES, spoken to Alice James, 1891

King George does not reign—he only sprinkles.

> JOSEPH HODGES CHOATE, when he was Ambassador to
> England, c. 1905

I know why the sun never sets on the British Empire. God wouldn't trust an Englishman in the dark.

> DUNCAN SPAETH

Never burn an uninteresting letter is the first rule of British aristocracy; never let a banality perish, but transcribe it and file it as a *bon mot.* The delight of the British aristocracy over a bit of commonsense, such as is quite ordinarily met with in other walks of life, has always been a marvel to those who have had the mental advantages of a humble origin. In the best British families, a word or two of commonsense is often preserved as an heirloom.

> FRANK MOORE COLBY, *The Colby Essays,* "A Note on the
> Literature of Malicious Exposure"

Suppose my neighbor's home catches fire, and I have a length of garden hose. . . . If he can take my garden hose . . . I may help him to put out the fire. Now what do I do? I don't say to him . . . "Neighbor, my garden hose cost me $15; you have to pay me $15 for it." . . . I don't want $15—I want my garden hose back after the fire is over.

> FRANKLIN D. ROOSEVELT, press conference, explaining
> Lend-Lease, 1940. Senator Burton K. Wheeler: "Lend-
> Lease would plow under every fourth American boy."

England was consciously refusing the twentieth century; knowing full well that they had gloriously created the nineteeth century and perhaps the twentieth century was going to be too many for them.

> GERTRUDE STEIN, *Paris, France,* 1940

This war is lost. . . . It is not within our power today to win the war for England, even though we throw the entire resources of our nation into the conflict.

> CHARLES A. LINDBERGH, April 19, 1941

Beneath this East River Drive [at East 25th Street] of the City of New York lie stones, brick, and rubble from the bombed City of Bristol. . . .

These fragments that once were homes shall testify while men love freedom to the resolution and fortitude of the people of Britain.

> STEPHEN VINCENT BENÉT, inscription for East River Drive,
> Manhattan

FRANCE

Every man has two countries, France and his own (*Chaque homme a
deux patries, la sienne et la France*).

> BENJAMIN FRANKLIN

France, freed from that monster, Bonaparte, must again become the most
agreeable country on earth. It would be the second choice of all whose
ties of family and fortune give a preference to some other one, and the
first choice of all not under those ties.

> THOMAS JEFFERSON, 1814

Good Americans, when they die, go to Paris.

> THOMAS GOLD APPLETON

He came down the rue de la Paix in the sun and, passing across the Tuileries and the river, indulged more than once—as if on finding himself
determined—in a sudden pause before the bookstalls of the opposite quay.
In the garden of the Tuileries he had lingered, on two or three spots, to
look; it was as if the wonderful Paris spring had stayed him as he roamed.
The prompt Paris morning struck its cheerful notes—in a soft breeze and
a sprinkled smell, in the light flit, over the garden-floor, of bare-headed
girls with the buckled strap of oblong boxes, in the type of ancient thrifty
persons basking betimes where terrace-walls were warm, in the blue-
frocked, brass-labelled officialism of humble rakers and scrapers, in the
deep references of a straight-pacing priest or the sharp ones of a white-
gaitered, red-legged soldier. He watched little brisk figures, figures whose
movement was as the tick of the great Paris clock, take their smooth diagonal from point to point; the air had a taste as of something mixed
with art, something that presented nature as a white-capped master-
chef. . . .

In the Luxembourg gardens he pulled up; here at last he found his
nook, and here, on a penny chair from which terraces, alleys, vistas, foun-

tains, little trees in green tubs, little women in white caps and shrill little girls at play all sunnily "composed" together, he passed an hour in which the cup of his impressions seemed truly to overflow.

HENRY JAMES, *The Ambassadors,* 1903

French is so poverty-stricken that about the only way a person can say anything intelligible is the right way.

ALBERT JAY NOCK, *A Journal of These Days,* 1934

On this tenth day of June, 1940, the hand that held the dagger has struck it into the back of its neighbor.

FRANKLIN D. ROOSEVELT, speech describing the Italian attack on France

The last time I see Paris will be on the day I die. The city was inexhaustible, and so is its memory.

ELLIOT PAUL, *The Last Time I Saw Paris,* 1942

RUSSIA

The sum of my certainty is that America has a very clear century of start over Russia, and that western Europe must follow us for a hundred years, before Russia can swing her flail over the Atlantic.

HENRY ADAMS, letter to Elizabeth Cameron, 1901

I am half crazy with fear that Russia is sailing straight into another French revolution which may upset all Europe and us too. A serious disaster to Russia might smash the whole civilized world. Other people see only the madness; I see only the ruin. Russia is completely off her head.

HENRY ADAMS, letter to Elizabeth Cameron, 1904

Our so-called civilization has shown its movement, even at the centre, arrested. It has failed to concentrate further. Its next effort may succeed, but it is more likely to be one of disintegration, with Russia for the eccentric on one side and America on the other.

HENRY ADAMS, letter to Brooks Adams

Ten Days That Shook the World.

> JOHN REED, title of book, 1919, an eyewitness account of
> the first days of the Bolshevik Revolution

Bolshevism is knocking at our gates. We can't afford to let it in. . . . We
have to organize ourselves against it and put our shoulders together and
hold fast.

> AL CAPONE

"So you've been over in Russia?" said Bernard Baruch, and I answered
very literally, "I have been over into the future, and it works." * This was
in Jo Davidson's studio, where Mr. Baruch was sitting for a portrait bust.
The sculptor asked if I wasn't glad to get back. I was. It was a mental
change that we had experienced, not physical. Bullitt asked in surprise
why it was that, having been so elated by the prospect of Russia, we were
so glad to be back in Paris. I thought it was because, though we had been
to heaven, we were so accustomed to our own civilization that we preferred hell. We were ruined; we could recognize salvation, but could not
be saved.

And, by the way, it was harder on the real reds than it was on us liberals. Emma Goldman, the anarchist who was deported to that socialist
heaven, came out and said it was hell. And the socialists, the American,
English, the European socialists, they did not recognize their own heaven.
As some wit put it, the trouble with them was that they were waiting at a
station for a local train, and an express tore by and left them there. My
summary of all our experiences was that it showed that heaven and hell
are one place, and we all go there. To those who are prepared, it is
heaven; to those who are not fit and ready, it is hell.

> LINCOLN STEFFENS, *Autobiography*, 1931

Certainly it was not made of flesh. And I have seen so many waxworks
which were actual (some ludicrous more horrible most both) so many
images whose very unaliveness could liberate Is, invent Being (or what
equally disdains life and unlife)—I have seen so very many better gods
or stranger, many mightier deeper puppets; everywhere and elsewhere
and perhaps in America and (for instance) in Coney Island.

> E. E. CUMMINGS, *Eimi,* concerning the embalmed body of
> Nicolai Lenin, in Red Square, Moscow

I had expected Moscow to be old and musty, but it is modern and ener-

---

* "Well, so does the atom bomb."—Max Nomad

getic. The people are better dressed and more prosperous-appearing, in general, than the people in Leningrad. The main business section, the "Center," is much like an American city. They have set out to rearrange the whole place, and already there are only little patches of the original Moscow of the Muscovite Tsars embedded in drab streets and crowded traffic: the jewel-box of the Kremlin with its needle-pointed gleaming gilt spires (which, since the Kirov shooting, visitors are not allowed to see); the shabby domes of St. Basil's in their big ugly bulbous mushroom-clump. St. Basil's, inside, is a labyrinth, lined with faded saints and angels which the authorities have done nothing to freshen, and plastered with aggressively glaring texts from Marx and Engels and Lenin which declare that religion is a fraud. Outside, the millions of stubby little people who have been flocking into the metropolis but who are not used to getting around in a city, are plunging about and bumping into one another. Moscow seems even to a New Yorker a terribly exhausting place. The tramcars are usually crowded, and the people hang onto the outside and fall off and get under the cars and have their legs and arms run over. And though the pace of Russian life is in general so much slower and less effortful than ours, their new mechanical means of locomotion seem sometimes to go to their heads. They rip around the streets in their Russian-made cars tooting wild defiant horns, like galloping Cossacks; and the escalators in their new little subway rush the passengers up and down at a speed unknown in any American city. Women and children scream; a first ride is a major adventure. When the subway was opened, Comrade Stalin, who can take it, rode the escalator twice in succession.

EDMUND WILSON, *U.S.S.R.—Idyll and Counter-Idyll,* 1936

The refusal of the British and Russian peoples to accept what appeared to be inevitable defeat was the great factor in the salvage of our civilization.

GEORGE C. MARSHALL, *Biennial Report of Chief of Staff of U.S. Army,* September 1, 1945

There are dictatorships that are not political, yet effective. One of them is that fear by which all Americans are hag-ridden. We are not a free people because, to a very large extent, Malenkov dictates what we shall do and especially what we shall not do. He does it by contraries, but he does it. Whatever Malenkov approves, that we must despise; whatever Malenkov hates, to that we must adhere. He has bound us, not with his Red army, but with the chains of our own fear; but he has bound us.

GERALD W. JOHNSON, *American Freedom and the Press*

THE EAST

The twentieth century will be American. American thought will dominate it. American progress will give it color and direction. American deeds will make it illustrious.

Civilization will never lose its hold on Shanghai. Civilization will never depart from Hong Kong. The gates of Peking will never again be closed to the methods of modern man. The regeneration of the world, physical as well as moral, has begun, and revolutions never move backwards.

> ALBERT J. BEVERIDGE, responding to the toast, "The Twentieth Century," 1900

The open door.

> JOHN HAY. On January 2, 1900, Hay, then Secretary of State, announced to the cabinet that he had completed negotiations for the "open door" in China.

The little brown brother.

> WILLIAM HOWARD TAFT, of the Filipinos when Commissioner of the Philippines, 1900. The phrase gave rise to the song,
>
> > He may be a brother to Big Bill Taft,
> > But he's not a brother to me.

We send missionaries to China so the Chinese can get to heaven, but we won't let them into our country.

> PEARL BUCK

With all of these changes in styles there is one fundamental attitude of the Chinese woman on the subject of clothes which has remained unchanged from the time of Cleopatra. She dresses to attract the admiration of men, and especially to hold the admiration of her husband. The foreign woman dresses for the benefit of her sisters, hoping that her new ensemble will be admired by her friends and acquaintances, nor would it be a matter of great regret on her part, if some should be made miserable through the extremity of their jealousy and envy. Whether or not her husband is pleased is a matter of relatively small importance. He has to pay for the gown anyway. The point of view of the Chinese woman is just the reverse. She dresses with the idea of pleasing her husband. Her prettiest dresses are worn in her own home. If she is admired by other women, she accepts the compliment with all the greater pleasure because she has not striven for it. I suppose the foreign woman has a lot more fun and excitement in her endeavours to outdress and outbeautify her sisters, but I am sure the Chinese wife has a much easier time of it when it comes to the problem of getting her dress allowance increased.

CARL CROW, *400,000,000 Customers*

We have a phrase in English, "straight from the horse's mouth."

JOSEPH CLARK GREW, address, Tokyo, October 19, 1939. This was the opening sentence of a speech in which Grew tried to indicate the feelings of the American people toward Japanese imperialism.

OTHERS

The Creator made Italy with designs by Michael Angelo.

SAMUEL L. CLEMENS ("MARK TWAIN"), *Innocents Abroad*

We want Perdicaris alive, or Raisuli dead.

JOHN HAY, cablegram to the Sultan of Morocco demanding the release of Ion Perdicaris, a native of Greece and a naturalized American, who had been captured and held for $70,000 ransom by Achmed Ben Mohammed Raisuli, a bandit chief in revolt against the Sultan, June, 1904

Sawdust Caesar.

GEORGE SELDES, title of book on Mussolini, 1932

In all of these comparisons between Samoan and American culture, many points are useful only in throwing a spotlight upon our own solutions, while in others it is possible to find suggestions for change. Whether or not we envy other peoples one of their solutions, our attitude towards our own solutions must be greatly broadened and deepened by a consideration of the way in which other peoples have met the same problems. Realising that our own ways are not humanly inevitable nor God-ordained, but are the fruit of a long and turbulent history, we may well examine in turn all of our institutions, thrown into strong relief against the history of other civilisations, and weighing them in the balance, be not afraid to find them wanting.

MARGARET MEAD, *Coming of Age in Samoa*

Life in Africa is like life in a ship—and the white men are the passengers.

NEGLEY FARSON, *Black Zoos*

IX. Our Proverbs

God looks after drunks, children, and Americans.

> Quoted as "an old saying" by James Truslow Adams, *Virginia Quarterly*, July, 1934

Jay-bird don't rob his own nes'.
Youk'n hide de fier, but w'at you gwine do wid de smoke?

> Joel Chandler Harris, *Plantation Proverbs*

Quicker than greased lightning.   Traced to 1833

As cold as the north side of a gravestone in Winter.   Traced to 1835

There's a nigger in the woodpile.   Traced to 1864 and probably older

Let's get down to brass tacks.   Traced to 1870

I picked a lemon in the garden of love.   Traced to 1895

Long-haired men and short-haired women.   Traced to 1920

He has ants in his pants.

> Popularized by Hugh S. Johnson, 1939. (In the form of "He has a breeze in his breech" it goes back to the seventeenth century.)

If you can't be good, be sanitary.   American version of an old saying

Curiosity killed the cat.   Not recorded in any English collection

Two's company, three's a crowd.

Home was never like this.

We're here today and gone tomorrow.

If you want to know what God thinks of money, look at the people he gives it to.

You have two chances—one of getting the germ and one of not.
   And if you get the germ you have two chances—one of getting the disease and one of not.

And if you get the disease you have two chances—one of dying and one of not.

And if you die—well, you still have two chances.

Don't kick a fellow when he's down.

Don't spit; remember the Johnstown flood.

Having wonderful time—wish you were here.

Lightning never strikes twice in the same place.

I am willing to try anything once.

Every man to his own poison.

Quit while you're ahead.

If you leave your umbrella at home, it is sure to rain.

If you don't like it here, why don't you go back where you came from?

In God we trust; all others pay cash.

Sweat and be saved.

There's always room at the top.

It's no worse than a bad cold.

Doctors keep you alive but keep you dying.

Don't take any wooden nickels.

Never trouble trouble till trouble troubles you.

Ain't nature grand?

It will never get well if you pick it.

When the water reaches the upper deck, follow the rats.

It will all come out in the wash.

Them as has, gits.

Fish or cut bait.

Nobody loves a fat man.

Love 'em and leave 'em.

No more chance than a snowball in Hell.

Blow your own horn—even if you don't sell a clam.

The final test of fame is to have a crazy person imagine he is you.

*X. As Others See Us: from Leif Ericson
to Sir Osbert Sitwell*

There was now much talk about voyages of discovery. Leif, the son of Eric the Red, of Brattahild, went to Biarni Heriulfson, and bought the ship of him, and engaged men for it, so that there were thirty-five men in all. Leif asked his father Eric to be the leader on the voyage, but Eric excused himself, saying that he was now pretty well stricken in years, and could not now, as formerly, hold out against all the hardships of the sea. Leif said that still he was the one of the family whom good fortune would soonest attend, and Eric gave in to Leif's request, and rode from home so soon as they were ready, and it was but a short way to the ship. The horse stumbled that Eric rode, and he fell off and bruised his foot. Then said Eric, "It is not ordained that I should discover more countries than that which we now inhabit, and we should make no further attempt in company." Eric went home to Brattahild, but Leif repaired to the ship, and his comrades with him. . . .

Now prepared they their ship, and sailed out into the sea when they were ready, and then found that land first which Biarni had found last. There sailed they to the land, and cast anchor, and put off boats and went ashore, and saw there no grass. Great icebergs were over all the up country, but like a plain of flat stones was all from the sea to the mountains, and it appeared to them that this land [Labrador or northern Newfoundland?] had no good qualities. . . .

Then went they on board, and after that sailed out to sea, and found another land. They sailed again to the land and cast anchor, then put off boats and went on shore. This land was flat and covered with wood, and white sands were far around where they went, and the shore was low. Then said Leif: "This land shall be named after its qualities, and called Markland [woodland—Cape Breton Island or Nova Scotia?]." They then immediately returned to the ship.

Now sailed they thence into the open sea with a northeast wind, and were two days at sea before they saw land, and they sailed thither and came to an island which lay to the eastward of the land, and went up there and looked around them in good weather, and observed that there was dew upon the grass. And it so happened that they touched the dew with their hands, and raised the fingers to the mouth, and they thought that they had never before tasted anything so sweet.

After that they went to the ship and sailed into a sound which lay between the island and a promontory. It was very shallow at ebb tide, and their ship stood up so that it was far to see from the ship to the water.

But so much did they desire to land that they did not give themselves time to wait until the water again rose under their ship, but ran at once on shore at a place where a river flows out of a lake. But so soon as the waters rose up under the ship, then took they boats, and rowed to the ship, and floated it up the river, and thence into the lake, and there cast anchor, and brought up from their ship their skin cots, and made their booths.

After this they took counsel and formed the resolution of remaining there for the winter, and built there large houses. There was no want of salmon either in the river or in the lake, and larger salmon than they had before seen. The nature of the country was, as they thought, so good that cattle would not require house feeding in winter, for there came no frost in winter, and little did the grass wither there. Day and night were more equal than in Greenland or Iceland, for on the shortest day the sun was above the horizon from half past seven in the forenoon till half past four in the afternoon. . . .

It happened one evening that a man of the party was missing, and this was Tyrker the German. . . . Leif now took his people severely to task, and prepared to seek for Tyrker, and took twelve men with him. But when they got a short way from the house, then came Tyrker towards them and was joyfully received. . . . Then said Leif to him: "Why were thou so late . . . and separated from the party?" He now spoke first for a long time in German, and rolled his eyes about to different sides, and twisted his mouth, but they did not understand what he said. After a time he spoke Norsk. "I have not been much farther off, but still I have something new to tell of; I found vines and grapes." "But is that true, my fosterer?" quoth Leif. "Surely is it true," replied he, "for I was bred up in a land where there is no want of either grapes or vines."

They slept for the night, but in the morning Leif said to his sailors: "We will now set about two things, in that the one day we gather grapes, and the other day cut vines and fell trees, so from thence will be a loading for my ship." And that was the counsel taken, and it is said their longboat was filled with grapes. Now was a cargo cut down for the ship, and when the spring came they got ready and sailed away; and Leif gave the land a name after its qualities, and called it Vineland.

> ANON., *The Voyages of the Northmen to America*, ed. Slater, Boston, 1877. Experts vary as to the identify of Vineland: it has been suggested that it might have been Newfoundland, the mouth of the St. Lawrence, Nova Scotia, northern New England, Cape Cod, Martha's Vineyard,

Rhode Island, New York, New Jersey (or Chesapeake Bay),
or Virginia. It might be noted that Tyrker was probably the
first European to get drunk on New World soil.

Whereas a certain controversy exists between the . . . lords, their constituents, as to what lands, of all those discovered in the ocean sea up to the
present day, the date of this treaty, pertain to each one of the said parts
respectively; therefore, for the sake of peace and concord, and for the
preservation of the relationship and love of the said King of Portugal for
the said King and Queen of Castile, Aragon, etc. it being the pleasure of
their Highnesses, they . . . covenanted and agreed that a boundary or
straight line be determined and drawn north and south, from pole to pole,
on the said ocean sea, from the Arctic to the Antarctic pole. This boundary
or line shall be drawn straight, as aforesaid, at a distant of three hundred
and seventy leagues west of the Cape Verde Islands, being calculated by
degrees. . . . And all lands, both islands and mainlands, found and discovered already, or to be found and discovered hereafter, by the said
King of Portugal and by his vessels on this side of the said line and bound
determined as above, toward the east, in either north or south latitude, on
the eastern side of the said bound, provided the said bound is not crossed,
shall belong to and remain in the possession of, and pertain forever to,
the said King of Portugal and his successors. And all other lands, both
island and mainlands, found or to be found hereafter . . . by the said
King and Queen of Castile, Aragon, etc. and by their vessels, on the western side of the said bound, determined as above, after having passed the
said bound toward the west, in either its north or south latitude, shall belong to . . . the said King and Queen of Castile, Leon, etc. and to their
successors.

The Treaty of Tordesillas, June 7, 1492

As soon as we had arrived at that island . . . I proceeded along its coast
towards the west for some distance; I found it so large and without perceptible end, that I believed it to be not an island, but the continental
country of Cathay; seeing, however, no towns or cities situated on the
sea-coast, but only some villages and rude farms, with whose inhabitants I
was unable to converse, because as soon as they saw us they took flight.

CHRISTOPHER COLUMBUS, letter on the discovery of America. He is describing Cuba, called by him Juana.

We ever held it certain that going toward the sunset we would find what
we desired.

CABEZA DE VACA, in Florida, 1528

Elizabeth, by the Grace of God of England, Fraunce and Ireland Queene, defender of the faith, &c. To all people to whome these presents shall come, greeting.

Knowe ye that of our especial grace, certaine science, and meere motion . . . we give and grant to our trustie and welbeloved servant *Walter Ralegh,* Esquire, and to his heires assignes for ever, free libertie and license from time to time, and at all times for ever hereafter, to discover, search, finde out, and view such remote, heathen and barbarous lands, countries, and territories, not actually possessed of any Christian Prince, nor inhabited by Christian People, as to him . . . shall seeme good.

QUEEN ELIZABETH, patent to Sir Walter Raleigh, 1584

O my America! My new-found-land!

JOHN DONNE, "To His Mistris Going to Bed"

And, cheerfully at sea,
Success you will entice,
    To get the pearl and gold,
    And ours to hold,
VIRGINIA,
Earth's only paradise.

MICHAEL DRAYTON, "To the Virginian Voyage"

IN The Name of God, Amen. We, whose names are underwritten, the Loyal Subjects of our dread Sovereign Lord King *James,* by the Grace of God, of *Great Britain, France,* and *Ireland,* King, *Defender of the Faith,* &c. Having undertaken for the Glory of God, and Advancement of the Christian Faith, and the Honour of our King and Country, a Voyage to plant the first colony in the northern Parts of Virginia; Do by these Presents, solemnly and mutually in the Presence of God and one another, covenant and combine ourselves together into a civil Body Politick, for our better Ordering and Preservation, and Furtherance of the Ends aforesaid; And by Virtue hereof do enact, constitute, and frame, such just and equal Laws, Ordinances, Acts, Constitutions, and Offices, from time to time, as shall be thought most meet and convenient for the general Good of the Colony; unto which we promise all due Submission and Obedience. In WITNESS whereof we have hereunto subscribed our names at *Cape Cod* the eleventh of *November,* in the Reign of our Sovereign Lord King *James* of *England, France,* and *Ireland,* the eighteenth and of *Scotland,* the fifty-fourth. *Anno Domini,* 1620.

The Mayflower Compact

Westward the course of empire takes its way;
The four first acts already past,
A fifth shall close the drama with the day:
Time's noblest offspring is the last.

GEORGE BERKELEY, "On the Prospect of Planting Arts and Learning in America"

I rejoice that America has resisted. Three millions of people, so dead to all the feelings of liberty, as voluntarily to submit to be slaves, would have been fit instruments to make slaves of the rest.

WILLIAM PITT, speech in Commons, 1766

I am willing to love all mankind, except an American.

SAMUEL JOHNSON, quoted by Boswell, *Life*

[The Americans] are a race of convicts, and ought to be thankful for anything we allow them short of hanging.

SAMUEL JOHNSON, *Ibid.*

Indeed, although in my travels I saw very good sites and beautiful country, I saw none which pleased me so much as this. And I think that if it could be well settled like Europe there would not be anything more beautiful in all the world, for it has best advantages for founding in it a most beautiful city with all the conveniences desired, by land as well as by sea, with that harbor so remarkable and so spacious, in which may be established shipyards, docks, and anything that might be wished.

FATHER PEDRO FONT, of San Francisco Harbor, in 1775

All protestantism, even the most cold and passive, is a form of dissent. But the religion most prevalent in our northern colonies [New England] is a refinement of the principle of resistance: it is the dissidence of dissent, and the protestantism of the Protestant religion.

EDMUND BURKE, "Speech on Conciliation with America," March 22, 1775

Young man, there is America—which at this day serves for little more than to amuse you with stories of savage men, and uncouth manners; yet shall, before you taste of death, show itself equal to the whole of that commerce which now attracts the envy of the world.

EDMUND BURKE, *Ibid.*

By the waters of Babylon we sit down and weep, when we think of thee, O America!

> HORACE WALPOLE, letter to Mason, 1775

The Huron and Iroquois forests are peopled with my friends; the despots of Europe and their courts, these to me are the savages.

> MARQUIS DE LAFAYETTE, in 1776

You cannot conquer America.

> WILLIAM PITT, speech in House of Commons, November 18, 1777

I cannot conclude without mentioning how sensibly I feel the dismemberment of America from this empire, and that I should be miserable indeed if I did not feel that no blame on that account can be laid at my door, and did I not also know that knavery seems to be so much the striking feature of its inhabitants that it may not in the end be an evil that they will become aliens to this kingdom.

> GEORGE III, letter to Shelburne, November 10, 1782

He snatched the lightning from heaven and the sceptre from tyrants. (*Eripuit coelo fulmen sceptrumque tyrannis.*)

> ANNE MARIE JACQUES TURGOT, inscription on Houdon's bust of Franklin

He defeated the Americans with great slaughter.

> Inscription on the tomb of Lord Cornwallis, in Westminster Abbey. The surrender of Cornwallis at Yorktown, October 17, 1781, virtually ended the Revolutionary War.

> America, you fare much better
> Than this old continent of ours
> No basalt rocks your land enfetters
> No ruined towers . . .
>> JOHANN WOLFGANG VON GOETHE, *Poems of Wisdom*

It is immensely difficult to create a country out of states without any community of religion and interests, states which have been peopled by different stocks, and are living on varied soils and under diverse climates. What link is there between a Frenchman of Louisiana, a Spaniard of

Florida, a German of New York, an Englishman of New England, Carolina, Georgia—all considered Americans? . . . How many centuries will
be needed to make these elements homogeneous?

VICOMTE DE CHATEAUBRIAND

The English know very well that the Americans would give their lives in
defense of their national soil, but that they dislike fighting a war away
from their homes. They have not yet reached the point where they can
seriously worry the English. Some day, perhaps, they will be the avengers
of the seas, but that day is still far off. The Americans will become great
slowly, or not at all.

NAPOLEON BONAPARTE, quoted by Fleury de Chaboulon,
Les Cents Jours, 1819

The freedom of the world depends on the health of America.

SIMÓN BOLÍVAR, quoted by Frank, *Nation,* June 19, 1954

In the four quarters of the globe, who reads an American book? or goes
to an American play? or looks at an American picture or statue? What
does the world yet owe to American physicians or surgeons? What new
substances have their chemists discovered? or what old ones have they
analyzed? What new constellations have been discovered by the telescopes
of Americans? What have they done in mathematics? Who drinks out of
American glasses? or eats from American plates? or wears American coats
or gowns? or sleeps in American blankets? Finally, under which of the
old tyrannical governments of Europe is every sixth man a slave, whom
his fellow creatures may buy, and sell, and torture?

SYDNEY SMITH, review of Seybert's *Annals of the United
States, Edinburgh Review,* January, 1820. Irwin Edman
noted, *Perspectives U.S.A.,* April 7, 1954: "Who reads an
American book? is no longer a rhetorical or contemptuous
or even relevant question. The rise of interest in American
studies all over the world is a barometer of the awareness
of American civilization."

Daniel Webster struck me much like a steamengine in trousers.

SYDNEY SMITH

To the United States of America to found at Washington, under the name of the Smithsonian Institution, an establishment for the increase and diffusion of knowledge among men.

> JAMES SMITHSON, bequest. The donor, an English chemist, died in 1829, but the money did not become available to the U.S. until 1835, when Smithson's nephew died without issue. Congress exhibited considerable reluctance to accept the gift, but largely through the efforts of John Quincy Adams it arrived on these shores in 1838 and was promptly invested in Arkansas State Bonds, which proved worthless. Congress made up the loss, however, and appropriated $500,000; the Institution was founded in 1846.

I know no country in which there is so little independence of mind and freedom of discussion as in America.

ALEXIS DE TOCQUEVILLE, 1831

If movement and the quick succession of sensations and ideas constitute life, here one lives a hundred fold more than elsewhere; all is here circulation, motion, and boiling agitation. Experiment follows experiment; enterprise succeeds to enterprise. Riches and poverty follow on each other's traces, and each in turn occupies the place of the other. . . . Fortunes last for a season: reputations, during the twinkling of an eye. An irresistible current sweeps away everything, grinds everything to powder, and deposits it again under new forms. Men change their houses, their climate, their trade, their condition, their party, their sect; the States change their laws, their officers, their constitutions. The soil itself, or at least the houses, partake of the universal instability. The existence of social order, in the bosom of this whirlpool seems a miracle, an inexplicable anomaly. One is tempted to think, that such a society, formed of heterogeneous elements, brought together by chance, and following each its own orbit according to the impulse of its own caprice or interest,—one would think, that after rising for one moment to the heavens, like a water-spout, such a society would inevitably fall flat in ruins the next; such is not, however, its destiny.

MICHEL CHEVALIER, *Society, Manners and Politics,* 1834

The great advantage of the Americans consists in their being able to commit faults which they may afterwards repair.

ALEXIS DE TOCQUEVILLE, *Democracy in America,* 1835

Sometimes the progress of man is so rapid that the desert reappears behind him. The woods stoop to give him a passage, and spring up again when he is past. It is not uncommon, in crossing the new states of the West, to meet with deserted dwellings in the midst of the wilds; the traveller frequently discovers the vestiges of a log house in the most solitary retreat, which bear witness to the power, and no less to the inconstancy, of man. . . .

I remember that in crossing one of the woodland districts that still cover the state . . . I reached the shores of a lake which was embosomed in forests coeval with the world. . . .

I was far from supposing that this spot had ever been inhabited, so completely did Nature seem to be left to herself; but when I reached the center of the isle, I thought that I discovered some traces of man. I then proceeded to examine the surrounding objects with care, and I soon perceived that a European had undoubtedly been led to seek a refuge in this place. . . . The logs which he had hastily hewn . . . had sprouted afresh; the very props were intertwined with living verdure. . . . I stood for some time in silent admiration for the resources of Nature and the littleness of Man; and when I was obliged to leave that enchanting solitude, I exclaimed with sadness, "Are ruins, then, already here?"

> ALEXIS DE TOCQUEVILLE, *Ibid.* John Gunther comments
> that "the history of the West has been in large part a race
> between man and his own ruins."

The time will . . . come when one hundred and fifty million men will be living in North America, equal in condition, all belonging to one family, owing their origin to the same cause, and, preserving the same civilization, the same language, the same religion, the same habits, the same manners, the same opinions, propagated under the same forms. The rest is uncertain, but this is certain; and it is a fact new to the world, a fact that the imagination strives in vain to grasp.

ALEXIS DE TOCQUEVILLE, *Ibid.*

There are at the present time two great nations in the world, which started from different points, but seem to tend toward the same end. I allude to the Russians and the Americans. Both of them have grown up unnoticed; and while the attention of mankind was directed elsewhere, they have suddenly placed themselves in the front rank among the nations, and the world learned their existence and their greatness at almost the same time.

All other nations seem to have nearly reached their natural limits, and they have only to maintain their power; but these are still in the act of growth. All the others have stopped, or continue to advance with extreme difficulty; these alone are proceeding with ease and celerity along a path to which no limit can be perceived. The American struggles against the obstacles that nature opposes to him; the adversaries of the Russian are men. The former combats the wilderness and savage life; the latter, civilization with all its arms. The conquests of the American are thus gained by the plowshare; those of the Russian by the sword. The Anglo-American relies upon personal interest to accomplish his ends and gives free scope to the unguided strength and common sense of the people; the Russian centers all the authority of society in a single arm. The principal instrument of the former is freedom; of the latter, servitude. Their starting-point is different and their courses are not the same; yet each of them seems marked out by the will of Heaven to sway the destinies of half the globe.

ALEXIS DE TOCQUEVILLE, *Ibid.*

The great advantage of the Americans is that they have arrived at a state of democracy without having to endure a democratic revolution; and that they are born equal, instead of becoming so.

ALEXIS DE TOCQUEVILLE, *Ibid.*

It is by the enjoyment of a dangerous freedom that the Americans learn the art of rendering the danger of freedom less formidable.

ALEXIS DE TOCQUEVILLE, *Ibid.*

Connecticut, the little yellow spot [on the map] that makes the clock-peddler, the schoolmaster, and the senator. The first, gives you time; the second, tells you what to do with it; and the third makes your law and your civilization.

ALEXIS DE TOCQUEVILLE, address at Fourth of July Celebration in Paris, 1835

While the republics of North America are new, the ideas of the people are old. While these republics were colonies, they contained an old people, living under old institutions, in a new country. Now they are a mixed people, infant as a nation, with a constant accession of minds from old countries, living in a new country, under institutions newly combined out of old elements. It is a case so singular, that the old world may well have patience for some time, to see what will arise. . . . The Americans have no national character as yet.

HARRIET MARTINEAU, *Society in America,* 1836

In America, the eager pursuit of wealth does not necessarily indicate a love of wealth for its own sake.

HARRIET MARTINEAU, Ibid.

Mr. Calhoun, the cast-iron man, looks as if he had never been born and could not be extinguished.

HARRIET MARTINEAU, A Retrospect of Western Travel, 1838

It is remarkable how very debased the language has become in a short period in America.

FREDERICK MARRYAT, A Diary in America, 1839

But what words shall describe the Mississippi, great father of waters, who (praise be to Heaven) has no young children like him! An enormous ditch, sometimes two or three miles wide, running liquid mud, six miles an hour; its strong and frothy current choked and obstructed everywhere by huge logs and whole forest trees . . . now rolling past like monstrous bodies, their tangled roots showing like matted hair . . . or wounded snakes. The banks low, the trees dwarfish, the marshes swarming with frogs, the wretched cabins few and far apart, their inmates hollow-cheeked and pale, mosquitoes penetrating into every crack and crevice of the boat, mud and slime on everything. . . .

For two days we toiled up this foul stream.

CHARLES DICKENS, American Notes, 1842

It would be impossible to get on anywhere in America, without a rocking-chair.

CHARLES DICKENS, Ibid.

How beautiful to think of lean tough Yankee settlers, tough as gutta-percha, with most *occult* unsubduable fire in their belly, steering over the Western Mountains to annihilate the jungle, and bring bacon and corn out of it for the Posterity of Adam.—There is no *Myth* of Athene or Herakles equal to this *fact*.

THOMAS CARLYLE, letter to Emerson, 1849

Either some Caesar or Napoleon will seize the reins of government with a strong hand, or your republic will be as fearfully plundered and laid waste by barbarians in the Twentieth Century as the Roman Empire was in the Fifth; with this difference, that the Huns and Vandals who ravaged the Roman Empire came from without, and that your Huns and

Vandals will have been engendered within your own country by your own institutions.

> Thomas Babington Macaulay, *letter to H. S. Randall,*
> May 23, 1857

I do not like the Americans of the lower orders. I am not comfortable among them. They tread on my corns and offend me. They make my daily life unpleasant. But I do respect them. I acknowledge their intelligence and personal dignity. I know that they are men and women worthy to be so called.

> Anthony Trollope, *North America,* 1862

I saw but one drunken man through all New England, and he was very respectable.

> Anthony Trollope, *Ibid.*

There is a grave misapprehension, both in the ranks of Her Majesty's Government and of Her Majesty's Opposition, as to what constitutes the true meaning of the American democracy. The American democracy is not made up of the scum of the great industrial cities of the United States, nor of an exhausted middle class that speculates in stocks and calls that progress. The American democracy is made up of something far more stable, that may ultimately decide the fate of the two Americas and of "Europe."

> Benjamin Disraeli, 1863

> That great people who may bless
> Or curse mankind: they have the might.

> George Meredith, 1867

Our society distributes itself into Barbarians, Philistines, and Populace; and America is just ourselves, with the Barbarians quite left out, and the Populace nearly.

> Matthew Arnold, *Culture and Anarchy,* 1869

[The American Revolution] was a vindication of liberties inherited and possessed. It was a conservative revolution.

> William Ewart Gladstone, "Kin Beyond the Sea," *North American Review,* September-October, 1878

The most wonderful work ever struck off at a given time by the brain and purpose of man.

> WILLIAM EWART GLADSTONE, of the U.S. Constitution

The Republican form of Government is the highest form of government; but because of this it requires the highest type of human nature—a type nowhere at present existing.

> HERBERT SPENCER, *The Americans*

A month [in Pittsburgh] would fortify anyone in committing suicide.

> HERBERT SPENCER, *Ibid.*

America is one long expectoration.

> OSCAR WILDE, newspaper interview, during his visit to America, 1882

There is no country in the world where machinery is so lovely as in America. I have always wished to believe that the line of strength and the line of beauty are one. That wish was realized when I contemplated American machinery. It was not until I had seen the waterworks at Chicago that I realized the wonders of machinery; the rise and fall of the steel rods, the symmetrical motion of great wheels is the most beautifully rhythmic thing I have ever seen.

> OSCAR WILDE, "Impressions of America," a lecture, September, 1883

The capital defect of life in America: namely, that compared with life in England it is so uninteresting, so without savour and without depth.

> MATTHEW ARNOLD, letter, written in 1886 during his second visit to America

In truth everything is against destruction in America, and against the sense of elevation to be gained through admiring and respecting it.

> MATTHEW ARNOLD, *Civilization in the United States,* 1888

The West may be called the most distinctly American part of America, because the points in which it differs from the East are the points in which America as a whole differs from Europe.

> JAMES BRYCE, *The American Commonwealth,* 1888

We have really everything in common with America nowadays, except, of course, language.

OSCAR WILDE, The Canterville Ghost, 1888

I met a very large and interesting family (in Philadelphia) named Scrapple, and I discovered a rather delicious native food they call biddle.

EDWARD VII

In America an hour is forty minutes.

German proverb

I do not think America is a good place in which to be a genius. A genius can never expect to have a good time anywhere, but America is about the last place in which life will be endurable at all for an inspired writer.

SAMUEL BUTLER, Note-Books: "Cash and Credit"

When good Americans die they go to Paris; when bad Americans die they go to America.

OSCAR WILDE, A Woman of No Importance, 1893

The youth of America is their oldest tradition. It has been going on now for three hundred years.

OSCAR WILDE, Ibid.

In America, the President reigns for four years, and journalism governs forever and ever.

OSCAR WILDE

The crude commercialism of America, its indifference to the poetical side of things, are entirely due to the country's having adopted as its national hero a man who, according to his own confession, was unable to tell a lie.

OSCAR WILDE

Every American bride is taken to Niagara Falls, and the sight of this stupendous water-fall must be one of the earliest, if not the keenest, disappointments in American married life.

OSCAR WILDE

America really was discovered by a dozen people before Columbus, but it always was successfully hushed up.

OSCAR WILDE

Enslaved, illogical, elate,
　　He greets the embarrassed gods, nor fears
To shake the iron hand of fate
　　Or match with destiny for beers.

RUDYARD KIPLING, "An American," 1894

[Button Punch is] compounded of the shavings of cherubs' wings, the glory of a tropical dawn, the red clouds of sunset, and fragments of lost epics by dead masters.

RUDYARD KIPLING, while visiting San Francisco. "Button
Punch" of course is a drink.

San Francisco is a mad city inhabited by perfectly insane people whose women are of a remarkable beauty.

RUDYARD KIPLING

Why does the Westerner spit? It can't amuse him, and it doesn't interest his neighbor.

RUDYARD KIPLING

I have struck a city—a real city—and they call it Chicago. . . . This place is the first American city I have encountered.

RUDYARD KIPLING

Remember that the men who stocked California in the 50's were physically, and as far as regards certain tough virtues, the pick of the earth. . . . It needs no little golden badge . . . to make the native son of the Golden West. Him I love because he is devoid of fear, carries himself like a man, and has a heart as big as his boots.

RUDYARD KIPLING

It is not good to be a Negro in the land of the free and the home of the brave.

RUDYARD KIPLING

Some of us regretted that he was an American, and therefore necessarily about fifty years out of date in his economics and sociology from the point of view of an older country; but only an American could have seen in a single lifetime the growth of the whole tragedy of civilization from the primitive forest clearing.

GEORGE BERNARD SHAW, of Henry George, c. 1895

The two things in America which seem to me most extraordinary are Niagara Falls and President Roosevelt.

JOHN MORLEY, 1904

The 100 per cent American is 99 per cent an idiot.

GEORGE BERNARD SHAW

The economic life means to the American a realizing of efforts which are in themselves precious. It is not the means to an end, but is its own end. . . . The merchant in Europe does not feel himself to be a free creator like the artist or scholar. . . . The American merchant works for money in exactly the sense that a great painter works for money; the high price which is paid for his picture is a very welcome indication of the general appreciation of his art.

HUGO MÜNSTERBERG, *The Americans,* 1904

The greatest liberty that man has taken with Nature.

JAMES BRYCE, of the Panama Canal

America is God's crucible, the Great Melting Pot, where all the races of Europe are reforming. Here you stand, goodfolk, think I, when I see them at Ellis Island, here you stand in your fifty groups with your fifty languages and histories and your fifty blood-hatreds and rivalries. But you won't long be like that, brothers, for these are the fires of God you've come to—these are the fires of God. A fig for your feuds and vendettas. Germans and Frenchmen, Irishmen and Englishmen, Jews and Russians, into the crucible with you all. God is making the American.

ISRAEL ZANGWILL, *The Melting Pot,* 1908

What you want [in Washington] is to have a city which every one who comes from Maine, Texas, Florida, Arkansas, or Oregon can admire as being finer and more beautiful than he had ever dreamed of before; something which makes him even more proud to be an American.

JAMES BRYCE, "The Nation's Capital," *National Geographic,* 1913

The American mind has long been honeycombed with moral impulse; it is very much what the German mind was up to the middle of the Nineteenth Century.

W. L. GEORGE, *The Intelligence of Woman,* 1916

There is no peace in Chicago. It is a city of terror and light, untamed.

W. L. GEORGE

The true America is the Middle West, and Columbus discovered nothing at all except another Europe.

W. L. GEORGE

New York is all the cities.

W. L. GEORGE

This war, like the next war, is a war to end war.

Attributed to DAVID LLOYD GEORGE, of World War I

The good Lord had only ten! (*Le bon Dieu n'avait que dix!*)

GEORGES CLEMENCEAU, on hearing that President Wilson had Fourteen Points

Consider the American continent! How simple it is! How broad! How large! How grand in design! A strip of coast, a range of mountains, a plain, a second range, a second strip of coast! That is all. Contrast the complexity of Europe, its lack of symmetry, its variety, irregularity, disorder and caprice! The geography of the two continents already foreshadows the differences in their civilizations.

G. LOWES DICKINSON, *A Modern Symposium*

The United States of America—the greatest potential force, material, moral, and spiritual, in the world.

G. LOWES DICKINSON, *The Choice Before Us*

Every time Europe looks across the Atlantic to see the American eagle, it observes only the rear end of an ostrich.

H. G. WELLS

[America is] the great problem child of humanity.

H. G. WELLS

James's critical genius comes out most tellingly in his mastery over, his baffling escape from, Ideas; a mastery and an escape which are perhaps the last test of a superior intelligence. He had a mind so fine that no idea could violate it.

T. S. ELIOT, *On Henry James*, 1918

James in his novels is like the best French critics in maintaining a point of view, a viewpoint untouched by the parasite idea. He is the most intelligent man of his generation.

T. S. ELIOT, *Ibid.*

You are right in your impression that a number of persons are urging me to come to the United States. But why on earth do you call them my friends?

GEORGE BERNARD SHAW, letter to Oswald Garrison Villard, August 4, 1921

Baseball has the great advantage over cricket of being sooner ended.

GEORGE BERNARD SHAW

The haughty American nation . . . makes the Negro clean its boots and then proves the . . . inferiority of the Negro by the fact that he is a bootblack.

GEORGE BERNARD SHAW

In America law and custom alike are based upon the dreams of spinsters.

BERTRAND RUSSELL

Where *is* this new bird called the true American? Show us the homunculus of the new era. Go on, show us him. Because all that is visible to the naked European eye, in America, is a sort of recreant European. We want to see this missing link of the next era.

D. H. LAWRENCE, *Studies in Classic American Literature*

All this Americanizing and mechanizing has been for the purpose of overthrowing the past. And now look at America, tangled in her own barbed wire, and mastered by her own machines. Absolutely got down by her own barbed wire of shalt-nots, and shut up fast in her own "productive" machines like millions of squirrels running in millions of cages. It is just a farce.

Now is your chance, Europe. Now let Hell loose and get your own back, and paddle your own canoe on a new sea, while clever America lies on her muck-heaps of gold, strangled in her own barbed wire of shalt-not ideals and shalt-not moralisms. While she goes out to work like millions of squirrels in millions of cages. Production!

Let Hell loose, and get your own back, Europe!

D. H. LAWRENCE, *Ibid.*

L'Amérique est pourrie avant d'être mûre. (America is rotten without ever having been ripe.)

> ANON., quoted by D. H. Lawrence, *Ibid.*

This awful Whitman. This post mortem poet. This poet with the private soul leaking out of him all the time. All his privacy leaking out in a sort of dribble, oozing into the universe.

> D. H. LAWRENCE, *Ibid.*

Whitman like a strange, modern, American Moses. Fearfully mistaken. And yet the great leader. . . . Ahead of all poets, pioneering into the wilderness of unopened life.

> D. H. LAWRENCE, *Ibid.*

> Oh, America, the sun sets in you.
> Are you the grave of our day?
> > D. H. LAWRENCE, "The Evening Land"

The great factor of the future is that vast, unthinking, unfeeling American people. . . . It is they who, with closed eyes, will impose their decision upon the whole world.

> WALTER RATHENAU, in conversation with André Gide

[American practicality] is that indomitable force, which knows and recognizes no obstacle, which by its businesslike perseverance washes away all and every impediment, which simply must go through with a job begun even if it is of minor importance, and without which any serious constructive work is impossible.

> JOSEPH STALIN, in 1924, quoted by Towster, *Political Power in the U.S.S.R.*

American women expect to find in their husbands a perfection that English women only hope to find in their butlers.

> W. SOMERSET MAUGHAM

Thought is barred in this city of Dreadful Joy and conversation is unknown.

> ALDOUS HUXLEY, of Los Angeles in 1926

The pilgrims leave no impression of personality on the mind. They were not "remarkable." Not one of them had compelling personal genius, or marked talent for the work in hand. They were plain men of moderate abilities, who, giving up all things, went to live in the wilds, at unknown cost to themselves, in order to preserve to their children a life in the soul.

> JOHN MASEFIELD, *Chronicles of the Pilgrims*

I like the Americans because they are healthy and optimistic.

> FRANZ KAFKA

For America, hitherto lying apart and self-contained, rather a region than a State, the parallelism of President and Congress which she derived from a theory of Montesquieu has, with her entry into world politics, become untenable, and must in times of real danger make way for formless powers such as those with which Mexico and South America have long been familiar.

> OSWALD SPENGLER, *The Decline of the West*, II, 1928

Democracy is talking itself to death. The people do not know what they want; they do not know what is the best for them. There is too much foolishness, too much lost motion. I have stopped the talk and the nonsense. I am a man of action. Democracy is beautiful in theory; in practice it is a fallacy. You in America will see that some day.

> BENITO MUSSOLINI, to Edwin L. James of the *New York Times*, 1928

Most Americans are born drunk . . . They have a sort of permanent intoxication from within, a sort of invisible champagne. . . . Americans do not need to drink to inspire them to do anything.

> G. K. CHESTERTON, *New York Times*, June 28, 1931

What a glorious garden of wonders the lights of Broadway would be to anyone lucky enough to be unable to read.

> G. K. CHESTERTON

To rouse their [the Americans'] eager interest, their distinguished consideration and their undying devotion, all that is necessary is to hold them up to the ridicule of the rest of the universe. Dickens won them to him forever by merciless projections of typical Americans as windbags, swindlers and assassins.

> GEORGE BERNARD SHAW, comment on award of Nobel Prize to Sinclair Lewis, 1931

When you came to examine the American Constitution, you found that it was not really a constitution, but a Charter of Anarchism. It was not an instrument of government: it was a guarantee to the whole American nation that it never should be governed at all. And that is exactly what the Americans wanted.

GEORGE BERNARD SHAW, address in New York, 1933

An American has no sense of privacy. He does not know what it means. There is no such thing in the country.

GEORGE BERNARD SHAW, *Ibid.*

THE AMERICANS ARE A QUEER PEOPLE: THEY CAN'T REST.

They have more time, more leisure, shorter hours, more holidays and more vacations than any other people in the world. But they can't rest. They rush up and down across their continent as tourists; they move about in great herds to conventions, they invade the wilderness, they flood the mountains, they keep the hotels full. But they can't rest. The scenery rushes past them. They learn it, but they don't see it. Battles and monuments are announced to them in a rubber neck bus. They hear them, but they don't get them. They never stop moving; they rush up and down as Shriners, Masons, Old Graduates, Bankers—they are a new thing each day, always rushing to a reunion or something.

So they go on rushing till the Undertaker gathers them in to a last Convention.

THE AMERICANS ARE A QUEER PEOPLE: THEY CAN'T READ.

They have more schools, and better schools, and spend more money on schools and colleges than all of Europe. But they can't read. They print more books in one year than the French print in ten. But they can't read. They cover their country with 100,000 tons of Sunday newspapers every week. But they don't read them. They're too busy. They use them for fires and to make more paper with. They buy eagerly thousands of new novels at two dollars each. But they only read page one. Their streets are full of huge signs. They won't look at them. Their street cars are filled with advertising; they turn their eyes away. Transparent colors, cartwheels and mechanical flares whirl and flicker in the crowded streets at night. No one sees them. Tons of circulars pour through the mails, through the houses and down the garbage chutes. The last American who sat down to read died in about the days of Henry Clay.

THE AMERICANS ARE A QUEER PEOPLE: THEY CAN'T DRINK.

All of the American nation is haunted. They have a fierce wish to be

sober: and they can't. They pass fierce laws against themselves, shut themselves up, chase themselves, shoot themselves: and they can't stay sober
and they can't drink. They have a furious idea that if they can ever get
sober, they can do big things. But they can't hold it. They got this mentality straight out of home life in Ohio, copied from the wild spree and
the furious repentance of the pioneer farmer. The nation keeps it yet. It
lives among red specters, rum devils, broken bottles, weeping children,
penitentiary cells, bar rooms and broken oaths. The last man who sat
down and drank a quiet glass of beer was found dead—dead for twenty
years—in Milwaukee.

THE AMERICANS ARE A QUEER PEOPLE: THEY CAN'T PLAY.

Americans rush to work as soon as they get up. They want their work
as soon as they wake. It is a stimulant: the only one they're not afraid of.
They used to open their offices at 10 o'clock: then at 9: then at 8: then
at 7. Now they never shut them. Every business in America is turning into
an open-all-day-and-night business. They eat all night, dance all night,
build buildings all night, make a noise all night. They can't play. They
try to, but they can't. They turn football into a fight: baseball into a lawsuit and yachting into machinery. They can't play. The little children
can't play: they use mechanical toys instead: toy cranes hoisting toys'
loads: toy machinery spreading a toy industrial depression of infantile
dullness. The grown-up people can't play: they use a mechanical gym-
nasium and a clockwork horse. They can't swim: they use a float; they
can't run: they use a car. They can't laugh: they hire a comedian and
watch him laugh.

THE AMERICANS ARE A QUEER PEOPLE: THEY DON'T GIVE A DAMN.

All the world criticizes them and they don't give a damn. All the world
writes squibs like this about them and they don't give a damn. Foreign
visitors come and write them up: they don't give a damn. Lecturers
lecture at them: they don't care. They are told they have no art, no
literature, and no soul. They never budge. Moralists cry over them, crim-
inologists dissect them, writers shoot epigrams at them, prophets foretell
the end of them, and they never move. Seventeen brilliant books analyze
them every month: they don't read them. The Europeans threaten to
unite against them: they don't mind. Equatorial Africa is dead sour on
them: they don't even know it. The Chinese look on them as full of oriental cunning; the English accuse them of British stupidity; the Scotch
call them close-fisted; the Italians say they are liars; the French think
their morals loose, and the Bolsheviks accuse them of Communism.

But that's all right. The Americans don't give a damn: don't need to: never did need to. That is their salvation.

STEPHEN LEACOCK, *A Neighbor Looks at America*

America is younger than Russia. I have always maintained, though in fear of exaggeration, that it is a primitive people camouflaged behind the latest inventions.

JOSÉ ORTEGA Y GASSET, *The Revolt of the Masses*

When we want to freshen our speech, we borrow from American—*poppycock, rambunctious, flip-flop, booster, good mixer.* All the expressive, ugly, vigorous slang which creeps into use among us, first in talk, later in writing, comes from across the Atlantic.

VIRGINIA WOOLF

The facts that we ought to realize, and that we ignore when we talk loftily about Americanisms, are that America is making a formidable contribution to the development of our language, and that all our attempts to reject that contribution will in the long run be vain.

EDWARD SHANKS

The psychological error lay in our conception of the American as a self-important boaster, a shoddy manufacturer of shoddy goods and an unscrupulous over-reacher in business, whose word could not be trusted. Such Americans there certainly were, but there is the other type of American, who is conspicuously efficient in all industrial and technical undertakings, the American who builds the highest houses, produces most motor-cars, attains record economic output, who built the Panama Canal and whose spirit of enterprise knows no bounds.

EWALD HERMANN AUGUST BANSE, *Germany Prepares for War,* 1934

The greatest American superstition is belief in facts.

COUNT HERMANN KEYSERLING

When you become used to never being alone, you may consider yourself Americanized.

ANDRÉ MAUROIS

I visited Chicago. It must be a very wicked city. Imagine, a friend of mine who lives there has two locks on his door!

E. M. FORSTER, in conversation, c. 1935

[Hitler] states that he could not, for anything in the world, live in a country like the U.S.A., whose conceptions of life are inspired by the most grasping commercialism and which does not love any of the loftiest expressions of the human spirit such as music.

> Count Ciano, *Diplomatic Papers*

After all, the 20th century is only the 19th speaking with a slightly American accent.

> Philip Guedalla

The true history of the United States is the history of transportation . . . in which the names of railroad presidents are more significant than those of Presidents of the United States.

> Philip Guedalla, *The Hundred Years*

Babylon piled on Imperial Rome.

> J. B. Priestley, of New York City

The American people have a genius for splendid and unselfish action, and into the hands of America God has placed the destinies of afflicted humanity.

> Pope Pius XII (Eugenio Pacelli), *Wisdom—Not Weapons of War*

That long [Canadian] frontier from the Atlantic to the Pacific Oceans, guarded only by neighborly respect and honorable obligations, is an example to every country and a pattern for the future of the world.

> Winston Churchill, speech in honor of R. B. Bennett, Canada Club, London, April 20, 1939

The British Empire and the United States will have to be somewhat mixed up together in some of their affairs for mutual and general advantage. For my own part, looking out upon the future, I do not view the process with any misgivings. I could not stop it if I wished; no one can stop it. Like the Mississippi, it just keeps rolling along. Let it roll. Let it roll on full flood, inexorable, irresistible, benignant, to broader lands and better days.

> Winston Churchill, tribute to the Royal Air Force, House of Commons, August 20, 1940

In ten most eventful years, the American political system has changed comparatively little and some of its most dramatic changes have been forced on it from the outside. It was Herr Hitler who both elected Mr. Roosevelt for a third term and nominated Mr. Wendell Willkie in 1940. But this is not the only proof of elasticity that the American system has given. We have only to compare the atmosphere of the United States to-day with the atmosphere of 1932 or 1922 to see what profound changes are possible even under an apparently rigid constitutional system and conservative national tradition. The scope of State and Federal government has been vastly enlarged. The relationship between State and Union has been transformed into an effective partnership. The dangerous strain imposed by the political activities of the Supreme Court has been relieved. And the United States has been provided, in its greatest crisis since 1861, with a chief who may have all the faults his critics impute to him, and yet has that quality which his most bitter enemies in Berlin and Tokio, if not in Chicago, freely credit to him, that power of foresight, of courage, of resolution, by whose presence or absence great political systems live or die.

There have been so few changes in the American system because, for all its defects, for all its inelegancies, it represents a unique success, the extension and maintenance of free institutions over a continental area and the creation at the same time of a national unity that has stood the severest tests. In 1789, the Constitution went into effect; it was designed, so the preamble states, to form "a more perfect union" and to "promote the general welfare." It has done both. The Roman lawyer remembered that *de minimis non curat praetor*. The statesman will not be too ready to condemn or mutilate, in deference to any theory, one of the great living political systems of the world. He will be to its virtues very kind and to its faults a little blind. A political analyst, like myself, has no business to be blind to the faults; but that will matter little as long as the basic truth is remembered, that the American political system has succeeded to a degree that would have surprised the most optimistic of those revolutionary leaders who made the dangerous and novel experiment in 1776 of bringing forth "a nation conceived in liberty and dedicated to the proposition that all men are created equal."

> DENIS BROGAN, *Government of the People,* "Preface to New
> (American) Edition," February 12, 1943

Recent events have made it probable that this epoch [of unquestioning acceptance of political theory] of American history is drawing to a close. The United States have now developed all the typical phenomena of European life. There is an hereditary leisured class, with much the same habits, though on an ampler scale, of a European aristocracy; there is a strong middle class whose access to favoured positions is becoming increasingly stereotyped; there is the characteristic proletariat of our great cities; and there is the division between urban and rural interests growing clearly before our eyes. The foreign observer can see without difficulty how the American Constitution could work without undue conflict in an epoch of remarkable growth. His problem is to understand whether the equilibrium it protects can be harmonized with the needs of an era in which, as in our own, the claims of property to a special position in the State are seriously challenged.

> HAROLD LASKI, *Government of the People* (Brogan), "Foreword," 1943

"Howdy, Stranger" is not a hostile greeting, and it was invented in America.

> DENIS BROGAN, *The American Character,* 1944

Any well-established village in New England or the northern Middle West could afford a town drunkard, a town atheist, and a few Democrats.

> DENIS BROGAN, *Ibid.*

A people that has licked a more formidable enemy than Germany or Japan, primitive North America . . . a country whose national motto has been "root, hog, or die."

> DENIS BROGAN, *Ibid.*

Man does not live by bread alone, even pre-sliced bread.

> DENIS BROGAN, *Ibid.*

In Franklin Roosevelt there died the greatest American friend we have ever known—and the greatest champion of freedom who has ever brought help and comfort from the new world to the old.

> WINSTON CHURCHILL, tribute to President Roosevelt, House of Commons, April 17, 1945

America is everywhere. For an isolationist nation it is remarkable how she gets about.

> EDWARD CRANKSHAW, *Russia and the Russians,* 1948

Not long ago I read several articles on the life of American workers. Gloomy pictures of capitalist realities appear before one's eyes. Unemployment is increasing constantly in the U.S.A. Wages are being cut and prices are rising and the standard of living of the toilers is deteriorating. It is a calamity if a worker becomes ill. He loses all possibility of receiving any means of existence, for there is no social insurance in the United States.

ANON., *Bloknot Agitatora,* a Soviet magazine, Jan., 1949

All that we Russians want is to drink, love, dance and live. The only country we fear is America, but we will fight you if necessary with our bare hands.

A young Russian lieutenant, after World War II

Les Américains en Amérique! (Americans in America!)

French Communist slogan, after World War II

The people of Hiroshima ask nothing of the world except that we be allowed to offer ourselves as an exhibit for peace. We ask only that enough peoples know what happened here and how it happened and why it happened, and that they work hard to see that it never happens again anywhere.

MAYOR HOMAI of Hiroshima, "Message to the American People," 1949. The message was accompanied by greetings from 106,000 citizens of Hiroshima.

The real end of the American year is not the thirty-first of December but the old festival of Labor Day. It is the day when the summer is put away . . . the lock turned for the last time on your private world of sun and sand and picnics and the pride of growing children. Labor Day brings you back to the world of schools and offices, to sniffling colds and insurance policies and taxes and radio commentators, to dark nights and the dark horizon of politics.

ALISTAIR COOKE, *One Man's America,* 1952

In Britain, one of the minor duties of good citizenship is not to disturb the private life of other citizens. In this country, it's the other way around —not to disturb other citizens who are enjoying their private life in public. . . . There are limits. Just the same, the decision of a Washington court of appeal not to let advertisers broadcast in public buses only shows how far you can go in America without being stopped.

ALISTAIR COOKE, *Ibid.*

For the newcomer there will be little concern about how he lived or what he was used to, or the kind of people he moved among. If he wants the same society in America he must buy his way into it. Not what you seem to be but what you prove you can do: that is still, for the stranger, the persistent pioneer requirement.

> ALISTAIR COOKE, *Ibid.*, "Letter to an Intending Immigrant"

You Americans are wrong in trying to force your methods on our country. You believe in theology, in sorcery, in witchcraft. For you, communism is a sin, and the Communists are witches to be burned. The fact is they are very simple, ordinary people. For fifteen years the Communists have pulled to their ranks the finest young people of France. France is such an old country, so much is rotten in it, and the Communist argument is so simple—to make an omelet, they say, you must smash eggs. So year after year the generous, the noble, the bold, the brilliant youth of a full generation has been drawn to it and been led by it to the final abomination which is communism. For the error of original decision in joining the Communists is so slight and the final consequences are so terrible. They, the young men of communism, are the truest victims, and the job is not to persecute them but to liberate them.

> PIERRE BERTAUX, quoted by White, *Fire in the Ashes,* 1953

America has saved the world.

> WINSTON CHURCHILL, to Adlai Stevenson, 1953

How the Great Democracies Triumphed, and so were able to Resume the Follies which had so nearly Cost Them their Life.

> WINSTON CHURCHILL, *Triumph and Tragedy,* 1953

American Christianity is too often institutional rather than personal . . . congealed into a block rather than grounded in individual conviction.

American Christians appear rather self-assured about their own efficiency so that God sometimes seems to be about as much dependent on them as they on God.

To some European Christians, the American churches occasionally appear to have two altars, one for the dollar and another for God.

American Christianity often looks confused, lacking a truly creedal structure, and seeming to have no very clear conception of the place and role of Jesus as Savior and Redeemer.

American Christianity looks very much divided even within the several official denominations, as among Methodists, Baptists and Lutherans, for example. Such divisions often appear to be determined more by sentiment than motivated by sound theological reasoning. . . .

The outlook of American Christianity often looks to us rather earth-bound, expecting the fulfillment of God's Kingdom here on earth—one might even say . . . in the U. S. A. . . .

Perhaps we are like the son who said Yes, but did not do what he had promised, while the Americans are like the other son who said No, but did go on to do the Father's will. Is it perhaps that the Americans are weak in thinking things out, but quick and firm to act, while we are sound in our reasoning, but weak to carry through?

> EIVIND BERGGRAV, Primate of Norway (Retired), *Christian Century*, September, 1953

When men are insecure, they are afraid. And it is neither God nor the physical universe the American fears, since he sees himself as the associate of the one and the master of the other. What he fears is his fellow man.

> FRANCIS L. K. HSU, *Americans and Chinese*, 1953

It is no exaggeration to say that the average American high school graduate knows very little about the rest of the world, especially Asia. Further, knowledgeable or not, his attitude toward other peoples is at best one of condescension and at worst one of contempt.

> FRANCIS L. K. HSU, *Ibid.*

In China the term "love," as it is used by Americans, has never been respectable. Up to modern times the term was scarcely used in Chinese literature. This is not to say that Chinese culture denied or glossed over the existence of sexual attraction, quite the contrary, but the American way of love would seem to the Chinese to be almost indistinct from what they term licentiousness.

> FRANCIS L. K. HSU, *Ibid.*

With the exception of a small group of Texans, Americans are particularly sensitive to the historical quality in the towns they visit. "If these walls had tongues," said my taxi driver in Hollywood as we passed a big hotel, "they could tell a story. That building must be twenty-five years old."

> STEPHEN POTTER, "One-Upmanship on the Thames," *New York Times Magazine*, May 17, 1953

I have observed . . . that in his attitude toward food the American reveals significant aspects of his character. The endemic waste, the exclusive reliance upon the grocer and the butcher for all his culinary needs, the obliviousness to what grows freely in the environment—do not these reflect his indifference to frugality as a virtue, and his subservience to what I have called the quantitative fallacy? . . . In a land that idolizes the Rockefellers and the Fords, the growing of a carrot and a cabbage seems a trifling occupation—unless, perhaps, they can be exhibited as the *biggest* carrot and the *biggest* cabbage ever grown anywhere.

There is yet no evidence that the experience of the war years has had the salutary effect for which some of us had hoped. The American still wastes and continues to trample underfoot whatever does not measure up to his gigantic illusions. He does not yet perceive the consequences of having used with reckless imprudence the precious yield of the good earth; he does not realize that the quantitative analysis of value is fundamentally deceptive; nor does he yet see with any clarity that, in his uncritical devotion to big things, he has neglected the trifles which, in their totality, constitute a principal ingredient in human happiness.

> Angelo Pelligrini, "The Unprejudiced Palate," *New York Times Book Review,* June 7, 1953

Perhaps the essence of the American outlook lies in the insistence that a target that has been realistically established can and must be achieved. The difficulties that inevitably occur are regarded not as inevitable strokes of fate which make delay inevitable but simply as difficulties which will probably be overcome with energy and persistence. This attitude is an infectious one.

> Report of British Institute of Management on American construction of a refinery in Britain, 1954

Senator McCarthy this afternoon achieved what General Burgoyne and General Cornwallis never achieved—the surrender of the American Army.

> The London *Times,* February 26, 1954. The reference is to the McCarthy-Stevens episode.

Many Americans talk about fishing with the suspicious insistence with which middle-aged Frenchmen with stomach trouble talk about food and middle-aged Italians talk about love.

> Luigi Barzini, Jr., *Americans Are Alone in the World*

Intellectuals want, more than anything else, to be taken seriously, and Communism is the sole party to grant them any importance—if only by putting them in prison. It is the United States which takes intellectuals the least seriously—even while paying them fortunes.

RAYMOND ARON, *Le Figaro,* Paris, February, 1954

To the Europeans an American recession, even a small one, is no longer an economic process. It has become a moral crime. Few seem to remember that the American economy, for all its mistakes, has recently saved the world from ruin. The Russians remember, with regret.

BRUCE HUTCHINSON, *Canada's Lonely Neighbour,* 1954

It is worth saying once again that no nation has ever come into the possession of such powers for good or ill, for freedom or tyranny, for friendship or enmity among the peoples of the world, and that no nation in history has used those powers, by and large, with greater vision, restraint, responsibility and courage.

The London *Times,* March, 1954

Nothing could ever squeeze the vast eruptions and gigantic cataclysms, the enormous joys and sorrows of the North American territories into any but the heroic mold. . . . Look up into the sky above America! . . . No man would be a slave, no man would barter his freedom under such a canopy!

OSBERT SITWELL, *The Four Continents,* 1955

BOOK TWO

* * * * * * * * * * * *

POETS AND VERSIFIERS

* *INTRODUCTION* *

What follows should not be judged as a comprehensive collection or even selection of the best American verse. While a great many entire poems are included, there are also a great many "short takes," even single lines on occasion torn pitilessly from their context. No poet should be judged by such samples, but only by his whole life work, which this anthology makes no claim to represent. It is not intended for the scholar or even the assiduous reader of poetry. It *is* intended for Americans who do not ordinarily read verse, but who are willing to become aware of the treasures our American bards have left us, whether in popular song, in light verse or in full-dress poetry.

Our only claim is to have here assembled the lines, the passages and the whole short poems or songs that are remembered, whether precisely or vaguely, by most of us; or which are now in the process of becoming part of what we will remember; or what the editors believe will soon come to be remembered; or what, in some cases, they would like to be remembered. Perhaps half of the total is generally familiar, the other half familiar in varying degrees to different groups of readers.

Though there is much overlapping, still a distinction may be drawn between being part of the literature and part of the language. Only by rather relaxed standards can we call "The Children's Hour" literature; but it occupies a pleasant and probably permanent place in our American language, and most of it is therefore here included. Perhaps fifteen per cent of the verse that follows is of this order: part of our idiom, no longer subject to sophisticated evaluation, any more than are our mothers and fathers. But we have cleared out a great deal of mediocre nineteenth-century verse that most anthologies, decade after decade, piously commemorate. We hope these omissions will cause no reader pain.

Book Two is more nearly patterned after the traditional volume of reference than is either of its fellows. It is not primarily experimental, and lovers of modern verse will note the absence of much that is rare and beautiful. There is little doubt, for example, that Conrad Aiken and Wallace Stevens are finer poets than Edgar Allan Poe, but you will find more Poe here than Stevens or Aiken, though the latter are represented by those passages which have already begun to form part of our heritage. Poe, however, for all his jingly quality, or perhaps because of it, is familiar

542

in excerpts to millions, and is valued for certain qualities that will keep him alive for several generations to come. Perhaps his lines say little, but they are *telling* lines nonetheless.

After a generation or two have passed it may well be that Marianne Moore or E. E. Cummings will have become as much a part of us as is Longfellow; but that time is not yet, and it is not the primary function of this book to anticipate the verdicts of posterity. On the other hand, wherever it is apparent that a contemporary poet has already become part of the common stock, almost of our households, he is represented copiously. This is true, for example, of Robert Frost. It is true to a lesser degree of Emily Dickinson. It would have been true of T. S. Eliot had we been able to persuade ourselves that he was, beyond the circumstance of his birth, an American.

The reader will note that Whitman, naturally a sprawler, occupies more space than any other poet. His case is especially interesting. He is our nearest approach to a national bard. At any rate that was his own conception of his mission and so powerful a propagandist is he that we have come to accept his valuation of himself. The greatness of Whitman is, I think, established beyond cavil, even such eloquent cavil as Santayana's. But he has never been able to win for himself that audience of "powerful uneducated persons" he had in mind. His influence is greater than that of any other American poet, but it is an influence that works largely by indirection, through later writers.

On the other hand, hundreds of thousands of Americans who have never read and perhaps never will read Whitman are unconsciously aware of him, not only through the writers he has affected, but because he is one of the most memorable phrase-makers in the language. He is a poet in the original sense of the word; that is he is a maker, a language-coiner. In these pages we supply a virtual anthology of Whitman, not merely because we admire him, but because you can hardly read any fifty lines of him without coming across a phrase almost as familiar as many from Shakespeare or Pope.

I hear America singing. I celebrate myself. I loaf and invite my soul. I wear my hat as I please indoors or out. I find no sweeter fat than sticks to my bones. I am the man, I suffered, I was there. Do I contradict myself? Very well then I contradict myself. Passage to India. I sound my barbaric yawp over the roofs of the world. A woman waits for me. When I give I give myself. The long brown path before me leading wherever I choose. The never-ending audacity of elected persons. Pioneers! O Pioneers! Out of the cradle endlessly rocking. When lilacs last in the dooryard bloomed. O Captain! My Captain! Who touches this, touches a man. I think I could turn and live with animals. A great city is that which has the greatest men and women.

I have omitted the quotation marks around these lines because those marks have long since ceased to exist in our minds and memories. It is not Whitman's message (at least not yet) that has become a part of us. It is his lingo.

Perhaps I have over-emphasized the traditional pattern of Book Two. Let me redress the balance. The editors take satisfaction in a few items that may hold a certain novelty for a good many readers: the careful selection of Indian verse, some of it very beautiful indeed; the inclusion of William J. Grayson, reminding us that the whole truth is not to be found in *Uncle Tom's Cabin;* Trumbull Stickney's lovely "Mnemosyne," which does not merit oblivion; and others that we leave the reader to discover for himself.

The second part of Book Two is devoted to light verse. In this delightful field, particularly during the last twenty-five years, Americans have achieved a commanding position, outdistancing the English, whose mastery reached its peak during the nineteenth century. There are fuller collections of American light verse in print (the reader must bear in mind the limitations of space) but we believe most of our poets of comedy and light satire are fairly represented, from Ben Franklin to Phyllis McGinley. Most of the old favorites are here. With respect to what it grins or smiles at, mankind is conservative.

The editors wish that the "Anonymous" section of light verse could have been ampler, for some of the most amusing things ever written by Americans bear no sign of individual authorship. One comes with joy upon so delightful a bit as the first mention (1744) of baseball:

> The ball once struck off,
>   Away flies the boy
> To the next destined post,
>   And then home with joy.

or that nugget of Shaker wisdom:

> Leave the flurry
> To the masses;
> Take your time
> And shine your glasses.

In making our selections, whether grave or gay, we juggled, rather precariously, several criteria: familiarity, intrinsic excellence, our own taste. And one other: read-aloudability. I am a firm believer in the old-fashioned practice of reading aloud in the home. I am even of opinion that the practice has a genuine cementing or centripetal force. Most of the poetry here included, particularly the light verse, is suitable for such reading, and requires no special histrionic talents. Try Ogden Nash or Robert Frost on the family circle sometime. It is surprising what stiff competition you will find yourself putting up against the currently popular TV entertainers.

The third section of Book Two is called The Songs We Sing. These are printed not in the order of the authors' birth dates, as with the two preceding sections, but roughly in order of publication. This puts together all the songs of a given period, thus providing a kind of sketchy lyric history of the country's career.

Songs, even Tin-Pan Alley songs, often come from something deep in us, circulate like the very air we breathe, and then sink back in us, never to be forgotten. A single line will call forth a whole era. In seven syllables "Brother, can you spare a dime" revives a terrible time. Our songs are peculiarly rich in this quality of evocation, whether they be folk songs or brash commercial products.

They are also notable for their beauty. "Floating like a vapor on the soft summer air" is not Keats, but is poetry nonetheless. Dreiser's "Through the sycamores the candle lights are gleaming/On the banks of the Wabash far away" could not be better phrased: all of our homesickness is there.

Nostalgia is one of the hallmarks of our popular songs. That is natural enough, for we are a people on the move and always have been. It is as if in these sorrowful retrospective ditties we were compensating for our violent faith in progress and our almost dogmatic future-mindedness. Indeed it is possible to say that there is less tragic feeling in our serious verse than in our simplest folk songs. This sense of loss, of something missing, rises to its perfect expression in the Negro spiritual. The Negro somehow speaks for all of us: "Sometimes I feel like a motherless child/A long way from home." What a great deal of Thomas Wolfe could be compressed into those two lines!

But there is jollity and wit and high-hearted brass-band patriotism here too; and social protest; and a simple kind of romantic feeling which our serious verse and our prose express but poorly; and tag-lines—"I wonder who's kissing her now"—that have wonderful economy of expression.

Whether the reader fixes his attention on our songs, our light verse, or our more serious poetry, he will discover, if he does his reading in large gulps, a progression (there are exceptions) from the simple to the more complex, or sometimes merely more sophisticated. Our early simplicity, so pure and pleasing in a Longfellow or a Whittier, degenerates in our day into the platitudes of an Eddie Guest. We no longer seem to produce poets who are at once sound and universally popular. Or it may be that a lyricist like Oscar Hammerstein now fills the place once occupied by a Longfellow, in which case it is short-sighted of us to deny him the formal title of poet.

The change in our verse is not only toward complexity of form, but toward complexity of feeling. Poets, despite their seeming remoteness from practical affairs, are actually the finest reflecting mirrors of the time. A

Wallace Stevens differs from a William Cullen Bryant partly because his America is different. Its older certainties are being questioned; some are vanishing entirely; and the poet feels this, though the words he uses to express his feeling may seem strange to some of us. A sense of the challenge facing the modern poet will help us to understand him and encourage us to persist in deciphering what at first glance appears to be a private language.

The probability is that we are living in a major poetical period. But so far only a few modern American poets have broken through to a large audience: Frost and Robinson of an older generation, Benét—who else? It is a serious mistake on our part to let rust in us—and particularly in our children—the faculty of enjoying poetry. The editors hope that the pages following will become as well-worn and thumb-marked and dog-eared as any in this book.

C. F.

I. Memorable Passages from Serious Verse

O Great Spirit!
Thou hast made this lake;
Thou hast also created us as Thy
    children;
Thou art able to make this water calm
Until we have safely passed over.

      "Voyager's Prayer," Chippewa

The voice that beautifies the land!
The voice above,
The voice of the thunder,
Among the dark clouds
Again and again it sounds,
The voice that beautifies the land.

The voice that beautifies the land!
The voice below,
The voice of the grasshopper,
Among the flowers and grasses
Again and again it sounds,
The voice that beautifies the land.

      "The Voice That Beautifies the
      Land," Navaho, translated by
      Washington Matthews, 1877

Stenatleha, you are good, I pray for
    long life.
I pray for your good looks.
I pray for good breath.
I pray for good speech.
I pray for feet like yours to carry me
    through a long life.
I pray for a life like yours.
I walk with people; ahead of me all is
    well.
I pray for people to smile as long as I
    live.
I pray to live long.
I pray, I say, for a long life to live
    with you where the good people
    are.
I live in poverty.
I wish the people there to speak of
    goodness and to talk to me.
I wish you to divide your good things
    with me as a brother.

Ahead of me is goodness; lead me on.

      "Medicine Song," Apache,
      translated by Edward S. Curtis,
      The North American Indian.
      Stenatleha: "Woman with par-
      ents—goddess of creation."

How joyous his neigh!
Lo, the Turquoise Horse of Johano-ai,
    How joyous his neigh,
There on precious hides outspread
    standeth he;
    How joyous his neigh,
There on tips of fair fresh flowers
    feedeth he;
    How joyous his neigh,
There of mingled waters holy drinketh
    he;
    How joyous his neigh,
There he spurneth dust of glittering
    grains;
    How joyous his neigh,
There in midst of sacred pollen hid-
    den, all hidden he;
    How joyous his neigh,
There his offspring many grow and
    thrive for evermore;
    How joyous his neigh!

      "Song of the Horse," Navaho.
      Johano-ai is the sun-god of the
      Navahos. He "pastures his
      herds on flower-blossoms and
      gives them to drink of the min-
      gled waters. These are holy
      waters, waters of all kinds,
      spring-water, snow-water, hail-
      water and water from the four
      quarters of the world. The
      Navahos use such waters in
      their rites. When the horse of
      the sun-god goes, he raises, not
      dust, but 'pitistchi,' glittering
      grains of mineral such as are
      used in religious ceremonies;
      and when he rolls, and shakes
      himself, it is shining pitistchi

that flies from him. When he
runs, the sacred pollen offered
to the sun-god is all about him,
like dust, so that he looks like
a mist; for the Navahos sometimes say that the mist on the
horizon is the pollen that has
been offered to the gods." *The
Indian's Book*. The constantly
repeated line is, in the original,
"Nizho'ko ani—hiye!"

Weep not for me, Loved Woman,
Should I die;
But for yourself be weeping!

Weep not for warriors who go
Gladly to battle.
Theirs to revenge
Fallen and slain of our people;
Theirs to lay low
All our foes like them,
Death to make, singing.

Weep not for warriors,
But weep for women!
Oh, weep for women!

Theirs to be pitied
Most of all creatures,
Whose men return not!
How shall their hearts be stayed
When we are fallen?

Weep not for me, Loved Woman,
For yourself alone be weeping!
> "Warrior's Song," translated by
> Mary Austin, *The American
> Rhythm*

With beauty before me, I walk.
With beauty behind me, I walk.
With beauty below me, I walk.
With beauty above me, I walk.
With beauty all around me, I walk.

.   .   .   .

It is finished in beauty.
> Navaho chant

Look as they rise, rise
Over the line where sky meets the
    earth;
Pleiades!
Lo! They ascending, come to guide us,
Leading us safely, keeping us one;
Pleiades,
Teach us to be, like you, united.
> "Song to the Pleiades," Paw-
> nee, translated by Alice C.
> Fletcher, *The Hako*

Crow Indian,
You must watch your horse.
A horse thief often am I.
> Sioux warning to the foe

Newborn, on the naked sand
Nakedly lay it.
Next to the earth mother,
That it may know her;
Having good thoughts of her, the food
    giver.

Newborn, we tenderly
In our arms take it,
Making good thoughts.
House-god, be entreated,
That it may grow from childhood to
    manhood,
Happy, contented;
Beautifully walking
The trail to old age.
Having good thoughts of the earth its
    mother,
That she may give it the fruits of her
    being.
Newborn, on the naked sand
Nakedly lay it.
> "Song for the Newborn,"
> Pueblo, translated by Mary
> Austin, *The American Rhythm*

In old age wandering on a trail of
beauty, lively may I walk.
> Navaho night chant

My baby boy, my little baby boy, my
    little son,

You will put a sealing-spear into your
    canoe without knowing what use
    you make of it when you are a
    man.

                    Nootka song

Early I rose
In the blue morning;
My love was up before me,
It came running up to me from the
    doorways of the Dawn.

On Papago Mountain
The dying quarry
Looked at me with my love's eyes.
        "Papago Love Song," trans-
        lated by Mary Austin, *The
        American Rhythm*

Lovely! See the cloud, the cloud ap-
    pear!
Lovely! See the rain, the rain draw
    near!
  Who spoke?
'Twas the little corn-ear
High on the tip of the stalk
Saying while it looked at me
  Talking aloft there—
"Ah, perchance the floods
  Hither moving—
Ah, may the floods come this way!"
        "Corn-Grinding Song," Zuni,
        sung by the youths while the
        maidens grind the corn

The clear sky,
The green fruitful earth is good;
But peace among men is better.
        "Wawan Song," Omaha, trans-
        lated by Alice C. Fletcher, *The
        Omaha Tribe,* 1907

The poor little bee
That lives in the tree,
The poor little bee
That lives in the tree

Has only one arrow
In his quiver.
        "Ka-Ni-Ca Song," translated
        by James Powell, from *Amer-
        ican Indian Love Lyrics and
        Other Verse*

As my eyes search the prairie,
I feel the summer in the spring.
        "A Song of Spring," Chippewa,
        translated by Frances Dens-
        more

Screaming the night away,
With his great wing feathers
Swooping the darkness up;
I hear the Eagle-bird
Pulling the blanket back
Off from the eastern sky.
        "The Invitation Song," part V,
        Iroquois, translated by Harriet
        Maxwell Converse, *Myths and
        Legends of the New York State
        Iroquois*

Truly buzzards
Around my sky are circling!
For my soul festers,
And an odor of corruption
Betrays me to disaster.

Meanness, betrayal and spite
Come flockwise,
To make me aware
Of sickness and death within me.
My sky is full of the dreadful sound
Of the wings of unsuccesses.
        "Glyphs III," translated by
        Mary Austin, *The American
        Rhythm*

ROGER WILLIAMS
•

God makes a path, provides a guide,
    And feeds in wildernesse!
His glorious name while breath re-
    mains,

O that I may confesse.
Lost many a time, I have had no
    guide,
    No house but hollow tree!
In stormy winter night no fire,
    No food, no company.

In him I have found a house, a bed,
    A table, company;
No cup so bitter but's made sweet
    When God shall sweetning be.
                    "God Makes a Path"

ANNE BRADSTREET
•

The stones and trees, insensible to
    time,
Nor age nor wrinkle on their front are
    seen;
If Winter come, and greenness then do
    fade,
A Spring returns, and they more
    youthful made;
But man grows old, lies down, remains
    where once he's laid.
                    "Contemplations," 1650

ANONYMOUS
•

In Adam's fall
We sinned all.
        New England Primer, "A,"
        1673

Zaccheus he
Did climb the tree
Our Lord to see.
                    Ibid., "Z"

Now I lay me down to sleep,
I pray thee, Lord, my soul to keep;
If I should die before I wake,
I pray thee, Lord, my soul to take.
                    Ibid., 1814

EDWARD TAYLOR
•

For in Christs Coach Saints sweetly
    sing,
As they to glory ride therein.
        "The Joy of Church Fellow-
        ship Rightly Attended"

This Bread of Life dropt in thy mouth
    doth Cry:
Eate, Eate me, Soul, and thou shalt
    never dy.
        "Sacramental Meditations,"
        VIII

Who Spread its Canopy? Or Curtains
    Spun?
Who in this Bowling Alley bowld the
    Sun?
        "God's Determinations Touch-
        ing His Elect"

PHILIP FRENEAU
•

In spite of all the learned have said,
    I still my old opinion keep;
The posture that we give the dead
    Points out the soul's eternal sleep.
            "The Indian Burying Ground"

WILLIAM J. GRAYSON
•

There Stowe, with prostituted pen, as-
    sails
One half her country in malignant
    tales;
Careless, like Trollope, whether truth
    she tells,
And anxious only how the libel sells,
To slander's mart she furnishes sup-
    plies,
And feeds its morbid appetite for lies
On fictions fashioned with malicious
    art,
The venal pencil, and malignant heart,
With fact distorted, inference un-
    sound,

Creatures in fancy, not in nature
found—
Chaste Quadroon virgins, saints of sa-
ble hue,
Martyrs, than zealous Paul more tried
and true,
Demoniac monsters, sentimental slaves,
Mulatto cavaliers, and Creole knaves—
Monsters each portrait drawn, each
story told!

The Hireling and the Slave,
Part I, 1854

Where hireling millions toil, in doubt
and fear,
For food and clothing all the weary
year,
Content and grateful if their masters
give
The boon they beg—to labor and to
live;
While dreamers task their idle wits to
find
A short-hand method to enrich mankind,
And Fourier's scheme or Owen's plans
entice
Expectant thousands with some deep
device
For raising wages, for abating toil,
And reaping crops from ill-attended
soil:
If, while the anxious multitudes ap-
pear,
Now glad with hope, now yielding to
despair,
A seraph form, descending from the
skies,
In mercy sent, should meet their won-
d'ring eyes,
And, smiling, offer to each suppliant
there
The promised good that fills the la-
borer's prayer—
Food, clothing, freedom from the
wants, the cares,
The pauper hireling ever feels or fears;

And, at their death, these blessings to
renew,
Their wives and children may enjoy
them too,
That, when disease or age their
strength impairs,
Subsistence and a home should still be
theirs—
What wonder would the gracious boon
impart,
What grateful rapture swell the peasant's heart!
How freely would the hungry list'ners
give
A life-long labor thus secure to live!

And yet the life, so unassailed by care,
So blessed with moderate work, with
ample fare,
With all the good the starving pauper
needs,
The happier slave on each plantation
leads;
Safe from harassing doubts and an-
nual fears,
He dreads no famine in unfruitful
years;
If harvests fail from inauspicious skies,
The master's providence his food sup-
plies;
No paupers perish here for want of
bread,
Or lingering live, by foreign bounty
fed;
No exiled trains of homeless peasants
go,
In distant climes, to tell their tales of
woe:
Far other fortune, free from care and
strife,
For work, or bread, attends the Ne-
gro's life,
And Christian slaves may challenge as
their own,
The blessings claimed in fabled states
alone—
The cabin home, not comfortless,
though rude,
Light daily labor, and abundant food,

The sturdy health that temperate hab-
    its yield,
The cheerful song that rings in every
    field,
The long, loud laugh, that freemen
    seldom share,
Heaven's boon to bosoms unap-
    proached by care,
And boisterous jest and humor unre-
    fined,
That leave, though rough, no painful
    sting behind;
While, nestling near, to bless their
    humble lot,
Warm social joys surround the Negro's
    cot,
The evening dance its merriment im-
    parts,
Love, with his rapture, fills their
    youthful hearts,
And placid age, the task of labor done,
Enjoys the summer shade, the winter
    sun,
And, as through life no pauper want
    he knows,
Laments no poor-house penance at its
    close.

                Ibid., Part II

FITZ-GREENE HALLECK
·

Green be the turf above thee,
    Friend of my better days!
None knew thee but to love thee,
    Nor named thee but to praise.
      "On the Death of Joseph Rod-
      man Drake"

WILLIAM CULLEN BRYANT
·

So live, that when thy summons comes
    to join
The innumerable caravan, which
    moves
To that mysterious realm, where each
    shall take

His chamber in the silent halls of
    death,
Thou go not, like the quarry-slave at
    night,
Scourged to his dungeon, but, sus-
    tained and soothed
By an unfaltering trust, approach thy
    grave
Like one who wraps the drapery of his
    couch
About him, and lies down to pleasant
    dreams.
              "Thanatopsis"

Whither, midst falling dew,
While glow the heavens with the last
    steps of day,
Far, through their rosy depths, dost
    thou pursue
Thy solitary way?
         "To a Waterfowl"

The melancholy days have come, the
    saddest of the year,
Of wailing winds, and naked woods,
    and meadows brown and sear.
      "The Death of the Flowers"

These are the gardens of the Desert,
    these
The unshorn fields, boundless and
    beautiful,
For which the speech of England has
    no name—
The Prairies.
           "The Prairies"

Truth, crushed to earth, shall rise
    again;
    Th' eternal years of God are hers;
But Error, wounded, writhes in pain,
    And dies among her worshippers.
         "The Battle-Field"

JOSEPH RODMAN DRAKE
·

When Freedom, from her mountain
    height,

Unfurled her standard to the air,
She tore the azure robe of night,
    And set the stars of glory there;
She mingled with its gorgeous dyes
The milky baldric of the skies,
And striped its pure, celestial white
With streakings of the morning light;
Then from his mansion in the sun,
She called her eagle bearer down,
And gave into his mighty hand
The symbol of her chosen land.
                    "The American Flag"

GEORGE POPE MORRIS
•
Woodman, spare that tree!
    Touch not a single bough!
In youth it sheltered me,
    And I'll protect it now.
            "Woodman, Spare That Tree!"

A song for our banner! The watch-
    word recall
Which gave the Republic her station:
"United we stand, divided we fall!"
It made and preserves us a nation!

The union of lakes, the union of lands,
The union of States none can sever,
The union of hearts, the union of
    hands,
And the flag of our Union forever!
                "The Flag of Our Union"

RALPH WALDO EMERSON
•
Good-bye, proud world! I'm going
    home;
Thou art not my friend; I am not
    thine.
                    "Good-Bye"

I like a church; I like a cowl;
I love a prophet of the soul;
And on my heart monastic aisles

Fall like sweet strains, or pensive
    smiles;
Yet not for all his faith can see,
Would I that cowled churchman be.
.   .   .   .

The hand that rounded Peter's dome,
And groined the aisles of Christian
    Rome,
Wrought in a sad sincerity;
Himself from God he could not free;
He builded better than he knew;—
The conscious stone to beauty grew.
                    "The Problem"

. . . The mad wind's night-work,
The frolic architecture of the snow.
                "The Snow-Storm"

I think no virtue goes with size.
                "The Titmouse"

He who has a thousand friends has
    not a friend to spare,
And he who has one enemy will meet
    him everywhere.
                "From the Persian"

In May, when sea-winds pierced our
    solitudes,
I found the fresh Rhodora in the
    woods,
Spreading its leafless blooms in a damp
    nook,
To please the desert and the sluggish
    brook.
The purple petals, fallen in the pool,
Made the black water with their
    beauty gay;
Here might the red-bird come his
    plumes to cool,
And court the flower that cheapens
    his array.
Rhodora! if the sages ask thee why
This charm is wasted on the earth and
    sky,
Tell them, dear, that if eyes were
    made for seeing,

Then Beauty is its own excuse for be-
    ing:
Why thou wert there, O rival of the
    rose!
I never thought to ask, I never knew:
But, in my simple ignorance, suppose
The self-same Power that brought me
    there brought you.
> "The Rhodora: On Being
> Asked, Whence Is the Flower?"

The mountain and the squirrel
Had a quarrel;
And the former called the latter "Lit-
    tle Prig."
But he replied,
"You are doubtless very big;
But all sorts of things and weather
Must be taken in together,
To make up a year
And a sphere.

.   .   .   .

Talents differ; all is well and wisely
    put;
If I cannot carry forests on my back,
Neither can you crack a nut."
> "The Mountain and the Squir-
> rel"

A subtle chain of countless rings
The next unto the farthest brings;
The eye reads omens where it goes,
And speaks all languages the rose;
And, striving to be man, the worm
Mounts through all the spires of form.
> "Nature"

Give all to love:
Obey thy heart;
Friends, kindred, days,
Estate, good fame,
Plans, credit, and the Muse—
Nothing refuse.

.   .   .   .

Heartily know,
When half-gods go,
The gods arrive.
> "Give All to Love"

'Tis the day of the chattel,
Web to weave, and corn to grind;
Things are in the saddle,
And ride mankind.

There are two laws discrete,
Not reconciled,—
Law for man, and law for thing;
The last builds town and fleet,
But it runs wild,
And doth the man unking.
> "Ode Inscribed to W. H.
> Channing"

By the rude bridge that arched the
    flood,
    Their flag to April's breeze unfurled,
Here once the embattled farmers
    stood,
    And fired the shot heard 'round the
    world.
> "Concord Hymn"

God said, I am tired of kings,
I suffer them no more;
Up to my ear the morning brings
The outrage of the poor.
> "Boston Hymn"

When the Church is social worth,
When the state house is the hearth
Then the perfect State is come,
The republican at home.
> *Essays: Second Series,* "Poli-
> tics"

So nigh is grandeur to our dust,
    So near is God to man,
When Duty whispers low, *Thou must,*
    The youth replies, *I can.*
> "Voluntaries"

If the red slayer think he slays,
    Or if the slain think he is slain,
They know not well the subtle ways
    I keep, and pass, and turn again.

Far or forgot to me is near;
  Shadow and sunlight are the same;
The vanished gods to me appear;
  And one to me are shame and fame.

They reckon ill who leave me out;
  When me they fly, I am the wings;
I am the doubter and the doubt,
  And I the hymn the Brahmin sings.

The strong gods pine for my abode,
  And pine in vain the sacred Seven;
But thou, meek lover of the good!
  Find me, and turn thy back on
    heaven.
                    "Brahma"

i

There is no great and no small
To the Soul that maketh all:
And where it cometh, all things are;
And it cometh everywhere.

ii

I am owner of the sphere,
Of the seven stars and the solar year,
Of Caesar's hand, and Plato's brain,
Of Lord Christ's heart, and Shake-
    speare's strain.
            "The Informing Spirit"

This losing is true dying,
This is lordly man's down-lying,
This is slow but sure declining,
Star by star his world resigning.
                    "Threnody"

It is time to be old,
To take in sail:—
The god of bounds,
Who sets to seas a shore,
Came to me in his fatal rounds,
And said: "No more!"
                    "Terminus"

WILLIAM GILMORE SIMMS
•

We follow where the Swamp Fox
    guides,
  His friends and merry men are we.
                    "The Swamp Fox"

HENRY WADSWORTH LONGFELLOW
•

Tell me not, in mournful numbers,
  Life is but an empty dream!—
For the soul is dead that slumbers,
  And things are not what they seem.

Life is real! Life is earnest!
  And the grave is not its goal;
Dust thou art, to dust returnest,
  Was not spoken of the soul.

.   .   .   .   .   .

Art is long, and Time is fleeting,
  And our hearts, though stout and
    brave,
Still, like muffled drums, are beating
  Funeral marches to the grave.

In the world's broad field of battle,
  In the bivouac of Life,
Be not like dumb, driven cattle!
  Be a hero in the strife!

.   .   .   .   .   .

Lives of great men all remind us
  We can make our lives sublime,
And, departing, leave behind us
  Footprints on the sands of time;

.   .   .   .   .   .

Let us, then, be up and doing,
  With a heart for any fate;
Still achieving, still pursuing,
  Learn to labor and to wait.
                    "A Psalm of Life"

"That's what I always say; if you wish
    a thing to be well done
You must do it yourself, you must not
    leave it to others!"
            *The Courtship of Miles Stand-
            ish,* Captain Standish to John
            Alden

Archly the maiden smiled, and, with
    eyes overrunning with laughter,
Said, in a tremulous voice, "Why don't
    you speak for yourself, John?"
                          Ibid.

It was the schooner Hesperus,
    That sailed the wintry sea;
And the skipper had taken his little
    daughter,
To bear him company.

.   .   .   .   .   .

And fast through the midnight dark
    and drear,
    Through the whistling sleet and
    snow,
Like a sheeted ghost, the vessel swept
    Towards the reef of Norman's Woe.

.   .   .   .

Such was the wreck of the Hesperus,
    In the midnight and the snow!
Christ save us all from a death like
    this
    On the reef of Norman's Woe!
        "The Wreck of the Hesperus"

Under a spreading chestnut tree
    The village smithy stands;
The smith, a mighty man is he,
    With large and sinewy hands;
And the muscles of his brawny arms
    Are strong as iron bands.

.   .   .   .   .   .

    He earns whate'er he can,
And looks the whole world in the face,
    For he owes not any man.

.   .   .   .   .   .

Toiling,—rejoicing,—sorrowing,
    Onward through life he goes;
Each morning sees some task begin,
    Each evening sees it close;
Something attempted, something done,
    Has earned a night's repose.
          "The Village Blacksmith"

Be still, sad heart! and cease repining;

Behind the clouds is the sun still shin-
    ing;
Thy fate is the common fate of all,
Into each life some rain must fall,
    Some days must be dark and dreary.
              "The Rainy Day"

Standing, with reluctant feet,
Where the brook and river meet,
Womanhood and childhood fleet!
              "Maidenhood"

The shades of night were falling fast
As through an Alpine village passed
A youth, who bore, 'mid snow and ice,
A banner with the strange device,
    Excelsior!

.   .   .   .

A traveller, by the faithful hound,
Half-buried in the snow was found.
Still grasping in his hand of ice
That banner with the strange device,
    Excelsior!
              "Excelsior"

I stood on the bridge at midnight,
    As the clocks were striking the hour,
And the moon rose o'er the city,
    Behind the dark church-tower.
              "The Bridge"

The day is done, and the darkness
    Falls from the wings of Night,
As a feather is wafted downward
    From an eagle in his flight.

I see the lights of the village
    Gleam through the rain and the
    mist,
And a feeling of sadness comes o'er
    me,
    That my soul cannot resist:

A feeling of sadness and longing,
    That is not akin to pain,
And resembles sorrow only
    As the mist resembles the rain.
            "The Day Is Done"

. . . the bards sublime
Whose distant footsteps echo
  Through the corridors of Time.
Ibid.

And the night shall be filled with mu-
    sic
  And the cares that infest the day
Shall fold their tents, like the Arabs,
  And as silently steal away.
Ibid.

I shot an arrow into the air,
It fell to earth, I knew not where;
For, so swiftly it flew, the sight
Could not follow it in its flight.

I breathed a song into the air,
It fell to earth, I knew not where;
For who has sight so keen and strong,
That it can follow the flight of song?

Long, long afterward, in an oak
I found the arrow, still unbroke;
And the song, from beginning to end,
I found again in the heart of a friend.
"The Arrow and the Song"

This is the forest primeval. The murmuring pines and the hemlocks,
Bearded with moss, and in garments
  green, indistinct in the twilight,
Stand like Druids of old, with voices
  sad and prophetic,
Stand like harpers hoar, with beards
  that rest on their bosoms.
Loud from its rocky caverns, the deep-
  voiced neighboring ocean
Speaks, and in accents disconsolate answers the wail of the forest.
Evangeline, opening lines

Fear, that reigns with the tyrant, and
  envy, the vice of republics.
Ibid., "Part the First"

But a celestial brightness—a more
  ethereal beauty—

Shone on her face and encircled her
  form when, after confession,
Homeward serenely she walked with
  God's benediction upon her.
When she passed, it seemed like the
  ceasing of exquisite music.
Ibid.

Silently, one by one, in the infinite
  meadows of heaven,
Blossomed the lovely stars, the forget-
  me-nots of the angels.
Ibid.

"Build me straight, O worthy Master!
Staunch and strong, a goodly vessel,
That shall laugh at all disaster,
And with wave and whirlwind wres-
  tle!"
.   .   .   .
And see! she stirs!
She starts—she moves—she seems to
  feel
The thrill of life along her keel,
And, spurning with her foot the
  ground,
With one exulting, joyous bound,
She leaps into the ocean's arms!
"The Building of the Ship"

Thou, too, sail on, O Ship of State!
Sail on, O Union, strong and great!
Humanity with all its fears,
With all the hope of future years,
Is hanging breathless on thy fate!
.   .   .   .
Our hearts, our hopes, are all with
  thee,
Our hearts, our hopes, our prayers,
  our tears,
Our faith triumphant o'er our fears,
Are all with thee—are all with thee!
Ibid.

"Wouldst thou"—so the helmsman
  answered,
  "Learn the secret of the sea?

Only those who brave its dangers
  Comprehend its mystery!"
                    "The Secret of the Sea"

By the shores of Gitche Gumee,
By the shining Big-Sea-Water,
Stood the wigwam of Nokomis,
Daughter of the Moon, Nokomis.
            The Song of Hiawatha, "Hia-
            watha's Childhood"

Then the little Hiawatha,
Learned of every bird its language,
Learned their names and all their se-
  crets,
How they built their nests in Summer,
Where they hid themselves in Winter,
Talked with them whene'er he met
  them,
Called them "Hiawatha's Chickens."
                              Ibid.

From the waterfall he named her,
Minnehaha, Laughing Water.
            Ibid., "Hiawatha and Mudje-
            keewis"

Often I think of the beautiful town
  That is seated by the sea,
Often in thought go up and down
The pleasant streets of that dear old
  town,
    And my youth comes back to me.
    And a verse of a Lapland song
    Is haunting my memory still:
    "A boy's will is the wind's will,
And the thoughts of youth are long,
  long thoughts."

  .   .   .   .

I remember the black wharves and the
  slips,
  And the sea-tides tossing free,
And Spanish sailors with bearded lips,
And the beauty and mystery of the
  ships,
  And the magic of the sea.
                        "My Lost Youth"

Between the dark and the daylight,
  When the night is beginning to
    lower,
Comes a pause in the day's occupa-
  tions,
  That is known as the Children's
    Hour.

I hear in the chamber above me
  The patter of little feet,
The sound of a door that is opened
  And voices soft and sweet.

From my study I see in the lamplight,
  Descending the broad hall stair,
Grave Alice, and laughing Allegra
  And Edith with golden hair.

  .   .   .   .

I have you fast in my fortress,
  And will not let you depart,
But put you down into the dungeon
  In the round-tower of my heart.

And there will I keep you forever,
  Yes, forever and a day,
Till the walls shall crumble to ruin,
  And moulder in dust away!
                        "The Children's Hour"

Listen, my children, and you shall hear
Of the midnight ride of Paul Revere.
On the eighteenth of April, in Seventy-
  five;
Hardly a man is now alive
Who remembers that famous day and
  year.

He said to his friend, "If the British
  march
By land or sea from the tower to-night,
Hang a lantern aloft in the belfry arch
Of the North Church tower as a signal
  light,—
One, if by land, or two, if by sea;
And I on the opposite shore shall be,
Ready to ride and spread the alarm
Through every Middlesex village and
  farm,

For the country-folk to be up and to
arm."

.   .   .   .

That was all! And yet, through the
gloom and the light
The fate of a nation was riding that
night.
> *Tales of a Wayside Inn*, "The
> Landlord's Tale, Paul Revere's
> Ride"

Ships that pass in the night, and speak
each other in passing;
Only a signal shown and a distant
voice in the darkness;
So in the ocean of life we pass and
speak one another,
Only a look and a voice; then darkness again and a silence.
> *Ibid.*, "The Theologian's Tale,
> Elizabeth"

Not in the clamour of the crowded
street,
Not in the shouts and plaudits of the
throng,
But in ourselves, are triumph and defeat.
> "The Poets"

Consult the dead upon the things that
were,
But the living only on things that are.
> "The Golden Legend"

SAMUEL FRANCIS SMITH
•

My country, 'tis of thee,
Sweet land of liberty,
  Of thee I sing;
Land where my fathers died,
Land of the pilgrims' pride,
From every mountain side
  Let freedom ring.
> "America," July 4, 1831; the
> entire poem written in half an
> hour by the author at the age
> of twenty-four

OLIVER WENDELL HOLMES
•

Youth longs and manhood strives, but
age remembers,
Sits by the raked-up ashes of the past,
Spreads its thin hands above the whitening embers
That warm its creeping life-blood to
the last.
> "The Iron Gate"

Ay, tear her tattered ensign down!
Long has it waved on high,
And many an eye has danced to see
That banner in the sky;
Beneath it rung the battle shout,
And burst the cannon's roar;—
The meteor of the ocean air
Shall sweep the clouds no more.
> "Old Ironsides"

Build thee more stately mansions, O
my soul,
  As the swift seasons roll!
  Leave thy low-vaulted past!
Let each new temple, nobler than the
last,
Shut thee from heaven with a dome
more vast,
  Till thou at length art free,
Leaving thine outgrown shell by life's
unresting sea!
> "The Chambered Nautilus"

Alas for those that never sing,
  But die with all their music in them!
> "The Voiceless"

EDGAR ALLAN POE
•

Once upon a midnight dreary, while I
pondered, weak and weary,

Over many a quaint and curious vol-
    ume of forgotten lore,
While I nodded, nearly napping, sud-
    denly there came a tapping,
As of some one gently rapping, rapping
    at my chamber door.
"'Tis some visitor," I muttered, "tap-
    ping at my chamber door—
    Only this and nothing more."

Ah, distinctly I remember it was in the
    bleak December,
And each separate dying ember
    wrought its ghost upon the floor.
Eagerly I wished the morrow; vainly
    I had sought to borrow
From my books surcease of sorrow—
    sorrow for the lost Lenore,
For the rare and radiant maiden
    whom the angels name Lenore—
Nameless *here* for evermore.

.   .   .   .

"Take thy beak from out my heart,
    and take thy form from off my
    door!"
    Quoth the Raven, "Nevermore."

And the Raven, never flitting, still is
    sitting, still is sitting
On the pallid bust of Pallas just above
    my chamber door;
And his eyes have all the seeming of a
    demon's that is dreaming,
And the lamp-light o'er him streaming
    throws his shadow on the floor;
And my soul from out that shadow
    that lies floating on the floor
    Shall be lifted—nevermore!
                "The Raven"

The lady sleeps! Oh, may her sleep,
Which is enduring, so be deep!
Heaven have her in its sacred keep!
This chamber changed for one more
    holy,
This bed for one more melancholy,
I pray to God that she may lie

Forever with unopened eye,
While the pale sheeted ghosts go by!
             "The Sleeper"

If I could dwell where Israfel
Hath dwelt, and he where I,—
He might not sing so wildly well
A mortal melody,
While a bolder note than his might
    swell
From my lyre within the sky.
             "Israfel"

By a route obscure and lonely,
Haunted by ill angels only,
Where an Eidolon, named Night,
On a black throne reigns upright,
I have reached these lands but newly
From an ultimate dim Thule—
From a wild weird clime that lieth,
    sublime,
    Out of Space—out of Time.

Bottomless vales and boundless floods,
And chasms, and caves, and Titan
    woods,
With forms that no man can discover
For the tears that drip all over;
Mountains toppling evermore
Into seas without a shore;
Seas that restlessly aspire,
Surging, unto skies of fire;
Lakes that endlessly outspread
Their lone waters—lone and dead,—
Their still waters—still and chilly
With the snows of the lolling lily.

.   .   .   .

I have wandered home but newly
From this ultimate dim Thule.
             "Dream-Land"

The viol, the violet and the vine.

.   .   .   .

From a proud tower in the town
Death looks gigantically down.

.   .   .   .

But, lo, a stir is in the air!

The wave—there is a movement there,
As if the towers had thrust aside,
In slightly sinking, the dull tide,
As if their tops had feebly given
A void within the filmy Heaven.
The waves have now a redder glow;
The hours are breaking faint and low;
And when, amid no earthly moans,
Down, down that town shall settle
    hence,
Hell, rising from a thousand thrones,
Shall do it reverence.

"The City in the Sea"

And all my days are trances,
    And all my nightly dreams,
Are where thy grey eye glances,
    And where thy footstep gleams—
In what ethereal dances,
    By what eternal streams.

"To One in Paradise"

While the angels, all pallid and wan,
    Uprising, unveiling, affirm
That the play is the tragedy, "Man,"
    And its hero the Conqueror Worm.

"The Conqueror Worm"

In the greenest of our valleys
    By good angels tenanted,
Once a fair and stately palace—
    Radiant palace—reared its head.
In the monarch Thought's dominion,
    It stood there;
Never seraph spread a pinion
    Over fabric half so fair!

.   .   .   .

And travellers now, within that valley,
    Through the red-litten windows see
Vast forms, that move fantastically
    To a discordant melody;
While, like a ghastly rapid river,
    Through the pale door
A hideous throng rush out forever
    And laugh—but smile no more.

"The Haunted Palace"

Hast thou not torn the Naiad from
    her flood,
The Elfin from the green grass, and
    from me
The summer dream beneath the tam-
    arind tree?

"To Science"

Helen, thy beauty is to me
    Like those Nicean barks of yore
That gently, o'er a perfumed sea,
    The weary way-worn wanderer bore
    To his own native shore.

On desperate seas long wont to roam,
    Thy hyacinth hair, thy classic face,
Thy Naiad airs have brought me home
    To the glory that was Greece,
And the grandeur that was Rome.

Lo, in yon brilliant window-niche
    How statue-like I see thee stand,
    The agate lamp within thy hand,
Ah! Psyche, from the regions which
    Are holy land!

"To Helen"

It was many and many a year ago,
    In a kingdom by the sea,
That a maiden there lived whom you
    may know
    By the name of Annabel Lee;
And this maiden she lived with no
    other thought
Than to love and be loved by me.

I was a child and *she* was a child,
    In this kingdom by the sea;
But we loved with a love that was
    more than love—
    I and my Annabel Lee—
With a love that the winged seraphs
    of heaven
    Coveted her and me.

.   .   .   .

The moon never beams without bring-
    ing me dreams
Of the beautiful Annabel Lee;

And the stars never rise but I feel the
  bright eyes
Of the beautiful Annabel Lee;
And so, all the night-tide, I lie down
  by the side
Of my darling—my darling—my life
  and my bride,
  In the sepulchre there by the sea,
  In her tomb by the sounding sea.
                                "Annabel Lee"

Keeping time, time, time,
  In a sort of Runic rhyme,
To the tintinabulation that so musi-
  cally wells
From the bells, bells, bells, bells.
  .   .   .   .

They are neither man nor woman—
They are neither brute nor human,
        They are Ghouls.
                                 "The Bells"

Gaily bedight,
  A gallant knight,
In sunshine and in shadow,
  Had journeyed long,
  Singing a song,
In search of Eldorado.

But he grew old—
  This knight so bold—
And o'er his heart a shadow
  Fell as he found
  No spot of ground
This land of Eldorado?"

And, as his strength,
  Failed him at length,
He met a pilgrim shadow—
  "Shadow," said he,
  "Where can it be—
This land of Eldorado?"

"Over the Mountains
  Of the Moon,
Down the Valley of the Shadow,
  Ride, boldly ride,"

The shade replied,—
"If you seek for Eldorado."
                                 "Eldorado"

The skies they were ashen and sober,
  The leaves they were crispèd and
    sere—
  The leaves they were withering and
    sere;
It was night in the lonesome October
  Of my most immemorial year;

It was hard by the dim lake of Auber,
  In the misty mid region of Weir—
It was down by the dank tarn of Au-
  ber,
  In the ghoul-haunted woodland of
    Weir.

Here once, through an alley Titanic,
  Of cypress, I roamed with my
    Soul—
  Of cypress, with Psyche, my Soul.
  .   .   .   .

[We] were stopped by the door of a
  tomb—
  By the door of a legended tomb;
And I said: "What is written, sweet
  sister,
  On the door of this legended tomb?"
  She replied: "Ulalume—Ulalume—
  'Tis the vault of thy lost Ulalume!"
                                 "Ulalume"

The fever call'd "Living"
Is conquer'd at last.
                                 "For Annie"

JOHN GREENLEAF WHITTIER
                    •
For of all sad words of tongue or pen,
The saddest are these: "It might have
  been!"
                                 "Maud Muller"

Old Floyd Ireson, for his hard heart,

Tarred and feathered and carried in a
    cart
  By the women of Marblehead!
                "Skipper Ireson's Ride"

All else is gone; from those great eyes
  The soul has fled:
When faith is lost, when honor dies,
  The man is dead!

Then, pay the reverence of old days
  To his dead fame;
Walk backward, with averted gaze,
  And hide the shame!
          "Ichabod," May 2, 1850. Whit-
      tier supplied this note: "This
      poem was the outcome of the
      surprise and grief and forecast
      of evil consequences which I
      felt on reading the seventh of
      March speech of Daniel Web-
      ster in support of the 'compro-
      mise' and the Fugitive Slave
      Bill. No partisan or personal
      enmity dictated it. On the con-
      trary my admiration of the
      splendid personality and intel-
      lectual power of the great sena-
      tor was never stronger than
      when I laid down his speech,
      and, in one of the saddest mo-
      ments of my life, penned my
      protest . . . in tones of stern
      and sorrowful rebuke."
          I Samuel 4:21: "And she
      named the child Ichabod, say-
      ing, the glory is departed from
      Israel."

No slave-hunt in our borders—no pirate on our strand!
No fetters in the Bay State—no slave
  upon our land!
        "Massachusetts to Virginia,"
        1843

Up from the meadows rich with corn,
Clear in the cool September morn,

The clustered spires of Frederick stand
Green-walled by the hills of Maryland.
.   .   .   .

"Shoot, if you must, this old gray
    head,
But spare your country's flag," she
    said.
.   .   .   .

"Who touches a hair of yon gray head
Dies like a dog! March on!" he said.
           "Barbara Frietchie"

CHRISTOPHER CRANCH
•

We are columns left alone
Of a temple once complete.
               "Gnosis"

JAMES T. FIELDS
•

"We are lost!" the captain shouted,
As he staggered down the stairs.

But his little daughter whispered,
As she took his icy hand,
"Isn't God upon the ocean,
Just the same as on the land?"
         "Ballad of the Tempest"

ELLEN STURGIS HOOPER
•

I slept and dreamed that life was
    beauty,
I woke and found that life was duty.

HENRY DAVID THOREAU
•

Low-anchored cloud,
Newfoundland air,
Fountain-head and source of rivers,
Dew-cloth, dream-drapery,
And napkin spread by fays;
Drifting meadows of the air,

Where bloom the daisied banks and
    violets,
And in whose fenny labyrinth
The bittern booms and heron wades;
Spirit of lakes and seas and rivers,
Bear only perfumes and the scent
Of healing herbs to just men's fields.
                                    "Mist"

Light-winged Smoke! Icarian bird,
Melting thy pinions in thy upward
    flight,
Lark without song, and messenger of
    dawn,
Circling above the hamlets as thy nest;
Or else, departing dream, and shad-
    owy form
Of midnight vision, gathering up thy
    skirts;
By night star-veiling, and by day
Darkening the light and blotting out
    the sun;
Go thou my incense upward from this
    hearth,
And ask the gods to pardon this clear
    flame.
                                    "Smoke"

JAMES RUSSELL LOWELL
            •

Let liars fear, let cowards shrink,
    Let traitors turn away,
Whatever we have dared to think
    That dare we also say.

They are slaves who dare not be
In the right with two or three.
                        "Stanzas on Freedom"

Truth forever on the scaffold,
Wrong forever on the throne.
                        "The Present Crisis"

Here lies a Poet. Stranger, if to thee
    His claim to memory be obscure,
If thou wouldst learn how truly great
    was he,

Go, ask it of the poor.
                        "To the Memory of Hood"

Earth gets its price for what Earth
    gives us;
    The beggar is taxed for a corner to
        die in,
The priest hath his fee who comes and
    shrives us,
    We bargain for the graves we lie in;
At the devil's booth are all things sold,
Each ounce of dross costs its ounce of
    gold;
    For a cap and bells our lives we pay,
Bubbles we buy with a whole soul's
    tasking;
    'Tis heaven alone that is given
        away,
'Tis only God may be had for the ask-
    ing;
No price is set on the lavish summer;
June may be had by the poorest comer.

And what is so rare as a day in June?
    Then, if ever, come perfect days;
Then Heaven tries earth if it be in
    tune,
    And over it softly her warm ear lays.

.   .   .   .

The little bird sits at his door in the
    sun,
    Atilt like a blossom among the
        leaves,
And lets his illumined being o'errun
    With the deluge of summer it re-
        ceives;
His mate feels the eggs beneath her
    wings,
And the heart in her dumb breast flut-
    ters and sings;
He sings to the wide world, and she
    to her nest,—
In the nice ear of Nature which song
    is the best?
                        "The Vision of Sir Launfal"

When I was a beggarly boy,
    And lived in a cellar damp,

I had not a friend nor a toy,
  But I had Aladdin's lamp;
When I could not sleep for the cold,
  I had fire enough in my brain,
And builded, with roofs of gold,
  My beautiful castles in Spain!

Since then I have toiled day and night,
  I have money and power good store,
But I'd give all my lamps of silver
  bright,
  For the one that is mine no more;
Take, Fortune, whatever you choose,
  You gave, and may snatch again;
I have nothing 'twould pain me to
  lose,
  For I own no more castles in Spain!
                "Aladdin"

Our children shall behold his fame,
  The kindly-earnest, brave, fore-
    seeing man,
Sagacious, patient, dreading praise,
  not blame,
  New birth of our new soil, the first
    American.
      "Lincoln: Ode Recited at Har-
      vard Commemoration," July
      21, 1865

HERMAN MELVILLE
•
The ribs and terrors in the whale,
  Arched over me a dismal gloom,
While all God's sun-lit waves rolled by,
  And lift me deepening down to
    doom.
    Moby Dick, "Father Mapple's
    Hymn"

No utter surprise can come to him
  Who reaches Shakespeare's core;
That which we seek and shun is
  there—
  Man's final lore.
              Battle-Pieces

All wars are boyish and are fought by
  boys,
The champions and enthusiasts of the
  state.
      "The March into Virginia"

We elms of Malvern Hill
  Remember everything;
But sap the twig will fill;
Wag the world how it will,
  Leaves must be green in Spring.
          "Malvern Hill"

What now avails the pageant verse,
Trophies and arms with music borne?
Base is the world; and some rehearse
How noblest meet ignoble scorn.
          "On Camoens"

Found a family, build a state,
The pledged event is still the same:
Matter in end will never abate
His ancient brutal claim.

Indolence is heaven's ally here,
And energy the child of hell:
The Good Man pouring from his
  pitcher clear
But brims the poisoned well.
      "Fragments of a Lost Gnostic
      Poem of the Twelfth Century"

O the navies old and oaken,
O, the Temeraire no more!
        "The Temeraire"

Marquesas and glenned isles that be
Authentic Edens in a Pagan sea.
          "To Ned"

I remember Taff the Welshman when
  he sank.
And his cheek it was like the budding
  pink.
But me they'll lash me in hammock,
  drop me deep.
Fathoms down, fathoms down, how
  I'll dream fast asleep.

I feel it stealing now. Sentry, are you
    there?
Just ease these darbies at the wrist,
And roll me over fair.
I am sleepy, and the oozy weeds about
    me twist.

       Billy Budd, Foretopman, "Billy
       in the Darbies"

WALT WHITMAN

•

Leaves of Grass.
         Title of book, 1855

One's-self I sing, a simple separate
    person,
Yet utter the word Democratic, the
    word En-Masse.
         "One's-Self I Sing"

Me imperturbe, standing at ease in
    Nature.
         "Me Imperturbe"

I hear America singing, the varied
    carols I hear,
Those of mechanics, each one singing
    his as it should be blithe and
    strong,
The carpenter singing his as he meas-
    ures his plank or beam,
The mason singing his as he makes
    ready for work, or leaves off work,
The boatman singing what belongs to
    him in his boat, the deckhand
    singing on the steamboat deck,
The shoemaker singing as he sits on
    his bench, the hatter singing as he
    stands,
The wood-cutter's song, the plough-
    boy's on his way in the morning,
    or at noon intermission or at sun-
    down,
The delicious singing of the mother, or
    of the young wife at work, or of
    the girl sewing or washing,

Each singing what belongs to him or
    her and to none else,
The day what belongs to the day—at
    night the party of young fellows,
    robust, friendly,
Singing with open mouths their strong
    melodious songs.
        "I Hear America Singing"

I will put in my poems that with you
    is heroism upon land and sea,
And I will report all heroism from an
    American point of view.
        "Starting from Paumanok"

I celebrate myself, and sing myself,
And what I assume you shall assume
For every atom belonging to me as
    good belongs to you.

I loafe and invite my soul,
I lean and loafe at my ease, observing
    a spear of summer grass.

.   .   .   .   .   .

There was never any more inception
    than there is now,
Nor any more youth or age than there
    is now,
And will never be any more perfection
    than there is,
Nor any more heaven or hell than
    there is now.

.   .   .   .   .   .

Welcome is every organ and attribute
    of me, and of any man hearty and
    clean,

Not an inch or a particle of an inch is
    vile, and none shall be less famil-
    iar than the rest.

.   .   .   .   .   .

A child said *What is the grass?* fetch-
    ing it to one with full hands;
How could I answer the child? I do
    not know what it is any more
    than he.

I guess it must be the flag of my disposition out of hopeful green stuff
woven.

Or I guess it is the handkerchief of
the Lord,
A scented gift and remembrancer designedly dropt,
Bearing the owner's name somewhere
in the corners, that we may see
and remark, and say *Whose?*

. . . .

And now it seems to me the beautiful
uncut hair of graves.

. . . .

Has anyone supposed it lucky to be
born?
I hasten to inform him or her it is just
as lucky to die, and I know it.

. . . .

I am enamour'd of growing out-doors,
Of men that live among cattle or taste
of the ocean or woods,
Of the builders and steerers of ships
and the wielders of axes and
mauls, and the drivers of horses,
I can eat and sleep with them week
in and week out.

. . . .

I resist anything better than my own
diversity,
Breathe the air but leave plenty after
me,
And am not stuck up, and am in my
place.

. . . .

This hour I tell things in confidence,
I might not tell everybody, but I will
tell you.

. . . .

Who goes there? hankering, gross,
mystical, nude;
How is it I extract strength from the
beef I eat?

. . . .

Whimpering and truckling fold with
powders for invalids, conformity
goes to the fourth-remov'd,
I wear my hat as I please indoors or
out.

. . . .

Having pried through the strata, ana-
lysed to a hair, counsel'd with
doctors and calculated close,
I find no sweeter fat than sticks to my
bones.

. . . .

Night of South winds—night of the
large few stars!
Still nodding night—mad naked summer night.

. . . .

What behaved well in the past or be-
haves well to-day is not such a
wonder,
The wonder is always and always how
there can be a mean man or an
infidel.

. . . .

Endless unfolding of words of ages!
And mine a word of the modern, the
word En-Masse.

. . . .

Walt Whitman, a kosmos, of Manhattan the son,
Turbulent, fleshy, sensual, eating,
drinking and breeding,
No sentimentalist, no stander above
men and women or apart from
them,
No more modest than immodest.

. . . .

I speak the pass-word primeval, I give
the sign of democracy,
By God! I will accept nothing which
all cannot have their counterpart
of on the same terms.

. . . .

I believe a leaf of grass is no less than
the journey-work of the stars,

And the pismire is equally perfect, and
a grain of sand, and the egg of
the wren,
And the tree-toad is a chef-d'oeuvre
for the highest,
And the running blackberry would
adorn the parlors of heaven,
And the narrowest hinge in my hand
puts to scorn all machinery,
And the cow crunching with de-
press'd head surpasses any statue,
And a mouse is miracle enough to
stagger sextillions of infidels.

.   .   .   .   .   .

I think I could turn and live with animals, they are so placid and self-
contain'd,
I stand and look at them long and
long.
They do not sweat and whine about
their condition,
They do not lie awake in the dark and
weep for their sins,
They do not make me sick discussing
their duty to God,
Not one is dissatisfied, not one is de-
mented with the mania of owning
things,
Not one kneels to another, nor to his
kind that lived thousands of years
ago,
Not one is respectable or unhappy
over the whole earth.

.   .   .   .   .   .

All this I swallow, it tastes good, I like
it well, it becomes mine,
I am the man, I suffered, I was there.

.   .   .   .   .   .

Agonies are one of my changes of garments,
I do not ask the wounded person how
he feels, I myself become the
wounded person.

.   .   .   .   .   .

Earth! you seem to look for something
at my hands,

Say, old top-knot, what do you want?

.   .   .   .   .   .

Behold, I do not give lectures or a
little charity,
When I give I give myself.

.   .   .   .   .   .

On women fit for conception I start
bigger and nimbler babes,
(This day I am jetting the stuff of far
more arrogant republics.)

.   .   .   .   .   .

I know perfectly well my own egotism,
Know my omnivorous lines and must
not write any less,
And would fetch you whoever you are
flush with myself.

.   .   .   .   .   .

It is time to explain myself—let us
stand up.

What is known I strip away,
I launch all men and women forward
with me into the Unknown.

.   .   .   .   .   .

Shoulder your duds dear son, and I
will mine, and let us hasten forth,
Wonderful cities and free nations we
shall fetch as we go.

.   .   .   .   .   .

I am the teacher of athletes,
He that by me spreads a wider breast
than my own proves the width of
my own,
He most honors my style who learns
under it to destroy the teacher.

.   .   .   .   .   .

I have said that the soul is not more
than the body,
And I have said that the body is not
more than the soul,
And nothing, not God, is greater to
one than one's self is.

.   .   .   .   .   .

And I say to mankind, Be not curious
about God,

For I who am curious about each am
not curious about God,
(No array of terms can say how much
I am at peace about God and
about death.)

I hear and behold God in every object, yet understand God not in
the least,
Nor do I understand who there can be
more wonderful than myself.

Why should I wish to see God better
than this day?
I see something of God each hour of
the twenty-four, and each moment then,

In the faces of men and women I see
God, and in my own face in the
glass,
I find letters from God dropped in the
street—and every one is signed by
God's name,   ·
And I leave them where they are, for
I know that wheresoe'er I go,
Others will punctually come forever
and ever.

.   .   .   .

Do I contradict myself?
Very well then I contradict myself,
(I am large, I contain multitudes.)

.   .   .   .

The spotted hawk swoops by and ac-
cuses me, he complains of my gab
and my loitering.

I too am not a bit tamed, I too am
untranslatable,
I sound my barbaric yawp over the
roofs of the world.

.   .   .   .

I bequeath myself to the dirt to grow
from the grass I love,
If you want me again look for me under your boot-soles.

"Song of Myself"

I Sing the Body Electric.

Title of poem

A woman waits for me, she contains
all, nothing is lacking.

"A Woman Waits for Me"

Once I Pass'd Through a Populous
City.

Title of poem

Facing West from California's shores,
Inquiring, tireless, seeking what is yet
unfound,
I, a child, very old, over waves, toward
the house of maternity, the land
of migrations, look afar,
Look off the shores of my Western sea,
the circle almost circled;
For starting westward from Hindustan,
from the vales of Kashmere,
From Asia, from the north, from the
God, the sage, and the hero,
From the south, from the flowery pen-
insulas and the spice islands,
Long having wander'd since, round
the earth having wander'd,
Now I face home again, very pleas'd
and joyous,
(But where is what I started for so
long ago?
And why is it yet unfound?)

"Facing West from California's
Shores"

Resolv'd to sing no songs to-day but
those of manly attachment,
Projecting them along the substantial
life,
Bequeathing hence types of athletic
love,
Afternoon this delicious Ninth-month
in my forty-first year,
I proceed for all who are or have been
young men,
To tell the secret of my nights and
days,
To celebrate the need of comrades.

"In Paths Untrodden"

The institution of the dear love of
comrades.

"I Hear It Was Charged
Against Me"

I dream'd in a dream I saw a city invincible to the attacks of the
whole of the rest of the earth,
I dream'd that was the new city of
Friends.

"I Dream'd in a Dream"

Afoot and light-hearted I take to the
open road,
Healthy, free, the world before me,
The long brown path before me leading wherever I choose.

Henceforth I ask not good fortune, I
myself am good fortune.

.   .   .   .

O public road, I say back I am not
afraid to leave you, yet I love you,
You express me better than I can express myself,
You shall be more to me than my
poem.

I think heroic deeds were all conceiv'd
in the open air, and all free poems
also,
I think I could stop here myself and
do miracles,
I think whatever I shall meet on the
road I shall like, and whoever be-
holds me shall like me,
I think whoever I see must be happy.

.   .   .   .

Have the past struggles succeeded?
What has succeeded? yourself? your
nation? Nature?
Now understand me well—it is provided in the essence of things that
from any fruition of success, no
matter what, shall come forth
something to make a greater
struggle necessary.

.   .   .   .

Camerado, I give you my hand!
I give you my love more precious than
money,
I give you myself before preaching or
law;
Will you give me yourself? will you
come travel with me?
Shall we stick by each other as long
as we live?

"Song of the Open Road"

A great city is that which has the
greatest men and women.
If it be a few ragged huts it is still the
greatest city in the whole world.

.   .   .   .

Where the populace rise at once
against the never-ending audacity
of elected persons.

.   .   .   .

Where the city of the faithfulest
friends stands,
Where the city of the cleanliest of the
sexes stands,
Where the city of the healthiest fathers
stands,
Where the city of the best-bodied
mothers stands,
There the great city stands.

"Song of the Broad-Axe"

Youth, large, lusty, loving—youth full
of grace, force, fascination,
Do you know that Old Age may come
after you with equal grace, force,
fascination?

"Youth, Day, Old Age and
Night"

Come my tan-faced children,
Follow well in order, get your weap-
ons ready,
Have you your pistols? Have you your
sharp-edged axes?
Pioneers! O Pioneers!

"Pioneers! O Pioneers!"

Out of the cradle endlessly rocking,
Out of the mocking-bird's throat, the musical shuttle,
Out of the Ninth-month midnight . . .
.   .   .   .
The white arms out in the breakers tirelessly tossing . . .

> "Out of the Cradle Endlessly Rocking"

When I heard the learn'd astronomer,
When the proofs, the figures, were ranged in columns before me,
When I was shown the charts and diagrams, to add, divide, and measure them,
When I sitting heard the astronomer where he lectured with much applause in the lecture-room,
How soon unaccountable I became tired and sick,
Till rising and gliding out I wander'd off by myself,
In the mystical moist night-air, and from time to time,
Look'd up in perfect silence at the stars.

> "When I Heard the Learn'd Astronomer"

Silent and amazed even when a little boy,
I remember I heard the preacher every Sunday put God in his statements,
As contending against some being or influence.

> "A Child's Amaze"

By the bivouac's fitful flame,
A procession winding around me, solemn and sweet and slow—but first I note,
The tents of the sleeping army, the fields' and woods' dim outline,
The darkness lit by spots of kindled fire, the silence,
Like a phantom far or near an occasional figure moving,
The shrubs and trees, (as I lift my eyes they seem to be stealthily watching me),
While wind in procession thoughts, O tender and wondrous thoughts,
Of life and death, of home and the past and loved, and of those that are far away;
A solemn and slow procession there as I sit on the ground,
By the bivouac's fitful flame.

> "By the Bivouac's Fitful Flame"

As toilsome I wander'd Virginia's woods,
To the music of rustling leaves kick'd by my feet (for 'twas autumn)
I mark'd at the foot of a tree the grave of a soldier;
Mortally wounded he and buried on the retreat, (easily all could I understand,)
The halt of the mid-day hour, when up! no time to lose—yet this sign left,
On a tablet scrawl'd and nail'd on the tree by the grave,
Bold, cautious, true, and my loving comrade.

Long, long I muse, then on my way go wandering,
Many a changeful season to follow, and many a scene of life,
Yet at times through changeful season and scene, abrupt, alone, or in the crowded street,
Comes before me the unknown soldier's grave, comes the inscription rude in Virginia's woods,
Bold, cautious, true, and my loving comrade.

> "As Toilsome I Wandered Virginia's Woods"

Word over all, beautiful as the sky,

Beautiful that war and all its deeds of
    carnage must in time be utterly
    lost,
That the hands of the sisters Death
    and Night incessantly softly wash
    again, and ever again, this soil'd
    world;
For my enemy is dead, a man divine
    as myself is dead,
I look where he lies white-faced and
    still in the coffin—I draw near,
Bend down and touch lightly with my
    lips the white face in the coffin.
                    "Reconciliation"

When lilacs last in the dooryard
    bloom'd,
And the great star early droop'd in the
    western sky in the night,
I mourn'd—and yet shall mourn with
    ever-returning spring.

Ever-returning spring, trinity sure to
    me you bring,
Lilac blooming perennial and droop-
    ing star in the west,
And thought of him I love.

.   .   .   .

Coffin that passes through lanes and
    streets,
Through day and night with the great
    cloud darkening the land,
With the pomp of the inloop'd flags
    with the cities draped in black,
With the show of the States them-
    selves as of crape-veil'd women
    standing,
With processions long and winding
    and the flambeaus of the night,
With the countless torches lit, with the
    silent sea of faces and the un-
    bared heads,
With the waiting depot, the arriving
    coffin, and the sombre faces,
With dirges through the night, with
    the thousand voices rising strong
    and solemn,

With all the mournful voices of the
    dirges pour'd around the coffin,
The dim-lit churches and the shud-
    dering organs—where amid these
    you journey,
With the tolling tolling bells' perpetual
    clang,
Here, coffin that slowly passes,
I give you my sprig of lilac.

.   .   .   .

Lo, body and soul—this land,
My own Manhattan with spires, and
    the sparkling and hurrying tides,
    and the ships,
The varied and ample land, the South
    and the North in the light, Ohio's
    shores and flashing Missouri,
And ever the far-spreading prairies
    covered with grass and corn.

.   .   .   .

Come lovely and soothing death,
Undulate round the world, serenely
    arriving, arriving,
In the day, in the night, to all, to each,
Sooner or later delicate death.

Praised be the fathomless universe,
For life and joy, and for objects and
    knowledge curious,
And for love, sweet love—but praise!
    praise! praise!
For the sure-enwinding arms of cool-
    enfolding death.

Dark mother always gliding near with
    soft feet,
Have none chanted for thee a chant
    of fullest welcome?
Then I chant it for thee, I glorify thee
    above all,
I bring thee a song that when thou
    must indeed come, come unfalter-
    ingly.

Approach, strong deliveress!
When it is so, when thou hast taken
    them, I joyously sing the dead,

Lost in the loving floating ocean of thee,
Laved in the flood of thy bliss, O death.

From me to thee glad serenades,
Dances for thee I propose, saluting thee, adornments and feastings for thee,
And the sights of the open landscapes and the high-spread sky are fitting,
And life and the fields, and the huge and thoughtful night.
The night in silence under many a star,
The ocean shore and the husky whispering wave whose voice I know,
And the soul turning to thee, O vast and well-veiled death,
And the body gratefully nestling close to thee.
Over the tree-tops I float thee a song,
Over the rising and sinking waves, over the myriad fields and the prairies wide,
Over the dense-packed cities all and the teeming wharves and ways,
I float this carol with joy, with joy to thee, O death.
"When Lilacs Last in the Dooryard Bloomed"

O Captain! my Captain! our fearful trip is done;
The ship has weather'd every rack; the prize we sought is won;
The port is near, the bells I hear, the people all exulting,
While follow eyes the steady keel, the vessel grim and daring;
But O heart! heart! heart!
O the bleeding drops of red,
Where on the deck my Captain lies,
Fallen cold and dead.
"O Captain! My Captain!"

These States are the amplest poem,

Here is not merely a nation but a teeming Nation of nations.

. . . .

Underneath all, individuals,
I swear nothing is good to me now that ignores individuals.
"By Blue Ontario's Shore"

There was a child went forth every day,
And the first object he look'd on, that object he became,
And that object became part of him for the day or a certain part of the day,
Or for many years or stretching cycles of years.
"There Was a Child Went Forth"

Passage, immediate Passage! the blood burns in my veins!
Away, O soul, hoist instantly the anchor!
Cut the hawsers—haul out—shake out every sail!
Have we not stood here like trees in the ground long enough?
Have we not grovel'd here long enough, eating and drinking like mere brutes?
Have we not darken'd and dazed ourselves with books long enough?
"Passage to India"

A noiseless patient spider,
I mark'd, where, on a little promontory, it stood, isolated;
Mark'd how, to explore the vacant, vast surrounding,
It launch'd forth filament, filament, filament, out of itself;
Ever unreeling them—ever tirelessly speeding them.

And you, O my Soul, where you stand,
Surrounded, surrounded, in measureless oceans of space,

Ceaselessly musing, venturing, throwing,—seeking the spheres, to connect them;
Till the bridge you will need, be form'd—till the ductile anchor hold;
Till the gossamer thread you fling, catch somewhere, O my Soul.

"A Noiseless Patient Spider"

Years of the modern! years of the unperform'd!
Your horizon rises, I see it parting away for more august dramas,
I see not America only, not only Liberty's nation but other nations preparing,
I see tremendous entrances and exits, new combinations, the solidarity of races,
I see that force advancing with irresistible power on the world's stage.

"Years of the Modern"

Camerado, this is no book,
Who touches this, touches a man.

"So Long"

Good-bye My Fancy.

Title of poem

GEORGE HENRY BOKER
•

Close his eyes; his work is done.
    What to him is friend or foeman,
Rise of moon, or set of sun,
    Hand of man, or kiss of woman?
        Lay him low, lay him low,
        In the clover or the snow!
        What cares he? he cannot know:
            Lay him low!

"Dirge for a Soldier"

BAYARD TAYLOR
•

Till the sun grows cold,

And the stars are old,
And the leaves of the Judgment Book unfold.

"Bedouin Song"

FRANCIS MILES FINCH
•

Under the sod and the dew,
    Waiting the judgment day;—
Under the one, the Blue;
    Under the other, the Gray.

"The Blue and the Gray"

HENRY TIMROD
•

Hath not the morning dawned with added light?
And shall not evening call another star
Out of the infinite regions of the night,
To mark this day in Heaven? At last, we are
A nation among nations; and the world
Shall soon behold in many a distant port
    Another flag unfurled!

"Ethnogenesis," written during the meeting of the first Southern Congress, at Montgomery, February, 1861. Timrod was known as the "Laureate of the Confederacy."

Stoop, angels, hither from the skies!
    There is no holier spot of ground
Than where defeated valor lies,
    By mourning beauty crowned!

"Ode Sung on the Occasion of Decorating the Graves of the Confederate Dead," at Magnolia Cemetery, Charleston, South Carolina, 1867

EMILY DICKINSON

•

There is no frigate like a book
  To take us lands away,
Or any coursers like a page
  Of prancing poetry.
  "There Is No Frigate Like a
  Book"

To make a prairie it takes a clover and
  one bee,—
And revery.
The revery alone will do
If bees are few.
  "To Make a Prairie"

The pedigree of honey
Does not concern the bee;
A clover, any time, to him
Is Aristocracy.
  "The Pedigree of Honey"

The red upon the hill
Taketh away my will;
If anybody sneer,
Take care, for God is here,
That's all.
  "The Red upon the Hill"

I never saw a moor.
  I never saw the sea;
Yet know I how the heather looks,
  And what a wave must be.

I never talked with God,
  Nor visited in heaven;
Yet certain am I of the spot
  As if the chart were given.
  "I Never Saw a Moor"

How dreary to be somebody!
How public, like a frog
To tell your name the livelong day
To an admiring bog!
  "How Dreary to Be Some-
  body!"

We never know how high we are
  Till we are called to rise;
And then, if we are true to plan,
  Our statures touch the skies.

The heroism we recite
  Would be a daily thing,
Did not ourselves the cubits warp
  For fear to be a king.
  "We Never Know How High
  We Are"

I like to see it lap the miles,
And lick the valleys up,
And stop to feed itself at tanks;
And then, prodigious, step

Around a pile of mountains,
And, supercilious, peer
In shanties by the sides of roads;
And then a quarry pare

To fit its sides, and crawl between,
Complaining all the while
In horrid, hooting stanza;
Then chase itself down hill

And neigh like Boanerges;
Then, punctual as a star,
Stop—docile and omnipotent—
At its own stable door.
  "I Like to See It Lap the
  Miles"

A narrow fellow in the grass
Occasionally rides;
You may have met him—did you not?
His notice sudden is.

·   ·   ·   ·   ·   ·   ·

Several of nature's people
I know, and they know me;
I feel for them a transport
Of cordiality;

But never met this fellow,
Attended or alone,

Without a tighter breathing,
And zero at the bone.
        "A Narrow Fellow in the
    Grass"

I started early, took my dog,
And visited the sea;
The mermaids in the basement
Came out to look at me,

And frigates in the upper floor
Extended hempen hands,
Presuming me to be a mouse
Aground, upon the sands.

But no man moved me till the tide
Went past my simple shoe,
And past my apron and my belt,
And past my bodice too,

And made as he would eat me up
As wholly as a dew
Upon a dandelion's sleeve—
And then I started too.

And he—he followed close behind;
I felt his silver heel
Upon my ankle,—then my shoes
Would overflow with pearl.

Until we met the solid town,
No man he seemed to know;
And bowing with a mighty look
At me, the sea withdrew.
                    "I Started Early"

Alter? When the hills do.
Falter? When the sun,
Question if his glory
Be the perfect one.

Surfeit? When the daffodil
Doth of the dew:
Even as herself, O friend!
I will of you!
                        "Alter?"

Much madness is divinest sense

To a discerning eye;
Much sense the starkest madness.
'Tis the majority
In this, as all, prevails.
Assent, and you are sane;
Demur,—you're straightway danger-
    ous,
And handled with a chain.
        "Much Madness Is Divinest
    Sense"

So we must keep apart,
You there, I here,
With just the door ajar
That oceans are,
And prayer,
And that pale sustenance,
Despair!
                "I Cannot Live with You"

I had no time to hate, because
The grave would hinder me.
And life was not so ample I
Could finish enmity.

Nor had I time to love; but since
Some industry must be,
The little toil of love, I thought,
Was large enough for me.
                "I Had No Time to Hate"

Elysium is as far as to
The very nearest room,
If in that room a friend await
Felicity or doom.

What fortitude the soul contains,
That it can so endure
The accent of a coming foot,
The opening of a door!
                                "Elysium"

The soul selects her own society,
Then shuts the door;
On her divine majority
Obtrude no more.

Unmoved, she notes the chariot's
    pausing

At her low gate;
Unmoved, an emperor is kneeling
Upon her mat.

I've known her from an ample nation
Choose one;
Then close the valves of her attention
Like stone.
> "The Soul Selects Her Own
> Society"

There's a certain slant of light,
On winter afternoons,
That oppresses, like the weight
Of cathedral tunes.

Heavenly hurt it gives us,
We can find no scar,
But internal difference
Where the meanings are.

None may teach it anything,
'Tis the seal, despair,—
An imperial affliction
Sent us of the air.

When it comes, the landscape listens,
Shadows hold their breath;
When it goes, 'tis like the distance
On the look of death.
> "There's a Certain Slant of
> Light"

A light exists in spring
Not present in the year
At any other period.
When March is scarcely here

A color stands abroad
On solitary hills
That science cannot overtake,
But human nature feels.

It waits upon the lawn;
It shows the furthest tree
Upon the furthest slope we know;
It almost speaks to me.

Then, as horizons step,
Or noons report away,
Without the formula of sound,
It passes, and we stay:

A quality of loss
Affecting our content,
As trade had suddenly encroached
Upon a sacrament.
> "A Light Exists in Spring"

Drowning is not so pitiful
    As the attempt to rise.
Three times, 'tis said, a sinking man
    Comes up to face the skies,
And then declines forever
    To that abhorred abode
Where hope and he part company—
    For he is grasped of God.
The Maker's cordial visage,
    However good to see,
Is shunned, we must admit it,
    Like an adversity.
> "Drowning Is Not So Pitiful"

The bustle in the house
The morning after death
Is solemnest of industries
Enacted upon earth;—
The sweeping up the heart
And putting love away
We shall not want to use again
Until eternity.
> "The Bustle in the House"

Because I could not stop for Death,
He kindly stopped for me;
The carriage held but just ourselves,
And Immortality.

We slowly drove, he knew no haste,
And I had put away
My labor and my leisure, too,
For his civility.

We passed the school where children
    played,
Their lessons scarcely done;

We passed the fields of gazing grain,
We passed the setting sun.

We paused before a house that seemed
A swelling of the ground;
The roof was scarcely visible,
The cornice but a mound.

Since then, 'tis centuries; but each
Feels shorter than the day
I first surmised the horses' heads
Were toward eternity.
            "Because I Could Not Stop for
            Death"

This quiet dust was Gentlemen and
      Ladies,
      And Lads and Girls;
Was laughter and ability and sighing,
      And frocks and curls.
This passive place a Summer's nimble
      mansion,
      Where Blooms and Bees
Fulfilled their Oriental Circuit,
      Then ceased like these.
                  "This Quiet Dust"

I died for beauty, but was scarce
Adjusted in the tomb,
When one who died for truth was lain
In an adjoining room.

He questioned softly why I failed?
"For beauty," I replied.
"And I for truth—the two are one;
We brethren are," he said.

And so, as kins-men met a-night,
We talked between the rooms,
Until the moss had reached our lips,
And covered up our names.
                  "I Died for Beauty"

Presentiment is that long shadow on
      the lawn
Indicative that suns go down;
The notice to the startled grass

That darkness is about to pass.
                  "Presentiment"

No one of all the purple host
Who took the flag today
Can tell the definition,
So clear, of victory,

As he, defeated, dying,
On whose forbidden ear
The distant strains of triumph
Break, agonized and clear.
            "Success Is Counted Sweetest"

After great pain a formal feeling
      comes.
                  First line of poem

THOMAS BAILEY ALDRICH
•
                        O Cruel Time,
Whose breath sweeps mortal things
      away,
   Spare long this image of his prime,
That others standing in the place
   Where save as ghosts we come no
      more,
May know what sweet, majestic face
   The gentle Prince of Players wore.
            "On Sargent's Portrait of Booth
            at the Players'"

BRET HARTE
•
What was it the Engines said,
Pilots touching, head to head
Facing on a single track,
Half a world behind each back?
            "What the Engines Said," of
            the meeting of the two lines of
            the Union Pacific, Promontory
            Point, Utah, May 10, 1869, the
            first transcontinental railroad
            link

JOHN BURROUGHS

•

In sorrow he learned this truth—
One may return to the place of his
birth,
He cannot go back to his youth.

WILLIAM VAUGHN MOODY

•

Are we the eagle nation Milton saw
Mewing its mighty youth,
Soon to possess the mountain wings of
truth,
And be a swift familiar of the sun . . .
Or have we but the talons and the
maw,
And for the abject likeness of our
heart
Shall some less lordly bird be set
apart?—
Some gross-billed wader where the
swamps are fat?
Some gorger in the sun? Some prowler
with the bat?
> "An Ode in Time of Hesita-
tion"

WILLIAM TUCKEY MEREDITH

•

Oh! while Atlantic's breast
Bears a white sail,
While the Gulf's towering crest
Tops a green vale,
Men thy bold deeds shall tell,
Old Heart of Oak,
Daring Dave Farragut,
Thunderbolt stroke!
> "Farragut"

JAMES RYDER RANDALL

•

The despot's heel is on thy shore,
Maryland!
His torch is at thy temple door,
Maryland!

Avenge the patriotic gore
That flecked the streets of Baltimore,
And be the battle-queen of yore,
Maryland! My Maryland!
> "My Maryland," written when
Union troops attacked Balti-
more, April 26, 1861

THOMAS B. REED

•

The terrible rumble, grumble and roar
Telling the battle was on once more—
And Sheridan twenty miles away!
> "Sheridan's Ride"

AMBROSE BIERCE

•

A little heap of dust,
A little streak of rust,
A stone without a name—
Lo! hero, sword and fame!

SIDNEY LANIER

•

As the marsh-hen secretly builds on
the watery sod,
Behold I will build me a nest on the
greatness of God:
I will fly in the greatness of God as
the marsh-hen flies
In the freedom that fills all the space
'twixt the marsh and the skies:
By so many roots as the marsh-grass
sends in the sod
I will heartily lay me a-hold on the
greatness of God:
Oh, like to the greatness of God is the
greatness within
The range of the marshes, the liberal
marshes of Glynn.
> "The Marshes of Glynn"

Into the woods my Master went,
Clean forspent, forspent.
Into the woods my Master came,

Forspent with love and shame,
But the olives they were not blind to
    Him;
The little gray leaves were kind to
    Him;
The thorn-tree had a mind to Him,
When into the woods He came.

Out of the woods my Master went,
And He was all content.
Out of the woods my Master came,
Content with death and shame.
When Death and Shame would woo
    Him last,
From under the trees they drew Him
    last:
'Twas on a tree they slew Him—last
When out of the woods He came.

    "A Ballad of the Trees and the
    Master"

H. Antoine D'Arcy

•

'Twas a balmy summer evening, and a
    goodly crowd was there,
Which well-nigh filled Joe's barroom
    on the corner of the square,
And as songs and witty stories came
    through the open door
A vagabond crept slowly in and posed
    upon the floor.
.   .   .   .

Another drink, and with chalk in hand
    the vagabond began
To sketch a face that well might buy
    the soul of any man.
Then, as he placed another lock upon
    the shapely head,
With a fearful shriek, he leaped and
    fell across the picture—dead.

    "The Face on the Barroom
    Floor"

John Boyle O'Reilly

•

The organised charity, scrimped and
    iced,
In the name of a cautious, statistical
    Christ.

                        "Charity"

Will Carleton

•

Over the hill to the poorhouse I'm
    trudgin' my weary way.
    "Over the Hill to the Poor-
    house"

Emma Lazarus

•

Give me your tired, your poor,
Your huddled masses, yearning to
    breathe free,
The wretched refuse of your teeming
    shore.
Send these, the homeless, tempest
    tossed, to me;
I lift my lamp beside the golden door.
    Inscription on Statue of Lib-
    erty, New York Harbor

Rosa Hartwick Thorpe

•

Curfew Must Not Ring To-Night.
                Title and refrain

Edwin Markham

•

Bowed by the weight of centuries he
    leans
Upon his hoe and gazes on the ground,
The emptiness of ages in his face,
And on his back the burden of the
    world.
Who made him dead to rapture and
    despair,
A thing that grieves not and that never
    hopes,
Stolid and stunned, a brother to the
    ox?

Who loosened and let down this brutal
jaw?
Whose was the hand that slanted back
this brow?
Whose breath blew out the light within
this brain?

. . . .

O masters, lords, and rulers in all
lands,
Is this the handiwork you give to God?

. . . .

O masters, lords, and rulers in all
lands,
How will the Future reckon with this
Man?
How answer his brute question in that
hour
When whirlwinds of rebellion shake
all shores?
How will it be with kingdoms and with
kings—
With those who shaped him to the
thing he is—
When this dumb Terror shall rise to
judge the world,
After the silence of the centuries?

"The Man with the Hoe"

He drew a circle that shut me out—
Heretic, rebel, a thing to flout.
But Love and I had the wit to win:
We drew a circle that took him in.

"Outwitted"

Lizette Woodworth Reese
•

When I consider life and its few
years—
A wisp of fog betwixt us and the sun;
A call to battle and the battle done
Ere the last echo dies within our ears;
A rose choked in the grass; an hour of
fears;
The gusts that past a darkening shore
do beat;
A burst of music down an unlistening
street—

I wonder at the idleness of tears.
Ye, old, old dead, and ye of yester-
night,
Chieftains and bards and keepers of
the sheep;
By every cup of sorrow that you had,
Loose me from tears, and make me see
aright
How each hath back what once he
stayed to weep;
Homer his sight, David his little lad!

"Tears"

Sam Walter Foss
•

Why should I sit in the scorner's seat,
Or hurl the cynic's ban?
Let me live in my house by the side of
the road
And be a friend to man.

"The House by the Side of the
Road"

Henry Holcomb Bennett
•

Hats off!
Along the street there comes
A blare of bugles, a ruffle of drums,
A flash of color beneath the sky:
Hats off!
The flag is passing by!

"The Flag Goes By"

George Santayana
•

O world, thou choosest not the better
part!
It is not wisdom to be only wise,
And on the inward vision close the
eyes,
But it is wisdom to believe the heart.
Columbus found a world and had no
chart,
Save one that faith deciphered in the
skies;

To trust the soul's invincible surmise
Was all his science and his only art.
Our knowledge is a torch of smoky
  pine
That lights the pathway but one step
  ahead
Across a void of mystery and dread.
Bid, then, the tender light of faith to
  shine
By which alone the mortal heart is led
Unto the thinking of the thought di-
  vine.

                                    "Faith"

As in the midst of battle there is room
For thoughts of love, and in foul sin
  for mirth;
As gossips whisper of a trinket's worth
Spied by the death-bed's flickering
  candle-gloom;
As in the crevices of Caesar's tomb
The sweet herbs flourish on a little
  earth:
So in this great disaster of our birth
We can be happy, and forget our
  doom.
For morning, with a ray of tenderest
  joy
Gilding the iron heaven, hides the
  truth,
And evening gently woos us to employ
Our grief in idle catches. Such is
  youth;
Till from that summer's trance we
  wake, to find
Despair before us, vanity behind.

                                    Sonnet

RICHARD HOVEY
•

I do not know beneath what sky
  Nor on what seas shall be thy fate;
I only know it shall be high,
  I only know it shall be great.

                        "Unmanifest Destiny"

EDGAR LEE MASTERS
•

And I say to you, Spoon River,
And to you, O republic,
Beware of the man who rises to power
From one suspender.

        Spoon River Anthology, "John
        Hancock Otis"

Listen to me, ye who live in the senses
And think through the senses only:
Immortality is not a gift,
Immortality is an achievement;
And only those who strive mightily
Shall possess it.

        Ibid., "The Village Atheist"

Often you asked me,
"What is the use of knowing the evil
  in the world?"
I am out of your way now, Spoon
  River,
Choose your own good and call it
  good.
For I could never make you see
That no one knows what is good
Who knows not what is evil;
And no one knows what is true
Who knows not what is false.

        Ibid., "Seth Compton"

God! ask me not to record your won-
  ders,
I admit the stars and the suns
And the countless worlds.
But I have measured their distances
And weighed them and discovered
  their substances.
I have devised wings for the air,
And keels for water,
And horses of iron for the earth.
.   .   .   .
I have written the *Iliad* and *Hamlet;*
And I have explored your mysteries,
And searched for you without ceasing,
And found you again after losing you
In hours of weariness—
And I ask you:

How would you like to create a sun
And the next day have the worms
Slipping in and out between your fingers?

> *Ibid.,* "Schofield Huxley"

Seeds in a dry pod, tick, tick, tick,
Tick, tick, tick, like mites in a quarrel—
Faint iambics that the full breeze wakens—
But the pine tree makes a symphony thereof.
Triolets, villanelles, rondels, rondeaus,
Ballades by the score with the same old thought:
The snows and the roses of yesterday are vanished;
And what is love but a rose that fades?
Life all around me here in the village:
Tragedy, comedy, valor and truth,
Courage, constancy, heroism, failure—
All in the loom, and oh what patterns!
Woodlands, meadows, streams and rivers—
Blind to all of it all my life long.
Triolets, villanelles, rondels, rondeaus,
Seeds in a dry pod, tick, tick, tick,
Tick, tick, tick, what little iambics,
While Homer and Whitman roared in the pines!

> *Ibid.,* "Petit, the Poet"

Degenerate sons and daughters,
Life is too strong for you—
It takes life to love Life.

> *Ibid.,* "Lucinda Matlock"

I am Ann Rutledge who sleeps beneath these weeds.
Beloved of Abraham Lincoln,
Wedded to him, not through union,
But through separation.
Bloom forever, O Republic,
From the dust of my bosom.

> *Ibid.,* "Ann Rutledge." There
> is no evidence that Lincoln ever
> loved Ann Rutledge.

EDWIN ARLINGTON ROBINSON
•

You are a friend then, as I make it out,
Of our man Shakespeare, who alone of us
Will put an ass's head in Fairyland.

.   .   .   .

"Your fly will serve as well as anybody.
And what's his hour? He flies, and flies, and flies,
And in his fly's mind has a brave appearance;
And then your spider gets him in his net,
And eats him up and hangs him up to dry.
That's Nature, the kind mother of us all.
And then your slattern housemaid swings her broom,
And where's your spider? And that's Nature, also.
It's Nature, and it's Nothing. It's all Nothing.
It's all a world where bugs and emperors
Go singularly back to the same dust,
Each in his time; and the old, ordered stars
That sang together, Ben, will sing the same
Old stave to-morrow."

> "Ben Jonson Entertains a Man
> from Stratford"

If after all that we have lived and thought,
All comes to Nought—
If there be nothing after Now,
And we be nothing anyhow,
And we know that—why live?
'Twere sure but weaklings' vain distress
To suffer dungeons where so many doors
Will open on the cold eternal shores
That look sheer down

To the dark tideless floods of Nothing-
ness
Where all who know may drown.

> "The Man Against the Sky"

I don't say what God is, but it's a
name
That somehow answers us when we
are driven
To feel and think how little we have
to do
With what we are.

> "King Jasper"

> . . . No God,
No Law, no purpose, could have
hatched for sport
Out of warm water and slime, a war
for life
That was unnecessary, and far better
Had never been—if man, as we behold
him,
Is all it means.

> *Ibid.*

Let us, the Children of the Night,
Put off the cloak that hides the scar!—
Let us be Children of the Light,
And tell the ages what we are!

> "The Children of the Night"

Here where the wind is always north-
north-east
And children learn to walk on frozen
toes,
Wonder begets an envy of all those
Who boil elsewhere with such a lyric
yeast
Of love that you will hear them at a
feast
Where demons would appeal for some
repose,
Still clamoring where the chalice over-
flows
And crying wildest who have drunk
the least.

Passion is here a soilure of the wits,

We're told, and Love a cross for them
to bear;
Joy shivers in the corner where she
knits
And Conscience always has the rock-
ing chair,
Cheerful as when she tortured into fits
The first cat that was ever killed by
Care.

> "New England"

He comes, and probably for years
  Will he be coming yet,—
Familiar as an old mistake,
  And futile as regret.

> "Bewick Finzer"

His words were magic and his heart
  was true,
  And everywhere he wandered he
  was blessed.
Out of all ancient men my childhood
  knew
  I choose him and I mark him for
  the best.
Of all authoritative liars, too,
  I crown him loveliest.

> "Uncle Ananias"

For we were not as other men:
'Twas ours to soar and his to see:
But we are coming down again,
And we shall come down pleasantly;
Nor shall we longer disagree
On what it is to be sublime,
But flourish in our perigee
And have one Titan at a time.

> "The Master," supposed to
> have been written not long
> after the Civil War

Go to the western gate, Luke Haver-
gal,
There where the vines cling crimson
  on the wall,
And in the twilight wait for what will
  come.

> "Luke Havergal"

Miniver Cheevy, child of scorn,
   Grew lean while he assailed the sea-
   sons;
He wept that he was ever born,
   And he had reasons.

.   .   .   .

Miniver Cheevy, born too late,
   Scratched his head and kept on
   thinking;
Miniver coughed, and called it fate,
   And kept on drinking.
"Miniver Cheevy"

Whenever Richard Cory went down
   town,
We people on the pavement looked at
   him:
He was a gentleman from sole to
   crown,
Clean favored, and imperially slim.

And he was always quietly arrayed,
And he was always human when he
   talked;
But still he fluttered pulses when he
   said,
"Good morning," and he glittered
   when he walked.

And he was rich—yes, richer than a
   king—
And admirably schooled in every
   grace.
In fine, we thought that he was everything
To make us wish that we were in his
   place.

So on we worked, and waited for the
   light,
And went without the meat, and
   cursed the bread;
And Richard Cory, one fine summer
   night,
Went home and put a bullet through
   his head.
"Richard Cory"

There was not much that was ahead
   of him,
And there was nothing in the town below—
Where strangers would have shut the
   many doors
That many friends had opened long
   ago.
"Mr. Flood's Party"

Whether or not we read him, we can
   feel
From time to time the vigor of his
   name
Against us like a finger for the shame
And emptiness of what our souls reveal
In books that are as altars where we
   kneel
To consecrate the flicker, not the
   flame.
"George Crabbe, Poet to Poet"

For, dear me, why abandon a belief
Merely because it ceases to be true?
Cling to it long enough, and not a
   doubt
It will turn true again, for so it goes.
Most of the change we think we see in
   life
Is due to truths being in and out of
   favour.
"The Black Cottage"

Stephen Crane

Tradition, thou art for suckling chil-
   dren,
Thou art the enlivening milk for
   babes;
But no meat for men is in thee.
Then—
But, alas, we are all babes.
"Tradition"

A man said to the universe,
"Sir, I exist!"

"However," replied the universe,
"The fact has not created in me
A sense of obligation."

"The Man"

In the desert I saw a creature, naked,
    bestial,
Who, squatting upon the ground, held
    his heart in his hand
And ate of it. I said, "Is it good,
    friend?"
"It is bitter—bitter," he answered;
    "But I like it
Because it is bitter, and because it is
    my heart."

"The Heart"

Do not weep, maiden, for war is kind.
Because your lover threw wild hands
    toward the sky
And the affrighted steed ran on alone,
Do not weep.
War is kind.

"War Is Kind"

I stood upon a high place,
And saw, below, many devils
Running, leaping,
And carousing in sin.
One looked up, grinning,
And said, "Comrade! Brother!"

"I Stood Upon a High Place"

The wayfarer,
Perceiving the pathway to truth,
Was struck with astonishment.
It was thickly grown with weeds.
"Ha," he said,
"I see no one has passed here
In a long time."
Later he saw that each weed
Was a singular knife.
"Well," he mumbled at last,
"Doubtless there are other roads."

"The Wayfarer"

ARTHUR CHAPMAN
•

Out where the handclasp's a little
    stronger,
Out where the smile dwells a little
    longer,
That's where the West begins.

"Out Where the West Begins"

AMY LOWELL
•

Sappho would speak, I think, quite
    openly,
And Mrs. Browning guard a careful
    silence,
But Emily would set doors ajar and
    slam them
And love you for your speed of ob-
    servation.

"The Sisters"

I shall go
Up and down,
In my gown.
Gorgeously arrayed,
Boned and stayed.
And the softness of my body will be
    guarded from embrace
By each button, hook, and lace.
For the man who should loose me is
    dead,
Fighting with the Duke in Flanders,
In a pattern called a war.
Christ! What are patterns for?

"Patterns"

You are beautiful and faded,
Like an old opera tune
Played upon a harpsichord.

"A Lady"

ALICE DUER MILLER
•

I am American bred,
    I have seen much to hate here—
    much to forgive,

SERIOUS VERSE: STEIN—FROST

But in a world where England is finished and dead,
  I do not wish to live.
> "The White Cliffs"

GERTRUDE STEIN
•

A rose is a rose is a rose.
I am Rose my eyes are blue
I am Rose and who are you
I am Rose and when I sing
I am Rose like anything.
> "I Am Rose"

Pigeons on the grass alas.
> *Four Saints in Three Acts,* 1934

TRUMBULL STICKNEY
•

Be still. The Hanging Gardens were a
  dream
That over Persian roses flew to kiss
The curled lashes of Semiramis.
Troy never was, nor green Skamander
  stream.
Provence and Troubadour are merest
  lies,
The glorious hair of Venice was a
  beam
Made within Titian's eye. The sunsets
  seem,
The world is very old and nothing is.
> "Be Still"

It's autumn in the country I remember.

How warm a wind blew here about
  the ways!
And shadows on the hillside lay to
  slumber
During the long sun-sweetened sum-
  mer-days.

It's cold abroad the country I remember.

The swallows veering skimmed the
  golden grain
At midday with a wing aslant and
  limber;
And yellow cattle browsed upon the
  plain.

It's empty down the country I remember.

I had a sister lovely in my sight:
Her hair was dark, her eyes were very
  somber;
We sang together in the woods at
  night.

It's lonely in the country I remember.

The babble of our children fills my
  ears,
And on our hearth I stare the perished
  ember
To flames that show all starry thro'
  my tears.

It's dark about the country, I remember.
> "Mnemosyne"

ROBERT FROST
•

I'm going out to clean the pasture
  spring;
I'll only stop to rake the leaves away
(And wait to watch the water clear,
  I may):
I sha'n't be gone long.—You come too.

I'm going out to fetch the little calf
That's standing by the mother. It's so
  young
It totters when she licks it with her
  tongue.
I sha'n't be gone long.—You come too.
> "The Pasture"

The fact is the sweetest dream that
  labor knows.

My long scythe whispered and left the hay to make.

"Mowing"

We make ourselves a place apart
  Behind light words that tease and flout,
But oh, the agitated heart
  Till someone find us really out.

'T is pity if the case require
  (Or so we say) that in the end
We speak the literal to inspire
  The understanding of a friend.

But so with all, from babes that play
  At hide-and-seek to God afar,
So all who hide too well away
  Must speak and tell us where they are.

"Revelation"

"Men work together," I told him from the heart,
"Whether they work together or apart."

"The Tuft of Flowers"

My apple trees will never get across
And eat the cones under his pines, I tell him.
He only says, "Good fences make good neighbors."

"Mending Wall"

Before I built a wall I'd ask to know
What I was walling in or walling out,
And to whom I was like to give offence.
Something there is that doesn't love a wall,
That wants it down!

Ibid.

"Home is the place where, when you have to go there,
They have to take you in."

"I should have called it

Something you somehow haven't to deserve."

"The Death of the Hired Man"

My long two-pointed ladder's sticking through a tree
Toward heaven still,
And there's a barrel that I didn't fill
Beside it, and there may be two or three
Apples I didn't pick upon some bough.
But I am done with apple-picking now.
Essence of winter sleep is on the night,
The scent of apples: I am drowsing off.
I cannot rub the strangeness from my sight
I get from looking through a pane of glass
I skimmed this morning from the drinking trough
And held against the world of hoary grass.
It melted, and I let it fall and break.
But I was well
Upon my way to sleep before it fell,
And I could tell
What form my dreaming was about to take.
Magnified apples appear and disappear,
Stem end and blossom end,
And every fleck of russet showing clear.
My instep arch not only keeps the ache,
It keeps the pressure of a ladder-round.
I feel the ladder sway as the boughs bend.
And I keep hearing from the cellar bin
The rumbling sound
Of load on load of apples coming in.
For I have had too much
Of apple-picking: I am overtired
Of the great harvest I myself desired.

There were ten thousand thousand
    fruit to touch,
Cherish in hand, lift down, and not
    let fall.
For all
That struck the earth,
No matter if not bruised or spiked
    with stubble,
Went surely to the cider-apple heap
As of no worth.
One can see what will trouble
This sleep of mine, whatever sleep it is.
Were he not gone,
The woodchuck could say whether it's
    like his
Long sleep, as I describe its coming on,
Or just some human sleep.
               "After Apple-Picking"

        You've found out something.
The hand that knows his business
    won't be told
To do work better or faster—those
    two things.
               "The Code"

        I thought that only
Someone who lived in turning to fresh
    tasks
Could so forget his handiwork on
    which
He spent himself, the labor of his ax,
And leave it there far from a useful
    fireplace
To warm the frozen swamp as best it
    could
With the slow smokeless burning of
    decay.
               "The Wood-Pile"

Two roads diverged in a yellow wood,
And sorry I could not travel both
And be one traveler, long I stood
And looked down one as far as I could
To where it bent in the underbrush;

Then took the other, as just as fair,
And having perhaps the better claim,

Because it was grassy and wanted
    wear;
Though as for that the passing there
Had worn them really about the same,

And both that morning equally lay
In leaves no step had trodden black.
Oh, I kept the first for another day!
Yet knowing how way leads on to
    way,
I doubted if I should ever come back.

I should be telling this with a sigh
Somewhere ages and ages hence:
Two roads diverged in a wood, and
    I—
I took the one less traveled by,
And that has made all the difference.
               "The Road Not Taken"

There is a singer everyone has heard,
Loud, a mid-summer and a mid-wood
    bird,
Who makes the solid tree trunks sound
    again.
He says that leaves are old and that
    for flowers
Mid-summer is to spring as one to ten.
He says the early petal-fall is past
When pear and cherry bloom went
    down in showers
On sunny days a moment overcast;
And comes that other fall we name the
    fall.
He says the highway dust is over all.
The bird would cease and be as other
    birds
But that he knows in singing not to
    sing.
The question that he frames in all but
    words
Is what to make of a diminished thing.
               "The Oven Bird"

So was I once myself a swinger of
    birches;
And so I dream of going back to be.
It's when I'm weary of considerations,

And life is too much like a pathless
   wood
Where your face burns and tickles with
   the cobwebs
Broken across it, and one eye is weep-
   ing
From a twig's having lashed it open,
I'd like to get away from earth a while
And then come back to it and begin
   over.
May no fate wilfully misunderstand
   me
And half grant what I wish and snatch
   me away
Not to return. Earth's the right place
   for love:
I don't know where it's likely to go
   better.
I'd like to go by climbing a high birch
   tree,
And climb black branches up a snow-
   white trunk
Toward heaven, till the tree could
   bear no more,
But dipped its top and set me down
   again.
That would be good both going and
   coming back.
One could do worse than be a swinger
   of birches.

                         "Birches"

I wonder about the trees:
Why do we wish to hear
Forever the noise of these
More than another noise
So close to our dwelling-place?

               "The Sound of the Trees"

                         Do you know,
Considering the market, there are
   more
Poems produced than any other thing?
No wonder poets sometimes have to
   seem
So much more business-like than busi-
   ness men.

Their wares are so much harder to get
   rid of.

                         "New Hampshire"

She's one of the two best states in the
   Union.
Vermont's the other.

                              Ibid.

Some say the world will end in fire,
Some say in ice.
From what I've tasted of desire
I hold with those who favor fire.
But if it had to perish twice,
I think I know enough of hate
To say that for destruction ice
Is also great
And would suffice.

                         "Fire and Ice"

The way a crow
Shook down on me
The dust of snow
From a hemlock tree

Has given my heart
A change of mood
And saved some part
Of a day I had rued.

                         "Dust of Snow"

Nature's first green is gold;
Her hardest hue to hold.
Her early leaf's a flower;
But only so an hour.
Then leaf subsides to leaf.
So Eden sank to grief,
So dawn goes down to day.
Nothing gold can stay.

                    "Nothing Gold Can Stay"

Once when the snow of the year was
   beginning to fall,
We stopped by a mountain pasture to
   say, "Whose colt?"
A little Morgan had one forefoot on
   the wall,

The other curled at his breast. He
dipped his head
And snorted at us. And then he had
to bolt.
We heard the miniature thunder
where he fled,
And we saw him, or thought we saw
him, dim and grey,
Like a shadow against the curtain of
falling flakes.
"I think the little fellow's afraid of
the snow.
He isn't winter-broken. It isn't play
With the little fellow at all. He's running away.
I doubt if even his mother could tell
him, 'Sakes,
It's only weather.' He'd think she
didn't know!
Where is his mother? He can't be out
alone."
And now he comes again with a clat-
ter of stone
And mounts the wall again with
whited eyes
And all his tail that isn't hair up
straight.
He shudders his coat as if to shake off
flies.
"Whoever it is that leaves him out so
late,
When other creatures have gone to
stall and bin,
Ought to be told to come and take
him in."

"The Runaway"

Whose woods these are I think I know.
His house is in the village though;
He will not see me stopping here
To watch his woods fill up with snow.

My little horse must think it queer
To stop without a farmhouse near
Between the woods and frozen lake
The darkest evening of the year.

He gives his harness bells a shake

To ask if there is some mistake.
The only other sound's the sweep
Of easy wind and downy flake.

The woods are lovely, dark and deep,
But I have promises to keep,
And miles to go before I sleep,
And miles to go before I sleep.

"Stopping by Woods on a
Snowy Evening"

The shattered water made a misty din.
Great waves looked over others com-
ing in,
And thought of doing something to the
shore
That water never did to land before.
The clouds were low and hairy in the
skies,
Like locks blown forward in the gleam
of eyes.
You could not tell, and yet it looked
as if
The shore was lucky in being backed
by cliff,
The cliff in being backed by continent;
It looked as if a night of dark intent
Was coming, and not only a night, an
age.
Someone had better be prepared for
rage.
There would be more than ocean-
water broken
Before God's last *Put out the Light*
was spoken.

"Once by the Pacific"

That day she put our heads together,
Fate had her imagination about her,
Your head so much concerned with
outer,
Mine with inner, weather.

"Tree at My Window"

The sun was warm but the wind was
chill.
You know how it is with an April day:

When the sun is out and the wind is
     still,
You're one month on in the middle of
     May.
But if you so much as dare to speak,
A cloud comes over the sunlit arch,
A wind comes off a frozen peak,
And you're two months back in the
     middle of March.
"Two Tramps in Mud Time"

But yield who will to their separation,
My object in life is to unite
My avocation and my vocation
As my two eyes make one in sight.
Only where love and need are one,
And the work is play for mortal stakes,
Is the deed ever really done
For Heaven and the future's sakes.
Ibid.

They cannot scare me with their
     empty spaces
Between stars—no stars where no hu-
     man race is.
I have it in me so much nearer home
To scare myself with my own desert
     places.
"Desert Places"

I never dared be radical when young
For fear it would make me conserva-
     tive when old.
"Precaution"

Never ask of money spent
Where the spender thinks it went.
Nobody was ever meant
To remember or invent
What he did with every cent.
"The Hardship of Accounting"

You see the beauty of my proposal is
It needn't wait on general revolution.
I bid you to a one-man revolution—
The only revolution that is coming.
"Build Soil"

Don't join too many gangs. Join few if
     any.
Join the United States and join the
     family—
But not much in between unless a col-
     lege.
Ibid.

I'm liberal. You, you aristocrat
     Won't know exactly what I mean by
     that.
I mean so altruistically moral
     I never take my own side in a quar-
     rel.
"A Witness Tree"

She is as in a field a silken tent
At midday when a sunny summer
     breeze
Has dried the dew and all its ropes
     relent,
So that in guys it gently sways at ease,
And its supporting central cedar pole,
That is its pinnacle to heavenward
And signifies the sureness of the soul,
Seems to owe naught to any single
     cord,
But strictly held by none, is loosely
     bound
By countless silken ties of love and
     thought
To everything on earth the compass
     round,
And only by one's going slightly taut
In the capriciousness of summer air
Is of the slightest bondage made
     aware.
"The Silken Tent"

The land was ours before we were the
     land's.
She was our land more than a hun-
     dred years
Before we were her people. She was
     ours
In Massachusetts, in Virginia,
But we were England's, still colonials,

Possessing what we still were unpos-
    sessed by,
Possessed by what we now no more
    possessed.
Something we were withholding left
    us weak
Until we found out that it was our-
    selves
We were withholding from our land of
    living,
And forthwith found salvation in sur-
    render.
Such as we were we gave ourselves
    outright
(The deed of gift was many deeds of
    war)
To the land vaguely realizing west-
    ward,
But still unstoried, artless, unen-
    hanced,
Such as she was, such as she would
    become.
              "The Gift Outright"

I hold your doctrine of Memento
    Mori.
And were an epitaph to be my story
I'd have a short one ready for my own.
I would have written of me on my
    stone:
I had a lover's quarrel with the world.
              "The Lesson for Today"

I advocate a semi-revolution.
The trouble with a total revolution
(Ask any reputable Rosicrucian)
Is that it brings the same class up on
    top.
Executives of skillful execution
Will therefore plan to go half-way and
    stop.
Yes, revolutions are the only salves,
But they're one thing that should be
    done by halves.
              "A Semi-Revolution"

The play seems out for an almost in-
    finite run

Don't mind a little thing like the ac-
    tors fighting.
The only thing I worry about is the
    sun.
We'll be all right if nothing goes
    wrong with the lighting.
              "It Bids Pretty Fair"

Sarcastic Science she would like to
    know,
In her complacent ministry of fear,
How we propose to get away from here
When she has made things so we have
    to go
Or be wiped out. Will she be asked to
    show
Us how by rocket we may hope to steer
To some star off there say a half light-
    year
Through temperature of absolute
    zeró?
Why wait for Science to supply the
    how
When any amateur can tell it now?
The way to go away should be the
    same
As fifty million years ago we came—
If anyone remembers how that was.
I have a theory, but it hardly does.
              "Why Wait for Science"

Job says there's no such thing as
    Earth's becoming
An easier place for man to save his
    soul in.
Except as a hard place to save his
    soul in,
A trial ground where he can try him-
    self
And find out whether he is any good,
It would be meaningless. It might as
    well
Be Heaven at once and have it over
    with.
             A Masque of Reason

It's God.
I'd have known Him by Blake's pic-
    ture anywhere.

SHERWOOD ANDERSON

•

I am a child, a confused child in a
  confused world.

Mid-American Chants, "Chicago"

SARAH N. CLEGHORN

•

The golf links lie so near the mill
  That almost every day
The laboring children can look out
  And see the men at play.

"The Golf Links"

ADELAIDE CRAPSEY

•

These be
Three silent things:
The falling snow . . . the hour
Before the dawn . . . the mouth of
  one
Just dead.

"Triad"

Just now,
Out of the strange
Still dusk . . . as strange, as still . . .
A white moth flew. Why am I grown
So cold?

"The Warning"

"Why do
You thus devise
Evil against her?" "For that
She is beautiful, delicate.
Therefore."

"Susanna and the Elders"

CARL SANDBURG

•

The fog comes
on little cat feet.
It sits looking

over the harbor and city
on silent haunches
and then moves on.

"Fog"

Hog-butcher for the World,
Tool-maker, Stacker of Wheat,
Player with Railroads and the Nation's Freight-handler;
Stormy, husky, brawling,
City of the Big Shoulders.

"Chicago"

I speak of new cities and new people.
I tell you the past is a bucket of ashes.
I tell you yesterday is a world gone
  down,
  A sun dropped into the West.
I tell you there is nothing in the world
  only an ocean of tomorrows, a sky
  of tomorrows.

"Prairie"

Pile the bodies high at Austerlitz and
  Waterloo.
Shovel them under and let me work—
  I am the grass; I cover all.

And pile them high at Gettysburg
And pile them high at Ypres and Verdun.
Shovel them under and let me work.
Two years, ten years, and the passengers ask the conductor:
    What place is this?
    Where are we now?
    I am the grass.
    Let me work.

"Grass"

When Abraham Lincoln was shoveled
  into the tombs, he forgot the copperheads and the assassin . . . in
  the dust, in the cool tombs.

And Ulysses Grant lost all thought of
  con men and Wall Street, cash

and collateral turned ashes . . .
in the dust, in the cool tombs.

Pocahontas' body, lovely as a poplar,
sweet as a red haw in November
or a pawpaw in May, did she
wonder? does she remember?
. . . in the dust, in the cool
tombs?

Take any streetful of people buying
clothes and groceries, cheering a
hero or throwing confetti and
blowing tin horns . . . tell me if
the lovers are losers . . . tell me
if any get more than the lovers
. . . in the dust . . . in the cool
tombs.

"Cool Tombs"

Why is there always a secret singing
When a lawyer cashes in?
Why does a hearse horse snicker
Hauling a lawyer away?

"The Lawyers Know Too
Much"

They put up big wooden gods.
Then they burned the big wooden
gods
And put up brass gods and
Changing their minds suddenly
Knocked down the brass gods and put
up
A dough-face god with gold ear-rings.
The poor mutts, the pathetic slant
heads,
They didn't know a little tin god
Is as good as anything in the line of
gods,
Nor how a little tin god answers
prayer
And makes rain and brings luck
The same as a big wooden god or a
brass
Or dough-face god with golden ear-
rings.

"Manufactured Gods"

I won't take my religion from any man
who never works except with his
mouth and never cherishes any memory except
the face of the woman on the American
silver dollar.

"To a Contemporary Bunk-
shooter"

A father sees a son nearing manhood.
What shall he tell that son?
"Life is hard; be steel; be a rock."
And this might stand him for the
storms
and serve him for humdrum and monotony
and guide him among sudden betrayals
and tighten him for slack moments.
"Life is a soft loam; be gentle; go
easy."
And this too might serve him.
Brutes have been gentled where lashes
failed.
The growth of a frail flower in a path
up
has sometimes shattered and split a
rock.
A tough will counts. So does desire.
So does a rich soft wanting.
Without rich wanting nothing arrives.

The People, Yes

The free man willing to pay and struggle and die for the freedom of
himself and others
Knowing how far to subject himself to
discipline and obedience for the
sake of an ordered society free
from tyrants, exploiters and legal-
ized frauds—
This free man is a rare bird and when
you meet him take a good look at
him and try to figure him out because
Some day when the United States of
the Earth gets going and runs

smooth and pretty there will be more of him than we have now.

Ibid.

VACHEL LINDSAY

•

Sleep softly . . . eagle forgotten . . . under the stone.
Time has its way with you there, and the clay has its own.

.   .   .   .

To live in mankind is far more than to live in a name,
To live in mankind, far, far more than . . . to live in a name.

"The Eagle that Is Forgotten"

It is portentous, and a thing of state
That here at midnight, in our little town
A mourning figure walks, and will not rest,
Near the old court-house pacing up and down,

Or by his homestead, or in shadowed yards
He lingers where his children used to play,
Or through the market, on the well-worn stones
He stalks until the dawn-stars burn away.

.   .   .   .

The sins of all the war-lords burn his heart.
He sees the dreadnaughts scouring every main.
He carries on his shawl-wrapped shoulders now
The bitterness, the folly and the pain.

"Abraham Lincoln Walks at Midnight (in Springfield, Illinois)"

Fat black bucks in a wine-barrel room,
Barrel-house kings, with feet unstable,
Sagged and reeled and pounded on the table,
Pounded on the table,
Beat an empty barrel with the handle of a broom,
Hard as they were able.
Boom, boom, Boom,
With a silk umbrella and the handle of a broom,
Boomlay, boomlay, boomlay, Boom.

.   .   .   .

Then I saw the Congo, creeping through the black,
Cutting through the Jungle with a golden track.

"The Congo: A Study of the Negro Race"

Let not young souls be smothered out before
They do quaint deeds and fully flaunt their pride.
It is the world's one crime its babes grow dull,
Its poor are ox-like, limp and leaden-eyed.
Not that they starve, but starve so dreamlessly;
Not that they sow, but that they seldom reap;
Not that they serve, but have no gods to serve;
Not that they die, but that they die like sheep.

"The Leaden-Eyed"

MABEL DODGE LUHAN

•

White man, you know, 'way deep down in you,
The Indian is the better man.
Deeply you are ruined—spoiled—inferior—lost, lost!

Lorenzo in Taos

WALLACE STEVENS

•

Beauty is momentary in the mind—
The fitful tracing of a portal;
But in the flesh it is immortal.
"Peter Quince at the Clavier"

A tune upon the blue guitar
Of things exactly as they are.
"The Man with the Blue Gui-
tar"

Let be be finale of seem.
The only emperor is the emperor of
ice-cream.
"The Emperor of Ice-Cream"

Chieftain Iffucan of Azcan in caftan
Of tan with henna hackles, halt!

Damned universal cock, as if the sun
Was blackamoor to bear your blazing
tail.

Fat! Fat! Fat! Fat! I am the personal.
Your world is you. I am my world.

You ten-foot poet among inchlings.
Fat!
Begone! An inchling bristles in these
pines,

Bristles, and points their Appalachian
tangs,
And fears not portly Azcan nor his
hoos.
"Bantams in Pine-Woods"

Complacencies of the peignoir, and
late
Coffee and oranges in a sunny chair,
And the green freedom of a cockatoo
Upon a rug mingle to dissipate
The holy hush of ancient sacrifice.
She dreams a little, and she feels the
dark
Encroachment of that old catastrophe,
As a calm darkens among water-lights.

The pungent oranges and bright, green
wings
Seem things in some procession of the
dead,
Winding across wide water, without
sound.
The day is like wide water, without
sound,
Stilled for the passing of her dreaming
feet
Over the seas, to silent Palestine,
Dominion of the blood and sepulchre.
"Sunday Morning"

She says, "I am content when wakened
birds,
Before they fly, test the reality
Of misty fields, by their sweet ques-
tionings;
But when the birds are gone, and their
warm fields
Return no more, where, then, is para-
dise?"
Ibid.

We live in an old chaos of the sun,
Or old dependency of day and night,
Or island solitude, unsponsored, free,
Or that wide water, inescapable.
Deer walk upon our mountains, and
the quail
Whistle about us their spontaneous
cries;
Sweet berries ripen in the wilderness;
And, in the isolation of the sky,
At evening, casual flocks of pigeons
make
Ambiguous undulations as they sink,
Downward to darkness, on extended
wings.
Ibid.

GRANTLAND RICE

•

When the One Great Scorer comes to
write against your name—

He marks—not that you won or lost—
    but how you played the game.
                "Alumnus Football"

All wars are planned by old men
    In council rooms apart,
Who plan for greater armament
    And map the battle chart.

.   .   .   .

But where their sightless eyes stare out
    Beyond life's vanished joys,
I've noticed nearly all the dead
    Were hardly more than boys.
              "Two Sides of War"

HERMANN HAGEDORN
•

The bomb that fell on Hiroshima fell
    on America too.
It fell on no city, no munition plants,
    no docks.
It erased no church, vaporized no pub-
    lic buildings, reduced no man to
    his atomic elements.
But it fell, it fell.
It burst. It shook the land.
God, have mercy on our children.
God have mercy on America.
        "The Bomb that Fell on Amer-
        ica"

SARA TEASDALE
•

Strephon kissed me in the spring,
    Robin in the fall,
But Colin only looked at me
    And never kissed at all.

Strephon's kiss was lost in jest,
    Robin's lost in play,
But the kiss in Colin's eyes
    Haunts me night and day.
              "The Look"

EZRA POUND
•

The age demanded an image
Of its accelerated grimace,
Something for the modern stage,
Not, at any rate, an Attic grace;

Not, not certainly, the obscure reveries
Of the inward gaze;
Better mendacities
Than the classics in paraphrase!

The "age demanded" chiefly a mould
    in plaster,
Made with no loss of time,
A prose kinema, not, not assuredly,
    alabaster
Or the "sculpture" of rhyme.
        "The Age Demanded an Image"

Like a skein of loose silk blown against
    a wall
She walks by the railing of a path in
    Kensington Gardens,
And she is dying piece-meal of a sort
    of emotional anemia.

And round about her there is a rabble
Of the filthy, sturdy, unkillable in-
    fants of the very poor.
They shall inherit the earth.

In her is the end of breeding.
Her boredom is exquisite and exces-
    sive.
She would like someone to speak to
    her,
And is almost afraid that I will com-
    mit that indiscretion.
             "The Garden"

I make a pact with you, Walt Whit-
    man—
I have detested you long enough.
I come to you as a grown child
Who has had a pig-headed father;
I am old enough now to make friends.
It was you that broke the new wood,

Now is the time for carving.
We have one sap and one root—
Let there be commerce between us.

"A Pact"

The ant's a centaur in his dragon
world.
Pull down thy vanity, it is not man
Made courage, or made order, or
made grace,
Pull down thy vanity, I say pull
down.
Learn of the green world what can be
thy place
In scaled invention or true artistry,
Pull down thy vanity,
Paquin pull down!
The green cask has outdone your ele-
gance.

"Master thyself, then others shall thee
beare"
Pull down thy vanity
Thou art a beaten dog beneath the
hail,
A swollen magpie in a fitful sun,
Half black half white
Nor knowst'ou wing from tail
Pull down thy vanity
How mean thy hates
Fostered in falsity,
Pull down thy vanity,
Rathe to destroy, niggard in charity,
Pull down thy vanity,
I say pull down.

"Canto LXXXI"

ELINOR WYLIE

•

I love those skies, thin blue or snowy
gray,
Those fields sparse-planted, rendering
meagre sheaves;
That spring, briefer than apple-blos-
som's breath,
Summer, so much too beautiful to
stay,

Swift autumn, like a bonfire of leaves,
And sleepy winter, like the sleep of
death.

"Wild Peaches"

I was, being human, born alone;
I am, being woman, hard beset;
I live by squeezing from a stone
The little nourishment I get.

"Let No Charitable Hope"

Avoid the reeking herd,
Shun the polluted flock,
Live like that stoic bird,
The eagle of the rock.

The huddled warmth of crowds
Begets and fosters hate;
He keeps, above the clouds,
His cliff inviolate.

When flocks are folded warm,
And herds to shelter run,
He sails above the storm,
He stares into the sun.

If in the eagle's track
Your sinews cannot leap,
Avoid the lathered pack,
Turn from the steaming sheep.

If you would keep your soul
From spotted sight or sound,
Live like the velvet mole;
Go burrow under ground.

And there hold intercourse
With roots of trees and stones,
With rivers at their source,
And disembodied bones.

"The Eagle and the Mole"

Reason's a rabbit in a hutch,
And ecstasy's a were-wolf ghost;
But, O, beware the nothing-much
And welcome madness and the most!

"Nonsense Rhyme"

WILLIAM ROSE BENÉT

•

I flung my soul to the air like a falcon
flying.
I said, "Wait on! wait on! while I ride
below!
I shall start a heron soon
In the marsh beneath the moon—
A strange white heron, rising with sil-
ver on its wings,
Rising and crying
Wordless, wondrous things;
The secret of the stars, of the
world's heart-strings,
The answer to their woe.
Then stoop thou upon him, and grip
and hold him so."

"The Falconer of God"

JOHN GOULD FLETCHER

•

Over the roof-tops race the shadows of
clouds;
Like horses the shadows of clouds
charge down the street.

"Irradiations"

We more than others have the perfect
right
To see the cities like flambeaux flare
along the night.

We more than others have the right to
cast away
Thought like a withered leaf, since it
has served its day;

Since for this transient joy which not
for long can burn
Within our hearts, we gave up in return

Ten thousand years of holy magic
power
Drawn from the darkness to transcend
death's hour.

For every witch that died an electric
lamp shall flare,
For every wizard drowned, the clear
blue air

Shall roar with jazz-bands into listening ears;
For every alchemist who spent in vain
his years

Seeking the stone of truth, a motor-
horn
Shall scare the sheep that wander
among the corn.

And there shall be no more the spirits
of the deep,
Nor holy satyrs slumbering upon the
steep,

Nor angels at a manger or a cross.
Life shall go on; to ugly gain or loss;

Yet vaster and more tragic, till at last
This present too shall make part of the
past:—

Till all the joy and tragedy man knows
To-day, become stiff gravestones in
long rows:

Till none dare look on the mountains
ranked far,
And think, "These are the cast-off
leavings of some star."

"Song of the Moderns"

JOYCE KILMER

•

I think that I shall never see
A poem lovely as a tree.

A tree whose hungry mouth is pressed
Against the earth's sweet flowing
breast;

A tree that looks at God all day,

And lifts her leafy arms to pray;

A tree that may in summer wear
A nest of robins in her hair;

Upon whose bosom snow has lain;
Who intimately lives with rain.

Poems are made by fools like me,
But only God can make a tree.

> "Trees." Heywood Broun, *It Seems to Me,* 1933, complained that *"Trees* (if I have the name right) is one of the most annoying pieces of verse within my knowledge. The other one is Kipling's *If,* with third place reserved for Henley's *Invictus.*
>
> *"Trees* maddens me, because it contains the most insincere line ever written by mortal man. Surely the Kilmer tongue must have been not far from the Kilmer cheek when he wrote, 'Poems are made by fools like me.'"

ROBINSON JEFFERS

•

While this America settles in the
   mould of its vulgarity, heavily
   thickening to empire,
And protest, only a bubble in the mol-
   ten mass, pops and sighs out, and
   the mass hardens,

I sadly remember that the flower fades
   to make fruit, the fruit rots to
   make earth.
Out of the mother; and through the
   spring exultances, ripeness and
   decadence; and home to the
   mother.

You make haste on decay: not blame-
   worthy; life is good, be it stub-
   bornly long or suddenly

A mortal splendor: meteors are not
   needed less than mountains:
   shine, perishing republic.

But for my children. I would have
   them keep their distance from the
   thickening center; corruption
Never has been compulsory, when the
   cities lie at the monster's feet
   there are left the mountains.

And boys, be in nothing so moderate
   as in love of man, a clever servant, insufferable master.
There is the trap that catches noblest
   spirits, that caught—they say—
   God, when he walked on earth.

       "Shine, Perishing Republic"

. . . The beauty of modern
Man is not in the persons but in the
Disastrous rhythm, the heavy and mo-
   bile masses, the dance of the
Dream-led masses down the dark
   mountain.

            "Rearmament"

          It is good for man
To try all changes, progress and corruption, powers, peace and anguish, not to go down the dino-
   saur's way
Until all his capacities have been explored: and it is good for him
To know that his needs and nature are
   no more changed in fact in ten
   thousand years than the beaks of
   eagles.

         "The Beaks of Eagles"

It is not bad. Let them play.
Let the guns bark and the bombing-
   plane
Speak his prodigious blasphemies.
It is not bad, it is high time,
Stark violence is still the sire of all the
   world's values.

         "The Bloody Sire"

MARIANNE MOORE

•

I, too, dislike it: there are things that
    are important beyond all this
    fiddle.
  Reading it, however, with a perfect
    contempt for it, one discovers in
  it after all, a place for the genuine.
    Hands that can grasp, eyes
    that can dilate, hair that can rise
      if it must, these things are im-
      portant not because a

high-sounding interpretation can be
    put upon them but because
    they are
  useful. When they become so deriv-
    ative as to become unintelli-
    gible,
  the same thing may be said for all of
    us, that we
    do not admire what
    we cannot understand: the bat
      holding on upside down or in
      quest of something to

eat, elephants pushing, a wild horse
    taking a roll, a tireless wolf
    under
  a tree, the immovable critic twitch-
    ing his skin like a horse that
    feels a flea, the base-
  ball fan, the statistician—
    nor is it valid
      to discriminate against 'business
      documents and

school-books'; all these phenomena are
    important. One must make a
    distinction
  however: when dragged into promi-
    nence by half poets, the result
    is not poetry,
  nor till the poets among us can be
    'literalists of
    the imagination'—above
      insolence and triviality and can
      present

for inspection, imaginary gardens with
    real toads in them, shall we
    have
it. In the meantime, if you demand on
    the one hand,
the raw material of poetry in
    all its rawness and
  that which is on the other hand
    genuine, then you are interested
    in poetry.

                          "Poetry"

    The world's an orphan's home.
    Shall
  we never have peace without sor-
    row?
without pleas of the dying for
    help that won't come? O
quiet form upon the dust, I cannot
look and yet I must. If these great
    patient
    dyings—all these agonies
      and woundbearings and
      blood shed—
    can teach us how to live, these
    dyings were not wasted.

Hate-hardened heart, O heart of
    iron,
  iron is iron till it rust.
There never was a war that was
    not inward; I must
fight till I have conquered in myself
    what
causes war.
              "In Distrust of Merits"

My father used to say,
"Superior people never make long
    visits,
have to be shown Longfellow's grave
or the glass flowers at Harvard.
Self-reliant like the cat—
that takes its prey to privacy,
the mouse's limp tail hanging like a
    shoelace from its mouth—
they sometimes enjoy solitude,
and can be robbed of speech

by speech which has delighted them.
The deepest feeling always shows itself
  in silence;
not in silence, but restraint."
Nor was he insincere in saying, "Make
  my house your inn."
Inns are not residences.

                    "Silence"

At all events there is in Brooklyn
something that makes me feel at home.
              "A Carriage from Sweden"

JOHN CROWE RANSOM

Here lies a lady of beauty and high
  degree.
Of chills and fever she died, of fever
  and chills,
The delight of her husband, her aunts,
  an infant of three,
And of medicos marveling sweetly on
  her ills.

.   .   .   .   .   :   .

Sweet ladies, long may ye bloom, and
  toughly I hope ye may thole,
But was she not lucky? In flowers and
  lace and mourning,
In love and great honour we bade God
  rest her soul
After six little spaces of chill, and six
  of burning.
                    "Here Lies a Lady"

ALAN SEEGER

I have a rendezvous with Death
At some disputed barricade,
When Spring comes back with rustling
  shade
And apple-blossoms fill the air—
I have a rendezvous with Death
When Spring brings back blue days
  and fair.

It may be he shall take my hand
And lead me into his dark land
And close my eyes and quench my
  breath—
It may be I shall pass him still.
I have a rendezvous with Death
On some scarred slope of battered hill
When Spring comes round again this
  year
And the first meadow-flowers appear.

.   .   .   .

When Spring trips north again this
  year,
And I to my pledged word am true,
I shall not fail that rendezvous.
          "I Have a Rendezvous with
            Death"

CONRAD AIKEN

Why do you cry out, why do I like to
  hear you
Cry out, here in the dewless evening,
  sitting
Close, close together, so close that the
  heart stops beating
And the brain its thought? Wordless,
  worthless mortals
Stumbling, exhausted, in this wilderness
Of our conjoint destruction! Hear the
  grass
Raging about us! Hear the worms applaud!
Hear how the ripples make a sound of
  chaos!
Hear now, in these and the other
  sounds of chaos!
Hear now, in these and the other
  sounds of evening,
The first brute step of God!
                    "Sound of Breaking"

When trout swim down Great Ormond
  Street,
And sea-gulls cry above them lightly,

And hawthornes heave cold flagstones up
To blossom whitely,

Against old walls of houses there,
Gustily shaking out in moonlight
Their country sweetness on sweet air;
And in the sunlight,

By the green margin of that water,
Children dip white feet and shout,
Casting nets in the braided water
To catch the trout:

Then I shall hold my breath and die,
Swearing I never loved you; no,
"You were not lovely!" I shall cry,
"I never loved you so."

                        "Priapus and the Pool"

Music I heard with you was more than music,
And bread I broke with you was more than bread;
Now that I am without you, all is desolate;
All that was once so beautiful is dead.

                                   "Discordants"

MADELEINE SWEENEY MILLER
·

It isn't far to Bethlehem Town!
It's anywhere that Christ comes down
And finds in people's friendly face
A welcome and abiding place.
The road to Bethlehem runs right through
The homes of folks like me and you.

                    "How Far to Bethlehem?"

CHRISTOPHER MORLEY
·

For students of the troubled heart
Cities are perfect works of art.

                        "John Mistletoe"

Life is a game of whist,
Between Man and Nature
In which Nature knows all Man's cards.

                              "Handicapped"

And of all man's felicities
    The very subtlest one, say I,
Is when for the first time he sees
    His hearthfire smoke against the sky.

                "A Hallowe'en Memory"

The greatest poem ever known
Is one all poets have outgrown:
The poetry, innate, untold,
Of being only four years old.

                            "To a Child"

EDNA ST. VINCENT MILLAY
·

I like Americans.
You may say what you will, they are
    the nicest people in the world.
They sleep with their windows open.
Their bathtubs are never dry.
They are not grown up yet. They still
    believe in Santa Claus.

They are terribly in earnest.
But they laugh at everything. . . .

I like Americans.
They give the matches free. . . .

I like Americans.
They are the only men in the world,
    the sight of whom in their shirt-
    sleeves is not rumpled, embryonic
    and agonizing. . . .

I like Americans.
They carry such pretty umbrellas.
The Avenue de l'Opéra on a rainy day
    is just an avenue on a rainy day.
But Fifth Avenue on a rainy day is an
    old-fashioned garden under a
    shower. . . .

They are always rocking the boat.
I like Americans.
They either shoot the whole nickel, or
give up the bones.
You may say what you will, they are
the nicest people in the world.
"I Like Americans"

Oh, Prue she has a patient man,
And Joan a gentle lover,
And Agatha's Arth' is a hug-the-
hearth,—
But my true love's a rover!
"She Is Overheard Singing"

And if I loved you Wednesday,
Well, what is that to you?
I do not love you Thursday—
So much is true.
"Thursday"

O world, I cannot hold thee close
enough!
"God's World"

I would indeed that love were longer-
lived,
And oaths were not so brittle as they
are,
But so it is, and nature has contrived
To struggle on without a break thus
far,—
Whether or not we find what we are
seeking
Is idle, biologically speaking.
Sonnet

My candle burns at both ends;
It will not last the night;
But, ah, my foes, and, oh, my friends—
It gives a lovely light.
Figs from Thistles, "First Fig"

Safe upon the solid rock the ugly
houses stand:
Come and see my shining palace built
upon the sand!
Ibid., "Second Fig"

My heart is warm with the friends I
make,
And better friends I'll not be knowing;
Yet there isn't a train I wouldn't take
No matter where it's going.
"Travel"

Euclid alone
Has looked on Beauty bare. Fortunate
they
Who, though once only and then but
far away,
Have heard her massive sandal set on
stone.
"Euclid Alone Has Looked on
Beauty Bare"

The soul can split the sky in two,
And let the face of God shine through.
But East and West will pinch the heart
That cannot keep them pushed apart;
And he whose soul is flat—the sky
Will cave in on him by and by.
"Renascence"

Love is not all; it is not meat nor drink
Nor slumber nor a roof against the
rain,
Nor yet a floating spar to men that
sink.
"Fatal Interview"

What lips my lips have kissed, and
where, and why,
I have forgotten, and what arms have
lain
Under my head till morning; but the
rain
Is full of ghosts tonight, that tap and
sigh
Upon the glass and listen for reply;
And in my heart there stirs a quiet
pain
For unremembered lads that not
again
Will turn to me at midnight with a
cry.

Thus in the winter stands the lonely
tree,
Nor knows what birds have vanished
one by one,
Yet knows its boughs more silent than
before:
I cannot say what loves have come
and gone;
I only know that summer sang in me
A little while, that in me sings no
more.
"What Lips My Lips Have
Kissed"

Death devours all lovely things;
Lesbia with her sparrow
Shares the darkness,—presently
Every bed is narrow.
"Passer Mortuus Est"

Down, down, down into the darkness
of the grave
Gently they go, the beautiful, the tender, the kind;
Quietly they go, the intelligent, the
witty, the brave.
I know. But I do not approve. And I
am not resigned.
"Dirge Without Music"

ARCHIBALD MacLEISH

•

It is a strange thing—to be an American.
Neither an old house it is with the air
Tasting of hung herbs and the sun returning
Year after year to the same door and
the churn,
Making the same sound in the cool of
the kitchen
Mother to son's wife, and the place
to sit
Marked in the dusk by the worn stone
at the wellhead—
That—nor the eyes like each other's
eyes and the skull

Shaped to the same fault and the
hands' sameness.
Neither a place it is nor a blood name.

America is West and the wind blow-
ing.
America is a great word and the snow,
A way, a white bird, the rain falling,
A shining thing in the mind and the
gulls' call.
America is neither a land nor a people,
A word's shape it is, a wind's sweep—
America is alone: many together,
Many of one mouth, of one breath,
Dressed as one—and none brothers
among them:
Only the taught speech and the aped
tongue.
America is alone and the gulls calling.
"American Letter: For Gerald
Murphy"

Believe
America is promises to
Take!
America is promises to
Us
To take them
Brutally
With love but take them.

Oh believe this!
"America Was Promises"

The brotherhood is not by the blood
certainly.
But neither are men brothers by speech
—by saying so:
Men are brothers by life lived and are
hurt for it.

.   .   .   .

Brotherhood here in the strange world
is the rich and
Rarest giving of life and the most val-
ued,
Not to be had for a word or a week's
wishing.
"Speech to Those Who Say
Comrade"

A poem should be palpable and mute
As a globed fruit

.   .   .   .   .   .

A poem should be equal to:
Not true

.   .   .   .

A poem should not mean
But be.

"Ars Poetica"

Beauty is that Medusa's head
Which men go armed to seek and
   sever.

It is most deadly when most dead,
And dead will stare and sting forever.

"Beauty"

And here face down beneath the sun
And here upon earth's noonward
   height
To feel the always coming on
The always rising of the night

To feel creep up the curving east
The earthly chill of dusk and slow
Upon those under lands the vast
And ever climbing shadow grow

And strange at Ecbatan the trees
Take leaf by leaf the evening strange
The flooding dark about their knees
The mountains over Persia change

And now at Kermanshah the gate
Dark empty and the withered grass
And through the twilight now the late
Few travelers in the westward pass

And Baghdad darken and the bridge
Across the silent river gone
And through Arabia the edge
Of evening widen and steal on

And deepen on Palmyra's street
The wheel rut in the ruined stone
And Lebanon fade out and Crete
High through the clouds and over-
   blown

And over Sicily the air
Still flashing with the landward gulls
And loom and slowly disappear
The sails above the shadowy hulls

And Spain go under and the shore
Of Africa the gilded sand
And evening vanish and no more
The low pale light across that land

Nor now the long light on the sea

And here face downward in the sun
To feel how swift how secretly
The shadow of the night comes
   on. . . .

"You, Andrew Marvell"

At twenty, stooping round about,
I thought the world a miserable place,
Truth a trick, faith in doubt,
Little beauty, less grace.

Now at sixty what I see,
Although the world is worse by far,
Stops my heart in ecstasy.
God, the wonders that are there!

"With Age Wisdom"

E. E. CUMMINGS

•

i spill my bright incalculable soul.
"O thou to whom the musical
white spring"

"next to of course god america i
love you land of the pilgrims' and so
   forth oh
say can you see by the dawn's early my
country 'tis of centuries come and go
and are no more what of it we should
   worry
in every language even deafanddumb
thy sons acclaim your glorious name
   by gorry
by jingo by gee by gosh by gum
why talk of beauty what could be more
   beaut-

iful than these heroic happy dead
who rushed like lions to the roaring
    slaughter
they did not stop to think they died
    instead
then shall the voice of liberty be
    mute?"
He spoke. And drank rapidly a glass
    of water.
    "next to of course God America i"

                    We doctors know

a hopeless case if—listen: there's a hell
of a good universe next door; let's go
    "pity this busy monster, man-
    unkind"

I'd rather learn from one bird how to
    sing
than teach ten thousand stars how
    not to dance
    "you shall above all things be
    glad and young."

Kind Christ, this world is all aleak;
and lifepreservers there are none:
and waves which only He may walk
Who dares to call Himself a man.
    "Jehovah buried, Satan dead,"

(While you and i have lips and voices
    which
are for kissing and to sing with
who cares if some oneeyed son of a
    bitch
invents an instrument to measure
    Spring with?
    "voices to voices, lip to lip"

i like my body when it is with your
body. It is so quite new a thing.
Muscles better and nerves more.
i like my body. i like what it does,
i like its hows. i like to feel the spine
of your body and its bones, and the
    trembling
-firm-smooth ness and which i will
again and again and again

kiss, i like kissing this and that of you,
i like, slowly stroking the, shocking
    fuzz
of your electric fur, and what-is-it
    comes
over parting flesh . . . And eyes big
    love-crumbs,

and possibly i like the thrill

of under me you so quite new
    "i like my body when it is with
    your"

All in green went my love riding
on a great horse of gold
into the silver dawn.
    "All in green went my love
    riding"

GENEVIEVE TAGGARD
                    •
The words in the books are not true
If they do not act in you.
                    "Life of the Mind"

MARK VAN DOREN
                    •
Grass nibbling inward
    Like green fire.
                    "Former Barn Lot"

Anywhere beauty is,
All men smile;
Except its prophets;
And they fall.
                    "Beauty Is"

Remembered gaiety hurts mind and
    heart
As present pain is impotent to do.
                    "Remembered Gaiety"

Wit is the only wall
Between us and the dark.
                    "Wit"

Envy the young who have no words at
 all,
And the old, for they have had them.
                    "Envy the Old"

The father of the family, stoop-shoul-
 dered,
Has now another pride:
Not to mind much if his unspeakable
 authority
By smiles has died.
                    "Another Pride"

The animals will never know;
Could not find out; would scarcely
 care
That all their names are in our books,
And all their images drawn bare.
                    "If They Spoke"

Wait not, my soul, on circumstance;
It does not wait for you.
It nibbles at you now, and will
Devour you; I say true.
                    "Soul and Circumstance"

      But the child that was crying—
He is a beautiful, strange boy.
He is little and weak, this lord of the
 world,
   But oh, too strong, too strong to
 destroy.
                    "Dialogue in December"

When the world ends it is too much to
 hope,
And yet I do, that neither knife nor
 rope,
Nor sudden flame, nor worse than
 sudden freeze,
Is executioner. No less than these
Implacable, what if gold autumn came
And stayed till it was weary—spread
 the same
Cool hectic over waters and wild
 boughs
That now arrives for but a week's ca-
 rouse;

Then winter? What if such a wonder
 fall
Kept on as if it were the end, the all?
What if it were, and centuries of red
So flushed each field and roof and
 river bed
That death itself lay down, and noth-
 ing died
Till all things did, beneath a shower as
 wide
As oceans of together-dropping leaves?
What if it were, and still no late re-
 prieves
Canceled the utter end? I do not keep
That hope; and yet I dream of this
 slow sleep,
This indolent, this all but evermore
October such as never came before.
                    "When the World Ends"

LOUISE BOGAN

•

Come drunks and drug-takers; come,
 perverts unnerved!
Receive the laurel, given, though late,
 on merit; to whom and wherever
 deserved.

Parochial punks, trimmers, nice people, joiners true-blue,
Get the hell out of the way of the
 laurel. It is deathless. And it isn't
 for you.
                "Several Voices out of a Cloud"

Women have no wilderness in them,
They are provident instead,
Content in the tight hot cell of their
 hearts
To eat dusty bread.
                    "Women"

STEPHEN VINCENT BENÉT

•

When Daniel Boone goes by at night
The phantom deer arise

And all lost, wild America
Is burning in their eyes.

    "Daniel Boone, 1797–1889"

Remember that when you say
"I will have none of this exile and this
 stranger
For his face is not like my face and his
 speech is strange,"
You have denied America with that
 word.

      "Western Star"

I have fallen in love with American
 names,
The sharp names that never get fat,
The snakeskin-titles of mining-claims,
The plumed war-bonnet of Medicine
 Hat,
Tucson and Deadwood and Lost Mule
 Flat.

      "American Names"

Oh yes, I know the faults and the
 other side;
The lyncher's rope, the bought justice,
 the wasted land,
The scale on the leaf, the borers in
 the corn,
The finks with their clubs, the gray
 sky of relief,
All the long shame of our hearts and
 the long disunion.
I am merely remarking—as a country
 we try.
As a country, I think we try.

     "Nightmare at Noon"

American muse, whose strong and di-
 verse heart
So many men have tried to understand
But only made it smaller with their art,
Because you are as varied as your land

As mountainous-deep, as flowered with
 blue rivers,
Thirsty with deserts, buried under
 snows,

As native as the shape of Navaho
 quivers,
And native, too, as the sea-voyaged
 rose.
Swift runner, never captured or subdued,
Seven-branched elk beside the mountain stream,
That half a hundred hunters have pursued
But never matched their bullets with
 the dream,

Where the great huntsmen failed, I
 set my sorry
And mortal snare for your immortal
 quarry.

You are the buffalo-ghost, the bron-
 cho-ghost
With dollar-silver in your saddle-horn,
The cowboys riding in from Painted
 Post,
The Indian arrow in the Indian corn.

And you are the clipped velvet of the
 lawns
Where Shropshire grows from Massa-
 chusetts sods,
The grey Maine rocks, and the war-
 painted dawns
That break above the Garden of the
 Gods;

The prairie-schooners crawling toward
 the ore,
And the cheap car parked by the sta-
 tion-door.

Where the skyscrapers lift their foggy
 plumes
Of stranded smoke out of a stony
 mouth
You are that high stone and its arro-
 gant fumes,
And you are the ruined gardens in the
 South,

And bleak New England farms, so
winter-white
Even their roofs look lonely, and the
deep
The middle grainland where the wind
of night
Is like all blind earth sighing in her
sleep:

A friend, an enemy, a sacred hag
With two tied oceans in her medicine-
bag.

They tried to fit you with an English
song
And clip your speech into the English
tale.
But even from the first the words went
wrong,
The catbird pecked away the nightingale.

The homesick men begot high-cheek-
boned things
Whose wit was whittled with a different sound,
And Thames and all the rivers of the
kings
Ran into Mississippi and were
drowned.

They planted England with a stubborn
trust,
But the cleft dust was never English
dust.

Stepchild of every exile from content
And all the disavouched, hard-bitten
pack
Shipped overseas to steal a continent
With neither shirts nor honor to their
back:

Pimping grandee and rump-faced regi-
cide,
Apple-cheeked younkers from a wind-
mill-square,
Puritans stubborn as the nails of Pride,

Rakes from Versailles and thieves from
County Clare,

The black-robed priests who broke
their hearts in vain
To make you God and France or God
and Spain.

These were your lovers in your buck-
skin-youth.
And each one married with a dream
so proud
He never knew it could not be the
truth
And that he coupled with a girl of
cloud.

And now to see you is more difficult
yet
Except as an immensity of wheel
Made up of wheels, oiled with inhuman sweat
And glittering with the heat of ladled
steel.

All these you are, and each is partly
you,
And none is false, and none is wholly
true.
John Brown's Body, "Invoca-
tion"

Lincoln, six feet one in his stocking
feet,
The lank man, knotty and tough as a
hickory rail,
Whose hands were always too big for
white-kid gloves,
Whose wit was a coonskin sack of dry,
tall tales,
Whose weathered face was homely as
a plowed field.
Ibid.

ROSEMARY BENÉT
•

If Nancy Hanks
Came back as a ghost,

Seeking news
Of what she loved most,
She'd ask first
"Where's my son?
What's happened to Abe?
What's he done?

"Poor little Abe,
Left all alone
Except for Tom,
Who's a rolling stone;
He was only nine
The year I died.
I remember still
How hard he cried.

"Scraping along
In a little shack,
With hardly a shirt
To cover his back,
And a prairie wind
To blow him down,
Or pinching times
If he went to town.

"You wouldn't know
About my son?
Did he grow tall?
Did he have fun?
Did he learn to read?
Did he get to town?
Do you know his name?
Did he get on?"

"Nancy Hanks"

MALCOLM COWLEY

•

Now the dark waters at the bow
fold back, like earth against the plow;
foam brightens like the dogwood now
    at home, in my own country.

"My Own Country"

AMELIA EARHART PUTNAM

•

Courage is the prize that life exacts
    for granting peace.

The soul that knows it not, knows no
    release
From little things;
Knows not the livid loneliness of fear,
Nor mountain heights where bitter joy
    can hear
The sound of wings.

"Courage"

HENRY MORTON ROBINSON

•

God of the hidden purpose,
Let our embarking be
The prayer of proud men asking
Not to be safe, but free.

"God of the Hidden Purpose"

HART CRANE

•

It was a kind and northern face
That mingled in such exile disguise
The everlasting eyes of Pierrot
And, of Gargantua, the laughter.

"Praise for an Urn: In Memo-
    riam: Ernest Nelson"

Often beneath the wave, wide from
    this ledge
The dice of drowned men's bones he
    saw bequeath
An embassy. Their numbers as he
    watched,
Beat on the dusty shore and were ob-
    scured.

And wrecks passed without sound of
    bells,
The calyx of death's bounty giving
    back
A scattered chapter, lived hieroglyph,
The portent wound in corridors of
    shells.

Then in the circuit calm of one vast
    coil,
Its lashings charmed and malice rec-
    onciled,

Forested eyes there were that lifted
  altars;
And silent answers crept across the
  stars.

Compass, quadrant and sextant contrive
No farther tides. . . . High in the
  azure steeps
Monody shall not wake the mariner.
This fabulous shadow only the sea
  keeps.
                "At Melville's Tomb"

O Thou steeled Cognizance whose leap
  commits
The agile precincts of the lark's return.
                "The Bridge"

Russell Davenport

•

America lives in her simple homes:
The weathered door, the old wisteria
  vine,
The dusty barnyard where the rooster
  roams,
The common trees like elm and oak
  and pine:
In furniture for comfort, not for looks,
In names like Jack and Pete and Caro-
  line,
In neighbors you can trust, and honest
  books,
And peace, and hope, and opportunity.
She lives like destiny in Mom, who
  cooks
On gleaming stoves her special fricas-
  see,
And hams and cakes and endless apple
  pies.
She lives in Pop, the family referee,
Absorbing Sunday news with heavy
  eyes;
And in the dog, and in the shouting
  kids
Returning home from school, to mem-
  orize

The history of the ancient pyramids.
And still she lives in them when dark-
  ness wakes
The distant smells and infinite katy-
  dids,
And valleys seem like black and fear-
  some lakes
Guarded by windows of American
  light,
While in the wind the family maple
  rakes
The lucent stars westward across the
  night.
And still, however far her sons may go,
To venture or to die beyond her sight,
These little windows shine incognito
Across incredulous humanity;
That all the peoples of the earth may
  know
The embattled destination of the
  free—
Not peace, not rest, not pleasure—but
  to dare
To face the axiom of democracy:
Freedom is not to limit, but to share;
And freedom here is freedom every-
  where.
                My Country

Allen Tate

•

Row after row with strict impunity
The headstones yield their names to
  the element,
The wind whirrs without recollection;
In the riven troughs the splayed leaves
Pile up, of nature the casual sacra-
  ment
To the seasonal eternity of death,
Then driven by the fierce scrutiny
Of heaven to their business in the vast
  breath,
They sough the rumor of mortality.
                "Ode to the Confederate Dead"

Oscar Williams

•

One morning the world woke up and
there was no news.
    "One Morning the World
Woke Up"

Frances Frost

•

This is the place where fishermen
    stride up the cobbled hill again
    and scan the faint-starred skies,

where doors stand open to lilac-shine
    and supper-drift blows warm and
    fine
    and windows have seaward eyes.
            "Sea Town"

Frederic Prokosch

•

No one dies cleanly now.
All, all of us rot away:
No longer down the wood
Angelic shapes delight
The innocent and gay.
Poisonous things are spared,
The gifted are the sad
And solitude breeds hate.
Yellow is every bough,
No one dies cleanly now.
            "Eclogue"

Karl Shapiro

•

Underneath this wooden cross there
    lies
A Christian killed in battle. You who
    read,
Remember that this stranger died in
    pain;

And passing here, if you can lift your
    eyes
Upon a peace kept by a human creed,
Know that one soldier has not died in
    vain.
         "Elegy for a Dead Soldier"

To hurt the Negro and avoid the Jew
Is the curriculum.
             "University"

Yet you who saved neither yourselves
    nor us
Are equally with those who shed the
    blood
The heroes of our cause. Your con-
    science is
What we come back to in the armi-
    .'tice.
     "The Conscientious Objector"

Delmore Schwartz

•

Save postage stamps or photographs,
But save your soul! Only the past is
    immortal.
         "The Repetitive Heart"

Thomas Merton

•

When all the men of war are shot
And flags have fallen into dust,
Your cross and mine shall tell men still
Christ died on each, for both of us.

For in the wreckage of your April
    Christ lies slain,
And Christ weeps in the ruins of my
    spring:
The money of Whose tears shall fall
Into your weak and friendless hand,
And buy you back to your own land:
The silence of Whose tears shall fall
Like bells upon your alien tomb.

Hear them and come: they call you
    home.

      "For My Brother: Reported
    Missing in Action, 1943"

JAMES BROUGHTON
•

Come dally me, darling, dally me with
    kisses,
loiter me with lingers while the Romes
    all burn.

      Botteghe Oscura, Volume XII,
    1953

RANDALL JARRELL
•

From my mother's sleep I fell into the
    State
And I hunched in its belly till my wet
    fur froze.
Six miles from earth, loosed from its
    dream of life,
I woke to black flak and the night-
    mare fighters.
When I died they washed me out of
    the turret with a hose.

      "The Death of a Turret Gun-
    ner"

II. The Poets of Laughter: Light Verse

Benjamin Franklin

•

Here Skugg lies snug
As a bug in a rug.
>Letter to Miss Georgiana Shipley, September, 1772

Jack eating rotten cheese, did say,
Like Samson I my thousands slay:
I vow, quoth Roger, so you do.
And with the self-same weapon too.

Joel Barlow

•

Let the green succotash with thee contend;
Let beans and corn their sweetest juices blend;
Let butter drench them in its yellow tide,
And a long slice of bacon grace their side;
Not all the plate, how famed soe'er it be,
Can please my palate like a bowl of thee.
Some talk of hoe-cake, fair Virginia's pride!
Rich johnny-cake this mouth has often tried;
Both please me well, their virtues much the same,
Alike their fabric, as allied their fame,
Except in dear New England, where the last
Receives a dash of pumpkin in the paste,
To give it sweetness and improve the taste.
But place them all before me, smoking hot,
The big, round dumpling, rolling from the pot;
The pudding of the bag, whose quivering breast,
With suet lined, leads on the Yankee feast;
The charlotte brown, within whose crusty sides
A belly soft and pulpy apple hides;
The yellow bread whose face like amber glows,
And all of Indian that the bakepan knows—
You tempt me not; my favorite greets my eyes,
To that loved bowl my spoon by instinct flies.
>"The Hasty Pudding"

John Trumbull

•

No man e'er felt the halter draw,
With good opinion of the law.
>"M'Fingal"

Were there no fools beneath the skies,
What were the trick of being wise?
>*Ibid.*

Clement C. Moore

•

'Twas the night before Christmas, when all through the house,
Not a creature was stirring—not even a mouse:
The stockings were hung by the chimney with care,
In hopes that Saint Nicholas soon would be there.
>"A Visit from St. Nicholas"

SARAH J. HALE

•

Mary had a little lamb,
Its fleece was white as snow;
And everywhere that Mary went
The lamb was sure to go.

"Mary's Little Lamb"

LYDIA MARIA CHILD

•

Over the river and through the wood,
To grandfather's house we go;
The horse knows the way
To carry the sleigh
Through the white and drifted snow.

.   .   .   .

Over the river and through the
wood—
Now grandmother's cap I spy!
Hurrah for the fun!
Is the pudding done?
Hurrah for the pumpkin pie!

"Thanksgiving Day"

HENRY WADSWORTH LONGFELLOW

•

Very good in its way
Is the Verzenay,
Or the Sillery soft and creamy;
But Catawba wine
Has a taste more divine,
More dulcet, delicious, and dreamy.

"Catawba Wine"

There was a little girl
Who had a little curl
Right in the middle of her forehead,
When she was good
She was very, very good,
But when she was bad she was horrid.

"There Was a Little Girl"

OLIVER WENDELL HOLMES

•

Have you heard of the wonderful one-
hoss shay,

That was built in such a logical way
It ran a hundred years to a day?

"The Deacon's Masterpiece"

JOHN GODFREY SAXE

•

It was six men of Indostan
To learning much inclined,
Who went to see the Elephant
(Though all of them were blind);
That each by observation
Might satisfy his mind.

"The Blind Men and the Elephant"

I like the lad who, when his father
thought
To clip his morning nap by hackneyed
phrase
Of vagrant worm by early songster
caught,
Cried, "Served him right!—it's not at
all surprising;
The worm was punished, sir, for early
rising!"

"The Tables Turned"

HENRY WHEELER SHAW
("JOSH BILLINGS")

•

Thrice is he armed that hath his quarrel just;
And four times he who gets his fist in
fust.

•

I hate to be a kicker, I always long for
peace,
But the wheel that does the squeaking,
is the one that gets the grease.

JAMES RUSSELL LOWELL

•

Ez fur war, I call it murder—
There you hev it plain an' flat;
I don't want to go no furder

Than my Testyment fer that;
God hez sed so plump an' fairly,
 It's es long ez it is broad,
An' you've gut to git up airly
 Ef you want to take in God.
> *The Biglow Papers,* "No. 1, A
> Letter, etc."

Ain't it cute to see a Yankee
 Take sech everlastin' pains,
All to git the Devil's thankee
 Helpin' on 'em weld their chains?
Wy, it's jest ez clear ez figgers,
 Clear ez one an' one make two,
Chaps that make black slaves o' nig-
 gers
 Want to make white slaves o' you.
> *Ibid.*

Guvener B. is a sensible man;
 He stays to his home an' looks arter
 his folks;
He draws his furrer ez straight ez he
 can,
 An' into nobody's tater-patch
 pokes;—
 But John P.
 Robinson he
Sez he wunt vote fer Guvener B.
> *Ibid.,* "What Mr. Robinson
> Thinks"

I du believe in Freedom's cause,
 Ez fur away ez Payris is;
I love to see her stick her claws
 In them infarnal Phayrisees;
It's wal enough agin a king
 To dror resolves an' triggers,—
But libbaty's a kind o' thing
 That don't agree with niggers.
> *Ibid.,* "The Pious Editor's
> Creed"

God makes sech nights, all white an'
 still
 Fur'z you can look or listen,

Moonshine an' snow on field an' hill,
 All silence an' all glisten.
> *Ibid.,* "The Courtin'"

In creating, the only hard thing's to
 begin;
A grass-blade's no easier to make than
 an oak.
> "A Fable for Critics"

For though he builds glorious temples,
 'tis odd
He leaves never a doorway to get in a
 god.
> *Ibid.,* of Emerson

There comes Poe, with his raven, like
 Barnaby Rudge,
Three-fifths of him genius and two-
 fifths sheer fudge.
> *Ibid.*

In vain we call old notions fudge,
 And bend our conscience to our
 dealing;
The Ten Commandments will not
 budge,
 And stealing will continue stealing.
> "International Copyright."
> This is the motto of the Amer-
> ican Copyright League (No-
> vember 20, 1885).

George Martin Lane

•

A guest then says, quite ill at ease,
"A piece of bread, sir, if you please."
The waiter roars it through the hall:
"We don't give bread with one Fish-
 ball!"
> "One Fish-Ball"

Charles Godfrey Leland

•

Hans Breitmann gife a barty—
 Where ish dat barty now!
> "Hans Breitmann's Party"

JOHN TOWNSEND TROWBRIDGE

•

The birds can fly,
An' why can't I?
> "Darius Green and His Flying-
> Machine"

CHARLES GRAHAM HALPINE

•

When asked what State he hails from,
    Our sole reply shall be,
He comes from Appomattox
    And its famous apple tree.
> "U. S. Grant." Roscoe Conkling
> quoted the phrase in a speech
> putting Grant's name in nomi-
> nation for a third term, 1880,
> but Garfield won the nomina-
> tion and the Presidency.

ANONYMOUS

•

Conductor, when you receive a fare,
Punch in the presence of the passen-
    jare!
A blue trip slip for an eight-cent fare,
A buff trip slip for a six-cent fare,
A pink trip slip for a three-cent fare,
Punch in the presence of the passen-
    jare!

.   .   .   .

Punch, brothers! punch with care!
Punch in the presence of the passen-
    jare!
> Quoted by Mark Twain

BRET HARTE

•

I reside at Table Mountain, and my
    name is Truthful James;
I am not up to small deceit, or any
    sinful games.

.   .   .   .

And he smiled a kind of sickly smile,
    and curled up on the floor,

And the subsequent proceedings inter-
    ested him no more.
> "The Society upon the Stanis-
> laus"

Which I wish to remark—
    And my language is plain—
That for ways that are dark
    And for tricks that are vain,
The heathen Chinee is peculiar.
> "Plain Language from Truth-
> ful James"

JOHN MILTON HAY

•

I'll hold her nozzle agin the bank
    Till the last galoot's ashore.
> "Jim Bludso of the Prairie
> Belle"

He never flunked, and he never lied,—
    I reckon he never knowed how.

.   .   .   .

He seen his duty, a dead-sure thing,—
    And went for it thar and then;
And Christ ain't a-going to be too hard
    On a man that died for men.
> *Ibid.*

EDWARD ROWLAND SILL

•

At the punch-bowl's brink,
Let the thirsty think
What they say in old Japan:

First the man takes a drink;
Then the drink takes a drink;
Then the drink takes the man.
> "In Japan"

AMBROSE BIERCE

•

Don't steal; thou'lt never thus compete
Successfully in business. Cheat.
> *The Devil's Dictionary*

J. I. C. CLARKE

•

Well here's to the Maine, and I'm
sorry for Spain,
Said Kelly and Burke and Shea.
"The Fighting Race"

GEORGE T. LANIGAN

•

A squeak's heard in the orchestra
As the leader draws across
The intestines of the agile cat
The tail of the noble horse.
"The Fiddle"

JAMES WHITCOMB RILEY

•

An' all us other children, when the
supper things is done,
We set around the kitchen fire an'
has the mostest fun
A-listen' to the witch tales 'at Annie
tells about,
An' the gobble-uns 'at gits you
Ef you
Don't
Watch
Out!
"Little Orphant Annie"

O, it sets my heart a clickin' like the
tickin' of a clock,
When the frost is on the punkin and
the fodder's in the shock.
"When the Frost Is on the
Punkin"

EUGENE FIELD

•

But I, when I undress me
Each night, upon my knees
Will ask the Lord to bless me
With apple pie and cheese.
"Apple Pie and Cheese"

When I demanded of my friend what
viands he preferred,
He quoth: "A large cold bottle, and a
small hot bird."
"The Bottle and the Bird"

So now, in the prime of my manhood,
I polish this lyric gem
For the uses of all good fellows who
are thirsty at five a. m.,
But especially for those fellows who
have known the pleasing thrall
Of the clink of the ice in the pitcher
the boy brings up the hall.
"The Clink of the Ice"

The little toy dog is covered with dust,
But sturdy and staunch it stands;
And the little toy soldier is red with
rust,
And his musket molds in his hands.
Time was when the little toy dog was
new
And the soldier was passing fair,
And that was the time when our Little
Boy Blue
Kissed them and put them there.
"Little Boy Blue"

I never lost a little fish—
Yes, I am free to say,
It always was the biggest fish
I caught that got away.
"Fishing"

HENRY CUYLER BUNNER

•

Behold the deeds that are done of Mrs.
Jones!
"Behold the Deeds!"

BEN KING

•

Nothing to do but work,
Nothing to eat but food,

Nothing to wear but clothes
　　To keep one from going nude.
　　　　　　　"The Pessimist"

FRANK L. STANTON

Sweetest li'l feller, everybody knows;
Dunno what to call him, but he's
　　mighty lak' a rose;
Lookin' at his mammy wid eyes so
　　shiny blue
Mek' you think that Heav'n is comin'
　　clost ter you.
　　　　　　　"Mighty Lak' a Rose"

J. C. BOSSIDY

And this is good old Boston,
The home of the bean and the cod,
Where the Lowells talk to the Cabots,
And the Cabots talk only to God.
　　　　　"On the Aristocracy of Har-
　　　　　vard"

FRED NEWTON SCOTT

This of our tale is the short and the
　　long,
　　　I'm Romeo! I'm Juliet!
Here is the moral that goes with the
　　song,
　　　I'm Romeo, Juliet!
Lovers, we warn you of daggers be
　　wary,
Don't buy your drinks of an apothe-
　　cary,
Don't stab yourselves in the left pul-
　　monary,
　　　I'm Romeo, Juliet!
　　　　　　　"Romeo and Juliet"

HARRY B. SMITH

My Angeline! My Angeline!
Why didst disturb my mind serene?

My well-belovéd circus queen,
My Human Snake, my Angeline!
　　　　　　　"My Angeline!"

Oh! it's perfectly true you can beat a
　　tattoo,
　　But you can't beat a tattooed man.
　　　　　　　"The Tattooed Man"

JOHN KENDRICK BANGS

I think mankind by thee would be less
　　bored
If only thou wert not thine own re-
　　ward.
　　　　　　　"A Hint to Virtue"

FREDERICK SCHEETZ JONES

Here's to the town of New Haven,
　　The Home of the Truth and the
　　　Light,
Where God talks to Jones in the very
　　same tones
　　That he uses with Hadley and
　　　Dwight.
　　　　　　　"New Haven"

OLIVER HERFORD

Well I recall how first I met
Mark Twain—an infant barely three
Rolling a tiny cigarette
While cooing on his nurse's knee.
　　　　　"Mark Twain: A Pipe Dream"

Some take their gold in minted mould,
And some in harps hereafter,
But give me mine in tresses fine,
And keep the change—in laughter.
　　　　　　　"God Made Them"

The bubble winked at me, and said,
"You'll miss me brother, when you're
　　dead."
　　　　　"Toast: The Bubble Winked"

Here's to the man who invented stairs
And taught our feet to soar!
He was the first who ever burst
Into a second floor.

The world would be downstairs to-day
Had he not found the key;
So let his name go down to fame,
Whatever it may be.

"Stairs"

ERNEST L. THAYER

•

There was ease in Casey's manner as
    he stepped into his place;
There was pride in Casey's bearing,
    and a smile on Casey's face.

And when, responding to the cheers,
    he lightly doffed his hat,
No stranger in the crowd could doubt
    'twas Casey at the bat.

. . . .

There is no joy in Mudville—mighty
    Casey has struck out.

"Casey at the Bat"

RICHARD HOVEY

•

O, Eleazar Wheelock was a very pious
    man;
He went into the wilderness to teach
    the Indian,
With a Gradus ad Parnassum, a Bible,
    and a drum,
And five hundred gallons of New Eng-
    land rum.

"Eleazar Wheelock"

For it's always fair weather
When good fellows get together.

"Song in Spring"

ROBERT LOVEMAN

•

It is not raining rain to me,
    It's raining daffodils;
In every dimpled drop I see
    Wild flowers on the hills.

. . . .

A health unto the happy!
    A fig for him who frets!—
It is not raining rain to me,
    It's raining violets.

"April Rain"

J. GORDON COOGLER

•

Alas, for the South! Her books have
    grown fewer—
She never was much given to litera-
    ture.

GEORGE ADE

•

Last night at twelve I felt immense,
But now I feel like thirty cents.

. . . .

It is no time for mirth and laughter,
The cold, gray dawn of the morning
    after.

The Sultan of Sulu, "Remorse"

GELETT BURGESS

•

I never saw a Purple Cow,
    I never hope to see one;
But I can tell you anyhow
    I'd rather see than be one.

"The Purple Cow"

Ah, yes! I wrote the "Purple Cow"—
    I'm sorry, now, I wrote it!
But I can tell you anyhow,
    I'll kill you if you quote it!

•

I wish that my room had a floor;

I don't so much care for a door,
  But this walking around
  Without touching the ground
Is getting to be quite a bore.

•

There was a young lady of Lynn,
Who was deep in original sin;
  When they said, "Do be good,"
  She said, "Would if I could!"
And straightway went at it ag'in.

•

I'd rather have fingers than toes;
I'd rather have ears than a nose;
  And as for my hair
  I'm glad it's all there,
I'll be awfully sad when it goes.

BERT LESTON TAYLOR ("B.L.T.")

•

When quacks with pills political would
    dope us,
  When politics absorbs the livelong
    day,
I like to think about the star Canopus,
  So far, so far away!

.   .   .   .

When men are calling names and mak-
    ing faces,
  And all the world's ajangle and
    ajar,
I meditate on interstellar spaces
  And smoke a mild seegar.

.   .   .   .

A star that has no parallax to speak of,
  Conduces to repose.
                              "Canopus"

ELLIS PARKER BUTLER

•

Three millions yearly for manure
But not one cent for literature.
                                "Iowa"

STRICKLAND GILLILAN

•

Adam
Had 'em.
        "Lines on the Antiquity of Mi-
            crobes"

ARTHUR GUITERMAN

•

Don't tell your friends about your in-
    digestion:
"How are you!" is a greeting, not a
    question.
                          A Poet's Proverbs

Ability will see a Chance and snatch it.
Who has a Match will find a Place to
    scratch it.
                                    Ibid.

CLARENCE DAY

•

Might and Right are always fighting.
In our youth it seems exciting.
Right is nearly always winning.
Might can hardly keep from grinning.
                          "Might and Right"

Farewell, my friends—farewell and
    hail!
I'm off to seek the Holy Grail.
  I cannot tell you why.
Remember, please, when I am gone,
'Twas Aspiration led me on.
Tiddledy-widdlely tootle-oo,
All I want is to stay with you,
  But here I go. Good-bye.
                          "Farewell, My Friends"

When eras die, their legacies
  Are left to strange police.
Professors in New England guard
  The glory that was Greece.
                          "When Eras Die"

Robert W. Service

•

There are strange things done in the
    midnight sun
By the men who moil for gold;
The Arctic trails have their secret
    tales
That would make your blood run cold;
The Northern Lights have seen queer
    sights,
But the queerest they ever did see
Was that night on the marge of Lake
    Lebarge
I cremated Sam McGee.
        "The Cremation of Sam Mc-
        Gee"

A bunch of the boys were whooping it
    up in the Malamute saloon;
The kid that handles the music-box
    was hitting a jag-time tune;
Back of the bar, in a solo game, sat
    Dangerous Dan McGrew;
And watching his luck was his light-o'-
    love, the lady that's known as
    Lou.
        "The Shooting of Dan Mc-
        Grew"

Arthur W. Bell

•

As man and his motor have brought it
    about,
The angler must learn, if he hopes to
    take trout,
Two dominant factors in fisherman's
    luck:
The schedule and route of the hatch-
    ery truck.
        "Modern Times"

Hughes Mearns

•

As I was going up the stair
I met a man who wasn't there.

He wasn't there again to day.
I wish, I wish he'd stay away!
        "Antigonish"

William F. Kirk

•

Ef yu vant someteng yust lak anyel
    fude,
Yu try stewed prunes. By yiminy! dey
    ban gude.
        "Sonnet on Stewed Prunes"

Don Marquis

•

if monkey glands
did restore your youth
what would you do
with it
question mark
just what you did before
interrogation point
yes i thought so
exclamation point
        "certain maxims of archy"

prohibition makes you
want to cry
into your beer and
denies you the beer
to cry into
          Ibid.

every cloud
has its silver
lining but it is
sometimes a little
difficult to get it to
the mint
          Ibid.

i have often noticed that
ancestors never boast
of the descendants who boast
of ancestors i would rather
start a family than finish

one blood will tell but
often it tells too much
              "a roach of the taverns"

my youth i shall never forget
but there s nothing i really regret
wotthehell wohtthehell
there s a dance in the old dame yet
toujours gai toujours gai
the things that i had not ought to
i do because i ve gotto
wotthehell wotthehell
and i end with my favorite motto
toujours gai toujours gai
              "the song of mehitabel"

The great open spaces
where cats are cats.

CARL SANDBURG
•

They have yarns
Of a skyscraper so tall they have to
    put hinges
On the two top stories so as to let the
    moon go by.

.   .   .   .

Of pancakes so thin they had only one
    side.

.   .   .   .

Of a mountain railroad curve where
    the engineer in his cab can touch
    the caboose and spit in the con-
    ductor's eye,
Of a boy who climbed a cornstalk
    growing so fast he would have
    starved to death if they hadn't
    shot biscuits up to him.

.   .   .   .

Of the man so tall he must climb a
    ladder to shave himself,
Of the runt so teeny-weeny it takes
    two men and a boy to see him.

                          The People, Yes

DIXON L. MERRITT
•

A wonderful bird is the pelican!
His bill will hold more than his beli-
    can.
He can take in his beak
Enough food for a week
But I'm darned if I see how the heli-
    can.
                              "The Pelican"

THOMAS R. YBARRA
•

A Christian is a man who feels
Repentance on a Sunday
For what he did on Saturday
And is going to do on Monday.
                              "A Christian"

FRANKLIN PIERCE ADAMS
•

Christmas is over and Business is
    Business.
                    "For the Other 364 Days"

These are the saddest of possible
    words,
    "Tinker to Evers to Chance."
Trio of bear cubs, and fleeter than
    birds,
    "Tinker to Evers to Chance."
Ruthlessly pricking our gonfalon bub-
    ble,
Making a Giant hit into a double—
Words that are heavy with nothing but
    trouble:
    "Tinker to Evers to Chance."
                    "Baseball's Sad Lexicon"

Gosh! I feel like a real good cry!
Life, he says, is a cheat, a fake.
Well, I agree with the grouchy guy—
The best you get is an even break.
        "Ballade of Schopenhauer's
Philosophy"

On the 18th of April in '28
My Tim began to be corporate.
Be brave, my son, and speak the trut',
And I hope you'll like your baseball
    suit.
        "Happy Lifetime to You"

EDGAR A. GUEST
•

It takes a heap o' livin' in a house t'
    make it home.

WALTER HARD
•

He was sitting in the rocker
One spring day.
He'd just finished piling the wood in
    the shed.
A neighbor stopped his team in the
    dooryard.
"Well, Ezry, how you feelin' today?"
Ezra stopped rocking.
"Pretty good," he said in a throaty,
    tired voice.
"I been ailin' so much, I kinder got
    so's
I feel better when I'm sick
Than I do when I'm well."
        "A Health Note"

KEITH PRESTON
•

A modernist married a fundamentalist
    wife,
And she led him a catechism and
    dogma life.
        "Marital Tragedy"

Among our literary scenes,
Saddest this sight to me,
The graves of little magazines
That died to make verse free.
        "The Liberators"

Here lies beneath this mossy stone
  A politician who

Touched a live issue without gloves
  And never did come to.
        "Epitaph"

He must not laugh at his own wheeze:
A snuff box has no right to sneeze.

EZRA POUND
•

Tell me not in mournful wish-wash
Life's a sort of sugared dish-wash.
        "L'Homme Moyen Sensuel"

ISAAC GOLDBERG
•

Diplomacy is to do and say
The nastiest thing in the nicest way.
        "The Reflex"

EARNEST A. HOOTON
•

If you had lived to breed your kind
It would have had the sort of mind
That feeds upon the comic strips
And reads with movements of the lips.
        "Lines to Homo Somejerkten-
    sis." *

ROLAND YOUNG
•

And here's the happy, bounding flea—
You cannot tell the he from she.
The sexes look alike, you see;
But she can tell and so can he.
        "The Flea"

JOHN CROWE RANSOM
•

God have mercy on the sinner
Who must write without a dinner
  No gravy and no grub,

* The skull of a baby pithecanthropus,
found in Java, 1936

No pewter and no pub,
No belly and no bowels,
Only consonants and vowels.

"Survey of Literature"

SAMUEL HOFFENSTEIN

Breathes there a man with soul so
    tough
Who says two sexes aren't enough?

"The Sexes"

Babies haven't any hair;
Old men's heads are just as bare;—
Between the cradle and the grave
Lies a haircut and a shave.

"Songs of Faith in the Year
After Next"

CHRISTOPHER MORLEY

Genius, cried the commuter,
As he ran for the 8:13,
Consists of an infinite capacity
For catching trains.

"The Commuter"

MORRIS BISHOP

There I stood, and humbly scanned
    The Miracle that sense appals,
And I watched the tourists stand
    Spitting in Niagara Falls.

"Public Aid for Niagara Falls"

After the day is over
    And the passers-by are rare
The lights burn low in the barber-shop
    And the shades are drawn with care
To hide the haughty barbers
    Cutting each other's hair.

"The Tales the Barbers Tell"

There's a vaporish maiden in Harrison

Who longed for the love of a Saracen.
    But she had to confine her
    Intent to a Shriner
Who suffers, I fear, by comparison.

"Spilt Milk"

DOROTHY PARKER

They say of me, and so they should,
It's doubtful if I come to good.
I see acquaintances and friends
Accumulating dividends,
And making enviable names
In science, art, and parlor games.
But I, despite expert advice,
Keep doing things I think are nice,
And though to good I never come—
Inseparable my nose and thumb.

"Neither Bloody Nor Bowed"

Say my love is easy had,
    Say I'm bitten raw with pride,
Say I am too often sad—
    Still behold me at your side.

Say I'm neither brave nor young,
    Say I woo and coddle care,
Say the devil touched my tongue—
    Still you have my heart to wear.

But say my verses do not scan
And I get me another man!

"Fighting Words"

Men seldom make passes
At girls who wear glasses.

"News Item"

Prince, a precept I'd leave for you,
Coined in Eden, existing yet;
Skirt the parlor, and shun the zoo—
Women and elephants never forget.

"Ballade of Unfortunate Mammals"

He lies below, correct in cypress wood,

And entertains the most exclusive
worms.

        "The Very Rich Man"

Razors pain you;
Rivers are damp;
Acids stain you;
And drugs cause cramp.
Guns aren't lawful;
Nooses give;
Gas smells awful;
You might as well live.

        "Résumé"

By the time you swear you're his;
  Shivering and sighing,
And he vows his passion is
  Infinite, undying—
Lady, make a note of this:
  One of you is lying.

        "Unfortunate Coincidence"

Drink and dance and laugh and lie,
  Love, the reeling midnight through,
For tomorrow we shall die!
  (But, alas, we never do.)

        "The Flaw in Paganism"

For contrition is hollow and wraithful,
  And regret is no part of my plan,
And I think (if my memory's faithful)
  There was nothing more fun than a
  man!

        "The Little Old Lady in Lav-
        ender Silk"

Oh, life is a glorious cycle of song,
  A medley of extemporanea;
And love is a thing that can never go
  wrong;
  And I am Marie of Rumania.

        "Comment"

Some men break your heart in two,
  Some men fawn and flatter,

Some men never look at you;
  And that cleans up the matter.

        •

I'd rather flunk my Wasserman test
Than read a poem by Edgar A. Guest.

        Attributed to Miss Parker, who
        vehemently denies authorship

WESTBROOK PEGLER

        •

The thing we all love most about the
  glorious old United States of A.
Is that everybody, irregardless of creed
  or color, is entitled to have their
  say.
It makes no difference whether you
  are a member of the wealthy
  group,
Or if you are so poor all you have for
  your humble fare is soup.
It is just the same whether you are of
  socialist persuasion,
Or vegetarian or any other peculiar
  denomination,
Everybody is entitled to express their
  opinion in this wonderful free
  land of ours
From the rockbound coast of Maine
  to California's tropical bowers.

        "Fair Enough," August 30,
  1944

GRAHAM LEE HEMMINGER

        •

Tobacco is a dirty weed.
        I like it.
It satisfies no normal need.
        I like it.
It makes you thin, it makes you lean,
It takes the hair right off your bean.
It's the worst darn stuff I've ever seen.
        I like it.

        "Tobacco," first appeared in
        the Penn State *Froth,* Novem-
        ber, 1915

DAVID McCORD

•

By and by
God caught his eye.

"Epitaph for a Waiter"

The cod
Is odd.
The Cape Codder
Is odder.

"Cod"

The motto of the rabbit?
Amo, amas, amabbit.

"Bunny"

E. B. WHITE

•

Commuter—one who spends his life
In riding to and from his wife;
A man who shaves and takes a train,
And then rides back to shave again.

"The Commuter" from *The
Lady Is Cold*

In the sudden mirror in the hall
I saw not my own self at all,
I saw a most familiar face:
My father stood there in my place,
Returning, in the hall lamp's glare,
My own surprised and watery stare.
In thirty years my son shall see
Not himself standing there, but me.

"A Boy I Knew," *The Reader's
Digest*

OGDEN NASH

•

The dog is man's best friend.
He has a tail on one end.
Up in front he has teeth.
And four legs underneath.

.   .   .   .   .   .

Dogs display reluctance and wrath
If you try to give them a bath.
They bury bones in hideaways
And half the time they trot sideaways.

"An Introduction to Dogs"

Candy
Is dandy
But liquor
Is quicker.

"Reflection on Ice-Breaking"

Sure, deck your lower limbs in pants;
Yours are the limbs, my sweeting.
You look divine as you advance—
Have you seen yourself retreating?

"What's the Use?"

This is a song to celebrate banks,
Because they are full of money and
    you go into them and all you hear
    is clinks and clanks,
Or maybe a sound like the wind in the
    trees on the hills,
Which is the rustling of the thousand
    dollar bills.

"Bankers Are Just Like Everybody Else, Except Richer"

It is my duty, gentlemen, to inform
    you that women are dictators all,
    and I recommend to you this
    moral:
In real life it takes only one to make a
    quarrel.

"I Never Even Suggested It"

I think that I shall never see
A billboard lovely as a tree,
Perhaps, unless the billboards fall,
I'll never see a tree at all.

"Song of the Open Road"

They have such refined and delicate
    palates
That they can discover no one worthy
    of their ballots,
And then when some one terrible gets
    elected
They say, There, that's what I ex-
    pected!

"Election Day Is a Holiday"

One would be in less danger

From the wiles of the stranger
If one's own kin and kith
Were more fun to be with.
                    "Family Court"

The firefly's flame
Is something for which science has no
        name.
I can think of nothing eerier
Than flying around with an unidenti-
    fied glow on a person's posterior.
                        "The Firefly"

The turtle lives 'twixt plated decks
Which practically conceal its sex.
I think it clever of the turtle
In such a fix to be so fertile.
                        "The Turtle"

Some primal termite knocked on wood
    And tasted it, and found it good.
And that is why your Cousin May
    Fell through the parlor floor today.
                        "The Termite"

Children aren't happy with nothing to
        ignore,
And that's what parents were created
    for.
                        "The Parent"

A bit of talcum
Is always walcum.
                "Reflection on Babies"

Many an infant that screams like a
        calliope
Could be soothed by a little attention
    to its diope.
                "Pediatric Reflection"

Oh, a home as mute as a bell that's
        clapperless
Is forlorn as an Indian in Indianapolis.
                        "Little Feet"

The one-l lama,
He's a priest.
The two-l llama,

He's a beast.
And I will bet
A silk pajama
There isn't any
Three-l lllama.*
                        "The Lama"

Beneath this slab
John Brown is stowed.
He watched the ads
And not the road.
                "Lather As You Go"

The cow is of the bovine ilk;
One end is moo, the other, milk.
                        "The Cow"

The old men know when an old man
        dies.
                        "Old Men"

Sometimes with secret pride I sigh
To think how tolerant am I;
Then wonder which is really mine:
Tolerance, or a rubber spine?
                        "Yes and No"

How courteous is the Japanese;
He always says, "Excuse it, please."
He climbs into his neighbor's garden,
And smiles, and says, "I beg your par-
    don";
He bows and grins a friendly grin,
And calls his hungry family in;
He grins, and bows a friendly bow;
"So sorry, this my garden now."
                        "The Japanese"

A girl who is bespectacled
Don't even get her nectacled,
But safety pins and bassinets
Await the girl who fascinets.
                "Lines Written to Console
                Those Ladies Distressed by the
                Lines 'Men Never Make Passes,
                etc.' "

* The author's attention has been called
to a type of conflagration known as a
three-alarmer. Pooh.

A girl whose cheeks are covered with paint
Has an advantage with me over one whose ain't.
      "Biological Reflection"

Some one invented the telephone,
And interrupted a nation's slumbers,
Ringing wrong but similar numbers.
      "Look What You Did, Christopher"

There was a young belle of old Natchez
Whose garments were always in patchez.
  When comment arose
  On the state of her clothes,
She drawled, When Ah itchez, Ah scratchez!
      "Requiem"

There is something about a Martini,
A tingle remarkably pleasant;
A yellow, a mellow Martini;
I wish that I had one at present.
There is something about a Martini,
Ere the dining and dancing begin,
And to tell you the truth,
It is not the vermouth—
I think that perhaps it's the Gin.
      "A Drink with Something in It"

Well, who wants to be young, anyhow, any idiot born in the last forty years can be young, and besides forty-five isn't really old, it's right on the border;
At least, unless the elevator's out of order.
      "Let's Not Climb the Washington Monument Tonight"

I hardly suppose I know anybody who wouldn't rather be a success than a failure,
Just as I suppose every piece of crab-grass in the garden would much rather be an azalea,
And in celestial circles all the run-of-the-mill angels would rather be archangels or at least cherubim and seraphim,
And in the legal world all the little process-servers hope to grow up into great big bailiffim and sheriffim.
      "Kindly Unhitch That Star, Buddy"

PHYLLIS MCGINLEY
•

Of the small gifts of heaven,
It seems to me a more than equal share
At birth was given
To girls with curly hair.
Oh, better than being born with a silver ladle,
Or even with a caul on,
Is wearing ringlets sweetly from the cradle!
Slaves to no beauty salon,
Ladies whose locks grow prettier when moister
Can call the world their oyster.
      "Meditations During a Permanent Wave"

Snugly upon the equal heights
  Enthroned at last where she belongs,
She takes no pleasure in her Rights
  Who so enjoyed her Wrongs.
      "The Old Feminist"

Sticks and stones are hard on bones.
  Aimed with angry art,
Words can sting like anything.
  But silence breaks the heart.
      "A Choice of Weapons"

Love is a mischief,
Love is a brat.
Love is, admittedly, blind as a bat.

Aimless his arrows as bundles from the stork.
So I'm in love with
The City of New York.

. . . .

Too new for an empire, too big for its boots,
With cold steel cables where it might have roots,
With everything to offer and nothing to give,
It's a horrid place to visit but a fine place to live;

. . . .

Ah! some love Paris,
And some Purdue.
But love is an archer with a low I. Q.
A bold, bad bowman, and innocent of pity.
So I'm in love with
New York City.

"A Kind of Love Letter to New York"

RICHARD ARMOUR
•

Middle age
Is a time of life
That a man first notices
In his wife.

Light Armour, 1954

"TROUBADOUR"
•

Not always to the swift the race;
Nor to the strong the victory.
Not always to the pretty face
The man of wealth or poesy.

Not always to the bold, the fair;
Nor love from those we hold most dearly.
Not always nothing to a pair;
But pretty nearly.

"The Law of Averages"

ANONYMOUS
•

If fresh meat be wanting to fill up our dish,
We have carrots and turnips as much as we wish:
And if there's a mind for a delicate dish
We repair to the clam-banks, and there we catch fish.
Instead of pottage and puddings and custards and pies,
Our pumpkins and parsnips are common supplies;
We have pumpkins at morning and pumpkins at noon,
If it was not for pumpkins we should be undone.

If barley be wanting to make into malt,
We must be contented, and think it no fault;
For we can make liquor to sweeten our lips,
Of pumpkins and parsnips and walnut-tree chips.

"Forefathers' Song," in Massachusetts Historical Collection, supposedly taken from the lips of a ninety-six-year-old woman in 1785—but traced back to about 1630

The ball once struck off,
Away flies the boy
To the next destined post,
And then home with joy.

A Little Pretty Pocketbook, 1744. The quatrain is headed "Base Ball." This is supposed to be the first mention of baseball in print.

Since in a bed a man and maid
May bundle and be chaste,

It doth no good to burn up wood;
  It is a needless waste.

"New England Broadside in
  Defense of Bundling," c. 1786

Oh Burr, oh Burr, what hast thou
    done,
Thou hast shooted dead great Hamil-
    ton!
You hid behind a bunch of thistle,
And shooted him dead with a great
    hoss pistol!

  Poem dropped on Aaron Burr's
  doorstep and widely circulated.
  Burr killed Hamilton on the
  morning of July 11, 1804.

Leave the flurry
To the masses;
Take your time
And shine your glasses.

            Old Shaker verse

Voyager upon life's sea,
  To yourself be true,
And whate'er your lot may be,
  Paddle your own canoe.

  "Paddle Your Own Canoe,"
  published anonymously in the
  "Editor's Drawer" of *Harper's
  Monthly* for May, 1854, with
  prefatory note explaining that
  it was a "term in the West."
  The poem has been attributed
  to Sarah K. Bolton, Sarah
  Tittle and Edward P. Philpots.
  Notes and Queries, May 25,
  1901, p. 414, adds considerably
  to the confusion.

You can always tell the Irish,
  You can always tell the Dutch.
You can always tell a Yankee;
  But you cannot tell him much.

              •

I always eat peas with honey,
  I've done it all my life,

They do taste kind of funny,
But it keeps them on the knife.

              •

Nobody loves me, everybody hates me,
I'm going to eat some worms.
Big ones, round ones, little ones, slimy
    ones—
I'm going to eat some worms.

              •

Mary Ann has gone to rest,
Safe at last on Abraham's breast,
Which may be nuts for Mary Ann,
But is certainly rough on Abraham.

              •

Dey ketches little minners in de middle
    ob de sea,
An' you finds de smalles' possum up de
    bigges' kind o' tree.

              "Rev. Gabe Tucker's Remarks"

He may have done wrong but he
    thought he done right,
And he always was good to the poor.

              Ballad on Jim Fisk

Lizzie Borden took an ax
And gave her father forty whacks;
When she saw what she had done,
She gave her mother forty-one.

  "Lizzie Borden," sung to the
  tune of "Ta-Ra-Ra Boom-De-
  Ray." Miss Borden (1860–
  1927) was the daughter of a
  wealthy banker of Fall River,
  Massachusetts; after the discovery of the murdered bodies
  of her parents she became the
  central figure in a celebrated
  murder trial, 1892. She was
  finally acquitted.

What a wonderful bird the frog are—
When he stand he sit almost;
When he hop, he fly almost.
He ain't got no sense hardly;
He ain't got no tail hardly either.

When he sit, he sit on what he ain't
   got almost.
"The Frog"

I asked my mother for fifty cents
To see the elephant jump the fence;
He jumped so high
He reached the sky
And never came back till the Fourth
   of July.

•

John Wesley Gaines!
John Wesley Gaines!
Thou monumental mass of brains!
Come in, John Wesley—
For it rains.

    Mr. Gaines is believed to have
been a Congressman.

See the happy moron,
He doesn't give a damn!
I wish I were a moron—
My God! Perhaps I am!

    "The Moron," quoted in the
Journal of Heredity by its editor, Robert Cooke, who said he
took it from an English publication. Dorothy Parker denies
authorship, though the quatrain is often attributed to her.
    Another version:

I don't know what a moron is,
   And I don't give a damn.
I'm thankful that I am not
   one—
   My God! Perhaps I am!

    HENRY PRATT FAIR-
CHILD, "The Great Eco-
nomic Paradox," *Har-
per's Magazine,* May,
1932

Soldiers who wish to be a hero
Are practically zero,
But those who wish to be civilians,
Jesus, they run into the millions.

    Army latrine inscription,
quoted by Norman Rosten, *The
Big Road,* 1945

III. The Songs We Sing

Arranged as Far as Possible in Chronological Order

•

On Springfield Mountain there did
    dwell,
A comely youth I knew full well.

       "The Pesky Sarpent"

Rye whiskey, rye whiskey,
  Rye whiskey, I cry,
If you don't give me rye whiskey,
  I surely will die.

       "Rye Whiskey"

Ye monsters of the bubbling deep,
  Your Maker's praises shout,
Up from the sands, ye codlings, leap
  And wag your tails about.

    "Ye Monsters of the Bubbling
    Deep"

JOHN DICKINSON

•

Then join hand in hand, brave Americans all,—
By uniting we stand, by dividing we
  fall!

    "Liberty Song," Boston *Ga-
    zette,* July 18, 1768

JOSEPH HOPKINSON

•

Hail, Columbia! happy land!
Hail, ye heroes! heavenborn band!
Who fought and bled in Freedom's
  cause.

       "Hail, Columbia!"

EDWARD BANGS

•

Yankee Doodle, keep it up,
  Yankee Doodle dandy;

Mind the music and the step,
  And with the girls be handy.

Yankee Doodle came to town
  Riding on a pony;
Stuck a feather in his cap
  And called it Macaroni.

    "Yankee Doodle." Also attrib-
  uted to many others.

FRANCIS SCOTT KEY

•

Oh! say can you see by the dawn's
  early light
What so proudly we hailed at the
  twilight's last gleaming,
Whose broad stripes and bright stars,
  thro' the perilous fight,
O'er the ramparts we watched, were
  so gallantly streaming;
And the rocket's red glare, the bombs
  bursting in air,
Gave proof thro' the night that our
  flag was still there!
Oh! say, does that star-spangled banner yet wave,
O'er the land of the free and the home
  of the brave.

. . . .

Then conquer we must, for our cause
  it is just,—
And this be our motto,—"In God is
  our trust!"

    "The Star-Spangled Banner,"
  September 14, 1814

SAMUEL WOODWORTH

•

How dear to my heart are the scenes
  of my childhood,
When fond recollection presents them
  to view!

. . . .

The old oaken bucket, the iron-bound
bucket,
The moss-covered bucket that hung in
the well.
"The Old Oaken Bucket," 1818

EMMA WILLARD
•

Rocked in the cradle of the deep,
I lay me down in peace to sleep.
"Rocked in the Cradle of the
Deep"

JOHN HOWARD PAYNE
•

'Mid pleasures and palaces though we
may roam,
Be it ever so humble, there's no place
like home.
"Home Sweet Home" (from
the opera *Clari*)

ANONYMOUS
•

O the E-RI-E was a-risin'
And the gin was a-gettin' low,
And I scarcely think we'll git a drink
Till we get to Bufa-lo-o-o,
Till we get to Buffalo.
"The E-RI-E"

I've got a mule, her name is Sal,
Fifteen miles on the Erie Canal;
She's a good old worker and a good
old pal,
Fifteen miles on the Erie Canal.
We've hauled some barges in our day,
Filled with lumber, coal, and hay,
And we know ev'ry inch of the way
From Albany to Buffalo.
"The Erie Canal"

Ask any question in this town,
Of any one, by night or morn,

The answer will be always found
"Round Cape Horn."
.   .   .   .   .   .

Thus merchants, sailors, women, men,
The old, or children lately born,
To all you ask, reply again,—
"Round Cape Horn."

Now you who know, an answer give.
Do I stay here, or am I gone?
Tell me if I do surely live
"Round Cape Horn."
"Round Cape Horn"

Come all ye bold sailors
Who sail round Cape Horn,
Come all ye bold whalers
Who cruise round for sperm:
The captain has told us,
An' I hope 'twill prove true,
That there's plenty of sperm whales
Off the coast of Peru.
"The Coast of Peru"

Oh, Shenandoah, I long to hear you.
Away, you rolling river,
Oh Shenandoah, I love to hear you.
Away, I'm bound away
'Cross the wide Missouri.
"Shenandoah"

I was seeing Nellie home,
I was seeing Nellie home;
And 'twas from Aunt Dinah's quilting
party
I was seeing Nellie home.
"The Quilting Party"

HENRY WADSWORTH LONGFELLOW
•

Lord, let war's tempest cease,
Fold the whole world in peace
Under thy wings.
Make all the nations one,
All hearts beneath the sun,

Till Thou shalt reign alone,
Great King of Kings.
> Written for the tune of "Amer-
> ica"

THOMAS D. ("JIM CROW") RICE
•
Wheel about, turn about,
  Do jis so,
An' eberry time I wheel about
  I jump Jim Crow.
> "Jump Jim Crow"

STEPHEN COLLINS FOSTER
•
Gwine to run all night!
Gwine to run all day!
I'll bet my money on de bob-tail nag,
Somebody bet on de bay.
> "Camptown Races"

Weep no more, my lady,
  Oh! weep no more today!
We will sing one song for the old Ken-
  tucky Home,
  For the old Kentucky Home far
    away.
> "My Old Kentucky Home"

'Way down upon de Swanee Ribber,
  Far, far away,
Dere's where my heart is turning eb-
  ber;
  Dere's where de old folks stay.
All up and down the whole creation
  Sadly I roam,
Still longing for de old plantation,
  And for de old folks at home.
> "Old Folks at Home"

Old dog Tray's ever faithful,
  Grief cannot drive him away;
He is gentle, he is kind; I'll never,
  never find
  A better friend than old dog Tray.
> "Old Dog Tray"

Down in de corn-field
  Hear dat mournful sound:
All de darkies am a-weeping,—
  Massa's in de cold, cold ground.
> "Massa's in de Cold Cold
> Ground"

Oh! I dream of Jeanie with the light
  brown hair,
Floating, like a vapor, on the soft summer air.
> "Jeanie with the Light Brown
> Hair"

SEPTIMUS WINNER
("ALICE HAWTHORNE")
•
Listen to the mockingbird,
Still singing where the weeping wil-
  lows wave.
> "Listen to the Mockingbird,"
> 1855

ROBERT LOWRY
•
Shall We Gather at the River?
> Title and first line of hymn,
> 1856

Where is my wand'ring boy to-night?
> "Where Is My Boy Tonight?"

SARAH F. ADAMS
•
Nearer, my God, to Thee,
Nearer to Thee!
E'en though it be a cross
That raiseth me;
Still all my song shall be,
Nearer, my God, to Thee.
> "Nearer, My God, to Thee," c.
> 1856

JOHN H. HOPKINS

•

We three kings of Orient are;
Bearing gifts we traverse afar
Field and fountain, moor and moun-
   tain,
Following yonder star.
O Star of wonder,
Star of night,
Star with royal beauty bright,
Westward leading, still proceeding,
Guide us to Thy perfect light.

"We Three Kings," c. 1857

H. D. L. WEBSTER

•

The years creep slowly by, Lorena,
The snow is on the grass again;
The sun's low down the sky, Lorena,
The frost gleams where the flow'rs
   have been.
But the heart throbs on as warmly
   now,
As when the summer days were nigh;
Oh, the sun can never dip so low,
Adown affection's cloudless sky.

"Lorena," 1857

DANIEL DECATUR EMMETT

•

I wish I was in the land of cotton, old
   times there are not forgotten,
Look away, look away, look away,
   Dixie Land.
In Dixie Land where I was born in,
   early on a frosty mornin',
Look away, look away, look away,
   Dixie Land.

(Chorus)

Then I wish I was in Dixie, hooray!
   hooray!
In Dixie Land I'll take my stand to
   live and die in Dixie,
Away, away, away down South in
   Dixie,

Away, away, away down South in
   Dixie.

Old Missus marry Will de Weaber,
   Will-yum was a gay deceaber,
Look away, look away, look away,
   Dixie Land.
But when he put his arm around her,
   smiled as fierce as a forty pounder,
Look away, look away, look away,
   Dixie Land.

(Repeat *Chorus*)

Dars buckwheat cakes an' ingen bat-
   ter, makes you fat or a little fat-
   ter,
Look away, look away, look away,
   Dixie Land.
Den hoe it down and scratch your
   grabble, to Dixie's Land I'm
   bound to travel,
Look away, look away, look away,
   Dixie Land.

(Repeat *Chorus*)

"Dixie," 1859.
   On April 10, 1865, the news
of Lee's surrender reached
Washington and President Lincoln was called out of the
White House by a large crowd.
"I am very greatly rejoiced to
find," he said, "that an occasion
has occurred so pleasurable
that the people cannot restrain
themselves. [Cheers.] I suppose
that arrangements are being
made for some sort of a formal
demonstration, this, or perhaps,
tomorrow night. . . . If there
should be such a demonstration, I, of course, will be called
upon to respond, and I shall
have nothing to say if you dribble it all out of me before.
[Laughter and applause.] I see
you have a band of music with
you. [Voices, 'We have two or

three.'] I propose closing up this interview by the band performing a particular tune which I will name. Before this is done, however, I wish to mention one or two little circumstances connected with it. I have always thought 'Dixie' one of the best tunes I have ever heard. Our adversaries over the way attempted to appropriate it, but I insisted yesterday that we fairly captured it. [Applause.] I presented the opinion to the Attorney General, and he gave it as his legal opinion that it is our lawful prize. [Laughter and applause.] I now request the band to favor me with its performance."

ANONYMOUS

•

Old Abe Lincoln came out of the wilderness,
Down in Illinois.
        "Old Abe Lincoln," c. 1860

HARRY McCARTHY

•

We are a band of brothers
And native to the soil,
Fighting for our liberty,
With treasure blood and toil.
And when our rights were threaten'd
The cry rose near and far,
Hurrah for The Bonnie Blue Flag
That bears a single star!
Hurrah! Hurrah! For Southern rights hurrah!
Hurrah for the Bonnie Blue Flag
That bears a single star!
        "The Bonnie Blue Flag," c. 1861

MARIE RAVENEL

•

Somebody's darling, somebody's pride,
Who'll tell his mother where her boy died?
        "Somebody's Darling," c. 1861

JULIA WARD HOWE

•

Mine eyes have seen the glory of the coming of the Lord;
He is trampling out the vintage where the grapes of wrath are stored;
He hath loosed the fateful lightning of His terrible swift sword:
    His truth is marching on.

I have seen Him in the watch-fires of a hundred circling camps,
They have builded Him an altar in the evening dews and damps;
I can read His righteous sentence by the dim and flaring lamps:
    His truth is marching on.

I have read a fiery gospel writ in burnished rows of steel;
"As ye deal with my contemners so with you my grace shall deal;
Let the Hero, born of woman, crush the serpent with his heel,
    Since God is marching on!"

He has sounded forth the trumpet that shall never call retreat;
He is sifting out the hearts of men before his judgment seat.
O, be swift, my soul, to answer Him! be jubilant, my feet!
    Our God is marching on.

In the beauty of the lilies Christ was born across the sea,
With a glory in his bosom that transfigures you and me;
As He died to make men holy, let us die to make them free,

While God is marching on.

"Battle Hymn of the Republic." "I went to bed that night as usual and slept, according to my wont, quite soundly. I awoke in the gray of the morning twilight, and as I lay waiting for the dawn, the long lines of the desired poem began to twine themselves in my mind. Having thought out all the stanzas, I said to myself, 'I must get up and write these verses down, lest I fall asleep again and forget them.' So with a sudden effort I sprang out of bed and found in the dimness an old stump of a pen which I remembered to have used the day before. I scrawled the verses almost without looking at the paper. I had learned to do this when, on previous occasions, attacks of versification had visited me in the night and I feared to have recourse to a light lest I should wake the baby, who slept near me. I was always obliged to decipher my scrawl before another night should intervene, as it was only legible while the matter was fresh in my mind. At this time, having completed my writings, I returned to bed and fell asleep, saying to myself, 'I like this better than most things that I have written.' " *Reminiscences*, January, 1862

ANONYMOUS

•

John Brown's body lies a-mould'ring
in the grave,
John Brown's body lies a-mould'ring
in the grave,

John Brown's body lies a-mould'ring
in the grave,
But his soul goes marching on.

There are several versions of this famous song, which have been variously attributed to Charles Sprague Hall, Thomas Brigham Bishop, Frank E. Jerome, and others.

JAMES SLOAN GIBBONS

•

We Are Coming, Father Abraham,
Three Hundred Thousand More.
Song to aid in raising volunteer
Union Army, 1862

GEORGE F. ROOT

•

Yes, we'll rally round the flag, boys,
we'll rally once again,
Shouting the battle-cry of Freedom,
We will rally from the hillside, we'll
gather from the plain,
Shouting the battle-cry of Freedom.
"Battle Cry of Freedom"

Just before the battle, Mother,
I am thinking most of you.
"Just Before the Battle, Mother"

Tramp, tramp, tramp! the boys are
marching,
Cheer up, comrades, they will come
(they will come)
And beneath the starry flag we shall
breathe the air again
Of the free land in our own beloved
home.
"Tramp, Tramp, Tramp," c.
1863

ANONYMOUS

•

Weeping, sad and lonely,
Hopes and fears, how vain;

Yet praying
When this cruel war is over,
Praying that we meet again.
        "When This Cruel War Is
        Over," 1863

Save up your pennies and put away
    your rocks,
And you'll always have tobacco in
    your old tobacco box.
            "There Was an Old Soldier"

Shoo, fly, don't bother me,
I belong to Comp'ny G.
                                c. 1864

If de Debble do not ketch
Jeff Davis, dat infernal wretch,
An' roast and frigazee dat rebble,
What is de use of any Debble?
                    Negro Civil War song

De bottom rail's on de top
An we's gwine to keep it dar.
                                Ibid.

Missus in de big manse
Mammy in de yard
Missus holding her white hands
Mammy workin' hard.
White man in starched shirt setten in
    de shade
Laziest man God ever made.
                                Ibid.

ETHEL LYNN BEERS
•

"All quiet along the Potomac to-
    night,"
Where the soldiers lie peacefully
    dreaming.
And their tents in the rays of the clear
    Autumn moon,
And the light of the campfires are
    gleaming.
A tremulous sigh as the night wind

Through the forest leaves slowly is
    creeping,
While the stars up above, with their
    glittering eyes,
Keep guard over the army while sleep-
    ing.
All quiet along the Potomac tonight.
        "All Quiet Along the Potomac
        Tonight"

WALTER KITTREDGE
•

We're tenting tonight on the old
    camp-ground,
    Give us a song to cheer
Our weary hearts, a song of home
    And friends we love so dear.

Many are the hearts that are weary
    tonight,
    Wishing for the war to cease;
Many are the hearts looking for the
    right,
    To see the dawn of peace.
Tenting tonight, tenting tonight,
    Tenting on the old camp-ground.
            "We're Tenting Tonight"

HENRY CLAY WORK
•

Bring the good old bugle, boys, we'll
    sing another song;
Sing it with a spirit that will start the
    world along,
Sing it as we used to sing it—fifty
    thousand strong,
    As we were marching through Geor-
    gia.
"Hurrah! hurrah! we bring the Jubi-
    lee!
Hurrah! hurrah! the flag that makes
    you free!"
So we sang the chorus from Atlanta
    to the sea,

As we were marching through
    Georgia.
        "Marching Through Georgia,"
    1865

FATHER ABRAM J. RYAN
•

Furl that Banner for 'tis weary,
Round its staff 'tis drooping dreary,
Furl it, fold it, it is best.
For there's not a man to wave it,
And there's not a sword to save it
In the blood that heroes gave it,
And its foes now scorn and brave it,
Furl it, hide it, let it rest.

        "The Conquered Banner," a
    song of the Confederacy

INNES RANDOLPH
•

Oh, I'm a good old rebel, that's what
    I am,
And for this land of freedom, I don't
    give a damn;
I'm glad I fought agin her, I only wish
    we'd won,
And I ain't axed any pardon for any-
    thing I've done.

.   .   .   .

I hate the Constitution, this great re-
    public, too;
I hate the nasty eagle, and the uniform
    so blue;
I hate their glorious banner, and all
    their flags and fuss.
Those lying, thieving Yankees, I hate
    'em wuss and wuss.

.   .   .   .

I can't take up my musket and fight
    them now no mo',
But I'm not goin' to love 'em, and that
    is certain sho';
And I don't want no pardon for what
    I was or am,

I won't be reconstructed and I don't
    give a damn.
        "The Rebel," c. 1870. Edward
    VII referred to these verses as
    "that fine American song with
    the cusswords in it."

GEORGE W. JOHNSON
•

And now we are aged and gray, Mag-
    gie,
And the trials of life nearly done;
Let us sing of the days that are gone,
    Maggie,
When you and I were young.
        "When You and I Were
    Young, Maggie," c. 1865

GEORGE LEYBOURNE
•

He'd fly through the air with the
    greatest of ease,
This handsome young man on the fly-
    ing trapeze;
His movements were graceful, all girls
    he could please,
    And my love he has purloined away!
        "The Man on the Flying Tra-
    peze," 1868

HENRY CLAY WORK
•

Father, dear Father, come home with
    me now!
    The clock in the steeple strikes one.
You said you were coming right home
    from the shop
    As soon as your day's work was
    done.
                "Father, Dear Father"

Ninety years without slumbering
    Tick, tick, tick, tick.
His life-seconds numbering

Tick, tick, tick, tick.
It stopped short—never to go again—
When the old man died.

"Grandfather's Clock"

S. Fillmore Bennet

•

In the sweet by and by,
We shall meet on that beautiful shore.

"In the Sweet By and By"

Edward S. Ufford

•

Throw out the Life-Line!
Someone is drifting away;
Throw out the Life-Line!
Someone is sinking to day.

"Throw Out the Life-Line"

Phillips Brooks

•

O little town of Bethlehem,
How still we see thee lie!
Above thy deep and dreamless sleep
The silent stars go by;
Yet in thy dark streets shineth
The everlasting Light;
The hopes and fears of all the years
Are met in thee tonight.

"O Little Town of Bethlehem"

George W. Young

•

The Lips That Touch Liquor Must
Never Touch Mine.

Title and refrain, c. 1870

Brewster Higley

•

Home, home on the range,
Where the deer and the antelope
play;

Where seldom is heard a discouraging
word,
And the skies are not cloudy all day.

"The Western Home," 1873.
This, one of F. D. Roosevelt's
favorite songs, has been attributed to others, but Higley's
claim seems the most convincing.

Charles Edward Carryl

•

A capital ship for an ocean trip
Was the *Walloping Window-blind*—
No gale that blew dismayed her crew
Or troubled the captain's mind.
The man at the wheel was taught to
feel
Contempt for the wildest blow,
And it often appeared, when the
weather had cleared,
That he'd been in his bunk below.

"The Walloping Window-
Blind"

Eben E. Rexford

•

Darling, I am growing old;
Silver threads among the gold
Shine upon my brow today;
Life is fading fast away.

"Silver Threads Among the
Gold." In the seventies, Hart
P. Danks bought a batch of
poems from Rexford, editor of
a Wisconsin farm magazine, for
three dollars each. One of them
was "Silver Threads"; Danks
wrote a tune for it, and there
you are!

Roger Truhart

•

She's as graceful as a comet,
Smoother than a water fall,

It's the Western Combination,
Of the Wabash Cannon Ball.
> "The Wabash Cannon Ball," c.
> 1875

ANONYMOUS
•

De boll weevil is a little black bug
F'um Mexico, dey say,
He come to try dis Texas soil
An' thought he'd better stay,
A-lookin' for a home,
Jes' a-lookin' for a home,
A-lookin' for a home,
Jes' a-lookin' for a home.
> "Ballad of the Boll Weevil"

The farmer's the chief of the nation,
The oldest of nobles is he;
How blest beyond others his station;
From want and from envy how free;
His patent was granted in Eden
Long ages and ages ago;
O, the farmer, the farmer forever,
Three cheers for the plow, spade, and
   hoe.
> A Grange song of the seventies

How in hell can the old folks tell
It ain't gonna rain no more?
> "Ain't Gonna Rain No More"

Oh, the old gray mare, she ain't what
   she used to be,
Ain't what she used to be, ain't what
   she used to be.
The old gray mare, she ain't what she
   used to be,
Many long years ago.
> "The Old Gray Mare"

Fare thee well, fare thee well,
Fare thee well, my fairy fay,
For I'm off to Louisiana
For to see my Susyanna
Singin' Polly-wolly-doodle all the day.
> "Fare Thee Well"

Dey crucified my Lord,
An' He never said a mumblin' word.
Not a word—not a word—not a word.
> "Mumblin' Word"

I'm go'n' to lay down my sword and
   shield.
I ain' go'n' to study war no mo'.
> "Ain' Goin' Study War No
> Mo'"

Lord, I been down so long,
Down don't worry me.
> "Down Don't Worry Me"

Let the midnight special shine her
   light on me;
Let the midnight special
Shine her everloving light on me.
> "The Midnight Special"

Sometimes I feel like an eagle in de
   air.
Some-a dese mornin's bright an' fair
I'm goin' to lay down my heavy load;
Goin' to spread my wings an' cleave
   de air.
You may bury me in de east,
You may bury me in de west,
But I'll hear de trumpet sound
In-a dat mornin'.
> "In-a Dat Mornin'"

I know it, 'deed I know it,
Dese bones gwine rise again.
> "Dese Bones"

I know moon-rise, I know star-rise,
   I lay dis body down.
I walk in de moonlight, I walk in de
   starlight,
   To lay dis body down.
I walk in de graveyard, I walk throo
   de graveyard,
   To lay dis body down.
I lie in de grave an' stretch out my
   arms,
   I lay dis body down.

I go to de jedgment in de evenin' of
    de day,
  When I lay dis body down.
An' my soul an' your soul will meet in
    de day
    When I lay dis body down.
              "Lay Dis Body Down"

Sometimes I feel like a motherless
  child,
A long ways from home.
          "Motherless Child"

Oh, de Ribber of Jordan is deep and
  wide,
  One mo' ribber to cross.
       "One Mo' Ribber to Cross"

Go down, Moses,
'Way down in Egypt's land;
Tell ole Pharaoh—
Let my people go.
When Israel was in Egypt's land,
Let my people go;
Oppressed so hard they could not
  stand,
Let my people go.
         "Let My People Go"

I got shoes, you got shoes,
All o' God's chillun got shoes.
When I get to heab'n gonna put on
  my shoes,
Gonna walk all ovah God's Heab'n,
  Heab'n, Heab'n,
Ev'rybody talkin' 'bout heab'n ain't
  a-goin' dere;
Heab'n, Heab'n, I'm gonna walk all
  ovah God's Heab'n.
        "All o' God's Children"

Nobody knows the trouble I've seen,
Nobody knows but Jesus.
Nobody knows the trouble I've seen,
Glory, Hallelujah.
    "Nobody Knows the Trouble
  I've Seen"

Star in the east, star in the west,
Wish that star was in my breast,
Church, I know you go'n to miss me
  When I'm gone.
          "When I'm Gone"

De blues ain't nothin'
But a poor man's heart disease.
          "The Blues"

Oh, Lord, I want to be free, want to
  be free;
Rainbow round my shoulder, wings on
  my feet.
        "I Want to Be Free"

PERCY MONTROSE
•

In a cavern, in a canyon,
  Excavating for a mine,
Dwelt a miner, Forty-niner,
  And his daughter, Clementine.
Oh, my darling, oh my darling, oh my
  darling Clementine!
Thou art lost and gone forever, dread-
  ful sorry, Clementine.
    "My Darling Clementine," c.
1880

CLEMENT SCOTT
•

Oh, promise me that someday you
  and I
Will take our love together to some
  sky
Where we can be alone and faith renew,
And find the hollows where those flowers grew.
      "Oh, Promise Me," 1888

ANONYMOUS
•

I am bound for the promised land,
I'm bound for the promised land;

O who will come and go with me,
I am bound for the promised land.
                    Revival hymn of the 1880's

Whoopie ti yi yo, git along, little do-
    gies,
It's your misfortune, and none of my
    own.
Whoopie ti yi yo, git along, little do-
    gies,
For you know Wyoming will be your
    new home.
                    "Git Along, Little Dogies"

As I walked out in Laredo one day,
I spied a poor cowboy wrapped up in
    white linen,
Wrapped up in white linen as cold as
    the clay.
                    "The Cowboy's Lament"

Jesse had a wife to mourn for his life,
Three children, they were brave,
But that dirty little coward that shot
    Mr. Howard,
Has laid Jesse James in his grave.
                    "Jesse James," 1882

Frank Baker's my name, and a bache-
    lor I am.
I'm keeping old batch on an elegant
    plan.
You'll find me out west in the county
    of Lane,
A-starving to death on a government
    claim.
                    "The Lane County Bachelor"

We're marching together,
Our brave little band,
On the right side of temperance
We all take our stand.

We don't use tobacco
Because we all think,
That people who do so

Are likely to drink.
            Temperance song, late nine-
    teenth century

JOSEPH FLYNN
•

Down went McGinty to the bottom of
    the say,
And he must be very wet for they
    haven't found him yet,
But they say his ghost comes round the
    docks before the break of day,
Dress'd in his best suit of clothes.
        "Down Went McGinty," c.
    1889

JOHN W. KELLY
•

Slide, Kelly, Slide!
            Title and refrain, 1889

"Throw him down McCloskey," was
    to be their battle cry,
"Throw him down McCloskey, you
    can lick him if you try,"
And future generations, with wonder
    and delight,
Will read on hist'ry's pages of the
    great McCloskey fight.
        "Throw Him Down, McClos-
    key," c. 1889

CHARLES H. HOYT
•

The Bow'ry, the Bow'ry!
They say such things and they do such
    things
On the Bow'ry, the Bow'ry!
I'll never go there any more!
                    "The Bow'ry," 1891

HENRY J. SAYERS
•

A sweet Tuxedo girl you see,
Queen of swell society,

Fond of fun as fond can be,
When it's on the strict Q. T.
   Ta-ra-ra Boom-der-é. [repeated
   four times]
     "Ta-Ra-Ra Boom-Der-É,"
    1891

CHARLES K. HARRIS
•

Many a heart is aching, if you could
  read them all,
Many the hopes that have vanished,
  after the ball.
     "After the Ball," 1892

KATHERINE LEE BATES
•

O beautiful for patriot dream
  That sees beyond the years
Thine alabaster cities gleam
  Undimmed by human tears!
America! America!
  God shed His grace on thee
And crown thy good with brotherhood
  From sea to shining sea!
    "America the Beautiful," 1893

ANONYMOUS
•

I've been workin' on the railroad,
  All the live-long day,
I've been workin' on the railroad,
  Just to pass the time away.
    "I've Been Workin' on the
    Railroad," 1894

EDWARD B. MARKS
•

My mother was a lady like yours you
  will allow,
And you may have a sister, who needs
  protection now.
I've come to this great city to find a
  brother dear,

And you wouldn't dare insult me, Sir,
  If Jack were only here.
    "Mother Was a Lady," 1895

KERRY MILLS
•

A camp meeting took place, by the
  colored race;
Way down in Georgia.
There were folks large and small,
  lanky, lean, fat and tall,
At this great Georgia camp meeting.
When church was out, how the "sis-
  ters" did shout,
They were so happy.
But the young folks were tired and
  wished to be inspired,
And hired a big brass band.
    "At a Georgia Camp Meeting,"
  c. 1895

CHARLES K. HARRIS
•

Just break the news to Mother;
She knows how dear I love her,
And tell her not to wait for me,
For I'm not coming home;
Just say there is no other
Can take the place of Mother;
Then kiss her dear, sweet lips for me,
And break the news to her.
    "Break the News to Mother,"
  1896

JOE HAYDEN
•

When you hear those bells go ting-a-
  ling . . .
There'll be a hot time in the old town
  tonight.
    "There'll Be a Hot Time," 1896

D. A. ESTROM
•

Hail! Hail! The gang's all here!

What the hell do we care? What the
   hell do we care?
Hail! Hail! The gang's all here!
What the hell do we care now?

                          "Hail! Hail!" c. 1897

MONROE H. ROSENFELD

•

With All Her Faults I Love Her Still.
                          Title and refrain

Take back your gold, for gold can
   never buy me;
Take back your bride and promise
   you'll be true;
Give me the love, the love you would
   deny me;
Make me your wife, that's all I ask
   of you.

                "Take Back Your Gold," 1897

HARRY DACRE

•

Daisy, Daisy,
Give me your answer, do!
I'm half crazy,
All for the love of you!
It won't be a stylish marriage,
I can't afford a carriage,
But you'll look sweet
Upon the seat
Of a bicycle built for two!

         "Daisy Bell." Dacre was an
      English song writer who came
      to this country in the nineties.
      Bringing his bicycle, he was
      amazed to have to pay duty on
      it. A friend said, "Lucky for
      you it was not built for two,"
      and he had his song.

THEODORE DREISER

•

Oh, the moon is fair tonight along the
   Wabash,

From the fields there comes the breath
   of new-mown hay;
Through the sycamores the candle
   lights are gleaming
On the banks of the Wabash, far away.

         His brother, Paul Dresser, is
      credited with writing the song,
      but H. L. Mencken says Dreiser
      wrote the chorus, and curiously
      beautiful it is.

ANONYMOUS

•

Frankie and Johnny were lovers
O Lordy how they could love.
Swore to be true to each other,
True as the stars above.
He was her man, but he done her
   wrong.

.   .   .   .

This story has no moral,
This story has no end,
This story only goes to show
That there ain't no good in men.
He was her man, but he done her
   wrong.

         "Frankie and Johnny." The
      original ballad is said to have
      related the murder of Albert
      Brett by Frankie Baker, in St.
      Louis, 1899. Some versions
      have Frankie and Albert as the
      protagonists.

I been wanderin'
Early and late,
From New York City
To the Golden Gate,
And it looks like
I ain't never gonna
Cease my wanderin'.

                          "Wanderin'"

Pushing up the daisies,
Pushing up the daisies,
That's where we'll all be
One hundred years from now.

                          "On the Morgue"

I should worry, I should care,
I should marry a millionaire;
He should die, I should cry,
I should marry another guy.

> American children's song, probably from New York

From the halls of Montezuma
  To the shores of Tripoli
We fight our country's battles
  On the land as on the sea.

. . . .

If the Army and the Navy
  Ever look on Heaven's scenes,
They will find the streets are guarded
  by
  The United States Marines.

> "The Marines' Hymn"

Damn, damn, damn the Filipino.
Pock-marked khakiac ladrone; *
Underneath the starry flag
Civilize him with a Krag,
And return us to our own beloved
  home.

> Army song popular in the Philippines during commissionership of Taft, re guerrilla war with Aguinaldo, 1899–1902

Oh, why don't you work
Like other men do?
How the hell can I work
When there's no work to do?

  Hallelujah, I'm a bum.

  Hallelujah, bum again,
  Hallelujah, give us a handout
  To revive us again.

Oh, I love my boss
And my boss loves me,
And that is the reason
I'm so hungry.
  Halleujah, etc.

. . . .

  * Ladrone: from the Spanish *"ladrón"*
—a thief; highwayman.

When springtime does come,
O won't we have fun,
We'll throw up our jobs
And we'll go on the bum.
  Hallelujah, etc.

> "Hallelujah, I'm a Bum"

My sister she works in a laundry,
My father he fiddles for gin,
My mother she takes in washing,
My God, how the money rolls in!

> "My God, How the Money Rolls In"

I'm Jackhammer John, I'm a Jackhammer man;
Born with a Jackhammer in my hand!

I'm a Jackhammer Man from a Jackhammer town;
I built every port from the North Pole down.

. . . .

Hammered in the mill, hammered in the mines;
Been in jail about a thousand times.

> "Jackhammer Man"

In the Big Rock Candy Mountains,
There's a land that's fair and bright,
Where the handouts grow on bushes
And you sleep out ev'ry night,
Where the boxcars are all empty
And the sun shines ev'ry day—
Oh, the birds and the bees and the
  cigarette trees,
The rock-and-rye springs where the
  whangdoodle sings,
In the Big Rock Candy Mountains.

> "Big Rock Candy Mountain"

Round her waist, she wore a yellow
  ribbon;
  She wore it in the Springtime, and
    in the month of May;
And when I asked her why the hell
  she wore it,

She wore it for her lover who was
  far, far away.
> "The Yellow Ribbon"

The sons of the prophet are brave men
  and bold,
And quite unaccustomed to fear,
But the bravest by far in the ranks of
  the Shah
Was Abdul the Bulbul Amir.
> "Abdul the Bulbul Amir"

Then we'll sing of Lydia Pinkham,
And her love for the human race;
How she sold her veg'table compound
And the papers published her face.
> "Lydia Pinkham"

Oh, the eagles they fly high,
  In Mobile, in Mobile.
Oh, the eagles they fly high
  In Mobile.
    Oh, the eagles they fly high
    And they . . . right in your eye,
    It's a good thing cows don't fly,
  In Mobile.
> "Mobile"

Did you ever hear about Cocaine Lil?
She lived in Cocaine town on Cocaine
  hill,
She had a cocaine dog and a cocaine
  cat,
They fought all night with the cocaine
  rat.

.   .   .   .

On her headstone you'll find this refrain:
"She died as she lived, sniffing cocaine."
> "Cocaine Lil"

Take a whiff on me, take a whiff on
  me,
Hi, hi, baby, take a whiff on me,
Ho, ho, honey, take a whiff on me.
> "Take a Whiff on Me"

Oh, they chaw tobacco thin in Kansas.
Oh, they say that drink's a sin in
  Kansas.
> Kansas folksong

How dry I am! How dry I am!
Nobody knows how dry I am!
> "How Dry I Am!"

When I die
  Don't bury me at all.
Just pickle my bones
  In alcohol.
> "When I Die"

EDGAR SMITH
•

You may tempt the upper classes
With your villainous demi-tasses,
But, Heaven will protect the working-
  girl!
> "Heaven Will Protect the
> Working-Girl," 1899

JAMES W. BLAKE and
CHARLES LAWLOR
•

East side, West side,
All around the town,
The tots sing "Ring-a-Rosie,"
"London Bridge is falling down";
Boys and Girls together,
Me and Mamie O'Rourke,
Trip the light fantastic
On the sidewalks of New York.
> "The Sidewalks of New York,"
> c. 1900

WILL D. COBB
•

School-days, school-days, dear old
  Golden Rule days,
Readin' and 'ritin' and 'rithmetic,
Taught to the tune of a hick'ry stick.
> "School-Days"

WILLIAM B. GRAY
•

She is more to be pitied than cen-
sured,
She is more to be helped than despised,
She is only a lassie who ventured
On life's stormy path ill-advised.
Do not scorn her with words fierce and
bitter,
Do not laugh at her shame and down-
fall;
For a moment just stop and consider
That a man was the cause of it all.

"She Is More to Be Pitied than
Censured," c. 1900

JOHN PIERPONT
•

Jingle bells! Jingle bells! Jingle all the
way!
Oh! what fun it is to ride in a one-
horse open sleigh!

"Jingle Bells," c. 1900

A. B. STERLING
•

Strike up the band, here comes a
sailor,
Cash in his hand, just off a whaler;
Stand in a row, don't let him go;
Jack's a cinch, but every inch a sailor.

"Strike Up the Band," copyright 1900 (Renewed 1927),
1942 by Harry Von Tilzer Music Publishing Co. Used by permission of copyright proprietor.

REN SHIELDS
•

In the good old summer time,
In the good old summer time,
Strolling through the shady lanes
With your baby mine;
You hold her hand and she holds
yours,

And that's a very good sign
That she's your tootsey wootsey
In the good old summer time.

"In the Good Old Summer-
time," 1901, copyright by Edward B. Marks Music Corporation. Used by permission.

HUGHIE CANNON
•

Bill Bailey, Won't You Please Come
Home?

Title and refrain, 1902

RICHARD H. GIRARD
•

Sweet Adeline, My Adeline,
At night, dear heart, for you I pine.
In all my dreams, your fair face
beams;
You're the flower of my heart, Sweet
Adeline.

"Sweet Adeline." Copyright,
1903, by M. Witmark & Sons.
Reprinted by Permission.

EDDIE LEONARD
•

Ida, Sweet as Apple Cider.

Title and refrain, 1903

GEORGE M. COHAN
•

Give my regards to Broadway,
Remember me to Herald Square,
Tell all the gang at Forty-second
Street
That I will soon be there.

"Give My Regards to Broadway," copyright, 1904, F. A.
Mills. Renewed and assigned to
George M. Cohan Music Publishing Co., Inc., New York.

Always Leave Them Laughing When
you Say Good-bye.

> Title and refrain

I Guess I'll Have to Telegraph My
Baby.

> Title and refrain

BARTLEY C. COSTELLO
•

Here's Your Hat, What's Your Hurry?

> Title and refrain, 1904

VINCENT BRYAN
•

Come away with me, Lucile,
In my merry Oldsmobile,
Down the road of life we'll fly
Automobubbling you and I.
To the church we'll swiftly steal,
Then our wedding bells will peal,
You can go as far as you like with me,
In my merry Oldsmobile.

> "In My Merry Oldsmobile."
> Copyright, 1905, by M. Wit-
> mark & Sons. Reprinted by
> Permission.

JOHN EDWARD HAZZARD
•

Ain't It Awful, Mabel?

> Title and refrain, 1908

JAMES J. WALKER
•

Will you love me in December as you
do in May,
Will you love me in the good old fash-
ioned way?
When my hair has all turned gray,
Will you kiss me then and say,
That you love me in December as you
did in May?

> "Will You Love Me in Decem-
> ber as You Do in May?"

IRVING BERLIN
•

Come on and hear,
Come on and hear
Alexander's Ragtime Band.

> From the composition "Alex-
> ander's Ragtime Band." Copy-
> right, 1911, Irving Berlin.
> Copyright Renewed.

FRANK RAMSAY ADAMS and WILL M. HOUGH
•

I Wonder Who's Kissing Her Now?

> Title and refrain, 1912

WEBB M. OUNGST
•

Ev'ry time I come to town,
The boys keep kickin' my dawg
aroun';
Makes no difference if he is a houn',
They gotta quit kickin' my dawg
aroun'.

> Champ Clark campaign song,
> 1912

HENRY FINK
•

The Curse of an Aching Heart.

> Title and refrain, 1913

W. C. HANDY
•

I hate to see de evenin' sun go down,
'Cause my baby, he done lef' this town.
Feelin' tomorrow lak I feel today,
I'll pack my trunk, make my get away.

> St. Louis woman wid her diamond
> rings
> Pulls dat man roun' by her apron
> strings.

'Twant for powder an' for store
    bought hair
De man I love would not gone no-
    where.

Got de St. Louis Blues jes' as blue as
    I can be,
Dat man got a heart lak a rock cast
    in the sea,
Or else he wouldn't have gone so far
    from me.

        "The St. Louis Blues," 1914

JOE HILL

•

Work and pray,
Live on hay!
You'll get pie
In the sky,
When you die—
It's a lie.

        Attributed to. Song of the
        I.W.W., 1915

J. WILL CALLAHAN

•

There are smiles that make us happy,
There are smiles that make us blue.

        "Smiles," c. 1917

ALFRED BRYAN

•

I Didn't Raise My Boy to Be a Sol-
    dier.

        Title and refrain, 1914

GEORGE ASAF

•

What's the use of worrying?
    It never was worth while, so
Pack up your troubles in your old kit-
    bag,
    And smile, smile, smile.

        "Smile, Smile, Smile," 1915

LENA GUILBERT FORD

•

Keep the home fires burning,
While your hearts are yearning,
Though your lads are far away they
    dream of home.

      "Keep the Home Fires Burn-
      ing," 1915

GEORGE M. COHAN

•

Over there—over there—
Send the word, send the word over
    there—
That the Yanks are coming, the Yanks
    are coming,
The drums rumtumming ev'rywhere—
So prepare—say a pray'r—
Send the word, send the word to be-
    ware—
We'll be over, we're coming over,
And we won't come back till it's over
    over there.

      "Over There." Copyright, 1917.
      Copyright renewal, 1945, by
      Leo Feist, Inc. Used by special
      permission.

IRVING BERLIN

•

Oh! how I hate to get up in the morn-
    ing,
Oh! how I'd love to remain in bed;
    For the hardest blow of all
    Is to hear the bugle call,
"You've got to get up, you've got to
    get up,
You've got to get up this morning."
Some day I'm going to murder the
    bugler
    Some day they're going to find him
    dead.
    I'll amputate his reveille
    And step upon it heavily

And spend the rest of my life in bed.

> From the composition "Oh! How I Hate to Get Up in the Morning," copyright, 1918, Irving Berlin. Copyright Renewed.

SAM M. LEWIS and JOE YOUNG
·

How You Gonna Keep 'Em Down on the Farm After They've Seen Paree?

> Title and refrain, 1919

ANONYMOUS
·

The infantry, the infantry, with dirt behind the ears,
The infantry, the infantry, can drink their weight in beers;
The cavalry, the artillery and the God-damned engineers
Can never beat the infantry in a hundred thousand years.

·

Oh Mademoiselle from Armenteers
    Parleyvoo,
Oh Mademoiselle from Armenteers
    Parleyvoo,
Mademoiselle from Armenteers
Hasn't been kissed for forty years
    Hinkydinky parleyvoo.

> "Mademoiselle from Armenteers"

Every day we sign the pay-roll,
Every day we sign the pay-roll,
Every day we sign the pay-roll,
    But we never get a
        God-damned cent.

> "Every Day We Sign the Payroll," to the tune of "John Brown's Body"

You're in the army now,

You're not behind the plow;
You'll never get rich,
You son-of-a-bitch;
You're in the army now.

> "You're in the Army Now"

Uncle Sammy, he's got the infantry,
He's got the cavalry, he's got artillery,
And so, by gosh, we'll go to Germany,
Good-bye, Kaiser Bill.

> "Good-bye, Kaiser Bill"

LORENZ HART
·

Bulldogs run around New Haven,
    Harvard paints old Cambridge red;
Even poor old Philadelphia
    Really has a college, it is said.
Williamstown belongs to Williams,
    Princeton's Tiger stands at bay;
But old New York won't let the world
        forget
    That there's a college on Broadway!

> *Fly with Me*, "There's a College on Broadway," 1920

MAJOR EDMUND L. GRUBER
·

Then it's hi! hi! hee! in the field artillery,
Sound off your numbers loud and strong
Where e'er you go you will always know
That those caissons are rolling along.

> "The Caisson Song," 1921

GEORGE GERSHWIN
·

Rhapsody in Blue.

> Title of symphonic composition, 1923

JOHNNY BOYLE

•

Oh, give me a home
Where the millionaires roam,
And the dear little glamor girls play—
Where seldom is heard
An intelligent word,
And we round up the dollars all day.

> The Palm Beach theme song,
> c. 1925

JOSEPH McCARTHY

•

You made me love you,
I didn't want to do it.

> "You Made Me Love You," c.
> 1925

IRA GERSHWIN

•

A Babbitt met a Bromide on the avenue one day.
They held a conversation in their own
peculiar way.
They both were solid citizens—they
both had been around,
And as they spoke you clearly saw
their feet were on the ground:

.   .   .   .

Heigh ho! That's life!
What's new? Howza wife?
Gotta run! Oh, my!
Olive oil! Good bye!

> "Babbitt and Bromide." Copy-
> right, 1927, by New World
> Music Corporation. Reprinted
> by Permission.

It Ain't Necessarily So.

> *Porgy and Bess,* Title of song,
> 1935

I Got Plenty o' Nuttin'.

> *Ibid.,* title and refrain

GEORGE S. KAUFMAN, MORRIE RYSKIND and IRA GERSHWIN

•

She's the illegitimate daughter
Of an illegitimate son
Of an illegitimate nephew
Of Napoleon.

> *Of Thee I Sing,* 1931

E. Y. HARBURG

•

Brother, Can You Spare a Dime?

> Title and refrain, c. 1932

JACK YELLEN

•

Happy days are here again,
The skies above are clear again:
Let us sing a song of cheer again,
Happy days are here again!

> "Happy Days Are Here Again."
> Used as campaign song for
> Roosevelt, 1932

ANN RONELL

•

Who's Afraid of the Big, Bad Wolf?

> Title of song used in Disney's
> *Three Little Pigs,* 1933

JEROME KERN

•

Smoke Gets in Your Eyes.

> Title and refrain

IRVING BERLIN

•

There's No Business Like Show Business.

> From the composition "There's
> No Business Like Show Busi-
> ness." Copyright, 1946, Irving
> Berlin.

God bless America,
  Land that I love,
Stand beside her and guide her
  Through the night with a light from
    above;
From the mountains, to the prairies,
  To the oceans white with foam,
God bless America,
  My home sweet home!

I'm dreaming of a White Christmas,
Just like the ones I used to know.

Oscar Hammerstein II
                 •

Ol' Man River,
Dat Ol' Man River,
He mus' know sumpin'
But don' say nothin',
He jes' keep rollin',
He keeps on rollin' along.
He don' plant taters,
He don' plant cotton,
An' dem dat plants 'em
Is soon forgotten,
But Ol' Man River,
He jes' keeps rollin' along.
You an' me, we sweat an' strain,
Body all achin' and racked wid pain—
Tote dat barge!
Lif' dat bale!
Git a little drunk,
An' you land in jail. . . .
Ah git weary
An' sick of tryin';
Ah'm tired of livin'
An' skeered of dyin',

But Ol' Man River,
He jes' keep rollin' along.

The last time I saw Paris, her heart
  was young and gay,
I heard the laughter of her heart in
  every street café.

Oh, what a beautiful mornin'!
Oh, what a beautiful day!
I got a beautiful feelin'
Ev'rythin's goin' my way.

Ev'rythin's up to date in Kansas City.
They've gone about as fur as they c'n
  go.

There is nothin' like a dame—
Nothin' in the world!
There is nothin' you can name
That is anythin' like a dame.

I'm as corny as Kansas in August,
High as a flag on the Fourth of July!
If you'll excuse
An expression I use . . .
I'm in love with a wonderful guy!

ers and Oscar Hammerstein
2nd. Williamson Music, Inc.,
New York, N.Y., owner of publication and allied rights.

COLE PORTER
•

Night and day, you are the one,
Only you beneath the moon and un-
 der the sun—
Whether near to me or far
(It's no matter, darling, where you
 are)
 I think of you, night and day!

> "Night and Day." Copyright,
> 1932, by Harms, Inc. Reprinted
> by Permission.

It was great fun,
But it was just one
Of those things.

> "Just One of Those Things."
> Copyright, 1930, by Harms,
> Inc. Reprinted by Permission.

I get no kick from champagne.

Mere alcohol
Doesn't thrill me at all,
So tell me why should it be true
That I get a kick out of you?

> "I Get a Kick Out of You."
> Copyright, 1934, by Harms,
> Inc. Reprinted by Permission.

ABE BURROWS
•

The Girl with the Three Blue Eyes
 (What Makes Her Different?)
> Title and refrain

ANONYMOUS
•

We're the battling bastards of Bataan;
No mama, no papa, no Uncle Sam;
No aunts, no uncles, no cousins, no
 nieces;
No pills, no planes, no artillery pieces.
. . . And nobody gives a damn.

> Song sung during siege of Ba-
> taan, 1942

BOOK THREE

VARIOUS AMERICANS
ON THINGS IN GENERAL

* INTRODUCTION *

In a thousand years the United States as a political and social entity may have changed so much that many, perhaps most, of the words collected in Book One will puzzle our descendants, and seem as curious to them as the sentences of Magna Charta do to us. Even the Gettysburg Address may (one hopes not) require interpretation. What men say about their time and their country, however profound, runs the risk of becoming outmoded.

But what men say and feel about the world and mankind in general, if it be well and truly said and felt, may last longer. Einstein's statement, $E = mc^2$, will be just as interesting five millennia from now. So will Josiah Royce's remark: "Thinking is like loving and dying. Each of us must do it for himself." So will Emerson's "Every man is an impossibility until he is born." And so probably will Will Rogers' observation: "The girls are so beautiful. It's sad to think that twenty years from now, they'll all be five years older." Of course not all of Book Three attains this level of life expectancy.

We have attempted here to catch Americans in the act of thinking about things in general, rather than about their country or their fellow countrymen. We have tried to build up, piece by piece, a mosaic of the American mind, drawing our materials from the accumulation of two and a half centuries and from the words of theologians, public figures, businessmen, philosophers, historians, social scientists, educators, jurists, journalists, publicists, naturalists, explorers, travelers, scientists, inventors, doctors, psychologists, actors, musicians, painters, sculptors, architects, industrial designers, poets, playwrights, essayists, critics, novelists, and humorists.

The editors have a relaxed notion of the American mind. They do not believe professional thinkers to be the only ones that secrete valuable thoughts. There are few deeper sentences in this entire book than a casual remark made by the banker James A. Stillman when in 1913 he viewed the Armory Show of modern painting: "Something is wrong with the world. These men know." Therefore, while you will find in this section pages and pages of the profundities and brilliancies of Jefferson, Emerson, Thoreau, Santayana, William James, Justice Holmes, Henry Adams and other elevated minds, you will also come upon thousands of memorable words by less towering intellects, including Sam Goldwyn, Emily Post, Death Valley Scotty, W. C. Fields, Liberace, Helen Hokinson, Fred Allen and Groucho Marx. *The American Treasury* recognizes no intellectual class distinctions.

A great many of the names represented in Book Three are also to be found in Book One (We Look at Ourselves and Our Country). When Jonathan Edwards seems to be talking in his character of apologist for New England Calvinism, we drop him into Book One. When he seems to be talking out of his own uncommitted heart, we put him in Book Three. Sometimes the lines blur; we have used our best judgment.

As the reader leafs through Book Three, he may wish to note a few interesting saliencies. Starting from the beginning he will remark that we are not a race of theologians, or rather that our theological writing has not filtered down to the popular consciousness. We began with Jonathan Edwards and in a sense finished with him. Merely as a theological *writer* he has never been surpassed on this continent.

The more important statements of our Public Figures will be found scattered through Book One; but the section here devoted to them has its own odd interest. It is difficult to resist the conclusion that, merely as *minds,* our earlier Presidents have it all over our more recent ones. When you come to the utterances of Men of Business, note how trenchant they are: the bigger the man, the less he seems to use Madison Avenue gobble-degook. The section on Philosophers is notable particularly for the fresh, undated utterances of William James, so free of academic jargon, and for those of Santayana, the greatest master of the single sentence (after Thoreau) in our literature.

Among our historians study especially Henry Adams. Remark the chilling accuracy of the forecast contained in his letter to Brooks Adams in 1902, not to mention that of 1862. I like also Carl Becker's wry summary: "All that has happened to man in 506,000 years may be symbolized by this fact—he can, with ease and expedition, put his ancestors in cages."

Next come the Social Scientists. We take a mild satisfaction in retrieving from his little-read books some of the more pregnant remarks of William Graham Sumner, who invented the phrase "The Forgotten Man." There's a great deal of Mencken, too, in part because he represents a mocking, pessimistic slant which is not usually numbered (though it should be) among the qualities that make up the national character.

Educators and jurists are not generally thought of as vivid writers, and so it is gratifying to note how many of those we have collected express themselves with freshness and vigor—in the case of Holmes with mastery.

The division entitled Journalists and Publicists offers a mere sampling; it would have required at least another year of research to do the job satisfactorily—and then the necessary space would not have been available.

This is true of other sections, too, particularly XII (Men of Art) and XV (Critical Spirits). Here, all we could do was to indicate the variety of the minds engaged in these pursuits and to rescue from possible oblivion some of the best things that have come out of those minds. We felt it better to record a little of a lot of Americans rather than a great deal of just a few.

Section XIV, Essayists and Aphorists, is naturally one of the longest and most rewarding in this Book. We do not apologize for the many pages given over to Emerson and Thoreau: the best remains the best, even though in Emerson's case what we get on occasion is the clear phrasing of cloudy ideas. He, like Thoreau, never understood the paragraph; but how lightning-like are their sentences! To read Thoreau is in a sense not to read at all. He is not really writing "prose"; his books seem rather to be the by-product, almost the waste product, of living.

A large section is devoted to Tellers of Tales. The collection of snippets from novels and short stories may seem to some a dubious practice. We do not defend it as a substitute for reading the books. We do think, however, that there is a certain interest attaching to this airplane view of American fiction. It provides, for example, a quick way of measuring the astounding change in viewpoint between Washington Irving and James Jones. The two men are separated by far more than 150 years; in a way they are not even using the same language. The gulf is more marked in our fiction than it is in that of England or France, or even that of Russia, despite its revolution.

This anthology is particularly fortunate in that so many of our best novels contain passages, meditative or purple, that can without excessive violence be extracted from their context. This is notably true of Melville. I see nothing wrong in a familiarity with his more unforgettable short statements or descriptions, even if the reader goes no further. A good deal of Melville can be understood without a reading of his every word. The same is true of most of our major novelists—Hawthorne, Mark Twain, even—though this is less certain—Henry James.

We should, by the way, have wanted to include many representative passages from one of our finest storytellers, Willa Cather, but her posthumous wishes make it impossible to obtain permission to quote. I am sure her ghost will not haunt me, however, if I recall for the reader the one sentence (it is from *Shadows on the Rock*) that discloses the core of her delicate art: "There are all those early memories; one cannot get another set; one has only those."

The final section of Book Three and of *The American Treasury* is given over exclusively to laughter. Here we have one giant—Mark Twain —but his attendants are far from being pygmies. Even the old boys, such as Josh Billings and Artemus Ward and Bill Nye, are still funny if taken in small doses. (The editors have measured the doses carefully.) We are as a nation notably rich in pungent paragraphers, single-line men, such as Ed Howe, Kin Hubbard and Will Rogers, whose humor works close to the people and still retains the atmosphere of the cracker-barrel and the hot stove. When we come to our own time the tone seems to change, becoming engagingly zany with Robert Benchley and Frank Sullivan, and philosophical with James Thurber.

In general, humor fades quickly. We think everything in this section is still funny, but are prepared for vigorous demurrers.

C. F.

I. Men of God

John Wise

The Prime Immunity in Man's State, is that he is most properly the Subject of the Law of Nature. . . . The Second Great Immunity of Man is an Original Liberty Instampt upon his Rational Nature. He that intrudes upon this Liberty, Violates the Law of Nature. . . . The Third Capital Immunity belonging to Man's Nature, is an equality amongst Men.

1717

Jonathan Edwards

They say there is a young lady [in New Haven] who is beloved of that Great Being, who made and rules the world, and that there are certain seasons in which this Great Being, in some way or other invisible, comes to her and fills her mind with exceeding sweet delight, and that she hardly cares for anything, except to meditate on him—that she expects after a while to be received up where he is, to be raised up out of the world and caught up into heaven; being assured that he loves her too well to let her remain at a distance from him always. There she is to dwell with him, and to be ravished with his love and delight forever. Therefore, if you present all the world before her, with the richest of its treasures, she disregards it and cares for it not, and is unmindful of any pain or affliction. She has a strange sweetness in her mind, and singular purity in all her conduct; and you could not persuade her to do any thing wrong or sinful, if you would give her all the world, lest she should offend this Great Being. She is of a wonderful sweetness, calmness and universal benevolence of mind; especially after this Great God has manifested himself to her mind. She will sometimes go about from place to place, singing sweetly; and seems to be always full of joy and pleasure; and no one knows for what. She loves to be alone, walking in the fields and groves, and seems to have some one invisible always conversing with her.

> *A Personal Narrative*, 1739. The "young lady" referred to, incidentally, was Sarah Peabody, who was about thirteen at the time, and whom Edwards later married. God works in mysterious ways.

William Ellery Channing

A pure mind is free of the universe. It belongs to the church, the family of the pure, in all worlds. Virtue is no local thing. It is not honorable because born in this community or that, but for its independent, everlasting beauty. This is the bond of the universal church. No man can be excommunicated from it but by himself, by the death of goodness in his own breast.

The Church

I call that mind free which is jealous of its own freedom, which guards itself from being merged in others, which guards its empire over itself as nobler than the empire of the world.

The Free Mind

It is a greater work to educate a child, in the true and larger sense of the word, than to rule a state.

Sooner can the laws of the outward universe be repealed by human will, sooner can the sun be plucked from his sphere, than the idea of God can be erased from the human spirit, and His worship banished from the earth. All other wants of man are superficial. His animal wants are but for a day, and are to cease with the body. The profoundest of all human wants is the want of God.

If my barque sinks, 'tis to another sea.

ORESTES BROWNSON

There is no such thing as reforming the mass without reforming the individuals who compose it.

HENRY WARD BEECHER

No subtle manager or broker ever saw through a maze of financial embarrassments half so quick as a poor bookbuyer sees his way clear to pay for what he *must* have.

Star Papers, "Subtleties of Bookbuyers," 1855

If a man cannot be a Christian in the place where he is, he cannot be a Christian anywhere.

Life Thoughts

Doctrine is nothing but the skin of truth set up and stuffed.

Ibid.

In the ordinary business of life, industry can do anything which genius can do, and very many things which it cannot.

Proverbs from Plymouth Pulpit

The way the Spirit of God works with me makes it necessary that I should have something that I can clasp, and to me the Father is vague. I believe in a Father, but the definition of Him in my vision, is not to me what the portraiture of Christ is. . . . I cannot pray to the Father except through Christ. I pray to Christ. I must.

Never forget what a man says to you when he is angry.

MARY BAKER EDDY

I would no more quarrel with a man because of his religion than I would because of his art.

Miscellany

ROBERT G. INGERSOLL

An honest God is the noblest work of man.

The Gods, 1872

I would rather have been a French peasant and worn wooden shoes. I would rather have lived in a hut with a vine growing over the door and the grapes growing purple in the kisses of the Autumn sun. I would rather have been that poor peasant with my loving wife by my side, knitting as the day died out of the sky, with my children on my knee and their arms about me. I would rather have been that man and gone down to the tongueless silence of the dreamless dust than to have been that imperial impersonation of force and murder known as Napoleon the Great.

At the Tomb of Napoleon

If I owe Smith ten dollars, and God forgives me, that doesn't pay Smith.

Our hope of immortality does not come from any religions, but nearly all religions come from that hope.

PHILLIPS BROOKS

O, do not pray for easy lives. Pray to be stronger men. Do not pray for
tasks equal to your powers. Pray for powers equal to your tasks.

Going Up to Jerusalem

DWIGHT L. MOODY

Character is what you are in the dark.

Sermons

SHAILER MATHEWS

An epigram is a half-truth so stated as to irritate the person who believes
the other half.

WILLIAM A. ("BILLY") SUNDAY

Try praising your wife, even if it does frighten her at first.

MORDECAI FOWLER HAM

I like to tell people that just an outward appearance of being a Christian
isn't enough. You can't just quit drinking and think you're saved. You'll
just go to hell sober, that's all.

1954

HARRY EMERSON FOSDICK

Nothing in human life, least of all in religion, is ever right until it is
beautiful.

As I See Religion, 1932

God is not a cosmic bell-boy for whom we can press a button to get
things done.

Prayer

Hating people is like burning down your own home to get rid of a rat.

The Wages of Hate

The Sea of Galilee and the Dead Sea are made of the same water. It flows down, clear and cool, from the heights of Hermon and the roots of the cedars of Lebanon. The Sea of Galilee makes beauty of it, for the Sea of Galilee has an outlet. It gets to give. It gathers in its riches that it may pour them out again to fertilize the Jordan plain. But the Dead Sea with the same water makes horror. For the Dead Sea has no outlet. It gets to keep.

The Meaning of Service

When a man says he can get on without religion it merely means he has a kind of religion he can get on without.

Is it scientific? That question . . . has so cowed and scared religion that many modern-minded believers . . . instinctively throw up their hands at the mere whisper of it. . . . When a prominent scientist comes out strongly for religion, all the churches thank Heaven and take courage as though it were the highest possible compliment to God to have Eddington believe in Him.

JOHN HAYNES HOLMES

Priests are no more necessary to religion than politicians to patriotism.

Sensible Man's View of Religion

CHARLES FRANCIS POTTER

The bird of war is not the eagle but the stork.

Speech at Senate hearing on birth control, 1931

FULTON J. SHEEN

Science is a very valid and necessary way of knowing, but only of knowing those things which are subject to experimentation and to the methods of a laboratory. The great values of life such as justice, truth, and charity are beyond such an experimentation. No one yet has ever been able to put a mother's love into a test tube, and yet who will deny its reality? Nor can we throw a man into a caldron to boil to see if he gives forth the unmistakable green fumes of envy and jealousy.

Philosophies at War, 1943

Sooner or late philosophy must return to its Father's house, which is

Wisdom and Truth, and realize that as all fires mount toward the sun,
and all waters flow into the sea, so too all men must return to God, for
whom they were made and in whom they find their rest, their peace, their
perfection: their *rest,* for "Our hearts rest in Thee, O Lord"; their *peace,*
for peace is the tranquillity of order, and order is never tranquil unless
man loves God; their *perfection:* for in Him is found the plenitude of the
human heart's quest for Being, Truth and Love. A godless universe cannot exist for it cannot bear the sorrow of not knowing its Cause and its
Author; nor can a Godless humanity exist for it cannot bear the burden
of its own heart.

Joshua Loth Liebman

I have come to see over the span of years that the wider world just cannot
be dismissed and that man considered independent of his cosmic setting
can lead only to provincial pride or defiant despair. Man is not alone and
neither his mind nor his conscience nor his creative powers can be truly
understood if they are regarded as orphans without some universal Parent.
I have come to feel that the whole human story, with all its tragedy and
its triumph, is like a page torn from the middle of a book, without beginning or end—an undecipherable page, when cut out of its context. . . .
The context of man is the Power greater than man. The human adventure is part of a universal sonnet—one line in a deathless poem.

How Can I Believe in God Now? 1943

Thomas Merton

Despair is the absolute extreme of self-love. It is reached when a man
deliberately turns his back on all help from anyone else in order to taste
the rotten luxury of knowing himself to be lost.

Seeds of Contemplation, 1949

A humble man can do great things with an uncommon perfection because
he is no longer concerned about accidentals, like his own interests and
his own reputation, and therefore he no longer needs to waste his efforts
in defending them.

Ibid.

As soon as you begin to take yourself seriously and imagine that your virtues are important because they are yours, you become the prisoner of
your own vanity and even your best works will blind and deceive you.

Then, in order to defend yourself, you will begin to see sins and faults everywhere in the actions of other men. And the more unreasonable importance you attach to yourself and your own works, the more you will tend to build up your own idea of yourself by condemning other people. Some of the most virtuous men in the world are also the bitterest and most unhappy, because they have unconsciously come to believe that all their happiness depends on their being more virtuous than other men.

Ibid.

II. Public Figures

PRESIDENTS

•

John Adams

I would not give sixpence for a picture of Raphael or a statue of Phidias.

Thomas Jefferson

A lively and lasting sense of filial duty is more effectively impressed on the mind of a son or daughter by reading *King Lear,* than by all the dry volumes of ethics, and divinity, that ever were written.

Letter to Robert Skipworth, 1771

Ignorance is preferable to error; and he is less remote from the truth who believes nothing, than he who believes what is wrong.

Notes on the State of Virginia, 1781–82

I have never been able to conceive how any rational being could propose happiness to himself from the exercise of power over others.

Letter, 1811

I find the pain of a little censure, even when it is unfounded, is more acute than the pleasure of much praise.

Writings, VII

The greatest service which can be rendered any country is to add an useful plant to its culture.

It is the old practice of despots to use a part of the people to keep the rest in order.

John Quincy Adams

[The metric] system approaches to the ideal perfection of *uniformity* applied to weights and measures; and, whether destined to succeed, or doomed to fail, will shed unfading glory upon the age in which it was conceived, and upon the nation by which its execution was attempted, and has been in part achieved. In the progress of its establishment [in France], it has been often brought in conflict with the laws of physical and of moral nature; with the impenetrability of matter, and with the habits, passions, prejudices, and necessities of man. It has undergone various important modifications. It must undoubtedly still submit to others, before it can look for universal adoption. But if man upon earth be an improvable being; if that universal peace which was the object of a Saviour's mission, which is the desire of the philosopher, the longing of the philanthropist, the trembling hope of the Christian, is a blessing to which the futurity of mortal man has a claim of more than mortal promise; if the Spirit of Evil is, before the final consummation of things, to be cast down from his dominion over men, and bound in the chains of a thousand years, the foretaste here of man's eternal felicity; then this system of common instruments, to accomplish all the changes of social and friendly commerce, will furnish the links of sympathy between the inhabitants of the most distant regions; the metre will surround the globe in use as well as in multiplied extension; and one language of weights and measures will be spoken from the equator to the poles.

Report upon Weights and Measures, February, 1821

You will find hundreds of persons able to produce a crowd of ideas upon any subject for one who can marshal them to the best advantage.

My whole life has been a succession of disappointments. I can scarcely recollect an instance of success in anything that I ever undertook.

ANDREW JACKSON

One man with courage makes a majority.

MARTIN VAN BUREN

It is generally understood that the sun does rise in the East, but I am in the habit of sleeping late and of my own knowledge I could not say positively where it rises.

Attributed to

MILLARD FILLMORE

Let us remember that revolutions do not always establish freedom.

Address, 1853

ABRAHAM LINCOLN

Few can be induced to labor exclusively for posterity; and none will do it enthusiastically. Posterity has done nothing for us; and, theorize on it as we may, practically we should do very little for it, unless we are made to think we are at the same time doing something for ourselves.

> Address, Springfield, February 22, 1842

If any personal description of me is thought desirable, it may be said I am, in height, six feet four inches, nearly; lean in flesh, weighing on an average one hundred and eighty pounds; dark complexion, with coarse black hair and gray eyes. No other marks or brands recollected.

> "Autobiography" written in 1859

Why, Scripps, it is a great folly to attempt to make anything out of my early life. It can all be condensed into a single sentence you will find in Gray's Elegy—"The short and simple annals of the poor."

> To campaign biographer, 1860

Let us be diverted by none of these sophistical contrivances wherewith we are so industriously plied and belabored—contrivances such as groping for some middle ground between the right and the wrong; vain as the search for a man who should be neither a living man nor a dead man.

> Speech at New Haven, March 6, 1860

This man wants to work, so uncommon a want that I think it ought to be gratified.

> Memorandum, January 23, 1862

The Lord prefers common-looking people. That is the reason he makes so many of them.

> In his account of a dream, quoted by Hay, *Diary*, December 24, 1863

Yours of the 10th instant received. I am well acquainted with Mr. Blank and know his circumstances. First of all, he has a wife and baby. Together, they ought to be worth $50,000 to any man. Secondly, he has an office in which there is a table worth $1.50, and three chairs worth, say,

$1. Last of all, there is in one corner a large rat-hole which will bear looking into.

> Letter to a firm which had asked a credit reference. The letter has never been found among Lincoln's papers, and is probably a forgery.

Yes, we can doubtless gain your case for you; we can set a whole neighborhood at loggerheads; we can distress a widowed mother and her six fatherless children, and thereby get for you six hundred dollars to which you seem to have a legal claim, but which rightfully belongs, it appears to me, as much to the woman and her children as it does to you. You must remember, however, that some things legally right are not morally right. We shall not take your case, but we will give you a little advice for which we will charge you nothing. You seem to be a sprightly, energetic man. We would advise you to try your hand at making six hundred dollars in some other way.

> Advice to a client, reported by Herndon

Every man over forty is responsible for his face.

> To a cabinet member when the President was taken to account for turning down a job applicant because "I don't like his face"

A farce or a comedy is best played: a tragedy is best read at home.

> To John Hay, on seeing Edwin Booth in *The Merchant of Venice*

My father taught me to work; he did not teach me to love it.

No man has a good enough memory to be a successful liar.

Character is like a tree, and reputation like its shadow. The shadow is what we think of it; the tree is the real thing.

He reminds me of the man who murdered both his parents, and then, when sentence was about to be passed, pleaded for mercy on the grounds that he was an orphan.

I don't know who my grandfather was; I am much more concerned to know what his grandson will be.

> Quoted by Gross, *Lincoln's Own Stories*

My friend, you are half right.

> At a reception when a guest told him that "in my State they say that the welfare of the nation depends on God and Abraham Lincoln"

I laugh because I must not cry.

ULYSSES S. GRANT

I know only two tunes; one of them is "Yankee Doodle" and the other isn't.

THEODORE ROOSEVELT

It is not the critic who counts, not the man who points out how the strong man stumbled, or where the doer of deeds could have done them better. The credit belongs to the man who is actually in the arena; whose face is marred by dust and sweat and blood; who strives valiantly; who errs and comes short again and again; who knows the great enthusiasms, the great devotions, and spends himself in a worthy cause; who at the best knows in the end the triumph of high achievement; and who at the worst, if he fails, at least fails while daring greatly; so that his place shall never be with those cold and timid souls who know neither victory nor defeat.

Don't hit at all if it is honorably possible to avoid hitting; but *never* hit soft.

WOODROW WILSON

Benevolence or Justice? I don't care how benevolent the master is going to be, I will not live under a master.

The New Freedom, 1912

I fancy that it is just as hard to do your duty when men are sneering at you as when they are shooting at you.

Speech, May, 1914

I would never read a book if it were possible for me to talk half an hour with the man who wrote it.

CALVIN COOLIDGE

If you don't say anything, you won't be called on to repeat it.

I have never been hurt by anything J didn't say.

He said he was against it.

> On being asked what had been said by a clergyman who preached on sin

HERBERT HOOVER

A good many things go around in the dark besides Santa Claus.

Address, 1935

Well, on this side, certainly.

> To a friend who was riding with the President on a train and pointed out some sheep, saying "Those sheep have been sheared." Attributed also to Coolidge.

FRANKLIN D. ROOSEVELT

The ablest man I ever met is the man you think you are.

HARRY S. TRUMAN

There is nothing new in the world except the history you do not know.

DWIGHT D. EISENHOWER

Commanders are habitually different where they are called upon to deal with subjects that touch the human soul—aspiration, ideals, inner beliefs, affections, hatreds.

Crusade in Europe

OTHERS

•

WILLIAM PENN

He that has more knowledge than judgment, is made for another man's use more than his own.

Some Fruits of Solitude, 1693

Temper—Nothing does reason more right than the coolness of those who offer it. For truth often suffers more by the heat of its defenders than from the arguments of its opposers.

Ibid.

Jealousy is a kind of civil war in the soul, where judgment and imagination are at perpetual jars.

Ibid.

Whoever is right, the persecutor must be wrong.

Ibid.

If I am even with my enemy, the debt is paid; but if I forgive it, I oblige him for ever.

Ibid.

Much reading is an oppression of the mind, and extinguishes the natural candle, which is the reason of so many senseless scholars in the world.

Advice to His Children, 1699

They that love beyond the World cannot be separated by it. Death is but Crossing the World, as Friends do the Seas; they live in one another still.

It were better to be of no church, than to be bitter for any.

Men are generally more careful of the breed of their horses and dogs than of their children.

BENJAMIN FRANKLIN

The proud hate pride—in others.

Poor Richard's Almanac

Laws too gentle are seldom obeyed; too severe, seldom executed.

Ibid.

There are three faithful friends: an old wife, an old dog, and ready money.

Ibid.

Avarice and happiness never saw each other, how then should they become acquainted?

Ibid.

If your riches are yours, why don't you take them with you to t'other world?

Ibid.

Having been poor is no shame, but being ashamed of it, is.

Ibid.

Where there's marriage without love, there will be love without marriage.

Ibid.

A ship under sail and a big-bellied woman are the handsomest two things that can be seen common.

Ibid., 1735

All would live long, but none would be old.

Ibid., 1749

Doing an injury puts you below your enemy; revenging one makes you but even with him; forgiving it sets you above him.

Ibid.

Dost thou love life? Then do not squander time, for that is the stuff life is made of.

Ibid., 1757

Work as if you were to live 100 years. Pray as if you were to die To-morrow.

Ibid.

Experience keeps a dear school, yet fools will learn in no other.

Ibid.

It is hard for an empty sack to stand upright.

Ibid.

Three removes are as bad as a fire.

Ibid.

Never leave that till to-morrow which you can do to-day.

Ibid.

A single man has not nearly the value he would have in a state of union. He is an incomplete animal. He resembles the odd half of a pair of scissors.

Advice to a Young Man on the Choice of a Mistress, 1745

And lastly, they are so grateful!

Ibid., reasons for preferring an old to a young wife

If men are so wicked as we now see them with religion, what would they be if without it?

Letter, c. 1786

Our Constitution is in actual operation; everything appears to promise that it will last; but in this world nothing is certain but death and taxes.

Letter to M. Leroy, 1789

Persons of good sense, I have since observed, seldom fall into disputation, except lawyers, university men, and men of all sorts that have been bred at Edinborough.

Autobiography, 1818, 1867

The eyes of other people are the eyes that ruin us. If all but myself were blind, I should want neither fine clothes, fine houses, nor fine furniture.

Letter to Benjamin Vaughan

Your situation grieves me and I send you herewith a banknote for ten louis d'ors. I do not pretend to give such a sum; I only lend it to you. When you shall return to your country, you cannot fail of getting into some business that will in time enable you to pay all your debts. In that case, when you meet with another honest man in similar distress, you must pay by lending this sum to him, enjoining him to discharge the debt by a like operation when he shall be able and shall meet with another such opportunity. I hope it may thus go through many hands before it meets with a knave that will stop its progress. This is a trick of mine for doing a great deal of good with a little money. I am not rich enough to afford much in good works, and so am obliged to be cunning and make the most of a little. With best wishes for your future prosperity, I am, dear sir, your most obedient servant . . .

Letter to Benjamin Webb

Madame, I am waiting till the nights are longer.

To Madame Helvetius, who chided him for putting off a visit she expected

If the rascals knew the advantages of virtue they would become honest men out of rascality.

In conversation

If you would not be forgotten as soon as you are dead, either write things worth reading or do things worth writing.

If a man empties his purse into his head, no one can take it from him.

The most exquisite folly is made of wisdom spun too fine.

If a man could have half his wishes he would double his troubles.

There is much difference between imitating a good man, and counterfeiting him.

She laughs at everything you say. Why? Because she has fine teeth.

It is ill-manners to silence a fool, and cruelty to let him go on.

John Randolph

I am an aristocrat. I love liberty; I hate equality.

Aaron Burr

The rule of my life is to make business a pleasure, and pleasure my business.

Letter to Pichon

Alexander Hamilton

Real firmness is good for anything; strut is good for nothing.

Daniel Webster

Whatever makes men good Christians, makes them good citizens.

Speech at Plymouth, 1820

There is no refuge from confession but suicide; and suicide is confession.

Argument, 1830

One may live as a conqueror, a king or a magistrate; but he must die as a man.

William H. Seward

I know, and all the world knows, that revolutions never go backward.

Speech, 1858

Wendell Phillips

One, on God's side, is a majority.

John Hay

Love your neighbor but be careful of your neighborhood.

Thomas B. Reed

One, with God, is always a majority, but many a martyr has been burned at the stake while the votes were being counted.

Speech in the House, 1885

The only justification of rebellion is success.

Speech, 1878

JOHN L. SULLIVAN

A big man is a big man whether he's a president or a prizefighter.

Greeting to Theodore Roosevelt in the White House

WILLIAM JENNINGS BRYAN

Diplomacy is the art of keeping cool.

TIMOTHY ("BIG TIM") SULLIVAN

God and the People hate a chesty man.

DWIGHT MORROW

As I get older . . . I become more convinced that good government is not a substitute for self-government.

CYRUS CHING

I learned long ago never to wrestle with a pig. You get dirty, and besides the pig likes it.

HELEN KELLER

I who am blind can give one hint to those who see—one admonition to those who would make full use of the gift of sight: Use your eyes as if tomorrow you would be stricken blind. And the same method can be applied to the other senses. Hear the music of voices, the song of a bird, the mighty strains of an orchestra, as if you would be stricken deaf tomorrow. Touch each object you want to touch as if tomorrow your tactile sense would fail. Smell the perfume of flowers, taste with relish each morsel, as if tomorrow you could never smell and taste again. Make the most of every sense; glory in all the facets of pleasure and beauty which the world reveals to you through the several means of contact which Nature provides. But of all the senses, sight must be the most delightful.

Three Days to See

Were my Maker to grant me but one single glance through these sightless eyes of mine . . . I would without question or recall choose to see first a child, then a dog.

Ibid.

Douglas MacArthur

When I joined the army, even before the turn of the century, it was the fulfillment of all my boyhood hopes and dreams. . . . I still remember the refrain of one of the most popular barracks ballads of that day, which proclaimed most proudly that old soldiers never die; they just fade away. I now close my military career and just fade away.

Address before a joint meeting of Congress, April 19, 1951

James J. Walker

There are three things a man must do alone. Be born, die, and testify.

Most of the time.

His reply when asked if he was an actor

Hugh S. Johnson

There was never a war at arms that was not merely the extension of a preceding war of commerce grown fiercer until the weapons of commerce seemed no longer sufficiently deadly.

Radio broadcast for "World Peaceways," 1935

Joseph Warren Stilwell

Illegitimati Noli Carborundum. (Don't Let the Bastards Grind You Down.)

His motto

Eleanor Roosevelt

Up to a certain point it is good for us to know that there are people in the world who will give us love and unquestioned loyalty to the limit of their ability. I doubt, however, if it is good for us to feel assured of this without the accompanying obligation of having to justify this devotion by our behavior.

This Is My Story, 1937

No one can make you feel inferior without your consent.

The reason that fiction is more interesting than any other form of literature to those of us who really like to study people, is that in fiction the author can really tell the truth without hurting anyone and without humiliating himself too much.

Chester William Nimitz

A ship is always referred to as "she" because it costs so much to keep one in powder and paint.

Talk before the Society of Sponsors of the Navy, Feb., 1940

Fred M. Vinson

Wars are not "acts of God." They are caused by man, by man-made institutions, by the way in which man has organized his society. What man has made, man can change.

Wendell L. Willkie

I would rather lose in a cause that I know some day will triumph than to triumph in a cause that I know some day will fail.

III. Men of Business

JIM FISK

I worship in the Synagogue of the Libertines!

ANDREW CARNEGIE

No idol is more debasing than the worship of money.

At age thirty-five

J. P. MORGAN

Well, I don't know as I want a lawyer to tell me what I cannot do. I hire him to tell me how to do what I want to do.

To his associate, Judge Gary

A man always has two reasons for doing anything—a good reason and the real reason.

JAMES J. HILL

If you want to know whether you are destined to be a success or a failure in life, you can easily find out. The test is simple and is infallible. Are you able to save money? If not, drop out. You will lose.

JOHN D. ROCKEFELLER

Charles, I heard that you had been buying a cord of wood, and I went down to the cellar to look at it. *That* isn't a cord of wood. When I was a young fellow I used to cut a cord of wood, and I know what it looks like. I don't need a tape-measure to measure it with. They are cheating you.

To his son-in-law

JAMES A. STILLMAN

Something is wrong with the world. These men know.

Viewing the Armory Show of modern painting, N.Y., 1913

CHARLES M. SCHWAB

Personality is to man what perfume is to a flower.

Ten Commandments of Success

HENRY FORD

Records of old wars mean nothing to me. History is more or less bunk. It's tradition.

Newspaper interview, May, 1916

An idealist is a person who helps other people to be prosperous.

On the witness stand, 1919

Money is like an arm or a leg—use it or lose it.

Interview, *New York Times*, November 8, 1931

[Books] muss up my mind.

There is no place in civilization for the idler. None of us has any right to ease.

When a man dies, it means that a part has worn out.

You can't build up a reputation on what you are going to do.

Never give anything without strings attached.

Attributed to Ford by Harry Bennett, *We Never Called Him Henry*, 1951

OTTO H. KAHN

Those who love art and are truly susceptible to its spell, do die young in the sense that they remain young to their dying day.

A kike is a Jewish gentleman who has just left the room.

BERNARD BARUCH

We must get away from employment policies based on cold arithmetical averages and take advantage of the skills and judgment of older people. How hideous a mockery it would be if, as a result of advances in medicine, surgery, hygiene and higher living standards, older people were kept willing and able to work—but society deprived them of something useful to do.

Interview, New York *World-Telegram,* 1949

SAM GOLDWYN

Anyone who goes to a psychiatrist ought to have his head examined.

Attributed to

I'll give you a definite maybe.

Ibid.

Include me out.

Ibid.

In two words: im-possible.

Quoted by Alva Johnston, *The Great Goldwyn*

HENRY J. KAISER

When your work speaks for itself, don't interrupt.

HERBERT BAYARD SWOPE

I cannot give you the formula for success, but I can give you the formula for failure—which is: Try to please everybody.

Address, December 20, 1950

BRUCE BARTON

Conceit is God's gift to little men.

Conceit

ERIC JOHNSTON

The things a man believes most profoundly are rarely on the surface of his mind or on the tip of his tongue. Newly acquired notions, formulas learned by rote from books, decisions based on expediency, the fashionable ideas of the moment—these are right on top of the pile, ready to be sampled and displayed in bright after-dinner conversation. But the ideas that make up a man's philosophy of life are somewhere way down below.

America Unlimited

HENRY S. HASKINS

Taking counsel is worthwhile; not for the sake of the counsel, which is not worth a button to you in any case, but for the sake of seeing in your counselor's eye the flame of gladness at being important to somebody.

Meditations in Wall Street

The eyes, ears, nose, taste and touch are the only parts of our equipment that we can't rely on for complete and accurate information.

Ibid.

How gaily a man wakes in the morning to watch himself keep on dying.

Ibid.

The common mind reasons incorrectly from principles known to it, while genius reasons correctly from principles unknown to it.

Ibid.

Good behavior is the last refuge of mediocrity.

Ibid.

Modesty is most effective when its lowered lashes intimate that it has other moments.

Ibid.

On the whole, women pretty well resist the temptation to tempt.

Ibid.

Don't refuse to go on an occasional wild-goose chase; that is what wild geese are made for.

Ibid.

Expressions of concern for others is a dialect; thoughts concerning ourselves are the universal language.

Ibid.

The rare individual who has learned to govern himself is too fed up with the labor of it to want to govern anybody else.

Ibid.

Being a minute too late has led to some bright careers.

Ibid.

A man tries to give equal thanks to two people for equal benefits, but never succeeds; he is bound to resent one's help more than the other's.

Ibid.

It shocks the man with his feet on the ground to see a man with his head in the clouds pay a big income tax.

Ibid.

*IV. The Philosophers
from Charles Sanders Peirce to Mortimer Adler*

The visible world is but man turned inside out that he may be revealed to himself.

CHARLES SANDERS PEIRCE

Consider what effects, that might conceivably have practical bearings, we conceive the object of our conception to have. Then, our conception of these effects is the whole of our conception of the object.

Collected Papers

If a Pragmatist is asked what he means by "God," he can only say that just as long as acquaintance with a man of great character may deeply influence one's whole manner of conduct, so that a glance at his portrait may make a difference, just as almost living with Dr. Johnson enabled poor Boswell to write an immortal book and a really sublime book, just as long as study of the works of Aristotle may make him an acquaintance, so if contemplation and study of the physio-chemical universe can imbue a man with principles of conduct analogous to the influence of a great man's works or conversation, then that analogue of a mind—for it is impossible to say *any* human attribute is *literally* applicable—is what he means by "God."

Ibid.

All thinking is dialogic in form. Your self of one instant appeals to your deeper self for his assent.

Ibid.

Thought in action has for its only possible motive the attainment of Thought at rest.

Ibid.

Though the question of realism and nominalism has its roots in the technicalities of logic, its branches reach about our life. The question whether the *genus homo* has any existence except as individuals, is the question whether there is anything of more dignity, worth, and importance than individual happiness, individual aspirations, and individual life. Whether men really have anything in common, so that the community is to be considered as an end in itself, and if so, what the relative value of the two factors is, is the most fundamental practical question in regard to every public institution the constitution of which we have it in our power to influence.

WILLIAM JAMES

We are not only gregarious animals, liking to be in sight of our fellows, but we have an innate propensity to get ourselves noticed, and noticed favorably, by our kind. No more fiendish punishment could be devised, were such a thing physically possible, than that one should be turned loose in society and remain absolutely unnoticed by all the members thereof.

The Principles of Psychology, 1890

The great source of terror to infancy is solitude.

Ibid.

Could the young but realize how soon they will become mere walking bundles of habits, they would give more heed to their conduct while in the plastic stage. We are spinning our own fates, good or evil, and never to be undone. Every smallest stroke of virtue or of vice leaves its never so little scar. The drunken Rip Van Winkle, in Jefferson's play, excuses himself from every fresh dereliction by saying "It won't count this time!" Well, he may not count it, and a kind Heaven may not count it; but it is being counted none the less. Down among his nerve-cells and fibers the molecules are counting it, registering and storing it up to be used against him when the next temptation comes. Nothing we ever do is, in strict scientific literalness, wiped out. Of course, this has its good side as well as its bad one. As we become permanent drunkards by so many separate drinks, so we become saints in the moral, and authorities and experts in the practical and scientific spheres, by so many separate acts and hours of work. Let no youth have any anxiety about the upshot of his education, whatever the line of it may be. If he keep faithfully busy each hour of the working day, he may safely leave the final result to itself. He can with perfect certainty count on waking up some fine morning, to find himself one of the competent ones of his generation, in whatsoever pursuit he may have singled out. Silently, between all the details of his business, the *power of judging* in all that class of matter will have built itself up within him as a possession that will never pass away. Young people should know this truth in advance. The ignorance of it has probably engendered more discouragement and faint-heartedness in youths embarking on arduous careers than all other causes put together.

Ibid.

Habit is the enormous fly-wheel of society, its most precious conservative agent. It alone is what keeps us all within the bounds of ordinance. It dooms us all to fight out the battle of life upon the lines of our nurture or our early choice, and to make the best of a pursuit that disagrees, because there is no other for which we are fitted, and it is too late to begin again. It is well for the world that in most of us, by the age of thirty, the character has set like plaster, and will never soften again.

The great thing, then, in all education, is to make our nervous system our ally instead of our enemy. It is to fund and capitalize our acquisitions, and live at ease upon the interest of the fund. For this we must make automatic and habitual, as early as possible, as many useful actions as we can, and guard against the growing into ways that are likely to be disadvantageous to us, as one should guard against the plague. The more of the details of our daily life we can hand over to the effortless custody of automatism, the more our higher powers of mind will be set free for their own proper work. There is no more miserable human being than one in whom nothing is habitual but indecision. Full half the time of such a man goes to the deciding, or regretting, of matters which ought to be so ingrained in him as practically not to exist for his consciousness at all.

Ibid.

The hell to be endured hereafter, of which theology tells, is no worse than the hell we make for ourselves in this world by habitually fashioning our characters in the wrong way.

Ibid.

$$\text{Self-esteem} = \frac{\text{Success}}{\text{Pretensions}}$$

Psychology, Briefer Course, 1892

It must always remain an open question whether mystical states may not possibly be superior points of view, windows through which the mind looks out upon a more extensive and inclusive world.

The Will to Believe, 1897

These, then, are my last words to you: Be not afraid of life. Believe that life *is* worth living and your belief will help create the fact. The "scientific" proof that you are right may not be clear before the day of judgment (or some stage of being which that expression may serve to symbolize) is reached. But the faithful fighters of this hour, or the beings that then and there will represent them, may turn to the faint-hearted, who here decline to go on, with words like those with which Henry IV greeted the tardy Crillon after a great battle had been gained: "Hang yourself, brave Crillon! We fought at Arques, and you were not there!"

Ibid.

A man's religious faith (whatever more special items of doctrine it may involve) means for me essentially his faith in the existence of an unseen order of some kind in which the riddles of the natural order may be found explained. The bare assurance that this natural order is not ultimate but a mere sign or vision, the external staging of a many storied universe, in which spiritual forces have the last word and are eternal,—this bare assurance is to such men enough to make life seem worth living in spite of every contrary presumption suggested by circumstances on the natural plane. Destroy this inner assurance, however, vague as it is, and all the light and radiance of existence is extinguished for these persons at a stroke.

I confess that I do not see why the very existence of an invisible world may not in part depend on the personal response which any one of us may make to the religious appeal. God himself, in short, may draw vital strength and increase of very being from our fidelity. For my own part, I do not know what the sweat and blood and tragedy of this life mean, if they mean anything short of this. If this life be not a real fight, in which something is eternally gained for the universe by success, it is no better than a game of private theatricals from which one may withdraw at will. But it feels like a real fight,—as if there were something really wild in the universe which we, with all our idealities and faithfulnesses, are needed to redeem; and first of all to redeem our own hearts from atheisms and fears. For such a half-wild, half-saved universe our nature is adapted. The deepest thing in our nature is this dumb region of the heart in which we dwell alone with our willingnesses and our unwillingnesses, our faiths and fears. As through the cracks and crannies of caverns those waters exude from the earth's bosom which then form the fountainheads of springs, so in these crepuscular depths of personality the sources of all our outer deeds and decisions take their rise. Here is our deepest organ of communication with the nature of things; and compared with these concrete movements of our soul all abstract statements and scientific arguments—the veto, for example, which the strict positivist pronounces upon our faith—sound to us like mere chatterings of the teeth.

Ibid.

In human life, although we only see our world, yet encompassing (it) a still wider world may be there; and to believe in that world may be the most essential function that our lives in this world have to perform. The "scientific" life itself has much to do with maybes, and human life at large has everything to do with them. Not a victory is gained, not a deed of faithfulness or courage is done, except upon a maybe; not a service, not a sally of generosity, not a scientific exploration or experiment or text-book, that may not be a mistake. It is only by risking our persons from one hour to another that we live at all. And often enough our faith beforehand in an uncertified result is the only thing that makes the result come true.

Ibid., "Is Life Worth Living?"

The real world as it is given objectively at this moment is the sum total of all its beings and events now. But can we think of such a sum? Can we realize for an instant what a cross-section of all existence at a definite point of time would be? While I talk and the flies buzz, a sea-gull catches a fish at the mouth of the Amazon, a tree falls in the Adirondack wilderness, a man sneezes in Germany, a horse dies in Tartary, and twins are born in France. What does that mean? Does the contemporaneity of those events with one another, and with a million others as disjointed, form a rational bond between them, and unite them into anything that means for us a world? Yet just such a collateral contemporaneity, and nothing else, is the real order of the world. It is an order with which we have nothing to do but to get away from it as fast as possible. As I said, we break it: we break it into histories, and we break it into arts, and we break it into sciences; and then we begin to feel at home. We make ten thousand separate serial orders of it, and on any one of these we react as though the others did not exist. We discover among its various parts relations that were never given to sense at all (mathematical relations, tangents, squares, and roots and logarithmic functions), and out of an infinite number of these we call certain ones essential and lawgiving, and ignore the rest. Essential these relations are, but only *for our purpose,* the other relations being just as real and present as they; and our purpose is to *conceive simply* and to *foresee*.

                                        Ibid., "Reflex Action and Atheism"

The opposition between the men who have and the men who are is immemorial.

                                        The Varieties of Religious Experience, 1902

Prayer is religion in act; that is, prayer is real religion. It is prayer that distinguishes the religious phenomenon from such similar or neighboring phenomena as purely moral or esthetic sentiment. Religion is nothing if it be not the vital act by which the entire mind seeks to save itself by clinging to the principle from which it draws its life. This act is prayer, by which term I understand no vain exercise of words, no mere repetition of certain sacred formulae, but the very movement itself of the soul, putting itself in a personal relation of contact with the mysterious power— of which it feels the presence—it may be even before it has a name by which to call it. Whenever this interior prayer is lacking, there is no religion; wherever, on the other hand, this rises and stirs the soul, even in the absence of forms and doctrines, we have living religion.

                                        Ibid.

An idea, to be suggestive, must come to the individual with the force of a revelation.

                                        Ibid.

Happiness, like every other emotional state, has blindness and insensibility to opposing facts given it as its instinctive weapon for self-protection against disturbance.

                                        Ibid.

One hears of the mechanical equivalent of heat. What we now need to discover in the social realm is the moral equivalent of war: something heroic that will speak to men as universally as war does, and yet will be as compatible with their spiritual selves as war has proved itself to be incompatible.

                                        Ibid., "The Value of Saintliness"

What the more characteristically divine facts are, apart from the actual inflow of energy in the faith-state and the prayer-state, I know not. But the over-belief on which I am ready to make my personal venture is that they exist. The whole drift of my education goes to persuade me that the world of our present consciousness is only one out of many worlds of consciousness that exist, and that those other worlds must contain experiences which have a meaning for our life also; and that although in the main their experiences and those of this world keep discrete, yet the two become continuous at certain points, and higher energies filter in.

Ibid., "Conclusions"

Everyone knows what it is to start a piece of work, either intellectual or muscular, feeling stale—or *cold,* as an Adirondack guide once put it to me. And everybody knows what it is to "warm up" to his job. The process of warming up gets particularly striking in the phenomenon known as "second wind." On usual occasions we make a practice of stopping an occupation as soon as we meet the first effective layer (so to call it) of fatigue. We have then walked, played, or worked "enough," so we desist. That amount of fatigue is an efficacious obstruction on this side of which our usual life is cast. But if unusual necessity forces us to press onward, a surprising thing occurs. The fatigue gets worse up to a certain critical point, when gradually or suddenly it passes away, and we are fresher than before. We have evidently tapped a level of new energy, masked till then by the fatigue-obstacle usually obeyed. There may be layer after layer of this experience. A third and a fourth "wind" may supervene. Mental activity shows the phenomenon as well as physical, and in exceptional cases we may find, beyond the very extremity of fatigue-distress, amounts of ease and power that we never dreamed ourselves to own,—sources of strength habitually not taxed at all, because habitually we never push through the obstruction, never pass those early critical points.

Address, American Philosophical Society, 1906

The pragmatic method is primarily a method of settling metaphysical disputes that otherwise might be interminable. Is the world one or many? —fated or free?—material or spiritual?—here are notions either of which may or may not hold good of the world; and disputes over such notions are unending. The pragmatic method in such cases is to try to interpret each notion by tracing its respective practical consequences. What difference would it practically make to any one if this notion rather than that notion were true? If no practical difference whatever can be traced, then the alternatives mean practically the same thing, and all dispute is idle.

Whenever a dispute is serious, we ought to be able to show some practical difference that must follow from one side or the other's being right.

Pragmatism, "What Pragmatism Means," 1907

[Pragmatism is] the attitude of looking away from first things, principles, "categories," supposed necessities, and of looking towards last things, fruits, consequences, facts.

Ibid.

Pragmatically interpreted, pluralism or the doctrine that it is many means only that the sundry parts of reality *may be externally related.* Everything you can think of, however vast or inclusive, has on the pluralistic view a genuinely "internal" environment of sort or amount. Things are "with" one another in many ways, but nothing includes everything, or dominates over everything. The word "and" trails along after every sentence. Something always escapes. "Ever not quite" has to be said of the best attempts made anywhere in the universe at attaining all-inclusiveness. The pluralistic world is thus more like a federal republic than like an empire or a kingdom. However much may be collected, however much may report itself as present at any effective center of consciousness or action, something else is self-governed and absent and unreduced to unity.

A Pluralistic Universe, 1909

Pragmatism asks its usual question. "Grant an idea or belief to be true," it says, "what concrete difference will its being true make in any one's actual life? What experiences [may] be different from those which would obtain if the belief were false? How will the truth be realized? What, in short, is the truth's cash-value in experiential terms?" The moment pragmatism asks this question, it sees the answer. *True ideas are those that we can assimilate, validate, corroborate, and verify. False ideas are those that we cannot.* That is the practical difference it makes to us to have true ideas; that therefore is the meaning of truth, for it is all that truth is known as.

The Meaning of Truth, "Preface," 1909

If my reader can succeed in abstracting from all conceptual interpretation and lapse back into his immediate sensible life at this very moment, he will find it to be what some one has called a big blooming buzzing confusion, as free from contradiction in its "much-at-onceness" as it is all alive and evidently there.

Some Problems of Philosophy, "Precept and Concept," 1911

Who can decide offhand which is absolutely better, to live or to understand life? We must do both alternately, and a man can no more limit himself to either than a pair of scissors can cut with a single one of its blades.

Ibid.

Man, biologically considered . . . is the most formidable of all the beasts of prey, and indeed, the only one that preys systematically on its own species.

Memories and Studies, 1911

The stream of thinking is only a careless name for what, when scrutinized, reveals itself to consist chiefly of the stream of my breathing.

Essays in Radical Empiricism, 1912

Taken as it does appear, our universe is to a large extent chaotic. No one single type of connection runs through all the experiences that compose it. If we take space-relations, they fail to connect minds into any regular system. Causes and purposes obtain only among special series of facts. The self-relation seems extremely limited and does not link two different selves together. *Prima facie,* if you should liken the universe of absolute idealism to an aquarium, a crystal globe in which goldfish are swimming, you would have to compare the empiricist universe to something more like one of those dried human heads with which the Dyaks of Borneo deck their lodges. The skull forms a solid nucleus; but innumerable feathers, leaves, strings, beads, and loose appendices of every description float and dangle from it, and save that they terminate in it, seem to have nothing to do with one another. Even so my experiences and yours float and dangle, terminating, it is true, in a nucleus of common perception, but for the most part out of sight and irrelevant and unimaginable to one another. This imperfect intimacy, this bare relation of *withness* between some parts of the sum total of experience and other parts, is the fact that ordinary empiricism over-emphasizes against rationalism, the latter always tending to ignore it unduly. Radical empiricism, on the contrary, is fair to both the unity and the disconnection. It finds no reason for treating either as illusory. It allots to each its definite sphere of description, and agrees that there appear to be actual forces at work which tend, as time goes on, to make the unity greater.

Ibid.

Reason is one of the very feeblest of Nature's forces, if you take it at any one spot and moment. It is only in the very long run that its effects become perceptible. Reason assumes to settle things by weighing them against one another without prejudice, partiality, or excitement; but what affairs in the concrete are settled by is and always will be just prejudices, partialities, cupidities, and excitements. Appealing to reason as we do, we are in a sort of forlorn hope situation, like a small sandbank in the midst of a hungry sea ready to wash it out of existence. But sandbanks grow when the conditions favor; and weak as reason is, it has the unique advantage over its antagonists that its activity never lets up and that it presses always in one direction, while men's prejudices vary, their passions ebb and flow, and their excitements are intermittent. Our sandbank, I absolutely believe, is bound to grow—bit by bit it will get dyked and break-watered.

You know how opposed your whole "third manner" of execution is to the literary ideals which animate my crude and Orson-like breast, mine being to say a thing in one sentence as straight and explicit as it can be made, and then to drop it forever; yours being to avoid naming it straight, but by dint of breathing and sighing all round and round it, to arouse in the reader who may have had a similar perception already (Heaven help him if he hasn't!) the illusion of a solid object, made . . . wholly out of impalpable materials, air, and the prismatic interferences of light, ingeniously focused by mirrors upon empty space. But you *do* it, that's the queerness! . . . And so I say now, give us *one* thing in your older directer manner, just to show that, in spite of your paradoxical success in this unheard-of method, you *can* still write according to accepted canons. For gleams and innuendoes and felicitous verbal insinuations you are unapproachable, but the *core* of literature is solid. Give it to us *once* again! The bare perfume of things will not support existence, and the effect of solidity you reach is but perfume and simulacrum.

Letter to Henry James, May 4, 1907

Fear of life in one form or another is the great thing to exorcise; but it isn't reason that will ever do it. Impulse without reason is enough, and reason without impulse is a poor makeshift. I take it that no man is educated who has never dallied with the thought of suicide.

Letter to Benjamin Paul Blood

In general I don't see how an epigram, being a pure bolt from the blue, with no introduction or cue, gets itself written.

Letters

There is no bad weather. There are only good clothes.

A great many people think they are thinking when they are merely rearranging their prejudices.

Mankind does nothing save through initiatives on the part of inventors, great and small, and imitation by the rest of us—these are the sole factors active in human progress.

When we survey the whole field of religion, we find a great variety in the thoughts that have prevailed there; but feelings on the one hand, conduct on the other, are almost always the same, for Stoic, Christian, and Buddhist saints are practically indistinguishable in their lives.

JOSIAH ROYCE

Unless you can find some sort of loyalty, you cannot find unity and peace in your active living.

The Philosophy of Loyalty, 1908

Leaving all else out of account, this one great fact of suffering would be enough to make us doubt the worth of life. Contemplate a battlefield the first night after the struggle, contemplate here a vast company the equal of the population of a great town, writhing in agony, their groans sounding at a great distance like the roar of the ocean, their pain uneased for many hours, even death, so lavish of his favors all day, now refusing to comfort; contemplate this and then remember that as this pain is to the agony of the world, so is an electric spark drawn from the back of a kitten to the devastating lightning of many great storms; and now estimate if you can the worth of all but a few exceptional human lives. . . . Briefly and imperfectly I state the case for pessimism, not even touching the economical and social argument, drawn from a more special consideration of the conditions of human life. What shall we call it and whereunto shall it be likened? A vapor vanishing in the sun? No, that is not insignificant enough. A wave, broken on the beach? No, that is not unhappy enough. A soap bubble bursting into thin air? No, even that has rainbow hues. What then? Nothing but itself. Call it human life. You could not find a comparison more thoroughly condemning it.

Ibid.

Knowledge of the community is not love of the community. Love, when it comes, comes as from above. I can be genuinely in love with the community only in case I have somehow fallen in love with the universe.

The Problem of Christianity, 1913

Thinking is like loving and dying. Each of us must do it for himself.

JOHN DEWEY

Education is not infrequently defined as consisting in the acquisition of those habits that effect an adjustment of an individual and his environment. The definition expresses an essential phase of growth. But it is essential that adjustment be understood in its active sense of *control* of means for achieving ends. If we think of habit simply as a change wrought in the organism, ignoring the fact that this change consists in ability to effect subsequent changes in the environment, we shall be led to think of "adjustment" as a conformity to environment as wax conforms to the seal which impresses it. . . . Adaptation, in fine, is quite as much adaptation *of* the environment to our own activities as of our activities *to* the environment.

Democracy and Education, 1916

Philosophy recovers itself when it ceases to be a device for dealing with the problems of philosophers and becomes a method, cultivated by philosophers, for dealing with the problems of men.

"The Need for a Recovery of Philosophy," *Creative Intelligence,* 1917

The social, in its human sense, is the richest, fullest and most delicately subtle of any mode actually experienced.

"Social as a Category," *Monist,* 1928

Social facts are themselves natural facts.

Ibid.

Probably my experimentalism goes deeper than any other "ism."

Letter to Jim Cork

To me, faith means not worrying.

The discipline that is identical with trained power is also identical with freedom. . . . Genuine freedom, in short, is intellectual; it rests in the trained power of thought.

Complete adaptation to environment means death. The essential point in all response is the desire to control environment.

This intelligence-testing business reminds me of the way they used to weigh hogs in Texas. They would get a long plank, put it over a cross-bar, and somehow tie the hog on one end of the plank. They'd search all around till they found a stone that would balance the weight of the hog and they'd put that on the other end of the plank. Then they'd guess the weight of the stone.

George Santayana

A man's hatred of his own condition no more helps to improve it than hatred of other people tends to improve them.

The Life of Reason, "Reason in Common Sense," 1905

In Aristotle the conception of human nature is perfectly sound; everything ideal has a natural basis and everything natural an ideal development.

Ibid.

That life is worth living is the most necessary of assumptions, and, were it not assumed, the most impossible of conclusions.

Ibid.

Fanaticism consists in redoubling your effort when you have forgotten your aim.

Ibid.

The highest form of vanity is love of fame.

Ibid., "Reason in Society," 1905

. . . Friends are generally of the same sex, for when men and women agree, it is only in their conclusions; their reasons are always different. So that while intellectual harmony between men and women is easily possible, its delightful and magic quality lies precisely in the fact that it does not arise from mutual understanding, but is a conspiracy of alien essences and a kissing, as it were, in the dark. The human Race, in its intellectual life, is organized like the bees: the masculine soul is a worker, sexually atrophied, and essentially dedicated to impersonal and universal arts; the feminine is a queen, infinitely fertile, omnipresent in its brooding industry, but passive and abounding in intuitions without method and passions without justice. Friendship with a woman is therefore apt to be more or less than friendship: less, because there is no intellectual parity; more, because (even when the relation remains wholly dispassionate, as in respect to old ladies) there is something mysterious and oracular about a woman's mind which inspires a certain instinctive deference and puts it out of the question to judge what she says by masculine standards. She has a kind of sibylline intuition and the right to be irrationally *à propos*. There is a gallantry of the mind which pervades all conversation with a lady, as there is a natural courtesy towards children and mystics; but such a habit of respectful concession, marking as it does an intellectual alienation as profound, though not as complete, as that which separates us from the dumb animals, is radically incompatible with friendship.

Ibid.

Love is a brilliant illustration of a principle everywhere discoverable: namely, that human reason lives by turning the friction of material forces into the light of ideal goods. There can be no philosophic interest in disguising the animal basis of love, or in denying its spiritual sublimations, since all life is animal in its origin and all spiritual in its possible fruits.

Ibid.

Not to believe in love is a great sign of dulness.

Ibid.

It takes patience to appreciate domestic bliss; volatile spirits prefer unhappiness.

Ibid.

Plasticity loves new moulds because it can fill them, but for a man of sluggish mind and bad manners there is decidedly no place like home.

Ibid.

To delight in war is a merit in the soldier, a dangerous quality in the captain, and a positive crime in the statesman.

Ibid.

It is easier to make a saint out of a libertine than out of a prig.

Ibid., "Reason in Religion," 1905

Even the heretics and atheists, if they have had profundity, turn out after a while to be forerunners of some new orthodoxy. What they rebel against is a religion alien to their nature; they are atheists only by acci· dent, and relatively to a convention which inwardly offends them, but they yearn mightily in their own souls after the religious acceptance of a world interpreted in their own fashion.

Ibid.

Prayer is not a substitute for work; it is a desperate effort to work further and to be efficient beyond the range of one's powers.

Ibid.

Fashion is something barbarous, for it produces innovation without reason and imitation without benefit.

Ibid.

Nothing is so poor and melancholy as art that is interested in itself and not in its subject.

Ibid., "Reason in Art," 1905

An artist may visit a museum, but only a pedant can live there.

Ibid.

The best men in all ages keep classic traditions alive. These men have on their side the weight of superior intelligence, and, though they are few, they might even claim the weight of numbers, since the few of all ages, added together, may be more than the many who in any one age follow a temporary fashion.

Ibid.

There is a pathetic capacity in men to live nobly if only they would give one another the chance.

Ibid., "Reason in Science," 1906

Almost every wise saying has an opposite one, no less wise, to balance it.

Ibid.

The spectacle of inexorable change, the triumph of time, or whatever we may call it, has always been a favourite theme for lyric and tragic poetry, and for religious meditation. To perceive universal mutation, to feel the vanity of life, has always been the beginning of seriousness. It is the condition for any beautiful, measured, or tender philosophy. Prior to that, everything is barbarous, both in morals and in poetry; for until then mankind has not learned to renounce anything, has not outgrown the instinctive egotism and optimism of the young animal, and has not removed the centre of its being, or of its faith, from the will to the imagination.

Three Philosophical Poets, "Lucretius," 1910

The longing to be primitive is a disease of culture; it is Archaism in Morals. To be so preoccupied with vitality is a symptom of anaemia.

Winds of Doctrine, 1913

Our dignity is not in what we do, but what we understand. The whole world is doing things.

Ibid.

Few revolutionists would be such if they were heirs to a baronetcy.

Ibid.

Nothing can be meaner than the anxiety to live on, to live on anyhow and in any shape; a spirit with any honor is not willing to live except in its own way, and a spirit with any wisdom is not overeager to live at all.

Ibid. Ellen Glasgow, *The Woman Within,* 1954, terms this "the noblest passage in modern literature."

It is not worldly ecclesiastics that kindle the fires of persecution, but mystics who think they hear the voice of God.

New Republic, January 15, 1916

Comparison is the expedient of those who cannot reach the heart of the things compared.

Character and Opinion in the United States, 1920

My atheism, like that of Spinoza, is true piety toward the universe and denies only gods fashioned by men in their own image, to be servants of their human interests.

Soliloquies in England, 1922

Friendship is almost always the union of a part of one mind with a part of another; people are friends in spots.

Ibid.

The foolishness of the simple is delightful; only the foolishness of the wise is exasperating.

Ibid.

Repetition is the only form of permanence that nature can achieve.

Ibid., "Aversion from Platonism"

I have sometimes wondered at the value ladies set upon jewels: as centres of light, jewels seem rather trivial and monotonous. And yet there is an unmistakable spell about these pebbles; they can be taken up and turned over; they can be kept; they are faithful possessions; the sparkle of them, shifting from moment to moment, is constant from age to age. They are substances. The same aspects of light and colour, if they were homeless in space, or could be spied only once and irrecoverably, like fireworks, would have a less comfortable charm. In jewels there is the security, the mystery, the inexhaustible fixity proper to substance. After all, perhaps I can understand the fascination they exercise over the ladies; it is the same that the eternal feminine exercises over us. Our contact with them is unmistakable, our contemplation of them gladly renewed, and pleasantly prolonged; yet in one sense they are unknowable; we cannot fathom the secret of their constancy, of their hardness, of that perpetual but uncertain brilliancy by which they dazzle us and hide themselves. These qualities of the jewel and of the eternal feminine are also the qualities of substance and of the world. The existence of this world—unless we lapse for a moment into an untenable scepticism—is certain, or at least it is unquestioningly to be assumed. Experience may explore it adventurously, and science may describe it with precision; but after you have wandered up and down in it for many years, and have gathered all you could of its ways by report, this same world, because it exists substantially and is not invented, remains a foreign thing and a marvel to the spirit: unknowable as a drop of water is unknowable, or unknowable like a person loved.

"The Unknowable," a lecture, 1923

Scepticism is the chastity of the intellect, and it is shameful to surrender it too soon or to the first comer: there is nobility in preserving it coolly and proudly through a long youth, until at last, in the ripeness of instinct and discretion, it can be safely exchanged for fidelity and happiness.

Scepticism and Animal Faith, 1923

The brute necessity of believing something so long as life lasts does not justify any belief in particular.

Ibid.

The young man who has not wept is a savage, and the old man who will not laugh is a fool.

Dialogues in Limbo, 1925

That the end of life should be death may sound sad: yet what other end can anything have? The end of an evening party is to go to bed; but its use is to gather congenial people together, that they may pass the time pleasantly. An invitation to the dance is not rendered ironical because the dance cannot last forever; the youngest of us and the most vigorously wound up, after a few hours, has had enough of sinuous stepping and prancing. The transitoriness of things is essential to their physical being, and not at all sad in itself; it becomes sad by virtue of a sentimental illusion, which makes us imagine that they wish to endure, and that their end is always untimely; but in a healthy nature it is not so. What is truly sad is to have some impulse frustrated in the midst of its career, and robbed of its chosen object; and what is painful is to have an organ lacerated or destroyed when it is still vigorous, and not ready for its natural sleep and dissolution. We must not confuse the itch which our unsatisfied instincts continue to cause with the pleasure of satisfying and dismissing each of them in turn. Could they all be satisfied harmoniously we should be satisfied once for all and completely. Then doing and dying would coincide throughout and be a perfect pleasure.

Some Turns of Thought in Modern Philosophy, 1933

Between the laughing and the weeping philosopher there is no opposition: *the same facts* that make one laugh make one weep. No whole-hearted man, no sane art, can be limited to either mood.

Persons and Places, 1943

Liberalism, Protestantism, Judaism, positivism all have the same ultimate aim and standard. It is prosperity, or as Lutheran theologians put it, union with God at our level, not at God's level. The thing all these schools detest is the ideal of union with God at God's level, proper to asceticism, mysticism, Platonism, and pure intelligence, which insist on seeing things under the form of truth and of eternity.

Ibid.

I at least have found that old age is the time for happiness, even for enjoying in retrospect the years of youth that were so distracted in their day; and I seem to detect a certain sardonic defiance, a sort of pride, in the whining old beggars that look so wretched as they stretch out a trembling hand for a penny. They are not dead yet; they can hold together in spite of everything; and they are not deceived about *you,* you well-dressed young person. Your new shoes pinch you, and you are secretly racked by hopeless desires.

Ibid.

All beauties are to be honored, but only one embraced.

Ibid.

I call it reason because reason in my philosophy is only a harmony among irrational impulses.

The Middle Span, 1945

He told me his love-affairs, which were, as poetry should be, simple, sensuous, and short.

Ibid.

Concerning William James, I have made sundry scattered observations for the public without attempting a fair total portrayal of the man or of his philosophy: neither he nor his philosophy lent themselves to being summed up. But here, where I am portraying only my own impressions, I may add a word more about the feelings that he excited in me. I trusted his heart but I didn't respect his judgment. I admired his masculine directness, his impressionistic perceptions, and his picturesque words. I treasured his utterances on the medical side of things, such as that the best way to understanding the normal is to study the abnormal. All this belonged to his independent, radical, naturalistic temper, to his American sense of being just born into a world to be rediscovered. But he was really far from free, held back by old instincts, subject to old delusions, restless, spasmodic, self-interrupted: as if some impetuous bird kept flying aloft, but always stopped in mid-air, pulled back with a jerk by an invisible wire tethering him to a peg in the ground. The general agreement in America to praise him as a marvelous person, and to pass on, is justified by delight at the way he started, without caring where he went. In fact, he got no-where; and for that reason his influence could be great and beneficent over those who knew him, but soon seemed to become untraceable in the confused currents of the world. I, for instance, was sure of his goodwill and kindness, of which I had many proofs; but I was also sure that he never understood me, and that when he talked to me there was a manikin in his head, called G. S. and entirely fantastic, which he was addressing. No doubt I profited materially by this illusion, because he would have liked me less if he had understood me better; but the sense of that illusion made spontaneous friendship impossible. I was uncomfortable in his pres-ence. He was so extremely natural that there was no knowing what his nature was, or what to expect next; so that one was driven to behave and talk conventionally, as in the most artificial society. I found no foothold, I was soon fatigued, and it was a relief to be out again in the open, and alone.

Ibid.

Miracles are so called because they excite wonder. In unphilosophical minds any rare or unexpected thing excites wonder, while in philosophical minds the familiar excites wonder also, and the laws of nature, if we admit such laws, excite more wonder than the detached events. Each morning the sunrise excites wonder in the poet, and the order of the solar system excites it every night in the astronomer. Astronomy explains the sunrise, but what shall explain the solar system? The universe, which would explain everything, is the greatest of wonders, and a perpetual miracle.

The Idea of Christ in the Gospels, 1946

I remembered the judgment that my young friend Duer Irving had passed on Seville. Seville was nothing unless you had a horse and a love-affair, and then it was everything.

My Host the World, 1953

Catholicism is paganism spiritualised: it is fundamentally naturalistic; and the transcendental spirit and the wise statesman may accept Catholicism, where it naturally arises, as a good poetic symbol for the forces and the issues of human life in that phase; not, however, as a scientific revelation or a history of literal facts. Religion is valid poetry infused into common life. It is not revelation truer than perception or than science.

Ibid.

The contemporary world has turned its back on the attempt and even on the desire to live reasonably. The two great wars (so far) of the twentieth century were adventures in enthusiastic unreason. They were inspired by unnecessary and impracticable ambitions; and the "League" and the "United Nations," feebly set up by the victors, were so irrationally conceived that they at once reduced their victory to a stalemate. What is required for living rationally? I think the conditions may be reduced to two: First, self-knowledge, the Socratic key to wisdom; and second, sufficient knowledge of the world to perceive what alternatives are open to you and which of them are favourable to your true interests.

Now the contemporary world has plenty of knowledge of nature for its purposes, but its purposes show a positively insane abandonment of its true interests. You may say that the proletariat knows its interests perfectly; they are to work less and to earn more. Those are indeed its interests so long as it remains a proletariat: but to be a proletariat is an inhuman condition. Proletarians are human beings, and their first interest is to have a home, a family, a chosen trade, and freedom in practising it. And more particularly a man's true interest may exceptionally be not to have those things, but to wander alone like the rhinoceros; or perhaps to have a very special kind of home, family and occupation. There must be freedom of movement and vocation. There must be *Lebensraum* for the spirit.

There have always been beggars and paupers in the world, because there is bound to be a margin of the unfit, too bad or too good to keep in step with any well organised society; but that the great body of mankind should sink into a proletariat has been an unhappy effect of the monstrous growth of cities, made possible by the concentration of trade and the multiplication of industries, mechanised, and swelling into monopolies.

The natural state of mankind, before foreign conquerors dominate it or native ideologues reform it, is full of incidental evils; prophets have ample cause for special denunciations and warnings; yet there is, as in all animal economy, a certain nucleus of self-preserving instincts and habits, a normal constitution of society. Nature with its gods is the landlord of whose fields and woods they are local and temporary tenants; and with this invincible power they make prudent and far-seeing covenants. They know what is for their good and by what arts it might be secured. They live by agriculture, the hunting or breeding of animals, and such domestic arts as their climate and taste lead them to cultivate; and when a quarrel rises among them, or with strangers, they battle to preserve or to restore their free life, without more ambitious intentions. They are materially and morally rooted in the earth, bred in one land or one city. They are *civilised*. Wandering nations, with nothing of their own and working havoc wherever they go, are *barbarians*. Such "barbarians" were the proletariat of antiquity. When they occupied some civilised region without exterminating the natives, and established in the old strongholds a permanent foreign domination, they became half-civilised themselves, without shedding altogether the predatory and adventurous practices of their ancestors. This is the compound origin and nature of modern Western governments.

Varied, picturesque, and romantic mixtures of civilisation beneath and barbarism above have filled the history of Christendom, and produced beautiful transient arts, in which there was too little wisdom and too much fancy and fashion: think of Gothic architecture, or of manners, dress, poetry, and philosophy from the middle ages to our day. Civilisation had become more enterprising, plastic, and irresponsible, while barbarism seemed to retreat into sports, and into legal extravagances in thought and action. Intellectual chaos and political folly could thus come to co-exist strangely with an irresistible dominance of mechanical industry. The science that served this industrial progress by no means brought moral enlightenment. It merely enlarged acquaintance with phenomena and enabled clever inventors to construct all sorts of useful or superfluous machines. At first perhaps it was expected that science would make all both rich and free from material cares (two contradictory hopes) and would at the same time enlighten them at last about the nature of things, including their own nature, so that adequate practical wisdom would be secured together with fabulous material well-being.

This is the dream of the moderns, on which I found My Host boastfully running his establishment. He expected his guests also to act accordingly and to befuddle and jollify one another, so that all should convince themselves that they were perfectly happy and should advertise their Host's business wherever they went. Such forced enterprise, forced confidence, and forced satisfaction would never have sprung from domestic arts or common knowledge spontaneously extended. It was all artificial and strained, marking the inhuman domination of some militant class or sect. This society lacked altogether that essential trait of rational living, to have a clear, sanctioned, ultimate aim. The cry was for vacant freedom and indeterminate progress: *Vorwärts! Avanti! Onward! Full speed ahead!* without asking whether directly before you was not a bottomless pit.

Ibid.

Music bores me if I am sitting penned in among a crowd in a hot place, with bright artificial lights, and a general pretense at intelligent interest, whether such interest exists or not. It is too much like sitting through a service in a Protestant church. At the opera I can forget this discomfort because the impression, visual as well as auditory, is violent enough to hold my attention; but for pure music I desire the open air, solitude if possible, and liberty to move about and to go away. There is a wonderful sense of freedom in standing on one's two legs. It adds, in my feeling, to the sincere enjoyment of both nature and art. Music and landscape then come as a gift, not as a thing procured for a ticket that constitutes a promise and imposes a sort of pledge. I prefer that the beautiful should come upon me unannounced, and that it should leave me at liberty.

Ibid.

Never have I enjoyed youth so thoroughly as I have in my old age. In writing *Dialogues in Limbo, The Last Puritan,* and now all these descriptions of the friends of my youth and the young friends of my middle age, I have drunk the pleasure of life more pure, more joyful, than it ever was when mingled with all the hidden anxieties and little annoyances of actual living. Nothing is inherently and invincibly young except spirit. And spirit can enter a human being perhaps better in the quiet of old age and dwell there more undisturbed than in the turmoil of adventure. But it must be in solitude. I do not need or desire to hob-nob artificially with other old men in order to revisit them in their salad days, and to renew my own. In Rome, in the eternal city, I feel nearer to my own past, and to the whole past and future of the world, than I should in any cemetery or in any museum of relics. Old places and old persons in their turn, when spirit dwells in them, have an intrinsic vitality of which youth is incapable; precisely the balance and wisdom that comes from long perspectives and broad foundations. Everything shines then for the spirit by its own light in its own place and time; but not as it shone in its own restless eyes. For in its own eyes each person and each place was the centre of a universe full of threatening and tempting things; but old age, having less intensity at the centre has more clearness at the circumference, and knows that just because spirit, at each point, is a private centre for all things, no one point, no one phase of spirit is materially a public centre for all the rest. Thus recognition and honour flow out to all things, from the mind that conceives them justly and without egotism; and thus mind is reconciled to its momentary existence and limited vision by the sense of the infinite supplements that embosom it on every side.

Ibid.

No part of time is lost in eternity, only the haste and uncertainty of passing from one thing to another. I had not been ravaged by any hostile fate; my heart had simply uttered a warning against its own weakness. It had said to me: Cultivate imagination, love it, give it endless forms, but do not let it deceive you. Do not suffer it to oppress you with craving or with regret for the images that you may form of it. You will do the least harm and find the greatest satisfaction if, being furnished as lightly as possible with possessions, you live freely among ideas. To possess things and persons in ideas is the only pure good to be got out of them; to possess them physically or legally is a burden and a snare.

Ibid.

Before he sets out, the traveller must possess fixed interests and faculties, to be served by travel. If he drifted aimlessly from country to country he would not *travel* but only wander, ramble or tramp. The traveller must be somebody and come from somewhere, so that his definite character and moral traditions may supply an organ and a point of comparison for his observations. He must not go nosing about like a pedlar for profit or like an emigrant for a vacant lot. Everywhere he should show the discretion and maintain the dignity of a guest. Everywhere he should remain a stranger no matter how benevolent, and a critic no matter how appreciative. Were he a mere sensorium, without his own purposes, moral categories and points of reference, he might as well have left those variegated natives to lead their lives undisturbed and unvisited. They would have gone on the more comfortably without him, and he the more inexpensively without them, at home. The traveller should be an artist recomposing what he sees; then he can carry away the picture and add it to a transmissible fund of wisdom, not as further miscellaneous experience but as a corrected view of the truth.

Ibid.

Oaths are the fossils of piety.

The Absence of Religion in Shakespeare

Perhaps the only true dignity of man is his capacity to despise himself.

Introduction to . . . Spinoza

An artist is a dreamer consenting to dream of the actual world.

The arts may die of triviality, as they were born of enthusiasm.

Civilization is perhaps approaching one of those long winters which over-take it from time to time.

Life is not a spectacle or a feast; it is a predicament.

Piety to mankind must be three-fourths pity. To worship mankind as it is would be to deprive it of what alone makes it akin to the divine—its aspirations.

For an idea ever to be fashionable is ominous, since it must afterwards be always old-fashioned.

To understand oneself is the classic form of consolation; to elude oneself is the romantic.

Why should not things be largely absurd, futile and transitory? They are so, and we are so, and they and we go very well together.

A musical education is necessary for musical judgment. What most people relish is hardly music; it is, rather, a drowsy reverie relieved by nervous thrills.

Young poets on a slender experience sometimes reach the greatest heights and the greatest depths, finding nothing to intercept the impetuous flight of their spirits.

Poetry is religion which is no longer believed.

To be interested in the changing seasons is, in this middling zone, a hap-pier state of mind than to be hopelessly in love with Spring.

The basis of thought is vastly more elaborate than its deliverance. It takes a wonderful brain and exquisite senses to produce a few stupid ideas.

To substitute the society of ideas for that of things . . . is the sole path to happiness for the intellectual man, because the intellectual man cannot be satisfied with a world of perpetual change, defeat, and imperfection.

By Nature's kindly disposition most questions which it is beyond man's power to answer do not occur to him at all.

Those who cannot remember the past are condemned to repeat it.

Harry A. Overstreet

A person remains immature, whatever his age, as long as he thinks of himself as an exception to the human race.

The Mature Mind, 1949

When an adult peevishly protests that he didn't ask to be born, he overlooks the simple fact that nobody else did either.

Ibid.

Morris Raphael Cohen

The pearls which are dropped before real swine are likely to be imitation.

To his class

Will Durant

No man who is in a hurry is quite civilized.

The Life of Greece

Every form of government tends to perish by excess of its basic principle.

The right to nag is one of the consolations of matrimony.

Scott Buchanan

Science is an allegory that asserts that the relations between the parts of reality are similar to the relations between terms of discourse.

Poetry and Mathematics, 1929

The structures with which mathematics deals are more like lace, the leaves of trees, and the play of light and shadow on a human face, than they are like buildings and machines, the least of their representatives. The best proofs in mathematics are short and crisp like epigrams, and the longest have swings and rhythms that are like music. The structures of mathematics and the propositions about them are ways for the imagination to travel and the wings, or legs, or vehicles to take you where you want to go.

Ibid.

Every one ought to ask as many questions as he possibly can in this life, for when we die, those questions are answered which we have asked, and no others.

LEWIS MUMFORD

A city, properly speaking, does not exist by the accretion of houses, but by the association of human beings. When the accretion of houses reaches such a point of congestion that human association becomes difficult, the place ceases to be a city.

Sticks and Stones, 1924

Layer upon layer, past times preserve themselves in the city until life itself is finally threatened with suffocation; then, in sheer defense, modern man invents the museum.

The Culture of Cities, 1938

The final question is, "What kind of human being are we trying to produce?" Not the power, not the profit man, or the mechanical man, but the whole man must be the central actor in the new civilization.

New York Times, September 15, 1948

No one can understand the literature of the last half-century, its contradictions, its dehumanization, its preoccupation with violence, its increasing unintelligibility, who does not understand the great breach that the first World War effected in the human mind. While our visible monuments are still continuous with those of the nineteenth century, all our invisible landmarks have been defaced and demolished: "Over is under and close is apart."

We were born into the cocky, confident world of Bernard Shaw; and we have lived to understand sympathetically the life and confessions of

Saint Augustine. To interpret the literature of our period, we must realize
how time has been distorted for us by the meeting, within a generation,
of still youthful senescents and grimly senescent youths: it is the old who
are giddy and the young who are grave.

Seven Arts, "Mirror of a Violent Half Century"

IRWIN EDMAN

M. Platon's suggestion of a communion not of saints but of minds has
much to commend it. A communion is, as a matter of fact, only a sacramental way of speaking of a *coterie.* Such a communion of minds exists
in essence already and has always existed. There are humanists who are
friends in the spirit although they have never met, and Platonists who see
eye to eye, although they are as far apart as North Dakota and Beirut.
Everyone has had the sense, on making a chance acquaintance on a
steamer, at a professional meeting, in a country house, at a cocktail party
(where one is likely to make a mistake), of having known that person
always in essence and of two spirits' having for a long time been, unknown
to each other, travelling-companions on the same road. One has the sense
of having moved in parallel lines, of having touched the same beauties,
shared the same truths, or nourished the same errors, found light by or
aspired towards the same stars. *En route* to Italy I once met a civil engineer and in a small inn in New Hampshire, a Boston surgeon, who both
quoted to me my favorite passages of Santayana. There are no meetings
of such a society of communicants in identical objects of love, and most
of the members all their lives will never know each other. They are simply
mutually unknown communicants of the same gods.

Philosopher's Holiday, 1938

. . . I think, of all the moments I remember at philosophical gatherings,
the most memorable occurred in the Hague in the autumn of 1932 when
a Congress was being held to celebrate the three hundredth anniversary
of the birth of Spinoza. . . . The first evening was devoted to an address
by George Santayana. He read his essay called "Ultimate Religion." . . .
What I remember of the occasion is not simply the paper but the temper
of the reading. I had spoken often with Santayana before and had heard
him pass into eloquent soliloquy. I had heard legends of the great days of
his lectures at Harvard, when those who could understand understood,
and those who could not were convinced by the beauty of the language

and the elevation of the spirit of the man addressing them. It was the same here at the Hague. For there were many here who literally could not understand, who knew no English and certainly many—especially among the Germans and grammarians of philosophy—who, if they understood the literal words, must have found the doctrine strange and the poetry of the utterance ambiguous. But I have seldom seen an audience so rapt. Santayana read very slowly in his naturally clear and musical voice with its natural or artfully measured cadence. He read as if he were reading not simply an essay on "Ultimate Religion," but frankly, intensely, and after long brooding and reflection, his own ultimate religion. It was an act of piety to Spinoza and a confession of his own faith in which he invited all men of good-will and honest reflection to join him. It was not a routine reading of an academic tribute. The speaker was obviously aware of the occasion and what in essence it meant. Many of the audience must have gathered it from the tone and the look of absorption in the speaker. It was clear that at least one did. For there was sitting next to me a young German, deeply absorbed. When it was over, I asked him whether he had understood. "No," he replied, "I do not understand English, but it sounded so human and so beautiful, I am sure it was." He was right.

Ibid.

Mortimer J. Adler

All books will become light in proportion as you find light in them.

How to Read a Book, "Preface"

If we consider men and women generally, and apart from their professions or occupations, there is only one situation I can think of in which they almost pull themselves up by their bootstraps, making an effort to read better than they usually do. When they are in love and are reading a love letter, they read for all they are worth. They read every word three ways; they read between the lines and in the margins; they read the whole in terms of the parts, and each part in terms of the whole; they grow sensitive to context and ambiguity, to insinuation and implication; they perceive the color of words, the odor of phrases, and the weight of sentences. They may even take the punctuation into account. Then, if never before or after, they read.

Ibid.

He was no less anxious to teach than to learn. Since the truth belongs to no man, one has no right not to pass it on.

Of Professor Jerome Michael

There is no point in our ancestors speaking to us unless we know how to listen.

V. The Historians
from John Lothrop Motley to Dumas Malone

John Lothrop Motley

Give us the luxuries of life, and we will dispense with the necessities.

> Quoted by Holmes, *The Autocrat of the Breakfast Table*. Sometimes ascribed to Oscar Wilde, but Motley's claim is good.

Henry Adams

Man has mounted science, and is now run away with. I firmly believe that before many centuries more, science will be the master of man. The engines he will have invented will be beyond his strength to control. Some day science may have the existence of mankind in its power, and the human race may commit suicide by blowing up the world.

> Letter, 1862

Did you ever read Karl Marx? I think I never struck a book which taught me so much, and with which I disagreed so radically in conclusion.

> Letter to Charles Milnes Gaskell, 1894

I apprehend for the next hundred years an ultimate, colossal, cosmic collapse; but not on any of our old lines. My belief is that science is to wreck us, and that we are like monkeys monkeying with a loaded shell; we don't in the least know or care where our practically infinite energies come from or will bring us to. For myself, it is true; I know no care at all. But the faintest disturbance of equilibrium is felt throughout the solar system, and I feel sure that our power over energy has now reached a point where it just sensibly effects the old adjustment. It is mathematically certain to me that another thirty years of energy-development at the rate of the last century, must reach an *impasse*.

> Letter to Brooks Adams, 1902

One sees her personal presence on every side. Anyone can feel it who will only consent to feel like a child. Sitting here any Sunday afternoon, while the voices of the children are chanting in the choir—your mind held in the grasp of the strong lines and shadows of the architecture; your eyes flooded with the autumn tones of the glass; your ears drowned with the purity of the voices; one sense reacting upon another until sensation reaches the limit of its range—you, or any other lost soul, could, if you cared to look and listen, feel a sense beyond the human ready to reveal a sense divine that would make that world once more intelligible, and would bring the Virgin to life again, in all the depths of feeling which she shows here—in lines, vaults, chapels, colors, legends, chants—more eloquent than the prayerbook, more beautiful than the autumn sunlight.

Mont-Saint-Michel and Chartres, 1904

Pessimists are social bores. Optimists are intellectual idiots. If you want thorough work, always employ a pessimist. The optimist trusts to good luck; he gambles on his cards without calculating them. In the long run, in life, one has got to lose.

Letter to Elizabeth Cameron, 1905

From cradle to grave this problem of running order through chaos, direction through space, discipline through freedom, unity through multiplicity, has always been, and must always be, the task of education.

The Education of Henry Adams, 1907

Nothing in education is so astonishing as the amount of ignorance it accumulates in the form of inert facts.

Ibid.

A teacher affects eternity; he can never tell where his influence stops.

Ibid.

What one knows is, in youth, of little moment; they know enough who know how to learn.

Ibid.

Those who seek education in the paths of duty are always deceived by the illusion that power in the hands of a friend is an advantage to them.

Ibid.

A friend in power is a friend lost.

Ibid.

History is a tangled skein that one may take up at any point, and break when one has unravelled enough; but complexity precedes evolution.

Ibid.

Any schoolboy could see that man as a force must be measured by motion, from a fixed point. Psychology helped here by suggesting a unit—the point of history when man held the highest idea of himself in a unified universe. Eight or ten years of study had led Adams to think he might use the century 1150–1250 expressed in Amiens Cathedral and the Works of Thomas Aquinas, as the unit from which he might measure motion down to his own time, without assuming anything as true or untrue, except relation. The movement might be studied at once in philosophy and mechanics. Setting himself to the task, he began a volume which he mentally knew as "Mont-Saint-Michel and Chartres: A Study in Thirteenth-Century Unity." From that point he proposed to fix a position for himself, which he could label: "The Education of Henry Adams: A Study in Twentieth-Century Multiplicity." With the help of these two points of relation, he hoped to project his lines forward and backward indefinitely, subject to correction from anyone who should know better.

Ibid.

The movement from unity into multiplicity, between 1200 and 1900, was unbroken in sequence, and rapid in acceleration. Prolonged one generation longer, it would require a new social mind.

Ibid.

As he lay on Wenlock Edge, with the sheep nibbling the grass close about him as they or their betters had nibbled the grass—or whatever was there to nibble—in the Silurian kingdom of *Pteraspis,* he seemed to have fallen on an evolution far more wonderful than that of fishes. He did not like it; he could not account for it; and he determined to stop it. Never since the day of his *Limulus* ancestry had any of his ascendants thought thus. Their modes of thought might be many, but their thought was one. Out of his millions of millions of ancestors, back to the Cambrian mollusks, every one had probably lived and died in the illusions of Truths which did not amuse him, and which had never changed. Henry Adams was the first in an infinite series to discover and admit to himself that he really did not care whether truth was, or was not, true. He did not even care that it should be proved true, unless the process were new and amusing. He was a Darwinian for fun.

From the beginning of history, this attitude had been branded as criminal—worse than crime—sacrilege! Society punished it ferociously and justly, in self-defence. Mr. Adams the father looked on it as moral weakness; it annoyed him; but it did not annoy him nearly as much as it an-

noyed his son, who had no need to learn from Hamlet the fatal effect of
the pale cast of thought on enterprise great or small.

Ibid.

Historians undertake to arrange sequences,—called stories, or histories—
assuming in silence a relation of cause and effect. These assumptions, hidden in the depths of dusty libraries, have been astounding, but commonly
unconscious and childlike; so much so, that if any captious critic were to
drag them to light, historians would probably reply, with one voice, that
they had never supposed themselves required to know what they were
talking about. Adams, for one, had toiled in vain to find out what he
meant. He had even published a dozen volumes of American history for
no other purpose than to satisfy himself whether, by the severest process
of stating, with the least possible comment, such facts as seemed sure, in
such order as seemed rigorously consequent, he could fix for a familiar moment a necessary sequence of human movement. The result had satisfied
him as little as at Harvard College. Where he saw sequence, other men
saw something quite different, and no one saw the same unit of measure.
He cared little about his experiments and less about his statesmen, who
seemed to him quite as ignorant as himself and, as a rule, no more honest;
but he insisted on a relation of sequence, and if he could not reach it by
one method, he would try as many methods as science knew. Satisfied that
the sequence of men led to nothing and that the sequence of their society
could lead no further, while the mere sequence of time was artificial, and
the sequence of thought was chaos, he turned at last to the sequence of
force; and thus it happened that, after ten years' pursuit, he found himself lying in the Gallery of Machines at the Great Exposition of 1900,
historical neck broken by the sudden irruption of forces totally new.

Ibid.

The study of history is useful to the historian by teaching him his ignorance of women. . . . The woman who is known only through a man is
known wrong.

Ibid.

I am inclined to say now that the man who has attained 80 years has
achieved the most stupendous failure possible, because he has, at least in
my case, seemed to have got to the bottom of everything, and has left no

experience that has not failed. I find this reflection very consolatory, in the midst of all our public anxieties.

                                    Letter to Charles Milnes Gaskell, February 19, 1918

Reason can be only another phase of the energy earlier known as Instinct or Intuition; and if this be admitted as the stem-history of the Mind as far back as the eocene lemur, it must be admitted for all forms of Vital Energy back to the vegetables and perhaps even to the crystals. In the absence of any definite break in the series, all must be endowed with energy equivalent to will. . . . Already the anthropologists have admitted man to be specialized beyond hope of further variation, so that, as an energy, he must be treated as a weakened Will,—an enfeebled vitality,— a degraded potential. He cannot himself deny that his highest Will-power, whether individual or social, must have proved itself by his highest variation, which was incontrovertibly his act of transforming himself from a hypothetical eocene lemur,—whatever such a creature may have been,— into a man speaking elaborately inflected language. This staggering but self-evident certainty requires many phases of weakening Will-power to intervene in the process of subsidence into the reflective, hesitating, relatively passive stage called Reason; so that in the end, while at the same time refusing to admit a break in the series, the historian will have to define his profession as the science of human degradation.

                                    The Degradation of the Democratic Dogma, 1919

ALFRED THAYER MAHAN

Self-interest is not only a legitimate, but a fundamental cause for national policy: one which needs no cloak of hypocrisy . . . It is vain to expect governments to act continuously on any other ground than national interest.

JAMES HARVEY ROBINSON

One cannot but wonder at this constantly recurring phrase, "getting something for nothing," as if it were the peculiar and perverse ambition of disturbers of society. Except for our animal outfit, practically all we have is handed to us gratis. Can the most complacent reactionary flatter himself that he invented the art of writing or the printing press, or discovered his religious, economic and moral convictions, or any of the devices which supply him with meat and raiment or any of the sources of such pleasures as he may derive from literature or the fine arts? In short, civilization is little else than getting something for nothing.

The Mind in the Making, 1921

We find it hard to believe that other people's thoughts are as silly as our own, but they probably are.

Ibid.

The truest and most profound observations on Intelligence have in the past been made by the poets and, in recent times, by story-writers. They have been keen observers and recorders and reckoned freely with the emotions and sentiments. Most philosophers, on the other hand, have exhibited a grotesque ignorance of man's life and have built up systems that are elaborate and imposing, but quite unrelated to actual human affairs. They have almost consistently neglected the actual process of thought and have set the mind off as something apart to be studied by itself. *But no such mind, except from bodily processes, animal impulses, savage traditions, infantile impressions, conventional reactions, and traditional knowledge, ever existed,* even in the case of the most abstract of metaphysicians. . . . To the modern student of mind pure reason seems as mythical as the pure gold, transparent as glass, with which the celestial city is paved.

Ibid.

Most of our so-called reasoning consists in finding arguments for going on believing as we already do.

Ibid.

JAMES HENRY BREASTED

The fact that man possessed the capacity to rise from bestial savagery to civilization, at a time when it had *never before been done,* is the greatest fact in the history of the universe as known to us. For this amazing new capability, transcending merely physical development and the evolution of more efficient organs, disclosed a kind of buoyancy of the *human spirit,* never before displayed in the history of life on our planet. For the first time it demonstrated the ability of the creature man to rise. In so far then, as the career of life is known to terrestrial intelligence, the emergence of a creature capable of thus rising is, I repeat, the greatest fact in the universe.

The Conquest of Civilization

CARL BECKER

The significance of man is that he is that part of the universe that asks the question, What is the significance of Man? He alone can stand apart imaginatively and, regarding himself and the universe in their eternal aspects, pronounce a judgement: The significance of man is that he is insignificant and is aware of it.

Progress and Power, 1935

All that has happened to man in 506,000 years may be symbolized by this fact—he can, with ease and expedition, put his ancestors in cages.

Ibid.

O History, how many truths have been committed in thy name!

CHARLES A. BEARD

1. Whom the gods would destroy, they first make mad with power.
2. The mills of God grind slowly, but they grind exceeding small.
3. The bee fertilizes the flower it robs.
4. When it is dark enough, you can see the stars.

> Asked if he could summarize the lessons of history in a short book, he replied that he could do it in four sentences.

CHARLES A. and MARY BEARD

After suffering defeats in every direction, adepts in the application of the scientific method of human affairs, except perhaps the least sophisticated, fell into a state of bewilderment. Slowly it dawned on them that the human mind and the method employed were not competent to the appointed task, that omniscience was not vouchsafed mortals. Moreover, it was finally realized that if all human affairs were reduced to law, to a kind of terrestrial mechanics, a chief end of the quest, that is, human control over occurrences and actions, would itself become meaningless. Should mankind discover the law of its total historical unfolding, then it would be imprisoned in its own fate and powerless to change it; the past, present, and future would be revealed as fixed and beyond the reach of human choice and will. Men and women would be chained to their destiny as the stars and tides are to their routine. The difference between human beings and purely physical objects would lie in their poignant knowledge of their doom and of their helplessness in its presence. . . . The scientific method has been defeated, and must be defeated in the effort to reach the supreme goal—the reduction of large areas of human affairs to isolated groupings subject to unequivocal law; and were it to reach its impossible goal, victory would be defeat for mankind, that is, imprisonment in a doom actually foreknown.

The Open Door at Home, 1934

HENDRIK WILLEM VAN LOON

A human being with the mind of a sixteenth-century tradesman driving a Rolls-Royce is still a human being with the mind of a sixteenth-century tradesman.

CARL VAN DOREN

The first writers are first and the rest, in the long run, nowhere but in anthologies.

What Is American Literature?

Affection, indulgence and humor alike are powerless against the instinct of children to rebel. It is as essential to their minds and wills as exercise to their bodies. If they have no reasons for it they will invent them, like nations bound on war. It is hard to imagine families limp enough to be always at peace. Wherever there is character there will be conflict. The best that parents and children can hope for is that the wounds of their conflict may not be too deep or too lasting.

Three Worlds

I have never in my life thought things out, nor have I known anybody who ever did. I have always had to live them out, thinking as I went along.

Ibid.

The black melancholy of young men has many apparent causes, but the many are really one: that the young men wish and will more than they can do.

Ibid.

Dumas Malone

The hero is a man who has fought impressively for a cause of which we approve.

VI. The Social Scientists: Critics and Commentators

Shortsighted is the philosophy which counts on selfishness as the master motive of human action. It is blind to facts of which the world is full. It sees not the present, and reads not the past aright. If you would move men to action, to what shall you appeal? Not to their pockets, but to their patriotism; not to their selfishness, but to sympathy. Self-interest is, as it were, a mechanical force—potent, it is true; capable of wide results. But there is in human nature what may be likened to a chemical force; which melts and fuses and overwhelms; to which nothing seems impossible. "All that a man hath will he give for his life"—that is self-interest. But in loyalty to higher impulses men will give even life.

Progress and Poverty, 1879

There is nothing whatever to show that the men who today build and navigate and use such ships [that ply the ocean with a velocity of five or six hundred miles a day] are one whit superior in any physical or mental quality to their ancestors, whose best vessel was a coracle of wicker and hide. The enormous improvement which these ships show is not an improvement of human nature; it is an improvement of society—it is due to a wider and fuller union of individual efforts in accomplishment of common ends.

Ibid.

WILLIAM GRAHAM SUMNER

If you want war, nourish a doctrine. Doctrines are the most frightful tyrants to which men ever are subject, because doctrines get inside of a man's reason and betray him against himself. Civilized men have done their fiercest fighting for doctrines.

War, 1903

The four great motives which move men to social activity are hunger, love, vanity, and fear of superior powers.

Ibid.

The great stream of time and earthly things will sweep on just the same in spite of us. It bears with it now all the errors and follies of the past, the wreckage of all the philosophies, the fragments of all the civilizations, the wisdom of all the abandoned ethical systems, the debris of all the institutions, and the penalties of all the mistakes. It is only in imagination that we stand by and look at and criticize it and plan to change it. Every one of us is a child of his age and cannot get out of it. He is in the stream and is swept along with it. All his sciences and philosophies come to him out of it. Therefore the tide will not be changed by us. It will swallow up both us and our experiments. It will absorb the efforts at change and take them into itself as new but trivial components, and the great movement of tradition and work will go on unchanged by our fads and schemes. The things which will change it are the great discoveries and inventions, the new reactions inside the social organism, and the changes in the earth itself on account of changes in the cosmical forces. These causes will make of it just what, in fidelity to them, it ought to be. The men will be carried along with it and be made by it. The utmost they can do by their cleverness will be to note and record their course as they are carried along, which is what we do now, and is that which leads us to vain fancy that we can make or guide the movement. That is why it is the greatest folly of which a man can be capable, to sit down with a slate and pencil to plan out a new social world.

War and Other Essays, 1911

Motives and purposes are in the brain and heart of man. Consequences are in the world of fact.

The Forgotten Man

The state, it cannot too often be repeated, does nothing, and can give nothing, which it does not take from somebody.

Ibid.

Whenever A and B put their heads together and decide what A, B, and C must do for D, there is never any pressure on A and B. They consent to it and like it. There is rarely any pressure on D because he does not like it and contrives to evade it. The pressure all comes on C. Now, who is C? He is always the man who, if let alone, would make a reasonable use of his liberty without abusing it. He would not constitute any social problem at all and would not need any regulation. He is the Forgotten Man.

Ibid.

In the forum of reason and deliberation war never can be anything but a makeshift. . . . A statesman who proposes war as an instrumentality admits his incompetency; a politician who makes use of war as a counter in the game of parties is a criminal.

Essays, 1927

The great force for forging a society into a solid mass has always been war.

Ibid.

"Knowledge is power." Yes, that is what knowledge is. It is power and nothing more. As a power it is like wealth, talent, or any power, that is, it is without any moral element whatever. The moral question always comes in when we ask, in respect to the man who has power: What will he do with it?

Ibid.

To the individual . . . it is hard to realize that he is not needed here; that his existence, however interesting and important to himself, is of no consequence to the world; that if he had never been born he never would have been missed; that the men in all history who have proved by their life and works that the world did need them and could illy have spared them, are not more than a score or two.

Ibid.

Men never cling to their dreams with such tenacity as at the moment when they are losing faith in them, and know it, but do not dare to confess it to themselves.

Ibid.

I have never discarded beliefs deliberately. I left them in the drawer, and, after a while, when I opened it, there was nothing there at all.

Reminiscences

If we put together all that we have learned from anthropology and ethnology about primitive men and primitive society, we perceive that the first task of life is to live. Men begin with acts, not with thoughts.

The "strong" and the "weak" are terms which admit of no definition unless they are made equivalent to the industrious and the idle, the frugal and the extravagant. . . . If we do not like the survival of the fittest, we have only one possible alternative, and that is the survival of the unfittest. The former is the law of civilization; the latter is the law of anti-civilization.

EDWARD BELLAMY

Let but the famine-stricken nation assume the function it had neglected, and regulate for the common good the course of the life-giving stream [the production of goods flowing from the labor of men], and the earth would bloom like one garden, and none of its children lack any good thing.

Looking Backward, 2000–1887

THORSTEIN VEBLEN

The first requisite of a good servant is that he should conspicuously know his place. It is not enough that he knows how to effect certain desired mechanical results; he must, above all, know how to effect these results in due form. Domestic service might be said to be a spiritual rather than a mechanical function.

The Theory of the Leisure Class, 1899

Abstention from labor is not only an honorific or meritorious act, but it presently comes to be a requisite of decency. The insistence on property as the basis of reputability is very naive and very imperious during the early stages of the accumulation of wealth. Abstention from labor is the conventional evidence of wealth and is therefore the conventional mark of social standing; and this insistence on the meritoriousness of wealth leads to a more strenuous insistence on leisure. . . . According to well-established laws of human nature, prescription presently seizes upon this conventional evidence of wealth and fixes it in men's habits of thought as something that is in itself substantially meritorious and ennobling; while productive labor at the same time and by a like process becomes in a double sense intrinsically unworthy. Prescription ends by making labor not only disreputable in the eyes of the community, but morally impossible to the noble, freeborn man, and incompatible with a worthy life.

This tabu on labor has a further consequence in the industrial differentiation of classes. As the population increases in density and the predatory group grows into a settled industrial community, the constituted authorities and the customs governing ownership gain in scope and consistency.

It then presently becomes impracticable to accumulate wealth by simple seizure, and, in logical consistency, acquisition by industry is equally impossible for high-minded and impecunious men. The alternative open to them is beggary or privation. Wherever the canon of conspicuous leisure has a chance undisturbed to work out its tendency, there will therefore emerge a secondary, and in a sense spurious, leisure class—abjectly poor and living a precarious life of want and discomfort, but morally unable to stoop to gainful pursuits. . . . So, for instance, we are told of certain Polynesian chiefs, who, under the stress of good form, preferred to starve rather than carry their food to their mouths with their own hands. It is true, this conduct may have been due, at least in part, to an excessive sanctity or tabu attaching to the chief's person. The tabu would have been communicated by the contact of his hands, and so would have made anything touched by him unfit for human food. But the tabu is itself a derivative of the unworthiness or moral incompatibility of labor; so that even when construed in this sense the conduct of the Polynesian chiefs is truer to the canon of honorific leisure than would at first appear. A better illustration, or at least a more unmistakable one, is afforded by a certain king of France, who is said to have lost his life through an excess of moral stamina in the observance of good form. In the absence of the functionary whose office it was to shift his master's seat, the king sat uncomplaining before the fire and suffered his royal person to be toasted beyond recovery. But in so doing he saved his Most Christian Majesty from menial contamination.

Ibid.

The classics have scarcely lost in absolute value as a voucher of scholastic respectability, since for this purpose it is only necessary that the scholar should be able to put in evidence some learning which is conventionally recognized as evidence of wasted time.

Ibid.

In the case of those domestic animals which are honorific and are reputed beautiful, there is a subsidiary basis of merit that should be spoken of. Apart from the birds which belong in the honorific class of domestic animals, and which owe their place in this class to their non-lucrative character alone, the animals which merit particular attention are cats, dogs, and fast horses. The cat is less reputable than the other two just named, because she is less wasteful; she may even serve a useful end. At the same time the cat's temperament does not fit her for the honorific purpose. She lives with man on terms of equality, knows nothing of that relation of status which is the ancient basis of all distinctions of worth, honor, and repute, and she does not lend herself with facility to an invidious comparison between her owner and his neighbors. The exception to this last rule occurs in the case of such scarce and fanciful products as the Angora cat, which have some slight honorific value on the ground of expensiveness, and have, therefore, some special claim to beauty on pecuniary grounds.

The dog has advantages in the way of uselessness as well as in special gifts of temperament. He is often spoken of, in an eminent sense, as the friend of man, and his intelligence and fidelity are praised. The meaning of this is that the dog is man's servant and that he has the gift of an unquestioning subservience and a slave's quickness in guessing his master's mood. Coupled with these traits, which fit him well for the relation of status—and which must for the present purpose be set down as serviceable traits—the dog has some characteristics which are of a more equivocal aesthetic value. He is the filthiest of the domestic animals in his person and the nastiest in his habits. For this he makes up in a servile, fawning attitude towards his master, and a readiness to inflict damage and discomfort on all else. The dog, then, commends himself to our favor by affording play to our propensity for mastery, and as he is also an item of expense, and commonly serves no industrial purpose, he holds a well-assured place in men's regard as a thing of good repute. The dog is at the same time associated in our imagination with the chase—a meritorious employment and an expression of the honorable predatory impulse.

Standing on this vantage ground, whatever beauty of form and motion and whatever commendable mental traits he may possess are conventionally acknowledged and magnified. And even those varieties of the dog which have been bred into grotesque deformity by the dog-fancier are in good faith accounted beautiful by many. These varieties of dogs—and the like is true of other fancy-bred animals—are rated and graded in aesthetic value somewhat in proportion to the degree of grotesqueness and instability of the particular fashion which the deformity takes in the given case. For the purpose in hand, this differential utility on the ground of grotesqueness and instability of structure is reducible to terms of a greater scarcity and consequent expense. The commercial value of canine monstrosities, such as the prevailing styles of pet dogs both for men's and women's use, rests on their high cost of production, and their value to their owners lies chiefly in their utility as items of conspicuous consumption. Indirectly, through reflection upon their honorific expensiveness, a social worth is imputed to them; and so, by an easy substitution of words and ideas, they come to be admired and reputed beautiful. Since any attention bestowed upon these animals is in no sense gainful or useful, it is also reputable; and since the habit of giving them attention is consequently not deprecated, it may grow into an habitual attachment of great tenacity and of a most benevolent character. So that in the affection bestowed on pet animals the canon of expensiveness is present more or less remotely as a norm which guides and shapes the sentiment and selection of its object. The like is true . . . with respect to affection for persons also; although the manner in which the norm acts in that case is somewhat different.

Ibid.

The discipline of savage life has been by far the most protracted and probably the most exacting of any phase of culture in all the life-history of the race; so that by heredity human nature still is, and must indefinitely continue to be, savage human nature.

IRVING BABBITT

It is a quality of will that distinguishes man from physical nature and yet is natural in the sense that it is a matter of immediate perception and not of outer authority. The neglect of this quality of will by both utilitarians and sentimentalists has encouraged a sophistical definition of liberty—a type of liberty that owes its appeal to its flattery of spiritual indolence, perhaps the most fundamental human trait.

Democracy and Leadership, 1924

H. L. MENCKEN

A man's women folk, whatever their outward show of respect for his merit and authority, always regard him secretly as an ass, and with something akin to pity.

In Defence of Women, 1918

The smallest atom of truth represents some man's bitter toil and agony; for every ponderable chunk of it there is a brave truth-seeker's grave upon some lonely ash-heap and a soul roasting in hell.

Prejudices: First Series, 1919

The capacity for discerning the essential truth . . . is as rare among men

as it is common among crows, bullfrogs and mackerel. The man who
shows it is a man of quite extraordinary quality—perhaps even a man
downright diseased.

Ibid.

The impulse to create beauty is rather rare in literary men. . . . Far
ahead of it comes the yearning to make money. And after the yearning
to make money comes the yearning to make a noise.

Ibid.

To sum up:

1. The cosmos is a gigantic fly-wheel making 10,000 revolutions a
minute.

2. Man is a sick fly taking a dizzy ride on it.

3. Religion is the theory that the wheel was designed and set spinning
to give him the ride.

Ibid.

To die for an idea; it is unquestionably noble. But how much nobler it
would be if men died for ideas that were true!

Ibid.

The anthropomorphic theory of the world is made absurd by modern bi-
ology—but that is not saying, of course, that it will ever be abandoned by
the generality of men. To the contrary, they will cherish it in proportion
as it becomes more and more dubious. Today, indeed, it is cherished as
it was never cherished in the Ages of Faith, when the doctrine that man
was god-like was at least ameliorated by the doctrine that woman was
vile. What else is behind charity, philanthropy, pacifism, the uplift, all
the rest of the current sentimentalities? One and all, these sentimentalities
are based upon the notion that man is a glorious and ineffable animal,
and that his continued existence in the world ought to be facilitated and
insured. But this notion is obviously full of fatuity. As animals go, even in
so limited a space as our world, man is botched and ridiculous. Few other
brutes are so stupid or so cowardly. The commonest yellow dog has far
sharper senses and is infinitely more courageous, not to say more honest
and dependable. The ants and the bees are, in many ways, far more intelligent and ingenious; they manage their government with vastly less quarreling, wastefulness and imbecility. The lion is more beautiful, more
dignified, more majestic. The antelope is swifter and more graceful. The

ordinary house-cat is cleaner. The horse, foamed by labor, has a better smell. The gorilla is kinder to his children and more faithful to his wife. The ox and the ass are more industrious and serene. But most of all, man is deficient in courage, perhaps the noblest quality of them all. He is not only mortally afraid of all other animals of his own weight or half his weight—save a few that he has debased by artificial inbreeding—; he is even mortally afraid of his own kind—and not only of their fists and hooves, but even of their sniggers.

No other animal is so defectively adapted to its environment. The human infant, as it comes into the world, is so puny that if it were neglected for two days running it would infallibly perish, and this congenital infirmity, though more or less concealed later on, persists through life. Man is ill far more than any other animal, both in his savage state and under civilization. He has more different diseases and he suffers from them oftener. He is easily exhausted and injured. He dies more horribly and usually sooner. Practically all the other higher vertebrates, at least in their wild state, live longer and retain their faculties to a greater age. Here even the anthropoid apes are far beyond their human cousins. An orang-outang marries at the age of seven or eight, raises a family of seventy or eighty children, and is still as hale and hearty at eighty as a European at forty-five.

All the errors and incompetencies of the Creator reach their climax in man. As a piece of mechanism he is the worst of them all; put beside him, even a salmon or a staphylococcus is a sound and efficient machine. He has the worst kidneys known to comparative zoology, and the worst lungs, and the worst heart. His eye, considering the work it is called upon to do, is less efficient than the eye of an earthworm; an optical instrument maker who made an instrument so clumsy would be mobbed by his customers. Alone of all animals, terrestrial, celestial or marine, man is unfit by nature to go abroad in the world he inhabits. He must clothe himself, protect himself, swathe himself, armor himself. He is eternally in the position of a turtle born without a shell, a dog without hair, a fish without fins. Lacking his heavy and cumbersome trappings, he is defenseless even against flies. As God made him he hasn't even a tail to switch them off.

I now come to man's one point of unquestionable natural superiority: he has a soul. This is what sets him off from all other animals, and makes him, in a way, their master. The exact nature of that soul has been in dispute for thousands of years, but regarding its function it is possible to speak with some authority. That function is to bring man into direct contact with God, to make him aware of God, above all, to make him resemble God. Well, consider the colossal failure of the device. If we assume that man actually does resemble God, then we are forced into the impossible theory that God is a coward, an idiot and a bounder. And if we assume that man, after all these years, does *not* resemble God, then it appears at once that the human soul is as inefficient a machine as the human liver or tonsil, and that man would probably be better off, as the chimpanzee undoubtedly *is* better off, without it.

Such, indeed, is the case. The only practical effect of having a soul is that it fills man with anthropomorphic and anthropocentric vanities—in brief, with cocky and preposterous superstitions. He struts and plumes himself because he has this soul—and overlooks the fact that it doesn't work. Thus he is the supreme clown of creation, the *reductio ad absurdum* of animated nature. He is like a cow who believed that she could jump over the moon, and ordered her whole life upon that theory. He is like a bullfrog boasting eternally of fighting lions, of flying over the Matterhorn, of swimming the Hellespont. And yet this is the poor brute we are asked to venerate as a gem in the forehead of the cosmos. This is the worm we are asked to defend as God's favorite on earth, with all its millions of braver, nobler, decenter quadrupeds—its superb lions, its lithe and gallant leopards, its imperial elephants, its honest dogs, its courageous rats. This is the insect we are besought, at infinite trouble, labor and expense, to reproduce.

Prejudices: Third Series, 1922

The older I grow the more I distrust the familiar doctrine that age brings wisdom.

Ibid.

The double standard of morality will survive in this world so long as a woman whose husband has been lured away is favored with the sympathetic tears of other women, and a man whose wife has made off is laughed at by other men.

Ibid.

Marriage, as everyone knows, is chiefly an economic matter. But too often it is assumed that its economy concerns only the wife's hats; it also concerns, and perhaps more importantly, the husband's cigars. No man is genuinely happy, married, who has to drink worse whiskey than he used to drink when he was single.

Prejudices: Fourth Series, 1924

Nothing can come out of an artist that is not in the man.

Prejudices: Fifth Series, 1926

In the long run all battles are lost, and so are all wars.

A Mencken Chrestomathy, 1949

When women kiss it always reminds one of prize-fighters shaking hands.

Ibid.

Man weeps to think that he will die so soon; woman, that she was born so long ago.

Ibid.

Optimist:—The sort of man who marries his sister's best friend.

Ibid.

Women have simple tastes. They can get pleasure out of the conversation of children in arms and men in love.

Ibid.

The difference between a moral man and a man of honor is that the latter regrets a discreditable act even when it has worked.

Ibid.

Love is the delusion that one woman differs from another.

Ibid.

Husbands never become good; they merely become proficient.

Ibid.

Conscience is the inner voice that warns us somebody may be looking.

Ibid.

Men are the only animals that devote themselves, day in and day out, to making one another unhappy. It is an art like any other. Its virtuosi are called altruists.

Ibid.

Self-Respect:—The secure feeling that no one, as yet, is suspicious.

Ibid.

Wife:—One who is sorry she did it, but would undoubtedly do it again.

Ah, that the eugenists would breed a woman as capable of laughter as the girl of twenty, and as adept at knowing when not to laugh as the woman of thirty-five.

Opera in English is, in the main, just about as sensible as baseball in Italian.

Archbishop: a Christian ecclesiastic of a rank superior to that attained by Christ.

A church is a place in which gentlemen who have never been to heaven brag about it to persons who will never get there.

Let us not burn the universities—yet. After all, the damage they do might be worse. . . . Suppose Oxford had snared and disemboweled Shakespeare! Suppose Harvard had rammed its buttermilk into Mark Twain!

A superior man's struggle in the world is not with exterior lions, trusts, margraves, policemen, rivals in love, German spies, radicals and tornadoes, but with the obscure, atavistic impulses within him—the impulses, weaknesses and limitations that war with his notion of what life should be. Nine times out of ten he succumbs. Nine times out of ten he must yield to the dead hand. Nine times out of ten his aspiration is almost infinitely above his achievement. The result is that we see him sliding downhill— his ideals breaking up, his hope petering out, his character in decay. Character in decay is thus the theme of the great bulk of superior fiction.

Man makes love by braggadocio. Woman makes love by listening—once a woman passes a certain point in intelligence she finds it almost impossible to get a husband: she simply cannot go on listening without snickering.

The way to hold a husband is to keep him a little bit jealous. The way to lose him is to keep him a little bit more jealous.

A woman usually respects her father, but her view of her husband is mingled with contempt, for she is of course privy to the transparent devices by which she snared him.

A gentleman is one who never strikes a woman without provocation.

I go on working for the same reason that a hen goes on laying eggs.

Life is pleasant and I have enjoyed it, but I have no yearning to clutter up the Universe after it is over.

THOMAS BEER

Perhaps historians may yet discover that success is just a form of amusement, mostly sacred to those who have not brains enough to atttain it.

Hanna, 1929

ALVIN JOHNSON

It is commonly assumed that revolutions are periods of accelerated social evolution, but the assumption is doubtful.

LEWIS E. LAWES

Never give a man up until he has failed at something he likes.

PHILIP WYLIE

One thing is sure. The pulpit cannot beat prophylaxis. It failed to beat even golf. The age of innocence is done for.

Generation of Vipers, 1942

We're about to enter the age of flight before we've even developed a chair that a man can sit in comfortably.

MORTON CLURMAN

Every trade in every age has its special delusions, and a major affliction of social science today might be called the IBM fallacy. This delusion reflects the endemic conviction of 20th-century man that machines can do everything for him—including thinking. In the case of the social scientist it takes the form of a certainty that if you feed enough data through enough electrical circuits what you are looking for is bound to come out. The corollary of this hypothesis is the conviction that only a minimum of human cerebration need be combined with a maximum of electronics to produce miraculous results.

But little fallacies survive and multiply in the shadow of big ones. The belief in the omnipotent machine is supported by the idea that the social sciences can attain the same exactitude as the natural sciences, with help of the statistician and his machine. This idea, in turn, depends on a mistaken notion of how data are used in the natural sciences. Like the movie cowboy who is almost never seen herding cattle, the physicist or chemist is too often pictured collecting or processing data amid a jungle of laboratory gadgets, and seldom in that crucial act of scientific creation—thinking. The laboratory experiment, or natural observation, which are analogous to the collection and processing of data in the social sciences, are simply ways of verifying the scientist's hypothesis. They cannot create a hypothesis, only confirm one. Where that hypothesis comes from, God may know, but certainly no one else does. Where it doesn't come from, however, is a machine or any specific body of data. If it did, scientific creation would be possible for almost any high school boy.

Commentary, June, 1953

*VII. The Educators
from Horace Mann to Nathan Pusey*

Horace Mann

Be ashamed to die until you have won some victory for humanity!

> "Commencement Address," Antioch College, 1859

A house without books is like a room without windows.

Lost, yesterday, somewhere between sunrise and sunset, two golden hours, each set with sixty diamond minutes. No reward is offered for they are gone forever.

Charles W. Eliot

Electricity—carrier of light and power, devourer of time and space, bearer of human speech over land and sea, greatest servant of man, itself unknown.

> Inscription, Union Station, Washington, D.C.

A. Lawrence Lowell

Profound student of the social life of insects, who has shown that they also can maintain complex communities without the use of reason.

> Of William Morton Wheeler, conferring upon him the degree of Doctor of Science, Harvard, 1930

Universities are full of knowledge; the freshmen bring a little in and the seniors take none away, and knowledge accumulates.

Dealing with the concrete does not lead to knowledge of the abstract.

You can do a thing or you can get the credit for it, but you can't have both.

A tale is told of a man in Paris during the upheaval in 1848, who saw a friend marching after a crowd toward the barricades. Warning him that these could not be held against the troops, that he had better keep away, and asking why he followed these people, he received the reply, "I must follow them. I am their leader."

George Lyman Kittredge

My dear sir, who could examine me?
>When asked why, though he was such a great scholar, he did not have a Ph.D.

Charles Townsend Copeland

To eat is human; to digest, divine.

Charles D. McIver

When you educate a man you educate an individual; when you educate a woman you educate a whole family.
>Address, North Carolina College for Women

Nicholas Murray Butler

An expert is one who knows more and more about less and less.
>Robert M. Hutchins, *The Conflict in Education,* 1953, remarked that "in the United States we have discovered that [the specialist] can be a man who learns less and less about less and less."

One of the embarrassments of being a gentleman is that you are not permitted to be violent in asserting your rights.

Time was invented by Almighty God in order to give ideas a chance.

All the problems of the world could be settled easily if men were only willing to think. The trouble is that men very often resort to all sorts of devices in order not to think, because thinking is such hard work.

William Allan Neilson

Not one student in a thousand breaks down from overwork.

J. E. Spingarn

Men, women, and professors.

ALBERT GUÉRARD

Chivalry is the most delicate form of contempt.

Bottle in the Sea, 1954

LYMAN BRYSON

We are restless because of incessant change, but we would be frightened if change were stopped.

The Drive Toward Reason, 1954

We have provided for the survival of man against all enemies except his fellow man.

Ibid.

Youth thinks intelligence a good substitute for experience, and his elders think experience a substitute for intelligence.

Ibid.

JACOB VINER

Men are not narrow in their intellectual interests by nature; it takes special and vigorous training to accomplish that end.

A Modest Proposal for Some Stress on Scholarship in Graduate Training, 1953

JAMES BRYANT CONANT

Behold the turtle. He makes progress only when he sticks his neck out.

ROBERT M. HUTCHINS

I once knew a student who boasted that he had graduated from college without taking any course that was offered above the first floor.

The Conflict in Education, 1953

To destroy the Western tradition of independent thought it is not necessary to burn the books. All we have to do is to leave them unread for a couple of generations.

Ibid.

A college teaches; a university both teaches and learns.

It is not so important to be serious as it is to be serious about the important things. The monkey wears an expression of seriousness which would do credit to any college student, but the monkey is serious because he itches.

Too few have the courage of my convictions.

Whenever I feel like exercise, I lie down until the feeling goes away.

A. WHITNEY GRISWOLD

Wisdom and virtue cannot be forced from a crowd as eggs from chickens under electric lights. There is no such thing as general intelligence. There is only individual intelligence communicating itself to other individual intelligences. And there is no such thing as public morality. There is only a composite of private morality.

JACQUES BARZUN

Let us be clear about the role of the classics: they are worth studying as examples of *how* to think, not of *what* to think. We shall be acting most like Dante or Newton or Pascal if we think thoughts very different from theirs, but having the same potency for our times that their thoughts had for their times. This does not exclude adoption and adaptation of former wisdom, it merely stresses the need for rethinking against rehashing. The intellectual life justifies itself when, having embraced the common facts, it asks and answers the question, "What does it all mean?" There lies the true responsibility of the scholar—not to a ritual but to the reality of a subject.

Teacher in America, 1943

Pascal once said that all the trouble in the world was due to the fact that man could not sit still in a room. He must hunt, flirt, gamble, chatter. That is man's destiny and it is not to be quarreled with, but the educated man has through the ages found a way to convert passionate activity into a silent and motionless pleasure. He can sit in a room and not perish.

Life, October 16, 1950

Ideology is to genuine ideas what processed cheese is to the real thing.

God's Country and Mine, 1954

NATHAN M. PUSEY

The best teacher is not life, but the crystallized and distilled experience of the most sensitive, reflective, and most observant of our human beings, and this experience you will find preserved in our great books and nowhere else.

VIII. Words and Opinions
of Jurists and Lawyers

John Marshall

That the power of taxing [the bank] by the States may be exercised so as to destroy it, is too obvious to be denied. . . . That the power to tax involves the power to destroy [is] not to be denied.

McCulloch v. *Maryland,* 1819

Rufus Choate

History shows you prospects by starlight, or, at best, by the waning moon.

New England History

Chauncey Depew

A pessimist is a man who thinks all women are bad.
An optimist is a man who hopes they are.

I am not at all superstitious, but I would not sleep thirteen in a bed on a Friday night.

I get my exercise acting as pallbearer to my friends who exercise.

Oliver Wendell Holmes, Jr.

The life of the law has not been logic: it has been experience. The felt necessities of the time, the prevalent moral and political theories, intuitions of public policy, avowed or unconscious, even the prejudices which judges share with their fellow-men, have had a good deal more to do than the syllogism in determining the rules by which men should be governed. The law embodies the story of a nation's development through many centuries, and it cannot be dealt with as if it contained only the axioms and corollaries of a book of mathematics. In order to know what it is, we must know what it has been, and what it tends to become. We must alternately consult history and existing theories of legislation. But the most difficult labor will be to understand the combination of the two into new products at every stage. The substance of the law at any given time pretty nearly corresponds, so far as it goes, with what is then understood to be convenient; but its form and machinery, and the degree to which it is able to work out desired results, depend very much upon its past.

The Common Law, 1881

No man has earned the right to intellectual ambition until he has learned to lay his course by a star which he has never seen,—to dig by the divining rod for springs which he may never reach. In saying this, I point to that which will make your study heroic. For I say to you in all sadness of conviction, that to think great thoughts you must be heroes as well as idealists. Only when you have worked alone,—when you have felt around you a black gulf of solitude more isolating than that which surrounds the dying man, and in hope and in despair have trusted to your own unshaken will,—then only can you gain the secret isolated joy of the thinker, who knows that, a hundred years after he is dead and forgotten, men who have never heard of him will be moving to the measure of his thought,— the subtle rapture of a postponed power, which the world knows not because it has no external trappings, but which to his prophetic vision is more real than that which commands an army. And if this joy should not be yours, still it is only thus that you can know that you have done what it lay in you to do,—can say that you have lived, and be ready for the end.

"The Profession of the Law," Harvard lecture, 1886

There were few of the charts and lights for which one longed when I began. One found oneself plunged in a thick fog of details—in a black and frozen night, in which were no flowers, no spring, no easy joys. Voices of authority warned that in the crush of that ice any craft might sink. One heard Burke saying that law sharpens the mind by narrowing it. One heard in Thackeray of a lawyer bending all the powers of a great mind to a mean profession. One saw that artists and poets shrank from it as from an alien world. One doubted oneself how it could be worthy of the interest of an intelligent mind. And yet one said to oneself, law is human—it is a part of man, and of one world with the rest.

Address, 1897

The great act of faith is when man decides that he is not God.

To William James, 1907

If I am right it will be a slow business for our people to reach rational views, assuming that we are allowed to work peaceably to that end. But as I grow older I grow calm. If I feel what are perhaps an old man's apprehensions, that competition from new races will cut deeper than working men's disputes and will test whether we can hang together and can fight; if I fear that we are running through the world's resources at a pace that we cannot keep; I do not lose my hopes. I do not pin my dreams for the future to my country or even to my race. I think it probable that civilization somehow will last as long as I care to look ahead—perhaps with smaller numbers, but perhaps also bred to greatness and splendor by science. I think it not improbable that man, like the grub that prepares a chamber for the winged thing it never has seen but is to be—that man may have cosmic destinies that he does not understand. And so beyond the vision of battling races and an impoverished earth I catch a dreaming glimpse of peace.

The other day my dream was pictured to my mind. It was evening. I was walking homeward on Pennsylvania Avenue near the Treasury, and as I looked beyond Sherman's Statue to the west the sky was aflame with scarlet and crimson from the setting sun. But, like the note of downfall in Wagner's opera, below the sky line there came from little globes the pallid discord of the electric lights. And I thought to myself the *Götterdämmerung* will end, and from those globes clustered like evil eggs will come the new masters of the sky. It is like the time in which we live. But then I remembered the faith that I partly have expressed, faith in a universe not measured by our fears, a universe that has thought and more than thought inside of it, and as I gazed, after the sunset and above the electric lights, there shone the stars.

Speech, New York, February 15, 1913

The Common Law is not a brooding omnipresence in the sky, but the articulate voice of some sovereign or quasi-sovereign that can be identified.

1916

I used to say, when I was young, that truth was the majority vote of that nation that could lick all others. Certainly we may expect that the received opinion about the present war will depend a good deal upon which side wins (I hope with all my soul it will be mine), and I think that the statement was correct in so far as it implied that our test of truth is a reference to either a present or an imagined future majority in favor of our view. If, as I have suggested elsewhere, the truth may be defined as the system of my (intellectual) limitations, which gives it objectivity, it is the fact that I find my fellow man to a greater or less extent (never wholly) subject to the same *Can't Helps*. If I think that I am sitting at a table, I find that the other persons present agree with me; so if I say that the sum of the angles of a triangle is equal to two right angles. If I am in a minority of one, they send for a doctor or lock me up; and I am so far able to transcend the to me convincing testimony of my senses or my rea-

son as to recognise that if I am alone probably something is wrong with
my works.

Letter written during World War I

A word is not a crystal, transparent and unchanged, it is the skin of a
living thought and may vary greatly in color and content according to
the circumstances and the time in which it is used.

Towne vs. Eisner, 1918

A platitude has come home to me with *quasi* religious force. I was repining at the thought of my slow progress—how few new ideas I had or
picked up—when it occurred to me to think of the total of life and how
the greater part was wholly absorbed in living and continuing life—vic-
tuals—procreation—rest and eternal terror. And I bid myself accept the
common lot; an adequate vitality would say daily: "God—what a good
sleep I've had." "My eye, that was a dinner." "Now for a rattling walk—"
in short, realize life as an end in itself. Functioning is all there is—only
our keenest pleasure is in what we might call the higher sort. I wonder if
cosmically an idea is any more important than the bowels.

Letter to Sir Frederick Pollock, August 21, 1919

I dare say that I have worked off my fundamental formula on you that
the chief end of man is to frame general propositions and that no general
proposition is worth a damn.

Ibid., 1920

I repeat my old aphorism that everything is founded on the death of men
—society, which only changes the mode of killing—romance, to which
centuries, that is generations, of dead, on the memorial tablets of a great
war are necessary.

Letter to Harold Laski, January 14, 1920

[I have] faith in a universe that has thought and more than thought
inside of it. . . . I think it not improbable that man, like the grub that
prepares a chamber for the winged thing it has never seen but is to be,
that man may have cosmic destinies that he does not understand.

Collected Legal Papers, 1920

Philosophy does not furnish motives, but it shows men that they are not
fools for doing what they already want to do.

Ibid., "The Natural Law"

The ideas of the classics, so far as living, are our commonplaces. It is the modern books that give us the latest and most profound conceptions. It seems to me rather a lazy makeshift to mumble over the familiar.

Letter to C. C. Wu, 1925

It seems to me that the whole scheme of salvation depends on having a required modicum of intelligence. People are born fools and damned for not being wiser. I often say over to myself the verse, "O God, be merciful to me a fool," the fallacy of which to my mind (you won't agree with me) is in the "me," that it looks on man as a little God over against the universe, instead of as a cosmic ganglion, a momentary intersection of what humanly speaking we call streams of energy, such as gives white light at one point and the power of making syllogisms at another, but always an inseparable part of the unimaginable, in which we live and move and have our being, no more needing its mercy than my little toe needs mine. It would be well if the intelligent classes could forget the word sin and think less of being good. We learn how to behave as lawyers, soldiers, merchants, or what not by being them. Life, not the person, teaches conduct.

Letter to Sir Frederick Pollock, 1926

The riders in a race do not stop when they reach the goal. There is a little finishing canter before coming to a standstill. There is time to hear the kind voice of friends and to say to one's self: "The work is done." But just as one says that, the answer comes: "The race is over, but the work never is done while the power to work remains." The canter that brings you to a standstill need not be only coming to rest. It cannot be, while you still live. For to live is to function. That is all there is in living.

Radio address on his ninetieth birthday, March 8, 1931

Life seems to me like a Japanese picture which our imagination does not allow to end with the margin. We aim at the infinite and when the arrow falls to earth it is in flames.

February 29, 1932

I never read a Socialist yet from Karl Marx down, and I have read a number, that I didn't think talked drool. Nor do I expect to hear anything better from anyone who hopes to regenerate society via property.

Holmes-Laski Letters

The joy of life consists in the neglect of opportunities. . . . He who makes the most of himself doesn't make much.

Ibid.

An epitome of my life: my first book ends (designedly) with the word "explained"—my last with the word "unknown."

Ibid.

I have no respect for the passion for equality, which seems to me merely idealizing envy.

Ibid.

I think pragmatism an amusing humbug—like most of William James's speculations, as distinguished from his admirable and well written Irish perceptions of life. They all of them seem to me of the type of his answer to prayer in the subliminal consciousness—the spiritualist's promise of a miracle if you will turn down the gas. As I have said so often, all I mean by truth is what I can't help thinking.

Holmes-Pollock Letters

Only man among the creatures of the earth strives to penetrate the unknown and to understand the unknowable. . . . This endless aerial pursuit is our fate, as truly as to bear offspring or to toil for bread. This passion is as genuine and as self-justifying as any other.

Speech

Deep-seated preferences cannot be argued about—you cannot argue a man into liking a glass of beer—and therefore, when differences are sufficiently far-reaching, we try to kill the other man rather than let him have his way. But that is perfectly consistent with admitting that, so far as appears, his grounds are just as good as ours.

The joy of life is to put out one's power in some natural and useful or harmless way. There is no other. And the real misery is not to do this.

I think the best image for a man is an electric light—the spark feels isolated and independent but really is only a moment in a current.

The vindication of the obvious is sometimes more important than the elucidation of the obscure.

Historic continuity with the past is not a duty, it is only a necessity.

Any two philosophers can tell each other all they know in two hours.

I have always sought to guide the future—but it is very lonely sometimes trying to play God.

Oh, to be sixty again!

> Viewing a pretty girl at the age of eighty-seven. Attributed to Holmes.

Louis D. Brandeis

I never read anything on the immortality of the soul, and I admit having read but little on the subject, that convinced me of its truth. What surprises me is that men should be longing for an afterlife in which there would apparently be nothing to do except to delight in heaven's wonders. For, as the theologians have pictured the afterlife, man will be there *sine* body and his soul will rejoin the Deity. If this is so then intellectual pursuits will come to an end with bodily exertions, for, as a part of the Deity, man will be in possession of all knowledge, leaving nothing to occupy him except some kind of spiritual enjoyment. But enjoyment, I thought, was more pagan than Jewish or Christian.

> *The Words of Justice Brandeis,* 1953

Clarence Darrow

I do not consider it an insult, but rather a compliment to be called an agnostic. I do not pretend to know where many ignorant men are sure—that is all that agnosticism means.

> At Scopes trial, Dayton, Tennessee, July 13, 1925

Everybody is a potential murderer. I've never killed anyone, but I frequently get satisfaction reading the obituary notices.

> Interview, Chicago, April 18, 1937

There is no such thing as justice—in or out of court.

> *Ibid.,* April 18, 1936

I don't believe in God because I don't believe in Mother Goose.

I have suffered from being misunderstood, but I would have suffered a hell of a lot more if I had been understood.

BENJAMIN NATHAN CARDOZO

Not lightly vacated are the verdicts of quiescent years.

JOHN M. WOOLSEY

If Joyce did not attempt to be honest in developing the technique which he has adopted in "Ulysses" the result would be psychologically misleading and thus unfaithful to his chosen technique. Such an attitude would be artistically inexcusable.

It is because Joyce has been loyal to his technique and has not funked its necessary implications, but has honestly attempted to tell fully what his characters think about, that he has been the subject of so many attacks and that his purpose has been so often misunderstood and misrepresented. For his attempt sincerely and honestly to realize his objective has required him incidentally to use certain words which are generally considered dirty words and has led at times to what many think is a too poignant preoccupation with sex in the thoughts of his characters.

The words which are criticized as dirty are old Saxon words known to almost all men and, I venture, to many women, and are such words as would be naturally and habitually used, I believe, by the types of folk whose life, physical and mental, Joyce is seeking to describe. In respect of the recurrent emergence of the theme of sex in the minds of his characters, it must always be remembered that his locale was Celtic and his season Spring.

. . . I am quite aware that owing to some of its scenes "Ulysses" is a rather strong draught to ask some sensitive, though normal, persons to take. But my considered opinion, after long reflection, is that whilst in many places the effect of "Ulysses" on the reader undoubtedly is somewhat emetic, nowhere does it tend to be an aphrodisiac.

"Ulysses" may, therefore, be admitted into the United States.

Judgment in *U.S.* v. *One Book Called "Ulysses,"* 1933

FELIX FRANKFURTER

It simply is not true that war never settles anything.

ROBERT H. JACKSON

The idea that a State, any more than a corporation, commits crimes is a fiction. Crimes always are committed only by persons.

Opening remarks at trial of Nazi war leaders, Nuremberg

CURTIS BOK

We are a very moral nation, and our high divorce rate has little to do with it. The primary cause of divorce is marriage, not sexual irregularity, and divorce will not slacken until we learn better how to marry.

Radio talk, March 29, 1953

In the whole history of law and order the longest step forward was taken by primitive man, when, as if by common consent, the tribe sat down in a circle and allowed one man to speak at a time. An accused who is shouted down has no rights whatever. Unless people have an instinct for procedure, their conception of basic human rights is a waste of effort, and wherever we see a negation of those rights it can be traced to a lack, an inadequacy, or a violation of procedure. Hence procedure effectively comes first: the mechanics of argument and discovery are often set up before the rights they serve take full form in practice.

Address, National Book Awards, New York, Jan. 26, 1954

We are so fearful of other people's morals; they so seldom have the courage of our own convictions.

Commonwealth v. *Gordon*

FRANK J. DONAHUE

The book . . . acts like a soporific rather than an aphrodisiac. While conducive to sleep it is not conducive to a desire to sleep with a member of the opposite sex.

Deciding that *Forever Amber* was dull but not obscene and therefore could be sold in Massachusetts, 1947

IX. Journalists and Publicists

Thomas Paine

War involves in its progress such a train of unforeseen and unsupposed circumstances that no human being can calculate the end. It has but one thing certain, and that is to increase taxes.

Prospects on the Rubicon, 1787

A man may write himself out of reputation when nobody else can do it.

The Rights of Man, 1791–92

The world is my country, all mankind are my brethren, and to do good is my religion.

Ibid.

George D. Prentice

A dishonest critic, by severing passages from their context, may make the best book appear to condemn itself. A book, thus unfairly treated, may be compared to the laurel—there is honor in the leaves but poison in the extract.

Louisville *Journal*

Frederick S. Cozzens

Proverbs may be called the literature of the illiterate.

Sayings, Wise and Otherwise, 1880

Horace Greeley

The darkest hour of any man's life is when he sits down to plan how to get money without earning it.

Charles Dudley Warner

What a man needs in gardening is a cast-iron back, with a hinge in it.

My Summer in a Garden, 1870

Broad acres are a patent of nobility; and no man but feels more of a man in the world if he have a bit of ground that he can call his own. However small it is on the surface, it is four thousand miles deep; and that is a very handsome property.

Ibid.

The thing generally raised on city land is taxes.

Ibid.

Everybody talks about the weather, but nobody does anything about it.

> Attributed to, c. 1890. The sentence is not found in the files of the Hartford *Courant,* which Warner edited (1861–1900).

Anonymous

There was a blow. Somebody fell. We got up. Turning upon our antagonist, we then succeeded in winding his arms around our waist, and by a quick manoeuvre threw him on top of us, bringing our back at the same time in contact with the bed of the printing press. Then, inserting our nose between his teeth, and our hands in his hair, we had him.

> Attributed to an unnamed Iowa editor, c. 1885

Frank Church

Not believe in Santa Claus! You might as well not believe in fairies. . . . Nobody sees Santa Claus, but that is no sign there is no Santa Claus. The most real things in the world are those which neither children nor men can see. No Santa Claus! Thank God! he lives and he lives forever.

> "Is There a Santa Claus?", New York *Sun,* 1897

John Maxwell

Life is a god-damned stinking, treacherous game, and nine hundred and ninety-nine men out of every thousand are bastards.

> To Theodore Dreiser. Maxwell was copy editor of the Chicago *Globe* when Dreiser came to Chicago in 1892.

Elbert Hubbard

Bohème is not down on the map because it is not a money-order office.

The Philistine

It is not book learning young men need, nor instruction about this and that, but a stiffening of the vertebrae which will cause them to be loyal to a trust, to act promptly, concentrate their energies, do a thing—"carry a message to Garcia."

> "A Message to Garcia," first printed in *The Philistine*, 1900

Polygamy: An endeavor to get more out of life than there is in it.

> *Roycroft Dictionary and Book of Epigrams*, 1923

As a career, the business of an orthodox preacher is about as successful as that of a celluloid dog chasing an asbestos cat through Hell.

> *Ibid.*

There are two kinds of discontent in this world: the discontent that works, and the discontent that wrings its hands. The first gets what it wants, and the second loses what it had. There is no cure for the first but success, and there is no cure at all for the second.

> *Scrapbook*

One machine can do the work of fifty ordinary men. No machine can do the work of one extraordinary man.

Initiative is doing the right thing without being told.

Genius may have its limitations but stupidity is not thus handicapped.

Keep away from that wheelbarrow—what the hell do you know about machinery?

> Attributed to Hubbard by Eugene Manlove Rhodes

Arthur Brisbane

The fence around a cemetery is foolish, for those inside can't get out and those outside don't want to get in.

> *The Book of Today*, 1923

Tom Masson

"Be yourself!" is about the worst advice you can give to some people.

Hamlet is the tragedy of tackling a family problem too soon after college.

WILLIAM ALLEN WHITE

One grandmother will spoil a baby. Two working together will bring him up in the way he should go, for each will suspect the other of spoiling him and will check it.

Autobiography, 1946

JOHN W. RAPER

Dignity is the quality that enables a man who says nothing, does nothing and knows nothing to command a great deal of respect.

What This World Needs, 1954

If tombstones told the truth, everybody would wish to be buried at sea.

Ibid.

There is no sense in having an argument with a man so stupid he doesn't know you have the better of him.

Ibid.

If you wish to know whether or not you have been licked, turn around and count the number of persons following you.

Ibid.

Hit the ball over the fence and you can take your time going around the bases.

Ibid.

Do you wish to be remembered? Leave a lot of debts.

Ibid.

EMILY POST

If God intended for women to wear slacks, He would have constructed them differently.

MARY WILSON LITTLE

Men who make no pretensions to being good on one day out of seven are called sinners.

There is no pleasure in having nothing to do; the fun is in having lots to do and not doing it.

H. L. GOLD

You might say that humanity's slogan is, "The obvious we see eventually; the completely apparent takes longer."

Galaxy Science Fiction, April, 1953

FRANKLIN PIERCE ADAMS

An illness is upon me, yet none will grant me sympathies, albeit my head is like to brast and my brain is as it were a colliflower. My wife calleth me craven and saith, do I have a cold I fear lest it be my death. Which is true, for albeit I fear the Reaper not at all, yet is this life, imperfect though it be, so sweet I am loth to quit it, and am dizzy to think of all I may not see an hundred years hence.

Diary of Our Own Samuel Pepys, December 2, 1911

My heart is soft as any melon.

Ibid., December 28, 1911

Found this day many a gray hair on the left side of my head, and am growing old, as the song hath it, which thinking of, I to my harmonicka and play, very sweet and sad.

Ibid., April 2, 1912

This day cloudy and rainy. Meditating all the morning upon Life and its purpose, yet am come to no conclusion, save that it is worth its so-great cost.

Ibid., September 29, 1912

And I did read until my eyes were weary, and would have read longer, save for thinking of how old Samuel's eyes failed him in 1676, and for that I have no desire, forasmuch as there are so many things I am fain yet for seeing and so many more I have not yet seen at all.

Ibid., October 1, 1913

Those days [of Lincoln] seem full of greatness and romance and adventure, yet I doubt that they were as wonderful as our own days, here in the office, did we but know it.

Ibid., January 1, 1916

She very pretty and gay, and told me again she thought I was a good man, and was astonished it did not anger me, which it did not, but pleased me greatly.

Ibid., December 13, 1922

Lord! I hear a deal of arguing these days, yet never do I hear that anybody is convinced of anything he did not believe already. Nobody, that is, save myself, I being so fair-minded that anybody can convince me of anything, but some do say that is not fair-mindedness, but spinelessness.

Ibid., May 3, 1926

Two plus two are four when one is a child, and they will be four when one is dead; but it is not well to think that about life, for life and love and happiness and hatred vary from day to day, and even words mean one thing on Monday and another on Tuesday.

Ibid., June 15, 1926

As to knowing that my thoughts and feelings are to be read, that perturbs me no whit, forasmuch as no man in his writings can conceal the fact that he is a hero and a coward and a fool, and no matter how cunningly he writeth there are things he cannot conceal; and no matter how candidly he writeth, there are things he cannot exhibit or disclose.

Ibid., November 27, 1926

The average man is a great deal above the average.

Attributed to Adams by Adlai Stevenson, 1952

O. O. MᴄIɴᴛʏʀᴇ

There are no illegitimate children: there are only illegitimate parents.

Before the New York Legislature

Dᴀᴍᴏɴ Rᴜɴʏᴏɴ

It may be that the race is not always to the swift, nor the battle to the strong—but that's the way to bet.

Nothing between humans is one to three. In fact, I long ago came to the conclusion that all life is six to five against.

HEYWOOD BROUN

The ability to make love frivolously is the chief characteristic which distinguishes human beings from the beasts.

It Seems to Me, 1933

Hell is paved with great granite blocks hewn from the hearts of those who said, "I can do no other."

Syndicated column, January 20, 1934

Obscenity is such a tiny kingdom that a single tour covers it completely.

Repartee is what you wish you'd said.

PAUL ELDRIDGE

Man is ready to die for an idea, provided that idea is not quite clear to him.

FREDERICK LEWIS ALLEN

Romance cannot be put into quantity production—the moment love becomes casual, it becomes commonplace.

Only Yesterday, 1931

ELMER DAVIS

The Scottish scientist J. B. S. Haldane once said that the people who can make a positive contribution to human progress are few; that most of us have to be satisfied with merely staving off the inroads of chaos. That is a hard enough job—especially in these times, when those inroads are more threatening than they have been for a long time past. But if we can stave them off, and keep the field clear for the creative intelligence, we can feel that we have done our part toward helping the human race get ahead.

This I Believe

GERALD W. JOHNSON

Nothing changes more constantly than the past; for the past that influences our lives does not consist of what actually happened, but of what men believe happened.

American Heroes and Hero-Worship

BENJAMIN STOLBERG

An expert is a person who avoids the small errors as he sweeps on to the grand fallacy.

RICHARD MANEY

A critic is a gentleman who reports his prejudices and his preferences in such English as he is equipped with.

WESTBROOK PEGLER

I am a member of the rabble in good standing.

The Lynching Story

DOROTHY THOMPSON

The mother of a friend of mine died the other day. My friend's eleven-year-old daughter was sent away until after the funeral. She must be spared a knowledge of death. Is this not characteristic of our society? We treat death as if it were an aberration. Age approaches but beauticians, masseurs and gland specialists co-operate to keep alive the illusion that we are not really growing older. Anything that reminds us of the inescapable fact that we are to die seems morbid to us. Yet without the serene acceptance of death as inexorable we lose all the magic and wonder of life and live in constant unconscious fear. For only when one is no longer afraid to die is one no longer afraid at all. And only when we are no longer afraid do we begin to live in every experience, painful or joyous; to live in gratitude for every moment, to live abundantly.

New York *Herald Tribune*

HERBERT AGAR

Snobs talk as if they had begotten their own ancestors.

LILLIAN SMITH

To believe in something not yet proved and to underwrite it with our lives: it is the only way we can leave the future open. Man, surrounded by facts, permitting himself no surmise, no intuitive flash, no great hypothesis, no risk is in a locked cell. Ignorance cannot seal the mind and imagination more surely. To find the point where hypothesis and fact meet; the delicate equilibrium between dream and reality; the place where fantasy and earthy things are metamorphosed into a work of art; the hour when faith in the future becomes knowledge of the past; to lay down one's power for others in need; to shake off the old ordeal and get ready for the new; to question, knowing that never can the full answer be found; to accept uncertainties quietly, even our incomplete knowledge of God; this is what man's journey is about, I think.

The Journey, 1954

WALTER WINCHELL

Success is the reward of anyone who looks for trouble.

April 15, 1940

JOHN GUNTHER

The next morning the boys assembled early for the quarter-mile walk to the white-frame Deerfield church, arranging themselves four abreast in order of their height. I did not think Johnny could manage such a march. He shook us off and disappeared. The procedure is that the boys, reaching the church, line up behind the pews, and then walk one by one down the center aisle, as each name is called. Mr. Flynt, the president of the board of trustees, then shakes hands with each boy, giving him his diploma in the left hand. We explained that Johnny might not be able to grasp the smooth roll of diploma with his left fingers, and asked Mr. Flynt to try to slip it into his right hand instead. The boys began to march in slowly, and though Johnny should have been conspicuous with his white bandage, we did not see him and I was in an agony fearing that he had fallen out. Mr. Boyden, sweeping the assembly with his all-embracing sharp affectionate glance, caught Frances's eye and nodded to her reassuringly. One by one the names were called out, and each boy disassociated himself from the solid group and marched forward alone. The call was alphabetical, and by the time the G's were reached we were limp with suspense, since we did not know for sure that Johnny had even got into the church. As each

boy passed down the aisle, there was applause, perfunctory for some, pronounced for others. Gaines, Gillespie, Goodwin, Griffin, Gunther. Slowly,
very slowly, Johnny stepped out of the mass of his fellows and trod by us,
carefully keeping in the exact center of the long aisle, looking neither to
the left nor to the right, but straight ahead, fixedly, with the white bandage flashing in the light through the high windows, his chin up, carefully,
not faltering, steady, but slowly, so very slowly. The applause began and
then rose and the applause became a storm, as every single person in that
old church became whipped up, tight and tense, to see if he would make
it. The applause became a thunder, it rose and soared and banged, when
Johnny finally reached the pulpit. Mr. Flynt carefully tried to put the
diploma in his right hand, as planned. Firmly Johnny took it from right
hand to left, as was proper, and while the whole audience rocked now
with release from tension, and was still wildly, thunderously applauding,
he passed around to the side and, not seeing us, reached his place among
his friends.

> *Death Be Not Proud,* the story of his son who became ill of
> a brain tumor at age sixteen, and who died of it a month
> after graduation. His last words were to ask whether Har-
> vard had admitted him.

A. J. Liebling

The brain, like Rhenish wine, should be chilled, not iced, to be at its best.
Women, however, are best at room temperature.

The Honest Rainmaker, 1953

Earl Wilson

Modern women fall into two classes: those who make a home for a man
and those who make a man for a home.

Jimmy Cannon

I pity people who are in a hurry on Sunday morning.

Robert Capa

[War] is like an aging actress: more and more dangerous, and less and
less photogenic.

SYDNEY J. HARRIS

Almost every man looks more so in a belted trench coat.

Strictly Personal, 1953

The public will go for anything that's limited one to a customer. If polygamy were the law of the land, few persons would bother to marry at all.

Ibid.

VERN DOLLASE

Respectability is not a virtue, but an opinion.

BRUCE ELLIOTT

After they put the fifteen apes in front of the typewriters there was a long wait. The animals sat and looked at the machines, at the paper on the rollers. There was a long pause, then each ape, one after the other, leaned forward and typed a single, different word.

The experimenter waited a long, long time. But after the one flurry of activity, nothing happened. Finally, seeing that the apes had no intention of continuing, he went towards the typewriters.

The first ape had typed, NOW; the second had typed, IS; the third one, THE; the fourth, TIME; the fifth, FOR; the sixth ape, ALL; the seventh, GOOD; the eighth one, PARTIES; the ninth, TO; the tenth, COME; the eleventh, TO; the twelfth ape, THE; the thirteenth, AID; the fourteenth, OF; and the last ape had typed, MAN.

Fantasy and Science Fiction, February, 1951

JOE E. WELLS

Was there ever a grandparent, bushed after a day of minding noisy youngsters, who hasn't felt the Lord knew what He was doing when He gave little children to young people.

New York Times "Magazine," October 11, 1953

X. Outdoor Spirits

NATURALISTS

•

William Bartram

The alligator when full grown is a very large and terrible creature, and of prodigious strength, activity and swiftness in the water. I have seen them twenty feet in length, and some are supposed to be twenty-two or twenty-three feet. Their body is as large as a horse; their shape exactly resembles that of a lizard, except their tail, which is flat or cuneiform, being compressed on each side, and gradually diminishing from the abdomen to the extremity, which, with the whole body, is covered with horny plates or squamae, impenetrable when on the body of the live animal, even to a rifle ball, except about their head and just behind their forelegs or arms, where it is said they are only vulnerable. The head of a full grown one is about three feet, and the mouth opens nearly the same length; their eyes are small in proportion, and seem sunk deep in the head, by means of the prominency of the brows; the nostrils are large, inflated and prominent on the top, so that the head in the water resembles, at a distance, a great chunk of wood floating about. Only the upper jaw moves, which they raise almost perpendicular, so as to form a right angle with the lower one. In the fore-part of the upper jaw, on each side, just under the nostrils, are two very large, thick, strong teeth or tusks, not very sharp, but rather the shape of a cone: these are as white as the finest polished ivory, and are not covered by any skin or lips, and always in sight, which gives the creature a frightful appearance: in the lower jaw are holes opposite to these teeth, to receive them: when they clap their jaws together it causes a surprising noise, like that which is made by forcing a heavy plank with violence upon the ground, and may be heard at a great distance.

But what is yet more surprising to a stranger, is the incredible loud and terrifying roar, which they are capable of making, especially in the spring season, their breeding time. It most resembles very heavy distant thunder, not only shaking the air and waters, but causing the earth to tremble; and when hundreds and thousands are roaring at the same time, you can scarcely be persuaded, but that the whole globe is violently and dangerously agitated.

An old champion, who is perhaps absolute sovereign of a little lake or lagoon (when fifty less than himself are obliged to content themselves

803

with swelling and roaring in little coves round about) darts forth from the reedy coverts all at once, on the surface of the waters, in a right line; at first seemingly as rapid as lightning, but gradually more slowly until he arrives at the center of the lake, when he stops. He now swells himself by drawing in wind and water through his mouth, which causes a loud sonorous rattling in the throat for near a minute, but it is immediately forced out again through his mouth and nostrils, with a loud noise, brandishing his tail in the air, and the vapor ascending from his nostrils like smoke. At other times, when swollen to an extent ready to burst, his head and tail lifted up, he spins or twirls round on the surface of the water. He acts his part like an Indian chief when rehearsing his feats of war; and then retiring, the exhibition is continued by others who dare to step forth, and strive to excel each other, to gain the attention of the favorite female.

Travels through North and South Carolina, Georgia, East and West Florida, 1791

John Burroughs

I see the Nature Providence going its impartial way. I see drought and flood, heat and cold, war and pestilence, defeat and death, besetting man at all times, in all lands. I see hostile germs in the air he breathes, in the water he drinks, in the soil he tills. I see the elemental forces as indifferent toward him as toward ants and fleas. I see pain and disease and defeat and failure dogging his footsteps. I see the righteous defeated and the ungodly triumphant—this and much more I see; and yet I behold through the immense biological vista behind us the race of man slowly, oh, so slowly! emerging from its brute or semi-human ancestry into the full estate of man, from blind instinct and savage passion into the light of reason and moral consciousness. I behold the great scheme of evolution unfolding despite all the delays and waste and failures, and the higher forms appearing upon the scene. I see on an immense scale, and as clearly as in a demonstration in a laboratory, that good comes out of evil; that the impartiality of the Nature Providence is best; that we are made strong by what we overcome; that man is man because he is as free to do evil as to do good; that life is as free to develop hostile forms as to develop friendly; that power waits upon him who earns it; that disease, wars, the unloosened, devastating elemental forces have each and all played their part in developing and hardening man and giving him the heroic fiber.

Accepting the Universe

Few books and plenty of real things.

Indoor Studies

I was born with a chronic anxiety about the weather.

Is It Going to Rain?

It is always easier to believe than to deny. Our minds are naturally affirmative.

The Light of Day

JOHN MUIR

I soon learned to distinguish the pretty sparrow track from that of the magpie and lark with their three delicate branches and the straight scratch behind made by the back-curving claw, dragged loosely like a spur of a Mexican vaquero. The cushioned elastic feet of the hare frequently were seen mixed with the pattering scratchy prints of the squirrels. I was now wholly trackful. I fancied I could see the air whirling in dimpled eddies from sparrow and lark wings. Earthquake boulders descending in a song of curves, snowflakes glinting songfully hither and thither. "The water in music the oar forsakes." The air in music the wing forsakes. All things move in music and write it. The mouse, lizard, and grasshopper sing together on the Turlock sands, sing with the morning stars.

Letter to Mrs. Jeanne C. Carr, Yosemite, 1874

Oftentimes on a broad meadow near Dunbar we stood for hours enjoying their marvelous singing and soaring. From the grass where the nest was hidden the male would suddenly rise, as straight as if shot up, to a height of perhaps thirty or forty feet, and sustaining himself with rapid wingbeats, pour down the most delicious melody, sweet and clear and strong, overflowing all bounds, then suddenly he would soar higher again and again, ever higher and higher, soaring and singing until lost to sight even on perfectly clear days. . . . To test our eyes we often watched a [sky] lark until he seemed a faint speck in the sky and finally passed beyond the keenest-sighted of us all. "I see him yet!" we would cry, "I see him yet!" "I see him yet!" "I see him yet!" as he soared. And finally only one of us would be left to claim that he still saw him. At last he, too, would have to admit that the singer had soared beyond his sight, and still the music came pouring down to us in glorious profusion, from a height far above our vision, requiring marvelous power of wing and marvelous power of voice, for that rich, delicious, soft, and yet clear music was distinctly heard long after the bird was out of sight. Then, suddenly ceasing, the glorious singer would appear, falling like a bolt straight down to his nest, where his mate was sitting on the eggs.

The Story of My Boyhood and Youth, 1913

It has been said that trees are imperfect men, and seem to bemoan their imprisonment rooted in the ground. But they never seem so to me. I never saw a discontented tree. They grip the ground as though they liked it, and though fast rooted they travel about as far as we do. They go wandering forth in all directions with every wind, going and coming like ourselves, traveling with us around the sun two million miles a day, and through space heaven knows how fast and far!

The Wilderness World of John Muir, edited by Edwin Way Teale, 1954

Most civilized folks cry morbidness, lunacy upon all that will not weigh on Fairbanks's scales or measure to that seconds rod of English brass. But we know that much that is most real will not counterpoise cast-iron, or dent our human flesh.

Ibid.

This grand show is eternal. It is always sunrise somewhere; the dew is never all dried at once; a shower is forever falling; vapor is ever rising. Eternal sunrise, eternal sunset, eternal dawn and gloaming, on sea and continents and islands, each in its turn, as the round earth rolls.

Ibid.

How hard to realize that every camp of men or beast has this glorious starry firmament for a roof! In such places standing alone on the mountain-top it is easy to realize that whatever special nests we make—leaves and moss like the marmots and birds, or tents or piled stone—we all dwell in a house of one room—the world with a firmament for its roof—and are sailing the celestial spaces without leaving any track.

Ibid.

Most people are *on* the world, not in it—having no conscious sympathy or relationship to anything about them—undiffused, separate, and rigidly alone like marbles of polished stone, touching but separate.

Ibid.

The rugged old Norsemen spoke of death as *Heimgang*—home-going. So the snow-flowers go home when they melt and flow to the sea, and the rock-ferns, after unrolling their fronds to the light and beautifying the rocks, roll them up close again in the autumn and blend with the soil. Myriads of rejoicing living creatures, daily, hourly, perhaps every moment sink into death's arms, dust to dust, spirit to spirit—waited on, watched over, noticed only by their Maker, each arriving at its own Heaven-dealt destiny. All the merry dwellers of the trees and streams, and the myriad swarms of the air, called into life by the sunbeam of a summer morning, go home through death, wings folded perhaps in the last red rays of sunset of the day they were first tried. Trees towering in the sky, braving storms of centuries, flowers turning faces to the light for a single hour or day, having enjoyed their share of life's feast—all alike pass on and away under the law of death and love. Yet all are our brothers and they enjoy life as we do, share Heaven's blessings with us, die and are buried in hallowed ground, come with us out of eternity and return into eternity. "Our lives are rounded with a sleep."

Ibid.

I only went out for a walk and finally concluded to stay out until sundown, for going out, I found, was really going in.

Journal

Sir, an insect may sting a noble animal, but it is none the less an insect.

Come with me along the glaciers and see God making landscapes.

HENRY BESTON

We need another and a wiser and perhaps a more mystical concept of animals. Remote from universal nature, and living by complicated artifice, man in civilization surveys the creature through the glass of his knowledge and sees thereby a feather magnified and the whole image in distortion. We patronize them for their incompleteness, for their tragic fate of having taken form so far below ourselves. And therein we err, and greatly err. For the animal shall not be measured by man. In a world older and more complete than ours they move finished and complete, gifted with extensions of the senses we have lost or never attained, living by voices we shall never hear. They are not brethren, they are not underlings; they are other nations, caught with ourselves in the net of life and time, fellow prisoners of the splendor and travail of the earth.

The Outermost House: A Year of Life on the Great Beach of Cape Cod, 1928

Learn to reverence night and to put away the vulgar fear of it, for, with the banishment of night from the experience of man, there vanishes as well a religious emotion, a poetic mood, which gives depth to the adventure of humanity. By day, space is one with the earth and with man—it is his sun that is shining, his clouds that are floating past; at night, space is his no more. When the great earth, abandoning day, rolls up the deeps of the heavens and the universe, a new door opens for the human spirit, and there are few so clownish that some awareness of the mystery of being does not touch them as they gaze. For a moment of night we have a glimpse of ourselves and of our world islanded in its stream of stars—pilgrims of mortality, voyaging between horizons across the eternal seas of space and time. Fugitive though the instant be, the spirit of man is, during it, ennobled by a genuine moment of emotional dignity, and poetry makes its own both the human spirit and experience.

Ibid.

A year indoors is a journey along a paper calendar; a year in outer nature is the accomplishment of a tremendous ritual.

Ibid.

Gustav Eckstein

Rodents are the most abundant of all mammals in the world. Like the house rat, the house mouse came originally from the Orient and is the only terrestrial mammal that has successfully crossed the East Indies and reached Australia without man's help. But it also has not scorned man's help. It has followed his commerce lines, spread via them over the globe, gone into the most extreme climates, from pole to equator. Man by his large and choice brain has occupied the earth, and the house mouse, the field mouse, the house rat, the house fly, the bed bug, certain flukes, worms, mites, ticks, lice, fleas, all have followed man around, may, to that extent, be said to have acknowledged that large and choice brain, and to have cast in their lot with it.

Everyday Miracle, 1948

Joseph Wood Krutch

What man knows is everywhere at war with what he wants.

The Modern Temper, 1929

If the plays and the novels of today deal with littler people and less mighty emotions it is not because we have become interested in common-place souls and their unglamorous adventures but because we have come, willy-nilly, to see the soul of man as commonplace and its emotions as mean.

Ibid.

Metaphysics may be, after all, only the art of being sure of something that is not so, and logic only the art of going wrong with confidence.

Ibid.

Rhetoric takes no real account of the art in literature, and morality takes no account of the art in life.

Ibid.

It is not easy to live in that continuous awareness of things which alone is true living. Even those who make a parade of their conviction that sunset, rain, and the growth of a seed are daily miracles are not usually so impressed by them as they urge others to be. The faculty of wonder tires easily and a miracle which happens everyday is a miracle no longer, no matter how many times one tells oneself that it ought to be. Life would seem a great deal longer and a great deal fuller than it does if it were not for the fact that the human being is, by nature, a creature to whom *"O altitudo"* is much less natural than "So what!" Really to see something once or twice a week is almost inevitably to have to try—though, alas, not necessarily with success—to make oneself a poet.

The Desert Year, 1952

The first sound which even the unobservant stranger [to the American Southwest] is likely to notice, later in the morning or even in the middle of a hot afternoon, is a mysterious, almost threatening coo-uh-cuck-oo breaking the torrid stillness when everything else is quiet. Obviously, I said to myself when I heard it, an owl of some sort. But it turned out to be, of all unlikely things, a dove. White-winged dove is its popular name; it is extremely prevalent; and it loves to sit on the very tiptop of a saguaro. But why a dove, the most banal symbol of the inoffensive and the senti-mental, should choose to imitate possibly the fiercest, and certainly the most irascible, of birds I do not know. It hints at that most terrible of all imaginable anarchies; at that anarchy which, some say, haunted the mind of Shakespeare in *Lear;* the anarchy, I mean, in which everything would forget what is appropriate to its nature. Are the meek whom the dove symbolizes about to inherit the earth in an unexpected and horrible way—by turning rapacious and implacable? Will the lamb lie down with the lion—and bite him?

In human society, I sometimes suspect that something like that has already begun to happen.

Ibid.

I have met few men or women wholly country-bred and completely without experience of life in cities, with whom I felt entirely at home. About them there is nearly always something *farouche,* if not actually savage. At some time in the course of his experience, every man should rub shoulders with his fellows, experience the excitement of a metropolis' nervous activity; live close to the great, the distinguished, the famous, and the merely notorious—if for no other reason than because only so can he learn properly to discount them, or at least learn in what ways they are, and in what ways they are not, to be taken at their own and the world's valuation. Those who, for example, have never seen an author are likely to take books with the wrong kind of seriousness! Urbanity seems to be literally that: Something impossible to acquire except in cities. But one need not, and one should not, I think, spend a lifetime in getting it, for in that respect, as in so many others, the city pays a diminishing return. The years between 18 and 30 should be amply sufficient to polish anyone capable of being polished. If he is not urbane by then, something more drastic than mere residence in a city would seem to be called for. And if I have never felt entirely at home with anyone who never had any experience of cities, I can say much the same of those who have never had any other kind.

The Best of Two Worlds, 1953

To be reminded that one is very much like other members of the animal kingdom is often funny enough, though it is never, like being compared to a machine, merely humiliating. I do not too much mind being somewhat like a cat, a dog, or even a frog, but I resent having it said that even an electronic calculator is like me.

Ibid.

I feel both happier and more secure when I am reminded that I have the backing of something older and perhaps more permanent than I am—the something, I mean, which taught the flower to count five and the beetle to know that spots are more pleasing if arranged in a definite order. Some of the most important secrets are, they assure me, known to others besides myself.

Ibid.

In the thirteenth century, man was good enough at least to survive, and he would be good enough to survive now if things were as simple as they were then. We may think that we would hate to give up our "higher standard of living," but is that what we have really got—or is it only a higher standard of dying? What we ride toward at high speed may not be a more abundant life, but only a more spectacular death.

American Scholar, Spring, 1953

The cockroach and the bird were both here long before we were. Both could get along very well without us; although it is perhaps significant that of the two the cockroach would miss us most.

There is no such thing as a dangerous woman. There are only susceptible men.

Donald Culross Peattie

Life is adventure in experience, and when you are no longer greedy for the last drop of it, it means no more than that you have set your face, whether you know it or not, to the day when you shall depart without a backward look. Those who look backward longingly to the end die young, at whatever age.

An Almanac for Moderns, 1935

I say that it touches a man that his blood is sea water and his tears are salt, that the seed of his loins is scarcely different from the same cells in a seaweed, and that of stuff like his bones are coral made. I say that physical and biologic law lies down with him, and wakes when a child stirs in the womb, and that the sap in a tree, uprushing in the spring, and the smell of the loam, where the bacteria bestir themselves in darkness, and the path of the sun in the heaven, these are facts of first importance to his mental conclusions, and that a man who goes in no consciousness of them is a drifter and a dreamer, without a home or any contact with reality.

Ibid.

The time to hear bird music is between four and six in the morning.

Seven o'clock is not too late, but by eight the fine rapture is over, due, I suspect, to the contentment of the inner man that comes with breakfast; a poet should always be hungry or have a lost love.

Ibid.

It is natural that women should like the birds whose domestic affairs can be observed under the eaves; they love the sweetest singers, the brightest plumage, the species not too shy to be seen at close range. For them the waders and swimmers, the awkward of leg, the harsh of cry, the wild of soul, have seldom the same appeal. But that which flees from men, that will men have. Women of all people ought to understand this, but they do not, quite.

Ibid.

Rachel Carson

The sea lies all about us. The commerce of all lands must cross it. The very winds that move over the lands have been cradled on its broad expanse and seek ever to return to it. The continents themselves dissolve and pass to the sea, in grain after grain of eroded land. . . . In its mysterious past it encompasses all the dim origins of life and receives in the end, after, it may be, many transmutations, the dead husks of that same life. For all at last returns to the sea—the beginning and the end.

The Sea Around Us

Bertha Damon

He was somewhat of a philosopher, Tom was; a cat has to be, as have all animals who deal with people.

EXPLORERS AND TRAVELERS

•

Jim Bridger

I won't listen any more to the talk of a man who was mean enough to kill his mother.

Reading *Richard III*

RICHARD HENRY DANA

Nothing can compare with the *early breaking of day* upon the wide, sad ocean. There is something in the first grey streaks stretching along the Eastern horizon, and throwing an indistinct light upon the face of the deep, which creates a feeling of loneliness, of dread, and of melancholy foreboding, which nothing else in nature can give.

Two Years Before the Mast, 1840

The freshness and crispness of the raw onion, with the earthy taste, give it a great relish to one who has been a long time on salt provisions. We were perfectly ravenous after them. We ate them at every meal, by the dozen; and filled our pockets with them, to eat on the watch on deck. The chief use, however, of the fresh provisions was for the men with the scurvy. One was able to eat, and he soon brought himself to by gnawing upon raw potatoes; but the other, by this time, was hardly able to open his mouth; and the cook took the potatoes raw, pounded them in a mortar, and gave him the juice to suck. The strong earthy taste and smell of this extract of the raw potatoes at first produced a shuddering through his whole frame, and after drinking it, an acute pain, which ran through all parts of his body; but knowing by this that it was taking strong hold, he persevered, drinking a spoonful every hour or so, until, by the effect of this drink, he became so well as to be able to move about, and open his mouth enough to eat the raw potatoes and onions pounded into a soft pulp. This course soon restored his appetite and strength; and ten days after . . . so rapid was his recovery that, from lying helpless and almost hopeless in his berth, he was at the masthead, furling a royal.

Ibid.

It is always observable that the physical and exact sciences are the last to suffer under despotisms.

To Cuba and Back, 1859

Better to be driven out from among men than to be disliked of children.

MIKE FINK

What's the use of improvements? Where's the fun, the frolicking, the fighting? Gone! All gone!

Attributed to

"DEATH VALLEY SCOTTY"

I play to the gallery and keep two campfires ahead, and if I should die today just tell the world I had a run for my money.

> His own motto. He died January 6, 1953, at age eighty-one, known by no other name.

RICHARD E. BYRD

The day was dying, the night being born—but with great peace. Here were the imponderable processes and forces of the cosmos, harmonious and soundless. Harmony, that was it! That was what came out of the silence—a gentle rhythm, the strain of a perfect chord, the music of the spheres, perhaps.

It was enough to catch that rhythm, momentarily to be myself a part of it. In that instant I could feel no doubt of man's oneness with the universe. The conviction came that that rhythm was too orderly, too harmonious, too perfect to be a product of blind chance—that, therefore, there must be purpose in the whole and that man was part of that whole and not an accidental offshoot. It was a feeling that transcended reason; that went to the heart of man's despair and found it groundless. The universe was a cosmos, not a chaos; man was as rightfully a part of that cosmos as were the day and night.

Alone, 1928

A man doesn't begin to attain wisdom until he recognizes that he is no longer indispensable.

Ibid.

CHARLES A. LINDBERGH

We (that's my ship and I) took off rather suddenly. We had a report somewhere around four o'clock in the afternoon before that the weather would be fine, so we thought we would try it.

New York Times, May 23, 1927

I saw a fleet of fishing boats. . . . I flew down almost touching the craft and yelled at them, asking if I was on the right road to Ireland.

They just stared. Maybe they didn't hear me. Maybe I didn't hear them. Or maybe they thought I was just a crazy fool. An hour later I saw land.

Ibid.

I lean back in the wicker seat, running my eyes once more over the instruments. Nothing wrong there. They all tell the proper story. Even the tachometer needle is in place, with the engine idling. . . . I turn again to the problem of take-off. It will be slow at best. Can the engine stand such a long ground run at wide-open throttle, or will it overheat and start to miss?

Suppose I *can* hold the runway, suppose I *do* get off the ground—will fog close in and force me back? Suppose the ceiling drops to zero—I can't fly blind with this overload of fuel; but the wheels have doubtful safety factors for a landing. Shall I cut the switch and wait another day for confirmation of good weather? But if I leave now, I'll have a head start on both the Fokker and the Bellanca. Once in the air, I can nurse my engine all the way to Paris—there'll be no need to push it in a race. And the moon's past full—it will be three weeks to the next one; conditions then may be still worse.

Wind, weather, power, load—gradually these elements stop churning in my mind. It's less a decision of logic than of feeling, the kind of feeling that comes when you gauge the distance to be jumped between two stones across a brook. Something within you disengages itself from your body and travels ahead with your vision to make the test. You can feel it try the jump as you stand looking. Then uncertainty gives way to the conviction that it *can* or can't be done. Sitting in the cockpit, in seconds, minutes long, the conviction surges through me that the wheels *will* leave the ground, that the wings *will* rise above the wires, that it *is* time to start the flight.

I buckle my safety belt, pull goggles down over my eyes, turn to the men at the blocks, and nod. Frozen figures leap to action. A yank on the ropes—the wheels are free. . . .

The Spirit of St. Louis, 1954

A cushion of air lies close to the water. On it, wings glide more smoothly; the tail lifts higher, the waves flash by, and a plane races along with lessened effort. The *Spirit of St. Louis* is like a butterfly blown out to sea. How often I used to watch them, as a child, on the banks of the Mississippi, dancing up and down above the water, as I am dancing now; up and down with their own fancy and the currents of the air. But a touch of wing to water, and they were down forever, just as my plane would be. I saw dozens of them floating, broken and lifeless, in eddying currents near our shore. Why, I used to wonder, did they ever leave the safety of the land. But why have I?

Ibid.

I wonder if man ever escapes from worldly bonds so completely as when he flies alone above clouds at night. When there's no cloud layer beneath him, then, no matter how high he may ascend, he is still conscious of the surface of the earth by day and of its mass by night. While flying over clouds in daytime, there's something about the motherly warmth of the sun which imparts a feeling of the earth below. You sense it down there underneath, covered only by a layer of mist which may draw apart at any moment to leave the graceful contours of land or the flat, sparkling sea, clear and naked in sunlight.

By day, or on a cloudless night, a pilot may drink the wine of the gods, but it has an earthy taste; he's a god of the earth, like one of the Grecian deities who lived on worldly mountains and descended for intercourse with men. But at night, over a stratus layer, all sense of the planet may disappear. You know that down below, beneath that heavenly blanket, *is* the earth, factual and hard. But it's an intellectual knowledge; it's a knowledge tucked away in the mind; not a feeling that penetrates the body. And if at times you renounce experience and the mind's heavy logic, it seems that the world has rushed along on its orbit, leaving you alone, flying above a forgotten cloud bank, somewhere in the solitude of interstellar space.

Ibid.

In spite of my speed, the *Spirit of St. Louis* seems about to stall. My lack of feel alarms me. I've never tried to land a plane without feel before. I want to open the throttle wider, to glide faster, to tauten the controls still more. But—I glance at the dial—the needle points to eighty miles an hour. The *Spirit of St. Louis* is lightly loaded, with most of its fuel gone. Even at this speed I'll overshoot the lighted area before my tail skid strikes the ground. No, I'll have to pull the nose higher instead of pushing it down. I'll have to depend on the needle, on judgment more than instinct. I kick rudder and push the stick to one side, just to be sure —yes, controls are taut, there's plenty of speed. And feeling is not completely gone. I still have a little left. I can feel the skid and slip. But the edge of perception is dull, very dull. It's better to come in fast, even if I roll into that black area after I land. And it's better to come in high—there may be poles or chimneys at the field's edge—Never depend on obstruction lights—especially when you don't see any.

It's only a hundred yards to the hangars now—solid forms emerging from the night. I'm too high—too fast. Drop wing—left rudder—sideslip—Careful—mustn't get anywhere near the stall. I've never landed the *Spirit of St. Louis* at night before. It would be better to come in straight. But if I don't sideslip, I'll be too high over the boundary to touch my wheels in the area of light. That would mean circling again—Still too high. I push the stick over to a steeper slip, leaving the nose well down—Below the hangar roofs now—straighten out—A short burst of the engine—Over the lighted area—Sod coming up to meet me—Deceptive high lights and shadows—Careful—easy to bounce when you're tired—Still too fast—Tail too high—Hold off—Hold off—But the lights are far behind—The surface dims—Texture of sod is gone—Ahead, there's nothing but night—Give her the gun and climb for another try?—The wheels touch gently—off again—No, I'll keep contact—Ease the stick forward—Back on the ground—Off—Back—the tail skid too—Not a bad landing, but I'm beyond the light—can't see anything ahead—Like flying in fog—Ground loop?—No, still rolling too fast—might blow a tire—the field *must* be clear—Uncomfortable though, jolting into blackness—Wish I had a wing light—but too heavy on the take-off—Slower, now—slow enough to ground loop safely—left rudder—reverse it—stick over the other way—The *Spirit of St. Louis* swings around and stops rolling, resting on the solidness of earth, in the center of *Le Bourget*.

I start to taxi back toward the floodlights and hangars—But the entire field ahead is covered with running figures!

Ibid.

There must be pioneers and some of them get killed.

I'd rather fly than eat.

XI. Men of Science

SCIENTISTS AND INVENTORS

•

BENJAMIN FRANKLIN

As frequent mention is made in public papers from Europe of the success of the Philadelphia experiment for drawing the electric fire from clouds by means of pointed rods of iron erected on high buildings, etc., it may be agreeable to the curious to be informed, that the same experiment has succeeded in Philadelphia, though made in a different and more easy manner, which is as follows:

Make a small cross of two light strips of cedar, the arms so long as to reach to the four corners of a large thin silk handkerchief when extended; tie the corners of the handkerchief to the extremities of the cross, so you have the body of a kite; which being properly accommodated with a tail, loop, and string, will rise in the air, like those made of paper; but this being of silk, is fitter to bear the wet and wind of a thunder-gust without tearing. To the top of the upright stock of the cross is to be fixed a very sharp pointed wire, rising a foot or more above the wood. To the end of the twine, next the hand, is to be tied a silk ribbon, and where the silk and twine join, a key may be fastened. This kite is to be raised when a thunder-gust appears to be coming on, and the person who holds the string must stand within a door or window or under some cover, so that the silk ribbon may not be wet; and care must be taken that the twine does not touch the frame of the door or window. As soon as any of the thunder-clouds come over the kite, the pointed wire will draw the electric fire from them, and the kite, with all the twine, will be electrified, and the loose filaments of the string will stand out every way, and be attracted by an approaching finger. And when the rain has wet the kite and twine, so that it can conduct the electric fire freely, you will find it stream out plentifully from the key on the approach of your knuckle. At this key the phial may be charged; and from electric fire thus obtained, spirits may be kindled, and all the other electric experiments be performed, which are usually done by the help of a rubbed glass globe or tube, and thereby the sameness of the electric matter with that of lightning completely demonstrated.

Letter to Peter Collinson, 1752

[The balloon] appears, as you observe, to be a discovery of great importance, and what may possibly give a new turn to human affairs. Convincing sovereigns of the folly of wars may perhaps be one effect of it; since it will be impracticable for the most potent of them to guard his dominions. Five thousand balloons, capable of raising two men each, could not cost more than five ships of the line; and where is the prince who can afford so to cover his country with troops for its defence, as that ten thousand men descending from the clouds might not in many places do an infinite deal of mischief, before a force could be brought together to repel them?

Letter to Jan Ingenhousz, 1784

What good is a new-born baby?

When asked what good a balloon would be

Robert Fulton

The mechanic should sit down among levers, screws, wedges, wheels, etc., like a poet among the letters of the alphabet, considering them as the exhibition of his thoughts, in which a new arrangement transmits a new idea to the world.

Louis Agassiz

All these facts proclaim aloud the One God, whom man may know, adore, and love; and Natural History must, in good time, become the analysis of the thoughts of the Creator of the Universe, as manifested in the animal and vegetable kingdoms.

Essay on Classifications, 1857–62

It cannot be too soon understood that science is one, and that whether we investigate language, philosophy, theology, history, or physics, we are dealing with the same problems, culminating in the knowledge of ourselves. Speech is known only in connection with the organs of man, thought in connection with his brain, religion as the expression of his aspirations, history as the record of his deeds, and physical sciences as the laws under which he lives. Philosophers and theologians have yet to learn that a physical fact is as sacred as a moral principle. Our own nature demands from us this double allegiance.

"Evolution and the Permanence of Type," *Atlantic Monthly*, 1874

The study of Nature is intercourse with the Highest Mind. You should never trifle with Nature.

Agassiz at Penikese

Gentlemen, the world is older than we have been taught to think. Its age is as if one were gently to rub a silk handkerchief across Plymouth Rock once a year until it were reduced to a pebble.

To his classes each year

I cannot afford to waste my time making money.

BENJAMIN PEIRCE

Mathematics is the science which draws necessary conclusions.

Linear Associative Algebra, first sentence, 1870

JOSIAH WILLARD GIBBS

Mathematics is also a language.

At faculty meeting, Yale University, commenting on requests for more money for the Language Departments

The whole is simpler than its parts.

THOMAS A. EDISON

Everything comes to him who hustles while he waits.

Golden Book, April, 1931

I am long on ideas, but short on time. I expect to live to be only about a hundred.

Ibid.

I am not acquainted with any one who is happy.

Interview when an old man

My mind is incapable of conceiving such a thing as a soul. I may be in error, and man may have a soul; but I simply do not believe it.

Do We Live Again?

I don't live with the past. I am living for today and tomorrow.

I start where the last man left off.

There is no expedient to which a man will not go to avoid the real labor of thinking.

Genius is one per cent inspiration and ninety-nine per cent perspiration.

WILBUR WRIGHT

I do not believe [the airplane] will surplant surface transportation. I believe it will always be limited to special purposes. It will be a factor in war. It may have a future as a carrier of mail.

Interview, March, 1906

If a man is in too big a hurry to give up an error he is liable to give up some truth with it, and in accepting the arguments of the other man he is sure to get some error with it. . . . After I get hold of a truth I hate to lose it again, and I like to sift all the truth out before I give up an error.

ORVILLE WRIGHT

When my brother and I built and flew the first man-carrying flying machine, we thought that we were introducing into the world an invention which would make further wars practically impossible. That we were not alone in this thought is evidenced by the fact that the French Peace Society presented us with medals on account of our invention. We thought governments would realize the impossibility of winning by surprise attacks, and that no country would enter into war with another when it knew it would have to win by simply wearing out the enemy.

1917

EDWIN GRANT CONKLIN

When children are taught not merely to know things but particularly to know themselves, not merely how to do things but especially how to compel themselves to do things, they may be said to be really educated.

Heredity and Environment in the Development of Man

CHARLES FORT

I think we're property. I should say we belong to something. . . . That something owns this earth—all others warned off.

New Lands, 1923

CHARLES F. KETTERING

A friend of mine asked me, years ago, whether it was true that I went from Detroit to Dayton in four and a half hours without speeding. I said it was true and asked him to follow me the following Saturday when I was going home. This he did and we arrived in Dayton in four and a half hours without having passed the speed limit. My friend was mad when we got there. "You didn't take road 25," he said. Naturally, I had taken a shorter route which I had worked out on the map. I answered that whoever wants to get somewhere fast should never take road 25 but always a road of his own choosing.

Speech

A man must have a certain amount of intelligent ignorance to get any where.

My interest is in the future because I am going to spend the rest of my life there.

It's easy to build a philosophy. It doesn't have to run.

HANS ZINSSER

But it is a strange fact that the impractical among mankind are remembered. Why? Because of that quality which more than any other lends dignity to life: the instinct for happiness in understanding,—whether it be by intellectual or emotional perception,—which is the most incomprehensible of the attributes of mankind, and which neither the frugalities of individual nor the brutalities of national competition have ever succeeded in annihilating.

Rats, Lice and History, 1935

I remember one dark, rainy day when we buried a Russian doctor. . . . When the chanting procession finally disappeared over the hill, I was glad that the rain on my face obscured the tears that I could not hold back. I felt in my heart, then, that I never could or would be an observer, and that, whatever Fate had in store for me, I would always wish to be in the ranks, however humbly or obscurely; and it came upon me suddenly that I was profoundly happy in my profession, in which I would never aspire to administrative power or prominence so long as I could remain close, heart and hands, to the problems of disease.

ALBERT EINSTEIN

I never think of the future. It comes soon enough.

Interview, December, 1930

The true value of a human being is determined primarily by the measure and the sense in which he has attained liberation from the self.

My World-Picture, 1934

My dear young friends: I am glad to see you before me, a flourishing band of young people who have chosen applied science as a profession.

I could sing a hymn of praise with the refrain of the splendid progress in applied science that we have already made, and the enormous further progress that you will bring about. We are indeed in the era and also in the native land of applied science.

But it lies far from my thought to speak in this way. . . .

Why does this magnificent applied science, which saves work and makes life easier, bring us so little happiness? The simple answer runs—because we have not yet learned to make a sensible use of it.

In war, it serves that we may poison and mutilate each other. In peace it has made our lives hurried and uncertain. Instead of freeing us in great measure from spiritually exhausting labor, it has made men into slaves of machinery, who for the most part complete their monotonous long day's work with disgust, and must continually tremble for their poor rations.

You will be thinking that the old man sings an ugly song. I do it, however, with a good purpose, in order to point out a consequence.

It is not enough that you should understand about applied science in order that your work may increase man's blessings. *Concern for man himself and his fate must always form the chief interest of all technical endeavours, concern for the great unsolved problems of the organization of labor and the distribution of goods*—in order that the creations of our mind shall be a blessing and not a curse to mankind. Never forget this in the midst of your diagrams and equations.

Address to student body, California Institute of Technology

As long as there are sovereign nations possessing great power, war is inevitable.

Atlantic Monthly, November, 1945

The most beautiful and most profound emotion we can experience is the sensation of the mystical. It is the dower of all true science. He to whom this emotion is a stranger, who can no longer wonder and stand rapt in awe, is as good as dead. To know that what is impenetrable to us really exists, manifesting itself as the highest wisdom and the most radiant beauty which our dull faculties can comprehend only in their most primitive forms—this knowledge, this feeling is at the centre of true religiousness.

Out of My Later Years, 1950

The word imposition is never used where there is love.

To a sick friend who remonstrated that it was an "imposition" to have Einstein come and see him, 1953

Man usually avoids attributing cleverness to somebody else—unless it is an enemy.

Ideas and Opinions, 1954

If I would be a young man again and had to decide how to make my living, I would not try to become a scientist or scholar or teacher. I would rather choose to be a plumber or a peddlar, in the hope to find that modest degree of independence still available under present circumstances.

Interview, November 14, 1954

If my theory of relativity is proven successful, Germany will claim me as a German and France shall declare that I am a citizen of the world. Should my theory prove untrue, France will say that I am a German and Germany will declare that I am a Jew.

Address at the Sorbonne, Paris

God is clever but he is not dishonest.

It is the supreme art of the teacher to awaken joy in creative expression and knowledge.

Motto for the Astronomy Building, Pasadena Junior College, Pasadena, California

How do I work? I grope.

Isn't it strange that I who have written only unpopular books should be such a popular fellow.

$E = mc^2$, where E is the energy in ergs, m the mass in grams and c the velocity of light (that is, 3×10^{10} cm. per second).

No amount of experimentation can ever prove me right; a single experiment may at any time prove me wrong.

Of his Theory of Relativity

As far as the laws of mathematics refer to reality, they are not certain; and as far as they are certain, they do not refer to reality.

The supreme task of the physicist is to arrive at those universal elementary laws from which the cosmos can be built up by pure deduction. There is no logical path to these laws; only intuition, resting on sympathetic understanding of experience, can reach them.

The most incomprehensible thing about the universe is that it is comprehensible.

PERCY WILLIAMS BRIDGMAN

There is no adequate defense, except stupidity, against the impact of a new idea.

ERIC TEMPLE BELL

. . . even stranger things have happened; and perhaps the strangest of all is the marvel that mathematics should be possible to a race akin to the apes.

The Development of Mathematics, 1940

ROBERT MOSES

A tunnel is merely a tiled, vehicular bathroom smelling faintly of monoxide.

Art and Public Works, 1945

John Hodgdon Bradley

Minorities of men have already demonstrated—in laboratories, hospitals, churches and schools—a capacity for extending the welfare of men as individuals. Should majorities of men intelligently and sincerely attempt to extend the welfare of man as a species, who can say what dream might not possibly come true? It is not for the historian of life to say. Self-directed evolution, so far as he knows, is an adventure without precedent in a billion years.

Patterns of Survival, 1953

Fritz Zwicky

We first throw a little something into the skies, then a little more, then a shipload of instruments—then ourselves.

Of rocket experiments at White Sands, New Mexico

MEDICAL MEN

•

William James Mayo

It is not surgery that kills people; it is *delayed* surgery.

Attributed to

Logan Clendening

Faddists are continually proclaiming the value of exercise; four people out of five are more in need of rest than exercise.

Modern Methods of Treatment, 1924

Surgery does the ideal thing—it separates the patient from his disease. It puts the patient back to bed and the disease in a bottle.

Ibid.

Gregory Zilboorg

In other words, psychoanalysts relieve their patients from feeling guilty about things of which they are not guilty, and leave them with the sense of guilt about things of which they are guilty.

Psychoanalysis and Religion

HARRY STACK SULLIVAN

There is one thing I wish you to remember while you work under me. In the present state of society the patient is right and you are wrong.

Greeting new internes at his mental hospital

ERICH FROMM

The more the drive towards life is thwarted, the stronger is the drive towards destruction; the more life is realised, the less is the strength of destructiveness. *Destructiveness is the outcome of unlived life.*

Escape from Freedom

There is much less difference between a mystic faith in God and an atheist's rational faith in mankind than between the former's faith and that of a Calvinist whose faith in God is rooted in the conviction of his own powerlessness and in his fear of God's power.

Man for Himself

BENJAMIN M. SPOCK

What good mothers and fathers instinctively feel like doing for their babies is best after all.

The Common Sense Book of Baby and Child Care

XII. Men of Art

ACTORS AND MUSICIANS

•

PHINEAS TAYLOR BARNUM

Every crowd has a silver lining.

There's a sucker born every minute.

EDWIN BOOTH

An actor is a sculptor who carves in snow.

E. F. ALBEE

Never give a sucker an even break.

Often attributed to W. C. Fields

ARTURO TOSCANINI

God tells me how the music should sound, but *you* stand in the way!

To a trumpet player. Quoted in the *New York Times*,
April 11, 1954

I kissed my first woman and smoked my first cigarette on the same day;
I have never had time for tobacco since.

GEORGE M. COHAN

I don't care what they call me as long as they mention my name.

MARY GARDEN

Women marry because they don't want to work.

Newspaper interview

ISADORA DUNCAN

All my life I have struggled to make one authentic gesture.

W. C. FIELDS

There may be some things better than sex, and some things may be worse. But there is nothing exactly like it.

> Quoted by Fowler, *Minutes of the Last Meeting,* 1954

JOHN BARRYMORE

My wife was too beautiful for words, but not for arguments.

My wife is the kind of girl who'll not go anywhere without her mother, and her mother will go anywhere.

The only way to fight a woman is with your hat. Grab it and run.

SIGMUND ROMBERG

A love song is just a caress set to music.

CHARLIE CHAPLIN

Laughter is the tonic, the relief, the surcease for pain.

> Quoted by Huff, *Charles Chaplin,* 1951

The human race I prefer to think of as an underworld of gods. When the gods go slumming they visit the earth. You see, my respect for the human race is not one hundred per cent.

> *Ibid.*

EDDIE CANTOR

Everybody has two businesses—his own, and show business.

JUDITH ANDERSON

There is nothing enduring in life for a woman except what she builds in a man's heart.

> Interview, March 8, 1931

Louis Armstrong

This one's for you, Rex.

> To King George VI when Armstrong's band played a command performance

Humphrey Bogart

The only reason to have money is to tell any s.o.b. in the world to go to hell.

> *Time,* June 7, 1954

Tallulah Bankhead

There is less in this than meets the eye.

> At a revival of *Aglavaine and Selysette,* by Maeterlinck. Alexander Woollcott claims she said it to him, but so do half a dozen other people. At least they agree that she *said* it.

I am as pure as the driven slush.

Oscar Levant

Epigram: a wisecrack that has played Carnegie Hall.

I've given up reading books; I find it takes my mind off myself.

I'm a controversial figure. My friends either dislike me or hate me.

In my last movie I played an unsympathetic character—myself.

Milton Berle

There's no such thing as a new joke. All jokes are public domain. It's not the gag, it's how you deliver it.

Joseph L. Mankiewicz

The worst mistake we make is teaching children that money isn't everything.

> Interview, October, 1954

LIBERACE

What you said hurt me very much. I cried all the way to the bank.

> To critics who showed a certain lack of enthusiasm for his vastly successful concert at Madison Square Garden, New York, June, 1954

Bach, Beethoven, Paderewski . . . and my dentist.

> Listing his four greatest "inspirations"

AVA GARDNER

Men are necessary, definitely not evil.

> Interview, June, 1954

ARTISTS AND SCULPTORS

•

WASHINGTON ALLSTON

The most common disguise of envy is in the praise of what is subordinate.

> "Text for reflection" penciled on his studio wall

Fame . . . is only known to exist by the echo of its footsteps through congenial minds.

> *Ibid.*

The only competition worthy of a wise man is with himself.

> *Ibid.*

HORATIO GREENOUGH

By beauty I mean the promise of function, by action I mean the presence of function, by character I mean the record of function.

> *Artist's Creed*

[The one principle of structure is] the principle of adaptation of forms to functions.

> Lecture

An obelisk says but one word, *Here!* but it speaks very loud.

As remembered by Emerson, 1852

Here is my theory of structure: a scientific arrangement of spaces and forms [adapted] to functions and to site; an emphasis of features proportioned to the gradated importance in function; color and ornament to be decided and arranged and varied by strictly organic laws, having a distinct reason for each decision; the entire and immediate banishment of all make-believe.

Letter to Emerson

We build our church up into the sky against the gravitation, but 'tis only the *downward tendency* that holds it *fast*.

AUGUSTUS SAINT-GAUDENS

What garlic is to salad, insanity is to art.

JOHN SINGER SARGENT

Every time I paint a portrait I lose a friend.

EUGENE SPEICHER

There is a universal definition of a portrait. A portrait is a picture in which there's something wrong with the mouth.

HELEN HOKINSON

[Women] want to learn; they buy the best books. The fact that they are intelligent, educated women, seeing and commenting on things they do not fully understand, is what makes them humorous.

ARCHITECTS AND DESIGNERS

•

LOUIS SULLIVAN

Form follows function.

FREDERICK W. GOUDY

I am the voice of today, the herald of tomorrow.

I am type! Of my earliest ancestry neither history nor relics remain. The wedge-shaped symbols impressed in plastic clay in the dim past by Babylonian builders foreshadowed me. From them through the hieroglyphs of the ancient Egyptians, the lapidary inscriptions of the early Romans, down to the beautiful letters by the scribes of the Italian renaissance, I was in the making.

John Gutenberg was the first to cast me in metal. From his chance thought straying through an idle reverie—a dream most golden, the profound art of printing with movable types was born. Cold, rigid, implacable I may be, yet the first impress of my face brought the divine Word to countless thousands. I bring into the light of day the precious stores of knowledge and wisdom long hidden in the grave of ignorance.

I coin for you the enchanting tale, the philosopher's moralizing and the poet's vision. I enable you to exchange the irksome hours that come, at times, to every one, for sweet and happy hours with books—golden urns filled with all the manna of the past. In books I present a portion of the eternal mind caught in its progress through the world, stamped in an instant and preserved for eternity. Through me, Socrates and Plato, Chaucer and the bards become your faithful friends who ever surround and minister to you. I am the leaden army that conquers the world—I AM TYPE!

The Type Speaks

FRANK LLOYD WRIGHT

No house should ever be *on* any hill or on anything. It should be *of* the hill, belonging to it, so hill and house could live together each the happier for the other.

An Autobiography, 1932

The physician can bury his mistakes, but the architect can only advise his client to plant vines.

New York Times "Magazine," October 4, 1953

What is an expert? An expert is a man who has stopped thinking. He knows!

Form and function are one.

Raymond Loewy

Concerning any new thing, never consult the man whose life it is about to change.

New Yorker, February 27, 1954

XIII. Poets and Dramatists:
Viewpoints and Visions

ANNE BRADSTREET

Authority without wisdom is like a heavy ax without an edge, fitter to bruise than polish.

Meditations Divine and Morall

WILLIAM CULLEN BRYANT

By eloquence, I understand those appeals to our moral perceptions that produce emotion as soon as they are uttered. It is in these that the orator is himself affected with the feelings he would communicate, that his eyes glisten, and his frame seems to dilate, and his voice acquires an unwonted melody, and his sentences arrange themselves into a sort of measure and harmony, and the listener is chained in involuntary and breathless attention.

Lectures on Poetry, 1826

HENRY WADSWORTH LONGFELLOW

If we could read the secret history of our enemies we should find in each man's life sorrow and suffering enough to disarm all hostility.

Driftwood

If spring came but once in a century instead of once a year, or burst forth with the sound of an earthquake and not in silence, what wonder and expectation there would be in all hearts, to behold the miraculous change.

We often excuse our own want of philanthropy by giving the name of fanaticism to the more ardent zeal of others.

EDGAR ALLAN POE

With me poetry has been not a purpose, but a passion.

Poems, 1845, "Preface"

I am not more sure that my soul lives than I am that perverseness is one of the primitive impulses of the human heart—one of the indivisible primary faculties or sentiments which give direction to the character of Man.

"The Black Cat," 1845

Men have called me mad; but the question is not yet settled, whether madness is or is not the loftiest intelligence—whether much that is glorious—whether all that is profound—does not spring from disease of thought—from moods of mind exalted at the expense of the general intellect. . . .

Those who dream by day are cognizant of many things which escape those who dream only by night.

"Eleonora," 1845

No one point in its composition is referable either to accident or intuition . . . the work proceeded, step by step, to its completion with the precision and rigid consequence of a mathematical problem.

The Philosophy of Composition (commentary on his own poem, "The Raven"), 1846

A poem, in my opinion, is opposed to a work of science by having, for its *immediate* object, pleasure, not truth; to romance, by having for its object an *indefinite* instead of a *definite* pleasure, being a poem only so far as this object is attained; romance presenting perceptible images with definite, poetry with *in*definite sensations, to which end music is *essential,* since the comprehension of sweet sound is our most indefinite conception. Music, when combined with a pleasurable idea, is poetry; music without the idea is simply music; the idea without the music is prose from its very definitiveness.

On Poets and Poetry

I would define, in brief, the Poetry of words as *The Rhythmical Creation of Beauty.* Its sole arbiter is Taste. With the Intellect or with the Conscious, it has only collateral relations. Unless incidentally, it has no concern whatever either with Duty or with Truth. . . .

I hold that a long poem does not exist. I maintain that the phrase, "a long poem," is simply a flat contradiction in terms.

The Poetic Principle

No hero-worshipper can possess anything within himself.

Hero Worship

The tale proper affords the fairest field which can be afforded by the wide domains of mere prose, for the exercise of the highest genius. Were I bidden to say how this genius could be most advantageously employed for the best display of its powers, I should answer, without hesitation, "in the composition of a rhymed poem not to exceed in length what might be perused in an hour."

> *The Short Story* (a review of Hawthorne's *Twice-Told Tales*)

The plots of God are perfect. The Universe is a plot of God.

> *Eureka*

If any ambitious man have the fancy to revolutionize, at one effort, the universal world of human thought, human opinion, and human sentiment, the opportunity is his own—the road to immortal renown lies straight, open, and unencumbered before him. All that he has to do is to write and publish a very little book. Its title should be simple—a few plain words—*My Heart Laid Bare*. But—this little book must be *true to its title*.

> *The Impossibility of Writing a Truthful Autobiography*

This is emphatically the thinking age; indeed it may very well be questioned whether man ever substantially thought before.

JULIA WARD HOWE

You wrote me a lovely letter on my ninetieth birthday. . . . What I have done looks small to me, but I have tried a good deal for the best I have known. . . . Don't you think that the best things are already in view? The opportunities for women, the growing toleration and sympathy in religion, the sacred cause of peace? I have lived like Moses, to see the entrance into the Promised Land. How much is this to be thankful for! My crabbed hand shows how Time abridges my working powers, but I march to the brave music still.

> Letter to Mrs. Spofford, 1909

EMILY DICKINSON

Truth is so rare, it's delightful to tell it.

When I feel physically as if the top of my head were taken off I know *that* is poetry.

WALT WHITMAN

Books are to be called for and supplied on the assumption that the process

of reading is not a half-sleep, but in the highest sense an exercise, a gym-
nastic struggle; that the reader is to do something for himself.

Democratic Vistas, 1871

You must not know too much, or be too precise or scientific about birds
and trees and flowers and watercraft; a certain free margin, and even
vagueness—perhaps ignorance, credulity—helps your enjoyment of these
things.

Specimen Days, "Birds," 1882

To have great poets there must be great audiences too.

Notes Left Over, "Ventures, on an Old Theme." Masthead
motto of *Poetry,* October, 1912.

Language is not an abstract construction of the learned, or of dictionary
makers, but is something arising out of the work, needs, ties, joys, affections, tastes, of long generations of humanity, and has its bases broad and
low, close to the ground.

"Slang in America"

William Vaughn Moody

The sailors were lying about asleep in the fierce sun—except one, who had
heaved his boat on her side and was calking her. By him stood a man
dressed in a long dark robe of coarse stuff, bare-headed, talking earnestly
to the stooping sailor. I took him for a Greek priest, by reason of his long
hair and spiritual profile. There was something in the spare frame of the
man, the slight stoop of the shoulders, and the calm intensity of the attitude, which made my heart stop beating. Presently he turned to look at
me, and it was indeed He. This has happened to me twice now—once
before at Sorrento seven years ago.

Letter to Mrs. Brainard, Crete, 1902

Edwin Arlington Robinson

There are too many words in prose, and they take up altogether too much
room.

In conversation, 1912

Poetry is a language which tells us, through a more or less emotional
reaction, something that cannot be said.

Newspaper interview

The world is not a prison-house, but a spiritual kindergarten where be-wildered infants are trying to spell God with the wrong blocks.

GEORGE CABOT LODGE

When you are accustomed to anything, you are estranged from it.

ROBERT FROST

Writing free verse is like playing tennis with the net down.

Address, May, 1935

I never felt the call to be an expatriate. But I hold it to be the inalienable right of anybody to go to hell in his own way.

Address, Berkeley, California, December, 1935

The figure a poem makes. It begins in delight and ends in wisdom. The figure is the same as for love. No one can really hold that the ecstasy should be static and stand still in one place. It begins in delight, it inclines to the impulse, it assumes direction with the first line laid down, it runs a course of lucky events, and ends in a clarification of life—not necessarily a great clarification, such as sects and cults are founded on, but in a momentary stay against confusion. It has denouement. It has an outcome that though unforeseen was predestined from the first image of the original mood—and indeed from the very mood. . . .

More than once I should have lost my soul to radicalism if it had been the originality it was mistaken for by its young converts. Originality and initiative are what I ask for my country. For myself the originality need be no more than the freshness of a poem run in the way I have described: from delight to wisdom. The figure is the same as for love. Like a piece of ice on a hot stove the poem must ride on its own melting. A poem may be worked over once it is in being, but may not be worried into being Its most precious quality will remain its having run itself and carried away the poet with it. Read it a hundred times: it will forever keep its fresh-ness as a metal keeps its fragrance. It can never lose its sense of a meaning that once unfolded by surprise as it went.

Collected Poems, "Preface," 1949

A poem is best read in the light of all the other poems ever written. We read A the better to read B (we have to start somewhere; we may get very little out of A). We read B the better to read C, C the better to read

D, D the better to go back and get something more out of A. Progress is
not the aim but circulation. The thing is to get among the poems where
they hold each other apart in their places as the stars do.

Aforesaid, "Preface," 1954

[A poem is] never a put-up job. . . . It begins as a lump in the throat,
a sense of wrong, a homesickness, a loneliness. It is never a thought to
begin with. It is at its best when it is a tantalizing vagueness.

It is absurd to think that the only way to tell if a poem is lasting is to wait
and see if it lasts. The right reader of a good poem can tell the moment
it strikes him that he has taken an immortal wound—that he will never
get over it. That is to say, permanence in poetry as in love is perceived
instantly. It hasn't to wait the test of time. The proof of a poem is not
that we have never forgotten it, but we knew at sight we never could
forget it.

The *belief* in God is a relationship you enter into with Him to bring about
the future.

AVERY HOPWOOD

However late one gets to *Siegfried,* there seems always to be one more act.

EZRA POUND

Literature is news that stays news.

How to Read, 1931

Great literature is simply language charged with meaning to the utmost
possible degree.

Ibid.

There is no reason why the same man should like the same book at 18
and at 48.

The ABC of Reading, 1934

[Civilization is] an old bitch gone at the teeth.

ROBINSON JEFFERS

Civilization is a transient sickness

Humanity is the mold to break away from, the atom to be split.

Eugene O'Neill

The playwright of today must dig at the roots of the sickness of today as he feels it—the death of the old God and the failure of science and materialism to give any satisfactory new one of the surviving primitive, religious instinct to find a meaning for life in, and to comfort its fears of death with.

Letter to George Jean Nathan, c. 1925

Archibald MacLeish

The perversion of the mind is only possible when those who should be heard in its defense are silent.

The Irresponsibles, 1940

A man who lives, not by what he loves but what he hates, is a sick man.

E. E. Cummings

People who live in steel houses should pull down the lightning.

"Jottings," Harvard *Wake,* 1951

Great men burn bridges before they come to them.

Ibid.

Equality is what does not exist among mortals.

Ibid.

Mark Van Doren

The dullest man sees the most things as the same; the livest man sees the most differences, and a completely live man tends . . . to find in even random objects a precious order and degree of being, as if the universe were here only that it might contain them.

Review of Gerard Manley Hopkins

If the plays of Shakespeare had not been easy to write they would have been impossible.

Shakespeare, 1939

Poetry speaks for itself. But poets, curiously enough, do not; and so it is time that they be defended against the silent charge, all the more damning because it is so silent, that they are a special race of men and women, different from all other creatures of their kind and possessed of faculties which would make them, if we knew them, only too wonderful to live with, not to say too embarrassing.

The Private Reader, "What Is a Poet?" 1942

In times like these the artist thinks of the world. He also thinks of himself; but the world changes faster than he does, and his eye cannot but follow it as far into the future as thought will go. Perhaps the activity should have been chronic with him; perhaps he should not be startled now. The world was always changing; it will always be changing; and who should know this better than the artist? He has to know, too, that the world never changes—the same old place, for better or for worse, simply looks different to its successive inhabitants. It is indeed different, and yet the "it" remains. The work of any artist, when it means enough to matter, means exactly this; and if it is given to few artists to mean so much, it is likewise given to few men to understand the mysteries of permanence and change. Few men of any sort have understood them, and no man has done so perfectly. The problem of the artist, like that of the philosopher, is immemorial; and difficult; and strange.

Address at American Academy, 1951

The value of knowledge in the conflict of truth and error is an ideal value, since there is never enough knowledge to resolve the conflict, or at any rate to resolve it absolutely. It is enough to know that Pilate's question, "What is truth?" will always be impossible to answer to the satisfaction of every man. When this is known, then knowledge exists in the most humane of all its forms—the recognition that any man may be right.

Columbia Bicentennial Pamphlet, 1953

The important thing about a poem is the reader.

In conversation, 1953

ROBERT HILLYER

When poets go, grammarians arrive.

Letter to a Teacher of English

I believe in my survival after death. Like many others before me, I have experienced "intimations of immortality." I can no more explain these than the brown seed can explain the flowering tree. Deep in the soil in time's midwinter, my very stirring and unease seem a kind of growing pain toward June.

This I Believe

ROBERT E. SHERWOOD

The playwright's chief stock in trade is feelings, not facts.

*XIV. Essayists and Aphorists
from Emerson to E. B. White*

Amos Bronson Alcott

To be ignorant of one's ignorance is the malady of the ignorant.

Ralph Waldo Emerson

Our age is retrospective. It builds the sepulchres of the fathers. It writes biographies, histories, and criticism. The foregoing generations beheld God and nature face to face; we, through their eyes. Why should not we also enjoy an original relation to the universe?

Nature, opening lines, 1836

Man is a god in ruins.

Ibid.

Whenever a true theory appears, it will be its own evidence. Its test is that it will explain all phenomena. Now many are thought not only unexplained but inexplicable: as language, sleep, madness, dreams, beasts, sex.

Ibid.

This time, like all times, is a very good one, if we but know what to do with it.

The American Scholar, 1837

Meek young men grow up in libraries, believing it their duty to accept the views which Cicero, which Locke, which Bacon, have given; forgetful that Cicero, Locke, and Bacon were only young men in libraries when they wrote these books.

Ibid.

The unstable estimates of men crowd to him whose mind is filled with a truth, as the heaped waves of the Atlantic follow the moon.

Ibid.

Beware when the great God lets loose a thinker on this planet.

Essays: First Series, "Circles," 1841

Proverbs, like the sacred books of each nation, are the sanctuary of the intuitions.

Ibid., "Compensation"

The only way to have a friend is to be one.

> *Ibid.*, "Friendship"

Santa Croce and the Dome of St. Peter's are lame copies after a divine model. Strasburg Cathedral is a material counterpart of the soul of Erwin of Steinbach. The true poem is the poet's mind; the true ship is the ship-builder.

> *Ibid.*, "History"

Every revolution was once a thought in one man's mind, and when the same thought occurs to another man, it is the key to that era. Every reform was once a private opinion, and when it shall be a private opinion again it will solve the problem of the age.

> *Ibid.*

God offers to every mind its choice between truth and repose. Take which you please,—you can never have both.

> *Ibid.*, "Intellect"

We grant that human life is mean, but how did we find out that it is mean?

> *Ibid.*, "The Over-Soul"

Do what we can, summer will have its flies. If we walk in the woods, we must feed mosquitoes.

> *Ibid.*, "Prudence"

To believe your own thought, to believe that what is true for you in your private heart is true for all men—that is genius.

> *Ibid.*, "Self-Reliance"

Trust thyself: every heart vibrates to that iron string. Accept the place the divine providence has found for you, the society of your contemporaries, the connection of events. Great men have always done so, and confided themselves childlike to the genius of their age, betraying their perception that the absolutely trustworthy was seated at their heart, working through their hands, predominating in all their being. And we are now men, and must accept in the highest mind the same transcendent destiny; and not minors and invalids in a protected corner, not cowards fleeing before a revolution, but guides, redeemers, and benefactors, obeying the Almighty effort and advancing on Chaos and the Dark.

Ibid.

Society everywhere is in conspiracy against the manhood of every one of its members. Society is a joint-stock company, in which the members agree, for the better securing of his bread to each shareholder, to surrender the liberty and culture of the eater. The virtue in most request is conformity. Self-reliance is its aversion. It loves not realities and creators, but names and customs.

Whoso would be a man, must be a nonconformist. He who would gather immortal palms must not be hindered by the name of goodness, but must explore if it be goodness. Nothing is at last sacred but the integrity of your own mind.

Ibid.

In every work of genius we recognize our own rejected thoughts; they come back to us with a certain alienated majesty.

Ibid.

Every true man is a cause, a country, and an age; requires infinite spaces and numbers and time fully to accomplish his design; and posterity seem to follow his steps as a train of clients. A man Caesar is born, and for ages after we have a Roman Empire. Christ is born, and millions of minds so grow and cleave to his genius that he is confounded with virtue and the possible of man. An institution is the lengthened shadow of one man.

Ibid.

As men's prayers are a disease of the will, so are their creeds a disease of the intellect.

Ibid.

Every Stoic was a Stoic; but in Christendom where is the Christian?

Ibid.

A foolish consistency is the hobgoblin of little minds, adored by little statesmen and philosophers and divines. With consistency a great soul has simply nothing to do. He may as well concern himself with his shadow on the wall. Speak what you think now in hard words and to-morrow speak what to-morrow thinks in hard words again, though it contradict every

thing you said to-day.—'Ah, so you shall be sure to be misunderstood.'—
Is it so bad then to be misunderstood? Pythagoras was misunderstood, and
Socrates, and Jesus, and Luther, and Copernicus, and Galileo, and Newton, and every pure and wise spirit that ever took flesh. To be great is to
be misunderstood.

Ibid.

Nothing can bring you peace but yourself. Nothing can bring you peace
but the triumph of principles.

Ibid., last lines

I love and honor Epaminondas—but I do not wish to be Epaminondas.
I hold it more just to love the world of this hour, than the world of *his*
hour.

Ibid., "Spiritual Laws"

There are not in the world at any one time more than a dozen persons
who read and understand Plato—never enough to pay for an edition of
his works; yet to every generation these come duly down, for the sake of
those few persons, as if God brought them in his hand.

Ibid.

Literature is the effort of man to indemnify himself for the wrongs of his
condition.

W. S. Landor, 1842

The years teach much which the days never know.

Essays: Second Series, "Experience," 1844

Every man is an impossibility until he is born.

Ibid.

That which we call sin in others is experiment for us.

Ibid.

I am always insincere, as always knowing there are other moods.

Ibid., "Nominalist and Realist"

The religions of men are the ejaculations of a few imaginative men.

Ibid., "The Poet"

It is not metres, but a metre-making argument that makes a poem—a thought so passionate and alive that like the spirit of a plant or an animal it has an architecture of its own, and adorns nature with a new thing.

Ibid.

The birth of a poet is the principal event in chronology.

Ibid.

The etymologist finds the deadest word to have been once a brilliant picture. Language is fossil poetry. As the limestone of the continent consists of infinite masses of the shells of animalcules, so language is made up of images or tropes, which now, in their secondary use, have long ceased to remind us of their poetic origin.

Ibid.

Nobody would be a charlatan who could afford to be sincere.

Ibid., "Politics"

Every actual State is corrupt. Good men must not obey the laws too well.

Ibid.

When nature removes a great man, people explore the horizon for a successor; but none comes, and none will. His class is extinguished with him. In some other and quite different field, the next man will appear.

Representative Men, "Uses of Great Men," 1850

Every hero becomes a bore at last.

Ibid.

Is not marriage an open question, when it is alleged, from the beginning of the world, that such as are in the institution wish to get out, and such as are out wish to get in?

Ibid., "Montaigne"

Life is eating us up. We shall be fables presently. Keep cool: it will be all one a hundred years hence.

Ibid.

I can reason down or deny everything except this perpetual belly: feed he must and will, and I cannot make him respectable.

Ibid.

Our impatience of miles, when we are in a hurry; but it is still best that
a mile should have seventeen hundred and sixty yards.

Ibid., "Plato"

Classics which at home are drowsily read have a strange charm in a
country inn, or in the transom of a merchant brig.

English Traits, 1856

Every god is there sitting in his sphere. The young mortal enters the hall
of the firmament; there is he alone with them alone, they pouring on him
benedictions and gifts, and beckoning him up to their thrones. On the
instant, and incessantly, fall snowstorms of illusions. He fancies himself
in a vast crowd which sways this way and that, and whose movements and
doings he must obey; he fancies himself poor, orphaned, insignificant. The
mad crowd drives hither and thither, now furiously commanding this
thing to be done, now that. What is he that he should resist their will,
and think or act for himself? Every moment new changes and new showers of deceptions to baffle and distract him. And when, by and by, for an
instant, the air clears and the cloud lifts a little, there are the gods still
sitting around him on their thrones—they alone and with him alone.

Illusions, 1857

Our chief want in life is somebody who shall make us do what we can.

Conduct of Life, "Considerations by the Way," 1860

There is always a best way of doing everything, if it be to boil an egg.
Manners are the happy ways of doing things.

Ibid., "Culture"

The riddle of the age has for each a private solution.

Ibid., "Fate"

Coal is a portable climate.

Ibid., "Wealth"

The value of a dollar is, to buy just things; a dollar goes on increasing in
value with all the genius and virtue of the world. A dollar in a university
is worth more than a dollar in a jail; in a temperate, schooled, law-abid-
ing community than in some sink of crime, where dice, knives and arsenic
are in constant play.

Ibid.

If a man own land, the land owns him.

Ibid.

Shallow men believe in luck.

Ibid., "Worship"

The louder he talked of his honor, the faster we counted our spoons.

Ibid.

The solar system has no anxiety about its reputation.

Ibid.

We are born believing. A man bears beliefs, as a tree bears apples.

Ibid.

The three practical rules, then, which I have to offer, are: 1. Never read any book that is not a year old; 2. Never read any but the famed books; 3. Never read any but what you like.

Society and Solitude, "Books," 1870

Now that is the wisdom of a man, in every instance of his labor, to hitch his wagon to a star, and see his chore done by the gods themselves.

Ibid., "Civilization"

Plain living and high thinking.

Ibid., "Domestic Life"

We boil at different degrees.

Ibid., "Eloquence"

Few envy the consideration enjoyed by the oldest inhabitant.

Ibid., "Old Age"

'Tis the good reader that makes the good book; in every book he finds passages which seem confidences or asides hidden from all else and unmistakably meant for his ear; the profit of books is according to the sensibility of the reader; the profoundest thought or passion sleeps as in a mine, until it is discovered by an equal mind and heart.

Ibid., "Success"

An everlasting Now reigns in nature, which hangs the same roses on our bushes which charmed the Roman and the Chaldean in their hanging gardens.

Ibid., "Works and Days"

To inflict anyone with a compulsory interview of more than ten minutes indicates a crude state of civilization.

Letters and Social Aims, 1875

Next to the originator of a good sentence is the first quoter of it.

Ibid., "Quotation and Originality"

By necessity, by proclivity and by delight, we all quote.

Ibid.

What is a weed? A plant whose virtues have not yet been discovered.

Fortune of the Republic

Hospitality consists in a little fire, a little food, and an immense quiet.

Journal

The things taught in colleges and schools are not an education, but the means of education.

Ibid., July 15, 1831

Went yesterday to Cambridge and spent most of the day at Mount Auburn; got my luncheon at Fresh Pond, and went back again to the woods. After much wandering and seeing many things, four snakes gliding up and down a hollow for no purpose that I could see—not to eat, not for love, but only gliding.

Ibid., April 11, 1834

It is very easy in the world to live by the opinion of the world. It is very easy in solitude to be self-centered. But the finished man is he who in the midst of the crowd keeps with perfect sweetness the independence of solitude. I knew a man of simple habits and earnest character who never put out his hands nor opened his lips to court the public, and having survived several rotten reputations of younger men, Honor came at last and sat down with him upon his private bench from which he had never stirred.

Ibid., December 22, 1834

In all my lectures, I have taught one doctrine, namely, the infinitude of
the private man.

Ibid., 1840

A sleeping child gives me the impression of a traveller in a very far
country.

Ibid., September 16, 1840

You shall have joy, or you shall have power, said God; you shall not have
both.

Ibid., October, 1842

Poetry must be as new as foam, and as old as the rock.

Ibid., March, 1845

The blazing evidence of immortality is our dissatisfaction with any other
solution.

Ibid., July, 1855

Gentlemen, I have ventured to offer you these considerations upon the
scholar's place and hope, because I thought that standing, as many of
you now do, on the threshold of this College, girt and ready to go and
assume tasks, public and private, in your country, you would not be sorry
to be admonished of those primary duties of the intellect whereof you
will seldom hear from the lips of your new companions. You will hear
every day the maxims of a low prudence. You will hear that the first duty
is to get land and money, place and name. "What is this Truth you seek?
what is this Beauty?" men will ask, with derision. If nevertheless God have
called any of you to explore truth and beauty, be bold, be firm, be true.
When you shall say, "As others do, so will I: I renounce, I am sorry for
it, my early visions; I must eat the good of the land and let learning and
romantic expectations go, until a more convenient season;"—then dies
the man in you; then once more perish the buds of art, and poetry, and
science, as they have died already in a thousand thousand men. The hour
of that choice is the crisis of your history, and see that you hold yourself
fast by the intellect. It is this domineering temper of the sensual world
that creates the extreme need of the priests of science. . . . Be content
with a little light, so it be your own. Explore, and explore. Be neither
chided nor flattered out of your position of perpetual inquiry. Neither
dogmatize, nor accept another's dogmatism. Why should you renounce

your right to traverse the star-lit deserts of truth, for the premature comforts of an acre, house, and barn? Truth also has its roof, and bed, and board. Make yourself necessary to the world, and mankind will give you bread, and if not store of it, yet such as shall not take away your property in all men's possessions, in all men's affections, in art, in nature, in hope.

Oration, Dartmouth College

Perpetual modernness is the measure of merit in every work of art.

A hero is no braver than an ordinary man, but he is brave five minutes longer.

Life consists in what a man is thinking of all day.

Thought is of no country.

Old Age brings along with its ugliness the comfort that you will soon be out of it. . . . To be out of the war, out of debt, out of the drought, out of the blues, out of the dentist's hands, out of the second thoughts, mortifications, and remorses that inflict such twinges and shooting pains,—out of the next winter, the high prices, and company below your ambition,— surely these are soothing hints. And, harbinger of this, what an alleviation is sleep, which muzzles all these dogs for me every day.

Conversation is an art in which a man has all mankind for his competitor.

OLIVER WENDELL HOLMES

The axis of the earth sticks out visibly through the center of each and every town or city.

The Autocrat of the Breakfast Table, 1858

The world's great men have not commonly been great scholars, nor its great scholars great men.

Ibid.

Insanity is often the logic of an accurate mind overtasked.

Ibid.

Unpretending mediocrity is good, and genius is glorious; but a weak flavor of genius in an essentially common person is detestable.

Ibid.

How many people live on the reputation of the reputation they might have made!

Ibid.

Fame usually comes to those who are thinking about something else.

Ibid.

A weak mind does not accumulate force enough to hurt itself; stupidity often saves a man from going mad.

Ibid.

Conceit is just as natural a thing to human minds as a centre is to a circle.

Ibid.

When a resolute young fellow steps up to the great bully, the world, and takes him boldly by the beard, he is often surprised to find it comes off in his hand, and that it was only tied on to scare away timid adventurers.

Elsie Venner, 1861

What I call a good patient is one who, having found a good physician, sticks to him until he dies.

The Young Practitioner, 1871

I firmly agree that if the whole *materia medica* as now used, could be sunk to the bottom of the sea, it would be all the better for mankind and all the worse for the fishes.

Lecture to a medical society

I would give more for a good nurse to take care of me while I was alive than for the best pathologist that ever lived to cut me up after I was dead.

Revolutions are not made by men in spectacles.

When you write in prose you say what you mean. When you write in verse you say what you must.

Identification with a locality is a surer passport to immortality than cosmopolitanism is.

A child's education should begin at least a hundred years before he is born.

The foolishest book is a kind of leaky boat on a sea of wisdom; some of the wisdom will get in anyhow.

Men heap together the mistakes of their lives, and create a monster they call Destiny.

Apology is only egotism wrong side out.

Heredity is an omnibus in which all our ancestors ride, and every now and then one of them puts his head out and embarrasses us.

Pretty much all the honest truthtelling there is in the world is done by children.

HENRY DAVID THOREAU

What is time but the stuff delay is made of?

> Review of a book on utopias, 1843

Waldo, why are you *not* here?

> To Emerson, when Thoreau was in jail for not paying the
> Massachusetts poll-tax, 1843, and Emerson asked him why
> he was there

I have no designs on society, or nature, or God. I am simply what I am, or I begin to be that. I *live* in the *present*. I only remember the past, and anticipate the future. I love reform better than its modes. There is no history of how bad became better. I believe something, and there is nothing else but that. I know that I am. I know that another is who knows more than I, who takes interest in me, whose creature, and yet whose kindred, in one sense, am I. I know that the enterprise is worthy. I know that things work well. I have heard no bad news.

> Letter to Mr. B., March 27, 1848

Pursue, keep up with, circle round and round your life, as a dog does his master's chaise. Do what you love. Know your own bone; gnaw it, bury it, unearth it, and gnaw it still. Do not be too moral. You may cheat yourself out of much life so. Aim above morality. Be not simply good; be good for something. All fables, indeed, have their morals; but the innocent enjoy the story. Let nothing come between you and the light. Respect men and brothers only. When you travel to the Celestial City, carry no letter of introduction. When you knock, ask to see God,—none of the servants. In what concerns you much, do not think that you have companions: know that you are alone in the world.

Ibid.

Any man more right than his neighbors constitutes a majority of one already.

Civil Disobedience, 1849

I heartily accept the motto, "That government is best which governs least;" and I should like to see it acted up to more rapidly and systematically. Carried out, it finally amounts to this, which also I believe— "That government is best which governs not at all;" and when men are prepared for it, that will be the kind of government which they will have. Government is at best but an expedient; but most governments are usually, and all governments are sometimes, inexpedient.

Ibid.

I think that we should be men first, and subjects afterward. It is not desirable to cultivate a respect for the law, so much as for the right. The only obligation which I have a right to assume is to do at any time what I think right.

Ibid.

The opportunities of living are diminished in proportion as what are called the "means" are increased. The best thing a man can do for his culture when he is rich is to endeavor to carry out those schemes which he entertained when he was poor.

Ibid.

Action from principle, the perception and the performance of right, changes things and relations; it is essentially revolutionary, and does not consist wholly with anything which was. It not only divides States and churches, it divides families; ay, it divides the *individual,* separating the diabolical in him from the divine.

Ibid.

It takes two to speak the truth—one to speak, and another to hear.

A Week on the Concord and Merrimack Rivers, 1849

Tradition is a more interrupted and feebler memory.

Ibid.

Heal yourselves, doctors; by God I live.

Ibid.

The wisest man preaches no doctrines; he has no scheme; he sees no rafter, not even a cobweb, against the heavens. It is clear sky.

Ibid.

It is an important epoch when a man who has always lived on the east side of a mountain, and seen it in the west, travels around and sees it in the east. Yet the universe is a sphere whose center is wherever there is intelligence. The sun is not so central as a man.

Ibid.

The frontiers are not east or west, north or south; but wherever a man *fronts* a fact.

Ibid.

It is not easy to write in a journal what interests us at any time, because to write it is not what interests us.

Ibid.

If a person lost would conclude that after all he is not lost, he is not beside himself, but standing in his own old shoes on the very spot where he is, and that for the time being he will live there; but the places that have known him, *they* are lost—how much anxiety and danger would vanish. I am not alone if I stand by myself. Who knows where in space this globe is rolling? Yet we will not give ourselves up for lost, let it go where it will.

Ibid.

Priests and physicians should never look one another in the face. They have no common ground, nor is there any to mediate between them. When the one comes, the other goes. They could not come together without laughter, or a significant silence, for the one's profession is a satire on the other's, and either's success would be the other's failure. It is wonderful that the physician should ever die, and that the priest should ever live. Why is it that the priest is never called to consult with the physician? Is it because men believe practically that matter is independent of spirit?

But what is quackery? It is commonly an attempt to cure the diseases of a man by addressing his body alone. There is need of a physician who shall minister to both soul and body at once, that is, to man. Now he falls between two stools.

Ibid.

The finest workers in stone are not copper or steel tools, but the gentle touches of air and water working at their leisure with a liberal allowance of time.

Ibid.

Live your life, do your work, then take your hat.

Ibid.

Shad are still taken in the basin of Concord River, at Lowell, where they are said to be a month earlier than the Merrimack shad, on account of the warmth of the water. Still patiently, almost pathetically, with instinct not to be discouraged, not to be *reasoned* with, revisiting their old haunts, as if their stern fates would relent, and still met by the Corporation with its dam. Poor shad! where is thy redress? When Nature gave thee instinct, gave she thee the heart to bear thy fate? . . . I for one am with thee, and who knows what may avail a crowbar against that Billerica dam? . . . Who hears the fishes when they cry? It will not be forgotten by some memory that we were contemporaries. Thou shalt ere long have thy way up the rivers, up all the rivers of the globe, if I am not mistaken. Yea, even thy dull watery dream shall be more than realized. If it were not so, but thou wert to be overlooked at first and at last, then would I not take their heaven. Yes, I say so, who think I know better than thou canst. Keep a stiff fin, then, and stem all the tides thou mayst meet.

Ibid.

Methinks my own soul must be a bright invisible green.

Ibid.

There is no rule more invariable than that we are paid for our suspicions by finding what we suspected.

Ibid., "Friendship"

Even the utmost goodwill and harmony and practical kindness are not sufficient for Friendship, for Friends do not live in harmony merely, as some say, but in melody. We do not wish for Friends to feed and clothe

our bodies—neighbors are kind enough for that—but to do the like office
to our spirits.

Ibid.

We often forbear to confess our feelings, not from pride, but for fear that
we could not continue to love the one who required us to give such proof
of our affection.

Ibid.

The partridge loves peas, but not those that go with her into the pot.

Walking, probably written 1851

It is true, we are but faint-hearted crusaders, even the walkers, nowadays,
who undertake no persevering, never-ending enterprises. Our expeditions
are but tours, and come round again at evening to the old hearth-side from
which we set out. Half the walk is but retracing our steps. We should go
forth on the shortest walk, perchance, in the spirit of undying adventure,
never to return—prepared to send back our embalmed hearts only as
relics to our desolate kingdoms. If you are ready to leave father and
mother, and brother and sister, and wife and child and friends, and never
see them again—if you have paid your debts, and made your will, and
settled all your affairs, and are a free man, then you are ready for a walk.

Ibid.

It is not worth while to go round the world to count the cats in Zanzibar.

Walden, 1854

I went to the woods because I wished to live deliberately, to front only
the essential facts of life, and see if I could not learn what it had to teach,
and not, when I came to die, discover that I had not lived. I did not wish
to live what was not life, living is so dear; nor did I wish to practice
resignation, unless it was quite necessary. I wanted to live deep and suck
out all the marrow of life, to live so sturdily and Spartan-like as to put to
rout all that was not life, to cut a broad swath and shave close, to drive
life into a corner, and reduce it to its lowest terms, and, if it proved to
be mean, why then to get the whole and genuine meanness of it, and
publish its meanness to the world; or if it were sublime, to know it by
experience, and be able to give a true account of it in my next excursion.

Ibid.

Men frequently say to me, "I should think you would feel lonesome down there, and want to be nearer to folks, rainy and snowy days and nights especially." I am tempted to reply to such,—This whole earth which we inhabit is but a point in space. How far apart, think you, dwell the two most distant inhabitants of yonder star, the breadth of whose disk cannot be appreciated by our instruments? Why should I feel lonely? is not our planet in the Milky Way? This which you put seems to me not to be the most important question. What sort of space is that which separates a man from his fellows and makes him solitary? I have found that no exertion of the legs can bring two minds much nearer to one another. What do we want most to dwell near to? Not to many men surely, the depot, the post-office, the bar-room, the meeting-house, the school-house, the grocery, Beacon Hill, or the Five Points, where men most congregate, but to the perennial source of our life, whence in all our experience we have found that to issue, as the willow stands near the water and sends out its roots in that direction. This will vary with different natures, but this is the place where a wise man will dig his cellar.

Ibid.

I frequently tramped eight or ten miles through the deepest snow to keep an appointment with a beech tree, or a yellow birch, or an old acquaintance among the pines.

Ibid.

I would rather sit on a pumpkin, and have it all to myself, than to be crowded on a velvet cushion.

Ibid.

A man is rich in proportion to the number of things which he can afford to let alone.

Ibid.

The cost of a thing is the amount of what I will call life which is required to pay for it, immediately or in the long run.

Ibid.

Superfluous wealth can buy superfluities only. Money is not required to buy one necessary of the soul.

Ibid.

As for the Doing-good, that is one of the professions that are full. Moreover, I have tried it fairly, and, strange as it may seem, am satisfied that it does not agree with my constitution.

Ibid.

I had three chairs in my house: one for solitude, two for friendship, three for society.

Ibid.

The owner of the axe, as he released his hold on it, said that it was the apple of his eye; but I returned it sharper than I received it.

Ibid.

I have lived some thirty years on this planet, and I have yet to hear the first syllable of valuable or even earnest advice from my seniors.

Ibid.

Some circumstantial evidence is very strong, as when you find a trout in the milk.

Ibid.

I long ago lost a hound, a bay horse, and a turtle-dove, and am still on their trail. Many are the travellers I have spoken concerning them, describing their tracks and what calls they answered to. I have met one or two who have heard the hound, and the tramp of the horse, and even seen the dove disappear behind a cloud, and they seemed as anxious to recover them as if they had lost them themselves.

Ibid.

Beware of all enterprises that require new clothes.

Ibid.

I once had a sparrow alight upon my shoulder for a moment while I was hoeing in a village garden, and I felt that I was more distinguished by that circumstance than I should have been by any epaulet I could have worn.

Ibid.

Why is it that a bucket of water soon becomes putrid, but frozen remains sweet forever? It is commonly said that this is the difference between the affections and the intellect.

Ibid.

What a man thinks of himself, that it is which determines, or rather indicates, his fate.

Ibid.

As if you could kill time without injuring eternity.

Ibid.

If you stand right fronting and face to face to a fact, you will see the sun glimmer on both its surfaces, as if it were a cimeter, and feel its sweet edge dividing you through the heart and marrow, and so you will happily conclude your mortal career. Be it life or death, we crave only reality. If we are really dying, let us hear the rattle in our throats and feel cold in the extremities; if we are alive, let us go about our business.

Time is but the stream I go a-fishing in. I drink at it; but while I drink I see the sandy bottom and detect how shallow it is. Its thin current slides away, but eternity remains. I would drink deeper; fish in the sky, whose bottom is pebbly with stars. I cannot count one. I know not the first letter of the alphabet, I have always been regretting that I was not as wise as the day I was born. The intellect is a cleaver; it discerns and rifts its way into the secret of things. I do not wish to be any more busy with my hands than is necessary. My head is hands and feet. I feel all my best faculties concentrated in it. My instinct tells me that my head is an organ for burrowing, as some creatures use their snout and fore-paws, and with it I would mine and burrow my way through these hills. I think that the richest vein is somewhere hereabouts; so by the divining rod and thin rising vapors I judge; and here I will begin to mine.

Ibid.

The greater part of what my neighbors call good I believe in my soul to be bad, and if I repent of anything, it is very likely to be my good behavior. What demon possessed me that I behaved so well?

Ibid.

While men believe in the infinite, some ponds will be thought to be bottomless.

Ibid.

To be awake is to be alive. I have never met a man who was quite awake. How could I have looked him in the face?

Ibid.

It is life near the bone, where it is sweetest.

Ibid.

Love your life, poor as it is. You may perhaps have some pleasant, thrilling, glorious hours, even in a poorhouse. The setting sun is reflected as brightly from the windows of the almshouse as from the rich man's abode.

Ibid.

To him whose elastic and vigorous thought keeps pace with the sun, the day is a perpetual morning.

Ibid.

Thank Heaven, here is not all the world. . . . Yet we think that if rail fences are pulled down, and stone walls piled up on our farms, bounds are henceforth set to our lives and our fates decided. If you are chosen town clerk, forsooth, you cannot go to Tierra del Fuego this summer: but you may go to the land of infernal fire nevertheless. . . . What does Africa, what does the West stand for? Is not our own interior white on the chart? black though it may prove, like the coast, when discovered. Is it the source of the Nile, or the Niger, or the Mississippi, or a Northwest Passage around this continent, that we would find? . . . Be rather the Mungo Park, the Lewis and Clark and Frobisher, of your own streams and oceans; explore your own higher altitudes, with shiploads of preserved meats to support you, if they be necessary; and pile the empty cans sky-high for a sign. . . . Every man is the lord of a realm beside which the earthly empire of the Czar is but a petty state, a hummock left by the ice. . . . There are continents and seas in the moral world to which every man is an isthmus or an inlet, yet unexplored by him. . . . It is easier to sail many thousand miles through cold and storm and cannibals, in a government ship, with five hundred men and boys to assist one, than it is to explore the private sea, the Atlantic and Pacific Ocean of one's being alone.

Ibid.

Man's capacities have never been measured; nor are we to judge of what he can do by any precedents, so little has been tried.

Ibid.

There are a thousand hacking at the branches of evil to one who is striking at the root.

Ibid.

Philanthropy is almost the only virtue which is sufficiently appreciated by mankind.

Ibid.

For my part, I could easily do without the post office. I think that there are very few important communications made through it. To speak critically, I never received more than one or two letters in my life—I wrote this some years ago—that were worth the postage.

Ibid.

Simplify, simplify.

Ibid.

I learned this, at least, by my experiment: that if one advances confidently in the direction of his dreams, and endeavors to live the life which he has imagined, he will meet with a success unexpected in common hours. He will put some things behind, will pass an invisible boundary; new, universal, and more liberal laws will begin to establish themselves around and within him; or the old laws be expanded, and interpreted in his favor in a more liberal sense, and he will live with the license of a higher order of things. In proportion as he simplifies his life, the laws of the universe will appear less complex, and solitude will not be solitude, nor poverty poverty, nor weakness weakness. If you have built castles in the air, your work need not be lost; that is where they should be. Now put foundations under them.

Ibid.

Why should we be in such haste to succeed and in such desperate enterprises? If a man does not keep pace with his companions, perhaps it is because he hears a different drummer. Let him step to the music which he hears, however measured or far away.

Ibid.

I would have my thoughts, like wild apples, to be food for walkers, and will not warrant them to be palatable if tasted in the house.

Wild Apples, probably written 1858

I have been in the habit of going across your lots much oftener than is usual, as many of you, perhaps to your sorrow, are aware. Yet many of you, to my relief, have seemed not to be aware of it; and, when I came across you in some out-of-the-way nook of your farms, have inquired, with an air of surprise, if I were not lost, since you had never seen me in that part of the town or country before; when, if the truth were known, and it had not been for betraying my secret, I might with more propriety have inquired if *you* were not lost, since I had never seen *you* there before. I have several times shown the proprietor the shortest way out of his wood-lot.

"The Succession of Forest Trees," address read to the Middlesex Agricultural Society in Concord, September, 1860

In proportion as our inward life fails, we go more constantly and desperately to the post-office. You may depend on it, that the poor fellow who walks away with the greatest number of letters, proud of his extensive correspondence, has not heard from himself this long while.

"Life Without Principle," *Atlantic Monthly,* 1863

Almost any man knows how to earn money, but not one in a million knows how to spend it. If he had known so much as this, he would never have earned it.

Journal

The bluebird carries the sky on his back.

Ibid.

Think of cats, for instance. They are neither Chinese or Tartars. They do not go to school, nor read the Testament. . . . What sort of philosophers are we, who know absolutely nothing of the origin and destiny of cats?

Ibid.

I have been breaking silence these twenty-three years and have hardly made a rent in it. Silence has no end; speech is but the beginning of it.

Ibid.

There is no remedy for love but to love more.

Ibid., July 25, 1839

The sudden revolutions of these times and this generation have acquired a very exaggerated importance. They do not interest me much, for they are not in harmony with the longer periods of nature. The present, in any aspect in which it can be presented to the smallest audience, is always mean. God does not sympathize with the popular movements.

Ibid., January 7, 1842

How often must one feel, as he looks back on his past life, that he has gained a talent but lost a character!

Ibid., March 28, 1842

And then the frogs, bullfrogs; they are the more sturdy spirits of ancient wine-bibbers and wassailers, still unrepentant, trying to sing a catch in their Stygian lakes. They would fain keep up the hilarious good fellowship and all the rules of their old round tables, but they have waxed hoarse and solemnly grave and serious their voices, mocking at mirth, and their wine has lost its flavor and is only liquor to distend their paunches, and never comes sweet intoxication to drown the memory of the past, but mere saturation and water-logged dullness and distension. Still the most aldermanic, and with his chin upon a pad, which answers for a napkin to his drooling chaps, under the eastern shore quaffs a deep draught of the once scorned water, and passes round the cup with the ejaculation *tr-r-r-r-r-oonk, tr-r-r-r-r-oonk, tr-r-r-r-r-oonk!* and straightway comes over the water from some distant cove the selfsame password, where the next in seniority and girth has gulped down to his mark; and when the strain has made the circuit of the shores, then ejaculates the master of ceremonies with satisfaction *tr-r-r-r-r-oonk!* and each in turn repeats the sound, down to the least distended, leakiest, flabbiest paunched, that there be no mistake; and the bowl goes round again, until the sun dispels the morning mist, and only the patriarch is not under the pond, but vainly bellowing *troonk* from time to time, pausing for a reply.

Ibid., August, 1845

The poet is a man who lives at last by watching his moods. An old poet comes at last to watch his moods as narrowly as a cat does a mouse.

Ibid., August 28, 1851

Why I left the woods? I do not think that I can tell. . . . Perhaps it is none of my business, even if it is yours. . . . There was a little stagnation, it may be. About two o'clock in the afternoon the world's axle creaked as if it needed greasing. . . . Perhaps if I lived there much longer, I might live there forever. One would think twice before he accepted heaven on such terms. A ticket to Heaven must include tickets to Limbo, Purgatory, and Hell.

Ibid., 1851 (four years after leaving Walden Pond)

The youth gets together his materials to build a bridge to the moon, or perchance a palace or temple on the earth, and at length the middleaged man concludes to build a wood-shed with them.

Ibid., July 14, 1852

A writer who does not speak out of a full experience uses torpid words, wooden or lifeless words, such words as "humanitary," which have a paralysis in their tails.

Ibid.

I have now a library of nearly nine hundred volumes, over seven hundred of which I wrote myself.

> *Ibid.*, 1853. In 1849 he paid to have printed 1,000 copies of his first book, *A Week on the Concord and Merrimack Rivers;* four years later 706 copies were returned unsold.

To inherit property is not to be born—it is to be still-born, rather.

Ibid., March 13, 1853

How earthy old people become,—mouldy as the grave. Their wisdom smacks of the earth. There is no foretaste of immortality in it. They remind me of earthworms and mole crickets.

Ibid., August 16, 1853

On the evening of the 5th the body of a man was found in the river between Fair Haven Pond and Lee's, much wasted. How these events disturb our associations and tarnish the landscape! It is a serious injury done to a stream.

Ibid., April 13, 1854

The man I meet with is not often so instructive as the silence he breaks.

Ibid., January 7, 1857

Passed a very little boy in the street today, who had on a homemade cap of a woodchuck-skin, which his father or elder brother had killed and cured, and his mother or elder sister had fashioned into a nice warm cap. I was interested by the sight of it, it suggested so much of family history, adventure with the chuck, story told about it, not without exaggeration, the human parents' care of their young these hard times. Johnny was promised many times, and now the work has been completed . . . a perfect little idyl, as they say. The cap was large and round, big enough, you would say, for the boy's father, and had some kind of cloth visor stitched to it. The top of the cap was evidently the back of the woodchuck as it was expanded in breadth, contracted in length, and it was as fresh and handsome as if the woodchuck wore it himself. The great gray-tipped wind hairs were all preserved, and stood out above the brown only a little more loosely than in life. As if he put his head into the belly of the wood-chuck, having cut off his tail and legs and substituted a visor for the head. The little fellow wore it innocently enough, not knowing what he had on, forsooth, going about his small business pit-a-pat; and his black eyes sparkled beneath it when I remarked on its warmth, even as the wood-chuck's might have done. Such should be the history of every piece of clothing that we wear.

Ibid., February 28, 1860

Thank God, men cannot as yet fly, and lay waste the sky as well as the earth! We are safe on that side for the present.

Ibid., January 3, 1861

The highest law gives a thing to him who can use it.

Nations! What are nations? Tartars! and Huns! and Chinamen! Like in-sects they swarm. The historian strives in vain to make them memorable. It is for want of a man that there are so many men.

A man sits as many risks as he runs.

The poet is he that hath fat enough, like bears and marmots, to suck his claws all winter. He hibernates in this world, and feeds on his own mar-row. Alas, the poet too is, in one sense, a sort of dormouse gone into winter quarters of deep and serene thoughts, insensible to surrounding circumstances; his words are the relation of his oldest and finest memory, a wisdom drawn from the remotest experience. Other men lead a starved existence, meanwhile, like hawks that would fain keep on the wing and trust to pick up a sparrow now and then.

A sentence should read as if its author, had he held a plough instead of a pen, could have drawn a furrough deep and straight to the end.

Any fool can make a rule, and every fool will mind it.

Compliments and flattery oftenest excite my contempt by the pretension they imply; for who is he that assumes to flatter me? To compliment often implies an assumption of superiority in the complimenter. It is, in fact, a subtle detraction.

Read the best books first, or you may not have a chance to read them at all.

HENRY VAN DYKE

It is with rivers as it is with people: the greatest are not always the most agreeable nor the best to live with.

Little Rivers

AGNES REPPLIER

The clearsighted do not rule the world, but they sustain and console it.

Eight Decades, 1937

LOUISE IMOGEN GUINEY

Quotations (such as have point and lack triteness) from the great old authors are an act of filial reverence on the part of the quoter, and a blessing to a public grown superficial and external.

Scribner's Magazine, January, 1911

JOHN JAY CHAPMAN

There are lots of people who can't think seriously without injuring their minds. Their minds were not meant for this use, and so the more they think the feebler they grow.

The cure is simple.

Speak out opinions before you think—and before the other fellow speaks. Thus you will give your mind some chance of forming them in a natural way—unconsciously. Accustom yourself to not knowing what your opinions are till you have blurted them out, and thus find what they are. That's what talk is for.

To Henry James

A thing is not truth until it is so strongly believed in that the believer is convinced that its existence does not depend on him. This cuts off the pragmatist from knowing what truth is.

Essays

FRANK MOORE COLBY

Self-esteem is the most voluble of the emotions.

The Colby Essays, 1926

It is the rule among college presidents that the mental disturbance following any of their remarks shall be almost as imperceptible as if the remarks
had not been made. A mind that is not only calm itself, but the cause of
calm in others—that is the true college presidential ideal; and as a rule
it is realized, especially on public occasions.

Ibid.

He is annoyed by the senseless refusal of almost everybody to shape his
life in such a manner as will redound to the advantage of the beings who
will people the earth a hundred thousand years hence.

Ibid., of H. G. Wells

Every man ought to be inquisitive through every hour of his great adventure down to the day when he shall no longer cast a shadow in the sun.
For if he dies without a question in his heart, what excuse is there for his
continuance?

Ibid., "Simple Simon"

By rights, satire is a lonely and introspective occupation, for nobody can
describe a fool to the life without much patient self-inspection.

Ibid.

True satire is not the sneering substance that we know, but satire that
includes the satirist.

Ibid., "Satire and Teeth"

Something off your own bat (to use a coarse post-classic figure) is wanted
now and then. One learns little more about a man from the feats of his
literary memory than from the feats of his alimentary canal.

Ibid., "Quotation and Allusion"

The classics are not and never have been chiefly valuable as the means
of success. They are obviously valued as the means of escaping its consequences. They are not esteemed for getting one on in the modern world,
but for getting one pleasantly out of it.

Ibid., "Debates on the Classics"

Were it not for the presence of the unwashed and the half-educated, the formless, queer and incomplete, the unreasonable and absurd, the infinite shapes of the delightful human tadpole, the horizon would not wear so wide a grin.

Ibid., "Imaginary Obligations"

A "new thinker," when studied closely, is merely a man who does not know what other people have thought.

Ibid., "The Margin of Hesitation"

In public we say the race is to the strongest; in private we know that a lopsided man runs the fastest along the little side-hills of success.

Ibid., "Constrained Attitudes"

ALBERT JAY NOCK

As sheer casual reading-matter, I still find the English dictionary the most interesting book in our language.

Memoirs of a Superfluous Man, 1943

Money does not pay for anything, never has, never will. It is an economic axiom as old as the hills that goods and services can be paid for only with goods and services; but twenty years ago this axiom vanished from everyone's reckoning, and has never reappeared. No one has seemed in the least aware that everything which is paid for must be paid for out of production, for there is no other source of payment.

Ibid.

With Mark Hopkins on one end of a log and a student on the other, the student gets the best out of Hopkins and gets as much of it as he can absorb; the law of diminishing returns does not touch him. Add twenty students, and neither he nor the twenty gets the same thing; add two hundred, and it is luck if anybody gets anything remotely like the same thing. All Souls College, Oxford, planned better than it knew when it limited the number of its undergraduates to four; four is exactly the right number for any college which is really intent on getting results.

Ibid.

A man's country is where the things he loves are most respected.

Ibid.

CLARENCE DAY

The ant is knowing and wise; but he doesn't know enough to take a vacation. The worshipper of energy is too physically energetic to see that he cannot explore certain higher fields until he is still.

This Simian World, 1920

A sudden vision comes to me of one of the first far-away apemen who tried to use reason instead of instinct as a guide for his conduct. I imagine him, perched in a tree, torn between those two voices, wailing loudly at night by a river, in his puzzled distress.

My poor far-off brother!

Ibid.

If mankind ever is swept aside as a failure, what a brilliant and enterprising failure he at least will have been!

Ibid.

I thought of a photograph I had once seen, of a ship being torpedoed. There it was, the huge, finely made structure, awash in the sea, with tiny black spots hanging on to its sides—crew and passengers. The great ship, even while sinking, was so mighty, and those atoms so helpless. Yet, it was those tiny beings that had created the ship. They had planned it and built it and guided its bulk through the waves. They had also invented a torpedo that could rend it asunder.

Ibid.

It is possible that our race may be an accident, in a meaningless universe, living its brief life uncared-for, on this dark, cooling star; but even so— and all the more—what marvelous creatures we are! What fairy-story, what tale from the *Arabian Nights* of the jinns, is a hundredth part as wonderful as this true fairy-story of simians! It is so much more heartening, too, than the tales we invent. A universe capable of giving birth to many such accidents is—blind or not—a good world to live in, a promising universe.

And if there are no other such accidents, if we stand alone, if all the uncountable armies of planets are empty, or peopled by animals only, with no keys to thought, then we have done something so mighty, what may it not lead to! What powers may we not develop before the Sun dies! We once thought we lived on God's footstool; it may be a throne.

This is no world for pessimists. An amoeba on the beach, blind and helpless, a mere bit of pulp—that amoeba has grandsons today who read Kant and play symphonies. Will those grandsons in turn have descendants who will sail through the void, discover the foci of forces, the means to control them, and learn how to marshal the planets and grapple with space? Would it after all be any more startling than our rise from the slime?

No sensible amoeba would have ever believed for a minute that any of his most remote children would build and run dynamoes. Few sensible men of today stop to feel, in their hearts, that we live in the very same world where that miracle happened.

This world, and our racial adventure, are magical still.

Ibid.

It wasn't at all easy for Father to see that he had any faults; and if he did, it didn't even occur to him to ask God to forgive them. He forgave them himself. In his moments of prayer, when he and God tried to commune with each other, it wasn't his own shortcomings that were brought on the carpet, but God's.

He expected a great deal of God, apparently. Not that he wanted God's help, of course; or far less His guidance. No, but it seemed that God—like the rest of us—spoiled Father's plans. Father was always trying to bring this or that good thing to pass, only to find that there were obstacles in the way. These of course roused his wrath. He would call God's attention to such things. They should not have been there. He didn't actually accuse God of gross inefficiency, but when he prayed his tone was loud and angry, like that of a dissatisfied guest in a carelessly managed hotel.

God and My Father, 1932

It disgusted him when atheists attacked religion: he thought they were vulgar. But he also objected to have religion make demands upon him—he felt that religion too was vulgar, when it tried to stir up men's feelings. It had its own proper field of activity, and it was all right there, of course; but there was one place religion should let alone, and that was a man's soul. He especially loathed any talk of walking hand in hand with the Saviour. And if he ever found the Holy Ghost trying to soften his heart, he would have regarded the behavior as distinctly uncalled for; even ungentlemanly.

Ibid.

At the gate of Heaven, if there was any misunderstanding about his own ticket, Father counted on Mother to get him in. That was her affair.

Ibid.

Father declared he was going to buy a new plot in the cemetery, a plot all for himself. "And I'll buy one on a corner," he added triumphantly, "where I can get out!"

Mother looked at him, startled but admiring, and whispered to me, "I almost believe he could do it."

Life with Father, 1935

The world of books is the most remarkable creation of man. Nothing else that he builds ever lasts. Monuments fall. Nations perish. Civilizations grow old and die out. And after an era of darkness new races build others. But in the world of books are volumes that have seen this happen again and again, and yet live on, still young, still as fresh as the day they were written, still telling men's hearts of the hearts of men centuries dead.

JOHN ERSKINE

The lover of intelligence must be patient with those who cannot readily share his passion. Some pangs the mind will inflict upon the heart. It is a mistake to think that men are united by elemental affections. Our affections divide us. We strike roots in immediate time and space, and fall in love with our locality, the customs and the language in which we were brought up. Intelligence unites us with mankind, by leading us in sympathy to other times, other places, other customs; but first the prejudiced roots of affection must be pulled up. These are the old pangs of intelligence, which still comes to set a man at variance against his father, saying, "He that loveth father or mother more than me, is not worthy of me."

Yet, if intelligence begins in a pang, it proceeds to a vision. Through measureless time its office has been to make of life an opportunity, to make goodness articulate, to make virtue a fact. In history at least, if not yet in the individual, Plato's faith has come true, that sin is but ignorance, and knowledge and virtue are one. But all that intelligence has accomplished dwindles in comparison with the vision it suggests and warrants. Beholding this long liberation of the human spirit, we foresee, in every new light of the mind, one unifying mind, wherein the human race shall know its destiny and proceed to it with satisfaction, as an idea moves to its proper conclusion; we conceive of intelligence at last as the infinite order, wherein man, when he enters it, shall find himself.

The Moral Obligation to Be Intelligent, 1921

When you sit down to write a novel, you find you must have something besides characters and a plot; you must have a philosophy of life.

The Delight of Great Books, 1928

To me nature is everything that man is born to, and art is the difference he makes in it.

Gentle Reader, December, 1931

Music is the only language in which you cannot say a mean or sarcastic thing.

WILLIAM A. ORTON

If you keep your mind sufficiently open people will throw a lot of rubbish into it.

Everyman Amid the Stereotypes, 1946

CHRISTOPHER MORLEY

There is no squabbling so violent as that between people who accepted an idea yesterday and those who will accept the same idea tomorrow.

Religio Journalistici

High heels were invented by a woman who had been kissed on the forehead.

My theology, briefly, is that the universe was dictated but not signed.

Man: An ingenious arrangement of portable plumbing.

Lots of times you have to pretend to join a parade in which you're not really interested in order to get where you're going.

Life is a foreign language: all men mispronounce it.

It is all very well to wear a crown of thorns, indeed every sensitive person carries one in his heart. But there are times when it ought to be worn cocked over one ear.

Few girls are as well shaped as a good horse.

Dogs are born journalists: their voices are like extras of dismay.

No man is lonely while eating spaghetti—it requires so much attention.

ROGER WILLIAM RIIS

I admire the human race. I do, indeed. Everybody is running us down, these days, for the mess they say we have made here and there and everywhere. Pshaw! That's short-range stuff, a worm's-eye view of our world. Over the marching and abundant centuries, we haven't made any mess. Far from it!

. . . If [man] has limits, I do not see where they are. I do not think he has limits. I think he is a child of the universe who inherits eternity. I think he is wonderful, I am his devoted partisan, and I am proud indeed to be one of him.

I Admire the Human Race

DAVID McCORD

A pedestrian is a man in danger of his life; a walker is a man in possession of his soul.

E. B. WHITE

The sound of the sea is the most time-effacing sound there is. The centuries reroll in a cloud and the earth becomes young again when you listen, with eyes shut, to the sea—a young green time when the water and the land were just getting acquainted and had known each other for only a few billion years and the mollusks were just beginning to dip and creep in the shallows; and now man the invertebrate, under his ribbed umbrella, anoints himself with oil and pulls on his Polaroid glasses to stop the glare and stretches out his long brown body at ease upon a towel on the warm sand and listens.

The sea answers all questions, and always in the same way; for when you read in the papers the interminable discussions and the bickerings and the prognostications and the turmoil, the disagreements and the fateful decisions and the agreements and the plans and the programs and the threats and the counter threats, then you close your eyes and the sea dispatches one more big roller in the unbroken line since the beginning of the world and it combs and breaks and returns foaming and saying: "So soon?"

One Man's Meat, 1944

The possession of a dog today is a different thing from the possession of a dog at the turn of the century, when one's dog was fed on mashed potato and brown gravy and lived in a doghouse with an arched portal. Today a dog is fed on scraped beef and Vitamin B$_1$, and lives in bed with you.

Ibid.

The future . . . seems to me no unified dream but a mince pie, long in the baking, never quite done.

Ibid.

I sometimes doubt that a writer should refine or improve his workroom by so much as a dictionary: one thing leads to another and the first thing you know he has a stuffed chair and is fast asleep in it.

Ibid.

A poet dares be just so clear and no clearer; he approaches lucid ground warily, like a mariner who is determined not to scrape his bottom on anything solid. A poet's pleasure is to withhold a little of his meaning, to intensify by mystification. He unzips the veil from beauty, but does not remove it. A poet utterly clear is a trifle glaring. . . .

There is also the obscurity which is the result of the poet's wishing to appear mad, if only a little mad. This is rather common and rather dreadful. I know of nothing more distasteful than the work of a poet who has taken leave of his reason deliberately, as a commuter might of his wife. . . .

My quarrel with poets (who will be surprised to learn that a quarrel is going on) is not that they are unclear, but that they are too diligent. Diligence in a poet is the same as dishonesty in a bookkeeper. There are rafts of bards who are writing too much, too diligently, and too slyly. Few poets are willing to wait out their pregnancy—they prefer to have a premature baby and allow it to incubate after being safely laid in Caslon Old Style.

Ibid.

There is always the miracle of the by-products. Plane a board, the shavings accumulate around your toes ready to be chucked into the stove to kindle your fires (to warm your toes so that you can plane a board). Draw some milk from a creature to relieve her fulness, the milk goes to the little pig to relieve his emptiness. Drain some oil from a crankcase, and you smear it on the roosts to control the mites. The worm fattens on the apple, the young goose fattens on the wormy fruit, the man fattens on the young goose, the worm awaits the man. Clean up the barnyard, the pulverized dung from the sheep goes to improve the lawn (before a rain in autumn); mow the lawn next spring, the clippings go to the compost pile, with a few thrown to the baby chickens on the way; spread the compost on the garden and in the fall the original dung, after many vicissitudes, returns to the sheep in the form of an old squash. From the fireplace, at the end of a November afternoon, the ashes are carried to the feet of the lilac bush, guaranteeing the excellence of a June morning.

Ibid.

Up at 5:15 and after breakfast to the doctor's, the country seeming very beautiful and cheerful after a light fall of snow. I am always humbled by the infinite ingenuity of the Lord, who can make a red barn cast a blue shadow.

Ibid.

Most writers find the world and themselves practically interchangeable, and in a sense the world dies every time a writer dies, because, if he is any good, he has been wet nurse to humanity during his entire existence and has held earth close around him, like the little obstetrical toad that goes about with a cluster of eggs attached to his legs.

New Yorker, November 10, 1945

The time not to become a father is eighteen years before a world war.

The Second Tree from the Corner, 1953

The year ends on a note of pure experimentation. Dr. Fritz Zwicky last week tried to hurl some metal slugs out into space, free of the earth's gravitational pull. Dr. Zwicky stood in New Mexico and tossed from there. He was well equipped: he had a rocket that took the slugs for the first forty-mile leg of the journey and then discharged them at high velocity to continue on their own. The desire to toss something in a new way, to toss it to a greater distance, is fairly steady in men and boys. Boys stand on high bridges, chucking chips down wind, or they stand on the shore of a pond, tossing rocks endlessly at a floating bottle, or at a dead cat, observing closely every detail of their experiment, trying to make every stone sail free of the pull of past experience. Then the boys grow older, stand in the desert, still chucking, observing, wondering. They have almost exhausted the earth's possibilities and are going on into the empyrean to throw at the stars, leaving the earth's people frightened and joyless, and leaving some fellow scientists switching over from science to politics and hoping they have made the switch in time.

Ibid., "Experimentation"

One college president has remarked that in fifty years "only 5 per cent of the people will be reading." For this, of course, one must be prepared. But how prepare? To us it would seem that even if only one person out of a hundred and fifty million should continue as a reader, he would be the one worth saving, the nucleus around which to found a university. We think this not impossible person, this Last Reader, might very well stand in the same relation to the community as the queen bee to the colony of bees, and that the others would quite properly dedicate themselves wholly to his welfare, serving special food and building special accommodations. From his nuptial, or intellectual, flight would come the new race of men, linked perfectly with the long past by the unbroken chain of the intellect, to carry on the community. But it is more likely that our modern hive of bees, substituting a coaxial cable for spinal fluid, will try to perpetuate the race through audio-visual devices, which ask no discipline of the mind and which are already giving the room the languor of an opium parlor.

Reading is the work of the alert mind, is demanding, and under ideal conditions produces finally a sort of ecstasy. As in the sexual experience, there are never more than two persons present in the act of reading—the writer, who is the impregnator, and the reader, who is the respondent. This gives the experience of reading a sublimity and power unequalled by any other form of communication. It would be just as well, we think, if educators clung to this great phenomenon and did not get sidetracked, for although books and reading may at times have played too large a part in the educational process, that is not what is happening today. Indeed, there is very little true reading, and not nearly as much writing as one would suppose from the towering piles of pulpwood in the dooryards of our paper mills. Readers and writers are scarce, as are publishers and reporters. The reports we get nowadays are those of men who have not gone to the scene of the accident, which is always farther inside one's head than it is convenient to penetrate without galoshes.

Ibid., "The Future of Reading"

Of the home economists we have met in our lifetime, all had one trait in common: not one of them was at home.

Ibid., "The Home"

Photography is the most self-conscious of the arts. The act of photography has been glorified in the newspicture magazines, and even in the newspapers. Publisher and reader enjoy shoptalk together. The editor continually points to "best shots," or "newspicture of the week," confident that his clientele is following every move of the shutter. . . . In the writing profession, there is nothing that quite corresponds to this sort of camaraderie. We feel rather left out. Perhaps we make a mistake not to make more fuss about the mechanics of our writing. When we toss off a particularly neat ablative absolute, or kill a hanging participle in the last three seconds of play, maybe our editor should call the matter to the attention of the reader. A writer does a lot of work the reader isn't conscious of, and never gets any credit. This paragraph was exposed for eighteen minutes, in a semi-darkened room. The writer was leaning far out over his typewriter, thinking to beat the band.

Ibid., "Peaks in Journalism"

Anne Morrow Lindbergh

To write or to speak is almost inevitably to lie a little.

The Wave of the Future, 1940

Margaret Halsey

Since I have been a parent, I have noticed [one] major particular in which my daughter's early life has no kinship whatsoever with my early years. . . . The circumstance that when I and my contemporaries were four years old, it was not possible to make very much money out of children. There were no comic books, no radio, no television, and the movies were still in a fledgling state. Except for oatmeal and library books, children were not consumers.

The Folks at Home, 1953

Russell Lynes

The only graceful way to accept an insult is to ignore it; if you can't ignore it, top it; if you can't top it, laugh at it; if you can't laugh at it, it's probably deserved.

"The Art of Accepting," 1954

The art of acceptance is the art of making someone who has done you a small favor wish that he might have done you a greater one.

Ibid.

Never accept flattery as though it were a compliment, and never treat a compliment as though it were mere flattery.

Ibid.

A truly appreciative child will break, lose, spoil, or fondle to death any really successful gift within a matter of minutes.

Ibid.

NORMAN COUSINS

Modern Man is Obsolete.

Title of book, 1945

Belonging to a nation, man has nations that can speak for him. Belonging to a religion, man has religions that can speak for him. Belonging to an economic and social order, man has economic or political orders that can speak for him. But belonging to the human race, man is without a spokesman.

Who Speaks for Man?, 1953

Free will and determinism, I was told, are like a game of cards. The hand that is dealt you represents determinism. The way you play your hand represents free will.

This I Believe

ALAN BECK

Between the innocence of babyhood and the dignity of manhood we find a delightful creature called a boy. Boys come in assorted sizes, weights, and colors, but all boys have the same creed: To enjoy every second of every minute of every hour of every day and to protest with noise (their only weapon) when their last minute is finished and the adult males pack them off to bed at night.

Boys are found everywhere—on top of, underneath, inside of, climbing on, swinging from, running around, or jumping to. Mothers love them, little girls hate them, older sisters and brothers tolerate them, adults ignore them, and Heaven protects them. A boy is Truth with dirt on its face, Beauty with a cut on its finger, Wisdom with bubble gum in its hair, and the Hope of the future with a frog in its pocket.

When you are busy, a boy is an inconsiderate, bothersome, intruding jangle of noise. When you want him to make a good impression, his brain turns to jelly or else he becomes a savage, sadistic jungle creature bent on destroying the world and himself with it.

A boy is a composite—he has the appetite of a horse, the digestion of a sword swallower, the energy of a pocket-size atomic bomb, the curiosity of a cat, the lungs of a dictator, the imagination of a Paul Bunyan, the shyness of a violet, the audacity of a steel trap, the enthusiasm of a fire cracker, and when he makes something he has five thumbs on each hand.

He likes ice cream, knives, saws, Christmas, comic books, the boy across the street, woods, water (in its natural habitat), large animals, Dad, trains, Saturday mornings, and fire engines. He is not much for Sunday School, company, schools, books without pictures, music lessons, neckties, barbers, girls, overcoats, adults, or bedtime.

Nobody else is so early to rise, or so late to supper. Nobody else gets so much fun out of trees, dogs, and breezes. Nobody else can cram into one pocket a rusty knife, a half-eaten apple, three feet of string, an empty Bull Durham sack, two gum drops, six cents, a slingshot, a chunk of unknown substance, and a genuine supersonic code ring with a secret compartment.

A boy is a magical creature—you can lock him out of your workshop, but you can't lock him out of your heart. You can get him out of your study, but you can't get him out of your mind. Might as well give up— he is your captor, your jailer, your boss, and your master—a freckled-face, pint-sized, cat-chasing bundle of noise. But when you come home at night with only the shattered pieces of your hopes and dreams, he can mend them like new with the two magic words—"Hi, Dad!"

> *What Is a Boy?* Bert Wheeler read this on *This Is Show Business,* February 25, 1951, and sixty thousand requests for copies came in from the East Coast alone.

Eric Hoffer

Fear comes from uncertainty. When we are absolutely certain, whether of our worth or worthlessness, we are almost impervious to fear. Thus a feeling of utter unworthiness can be a source of courage.

> *The Passionate State of Mind,* 1955

There is perhaps in all misfits a powerful secret craving to turn the whole of humanity into misfits. Hence partly their passionate advocacy of a drastically new social order. For we are all misfits when we have to adjust ourselves to the wholly new.

> *Ibid.*

Pride is a sense of worth derived from something that is not organically part of us, while self-esteem derives from the potentialities and achievements of the self. We are proud when we identify ourselves with an imaginary self, a leader, a holy cause, a collective body or possessions. There is fear and intolerance in pride; it is sensitive and uncompromising. The less promise and potency in the self, the more imperative is the need for pride. The core of pride is self-rejection.

Ibid.

It is impossible to think clearly in understatements. Thought is a process of exaggeration. The refusal to exaggerate is not infrequently an alibi for the disinclination to think or praise.

Ibid.

The nonconformist is a more stable type than the conforming individual. It is the average man of today who shows the most striking differences from people of other ages and other civilizations. The rebel of today is twin brother of rebels in all ages and climes.

Ibid.

The fear of becoming a "has been" keeps some people from becoming anything.

Ibid.

XV. Critical Spirits

ART AND MUSIC CRITICS

•

JAMES G. HUNEKER

There is no disputing tastes—with the tasteless.

Variations, 1921

A critic is a man who expects miracles.

It's pretty—but is it Art?

Attributed to

BERNARD BERENSON

Ultimates in art criticism, if they exist, must be sought for in the life-enhancement that results from identifying oneself with the object enjoyed or putting oneself in its place. For the act of deciphering shapes in a given design, or pattern, or composition offers a satisfaction that is little more than mental, and scarcely at all life-enhancing. In order to be life-enhancing an object must appeal to the whole of one's being, to one's senses, nerves, muscles, viscera, and to one's feeling for direction, for support and weight, for balance, for stresses and counter-stresses, and for the minimum of space required for one's indispensable bodily autonomy—an autonomy so precious that to yield an iota of it is to be a lover, to be compelled to surrender even an inch is to be a de-individualized prisoner. How can you identify yourself or put yourself in the place of a cube? It is easier no doubt to imagine oneself a cylinder, but if that gave us joy, we should love factory chimneys, and late Turkish minarets, like those for instance of the Mohamet Ali Mosque on the Cairo citadel. I and most of my readers are too unsophisticated to understand what bodily pleasure may be derived from the diagonal. As for the pyramid, it has a suggestion of restful compactness, and benefits by the ease with which memory calls up Egypt and shapes that at Gizeh have overwhelmed us with pride in the audacity of mere men, like ourselves, who dared to build on the scale of the horizon, and to insert into the pell-mell of nature rational geometric shapes in harmonious contrast with it.

An object to be life-enhancing must be one with which we can not only identify ourselves, but identify ourselves more easily, completely, and happily than we do in ordinary conditions. In art the object must not arouse any of those wakeful cannibal appetites that can never be satisfied, not even by satiety. . . . It should not arouse us to action, although it cannot help influencing conduct; it should not affect any of our productive, reproductive, or transitive energies, but tune us like instruments—instruments for ecstasy.

Natural objects, whether animate or inanimate, because they stimulate activities that are greedy, predatory, or coldly analytical, entailing excitement and exhaustion, with the resulting feeling of lowered vitality, cannot be life-enhancing. To be life-enhancing, visible things—with which we are here concerned—must be presented in a way to make us feel that we are perceiving them more quickly, grasping them more deeply than we do ordinarily. The instantaneous result is an illusion of unwonted and unexpected ease of functioning, and its inseparable accompaniment the sense of heightened vitality, all of which we credit to the object so presented to us.

It follows that only works of art can be life-enhancing, for merely visible things by themselves are not—except where we have learnt to enjoy them as if they were already works of art, as is the case with landscape for many of us. We have been taught by assiduous if not always conscious looking at representations of landscape not only to enjoy *feeling* nature as some may instinctively, but to enjoy seeing it in terms of art.

Not all artifacts are life-enhancing. Some are and some are not. Why is this? What makes them so or not so?

When artifacts are not merely representations of shapes, whether in nature or in the mind, but have tactile values and movement, then only are they life-enhancing.

Aesthetics and History, 1948

The reader may become aware that the words "beauty" and "beautiful" rarely occur in this book. I have not avoided them deliberately, but art history is the history of art as an experience and is indifferent to questions of beauty. I tend to use either of them in connection with "natural" objects rather than with the representations of them. "Beautiful" is too comprehensive a word for our activity. It is used to express satisfaction with any activity. Thus I recall phrases like a "beautiful surgical opera-tion," a "beautiful solution" of a problem, a "beautiful trick," used with the same zest as a "beautiful woman," a "beautiful landscape," a "beauti-ful picture." For which reason among others I seldom allow myself to use the words "beauty" and "beautiful" when trying to appreciate as well as appraise a work of art.

Ibid.

All thinking, and analytic thinking in particular is, as compared with ex-perience, a fictitious process directed by our imperative urge to under-stand, and through understanding to enhance experience. Thinking is never more than trying to inscribe within a circle the polygon that comes nearest to coinciding with it.

Ibid.

Leo Stein

My ideal of a picture is that every part of it should oblige the looker-on who has any real sense for a whole to see the rest.

Journey into Self, 1950

To fail is human. We must *climb* mountains because we cannot live on the summits.

Ibid.

Inspiration soon dies and is with difficulty reborn, but ingenuity only sleeps and is easily awakened.

Ibid.

Boredom is an emptiness filled with insistence.

Ibid.

The actually probable is often the apparently impossible.

Ibid.

David Randolph

Parsifal is the kind of opera that starts at 6 o'clock. After it has been going three hours you look at your watch and it says 6.20.

DRAMA CRITICS

•

PERCY HAMMOND

Upon looking over this report, I find that I have knocked everything but the chorus girls' legs—but nature has anticipated me there.

Review of a musical

The human knee is a joint and not an entertainment.

GEORGE JEAN NATHAN

If acting is to be termed an art, it is, like the living picture, a freak art, an art with belladonna in its eyes and ever, even at its highest, a bit grotesque.

The Critic and the Drama, 1922

The fine drama or the fine piece of music does not make its auditor part of a crowd; it removes him, and every one else in the crowd, and makes him an individual. The crowd ceases to exist as a crowd; it becomes a crowd of units, of separate individuals. The dramas of Mr. Owen Davis make crowds; the dramas of Shakespeare make individuals.

Ibid.

Life, as I see it, is for the fortunate few—life with all its Chinese lanterns, and sudden, lovely tunes, and gay sadness. In so far as I have any philosophy at all, it is founded upon that theory. For the Nietzschean "Be hard!" I have no use, however. It savors too much of canon, thong and overly intense purpose. For myself, I substitute "Be indifferent." I was born indifferent and at forty I find myself unchanged in attitude. . . . Indignation does not make, and never has made, the world any better than has my own objectionable philosophy of contentful *laissez faire*. No great man from Jesus Christ to Stonewall Jackson has been fired by philosophical asperity and spleen. Rome, the greatest nation in history, was never indignant about anything. Nor has been or is the nation of tomorrow, Japan. The chronic indignation of France is rapidly driving her onto the rocks.

The World in Falseface, "Foreword," 1923

There are two kinds of dramatic critics: destructive and constructive. I am a destructive. There are two kinds of guns: Krupp and pop.

Ibid.

The beautiful day, the day of blue and gold and sunshine, is God's gift to the plain people; the bad day, the day of gloom and gray and rain, He has reserved for the exclusive pleasure of the aristocracy. The artist, the connoisseur of emotions, the philosopher—these have no use for the fair day: it distracts them, summons them from their introspection and solitude, calls them into the open. On such a day, work and those pleasures dear to men with a taste for the sequestered are impossible: the outside beckons too persuasively and too disconcertingly. But when the world is full of wet and fog and the monotony of rain, then the artist, the connoisseur of quiet, the philosophers and all their brothers are happy. For it is on such days, while the yokelry is melancholy because it cannot be eating dill pickles and cheese sandwiches on the roadsides, or riding in Fords through the Jersey swamps, or chasing little white gutta-percha balls across the grass with a repertoire of clubs, that men of soul and sadness revel in the happiness that only God's elect can comprehend.

Materia Critica, 1924

[La Duse possessed] that one thing every great actress has had, has and must have—something that may idiotically be described as a sad arm; that line of the arm that, when extended from the shoulder, has about it something of melancholy. The extended right arm of Eleonora Duse had in it all the tears of Tristan and Isolde.

Ibid.

Poetry is uncouth, unshaven, boisterous prose afflicted with a crying drunk. Through its empty prose head there flow suddenly unsteady visions of its boyhood home, the little red schoolhouse, its first sweetheart, and the first kiss in the field of daisies back of the old circus lot, and, passing its hand over its prosy, stubby face, it has a moment of alcoholic self-disesteem and of melancholy repentance for what it thinks it might have been and might have had—had things been other than they are—of an almost unreal happiness. It idiotically and boozily wants something it cannot have, something that, once gone, it can never recapture, and in this mood it sings its futile, foolish, groggy and sometimes very beautiful song.

Ibid.

The heart and soul of genius may be mad, but the mind of true genius is ever as clear as the heavens seen through pine trees.

Ibid.

The notion, held by certain artists, that an artist can most convincingly record emotion when he himself is from one romantic cause or another afire with emotion is directly kin to the notion that a drunken man makes the best bartender.

Ibid.

Good drama is anything that interests an intelligently emotional group of persons assembled together in an illuminated hall.

The Theatre of George Jean Nathan, 1926

My code of life and conduct is simply this: work hard; play to the allowable limit; disregard equally the good and bad opinion of others; never do a friend a dirty trick . . . never grow indignant over anything . . . live the moment to the utmost of its possibilities . . . and be satisfied with life always, but never with oneself.

Testament of a Critic, 1931

When a jackass brays, no one pays any attention to him, not even other jackasses. But when a lion brays like a jackass, even the lions in the neighborhood may be pardoned for exhibiting a little surprise.

Ibid.

Anyone can write the truth but, when everybody already knows it, it takes some nose-scratching to present it in a fashion that will make the reader believe he is getting it for the first time.

The Theatre Book of the Year, 1948

An optimist is the kind of person who believes a housefly is looking for a way to get out.

The Theater in the Fifties, 1953

The fact about many play revivals is that, far from reviving the plays, they rather make them mortally ill.

Ibid.

No chronically happy man is a trustworthy critic.

Ibid.

Criticism is the art wherewith a critic tries to guess himself into a share of the author's fame.

The House of Satan

BROOKS ATKINSON

In the ideal sense nothing is uninteresting; there are only uninterested people.

JOHN MASON BROWN

To many people dramatic criticism must seem like an attempt to tattoo soap bubbles.

Broadway in Review, 1940

Existence is a strange bargain. Life owes us little; we owe it everything. The only true happiness comes from squandering ourselves for a purpose.

WOLCOTT GIBBS

It only goes to show what God could do if he had the money.

When the new landscaping at Moss Hart's home on Long Island was pointed out to him. Frank Case, *Tales of a Wayward Inn,* attributes the remark to Gibbs, who denies authorship, putting the blame on Case himself.

LOUIS KRONENBERGER

In tragedy men aspire to more than they achieve; in comedy they pretend to more.

The Thread of Laughter, 1952

To what extent sex itself is a comic theme must naturally vary with the morality of a particular age: there are times when it seems shocking for a man ever to have a mistress; there are times when it seems even more shocking for a man never to have one.

Ibid.

Tragedy carves out in granite the fact that Character is Fate; but high comedy knows that everything is writ in water, that the real enemy, the real betrayer and barbarian, is Time.

Ibid.

LITERARY CRITICS

•

MARGARET FULLER

Man is not made for society, but society is made for man.

I accept the universe.

> Carlyle commented, "Gad! she'd better!"

JAMES RUSSELL LOWELL

There is nothing so desperately monotonous as the sea, and I no longer wonder at the cruelty of pirates.

> *Fireside Travels,* "At Sea," 1864

He who is firmly seated in authority soon learns to think security, and not progress, the highest lesson of statecraft.

> *Among My Books,* "New England Two Centuries Ago"

What a sense of security in an old book which Time has criticized for us!

> *My Study Windows,* "Library of Old Authors," 1871

Let us be of good cheer, however, remembering that the misfortunes hardest to bear are those which never come.

> *Democracy and Addresses,* 1886

Typewriters quotha! They are as bad as postal cards. Both of them are unclean things I have never touched. . . . I could never say what I would if I had to pick out my letters like a learned pig.

> Letter to Mrs. W. K. Clifford, June 11, 1889

The devil loves nothing better than the intolerance of reformers.

What men prize most is a privilege, even if it be that of chief mourner at a funeral.

If youth be a defect, it is one we outgrow only too soon.

Let no man write a line that he would not have his daughter read.

It is not the insurrections of ignorance that are dangerous, but the revolts of intelligence.

BRANDER MATTHEWS

A highbrow is a person educated beyond his intelligence.

GEORGE EDWARD WOODBERRY

A nation's poets are its true owners; and by the stroke of the pen they convey the title-deeds of its real possession to strangers and aliens.

WILLIAM LYON PHELPS

The only war I ever approved of was the Trojan war; it was fought over a woman and the men knew what they were fighting for.
Sermon, Riverside Church, New York City, June 25, 1933

This is the final test of a gentleman: his respect for those who can be of no possible service to him.

EDITH HAMILTON

There is a field where all wonderful perfections of microscope and telescope fail, all exquisite niceties of weights and measures, as well as that which is behind them, the keen and driving power of the mind. No facts however indubitably detected, no effort of reason however magnificently maintained, can prove that Bach's music is beautiful.
Witness to the Truth, 1948

HENRY SEIDEL CANBY

Skunk cabbages! a thousand sonnets died in that misnomer.
Meditations in the Woods

MARY M. COLUM

The art of aristocrats, the art of enriching life.

Max Eastman

Modernity is a poor thing to feel priggish about; it only makes you a more obvious mark for the prigs of a new modernity to sneer back at. No man can keep up with the times for more than seventy years, and after that his frantic efforts to do so look silly forever.

The Enjoyment of Laughter, 1936

I don't know why it is we are in such a hurry to get up when we fall down. You might think we would lie there and rest awhile.

Ibid.

A simple experiment will distinguish two types of human nature. Gather a throng of people and pour them into a ferryboat. By the time the boat has swung into the river you will find that a certain proportion have taken the trouble to climb upstairs, in order to be out on deck and see what is to be seen as they cross over. The rest have settled indoors, to think what they will do upon reaching the other side, or perhaps lose themselves in apathy and tobacco smoke. But leaving out those apathetic, or addicted to a single enjoyment, we may divide all the alert passengers on the boat into two classes—those who are interested in crossing the river, and those who are merely interested in getting across.

The Enjoyment of Poetry, 1939

Van Wyck Brooks

No one should ever publish a book until he has read it aloud to a woman. . . . Women are the arbiters of words, and we should listen to them because they live close to the meanings of words. Men become infatuated with words themselves. Women are closer to the general life, the source of good style, while men tend to live the particular life, the source of bad style. So women will never allow you to say "obfuscate" when "bewilder" will do just as well; and they shiver at words like "historicity" and will not be comforted if you use them.

A Chilmark Miscellany: Notes from a Journal

Whoever is accustomed to reading with a definite subject in mind cannot long endure desultory reading. A subject acts as a magnet attracting, in all one reads, the facts and the ideas that are relevant to it, and this creates an excitement in the mind that makes all purposeless reading tame and insipid. And yet what a pity this is, for it is desultory reading that develops one's taste. It is fortunate that when we are young we are unfocused.

"A Writer's Notebook," Nation, November 14, 1953

ELIZABETH DREW

Too often travel, instead of broadening the mind, merely lengthens the conversation.

JOHN CROWE RANSOM

All the poets famous in our tradition, or very nearly all, have been poets of a powerful moral cast.

So I shall try a preliminary definition of the poet's traditional function on behalf of society: he proposed to make virtue delicious. He compounded a moral effect with an aesthetic effect. The total effect was not a pure one, but it was rich, and relished highly. The name of the moral effect was goodness; the name of the aesthetic effect was beauty. Perhaps these did not have to co-exist, but the planners of society saw to it that they should; they called upon the artists to reinforce morality with charm.

The World's Body, 1938

J. DONALD ADAMS

How much words have in common with money! They too are counters of exchange; like money they are inflated and debased, put in circulation and withdrawn; they accumulate interest, they are coined, they grow smooth and blurred with usage; they are hoarded and they are spent lavishly; they can be counterfeit; they jingle and they ring true; they convince and they seduce; they are accepted (too often) at their face value; and they lend themselves easily (or I would not be writing these particular words) to speculation.

New York Times Book Review, 1951

BURTON RASCOE

What no wife of a writer can ever understand, no matter if she lives with him for twenty years, is that a writer is working when he's staring out of the window.

EDMUND WILSON

The young, usually subject to exaggerated enthusiasms, are today not enthusiastic—not enthusiastic, that is, about books: they merely approve or
disapprove when a book does or does not suit their politics. But, seriously,
I find it a pity that they do not learn to read for pleasure. They may presently find that an acquaintance with the great works of art and thought
is the only real insurance possible against the barbarism of the time.

The Shores of Light

To detective-story addicts, then, I say: Please do not write me any more
letters telling me that I have not read the right books. And to the seven
correspondents who are with me and who in some cases have thanked me
for helping them to liberate themselves from a habit which they recog-
nised as wasteful of time and degrading to the intellect but into which
they had been bullied by convention and the portentously invoked examples of Woodrow Wilson and André Gide—to these staunch and pure
spirits I say: Friends, we represent a minority, but Literature is on our
side. With so many fine books to be read, so much to be studied and
known, there is no need to bore ourselves with this rubbish. And with the
paper shortage pressing on all publication and many first-rate writers
forced out of print, we shall do well to discourage the squandering of this
paper that might be put to better use.

Classics and Commercials

KENNETH BURKE

The artist [in satire] is seeking simultaneously to take risks and escape
punishment for his boldness.

CHARLES S. POORE

It might be said of this author, that not only does he wear his heart on
his sleeve, but his glands as well.

New York Times Book Review, November, 1934

LIONEL TRILLING

Snobbery is pride in status without pride in function.

The Liberal Imagination, 1950

The poet is in command of his fantasy, while it is exactly the mark of the neurotic that he is possessed by his fantasy.

Ibid.

Some paradox of our natures leads us, when once we have made our fellow men the objects of our enlightened interest, to go on to make them the objects of our pity, then of our wisdom, ultimately of our coercion.

Ibid.

CLEANTH BROOKS

Wit is not only an acute perception of analogies; it is a lively awareness of the fact that the obvious attitude toward a given situation is not the only possible attitude. Because wit, for us, is still associated with levity, it may be well to state it in its most serious terms. The witty poet's glancing at other attitudes is not merely "play"—an attempt to puzzle or show off his acuteness of perception; it is possible to describe it as merely his refusal to blind himself to a multiplicity which exists.

The Well-Wrought Urn

XVI. Tellers of Tales
from Washington Irving to James Jones

How convenient it would be to many of our great men and great families of doubtful origin, could they have the privilege of the heroes of yore, who, whenever their origin was involved in obscurity, modestly announced themselves descended from a god.

Knickerbocker's History of New York, 1809

Man passes away, his name perishes from record and recollection; his history is as a tale that is told, and his very monument becomes a ruin.

The Sketch Book, 1819–20

Those men are most apt to be obsequious and conciliating abroad, who are under the discipline of shrews at home.

Ibid., "Rip Van Winkle"

A sharp tongue is the only edged tool that grows keener with constant use.

Ibid.

Even to this day they never hear a thunderstorm of a summer afternoon about the Kaatskill, but they say Hendrick Hudson and his crew are at their game of nine-pins; and it is a common wish of all hen-pecked husbands in the neighborhood, when life hangs heavy on their hands, that they might have a quieting draught out of Rip Van Winkle's flagon.

Ibid.

The sorrow for the dead is the only sorrow from which we refuse to be divorced.

Ibid., "Rural Funerals"

Whenever a man's friends begin to compliment him about looking young, he may be sure that they think he is growing old.

Bracebridge Hall, "Bachelors," 1822

There is a certain relief in change, even though it be from bad to worse; as I have found in travelling in a stage-coach, that it is often a comfort to shift one's position and be bruised in a new place.

Tales of a Traveller, "To the Reader," 1824

913

I am always at a loss to know how much to believe of my own stories.

Ibid.

NATHANIEL HAWTHORNE

The great want which mankind labors under at this present moment is sleep. The world should recline its vast head on the first convenient pillow and take an age-long nap.

Mosses from an Old Manse, 1846

Truth often finds its way to the mind close muffled in robes of sleep, and then speaks with uncompromising directness of matters in regard to which we practise an unconscious self-deception during our waking moments.

Ibid., "The Birthmark"

On the wall hung a row of portraits, representing the forefathers of the Bellingham lineage, some with armor on their breasts, and others with stately ruffs and robes of peace. All were characterized by the sternness and severity which old portraits so invariably put on; as if they were the ghosts, rather than the pictures, of departed worthies, and were gazing with harsh and intolerant criticism at the pursuits and enjoyments of living men.

At about the center of the oaken panels, that lined the hall, was suspended a suit of mail, not, like the pictures, an ancestral relic, but of most modern date. . . . There was a steel head-piece, a cuirass, a gorget, and greaves, with a pair of gauntlets and a sword hanging beneath; all, especially the helmet and breast-plate, so highly burnished as to glow with white radiance, and scatter an illumination everywhere about the floor. . . .

Little Pearl—who was as greatly pleased with the gleaming armor as she had been with the glittering frontispiece of the house—spent some time looking into the polished mirror of the breast-plate.

"Mother," cried she, "I see you here. Look! Look!"

Hester looked, by way of humoring the child; and she saw that, owing to the peculiar effect of the convex mirror, the scarlet letter was represented in gigantic and exaggerated proportions, so as to be greatly the most prominent feature of her appearance. In truth, she seemed absolutely hidden behind it. Pearl pointed upward, also, at a similar picture in the head-piece; smiling at her mother with the elfish intelligence that was so familiar an expression on her small physiognomy. That look of naughty merriment was likewise reflected in the mirror, with so much

breadth and intensity of effect, that it made Hester Prynne feel as if it
could not be the image of her own child, but of an imp who was seeking
to mold itself into Pearl's shape.

The Scarlet Letter, 1850

Among many morals which press upon us from the poor minister's miserable experience, we put only this into a sentence: "Be true! Be true! Be
true! Show freely to the world, if not your worst, yet some trait whereby
the worst may be inferred!"

Ibid.

Hester Prynne, gazing steadfastly at the clergyman, felt a dreary influence
come over her, but wherefore or whence she knew not; unless that he
seemed so remote from her own sphere, and utterly beyond her reach.
One glance of recognition, she had imagined, must needs pass between
them. She thought of the dim forest, with its little dell of solitude, and
love, and anguish, and the mossy tree-trunk, where, sitting hand in hand,
they had mingled their sad and passionate talk with the melancholy murmur of the brook. How deeply had they known each other then! And was
this the man? She hardly knew him now! He, moving proudly past, enveloped, as it were, in the rich music, with the procession of majestic and
venerable fathers; he, so unattainable in his worldly position, and still
more so in that far vista of his unsympathizing thoughts, through which
she now beheld him! Her spirit sank with the idea that all must have
been a delusion, and that, vividly as she had dreamed it, there could be
no real bond betwixt the clergyman and herself. And thus much of a
woman was there in Hester, that she could scarcely forgive him,—least of
all now, when the heavy footstep of their approaching Fate might be
heard, nearer, nearer, nearer!—for being able so completely to withdraw
himself from their mutual world; while she groped darkly, and stretched
forth her cold hands, and found him not.

Ibid.

I begin to suspect that a man's bewilderment is the measure of his wisdom.

The House of the Seven Gables, 1851

At the moment of execution—with the halter about his neck and while
Colonel Pyncheon sat on horseback, grimly gazing at the scene—Maule
had addressed him from the scaffold, and uttered a prophecy, of which
history as well as fireside tradition, has preserved the very words. "God,"

said the dying man, pointing his finger, with a ghastly look, at the undismayed countenance of his enemy, "God will give him blood to drink!"

Ibid.

But we strive in vain to put the idea into words. No adequate expression of the beauty and profound pathos with which it impresses us is attainable. This being, made only for happiness, and heretofore so miserably failing to be happy—his tendencies so hideously thwarted that, some unknown time ago, the delicate springs of his character, never morally or intellectually strong, had given way, and he was now imbecile—this poor forlorn voyager from the Islands of the Blest, in a frail bark, on a tempestuous sea, had been flung by the last mountain-wave of his shipwreck into a quiet harbor. There, as he lay more than half lifeless on the strand, the fragrance of an earthly rose-bud had come to his nostrils, and, as odours will, had summoned up reminiscences or visions of all the living and breathing beauty amid which he should have had his home. With his native susceptibility of happy influences, he inhales the slight ethereal rapture into his soul, and expires!

Ibid., the death of Clifford Pyncheon

This greatest moral consolation, which we derive from the transitoriness of all things—from the right of saying, in every conjunction,—"This, too, shall pass away."

The Marble Faun, 1860

We sometimes congratulate ourselves at the moment of waking from a troubled dream: it may be so the moment after death.

Journal, October 25, 1835

Four precepts: to break off customs; to shake off spirits ill-disposed; to meditate on youth; to do nothing against one's genius.

American Notebooks, October 25, 1836

Articulate words are a harsh clamor and dissonance. When man arrives at his highest perfection, he will again be dumb!

Ibid., April, 1841

I am glad you think my style plain. I never, in any one page or paragraph, aimed at making it anything else, or giving it any other merit—and I wish people would leave off talking about its beauty. If it have any, it is only pardonable as being unintentional. The greatest possible merit of style is, of course, to make the words absolutely disappear into the thought.

Letter to an editor, 1851

I wandered from hall to hall with a weary and heavy heart, wishing (Heaven forgive me!) that the Elgin Marbles and the frieze of the Parthenon were all burnt to lime. . . . The present is burthened too much with the past. We have not time, in our earthly existence, to appreciate what is warm with life, and immediately around us; yet we heap up all these old shells, out of which human life has long emerged, casting them off forever. I do not see how future ages are to stagger onward under all this dead weight, with the additions that will be continually made to it.

Notebooks, March, 1856 (in the British Museum)

Romance and poetry, ivy, lichens, and wall-flowers need ruin to make them grow.

The Marble Faun, "Preface," 1860

They have the pale tint of flowers that blossomed in too retired a shade— the coolness of a meditative habit, which diffuses itself through the feeling and observation of every sketch. Instead of passion there is sentiment; and, even in what purport to be pictures of actual life, we have allegory, not always so warmly dressed in its habiliments of flesh and blood as to be taken into the reader's mind without a shiver. Whether from lack of power, or an unconquerable reserve, the author's touches have often an effect of tameness; the merriest man can hardly contrive to laugh at his broadest humor; the tenderest woman, one would suppose, will hardly shed warm tears at his deepest pathos. The book, if you would see anything in it, requires to be read in the clear, brown, twilight atmosphere in which it was written.

Of *Twice-Told Tales,* his first book, fifteen years after it was published.

The greatest obstacle to being heroic is the doubt whether one may not be going to prove one's self a fool; the truest heroism is to resist the doubt, and the profoundest wisdom is to know when it ought to be resisted and when to be obeyed.

Labor is the curse of the world, and nobody can meddle with it without becoming proportionately brutified.

HARRIET BEECHER STOWE

The huge green fragment of ice on which she alighted pitched and creaked as her weight came on it, but she stayed there not a moment. With wild cries and desperate energy she leaped to another and still another cake;—stumbling—leaping—slipping—springing upwards again! Her shoes were gone—her stockings cut from her feet—while blood marked every step; but she saw nothing, felt nothing, till dimly, as in a dream, she saw the Ohio side, and a man helping her up the bank.

Uncle Tom's Cabin, Eliza's escape, 1851–52

"Shif'less!" said Miss Ophelia.

Ibid.

"Have you ever heard anything about God, Topsy?" The child looked bewildered, but grinned as usual.

"Do you know who made you?"

"Nobody, as I knows on," said the child, with a short laugh. . . . "I spect I grow'd."

Ibid.

I's so awful wicked there can't nobody do nothin' with me. I used to keep old Missis a swarin' at me half de time. I spects I's the wickedest crittur in the world.

Ibid. Topsy is speaking.

There is no death to such as thou, dear Eva! neither darkness nor shadow of death; only such a bright fading as when the morning star fades in the golden dawn.

Ibid.

If ever a woman feels proud of her lover, it is when she sees him as a successful public speaker.

Dred, 1864

HERMAN MELVILLE

That voyager steered his bark through seas, untracked before; ploughed his own path mid jeers; though with a heart that oft was heavy with the thought, that he might only be too bold, and grope where land was none.

So I . . .

But this new world here sought, is stranger far than his, who stretched his vans from Palos. It is the world of mind; wherein the wanderer may gaze round, with more of wonder than Balboa's band roving through the golden Aztec glades.

But fiery yearnings their own phantom-future make, and deem it present. So, if after all these fearful, fainting trances, the verdict be, the golden haven was not gained; yet, on bold quest thereof, better to sink in boundless deeps, than float on vulgar shoals; and give me, ye gods, an utter wreck, if wreck I do.

Mardi, 1848

As a man-of-war that sails through the sea, so this earth that sails through the air. We mortals are all on board a fast-sailing, never-sinking world-frigate, of which God was the ship-wright; and she is but one craft in a Milky-Way fleet, of which God is the Lord High Admiral. The port we sail from is forever astern. And though far out of sight of land, for ages and ages we continue to sail with sealed orders, and our last destination remains a secret to ourselves and our officers; yet our final haven was predestined ere we slipped from the stocks of creation.

Thus sailing with sealed orders, we ourselves are the repositories of the secret packet, whose mysterious contents we long to learn. There are no mysteries out of ourselves. But let us not give ear to the superstitious, gun-deck gossip about whither we may be gliding, for, as yet, not a soul on board of us knows—not even the commodore himself; assuredly not the chaplain; even our professor's scientific surmisings are in vain. On that point, the smallest cabin-boy is as wise as the captain. And believe not the hypochondriac dwellers below hatches, who will tell you, with a sneer, that our world-frigate is bound to no final harbour whatever; that our voyage will prove an endless circumnavigation of space. Not so. For how can this world-frigate prove our eventual abiding place, when, upon our first embarkation, as infants in arms, her violent rolling—in after life unperceived—makes every soul of us sea-sick? Does not this show, too, that the very air we here inhale is uncongenial, and only becomes endurable at last through gradual habituation, and that some blessed, placid haven, however remote at present, must be in store for us all?

White-Jacket, the last chapter, 1850

Call me Ishmael. Some years ago—never mind how long precisely—having little or no money in my purse, and nothing particular to interest me on shore, I thought I would sail about a little and see the watery part of the world. It is a way I have of driving off the spleen, and regulating the circulation. Whenever I find myself growing grim about the mouth; whenever it is damp, drizzly November in my soul; whenever I find my-self involuntarily pausing before coffin warehouses, and bringing up the rear of every funeral I meet; and especially whenever my hypos get such an upper hand of me, that it requires a strong moral principle to prevent me from deliberately stepping into the street, and methodically knocking people's hats off—then, I account it high time to get to sea as soon as I can. This is my substitute for pistol and ball. With a philosophical flourish Cato throws himself upon his sword; I quietly take to the ship. There is nothing surprising in this. If they but knew it, almost all men in their degree, some time or other, cherish very nearly the same feelings towards the ocean with me.

Moby Dick, opening paragraph, 1851

Once more. Say, you are in the country; in some high land of lakes. Take almost any path you please, and ten to one it carries you down in a dale, and leaves you there by a pool in the stream. There is magic in it. Let the most absent-minded of men be plunged in his deepest reveries—stand that man on his legs, set his feet a-going, and he will infallibly lead you to water, if water there be in all that region. Should you ever be athirst in the great American desert, try this experiment, if your caravan happen to be supplied with a metaphysical philosopher. Yes, as every one knows, meditation and water are wedded for ever.

Ibid., I

By reason of these things, then, the whaling voyage was welcome; the great flood-gates of the wonder-world swung open, and in the wild con-ceits that swayed me to my purpose, two and two there floated into my inmost soul, endless processions of the whale, and, mid most of them all, one grand hooded phantom, like a snow hill in the air.

Ibid.

For all men tragically great are made so through a certain morbidness. Be sure of this, O young ambition, all mortal greatness is but disease.

Ibid., XVI

A noble craft, but somehow a most melancholy! All noble things are touched with that.

Ibid.

Ship and boat diverged; the cold, damp night breeze blew between; a screaming gull flew overhead; the two hulls wildly rolled; we gave three heavy-hearted cheers, and blindly plunged like fate into the lone Atlantic.

Ibid., XXII

If ye touch at the islands, Mr. Flask, beware of fornication. Good-bye, good-bye!

Ibid., Captain Bildad's farewell to the *Pequod,* XXII

Know ye now, Bulkington? Glimpses do ye seem to see of that mortally intolerable truth; that all deep, earnest thinking is but the intrepid effort of the soul to keep the open independence of her sea; while the wildest winds of heaven and earth conspire to cast her on the treacherous, slavish shore?

But as in landlessness alone resides the highest truth, shoreless, indefinite as God—so, better is it to perish in that howling infinite, than be ingloriously dashed upon the lee, even if that were safety! For worm-like, then, oh! who would craven crawl to land! Terrors of the terrible! is all this agony so vain? Take heart, take heart, O Bulkington! Bear thee grimly, demigod! Up from the spray of thy ocean-perishing—straight up, leaps thy apotheosis!

Ibid., XXIII

For small erections may be finished by their first architects; grand ones, true ones, ever leave the copestone to posterity. God keep me from ever completing anything. This whole book is but a draught—nay, but the draught of a draught. Oh, Time, Strength, Cash, and Patience!

Ibid., XXXII

The White Whale swam before him as the monomaniac incarnation of all those malicious agencies which some deep men feel eating in them, till they are left living on with half a heart and half a lung. That intangible malignity which has been from the beginning; to whose dominion even the modern Christians ascribe one-half of the worlds; which the ancient Ophites of the east reverenced in their statue devil;—Ahab did not fall down and worship it like them; but deliriously transferring its idea to the abhorred white whale, he pitted himself, all mutilated, against it. All that most maddens and torments; all that stirs up the lees of things; all truth with malice in it; all that cracks the sinews and cakes the brain; all the subtle demonisms of life and thought; all evil, to crazy Ahab, were visibly

personified, and made practically assailable in Moby Dick. He piled upon
the whale's white hump the sum of all the general rage and hate felt by
his whole race from Adam down; and then, as if his chest had been a
mortar, he burst his hot heart's shell upon it.

Ibid., XLI

But not yet have we solved the incantation of this whiteness, and learned
why it appeals with such power to the soul; and more strange and far
more portentous—why, as we have seen, it is at once the most meaning
symbol of spiritual things, nay, the very veil of the Christian's Deity; and
yet should be as it is, the intensifying agent in things the most appalling
to mankind.

Is it that by its indefiniteness it shadows forth the heartless voids and
immensities of the universe, and thus stabs us from behind with the
thought of annihilation, when beholding the white depths of the milky
way? Or is it, that as in essence whiteness is not so much a color as the
visible absence of color, and at the same time the concrete of all colors;
is it for these reasons that there is such a dumb blankness, full of meaning,
in a wide landscape of snows—a colorless, all-color of atheism from which
we shrink? And when we consider that other theory of the natural philosophers, that all other earthly hues—every stately or lovely emblazoning—
the sweet tinges of sunset skies and woods; yea, and the gilded velvets of
butterflies, and the butterfly cheeks of young girls; all these are but subtile
deceits, not actually inherent in substances, but only laid on from without;
so that all deified Nature absolutely paints like the harlot, whose allure-
ments cover nothing but the charnel-house within; and when we proceed
further, and consider that the mystical cosmetic which produces every one
of her hues, the great principle of light, for ever remains white or colorless in itself, and if operating without medium upon matter, would touch
all objects, even tulips and roses, with its own blank tinge—pondering all
this, the palsied universe lies before us a leper; and like wilful travelers
in Lapland, who refuse to wear colored and coloring glasses upon their
eyes, so the wretched infidel gazes himself blind at the monumental white
shroud that wraps all the prospect around him. And of all these things
the Albino whale was the symbol. Wonder ye then at the fiery hunt?

Ibid., XLII

Consider the subtleness of the sea; how its most dreaded creatures glide
under water, unapparent for the most part, and treacherously hidden beneath the loveliest tints of azure. Consider also the devilish brilliance and
beauty of many of its most remorseless tribes, as the dainty embellished

shape of many species of sharks. Consider, once more, the universal can-
nibalism of the sea; all whose creatures prey upon one another, carrying
on eternal war since the world began.

Consider all this; and then turn to this green, gentle, and most docile
earth; consider them both, the sea and the land; and do you not find a
strange analogy to something in yourself? For as this appalling ocean surrounds the verdant land, so in the soul of man there lies one insular
Tahiti, full of peace and joy, but encompassed by all the horrors of the
half known life. God keep thee! Push not off from that isle, thou canst
never return!

Ibid., XLVIII

"Swim away from me, do ye?" murmured Ahab, gazing over into the
water. There seemed but little in the words, but the tone conveyed more
of deep helpless sadness than the insane old man had ever before evinced.
But turning to the steersman, who thus far had been holding the ship in
the wind to diminish her headway, he cried out in his old lion voice,—
"Up helm! Keep her off round the world!"

Round the world! There is much in that sound to inspire proud feelings; but whereto does all that circumnavigation conduct? Only through
numberless perils to the very point whence we started, where those that
we left behind secure, were all the time before us.

Were this world an endless plain, and by sailing eastward we could
forever reach new distances, and discover sights more sweet and strange
than any Cyclades or Islands of King Solomon, then there were promise
in the voyage. But in pursuit of those far mysteries we dream of, or in
tormented chase of that demon phantom that, some time or other, swims
before all human hearts; while chasing such over this round globe, they
either lead us on in barren mazes or midway leave us whelmed.

Ibid., LII

All men live enveloped in whale-lines. All are born with halters round
their necks; but it is only when caught in the swift, sudden turn of death,
that mortals realize the silent, subtle, ever-present perils of life.

Ibid., LX

To ensure the greatest efficiency in the dart, the harpooners of this world
must start to their feet from out of idleness, and not from out of toil.

Ibid., LXII

O Nature, and O soul of man! how far beyond all utterances are your
linked analogies! not the smallest atom stirs or lives on matter, but has
its cunning duplicate in mind.

Ibid., LXX

Now, had Tashtego perished in that head, it had been a very precious
perishing; smothered in the very whitest and daintiest of fragrant sperma-
cetti; coffined, hearsed, and tombed in the secret inner chamber and
sanctum sanctorum of the whale. Only one sweeter end can readily be
recalled—the delicious death of an Ohio honey-hunter, who seeking honey
in the crotch of a hollow tree, found such exceeding store of it, that leaning too far over, it sucked him in, so that he died embalmed. How many,
think ye, have likewise fallen into Plato's honey head, and sweetly perished there?

> *Ibid.,* LXXVII. Tashtego, one of the harpooners, had
> fallen into the whale's head as he was extracting the "fra-
> grant spermacetti"; he had almost drowned.

To produce a mighty book, you must choose a mighty theme. No great
and enduring volume can ever be written on the flea, though many there
be that have tried it.

Ibid., LXXIX

Both the ancestry and posterity of Grief go further than the ancestry and
posterity of Joy.

Ibid., CVI

When gliding by the Bashee Isles we emerged at last upon the great South
Sea; were it not for other things, I could have greeted my dear Pacific
with uncounted thanks, for now the long supplication of my youth was
answered; that serene ocean rolled eastwards from me a thousand leagues
of blue.

There is, one knows not what sweet mystery about this sea, whose
gently awful stirrings seem to speak of some hidden soul beneath; like
those fabled undulations of the Ephesian sod over the buried Evangelist
St. John. And meet it is, that over these sea-pastures, wide-rolling watery
prairies and Potters' Fields of all four continents, the waves should rise
and fall, and ebb and flow unceasingly; for here, millions of mixed shades
and shadows, drowned dreams, somnambulisms, reveries; all that we call

lives and souls, lie dreaming, dreaming, still; tossing like slumberers in their beds; the ever-rolling waves but made so by their restlessness.

To any imaginative Magian rover, this serene Pacific, once beheld, must ever after be the sea of his adoption. It rolls the midmost waters of the world, the Indian ocean and the Atlantic being but its arms. The same waves wash the moles of the new-built California towns, but yesterday planted by the recentest race of men, and lave the faded but still gorgeous skirts of Asiatic lands, older than Abraham; while all between float milky ways of coral isles, and low-lying, endless, unknown Archipelagoes, and impenetrable Japans. Thus this mysterious, divine Pacific zones the world's whole bulk about; makes all coasts one bay to it; seems the tide-beating heart of earth. Lifted by those eternal swells, you needs must own the seductive god, bowing your head to Pan.

Ibid., CXI

Moby Dick seeks thee not! It is thou, thou, that madly seekest him!

Ibid., Starbuck to Ahab, CXXXV

The harpoon was darted; the stricken whale flew forward; with igniting velocity the line ran through the groove;—ran foul. Ahab stooped to clear it; he did clear it; but the flying turn caught him round the neck, and voicelessly as Turkish mutes bowstring their victim, he was shot out of the boat, ere the crew knew he was gone. Next instant, the heavy eye-splice in the rope's final end flew out of the stark-empty tub, knocked down an oarsman, and smiting the sea, disappeared in its depths.

For an instant, the tranced boat's crew stood still; then turned. "The ship? Great God, where is the ship?" Soon they through dim, bewildering mediums saw her sidelong fading phantom, as in the gaseous Fata Morgana; only the uppermost masts out of water; while fixed by infatuation, or fidelity, or fate, to their once lofty perches, the pagan harpooners still maintained their sinking lookouts on the sea. And now, concentric circles seized the lone boat itself, and all its crew, and each floating oar, and every lance-pole, and spinning, animate and inanimate, all round and round in one vortex, carried the smallest chip of the Pequod out of sight.

But as the last whelmings intermixingly poured themselves over the sunken head of the Indian at the mainmast, leaving a few inches of the erect spar yet visible, together with long streaming yards of the flag, which calmly undulated, with ironical coincidings, over the destroying billows they almost touched;—at that instant, a red arm and a hammer hovered backwardly uplifted in the open air, in the act of nailing the flag faster and yet faster to the subsiding spar. A sky-hawk that tauntingly had followed the maintruck downward from its natural home among the stars, pecking at the flag, and incommoding Tashtego there; this bird now chanced to intercept its broad fluttering wing between the hammer and the wood; and simultaneously feeling that ethereal thrill, the submerged savage beneath, in his death-grasp, kept his hammer frozen there; and so the bird of heaven, with archangelic shrieks, and his imperial beak thrust upwards, and his whole captive form folded in the flag of Ahab, went down with his ship, which, like Satan, would not sink to hell till she had dragged a living part of heaven along with her, and helmeted herself with it.

Now small fowls flew screaming over the yet yawning gulf; a sullen white surf beat against its steep sides; then all collapsed, and the great shroud of the sea rolled on as it rolled five thousand years ago.

Ibid., the end of the last chapter

All this Earth is Love's affianced; vainly the demon Principle howls to stay the banns.

Pierre: or, The Ambiguities, 1852

Ah, if man were wholly made in heaven, why catch we hell-glimpses? Why in the noblest marble pillar that stands beneath the all-comprising vault, ever should we descry the sinister vein?

Ibid.

In those Hyperborean regions, to which enthusiastic Truth, and Earnestness, and Independence, will invariably lead a mind fitted by nature for profound and fearless thoughts, all objects are seen in a dubious, uncertain, and refracting light. Viewed through that rarefied atmosphere the most immemorially admitted maxims of men begin to slide and fluctuate, and finally become wholly inverted; the very heavens themselves being not innocent of producing this confounding effect, since it is mostly in the heavens themselves that these wonderful mirages are exhibited.

But the examples of many minds forever lost, like undiscoverable arctic explorers, amid those treacherous regions, warn us entirely away from them; and we learn that it is not for man to follow the trail of truth too far, since by so doing he entirely loses the directing compass of his mind; for arrived at the Pole, to whose barrenness only it points, there, the needle indifferently respects all points of the horizon alike.

Ibid.

It is not down on any map, true places never are.

The Piazza Tales, "The Encantadas," 1856

Those whom books will hurt will not be proof against events. If some books are deemed most baneful and their sale forbid, how, then, with deadlier facts, not dreams of doting men? Events, not books, should be forbid.

Ibid.

It is with fiction as with religion: it should present another world, and yet one to which we feel the tie.

The Confidence Man, 1857

That fiction, where every character can, by reason of its consistency, be comprehended at a glance, either exhibits but sections of character, making them appear for wholes, or else is very untrue to reality.

Ibid.

Billy stood facing aft. At the penultimate moment, his words, his only ones, words wholly unobstructed in the utterance were these—"God bless Captain Vere!" Syllables so unanticipated coming from one with the ignominious hemp about his neck—a conventional felon's benediction directed aft towards the quarters of honor; syllables too delivered in the clear melody of a singing-bird on the point of launching from the twig, had a phenomenal effect, not unenhanced by the rare personal beauty of the young sailor spiritualized now through late experiences so poignantly profound.

Without volition as it were, as if indeed the ship's populace were but the vehicles of some vocal current electric, with one voice from alow and aloft, came a resonant sympathetic echo—"God bless Captain Vere!" And yet at that instant Billy alone must have been in their hearts, even as he was in their eyes.

At the pronounced words and the spontaneous echo that voluminously rebounded them, Captain Vere, either through stoic self-control or a sort of momentary paralysis induced by emotional shock, stood erectly rigid as a musket in the ship-armorer's rack.

The hull deliberately recovering from the periodic roll to leeward was just regaining an even keel, when the last signal a preconcerted dumb one was given. At the same moment it chanced that the vapory fleece hanging low in the East, was shot through with a soft glory as of the fleece of the Lamb of God seen in mystical vision and simultaneously therewith, watched by the wedged mass of upturned faces, Billy ascended; and, ascending, took the full rose of the dawn.

> *Billy Budd, Foretopman,* 1924, Billy's execution

You must have plenty of sea-room to tell the Truth in.

> *Hawthorne and His Mosses,* 1850 (a review of *Mosses from an Old Manse*)

Genius, all over the world, stands hand in hand, and one shock of recognition runs the whole circle round.

> *Ibid.*

The reason the mass of men fear God, and at *bottom dislike* Him, is because they rather distrust His heart, and fancy Him all brain like a watch.

> Letter to Hawthorne, April, 1851

We incline to think that God cannot explain His own secrets, and that He would like a little information upon certain points Himself. We mortals astonish Him as much as He us. But it is this *Being* of the matter; there lies the knot with which we choke ourselves. As soon as you say *Me,* a *God,* a *Nature,* so soon you jump off from your stool and hang from the beam. Yes, that word is the hangman. Take God out of the dictionary, and you would have Him in the street.

> *Ibid.*

All men who say *yes,* lie; and all men who say *no,*—why, they are in the happy condition of judicious, unincumbered travellers in Europe; they cross the frontiers into Eternity with nothing but a carpet-bag,—that is to say, the Ego. Whereas those *yes*-gentry, they travel with heaps of baggage, and, damn them! they will never get through the Custom house.

> *Ibid.*

A sense of unspeakable security is in me this moment, on account of your having understood the book [*Moby Dick*]. I have written a wicked book, and feel spotless as the lamb.

> Letter to Hawthorne, November, 1851

What reputation Herman Melville has is horrible. Think of it. To go down to posterity as the man who lived among the cannibals.

> Letter

FRANK R. STOCKTON

He could open either door he pleased. . . . If he opened the one, there came out of it a hungry tiger, the fiercest and most cruel that could be procured, which immediately sprang upon him, and tore him to pieces, as a punishment for his guilt. . . . But if the accused person opened the other door, there came forth from it a lady, the most suitable to his years and station that his Majesty could select among his fair subjects. . . . The question of her decision is not one to be lightly considered, and it is not for me to set myself up as the one person able to answer it. And so I leave it with you all: Which came out of the opened door—the lady, or the tiger?

"The Lady or the Tiger," 1884

SAMUEL L. CLEMENS ("MARK TWAIN")

Well, *I* don't see no p'ints about that frog that's any better'n any other frog.

The Celebrated Jumping Frog of Calaveras County, 1867

Tom gave up the brush with reluctance in his face, but alacrity in his heart. And while the late steamer *Big Missouri* worked and sweated in the sun, the retired artist sat on a barrel in the shade close by, dangled his legs, munched his apple, and planned the slaughter of more innocents. There was no lack of material; boys happened along every little while; they came to jeer, but remained to whitewash. By the time Ben was fagged out, Tom had traded the next chance to Billy Fisher for a kite, in good repair; and when *he* played out, Johnny Miller bought in for a dead rat and a string to swing it with—and so on, and so on, hour after hour. And when the middle of the afternoon came, from being a poor poverty-stricken boy in the morning, Tom was literally rolling in wealth. He had besides the things before mentioned, twelve marbles, part of a jews'-harp, a piece of blue bottle-glass to look through, a spool cannon, a key that wouldn't unlock anything, a fragment of chalk, a glass stopper of a decanter, a tin soldier, a couple of tadpoles, six firecrackers, a kitten with only one eye, a brass door-knob, a dog-collar—but no dog—the handle of a knife, four pieces of orange-peel, and a dilapidated old window-sash.

He had had a nice, good, idle time all the while, plenty of company—and the fence had three coats of whitewash on it! If he hadn't run out of whitewash, he would have bankrupted every boy in the village.

Tom said to himself that it was not such a hollow world, after all. He had discovered a great law of human action, without knowing it—namely, that in order to make a man or a boy covet a thing, it is only necessary to make the thing difficult to attain. If he had been a great and wise philosopher, like the writer of this book, he would now have comprehended that Work consists of whatever a body is *obliged* to do, and that Play consists of whatever a body is not obliged to do. And this would help him to understand why constructing artificial flowers or performing on a treadmill is work, while rolling tenpins or climbing Mont Blanc is only amusement. There are wealthy gentlemen in England who drive four-horse passenger-coaches twenty or thirty miles on a daily line, in the summer, because the privilege costs them considerable money; but if they were offered wages for the service, that would turn it into work and then they would resign.

The boy mused awhile over the substantial change which had taken place in his worldly circumstances, and then wended toward headquarters to report.

The Adventures of Tom Sawyer, 1876

There's plenty of boys that will come hankering and gruvvelling around when you've got an apple, and beg the core off you; but when *they've* got one, and you beg for the core and remind them how you give them a core one time, they make a mouth at you and say thank you 'most to death, but there ain't-a-going to be no core.

Ibid.

You don't know me without you have read a book by the name of *The Adventures of Tom Sawyer;* but that ain't no matter. That book was made by Mr. Mark Twain, and he told the truth, mainly. There was things which he stretched, but mainly he told the truth.

The Adventures of Huckleberry Finn, opening lines, 1884

. . . *I* hadn't done nothing. But that's always the way; it don't make no difference whether you do right or wrong, a person's conscience ain't got no sense, and just goes for him *anyway.* If I had a yaller dog that didn't know no more than a person's conscience does I would pison him. It takes up more room than all the rest of a person's insides, and yet ain't no good, nohow. Tom Sawyer he says the same.

Ibid.

I never felt easy till the raft was two miles below there and out in the middle of the Mississippi. Then we hung up our signal lantern, and

judged that we was free and safe once more. I hadn't had a bite to eat
since yesterday, so Jim he got out some corn-dodgers and buttermilk, and
pork and cabbage and greens—there ain't nothing in the world so good
when it's cooked right—and whilst I eat my supper we talked and had a
good time. I was powerful glad to get away from the feuds, and so was
Jim to get away from the swamp. We said there warn't no home like a
raft, after all. Other places do seem so cramped up and smothery, but a
raft don't. You feel mighty free and easy and comfortable on a raft.

Ibid.

I read considerable to Jim about kings and dukes and earls and such, and
how gaudy they dressed, and how much style they put on, and called each
other your majesty, and your grace, and your lordship, and so on, 'stead
of mister; and Jim's eyes bugged out, and he was interested. He says:

"I didn't know dey was so many un um. I hain't hearn 'bout none un
um, skasely, but ole King Sollermun, onless you counts dem kings dat's
in a pack er k'yards. How much do a king git?"

"Get?" I says; "why, they get a thousand dollars a month if they want
it; they can have just as much as they want; everything belongs to them."

"*Ain'* dat gay? En what dey got to do, Huck?"

"*They* don't do nothing! Why, how you talk! They just set around."

"No; is dat so?"

"Of course it is. They just set around—except, maybe, when there's a
war; then they go to the war. But other times they just lazy around; or go
hawking—just hawking and sp— Sh!—d'you hear a noise?"

We skipped out and looked; but it warn't nothing but the flutter of a
steamboat's wheel away down, coming around the point; so we come back.

"Yes," says I, "and other times, when things is dull, they fuss with the
parlyment; and if everybody don't go just so he whacks their heads off.
But mostly they hang round the harem."

"Roun' de which?"

"Harem."

"What's de harem?"

"The place where he keeps his wives. Don't you know about the harem?
Solomon had one; he had about a million wives."

"Why, yes, dat's so; I—I'd done forgot it. A harem's a bo'd'n-house, I
reck'n. Mos' likely dey has rackety times in de nussery. En I reck'n de
wives quarrels considable; en dat 'crease de racket. Yit dey say Sollermun
de wises' man dat ever live'. I doan' take no stock in dat. Bekase why:
would a wise man want to live in de mids' er sich a blim-blammin' all de

time? No—'deed he wouldn't. A wise man 'ud take en buil' a biler-factry; en den he could shet *down* de biler-factry when he want to res'."

"Well, but he *was* the wisest man, anyway; because the widow she told me so, her own self."

"I doan' k'yer what de widder say, he *warn't* no wise man nuther. He had some er de dad-fetchedes' ways I ever see. Does you know 'bout dat chile dat he 'uz gwyne to chop in two?"

"Yes, the widow told me all about it."

"*Well*, den! Warn' dat de beatenes' notion in de worl'? You jes' take en look at it a minute. Dah's de stump, dah—dat's one er de women; heah's you—dat's de yuther one; I's Sollermun; en dish yer dollar bill's de chile. Bofe un you claims it. What does I do? Does I shin aroun' mongs' de neighbors en fine out which un you de bill *do* b'long to, en han' it over to de right one, all safe en soun', de way dat anybody dat had any gumption would? No; I take en whack de bill in *two,* en give half un it to you, en de yuther half to de yuther woman. Dat's de way Sollermun was gwyne to do wid de chile. Now I want to ast you: what's de use er dat half a bill?—can't buy noth'n wid it. En what use is a half a chile? I wouldn' give a dern for a million un um."

"But hang it, Jim, you've clean missed the point—blame it, you've missed it a thousand mile."

"Who? Me? Go 'long. Doan' talk to *me* 'bout yo' pints. I reck'n I knows sense when I sees it; en dey ain' no sense in sich doin's as dat. De 'spute warn't 'bout a half a chile, de 'spute was 'bout a whole chile; an de man dat think he kin settle a 'spute 'bout a whole chile wid a half a chile doan' know enough to come in out'n de rain. Doan' talk to me 'bout Sollermun, Huck, I knows him by de back."

"But I tell you you don't get the point."

"Blame de point! I reck'n I knows what I knows. En mine you, de *real* pint is down furder—it's down deeper. It lays in de way Sollermun was raised. You take a man dat's got on'y one or two chillen; is dat man gwyne to be waseful o' chillen? No, he ain't; he can't 'ford it. *He* know how to value 'em. But you take a man dat's got 'bout five million chillen runnin' roun' de house, en it's diffunt. *He* as soon chop a chile in two as a cat. Dey's plenty mo'. A chile er two, mo' er less, warn't no consekens to Sollermun, dad fetch him!"

I never see such a nigger. If he got a notion in his head once, there warn't no getting it out again. He was the most down on Solomon of any nigger I ever see. So I went to talking about other kings, and let Solomon slide. I told about Louis Sixteenth that got his head cut off in France long time ago; and about his little boy the dolphin, that would 'a' been a king, but they took and shut him up in jail, and some say he died there.

"Po' little chap."

"But some says he got out and got away, and come to America."

"Dat's good! But he'll be pooty lonesome—dey ain' no kings here, is dey, Huck?"

"No."

"Den he cain't git no situation. What he gwyne to do?"

"Well, I don't know. Some of them gets on the police, and some of them learns people how to talk French."

"Why, Huck, doan' de French people talk de same way we does?"

"*No*, Jim; you couldn't understand a word they said—not a single word."

"Well, now, I be ding-busted! How do dat come?"

"*I* don't know; but it's so. I got some of their jabber out of a book. S'pose a man was to come to you and say Polly-voo-franzy—what would you think?"

"I wouldn' think nuffn; I'd take en bust him over de head—dat is, if he warn't white. I wouldn't 'low no nigger to call me dat."

"Shucks, it ain't calling you anything. It's only saying, do you know how to talk French?"

"Well, den, why couldn't he say it?"

"Why, he *is* a-saying it. That's a Frenchman's *way* of saying it."

"Well, it's a blame ridicklous way, en I doan' want to hear no mo' 'bout it. Dey ain' no sense in it."

"Looky here, Jim; does a cat talk like we do?"

"No, a cat don't."

"Well, does a cow?"

"No, a cow don't, nuther."

"Does a cat talk like a cow, or a cow talk like a cat?"

"No, dey don't."

"It's natural and right for 'em to talk different from each other, ain't it?"

"Course."

"And ain't it natural and right for a cat and a cow to talk different from *us?*"

"Why, mos' sholy it is."

"Well, then, why ain't it natural and right for a *Frenchman* to talk different from us? You answer me that."

"Is a cat a man, Huck?"

"No."

"Well, den, dey ain't no sense in a cat talkin' like a man. Is a cow a man?—er is a cow a cat?"

"No, she ain't either of them."

"Well, den, she ain't got no business to talk like either one er the yuther of 'em. Is a Frenchman a man?"

"Yes."

"*Well*, den! Dad blame it, why doan' he *talk* like a man? You answer me *dat!*"

I see it warn't no use wasting words—you can't learn a nigger to argue. So I quit.

Ibid.

Tom's most well now, and got his bullet around his neck on a watch-guard for a watch, and is always seeing what time it is, and so there ain't nothing more to write about, and I am rotten glad of it, because if I'd 'a' knowed what a trouble it was to make a book I wouldn't 'a' tackled it, and ain't a-going to no more. But I reckon I got to light out for the territory ahead of the rest, because Aunt Sally she's going to adopt me and sivilize me, and I can't stand it. I been there before.

Ibid., final paragraph

Satan was accustomed to say that our race lived a life of continuous and uninterrupted self-deception. It duped itself from cradle to grave with shams and delusions which it mistook for realities, and this made its entire life a sham. Of the score of fine qualities which it imagined it had and was vain of, it really possessed hardly one. It regarded itself as gold, and was only brass. One day when he was in this vein he mentioned a detail—the sense of humor. I cheered up then, and took issue. I said we possessed it.

"There spoke the race!" he said; "always ready to claim what it hasn't got, and mistake its ounce of brass filings for a ton of gold-dust. You have a mongrel perception of humor, nothing more; a multitude of you possess that. This multitude see the comic side of a thousand low-grade and trivial things—broad incongruities, mainly; grotesqueries, absurdities, evokers of the horselaugh. The ten thousand high-grade comicalities which exist in the world are sealed from their dull vision. Will a day come when the race will detect the funniness of these juvenilities and laugh at them—and by laughing at them destroy them? For your race, in its poverty, has unquestionably one really effective weapon—laughter. Power, money, persuasion, supplication, persecution—these can lift at a colossal humbug—push it a little—weaken it a little, century by century; but only laughter can blow it to rags and atoms at a blast. Against the assault of laughter nothing can stand. You are always fussing and fighting with your other weapons. Do you ever use that one? No; you leave it lying rusting. As a race, do you ever use it at all? No; you lack sense and the courage."

The Mysterious Stranger, 1916

This poor little one-horse town.

"The Undertaker's Story"

Marriage—yes, it is the supreme felicity of life, I concede it. And it is also the supreme tragedy of life. The deeper the love, the surer the tragedy. And the more disconsolating when it comes.

Letter to Father Fitz-Simon, on being informed of his coming marriage

Life does not consist mainly—or even largely—of facts and happenings. It consists mainly of the storm of thoughts that is forever blowing through one's head.

Autobiography, 1924

I came in with Halley's Comet in 1835. It is coming again next year, and I expect to go out with it. It will be the greatest disappointment of my life if I don't go out with Halley's Comet. The Almighty has said, no doubt: "Now here are these two unaccountable freaks; they came in together, they must go out together."

Quoted by Paine, *Mark Twain, a Biography.* Mark Twain born November 30, 1835; perihelion for Halley's Comet, 1835, was November 16. For 1910 it was April 20; Mark Twain died April 21 of that year.

WILLIAM DEAN HOWELLS

Some people can stay longer in an hour than others can in a week.

BRET HARTE

It needed but a glance to show them Kentuck lying there, cruelly crushed and bruised, but still holding The Luck of Roaring Camp in his arms. As they bent over the strangely assorted pair, they saw that the child was cold and pulseless. "He is dead," said one. Kentuck opened his eyes. "Dead?" he repeated feebly. "Yes, my man, and you are dying too." A smile lit the eyes of the expiring Kentuck. "Dying!" he repeated, "he's a-taking me with him—tell the boys I've got the Luck with me now"; and the strong man, clinging to the frail babe as a drowning man is said to cling to a straw, drifted away into the shadowy river that flows forever to the unknown sea.

The Luck of Roaring Camp, 1868

Beneath this tree
Lies the body
of
John Oakhurst
Who struck a streak of bad luck
On the 23d of November 1850
and
Handed in his checks
On the 7th December 1850

Epitaph from *The Outcasts of Poker Flat*

HENRY JAMES

The deep well of unconscious cerebration.

The American, 1877

Cats and monkeys, monkeys and cats—all human life is there.

The Madonna of the Future, 1879

For himself, beyond doubt, the thing we were all so blank about was vividly there. It was something, I guessed, in the primal plan; something like a complex figure in a Persian carpet. He highly approved of this image when I used it, and he used another himself. "It's the very string," he said, "that my pearls are strung on!"

The Figure in the Carpet, 1896

Live all you can; it's a mistake not to. It doesn't so much matter what you do in particular so long as you have your life. If you haven't had that what *have* you had? I'm too old—too old at any rate for what I see. What one loses one loses; make no mistake about that. Still, we have the illusion of freedom; therefore don't, like me today, be without the memory of that illusion. I was either, at the right time, too stupid or too intelligent to have it, and now I'm a case of reaction against the mistake. Do what you like so long as you don't make it. For it *was* a mistake. Live, live!

> *The Ambassadors,* 1903. Lambert Strether is speaking. James said in his preface to this work that "the remarks to which he thus gives utterance contain the essence of *The Ambassadors.*"

Facing him, waving him away, she had taken another upward step; but he sprang to the side of the stairs, and brought his hand, above the bannister, down hard on her wrist. "Do you mean to tell me that I must marry a woman I hate?"

From her step she looked down into his raised face. "Ah you see it's not true that you're free!" She seemed almost to exult. "It's not true, it's not true!"

He only, at this, like a buffeting swimmer, gave a shake of his head and repeated his question: "Do you mean to tell me I must marry such a woman?"

Fleda gasped too; he held her fast. "No. Anything's better than that."

"Then in God's name what must I do?"

"You must settle that with Mona. You mustn't break faith. Anything's better than that. You must at any rate be utterly sure. She must love you —how can she help it? *I* wouldn't give you up!" said Fleda. She spoke in broken bits, panting out her words. "The great thing is to keep faith. Where's a man if he doesn't? If he doesn't he may be so cruel, so cruel!" Fleda repeated. "I couldn't have a hand in that, you know: that's my position—that's mine. You offered her marriage. It's a tremendous thing for her." Then looking at him another moment, "*I* wouldn't give you up!" she said again. He still had hold of her arm; she took in his blank dread. With a quick dip of her face she reached his hand with her lips, pressing them to the back of it with a force that doubled the force of her words. "Never, never, never!" she cried; and before he could succeed in seizing her she had turned away and, flashing up the stairs, got away from him even faster than she had got away at Ricks.

> *The Spoils of Poynton,* 1907. Edith Wharton, *A Backward Glance,* proclaims this one of the "two most famous kisses of literature," the other being in *Troilus and Cressida.*

There are two kinds of taste in the appreciation of imaginative literature: the taste for emotions of surprise and the taste for emotions of recognition.

> *Anthony Trollope,* 1883

The only classification of the novel that I can understand is into that which has life and that which has it not.

The Art of Fiction, 1884

The only obligation to which in advance we may hold a novel, without incurring the accusation of being arbitrary, is that it be interesting.

Ibid.

Experience is never limited, and it is never complete; it is an immense sensibility, a kind of huge spider-web of the finest silken threads suspended in the chamber of consciousness, and catching every air-borne particle in its tissue.

Ibid.

We must grant the artist his subject, his idea, his *donné;* our criticism is applied only to what he makes of it.

Ibid.

I have not the least hesitation in saying that I aspire to write in such a way that it would be impossible to an outsider to say whether I am at a given moment an American writing about England or an Englishman writing about America (dealing as I do with both countries,) and far from being ashamed of such an ambiguity I should be exceedingly proud of it, for it would be highly civilized.

Letter to William James, 1888

But I have the imagination of disaster—and see life as ferocious and sinister.

Letter to A. C. Benson, 1896

The modern madness, mere maniacal motion and extension.

1905

I'm always sorry when I hear of your reading anything of mine, and always hope you won't—you seem to me so constitutionally unable to "enjoy" it, and so condemned to look at it from a point of view remotely alien to mine in writing it, and to the conditions out of which, *as* mine, it has inevitably sprung—so that all the intentions that have been its main reason for being (with *me*) appear never to have reached you at all— and you appear even to assume that the life, the elements forming its subject-matter, deviate from felicity in not having an impossible analogy with the life of Cambridge.

Letter to William James, on The Golden Bowl

Dramatise it, dramatise it. Then, and not sooner, would one see.

Works (New York Edition), 1907–09

It is as difficult . . . to trace the dividing line between the real and the romantic as to plant a mile-stone between north and south; but I am not sure an infallible sign of the latter is not this rank vegetation of the "power" of bad people that good get into, or vice-versa. It is so rarely, alas, into *our* power that anyone gets!

The American, "Preface," 1907

Really, universally, relations stop nowhere, and the exquisite problem of the artist is eternally but to draw, by a geometry of his own, the circle within which they shall happily *appear* to do so. He is in the perpetual predicament that the continuity of things is the whole matter, for him, of comedy and tragedy; that this continuity is never, by the space of an instant or an inch, broken, and that, to do anything at all, he has at once intensely to consult and intensely to ignore it.

Roderick Random, "Preface," 1907

The fatal futility of Fact.

The Spoils of Poynton, "Preface," 1907

There is, I think, no more nutritive or suggestive truth . . . than that of the perfect dependence of the "moral" sense of a work of art on the amount of felt life concerned in producing it.

The Portrait of a Lady, "Preface," 1908

Small children have many more perceptions than they have terms to translate them; their vision is at any moment much richer, their apprehension even constantly stronger, than their prompt, their at all producible, vocabulary.

What Maisie Knew, "Preface," 1908

What it all came back to was, no doubt, something like *this* wisdom— that if you haven't, for fiction, the root of the matter in you, haven't the sense of life and the penetrating imagination, you are a fool in the very presence of the revealed and the assured; but that if you *are* so armed you are not really helpless, not without your resource, even before mysteries abysmal.

The Princess Cassamassima, "Preface," 1908

That odd law which somehow always makes the minimum of valid suggestion serve the man of imagination better than the maximum. The historian, essentially, wants more documents than he can really use; the dramatist only wants more liberties than he can really take.

The Aspern Papers, "Preface," 1909

The anomalous fact is that the theatre, so called, can flourish in barbarism, but that any *drama* worth speaking of can develop but in the air of civilization.

Letter to C. E. Wheeler, April 9, 1911

Summer afternoon—summer afternoon; to me those have always been the two most beautiful words in the English language.

To Edith Wharton

I *am* damned critical—for it's the only thing to be, and all else is damned humbug.

Quoted by Dupee, *James*

EDWARD NOYES WESTCOTT

They say a reasonable amount o' fleas is good fer a dog—keeps him from broodin' over bein' a dog, mebbe.

David Harum, a Story of American Life, 1898

Wa'al, if I've done anything I'm sorry for, I'm willin' to be forgi'n.

Ibid.

Do unto the other fellow the way he'd like to do unto you an' do it fust.

Ibid.

JOEL CHANDLER HARRIS

You er what you is, en you can't be no is-er.

Nights with Uncle Remus, 1883

Tar-baby ain't sayin' nuthin', en Brer Fox, he lay low.

Ibid.

We er sorter po'ly, Sis Tempy, I'm 'blige ter you. You know w'at de jay-burd say ter der squinch-owl! "I'm sickly but sassy."

Ibid.

SARAH ORNE JEWETT

A harbor, even if it is a little harbor, is a good thing, since adventures come into it as well as go out, and the life in it grows strong, because it takes something from the world and has something to give in return.

Country Byways, 1881

The thing that teases the mind over and over for years, and at last gets itself put down rightly on paper—whether little or great, it belongs to Literature.

EDGAR SALTUS

Society would be delightful were all women married and all men single.

OWEN WISTER

When you call me that, *smile!*

The Virginian, 1902

WILLIAM SIDNEY PORTER ("O. HENRY")

If men knew how women pass the time when they are alone, they'd never marry.

Memoirs of a Yellow Dog

EDITH WHARTON

A frivolous society can acquire dramatic significance only through what its frivolity destroys. Its tragic implications lie in its power of debasing people and ideals.

BOOTH TARKINGTON

Penrod was doing something very unusual and rare, something almost never accomplished except by colored people or by a boy in school on a spring day: he was doing really nothing at all. He was merely a state of being.

Penrod, 1914

They were upon their great theme: "When I get to be a man!" Being human, though boys, they considered their present state too commonplace to be dwelt upon. So, when the old men gather, they say: "When I was a boy!" It really is the land of nowadays that we never discover.

Ibid.

An ideal wife is any woman who has an ideal husband.

Looking Forward

FRANK NORRIS

But to Romance belongs the wide world for range, and the unplumbed depths of the human heart, and the mystery of sex, and the problems of life, and the black, unsearched penetralia of the soul of man. You, the indolent, must not always be amused. What matter the silken clothes, what matter the prince's houses? Romance, too, is a teacher, and if—throwing aside the purple—she wears the camel's-hair and feeds upon the locusts, it is to cry aloud unto the people, "Prepare ye the way of the Lord; make straight his path."

A Plea for Romantic Fiction, 1902

If the novel were not one of the most important factors of modern life; if it were not the completest expression of our civilization; if its influence were not greater than all the pulpits, than all the newspapers between the oceans, it would not be so important that its message be true.

The Responsibilities of the Novelist, 1903

STEPHEN CRANE

At last, they saw him stop and stand motionless. Hastening up, they perceived that his face wore an expression telling that he had at last found the place for which he had struggled. His spare figure was erect; his bloody hands were quietly at his side. He was waiting with patience for something that he had come to meet. He was at the rendezvous. They paused and stood, expectant.

There was a silence.

Finally, the chest of the doomed soldier began to heave with a strained motion. It increased in violence until it was as if an animal was within and was kicking and tumbling furiously to be free.

This spectacle of gradual strangulation made the youth writhe, and once as his friend rolled his eyes, he saw something in them that made him sink wailing to the ground. He raised his voice in a last supreme call.

"Jim—Jim—Jim—"

The tall soldier opened his lips and spoke. He made a gesture. "Leave me be—don't tech me—leave me be—"

There was another silence while he waited.

Suddenly his form stiffened and straightened. Then it was shaken by a prolonged ague. He stared into space. To the two watchers there was a curious and profound dignity in the firm lines of his awful face.

He was invaded by a creeping strangeness that slowly enveloped him. For a moment the tremor of his legs caused him to dance a sort of hideous hornpipe. His arms beat wildly about his head in an expression of implike enthusiasm.

His tall figure stretched itself to its full height. There was a slight rending sound. Then it began to swing forward, slow and straight, in the manner of a falling tree. A swift muscular contortion made the left shoulder strike the ground first.

The body seemed to bounce a little way from the earth. "God!" said the tattered soldier.

The youth had watched, spellbound, this ceremony at the place of meeting. His face had been twisted into an expression of every agony he had imagined for his friend.

He now sprang to his feet, and, going closer, gazed upon the pastelike face. The mouth was open and the teeth showed in a laugh.

As the flap of the blue jacket fell away from the body, he could see that the side looked as if it had been chewed by wolves.

The youth turned, with sudden, livid rage, toward the battlefield. He shook his fist. He seemed about to deliver a philippic.

"Hell—"

The red sun was pasted in the sky like a wafer.

The Red Badge of Courage, 1895

At times he regarded the wounded soldiers in an envious way. He conceived persons with torn bodies to be peculiarly happy. He wished that he, too, had a wound, a red badge of courage.

Ibid.

When the roof fell in, a great funnel of smoke swarmed toward the sky, as if the old man's mighty spirit, released from its body—a little bottle— had swelled like the genie of fable. The smoke was tinted rose-hue from the flames, and perhaps the unutterable midnights of the universe will have no power to daunt the colour of this soul.

> *The Veteran,* 1897. The old man is Fleming, the hero of *The Red Badge of Courage.*

None of them knew the colour of the sky.

> *The Open Boat,* first line, 1898

When it occurs to a man that nature does not regard him as important . . . he at first wishes to throw bricks at the temple, and he hates deeply the fact that there are no bricks and no temples.

> *Ibid.*

The correspondent did not know all that transpired afterward. When he achieved safe ground he fell, striking the sand with each particular part of his body. It was as if he had dropped from a roof, but the thud was grateful to him.

It seems that instantly the beach was populated with men with blankets, clothes, and flasks, and women with coffee-pots and all the remedies sacred to their minds. The welcome of the land to the men from the sea was warm and generous, but a still and dripping shape was carried slowly up the beach, and the land's welcome for it could only be the different and sinister hospitality of the grave.

When it came night, the white waves paced to and fro in the moon-light, and the wind brought the sound of the great sea's voice to the men on shore, and they felt that they could then be interpreters.

> *Ibid.,* last lines

Every sin is the result of a collaboration.

THEODORE DREISER

I acknowledge the Furies, I believe in them, I have heard the disastrous beating of their wings.

> To Grant Richards, in 1911

As I see him the utterly infinitesimal individual weaves among the mys-teries a floss-like and wholly meaningless course—if course it be. In short

I catch no meaning from all I have seen, and pass quite as I came, confused and dismayed.

When asked for a "credo," 1928

RUPERT HUGHES

Her face was her chaperone.

ELLEN GLASGOW

Women like to sit down with trouble as if it were knitting.

The Sheltered Life, 1932

The mob that would die for a belief seldom hesitates to inflict death upon any opposing heretical group.

I Believe

The only difference between a rut and a grave is their dimensions.

GERTRUDE STEIN

America is my country and Paris is my home town and it is as it has come to be. After all anybody is as their land and air is. Anybody is as the sky is low or high, the air heavy or clear and anybody is as there is wind or no wind there. It is that which makes them and the arts they make and the work they do and the way they eat and the way they drink and the way they learn and everything.

And so I am an American and I have lived half my life in Paris, not the half that made me but the half in which I made what I made.

An American and France, 1936

The future is not important any more.

Wars I Have Seen, 1945

One of the things that is most striking about the young generation is that they never talk about their own future, there are no futures for this generation, not any of them, and so naturally they never think of them. It is very striking, they do not live in the present, they just live, as well as they can, and they do not plan. It is extraordinary that whole populations have no projects for a future, none at all. It certainly is extraordinary, but it is certainly true.

Ibid.

We are always the same age inside.

The money is always there, but the pockets change; it is not in the same pockets after a change, and that is all there is to say about money.

FRANCES M. FORD

I think I can—I think I can—I think I can. . . . I thought I could—I thought I could—I thought I could.

The Little Engine That Could

SHERWOOD ANDERSON

I am a lover and have not found my thing to love.

Winesburg, Ohio, "Tandy," 1919

Everyone in the world is Christ and they are all crucified.

Ibid., "The Philosopher"

If I could be brave enough and live long enough I could crawl inside the life of every man, woman, and child in America. After I had gone within them I could be born out of them. I could become something the like of which has never been seen before. We would see then what America is like.

A New Testament, "A Poet," 1927

My feet are cold and wet. I have been walking too long on the bed of a river.

> Spoken to his secretary on November 27, 1912, whereupon he left the factory and wandered aimlessly about for four days until he was found in Cleveland by a pharmacist. He had had some sort of breakdown, and it is probably untrue that, as he later said, this was a conscious and intentional diversionary activity on his part. The strain was so great that he had to discontinue his business in Elyria, Ohio, and go to Cleveland.

JACK LONDON

I would rather be ashes than dust! I would rather that my spark should burn out in a brilliant blaze than it should be stifled by dry-rot. I would rather be a superb meteor, every atom of me in magnificent glow, than a sleepy and permanent planet. The proper function of man is to live, not to exist. I shall not waste my days in trying to prolong them. I shall use my time.

Quoted by Joan London, *Jack London and His Times*

JAMES BRANCH CABELL

Providence labors with quaint instruments, dilapidating Troy by means of a wooden rocking-horse, and loosing sin into the Universe through a half-eaten apple.

Cream of the Jest, 1917

Indeed, when I consider the race to which I have the honor to belong, I am filled with respectful wonder. . . . All about it flows and gyrates unceasingly the material universe,—an endless inconceivable jumble of rotary blazing gas and frozen spheres and detonating comets, where-through spins Earth like a frail midge. And to this blown molecule adhere what millions and millions of parasites just such as I am, begetting and dreaming and slaying and abnegating and toiling and making mirth, just as did aforetime those countless generations of our forebears, every one of whom was likewise a creature just such as I am! Were the human beings that have been subjected to confinement in flesh each numbered, as is customary in other penal institutes, with what interminable row of digits might one set forth your number, say, or mine?

Nor is this everything. For my reason, such as it is, perceives this race, in its entirety, in the whole outcome of its achievement, to be beyond all wording petty and ineffectual: and no more than thought can estimate the relative proportion to the material universe of our poor Earth, can thought conceive with what quintillionths to express that fractional part which I, as an individual parasite, add to Earth's negligible fretting by ephemerae.

And still—behold the miracle!—still I believe life to be a personal transaction between myself and Omnipotence; I believe that what I do is somehow of importance; and I believe that I am on a journey toward some very public triumph not unlike that of the third prince in the fairy-tale. . . . Even to-day I believe in this dynamic illusion. For that creed was the first great inspiration of the demi-urge,—man's big romantic idea of Chivalry, of himself as his Father's representative in an alien country; —and it is a notion at which mere fact and reason yelp denial unavailingly. For every one of us is so constituted that he knows the romance to be true, and corporal fact and human reason in this matter, as in divers others, to be the suborned and perjured witnesses of "realism."

Beyond Life, 1919

I shall marry in haste, and repeat at leisure.

Jurgen, 1919

A man possesses nothing certainly save a brief loan of his own body; and yet the body of man is capable of much curious pleasure.

Ibid.

The optimist proclaims that we live in the best of all possible worlds, and the pessimist fears this is true.

JOHN ERSKINE

Everything begins from loneliness.

Adam and Eve, 1927

DOROTHY CANFIELD FISHER

History is worth reading when it tells us truly what the attitude toward life was in the past.

Vermont Tradition, 1953

MARY HEATON VORSE

The art of writing is the art of applying the seat of the pants to the seat of the chair.

DAMON RUNYON

"But," Mindy says, "this is neither here nor there nor elsewhere."

Runyon à la Carte

RING LARDNER

Louis was saving for a rainy day and his wife had long ago given up praying for rain.

Anniversary, 1926

If he got stewed and fell in the gutter he'd catch a fish.

Horseshoes, 1926

Midge Kelly scored his first knockout when he was seventeen. The knockee was his brother Connie, three years his junior and a cripple. The purse was a half dollar given to the younger Kelly by a lady whose electric had just missed bumping his soul from his frail little body.

Champion, opening lines

The lease said about I and my fathers trip from The Bureau of Manhattan to our new home the soonest mended. In some way either he or I got balled up on the Grand Concorpse and next thing you know we was threatening to swoop down on Pittsfield.

"Are you lost daddy?" I arsked tenderly.

"Shut up," he explained.

The Young Immigrunts

I can't come—it's the children's night out and I have to stay home with the nurse.

He give her a look that you could have poured on a waffle.

Sinclair Lewis

God give me unclouded eyes and freedom from haste. God give me a quiet and relentless anger against all pretense and all pretentious work and all work left slack and unfinished. God give me a restlessness whereby I may neither sleep nor accept praise till my observed results equal my calculated results or in pious glee I discover and assault my error. God give me strength not to trust in God!

Arrowsmith, Martin Arrowsmith's prayer, 1925

I suspect that no competent and adequately trained writer ever, after his apprenticeship, uses the word "style" in regard to his own work. If he did, he would become so self-conscious that he would be quite unable to write. . . . The generic concept of "style," as something apart from, distinguishable from, the matter, the thought, the story, does not come to his mind.

He writes as God lets him. He writes—if he is good enough!—as Tilden plays tennis or as Dempsey fights, which is to say, he throws himself into

it with never a moment of the dilettante's sitting back and watching himself perform.

Types and Times in the Essay, 1932

I was walking once with Carl Van Doren up a trail in the Taconic Mountains, and over us we saw an eagle. In a hundred walks along that trail, I
had never seen an eagle before, and I have never seen one since.

The Great Recorder, an impression of Carl Van Doren

KENNETH ROBERTS

On every side of us are men who hunt perpetually for their personal
Northwest Passage, too often sacrificing health, strength and life itself to
the search; and who shall say they are not happier in their vain but hopeful quest than wiser, duller folks who sit at home, venturing nothing and,
with sour laughs, deriding the seekers for that fabled thoroughfare?

Northwest Passage, 1937

ELIZABETH MADOX ROBERTS

I used to think when I was a youngone, Jasper, that all the things you
read about or hear came to pass in some country, all in some country
somewheres. "Oh, Mary go and call the cattle home," and "Lady Nancy
died like it might be today," all in one country. . . . A country a far
piece off. Off past Tennessee somewheres. But now I know better and
know how the world is, a little.

The Time of Man, 1926

EDNA FERBER

Being an old maid is like death by drowning, a really delightful sensation
after you cease to struggle.

HERVEY ALLEN

Grow up as soon as you can. It pays. The only time you really live fully is
from thirty to sixty. . . . The young are slaves to dreams; the old servants
of regrets. Only the middle-aged have all their five senses in the keeping
of their wits.

Anthony Adverse, 1933

CHRISTOPHER MORLEY

If you have to keep reminding yourself of a thing, perhaps it isn't so.

Thunder on the Left, 1925

Pop used to say about the Presbyterians, it don't prevent them committing all the sins there are but it keeps them from getting any fun out of it.

Kitty Foyle, 1939

MARGARET CULKIN BANNING

She never quite leaves her children at home, even when she doesn't take them along.

HENRY MILLER

It may be that we are doomed, that there is no hope for us, *any of us;* but if that is so then let us set up a last agonizing, blood-curdling howl, a screech of defiance, a war-whoop! Away with lamentations! Away with elegies and dirges! Away with biographies and histories, and libraries and museums! Let the dead bury the dead. Let us living ones dance about the rim of the crater, a last expiring dance. But a dance!

Tropic of Cancer, 1934

PEARL BUCK

The sun beat down upon them, for it was early summer, and [O-lan's] face was soon dripping with her sweat. Wang Lung had his coat off and his back bare, but she worked with her thin garment covering her shoulders and it grew wet and covered her like skin. Moving together in a perfect rhythm, without a word, hour after hour, he fell into a union with her which took the pain from his labor. He had no articulate thought of anything; there was only this perfect sympathy of movement, of turning this earth of theirs over and over to the sun, this earth which formed their home and fed their bodies and made their gods. The earth lay rich and dark, and fell apart lightly under the points of their hoes. Sometimes they turned up a bit of brick, a splinter of wood. It was nothing. Some time, in some age, bodies of men and women had been buried there, houses had stood there, had fallen, and gone back into the earth. So would also their house, some time, return to the earth, their bodies also. Each had his turn at this earth. They worked on, moving together—together—producing the fruit of this earth—speechless in their movement together.

When the sun had set he straightened his back slowly and looked at the woman. Her face was wet and streaked with the earth. She was as brown as the very soil itself. Her wet, dark garments clung to her square body. She smoothed a last furrow slowly. Then in her usual plain way she said, straight out, her voice flat and more than usually plain in the silent evening air,

"I am with child."

Wang Lung stood still. What was there to say to this thing, then! She stooped to pick up a bit of broken brick and threw it out of the furrow. It was as though she had said, "I have brought you tea," or as though she had said, "We can eat." It seemed as ordinary as that to her! But to him—he could not say what it was to him. His heart swelled and stopped as though it met sudden confines. Well, it was their turn at this earth!

The Good Earth, 1931

I enjoy life because I am endlessly interested in people and their growth. My interest leads me continually to widen my knowledge of people, and this in turn compels me to believe that the normal human heart is born good. That is, it is born sensitive and feeling, eager to be approved and to approve, hungry for simple happiness and the chance to live. If through circumstances it is overcome by evil, it never becomes entirely evil. There remain in it elements of good, however recessive, which continue to hold the possibility of restoration.

I believe in human beings but my faith is without sentimentality. I know that in environments of uncertainty, fear and hunger, the human being is dwarfed and shaped without his being aware of it, just as the plant struggling under a stone does not know its own condition. But the power to spring up is inherent, and only death puts an end to it.

I feel no need for any other faith than my faith in human beings. Like Confucius of old, I am so absorbed in the wonder of earth and the life upon it that I cannot think of heaven and the angels. I have enough for this life. If there is no other life, then this one has been enough to make it worth being born, myself a human being.

This I Believe

ANITA LOOS

Gentlemen Prefer Blondes.

Title of novel, 1925

Gentlemen always seem to remember blondes.

Ibid.

A girl never really looks as well as she does aboard a steamship, or even a yacht.

Ibid.

J. P. MARQUAND

There is a certain phase in the life of the aged when the warmth of the heart seems to increase in direct proportion with the years. This is a time of life when a solicitous family does well to watch affectionately over the vagaries of its unattached relatives, particularly of those who are comfortably off.

The Late George Apley, 1937

I was just repeating what I had heard other people say. The queer thing is that what other people say is so often true, or partly true. If you are young, they say, sooner or later you get over it. They don't say that everything hurts more when you are young. I like to think of that when I hear people talking about lost youth. I am glad that I am through with it and won't be young again.

H. M. Pulham, Esq., 1941

Once I believed, and I fear many writers do still, that one only needed to travel about the world collecting "local color" in order to write of distant places like a Kipling or a Conrad. This, I venture to assert, is not the case. No matter how skilled the author is and no matter what exceptional material he may encounter, his short story or his novel, though accurate and even perceptive, will lack in final authority if he simply goes about the world observing and taking notes and then returning home to put them in finished form. Perhaps it is necessary to make the experiment oneself before realizing that one must have a living stake in the community in order to convey a deep impression of it to others.

Thirty Years, in a note to the story "Poor Paw," 1954

BEN HECHT

A man nearly always loves for other reasons than he thinks. A lover is apt to be as full of secrets from himself as is the object of his love from him.

A Child of the Century, 1954

A man who writes of himself without speaking of God is like one who identifies himself without giving his address.

Ibid.

I know that a man who shows me his wealth is like the beggar who shows me his poverty; they are both looking for alms from me, the rich man for the alms of my envy, the poor man for the alms of my guilt.

Ibid.

There is hardly one in three of us who live in the cities who is not sick with unused self.

Ibid.

KATHERINE ANNE PORTER

In the face of such shape and weight of present misfortune, the voice of the individual artist may seem perhaps of no more consequence than the whirring of a cricket in the grass; but the arts do live continuously, and they live literally by faith; their names and their shapes and their uses and their basic meanings survive unchanged in all that matters through times of interruption, diminishment, neglect; they outlive governments and creeds and the societies, even the very civilizations that produced them. They cannot be destroyed altogether because they represent the substance of faith and the only reality. They are what we find again when the ruins are cleared away.

Flowering Judas, "Introduction," June 21, 1940

Love must be learned, and learned again and again; there is no end to it. Hate needs no instruction, but waits only to be provoked.

The Days Before, 1952

JEAN TOOMER

When I speak, I am persuaded.

F. SCOTT FITZGERALD

The victor belongs to the spoils.

The Beautiful and the Damned, 1922

The caterwauling horns had reached a crescendo and I turned away and cut across the lawn toward home. I glanced back once. A wafer of moon was shining over Gatsby's house, making the night fine as before, and surviving the laughter and the sound of his still glowing garden. A sudden emptiness seemed to flow now from the windows and the great doors, endowing with complete isolation the figure of the host, who stood on the porch, his hand up in a formal gesture of farewell.

The Great Gatsby, 1925

Gatsby believed in the green light, the orgiastic future that year by year recedes before us. It eluded us then, but that's no matter—to-morrow we will run faster, stretch out our arms farther. . . . And one fine morning—

So we beat on, boats against the current, borne back ceaselessly into the past.

Ibid., last lines

In a real dark night of the soul it is always three o'clock in the morning.

Handle With Care

So what? This is what I think now: that the natural state of the sentient adult is a qualified unhappiness.

Passing It Together, 1936

Of course all life is a process of breaking down, but the blows that do the dramatic side of the work—the big sudden blows that come, or seem to come, from outside—the ones you remember and blame things on and, in moments of weakness, tell your friends about, don't show their effect all at once. There is another sort of blow that comes from within—that you don't feel until it's too late to do anything about it, until you realize with finality that in some regard you will never be as good a man again. The first sort of breakage seems to happen quick—the second kind happens almost without your knowing it but is realized suddenly indeed.

February, 1936

You can take your choice between God and Sex. If you choose both, you're a smug hypocrite; if neither, you get nothing.

The Crackup, 1945

The kiss originated when the first male reptile licked the first female reptile, implying in a subtle, complimentary way that she was as succulent as the small reptile he had for dinner the night before.

Ibid.

She's got to be a loyal, frank person if she's got to bitch everyone in the world to do it.

Ibid.

Women have only one role—their own charm—all the rest is mimicry.

Note-Books

Show me a hero and I will write you a tragedy.

Ibid.

All good writing is *swimming under water* and holding your breath.

Letter, undated

Begin with an individual, and before you know it you find that you have created a type; begin with a type, and you find that you have created—nothing.

The test of a first-rate intelligence is the ability to hold two opposed ideas in the mind, at the same time, and still retain the ability to function.

Men get to be a mixture of the charming mannerisms of the women they have known.

WILLIAM FAULKNER

The Negro met the first of the ladies at the front door and let them in, with their hushed, sibilant voices and their quick, curious glances, and then he disappeared. He walked right through the house and out the back and was not seen again.

The two female cousins came at once. They held the funeral on the second day, with the town coming to look at Miss Emily beneath a mass of bought flowers, with the crayon face of her father musing profoundly above the bier and the ladies sibilant and macabre; and the very old men —some in their brushed Confederate uniforms—on the porch and the lawn, talking of Miss Emily as if she had been a contemporary of theirs, believing that they had danced with her and courted her perhaps, confusing time with its mathematical progression, as the old do, to whom all the past is not a diminishing road but, instead, a huge meadow which no winter ever quite touches, divided from them now by the narrow bottleneck of the most recent decade of years.

Already we knew that there was one room in that region above stairs which no one had seen in forty years, and which would have to be forced. They waited until Miss Emily was decently in the ground before they opened it.

The violence of breaking down the door seemed to fill this room with pervading dust. A thin, acrid pall as of the tomb seemed to lie everywhere upon this room decked and furnished as for a bridal: upon the valance curtains of faded rose color, upon the rose-shaded lights, upon the dressing table, upon the delicate array of crystal and the man's toilet things backed with tarnished silver, silver so tarnished that the monogram was obscured. Among them lay a collar and tie, as if they had just been removed, which, lifted, left upon the surface a pale crescent in the dust. Upon a chair hung the suit, carefully folded; beneath it the two mute shoes and the discarded socks.

The man himself lay in the bed.

For a long while we just stood there, looking down at the profound and fleshless grin. The body had apparently once lain in the attitude of an embrace, but now the long sleep that outlasts love, that conquers even the grimace of love, had cuckolded him. What was left of him rotted beneath what was left of the night-shirt, had become inextricable from the bed in which he lay; and upon him and upon the pillow beside him lay that even coating of the patient and biding dust.

Then we noticed that in the second pillow was the indentation of a head. One of us lifted something from it, and leaning forward, that faint and invisible dust dry and acrid in the nostrils, we saw a long strand of iron-gray hair.

"A Rose for Emily"

It had been a gray day, a gray summer, a gray year. On the street old men wore overcoats, and in the Luxembourg Gardens as Temple and her father passed the women sat knitting in shawls and even the men playing croquet played in coats and capes, and in the sad gloom of the chestnut trees the dry click of balls, the random shouts of children, had that quality of autumn, gallant and evanescent and forlorn. From beyond the circle with its spurious Greek balustrade, clotted with movement, filled with a gray light of the same color and texture as the water which the fountain played into the pool, came a steady crash of music. They went on, passed the pool where the children and an old man in a shabby brown overcoat sailed toy boats, and entered the trees again and found seats. Immediately an old woman came with decrepit promptitude and collected four sous.

In the pavilion a band in the horizon blue of the army played Massenet and Scriabin, and Berlioz like a thin coating of tortured Tschaikovsky on a slice of stale bread, while the twilight dissolved in wet gleams from the branches, onto the pavilion and the sombre toadstools of umbrellas. Rich and resonant the brasses crashed and died in the thick green twilight, rolling over them in rich sad waves. Temple yawned behind her hand, then she took out a compact and opened it upon a face in miniature sullen and discontented and sad. Beside her her father sat, his hands crossed on the head of his stick, the rigid bar of his moustache beaded with moisture like frosted silver. She closed the compact and from beneath her smart new hat she seemed to follow with her eyes the waves of music, to dissolve into the dying brasses, across the pool and the opposite semicircle of trees where at sombre intervals the dead tranquil queens in stained marble mused, and on into the sky lying prone and vanquished in the embrace of the season of rain and death.

Sanctuary, the ending, 1931

Our tragedy today is a general and universal physical fear so long sustained by now that we can even bear it. There are no longer problems of the spirit. There is only the question: When will I be blown up? Because of this, the young man or woman writing today has forgotten the problems of the human heart in conflict with itself which alone can make good writing because only that is worth writing about, worth the agony and the sweat.

He must learn them again. He must teach himself that the basest of all things is to be afraid; and, teaching himself that, forget it forever, leaving no room in his workshop for anything but the old verities and truths of the heart, the old universal truths lacking which any story is ephemeral and doomed—love and honor and pity and pride and compassion and sacrifice. Until he does so, he labors under a curse. He writes not of love but of lust, or defeats in which nobody loses anything of value, of victories without hope, and, worst of all, without pity or compassion. His griefs grieve on no universal bones, leaving no scars. He writes not of the heart but of the glands.

Until he learns these things, he will write as though he stood among and watched the end of man. I decline to accept the end of man. It is easy enough to say that man is immortal simply because he will endure: that when the last ding-dong of doom has clanged and faded from the last worthless rock hanging tideless in the last red and dying evening, that even then there will still be one more sound: that of his puny inexhaustible voice, still talking. I refuse to accept this. I believe that man will not merely endure: he will prevail. He is immortal, not because he alone among creatures has an inexhaustible voice, but because he has a soul, a spirit capable of compassion and sacrifice and endurance. The poet's, the writer's, duty is to write about these things. It is his privilege to help man endure by lifting his heart, by reminding him of the courage and honor and hope and pride and compassion and pity and sacrifice which have been the glory of his past. The poet's voice need not merely be the record of man, it can be one of the props, the pillars to help him endure and prevail.

"Nobel Prize Speech," Stockholm, December, 1950

THORNTON WILDER

It seemed to Brother Juniper that it was high time for theology to take its place among the exact sciences, and he had long intended putting it there. What he had lacked hitherto was a laboratory. Oh, there had never been any lack of specimens; any number of his charges had met calamity —spiders had stung them; their lungs had been touched; their houses had burned down and things had happened to their children from which one averts the mind. But these occasions of human woe had never been quite fit for scientific examination. They had lacked what our good savants were later to call *proper control*. The accident had been dependent upon human error, for example, or had contained elements of probability. But this collapse of the bridge of San Luis Rey was a sheer Act of God. It afforded a perfect laboratory. Here at last one could surprise His intentions in a pure state.

You and I can see that coming from anyone but Brother Juniper this plan would be the flower of a perfect scepticism. It resembled the effort of those presumptuous souls who wanted to walk on the pavements of heaven and built the Tower of Babel to get there. But to our Franciscan there was no element of doubt in the experiment. He knew the answer. He merely wanted to prove it, historically, mathematically, to his converts —poor obstinate converts, so slow to believe that their pains were inserted into their lives for their own good.

The Bridge of San Luis Rey, 1927

"Even now," [Donna Clare] thought, "almost no one remembers Esteban and Pepita, but myself. Camila alone remembers her Uncle Pio and her son; this woman, her mother. But soon we shall die and all memory of those five will have left the earth, and we ourselves shall be loved for a while and forgotten. But the love will have been enough; all those impulses of love return to the love that made them. Even memory is not necessary for love. There is a land of the living and a land of the dead and the bridge is love, the only survival, the only meaning."

Ibid., last lines

Great talkers are so constituted that they do not know their own thoughts until, on the tide of their particular gift, they hear them issuing from their mouths.

The Woman of Andros, 1930

Of all the forms of genius, goodness has the longest awkward age.

Ibid.

The central movement of the mind is the desire for unrestricted liberty and . . . this movement is invariably accompanied by its opposite, a dread of the consequences of liberty.

The Ides of March, 1948

I think there is only one solitude greater than that of the military commander and of the head of the state and that is the poet's—for who can advise him in that unbroken succession of choices which is a poem? It is in this sense that responsibility is liberty; the more decisions that you are forced to make alone, the more you are aware of your freedom to choose. I hold that we cannot be said to be aware of our minds save under responsibility.

Ibid.

A slave is twice enslaved, once by his chains and once again by the glances that fall upon him and say "thou slave."

Ibid.

The trivial is only endurable from the lips of those who put an importance upon it.

Ibid.

Literature is the orchestration of platitudes.

"Literature"

ERNEST HEMINGWAY

They shot the six cabinet ministers at half-past six in the morning against the wall of a hospital. There were pools of water in the courtyard. There were dead leaves on the paving of the courtyard. It rained hard. All the shutters of the hospital were nailed shut. One of the ministers was sick with typhoid. Two soldiers carried him downstairs and out into the rain. They tried to hold him up against the wall but he sat down in a puddle of water. The other five stood very quietly against the wall. Finally the officer told the soldiers it was no good trying to make him stand up. When they fired the first volley he was sitting down in the water with his head on his knees.

> *In Our Time,* 1924, quoted by Edmund Wilson in a review of the book for the *Dial,* October, 1924. It was the first Hemingway criticism to appear in America.

It is awfully easy to be hard-boiled about everything in the daytime, but at night it is another thing.

> *The Sun Also Rises,* 1926

In the fall the war was always there, but we did not go to it any more. It was cold in the fall in Milan and the dark came very early. Then the electric lights came on, and it was pleasant along the streets looking in the windows. There was much game hanging outside the shops, and the snow powdered in the fur of the foxes and wind blew their tails. The deer hung stiff and heavy and empty, and small birds blew in the wind and the wind turned their feathers. It was a cold fall and the wind came down from the mountains.

> *Men Without Women,* "In Another Country," 1927

In the late summer of that year we lived in a house in a village that looked across the river and the plain to the mountains. In the bed of the river there were pebbles and boulders, dry and white in the sun, and the water was clear and swiftly moving and blue in the channels. Troops went by the house and down the road and the dust they raised powdered the leaves of the trees. The trunks of the trees too were dusty and the leaves fell early that year and we saw the troops marching along the road and the dust rising and the leaves, stirred by the breeze, falling and the soldiers marching and afterward the road bare and white except for the leaves.

> *A Farewell to Arms,* first paragraph, 1929

After I had got them out and shut the door and turned off the light it

wasn't any good. It was like saying good-by to a statue. After a while I
went out and left the hospital and walked back to the hotel in the rain.

Ibid., last lines

Kilimanjaro is a snow covered mountain 19,710 feet high, and it is said
to be the highest mountain in Africa. Its western summit is called by the
Masai "Ngaje Ngai," the House of God. Close to the western summit
there is the dried and frozen carcass of a leopard. No one has explained
what the leopard was seeking at that altitude.

"The Snows of Kilimanjaro," "motto," 1936

The world is a fine place and worth fighting for.

For Whom the Bell Tolls, 1940

He had sailed for two hours, resting in the stern and sometimes chewing
a bit of the meat from the marlin, trying to rest and to be strong, when
he saw the first of the two sharks.

"*Ay,*" he said aloud. There is no translation for this word and perhaps
it is just a noise such as a man might make, involuntarily, feeling the nail
go through his hands and into the wood.

The Old Man and the Sea, 1952

He could not talk to the fish anymore because the fish had been ruined
too badly. Then something came into his head.

"Half fish," he said. "Fish that you were. I am sorry that I went too
far out. I ruined us both. But we have killed many sharks, you and I, and
ruined many others. How many did you ever kill, old fish? You do not
have that spear on your head for nothing."

He liked to think of the fish and what he could do to a shark if he were
swimming free. I should have chopped the bill off to fight with them, he
thought. But there was no hatchet and then there was no knife.

But if I had, and could have lashed it to an oar butt, what a weapon.
Then we might have fought them together. What will you do now if they
come in the night? What can you do?

"Fight them," he said. "I'll fight them until I die."

Ibid.

There are some things which cannot be learned quickly, and time, which
is all we have, must be paid heavily for their acquiring. They are the very
simplest things and because it takes a man's life to know them the little

new each man gets from life is very costly and the only heritage he has to leave. Every novel which is truly written contributes to the total of knowledge which is there at the disposal of the next writer who comes, but the next writer must pay, always, a certain nominal percentage in experience to be able to understand and assimilate what is available in his birthright and what he must, in turn, take his departure from.

Death in the Afternoon, 1932

What is moral is what you feel good after and what is immoral is what you feel bad after.

Ibid.

Those people who identify themselves with animals, that is, the almost professional lovers of dogs, and other beasts, are capable of greater cruelty to human beings than those who do not readily identify themselves with animals.

Ibid.

A growing ecstasy or ordered, formal, passionate, increasing disregard for death. . . .

It is impossible to believe the emotional and spiritual intensity and pure, classic beauty that can be produced by a man, an animal, and a piece of scarlet serge draped over a stick.

Ibid.

The great thing is to last and get your work done and see and hear and learn and understand; and write when there is something that you know; and not before; and not too damned much after. Let those who want to save the world if you can get to see it clear and as a whole. Then any part you make will represent the whole if it's made truly. The thing to do is to work and learn to make it. No. It is not enough of a book, but still there were a few things to be said. There were a few practical things to be said.

Ibid.

All good books are alike in that they are truer than if they really happened and after you are finished reading one you will feel that all that happened to you and afterwards it all belongs to you: the good and the bad, the ecstasy, the remorse and sorrow, the people and the places and how the weather was. If you can get so you can give that to people, then you are a writer.

"Old Newsman Writes," *Esquire,* December, 1934

When you describe something that has happened that day the timeliness makes people see it in their own imagination. A month later that element of time is gone and your account would be flat and they would not see it in their minds nor remember it. But if you can make it up instead of describe it you can make it round and whole and solid and give it life. You create it, for good or bad. It is made, not described. It is just as true as the extent of your ability to make it and the knowledge you put into it.

"Monologue to the Maestro," *Esquire,* October, 1935

The first panacea for a mismanaged nation is inflation of currency; the second is war. Both bring a temporary prosperity; both bring a permanent ruin. But both are the refuge of political and economic opportunists.

Notes on the Next War, 1935

They wrote in the old days that it is sweet and fitting to die for one's country. But in modern war there is nothing sweet nor fitting in your dying. You will die like a dog and for no good reason.

Ibid.

Cowardice . . . is almost always simply a lack of ability to suspend the functioning of the imagination.

Men at War, "Introduction," 1942

When you go to war as a boy you have a great illusion of immortality. Other people get killed; not you. It can happen to other people; but not to you. Then when you are badly wounded the first time you lose that illusion and you know it can happen to you. After being severely wounded two weeks before my nineteenth birthday I had a bad time until I figured it out that nothing could happen to me that had not happened to all men before me. Whatever I had to do men had always done. If they had done it then I could do it too and the best thing was not to worry about it.

I was very ignorant at nineteen and had read little and I remember the sudden happiness and the feeling of having a permanent protecting talisman when a young British officer I met when in the hospital first wrote out for me, so that I could remember them, these lines: "By my troth, I care not: a man can die but once; we owe God a death . . . and let it go which way it will, he that dies this year is quit for the next." (Henry IV, Part 2, Act III, Scene 2)

Ibid.

Writing, at its best, is a lonely life. . . . [A writer] does his work alone and if he is a good enough writer he must face eternity, or the lack of it, each day. . . . How simple the writing of literature would be if it were only necessary to write in another way what has been well written. It is because we have had such great writers in the past that a writer is driven far out past where he can go, out to where no one can help him.

> Speech (read by U.S. ambassador) upon receipt of Nobel
> Prize for Literature, Stockholm, 1954

Portable Corona No. 3.

> When asked the name of his analyst

A writer's problem does not change. He himself changes and the world he lives in changes but his problem remains the same. It is always how to write truly and, having found what is true, to project it in such a way that it becomes a part of the experience of the person who reads it.

Prose is architecture, not interior decoration.

THOMAS WOLFE

. . . a stone, a leaf, an unfound door; of a stone, a leaf, a door. And of all the forgotten faces.

Naked and alone we came into exile. In her dark womb we did not know our mother's face; from the prison of her flesh have we come into the unspeakable and incommunicable prison of this earth.

Which of us has known his brother? Which of us has looked into his father's heart? Which of us has not remained forever prison-pent? Which of us is not forever a stranger and alone?

O waste of loss, in the hot mazes, lost, among the bright stars on this most weary unbright cinder, lost! Remembering speechlessly we seek the great forgotten language, the lost lane-end into heaven, a stone, a leaf, an unfound door. Where? When?

O lost, and by the wind grieved, ghost, come back again.

> *Look Homeward Angel,* 1929; a passage printed on the
> flyleaf opposite the opening page

There is no spectacle on earth more appealing than that of a beautiful woman in the act of cooking dinner for someone she loves.

The Web and the Rock, 1939

LANGSTON HUGHES

I have not seen nobody die in their presence, so I do not know how that roomer went except that he went in the night when he were alone by hisself. I would not want to go like that. I would want somebody with me. I want some woman to hold my hand, some slim tall sweet old gal . . . to say, "Baby, don't go! I do not *know* what I can do without you."

I would want somebody to miss me—even *before* I am gone. I want somebody to cry real loud, scream and let the neighbors know I am no longer here. I want my passing to be a main event. . . .

In fact, if there are more than one woman crying over me, I will be glad. If there are three or four, or seven, I would not care. Let the world, the rest of the womens in it, and everybody know that I have been here and gone, been in this world, and passed through, and left a mighty mourning. . . .

When I die, I would not like to die like that fellow in Baltimore with nobody to claim his body, nobody to lay out Five Hundred Dollars for a funeral, nobody to come and cry. Only a lonesome few roomers knowed when he were taken down the steps with his room door left open—and it were empty in there. Empty, empty, and quiet.

No, I would not want to be carried out that way, feet first. I would really like to walk down the steps, out to my own funeral—if I had to go at all. . . .

Not having been around people very much who are dying, I did not know until then how it felt to see somebody walking down the hall tonight, then not see them in the morning because they are gone. *Gone* with a big letter, *gone* with a capital *G.* I mean *solid and really* not-here-no-more—gone. Silent, with nobody to scream. . . .

The landlord said to his wife the next day, "Put that sign—ROOM FOR RENT—back in the window. But don't let nobody have that room unless they pay a full week in advance."

That's all anybody said after that roomer were gone. But one night somebody came and rung his bell, three times. He were not there.

Simple Takes a Wife, 1953

John Steinbeck

The concrete highway was edged with a mat of tangled, broken, dry grass, and the grass heads were heavy with oat beards to catch on a dog's coat, and foxtails to tangle in a horse's fetlocks, and clover burrs to fasten in sheep's wool; sleeping life waiting to be spread and dispersed, every seed armed with an appliance of dispersal, twisting darts and parachutes for the wind, little spears and balls of tiny thorns, and all waiting for animals and for the wind, for a man's trouser cuff or the hem of a woman's skirt, all passive but armed with appliances of activity, still, but each possessed of the anlage of movement.

The sun lay on the grass and warmed it, and in the shade under the grass the insects moved, ants and ant lions to set traps for them, grasshoppers to jump into the air and flick their yellow wings for a second, sow bugs like little armadillos, plodding restlessly on many tender feet. And over the grass at the roadside a land turtle crawled, turning aside for nothing, dragging his high-domed shell over the grass. His hard legs and yellow-nailed feet threshed slowly through the grass, not really walking, but boosting and dragging his shell along. The barley beards slid off his shell, and the clover burrs fell on him and rolled to the ground. His horny beak was partly open, and his fierce, humorous eyes, under brows like fingernails, stared straight ahead. He came over the grass leaving a beaten trail behind him, and the hill, which was the highway embankment, reared up ahead of him. For a moment he stopped, his head held high. He blinked and looked up and down. At last he started to climb the embankment. Front clawed feet reached forward but did not touch. The hind feet kicked his shell along, and it scraped on the grass, and on the gravel. As the embankment grew steeper and steeper, the more frantic were the efforts of the land turtle. Pushing hind legs strained and slipped, boosting the shell along, and the horny head protruded as far as the neck could stretch. Little by little the shell slid up the embankment until at last a parapet cut straight across its line of march, the shoulder of the road, a concrete wall four inches high. As though they worked independently the hind legs pushed the shell against the wall. The head upraised and peered over the wall to the broad smooth plain of cement. Now the hands, braced on top of the wall, strained and lifted, and the shell came slowly up and rested its front end on the wall. For a moment the turtle rested. A red ant ran into the shell, into the soft skin inside the shell, and suddenly head and legs snapped in, and the armored tail clamped in sideways. The red ant was crushed between body and legs. And one head of

wild oats was clamped into the shell by a front leg. For a long moment
the turtle lay still, and then the neck crept out and the old humorous
frowning eyes looked about and the legs and tail came out. The back legs
went to work, straining like elephant legs, and the shell tipped to an angle
so that the front legs could not reach the level cement plain. But higher
and higher the hind legs boosted it, until at last the center of balance
was reached, the front tipped down, the front legs scratched at the pavement, and it was up. But the head of wild oats was held by its stem
around the front legs.

Now the going was easy, and all the legs worked, and the shell boosted
along, waggling from side to side. A sedan driven by a forty-year-old
woman approached. She saw the turtle and swung to the right, off the
highway, the wheels screamed and a cloud of dust boiled up. Two wheels
lifted for a moment and then settled. The car skidded back onto the road,
and went on, but more slowly. The turtle had jerked into its shell, but
now it hurried on, for the highway was burning hot.

And now a light truck approached, and as it came near, the driver saw
the turtle and swerved to hit it. His front wheel struck the edge of the
shell, flipped the turtle like a tiddly-wink, spun it like a coin, and rolled
it off the highway. The truck went back to its course along the right side.
Lying on its back, the turtle was tight in its shell for a long time. But at
last its legs waved in the air, reaching for something to pull it over. Its
front foot caught a piece of quartz and little by little the shell pulled over
and flopped upright. The wild oat head fell out and three of the spear-
heads stuck in the ground. And as the turtle crawled on down the embankment, its shell dragged dirt over the seeds. The turtle entered a dust
road and jerked itself along, drawing a wavy shallow trench in the dust
with its shell. The old humorous eyes looked ahead, and the horny beak
opened a little. His yellow toe nails slipped a fraction in the dust.

The Grapes of Wrath, "The Turtle," 1939

Man, unlike any other thing organic or inorganic in the universe, grows
beyond his work, walks up the stairs of his concepts, emerges ahead of his
accomplishments.

Ibid.

This here ol' man jus' lived a life and jus' died out of it. I don't know
whether he was good or bad, but that don't matter much. He was alive,
an' that's what matters. An' now he's dead, an' that don't matter. Heard
a fella tell a poem one time, an' he says "All that lives is holy."

Ibid., "Sermon"

"It might be like this, Mac: When group-man wants to move, he makes a standard. 'God wills that we recapture the Holy Land'; or he says 'We fight to make the world safe for democracy'; or he says, 'We will wipe out social injustice with communism.' But the group doesn't care about the Holy Land, or Democracy, or Communism. Maybe the group simply wants to move, to fight, and uses these words simply to reassure the brains of individual men. . . ."

"How," asks Mac, "do you account for people like me, directing things, moving things? That puts your group-man out."

"You might be an effect as well as a cause, Mac. You might be an expression of group-man, a cell endowed with a special function, like an eye cell, drawing your force from group-man, and at the same time directing him, like an eye. Your eye both takes orders from and gives orders to your brain."

"This isn't practical," objects Mac. "What's all this kind of talk got to do with hungry men, with lay-offs and unemployment?"

"It might have a great deal to do with them. It isn't a very long time since tetanus and lockjaw were not connected. There are still primitives in the world who don't know children are the result of intercourse. Yes, it might be worth while to know more about group-man, to know his nature, his ends, his desires. They're not the same as ours. The pleasure we get in scratching an itch causes death to a great number of cells. Maybe group-man gets pleasure when individual men are wiped out in a way."

In Dubious Battle, 1936

They're down there now. God, Mac, you ought to of seen them. It was like all of them disappeared, and it was just one big animal, going down the road. Just all one animal . . .

The *animal* don't want the barricade. I don't know what it wants. Trouble is, guys that study people always think it's men, and it isn't men. It's a different kind of animal. It's as different from men as dogs are. Jim, it's swell when we can use it, but we don't know enough. When it gets started it might do anything.

Ibid.

I believe that there is one story in the world, and only one, that has frightened and inspired us, so that we live in a Pearl White serial of continuing thought and wonder. Humans are caught—in their lives, in their thoughts, in their hungers and ambitions, in their avarice and cruelty, and in their kindness and generosity too—in a net of good and evil. I think this is the only story we have and that it occurs on all levels of feeling

and intelligence. Virtue and vice were warp and woof of our first consciousness, and they will be the fabric of our last, and this despite any
changes we may impose on field and river and mountain, on economy and
manners. There is no other story. A man, after he has brushed off the dust
and chips of his life, will have left only the hard, clean question: Was it
good or was it evil? Have I done well—or ill?

East of Eden, 1952

Our species is the only creative species, and it has only one creative instrument, the individual mind and spirit of a man. Nothing was ever created
by two men. There are no good collaborations, whether in music, in art,
in poetry, in mathematics, in philosophy. Once the miracle of creation
has taken place, the group can build and extend it, but the group never
invents anything. The preciousness lies in the lonely mind of man.

Ibid.

A book is somehow sacred. A dictator can kill and maim people, can sink
to any kind of tyranny and only be hated, but when books are burned the
ultimate in tyranny has happened.

ERSKINE CALDWELL

Tobacco Road.

Title of novel, 1932

JAMES GOULD COZZENS

Colonel Ross breathed in his breath and blew it out softly. For himself,
for old Schlichter, for mankind, he could feel the same subduing mortifi-
cation. There never could be a man so brave that he would not sometime,
or in the end, turn part or all coward; or so wise that he was not, from
beginning to end, part ass if you knew where to look; or so good that
nothing at all about him was despicable. This would have to be accepted.
This was one of the limits of human endeavor, one of those boundaries of
the possible whose precise determining was, as General Nichols with his
ascetic air of being rid of those youthful illusions, viewing with no nonsense the Here and the Now, always saw it, the problem. If you did not
know where the limits were, how did you know that you weren't working
outside them? If you were working outside them you must be working in
vain. It was no good acting on a supposition that men could, for your
purpose, be what they did not have it in them to be; just as it was unwise

to beguile yourself, up there on top of the whirlwind, with the notion that the storm was going to have to do what you said.

Guard of Honor, 1948

NATHANAEL WEST

He sat in the window thinking. Man has a tropism for order. Keys in one pocket, change in another. Mandolins are tuned G D A E. The physical world has a tropism for disorder, entropy. Man against Nature . . . the battle of the centuries. Keys yearn to mix with change. Mandolins strive to get out of tune. Every order has within it the germ of destruction. All order is doomed, yet the battle is worth while.

Miss Lonelyhearts, 1933

SAUL BELLOW

There haven't been civilizations without cities. But what about cities without civilizations?

The Adventures of Augie March, 1953

HERMAN WOUK

I kid you not.

The Caine Mutiny, Captain Queeg's favorite phrase

CARSON MCCULLERS

The hearts of small children are delicate organs. A cruel beginning in this world can twist them into curious shapes. The heart of a child can shrink so that forever afterward it is hard and pitted as the seed of a peach. Or again, the heart of such a child may fester and swell until it is a misery to carry within the body, easily chafed and hurt by the most ordinary things.

The Member of the Wedding, 1946

JAMES JONES

They shook hands solemnly again, for the last time, split the last drink in Warden's bottle between them, threw the bottle in the weeds, squared their shoulders, and quietly passed out and went peacefully to sleep.

They were still there at two o'clock, stretched out in the middle of the gravel, when Weary Russell came ramming his weapons carrier down the road to take The Warden home.

. . . He got it stopped about three yards from Warden's oblivious feet. He climbed out and looked at them.

"Jesus Christ!" he whispered awfully. "Jesus Christ!"

Warden was clear out, sleeping peacefully happily, but he managed to shake some life back into Prewitt.

"Come on. Wake up, goddam it. You crazy bastard. Come on, you cant snow me, I know you aint dead. You got to help me load him in the back so I can get him back to the CP. If Dynamite ever found out about this he'd bust him sure."

"Dynamite cou'nt bust him," Prew said vaguely.

"He couldnt, 'ey?"

"Hell no," Prew scoffed. "Who'd he get to be First Sarnt?"

"I dont know," Weary said thoughtfully. "Maybe he could— Aw, to hell with that," he snarled. "Help me to get him loaded. What would you crazy dumb screwballs of done if it was someone else who came along? Why, I might of run over you and killed you both," he raged. "Come on, will you?" he pleaded disgustedly, "help me get him loaded."

. . . Between them they managed to half-carry half-drag the big man's lax body that was slippery as an eel around to the back of the truck. . . As soon as he was in Warden opened his eyes and grinned at them slyly. "Is that Russell?" he mumbled vaguely.

"Yeahr," Weary said disgustedly. "Russell the nursemaid. . ."

"En listen to me, Russell," Warden said. "I want you da zu sompin. I mean za du sompin. See?"

"Yeah?" said Weary learily. "What?"

Weary reared half up and looked around. Prewitt was already lolling in the rider's seat, asleep again. "I tell you," Warden whispered with all the quiet of a hissing locomotive. "I want you to drive ziz man home tiz bivouac. . . But that aint all: when you get him home, I want you to tell his corprl of the guard the Firs Sarnt says he is relieve from duty the rest of the night. For helping the Firs Sarnt on a private reconnaissance."

. . . "Okay, Top. But you sure demand a hell of a lot for a lousy god-dam Pfc."

"Cmere," Warden said and grabbed him by the arm. "Don't you know we got to look out for this man, Weary?" he whispered. "He's the best . . . soljer in the Compny." He paused thoughtfully. "The *only* . . . soljer in the Company," he amended.

"What is this?" Weary said. "A mutual backslapping society I stumbled into?"

"We got to take caref him while we can, see?" The warden told him urgently. "This man may not be with us for long, and we got to take caref this man. . . . You promise?" Warden said.

"Yeahr," said Weary Russell wearily. "I promise. Now go back to sleep."

"Okay then," Warden said contentedly. "But dont forget. Zvery important." He rolled over comfortably complacently in the dirty ribbed wood floor of the truckbed. "Because it may happen any day," he said.

Weary looked at him and shook his head and put the tailgate up and drove off down the gravel toward the bivouac, carrying two drunks, who both fatuously drunkenly imagined, that once in a dream somewhere, sometime, somespace, they had managed for a moment to touch another human soul and understand it.

From Here to Eternity, 1951

SHELBY FOOTE

Longevity conquers scandal every time.

Jordan County, 1954

XVII. Comic Spirits: The Wits and Humorists from Josh Billings to Groucho Marx

The crane is neither flesh, beast, nor fowl, but a sad mixtur ov all these things.

He mopes along the brinks of kreeks and wet places, looking for sumthing he haz lost.

He haz a long bill, long wings, long legs, and iz long all over.

When he flies thru the air, he is az graceful az a windmill, broke loose from its fastenings.

"The Crane"

The duk iz a kind ov short-legged hen.

They kan sale on the water as eazy as a grease spot.

Duks have a broad bill which enables them tew eat their food without enny spoon.

Thare ain't any room on the outside of a duk for enny more feathers.

The duk don't kro like a rooster, but quaks like a duk.

"The Duk"

Waiting to be whipped iz the most uninteresting period of boyhood life.

Proverbial Philosophy

No man is so poor that he can't afford to keep one dog, and I've seen them so poor they could afford to keep three.

There are but few men who have character enough to lead a life of idleness.

My son, observe the postage stamp! Its usefulness depends upon its ability to stick to one thing until it gets there.

In the whole history of the world there is but one thing that money cannot buy—the wag of a dog's tail.

The power of oratory lays more in the manner than in the matter. You can't reduce it to writing any more than you can play a streak of lightning on a hand organ.

Nature never makes any blunders; when she makes a fool she means it.

It is a very delicate job to forgive a man, without lowering him in his estimation, and yours too.

The trouble with most folks isn't so much their ignorance, as knowing so many things that ain't so.

Laughing is the sensation of feeling good all over, and showing it principally in one spot.

There iz two things in this life for which we are never fully prepared; and this iz twins.

Adam invented love at first sight, one of the greatest labor-saving machines the world ever saw.

Politeness looks well in every man, except an undertaker.

If anyone asks you why you got married tell him you *don't recollect.*

The mule is half horse and half jackass, and then comes to a full stop, nature discovering her mistake.

One of the best temporary cures for pride and affectation is seasickness: a man who wants to vomit never puts on airs.

I don't care how much a man talks, if he only says it in a few words.

As scarce as truth is, the supply has always been in excess of the demand.

Man without woman would be as stupid a game as playing checkers alone.

The recipe for making a good proverb is, take one gallon of truth, boil it down to a pint, sweeten with kindness and lay away to cool.

The thinner the ice, the more anxious is everyone to see if it will bear.

When a man comes to me for advice, I find out the kind of advice he wants, and I give it to him.

If the animals had reason, they would act just as ridiculous as we menfolks do.

CHARLES FARRAR BROWNE ("ARTEMUS WARD")

An amoozin little cuss.

Artemus Ward: His Book, 1862. Of his kangaroo.

Let us all be happy, and live within our means, even if we have to borrow the money to do it.

Natural History

Why is this thus? What is the reason of this thusness?

Moses, the Sassy

I am happiest when I am idle. I could live for months without performing any kind of labor, and at the expiration of that time I should feel fresh and vigorous enough to go right on in the same way for numerous more months.

Pyrotechny, III

SAMUEL L. CLEMENS ("MARK TWAIN")

They spell it Vinci and pronounce it Vinchy; foreigners always spell better then they pronounce.

The Innocents Abroad, 1869

If there is one thing in the world that will make a man peculiarly and insufferably self-conceited, it is to have his stomach behave itself, the first day at sea, when nearly all his comrades are sick.

Ibid.

[You are as] ignorant as the unborn babe! ignorant as unborn *twins!*

Roughing It, 1872

Delicacy—a sad, false delicacy—robs literature of the best two things among its belongings: family-circle narrative and obscene stories.

Letter to W. D. Howells, September 19, 1877

On this up trip [up the Mississippi] I saw a little towhead (infant island) half a mile long, which had been formed during the past nineteen years. Since there was so much time to spare that nineteen years of it could be devoted to the construction of a mere towhead, where was the use, originally, in rushing this whole globe through in six days? It is likely that if more time had been taken, in the first place, the world would have been made right, and this ceaseless improving and repairing would not be necessary now. But if you hurry a world or a house, you are nearly sure to find out by and by that you have left out a towhead, or a broom-closet, or some other little convenience, here and there, which has got to be supplied, no matter how much expense or vexation it may cost.

Life on the Mississippi, 1883

All you need in this life is ignorance and confidence, and then success is sure.

Letter to Mrs. Foote, December 2, 1887

One thing at a time is my motto—and just play that thing for all it is worth, even if it's only two pair and a jack.

A Connecticut Yankee in King Arthur's Court, 1889

Adam and Eve had many advantages, but the principal one was that they escaped teething.

The Tragedy of Pudd'nhead Wilson, "Pudd'nhead Wilson's Calendar," 1894

The holy passion of Friendship is of so sweet and steady and loyal and enduring a nature that it will last through a whole lifetime, if not asked to lend money.

Ibid.

Training is everything. The peach was once a bitter almond; cauliflower is nothing but cabbage with a college education.

Ibid.

Whoever has lived long enough to find out what life is, knows how deep a debt of gratitude we owe to Adam, the first great benefactor of our race. He brought death into the world.

Ibid.

It were not best that we should all think alike; it is difference of opinion that makes horseraces.

Ibid.

As to the adjective, when in doubt, strike it out.

Ibid.

One of the striking differences between a cat and a lie is that the cat has only nine lives.

Ibid.

Consider well the proportions of things. It is better to be a young June-bug than an old bird of paradise.

Ibid.

Everything human is pathetic. The secret source of Humor itself is not joy but sorrow. There is no humor in heaven.

Following the Equator, 1897

We should be careful to get out of an experience only the wisdom that is in it—and stop there; lest we be like the cat that sits down on a hot stove-lid. She will never sit down on a hot stove-lid again—and that is well; but also she will never sit down on a cold one any more.

Ibid.

Be good and you will be lonesome.

Ibid.

There are several good protections against temptation, but the surest is cowardice.

Ibid., "Pudd'nhead Wilson's New Calendar"

Noise proves nothing. Often a hen who has merely laid an egg cackles as if she had laid an asteroid.

Ibid.

To be good is noble; but to show others how to be good is nobler and no trouble.

Ibid.

There isn't a Parallel of Latitude but thinks it would have been the Equator if it had had its rights.

Ibid.

Man is the only animal that blushes. Or needs to.

Ibid.

Grief can take care of itself, but to get full value of a joy you must have somebody to divide it with.

Ibid.

ADAM (at Eve's grave) : Wherever she was, *there* was Eden.

Eve's Diary, 1906

I conceive that the right way to write a story for boys is to write so that it will not only interest boys but strongly interest any man *who has ever been a boy.* That immensely *enlarges the audience.*

Letters, 1917

Heaven for climate, and hell for society.

Speeches, 1923

By and by when each nation has 20,000 battleships and 5,000,000 soldiers we shall all be safe and the wisdom of statesmanship will stand confirmed.

More Maxims of Mark, 1927

Never tell the truth to people who are not worthy of it.

Ibid.

You can straighten a worm, but the crook is in him and only waiting.

Ibid.

When in doubt, tell the truth.

Notebook, 1935

What a good thing Adam had—when he said a thing he knew nobody had said it before.

Ibid.

It is not in the least likely that any life has ever been lived which was not a failure in the secret judgment of the person who lived it.

Ibid.

Well enough for old folks to rise early, because they have done so many mean things all their lives they can't sleep anyhow.

Ibid.

If Christ were here now there is one thing he would not be—a Christian.

Ibid.

When we remember that we are all mad, the mysteries disappear and life stands explained.

Ibid.

Good breeding consists in concealing how much we think of ourselves and how little we think of the other person.

Ibid.

Of the delights of *this* world man cares *most* for sexual intercourse. He will go any length for it—risk fortune, character, reputation, life itself. And what do you think he has done? In a thousand years you would never guess—*He has left it out of his heaven! Prayer takes its place.*

Ibid.

One of the proofs of the immortality of the soul is that myriads have believed it. They also believed the world was flat.

Ibid.

My books are water: those of the great geniuses are wine. Everybody drinks water.

Ibid.

Keep away from people who try to belittle your ambitions. Small people always do that, but the really great make you feel that you, too, can become great.

Morally We Roll Along, 1938

I'm quite sure that . . . I have no race prejudices, and I think I have no color prejudices nor creed prejudices. Indeed, I know it. I can stand any society. All I care to know is that a man is a human being—that is enough for me; he can't be any worse.

Concerning the Jews

Of course, Satan has some kind of case, it goes without saying. It may be a poor one, but that is nothing; that can be said about any one of us. . . . We may not pay him reverence for that would be indiscreet; but we can at least respect his talents. A person who has for untold centuries maintained the imposing position of spiritual head of four fifths of the human race, and political head of the whole of it, must be granted the possession of executive abilities of the loftiest order. . . . I would like to see him. I would rather see him and shake him by the tail than any other member of the European Concert.

Ibid.

Don't . . . meddle with old unloaded firearms; they are the most deadly and unerring things that have ever been created by man. You don't have to have a rest, you don't have to have any sights on the gun, you don't have to take aim, even. No, you just pick out a relative and bang away, and you are sure to get him. A youth who can't hit a cathedral at thirty yards with a Gatling gun in three-quarters of an hour, can take up an old empty musket and bag his grandmother every time, at a hundred.

Advice to Youth

Go to bed early, get up early—this is wise. Some authorities say get up with the sun; some others say get up with one thing, some with another. But a lark is really the best thing to get up with. It gives you a splendid reputation with everybody to know that you get up with the lark; and if you get the right kind of lark, and work at him right, you can easily train him to get up at half past nine, every time—it is no trick at all.

Ibid.

What a man sees in the human race is merely himself in the deep and honest privacy of his own heart. Byron despised the race because he despised himself. I feel as Byron did, and for the same reason.

From a marginal note

Get your facts first, and then you can distort 'em as much as you please.

Ignorant people think it's the noise which fighting cats make that is so aggravating, but it ain't so; it's the sickening grammar they use.

After forty we lose friends and make only acquaintances.

Always do right. This will gratify some people, and astonish the rest.

Let us not be too particular; it is better to have old second-hand diamonds than none at all.

When I was a boy of fourteen, my father was so ignorant I could hardly stand to have the old man around. But when I got to be twenty-one, I was astonished at how much the old man had learned in seven years.

The difference between the right word and the almost right word is the difference between lightning and the lightning bug.

AMBROSE BIERCE

Absolute monarchy, *n.* One in which the monarch does as he pleases as long as he pleases the assassins.

Acquaintance, *n.* A person whom we know well enough to borrow from, but not well enough to lend to.

Adage, *n.* Boned wisdom for weak teeth.

Barometer, *n.* An ingenious instrument which indicates what kind of weather we are having.

Bore, *n.* A person who talks when you want him to listen.

Brain, *n.* An apparatus with which we think that we think.

Conservative, *n.* A statesman who is enamoured of existing evils, as distinguished from the Liberal, who wishes to replace them with others.

Corporation, *n.* An ingenious device for obtaining individual profit without individual responsibility.

Coward, *n.* One who in a perilous emergency thinks with his legs.

Cynic, *n.* A blackguard whose faulty vision sees things as they are, not as they ought to be.

Edible, *adj.* Good to eat, and wholesome to digest, as a worm to a toad, a toad to a snake, a snake to a pig, a pig to a man, and a man to a worm.

Envy, *n.* Emulation adapted to the meanest capacity.

Faith, *n.* Belief without evidence in what is told by one who speaks without knowledge, of things without parallel.

Habit, *n.* A shackle for the free.

Hospitality, *n.* The virtue which induces us to feed and lodge certain persons who are not in need of food and lodging.

Lawsuit, *n.* A machine which you go into as a pig and come out of as a sausage.

Marriage, *n.* The state or condition of a community consisting of a master, a mistress, and two slaves, making, in all, two.

Mayonnaise, *n.* One of the sauces which serve the French in place of a state religion.

Me, *pro.* The objectionable case of I. The personal pronoun in English has three cases, the dominative, the objectionable and the oppressive. Each is all three.

Ocean, *n.* A body of water occupying about two-thirds of a world made for man—who has no gills.

Once, *adv.* Enough.

Opposition, *n.* In politics the party that prevents the Government from running amuck by hamstringing it.

Painting, *n.* The art of protecting flat surfaces from the weather and exposing them to the critic.

Pilgrim, *n.* A traveler that is taken seriously.

Revolution, *n.* In politics, an abrupt change in the form of misgovernment.

Self-evident, *adj.* Evident to one's self and to nobody else.

Telescope, *n.* A device having a relation to the eye similar to that of the telephone to the ear, enabling distant objects to plague us with a multitude of needless details. Luckily it is unprovided with a bell summoning us to the sacrifice.

To be positive. To be mistaken at the top of one's voice.

The Devil's Dictionary, 1906, 1911

In each human heart are a tiger, a pig, an ass, and a nightingale. *Diversity of character* is due to their unequal activity.

If you would be accounted great by your contemporaries, be not too much greater than they.

Our vocabulary is defective; we give the same name to woman's lack of temptation and man's lack of opportunity.

Here's to woman! Would that we could fall into her arms without falling into her hands.

Women and foxes, being weak, are distinguished by superior tact.

You are not permitted to kill a woman who has injured you, but nothing forbids you to reflect that she is growing older every minute. You are avenged 1440 times a day.

Eugene Field

Here we have a baby. It is composed of a bald head and a pair of lungs.

The Denver Tribune Primer, 1882

Edgar Wilson ("Bill") Nye

I rise from bed the first thing in the morning not because I am dissatisfied with it, but because I cannot carry it with me during the day.

I'm told that Wagner's music is better than it sounds.

We owe it to our country to pay our taxes without murmuring; the time to get in our fine work is on the valuation.

Winter lingered so long in the lap of Spring that it occasioned a great deal of talk.

There are just two people entitled to refer to themselves as "we"; one is a newspaper editor and the other is the fellow with a tapeworm.

Edgar W. ("Ed") Howe

A really busy person never knows how much he weighs.

Country Town Sayings, 1911

A man should be taller, older, heavier, uglier, and hoarser than his wife.

Ibid.

The long and the short of it is, whoever catches the fool first is entitled to shear him.

Ventures in Common Sense, 1919

There are no mysteries. Where does the wind come from? It doesn't matter: we know the habits of the wind after it arrives.

Ibid.

Poets are prophets whose prophesying never comes true.

Ibid.

The thief pretends to practice the habits of respectable men; fallen women, when in public, try to behave as decent women do. Virtue must be valuable, if men and women of all degrees pretend to have it.

Ibid.

With women, men are the enemy; I suppose they abuse them as a nation abuses a people with whom it is at war, with old stories told in other wars.

Ibid.

Many of the optimists in the world don't own a hundred dollars, and because of their optimism never will.

The Blessing of Business

No man's credit is as good as his money.

Sinner Sermons

A fairly decent man does not need a state or national law to keep him straight; his competitors and patrons usually tend to that.

The most natural man in a play is the villain.

When a man says money can do everything, that settles it; he hasn't any. You can throw most men off their feet by crowding them.

A woman is as old as she looks before breakfast.

The difference between a good woman and a bad one is that a bad woman raises hell with a good many men, while a good woman raises hell with only one.

The history of mankind is one long record of giving revolution another trial, and limping back at last to sanity, safety, and work.

When people hear good music, it makes them homesick for something they never had and never will have.

You may talk all you please about patriotism and religion, but a right good love affair moves a man more than anything else.

What people say behind your back is your standing in the community.

Instead of loving your enemies, treat your friends a little better.

When a man dies, and his kin are glad of it, they say, "He is better off."

If a man should suddenly be changed to a woman, he couldn't get his clothes off.

Charles A. Munn

[A gentleman is] a man who for three generations has pronounced "to-may-to" "to-mah-to."

John Armstrong Chaloner

Who's loony now?

> Committed to an asylum upon his divorce in 1896, Chaloner sent the above telegram to his brother when the latter was divorced, 1911.

Oliver Herford

The crab, more than any of God's creatures, has formulated the perfect philosophy of life. Whenever he is confronted by a great moral crisis in life, he first makes up his mind what is right, and then goes sideways as fast as he can.

No one knows the worth of a woman's love till he sues for alienation.

I don't recall your name, but your manners are familiar.

My wife has a whim of iron.

Women's minds are cleaner than men's; they change them more often.

When Bennett published his first novel—*Buried Alive*—I reviewed it for the New York *Times;* and that review so prejudiced me against the man that I never read another word he wrote.

What is my loftiest ambition? I've always wanted to throw an egg into an electric fan.

GEORGE ADE

Never put off until To-morrow what should have been Done early in the Seventies.

Forty Modern Fables, "The Third and Last Call"

A rolling stone gathers no moss and therefore will not be derided as a moss-back. Roll as much as possible.

True Bills

The shorter the hours, the larger the income. Don't get into the habit of putting in long hours or you may be set down into a permanent subordinate position.

Ibid.

An ounce of prevention is worth a pound of cure and costs more.

Ibid.

Early to bed, early to rise, and you will meet very few prominent people.

BERT LESTON TAYLOR ("B.L.T.")

A bore is a man who, when you ask him how he is, tells you.

The So-Called Human Race, 1922

FINLEY PETER DUNNE ("MR. DOOLEY")

When ye build yer triumphal arch to yer conquerin' hero, Hinnissey, build it out of bricks so the people will have somethin' convanient to throw at him as he passes through.

Fame

A woman is as old as she looks to a man that likes to look at her.

Old Age

"How long wud you like to live?" asked Mr. Hennessy.

"Well," said Mr. Dooley, "I wuddn't want to have me life prolonged till I become a nuisance. I'd like to live as long as life is bearable to me an' as long afther that as I am bearable to life, an' thin I'd like a few years to think it over."

Mr. Dooley at His Best

Many a man that cudden't direct ye to th' dhrug store on th' corner whin he was thirty will get a respectful hearin' whin age has further impaired his mind. . . . "Why," said Mr. Hennessy, "ye'd give annythin' to be twinty-five agin."

"I widdn't," said Mr. Dooley. "Why shud I want to grow old again?"

Ibid.

"D'ye think th' colledges has much to do with th' progress iv th' wurruld?" asked Mr. Hennessy. "D'ye think," sais Mrs. Dooley, "'tis th' mill that makes th' wather run?"

Colleges and Degrees

You can lead a man up to the university, but you can't make him think.

It don't make much difference what you study, so long as you don't like it.

Be thankful f'r what ye have not, Hinnissy—'tis the only safe rule.

I think if people marry it ought to be for life; the laws are altogether too lenient with them.

Trust everybody, but cut the cards.

I wonder why ye can always read a doctor's bill an ye niver can read his purscription.

Frank McKinney ("Kin") Hubbard

Mr. an' Mrs. Tipton Bud, who have been quarantined fer two weeks, have both applied fer a divorce.

Abe Martin's Pump

"Well, sir, it wuz th' best I could do at that time," said ole Dan Moss, when asked how in the world he ever happened t' marry his uncle's widder.

Barbed Wire

Talk about hard luck, Mrs. Ike Lark has got an exclusive piece o' gossip, but nobuddy t'stay with her children while she puts it out.

Ibid.

A bee is never as busy as it seems; it's just that it can't buzz any slower.

We like little children because they tear out as soon as they get what they want.

It's th' good loser that finally loses out.

After a fellow gets famous it doesn't take long for someone to bob up that used to sit by him in school.

No one can feel as helpless as the owner of a sick goldfish.

The fellow that owns his own home is always just coming out of a hardware store.

Th' trouble with walkin' in a pe-rade is that life seems so dull an' colorless afterward.

Nothin' upsets a woman like somebuddy gittin' married she didn't even know had a beau.

Things'll never run very smooth in a home where th' husband pulls his watch out in th' kitchen.

You can't git along with th' best woman that ever lived after th' bureau drawers swell.

Married life ain't so bad after you get so you can eat the things your wife likes.

Th' easier somethin's prepared th' less a husband likes it.

Miss Fawn Lippincut says she wouldn' marry th' best man on earth, but we supposed she wuz much younger.

Two homely people allus seem t' be so genuinely glad t' git t'gether.

Money never made a fool of anybody; it only shows 'em up.

When a fellow says, "It ain't the money but the principle of the thing," it's the money.

No matter how a dun is addressed it allus reaches you.

Stew Nugent has decided t' go t' work till he kin find somethin' better.

The hardest thing is writing a recommendation for someone we know.

If there's anything a dentist hates it's a droopin' mustache.

We're all pretty much alike when we get out of town.

Very often the quiet feller has said all he knows.

It hain't a bad plan t' keep still occasionally even when you know what you're talkin' about.

She treated her hired girl like one of the family—so she quit.

The fellow that tries to commit suicide with a razor, and fails, would fail at anything.

Miss Eloise Moots has resigned from th' Monarch 5 & 10, and'll give her whole time t' her hair.

We now have 7,000 beauty preparations, or about 889 for each beauty.

Some people are so sensitive that they feel snubbed if an epidemic overlooks them.

Ever' once in a while some feller without a single bad habit gets caught.

It makes no difference what it is, a woman will buy anything she thinks a store is losing money on.

It would be a swell world if everybody was as pleasant as the fellow who's trying to skin you.

Th' hardest thing t' stop is a temporary chairman.

Th' worst sensation I know is gittin' up in th' night an' steppin' on a toy train o' cars.

Atlas had a great reputation, but I'd like to have seen him try to carry a mattress upstairs.

One good thing about having one suit of clothes—you've always got your pencil.

When Lem Moon was acquitted fer the murder of his wife and Judge Pusey asked him if he had anything t' say, he replied: "I never would have shot her if I'd knowed I'd have t' go thru so much red tape."

Nobody ever forgets where he buried a hatchet.

FRANK WARD O'MALLEY

Life is just one damned thing after another.
                                          Attributed also to Elbert Hubbard

IRVIN S. COBB

I hope it's nothing trivial.
               On hearing that his boss, Charles S. Chapin of the *World,*
               was ill

Epitaph: a belated advertisement for a line of goods that has been permanently discontinued.

WILSON MIZNER

The worst tempered people I've ever met were people who knew they were wrong.

Be sure it's light, then go to bed.

I hate careless flattery, the kind that exhausts you in your effort to believe it.

A sucker is born every minute, and two to take him.

Life's a tough proposition but the first hundred years are the hardest.

The only time most women give their orating husbands undivided attention is when the old boys mumble in their sleep.

Popularity is exhausting. The life of the party almost always winds up in a corner with an overcoat over him.

A good listener is not only popular everywhere, but after a while he knows something.

When you take stuff from one writer, it's plagiarism; but when you take it from many writers, it's research.

To my embarrassment I was born in bed with a lady.

He's so crooked he'd steal two left shoes.

There is something about a closet that makes a skeleton terribly restless.

We all have something to fall back on, and I never knew a phony who didn't land on it eventually.

Have my coffin fit well around the shoulders.

Be nice to people on your way up because you'll meet 'em on your way down.

Also attributed to Jimmy Durante

DON MARQUIS

Of middle age the best that can be said is that a middle-aged person has likely learned how to have a little fun in spite of his troubles.

The Almost Perfect State, 1927

Middle age is the time when a man is always thinking that in a week or two he will feel as good as ever.

Ibid.

Between the years of ninety-two and a hundred and two, however, we shall be the ribald, useless, drunken outcast person we have always wished to be. We shall have a long white beard and long white hair; we shall not walk at all, but recline in a wheel chair and bellow for alcoholic beverages; in the winter we shall sit before the fire with our feet in a bucket of hot water, with a decanter of corn whiskey near at hand, and write ribald songs against organized society; strapped to one arm of our chair will be a forty-five caliber revolver, and we shall shoot out the lights when we want to go to sleep, instead of turning them off; when we want air we shall throw a silver candlestick through the front window and be damned to it; we shall address public meetings to which we have been invited because of our wisdom in a vein of jocund malice. We shall . . . but we don't wish to make anyone envious of the good time that is coming to us . . . we look forward to a disreputable, vigorous, unhonoured, and disorderly old age.

Ibid.

All religion, all life, all art, all expression come down to this, to the effort of the human soul to break through its barrier of loneliness, of intolerable loneliness, and make some contact with another seeking soul, or with what all souls seek, which is (by any name) God.

Chapters for the Orthodox, XI, 1934

i have noticed that when chickens quit quarrelling over their food they often find that there is enough for all of them i wonder if it might not be the same way with the human race

archy s life of mehitabel

procrastination is the art of keeping up with yesterday

"certain maxims of archy"

I've conquered that god-damned will power of mine. Gimme a double scotch.

Coming into a bar after being a month "on the wagon."
Quoted by E. B. White, *The Second Tree from the Corner.*

If you want to get rich from writing, write the sort of thing that's read by persons who move their lips when they're reading to themselves.

If you make people think they're thinking, they'll love you; but if you really make them think, they'll hate you.

Nobody has any sympathy for a hen because she is not beautiful, while everyone gets sentimental over the oriole and says how shocking to kill the lovely thing.

Young man, if she asks you if you like her hair that way, beware; the woman has already committed matrimony in her heart.

There are three kinds of limericks; limericks to be told when ladies are present; limericks to be told when ladies are absent but clergymen are present—and limericks.

An idea that is not dangerous is unworthy of being called an idea at all.

An Idea isn't responsible for the people who believe in it.

If you go to sleep while you are loafing, how are you going to know you are loafing?

Will Rogers

A comedian can only last till he either takes himself serious or his audience takes him serious.

Syndicated article, June 28, 1931

The girls are so beautiful. It's sad to think that twenty years from now, they'll all be five years older.

There is nothing so stupid as an educated man, if you get off the thing that he was educated in.

I always like to hear a man talk about himself because then I never hear anything but good.

Everybody is ignorant, only on different subjects.

So live that you wouldn't be ashamed to sell the family parrot to the town gossip.

I never met a man I didn't like.

WILL CUPPY

Let's not be too quick to blame the human race for everything. A great many species of animals became extinct before man ever appeared on earth.

How to Become Extinct, 1941

The Dodo never had a chance. He seems to have been invented for the sole purpose of becoming extinct and that was all he was good for.

Ibid.

Orang-utans teach us that looks are not everything but darned near it.

Frogs will eat red-flannel worms fed to them by biologists. This proves a great deal about both parties concerned.

ROBERT QUILLEN

Violent exercise is like a cold bath. You think it does you good because you feel better when you stop it.

Another good reducing exercise consists in placing both hands against the table edge and pushing back.

A hick town is one where there is no place to go where you shouldn't be.

ALEXANDER WOOLLCOTT

All the things I really like to do are either immoral, illegal, or fattening.

Doctors want to keep you alive. I want to *live*.

To Dorothy Gish, shortly before his death

ROBERT BENCHLEY

The easiest way to make a monkey out of a man is to quote him. That remark, in itself, quoted as it stands wouldn't make much sense.

My Ten Years in a Quandary, 1936

Great literature must spring from an upheaval in the author's soul. If that upheaval is not present then it must come from the works of any other author which happen to be handy and easily adapted.

Ibid.

The biggest obstacle to professional writing today is the necessity for changing a typewriter ribbon.

Chips Off the Old Benchley, "Learn to Write," 1949

To you young men who only recently were graduated from our various institutions of learning (laughter), I would bring a message, a message of warning and yet, at the same time, a message of good cheer. Having been out in the world a whole month, it is high time that you learned something about the Facts of Life, something about how wonderfully Nature takes care of the thousand and one things which go to make up what some people jokingly call our "sex" life. I hardly know how to begin. Perhaps "Dear Harry" would be as good a way as any.

You all have doubtless seen, during your walks in the country, how the butterflies and bees carry pollen from one flower to another? It is very dull and you should be very glad that you are not a bee or a butterfly, for where the fun comes in *that* I can't see. However, they think that they are having a good time, which is all that is necessary, I suppose. Some day a bee is going to get hold of a real book on the subject, and from then on there will be mighty little pollen-toting done or I don't know my bees.

Well, anyway, if you have noticed carefully how the bees carry pollen from one flower to another (and there is no reason why you should have noticed carefully as there is nothing to see), you will have wondered what connection there is between this process and that of animal reproduction. I may as well tell you right now that there is no connection at all, and so your whole morning of bee-stalking has been wasted.

We now come to the animal world. Or rather, first we come to One Hundred and Twenty-fifth Street, but you don't get off there. The animal world is next, and off you get. And what a sight meets your eyes! My, my! It just seems as if the whole world were topsy-turvy.

The next time you are at your grocer's buying gin, take a look at his eggs. They really are some hen's eggs, but they belong to the grocer now, as he has bought them and is entitled to sell them. So they really *are* his eggs, funny as it may sound to anyone who doesn't know. If you will look at these eggs, you will see that each one is *almost* round, but not *quite*. They are more of an "egg-shape." This may strike you as odd at first, until you learn that this is Nature's way of distinguishing eggs from large golf balls. You see, Mother Nature takes no chances. She used to, but she learned her lesson. And that is a lesson that all of you must learn as well. It is called Old Mother Nature's Lesson, and begins on page 145.

Now, these eggs have not always been like this. That stands to reason. They once had something to do with a hen or they wouldn't be called hen's eggs. If they are called duck's eggs, that means that they had something to do with a duck. Who can tell me what it means if they are called "ostrich's eggs"? . . . That's right.

But the egg is not the only thing that had something to do with a hen. Who knows what else there was? . . . That's right.

Now the rooster is an entirely different sort of bird from the hen. It is very proud and has a red crest on the top of his head. This red crest is put there by Nature so that the hen can see the rooster coming in a crowd and can hop into a taxi or make a previous engagement if she wants to. A favorite dodge of a lot of hens when they see the red crest of the rooster making in their direction across the barnyard is to work up a sick headache. One of the happiest and most contented roosters I ever saw was one who had had his red crest chewed off in a fight with a dog. He also wore sneakers.

But before we take up this phase of the question (for it is a question), let us go back to the fish kingdom. Fish are probably the worst example that you can find; in the first place, because they work under water, and in the second, because they don't know anything. You won't find one fish in a million that has enough sense to come in when it rains. They are just stupid, that's all, and nowhere is their stupidity more evident than in their sex life.

Take, for example, the carp. The carp is one of the least promising of all the fish. He has practically no forehead and brings nothing at all to a conversation. Now the mother carp is swimming around some fine spring day when suddenly she decides that it would be nice to have some children. So she makes out a deposit slip and deposits a couple million eggs on a rock (all this goes on *under* water, mind you, of all places). This done, she adjusts her hat, powders her nose, and swims away, a woman with a past.

It is not until all this is over and done with that papa enters the picture, and then only in an official capacity. Papa's job is very casual. He swims over the couple of million eggs and takes a chance that by sheer force of personality he can induce half a dozen of them to hatch out. The remainder either go to waste or are blacked up to represent caviar.

So you will see that the sex life of a fish is nothing much to brag about. It never would present a problem in a fish community as it does in ours.

No committees ever have to be formed to regulate it, and about the only way in which a fish can go wrong is through drink or stealing. This makes a fish's life highly unattractive, you will agree, for, after a time, one would get very tired of drinking and stealing.

We have now covered the various agencies of Nature for populating the earth with the lesser forms of life. We have purposely omitted any reference to the reproduction of those unicellular organisms which reproduce by dividing themselves up into two, four, eight, etc., parts without any outside assistance at all. This method is too silly even to discuss.

We now come to colors. You all know that if you mix yellow with blue you get green. You also get green if you mix cherries and milk. (Just kidding. Don't pay any attention.) The derivation of one color from the mixture of two other colors is not generally considered a sexual phenomenon, but that is because the psychoanalysts haven't got around to it yet. By next season it won't be safe to admit that you like to paint, or you will be giving yourself away as an inhibited old uncle-lover and debauchee. The only thing that the sex-psychologists can't read a sexual significance into is trap-shooting, and they are working on that now.

All of which brings us to the point of wondering if it *all* isn't a gigantic hoax. If the specialists fall down on trap-shooting, they are going to begin to doubt the whole structure which they have erected, and before long there is going to be a reaction which will take the form of an absolute negation of sex. An Austrian scientist has already come out with the announcement that there is no such thing as a hundred per cent male or a hundred per cent female. If this is true, it is really a big step forward. It is going to throw a lot of people out of work, but think of the money that will be saved!

And so, young men, my message to you is this: Think the thing over very carefully and examine the evidence with fair-minded detachment. And if you decide that, within the next ten years, sex is going out of style, make your plans accordingly. Why not be pioneers in the new movement?

> "A Talk to Young Men: Graduation Address on the Decline of Sex"

Some time ago, in this space, I attempted to cheer up others, who felt Life closing in on them with nothing accomplished, by writing that Napoleon never saw a steamboat until he was fifty-eight and that Mozart never wrote a bar of music until he was ninety.

A very pleasant lady correspondent has written in to ask me if there has not been some mistake. She has always understood, she says, that

Mozart died at the age of thirty-five and that he began to compose at the age of four.

I don't believe that we can be thinking of the same Mozart. The Mozart that I meant was Arthur Mozart, who lived at 138th street until he died, in 1926, at the age of ninety-three.

This Mozart that I referred to was a journeyman whistler, who went about from place to place, giving bird calls and just plain whistles. He was a short, dark man, with a mustache in which everyone claimed he carried a bird. After his death this was proven to be a canard. (This is not a pun on the French word for "duck." He didn't carry a duck there, either.)

Up until the age of ninety, however, Arthur had never composed anything for himself to whistle, always relying on the well-known bird calls and popular airs of the day. That is, they were popular until Arthur gave them a workout.

But just before his ninetieth birthday, the Mozarts got together and decided that "Grampa Arthur," as they called him, ought to unbelt with a little something for posterity. So they gave him a pitch-pipe, and stood around waiting for him to swallow it.

But, instead of swallowing it, Mozart went into the next room and worked up a fairly hot number for woodwinds and brasses, called *Opus No. 1*, because it was such hard work. It was a steal from Debussy, but the cadenzas were Mozart's. He also went into the coda right after the first six bars.

This Arthur Mozart is the one I had reference to in my article. The Mozart that my correspondent refers to was evidently a prodigy of some sort, if he composed at the age of four. He also must have worked on one of the night-club pianos like Harry Richman's. Maybe it was Harry Richman!

All this shows what comes of not giving initials when you mention a name in print. But how was I to know that there were two Mozarts who were composers?

"Back to Mozart"

A dog teaches a boy fidelity, perseverance, and to turn around three times before lying down.

"Your Boy and His Dog"

It is often difficult to tell whether a maxim means something, or something means maxim.

"A Maxim from the Chinese"

Tell us your phobias and we will tell you what you are afraid of.

"Phobias"

It took me fifteen years to discover I had no talent for writing, but I couldn't give it up because by that time I was too famous.

It was one of those plays in which all the actors unfortunately enunciated very clearly.

Don Herold

Conversation is the slowest form of human communication.

Slow down the muscles and stir up the mind.

It is a good thing that life is not as serious as it seems to a waiter.

There is nobody so irritating as somebody with less intelligence and more sense than we have.

There's one thing about baldness: it's neat.

Moralizing and morals are two entirely different things and are always found in entirely different people.

Work is a form of nervousness.

George S. Kaufman

When I was born, I owed twelve dollars.

One man's Mede is another man's Persian.

Samuel Hoffenstein

What a lucky thing the wheel was invented before the automobile; otherwise, can you imagine the awful screeching?

Frank Sullivan

Francis John Sullivan is that rara avis, a native of Saratoga Springs, where he was born in 1892, the son of Lotta Crabtree and Harold W.

Ross. He made his first appearance on the stage two months later playing Fleance to Mme. Modjeska's Lady Macbeth. A promising stage career was terminated soon afterward when during a performance at Harmanus Bleecker Hall in Albany, Mrs. Modjeska dropped the budding Fleance on his head. The next day Sullivan became a humorist and startled the literary world with his brilliant novel of a man's love for the woman he loves, *What Makes Martin Chuzzlewit Run?* ("Could not put it down."—Hamilton Wright Mabie. "Held me from start to finish."—Brander Matthews. "Perfectly corking but lacks an index."—James Gibbons Huneker.)

Frank is five feet six inches high and about the same across and sleeps in the raw. His pupils dilate normally but his mainspring needs tightening. He spent the summer of 1910 pasting labels on bottles of Saratoga water. We shall see later how this affected the campaign of 1912.

"Autobiography" (in its entirety) supplied to *Vogue*

DOROTHY PARKER

His voice was as intimate as the rustle of sheets.

Where does she find them?
> On being told that a certain lady was "awfully kind to her inferiors"

How can they tell?
> On hearing that Coolidge had died. Also attributed to Wilson Mizner.

FRED ALLEN

The penguin flies backwards because he doesn't care to see where he's going, but wants to see where he's been.

How much would you charge to haunt a house?
> Addressed to a gaunt and wild-haired cello-player in the pit while Allen was playing in a vaudeville house in Toledo, Ohio

He has an impediment in his reach.
> Of a tightwad

I like long walks, especially when they are taken by people who annoy me.

JAMES THURBER

The War Between Men and Women.

Title of cartoon series

Well, who made the magic go out of our marriage—you or me?

Cartoon caption, New Yorker

With you I've known peace, Lida, and now you say you're going crazy.

Ibid.

Well, if I called the wrong number, why did you answer the phone?

Ibid.

I love the idea of there being two sexes, don't you?

Ibid.

He knows all about art, but he doesn't know what he likes.

Ibid.

Captain Mitty stood up and strapped on his huge Webley-Vickers automatic. "It's forty kilometers through hell, sir," said the sergeant. Mitty finished one last brandy. "After all," he said softly, "what isn't?"

"The Secret Life of Walter Mitty"

Once upon a sunny morning a man who sat in a breakfast nook looked up from his scrambled eggs to see a white unicorn with a gold horn quietly cropping the roses in the garden. The man went up to the bedroom where his wife was still asleep and woke her. "There's a unicorn in the garden," he said. "Eating roses." She opened one unfriendly eye and looked at him. "The unicorn is a mythical beast," she said, and turned her back on him. The man walked slowly downstairs and out into the garden. The unicorn was still there; he was now browsing among the tulips. "Here, unicorn," said the man, and he pulled up a lily and gave it to him. The unicorn ate it gravely. With a high heart, because there was a unicorn in his garden, the man went upstairs and roused his wife again. "The unicorn," he said, "ate a lily." His wife sat up in bed and looked at him, coldly. "You are a booby," she said, "and I am going to have you put in the booby-hatch." The man, who had never liked the words "booby" and "booby-hatch," and who liked them even less on a shining morning when there was a unicorn in the garden, thought for a moment. "We'll see about that," he said. He walked over to the door. "He has a golden horn in the middle of his forehead," he told her. Then he went back to the garden to watch the unicorn; but the unicorn had gone away. The man sat down among the roses and went to sleep.

As soon as the husband had gone out of the house, the wife got up and dressed as fast as she could. She was very excited and there was a gloat in her eye. She telephoned the police and she telephoned a psychiatrist; she told them to hurry to her house and bring a strait-jacket. When the police and the psychiatrist arrived they sat down in chairs and looked at her, with great interest. "My husband," she said, "saw a unicorn this morning." The police looked at the psychiatrist and the psychiatrist looked at the police. "He told me it ate a lily," she said. The psychiatrist looked at the police and the police looked at the psychiatrist. "He told me it had a golden horn in the middle of its forehead," she said. At a solemn signal from the psychiatrist, the police leaped from their chairs and seized the wife. They had a hard time subduing her, for she put up a terrific struggle, but they finally subdued her. Just as they got her into the strait-jacket, the husband came back into the house.

"Did you tell your wife you saw a unicorn?" asked the police. "Of course not," said the husband. "The unicorn is a mythical beast." "That's all I wanted to know," said the psychiatrist. "Take her away. I'm sorry, sir, but your wife is as crazy as a jay bird." So they took her away, cursing and screaming, and shut her up in an institution. The husband lived happily ever after.

Moral: Don't count your boobies until they are hatched.

                        Fables for Our Time, "The Unicorn in the Garden"

In the woods of the Far West there once lived a brown bear who could take it or let it alone. He would go into a bar where they sold mead, a fermented drink made of honey, and he would have just two drinks. Then he would put some money on the bar and say, "See what the bears in the back room will have," and he would go home. But finally he took to drinking by himself most of the day. He would reel home at night, kick over the umbrella stand, knock down the bridge lamps, and ram his elbows through the windows. Then he would collapse on the floor and lie there until he went to sleep. His wife was greatly distressed and his children were very frightened.

At length the bear saw the error of his ways and began to reform. In the end he became a famous teetotaler and a persistent temperance lecturer. He would tell everybody that came to his house about the awful effects of drink, and he would boast about how strong and well he had become since he gave up touching the stuff. To demonstrate this, he would stand on his head and on his hands and he would turn cartwheels in the house, kicking over the umbrella stand, knocking down the bridge lamps, and ramming his elbows through the windows. Then he would lie down on the floor, tired by his healthful exercise, and go to sleep. His wife was greatly distressed and his children were very frightened.

Moral: You might as well fall flat on your face as lean over too far backward.

Ibid., "The Bear That Could Let It Alone"

One afternoon a big wolf waited in a dark forest for a little girl to come along carrying a basket of food to her grandmother. Finally a little girl did come along and she was carrying a basket of food. "Are you carrying that basket to your grandmother?" asked the wolf. The little girl said yes, she was. So the wolf asked her where her grandmother lived and the little girl told him and he disappeared into the wood.

When the little girl opened the door of her grandmother's house she saw that there was somebody in bed with a nightcap and nightgown on. She had approached no nearer than twenty-five feet from the bed when she saw that it was not her grandmother but the wolf, for even in a nightcap a wolf does not look any more like your grandmother than the Metro-Goldwyn lion looks like Calvin Coolidge. So the little girl took an automatic out of her basket and shot the wolf dead.

Moral: It is not so easy to fool little girls nowadays as it used to be.

Ibid., "The Little Girl and the Wolf"

Once upon a time there was a bird sanctuary in which hundreds of Baltimore orioles lived together happily. The refuge consisted of a forest entirely surrounded by a high wire fence. When it was put up, a pack of foxes who lived nearby protested that it was an arbitrary and unnatural boundary. However, they did nothing about it at the time because they were interested in civilizing the geese and ducks on the neighboring farms. When all the geese and ducks had been civilized, and there was nothing else left to eat, the foxes once more turned their attention to the bird sanctuary. Their leader announced that there had once been foxes in the sanctuary but that they had been driven out. He proclaimed that Baltimore orioles belonged in Baltimore. He said, furthermore, that the orioles in the sanctuary were a continuous menace to the peace of the world. The other animals cautioned the foxes not to disturb the birds in their sanctuary.

So the foxes attacked the sanctuary one night and tore down the fence that surrounded it. The orioles rushed out and were instantly killed and eaten by the foxes.

The next day the leader of the foxes, a fox from whom God was receiving daily guidance, got upon the rostrum and addressed the other foxes. His message was simple and sublime. "You see before you," he said, "another Lincoln. We have liberated all those birds!"

Moral: Government of the orioles, by the foxes, and for the foxes, must perish from the earth.

Ibid., "The Birds and the Foxes"

A young and impressionable moth once set his heart on a certain star. He told his mother about this and she counselled him to set his heart on a bridge lamp instead. "Stars aren't the thing to hang around," she said; "lamps are the thing to hang around." "You get somewhere that way," said the moth's father. "You don't get anywhere chasing stars." But the moth would not heed the words of either parent. Every evening at dusk when the star came out he would start flying toward it and every morning at dawn he would crawl back home worn out with his vain endeavor. One day his father said to him, "You haven't burned a wing in months, boy, and it looks to me as if you were never going to. All your brothers have been badly burned flying around street lamps and all your sisters have been terribly singed flying around house lamps. Come on, now, get out of here and get yourself scorched! A big strapping moth like you without a mark on him!"

The moth left his father's house, but he would not fly around street lamps and he would not fly around house lamps. He went right on trying to reach the star, which was four and one-third light years, or twenty-five trillion miles, away. The moth thought it was just caught in the top branches of an elm. He never did reach the star, but he went right on trying, night after night, and when he was a very, very old moth he began to think that he really had reached the star and he went around saying so. This gave him a deep and lasting pleasure, and he lived to a great old age. His parents and his brothers and sisters had all been burned to death when they were quite young.

Moral: Who flies afar from the sphere of our sorrow is here today and here tomorrow.

Ibid., "The Moth and the Star"

Early to rise and early to bed makes a male healthy and wealthy and dead.

Ibid., "The Shrike and the Chipmunks"

You can fool too many of the people too much of the time.

> *Ibid.*, "The Owl Who Was God"

Humor is emotional chaos remembered in tranquillity.

Unfortunately, I have never been able to maintain a consistent attitude toward life or reality, or toward anything else. This may be entirely due to nervousness.

Groucho Marx

I never forget a face, but in your case I'll make an exception.

I do not care to belong to a club that accepts people like me as members.

> Letter of resignation

Do you mind if I don't smoke?

> Placing a cigar in his pocket

Bennett Cerf

Time wounds all heels.

> Attributed to

Arthur ("Bugs") Baer

If you do big things they print your face, and if you do little things they only print your thumbs.

You can take a boy out of the country but you can't take the country out of a boy.

It was as helpful as throwing a drowning man both ends of a rope.

A good neighbor is a fellow who smiles at you over the back fence but doesn't climb over it.

John Gould

Next to scalding a hog, there's as much getting Ready to a wedding as anything.

SAM LEVENSON

My mother got up every morning at 5 A.M., no matter what time it was.

We usually meet all of our relatives only at funerals where somebody always observes: "Too bad we can't get together more often."

When I was a boy I used to do what my father wanted. Now I have to do what my boy wants. My problem is: When am I going to do what I want?

A Genius: A stupid kid with very happy grandparents.

Mama used to say: "I wish I were dead so I could see how you could get along without me."

Papa once came home from work and announced: "You promise you won't laugh? The Boss died."

ROBERT HANLON

A cynic is a man who makes carbon copies of his love letters.

ANONYMOUS

All I want of you is a little see-vility, and that of the commonest god-damndest kind.

> New Bedford folk saying, supposed to have been said by the mate of a whaler to his ill-humored captain. There is a traditional reply, repudiated by New Bedford authorities. The captain answered: "All I want out of you is silence, and damn little of that."

My friends, money is not all. It is not money that will mend a broken heart or reassemble the fragments of a dream. Money cannot brighten the hearth nor repair the portals of a shattered home. (Pause.) I refer, of course, to Confederate money.

> Often attributed to "Judge Kelly of Chicago"

I now bid you a welcome adoo.

Artemus Ward: His Book

* ENVOI *

Talking about America is a baffling business because nothing you can think of saying is quite untrue. It's like talking about Life, or Human Nature. Providence seems to have laid out the country to be a happy hunting ground for generalizers, as *The American Treasury* demonstrates *passim.*

To this generalization itself, however, there is an exception. One thing we cannot say. We cannot say we are a settled people. Indeed, we are all Original non-Settlers. The thirteen hundred voices rumorous within these covers sound an obvious note of diversity. But they also sound a note a bit harder to identify, a note of the tentative, of the unfinished, perhaps even of the unfinishable. We seem to be able to manufacture everything except a national character guaranteed not to change its shape under any conditions.

We don't even boast an acceptable symbol. John Bull is a man, Uncle Sam a cartoon. Take Churchill: it's fair enough to say that he embodies most major English traits, including a touch of Shakespearean imagination. But no living American even vaguely sums us up. Recite the first dozen contemporary names that leap to your mind: President Eisenhower, Senator McCarthy, Bishop Sheen, Bernard Baruch, Eleanor Roosevelt, Irving Berlin, Robert Frost, Louis Wolfson, Marilyn Monroe, James Petrillo, Adlai Stevenson, Arthur Godfrey. Can you affirm that any one is a more "representative" American than any other? Or close your eyes and summon up a dozen familiar types: the conscientious public servant, the village schoolmarm, Donald Duck, the man in the gray flannel suit, Senator Claghorn, the late George Apley, the hillbilly, Arrowsmith, the joiner, the ward politician, the D.A.R. patriot, the Tin Pan Alley song-plugger. What do they have in common? Not much. Only American-ness. Vague. Mystical. Roll your own adjectives.

We have less sense of identity, which is something fixed, than of community, which is something growing. We are unjelled, unresolved, un-grooved. Perhaps it is a panicky sense of our unfinishedness that inclines some of us toward standardized behavior, that easy alternative to the forging of a national character. The same panic leads us to cry out *against* standardization. This oscillation is nothing new. It can be traced

1011

back at least a hundred years; our book supplies plenty of examples. In fact, it's a standardized oscillation.

It was an American who said, "It is a strange thing to be an American." No Frenchman, Englishman, German would speak thus of himself. He is used to being what he is. We are not used to being what we are because we're not sure we know what we are. It is a strange thing to be an American because our goals are neither achieved, as with the English, nor pre-determined, as with the Communists. We are sure we can solve any problem but as yet have not finally selected the problems to be solved. We are in a state of creative irresolution, like a bright college graduate who doesn't know what he wants to do.

It is a strange thing to be an American because we are the product of never-relaxing tensions. In the first place, we started oddly. No other country ever had a birth trauma like ours. Most nations, like Topsy, just grow. We declared ourselves existent by virtue of an act of will. This is such an unnatural way to begin life that it is no wonder we have been nervous ever since.

Furthermore at the very outset, instead of acting like healthy, mindless infants, we wrote the Declaration of Independence and the Constitution of the United States. We were set in transit by a bunch of calm-eyed intellectuals. But most of us were not and are not intellectuals. In consequence we have ever since been at mild cross purposes with our own origins. If we could repudiate these origins, things might be simpler. But, veneration of the Founding Fathers being our only state religion, we don't want to. Yet at times we feel it all might have been a little easier if we had been founded by regular guys, say folks like Andy Jackson, rather than by a parcel of literary fellers, like Jefferson and Adams. How much more comforting to hooray for Davy Crockett, who shot real bears with real bullets, than to study James Madison, who merely helped to make a nation with a few thousand words on paper. It's no cinch to be an American. You have to live up to a lot of ancestry, and some of it hardly seems like blood kin.

The Englishman is satisfied, with some reason, to be what he is. The Russian is satisfied, presumably, to be what he is ordered to be. The American shifts around uneasily between complacency and self-distrust. Like a beginner in a poker session he is all grins at the hand he has just scooped up—until he recollects that the game isn't over. One moment he is exasperated that provincial foreigners should prefer wine to a real drink like Coca-Cola. The next moment he is issuing to himself the severest calls to greatness.

Five minutes after we started on July 4, 1776, we were placed in the embarrassing position of leading the world, at least on the level of political thought. But we were also placed in the position of being compelled to solve quickly a host of down-to-earth practical problems, including the physical conquest of a continent. It is this curious situation, basically still unaltered, that is responsible for at least two seemingly contradictory strains in the national temperament. We are at once messiahs and self-interested hermits.

Far back in colonial times William Bradford spoke for us when he said, "The light here kindled has shone unto many." He and his people then proceeded to do a good many things rather remote from light-kindling, including killing Indians, growing squash, and trading fairly sharply. Ever since Bradford's day we have felt that we had caught hold of a good idea about how men should live together, an idea we wanted the rest of mankind to know about, an idea of which we were merely the lucky trustees. On the other hand, we were too busy to do much day-to-day evangelism. We had a living to make, the job was interesting, and all we asked was to be let alone. The resultant of these two lines of force has been the continuous production of the purest idealism and the acutest horse sense. Often (this is what confuses foreigners—and understandably, for it confuses us too) the two live successfully in the same man. That's why Lincoln is our Joan of Arc.

We want to hoe our own garden patch and in our spare time save, or at least help, the world. Every great American has recognized the split in us, for he recognized it in himself first. "We have a great ardor for gain; but we have a deep passion for the rights of man." The two parts of Woodrow Wilson's sentence share the same passionate intensity. The conjunction "but" binds and at the same time separates. Put it another way: Americans will become a hundred per cent world-minded only on the day when every one of us feels world-mindedness to be not merely noble but also sensible. We will stop distrusting our messianism when messianism looks good on the balance sheet. Until then we do our bewildered best to hold in our minds (to borrow F. Scott Fitzgerald's fine phrase) two opposed ideas at the same time. We have never had a less starry-eyed President than Dwight Eisenhower. But catch him off guard and what does he say? He says he won't have any man a slave to any other man—"Now that is all there is to it."

"One of those damn literary fellers," remarked Simon Cameron when R. H. Dana was being considered for a political appointment. No one remembers Simon Cameron and every schoolboy has read *Two Years Before the Mast.* But Cameron was speaking for us too, speaking for our practical distrust of the "impractical" in us. American utterance is, as the logicians say, dialectical through and through. We are forever talking back at ourselves. That is what makes this book so interesting. It is also what makes it poor both in the literature of solitary meditation, and in that of dogmatic philosophical system-building.

We want to make money, and when we have made it we discover that what we really want is to make money make something else. We have now reached the point where we actually want it to make ideas, good ideas, such as universal peace and decent leisure and hitherto unconceived-of comfort. We're a mighty peculiar people.

The opposition in us is shadowed in our literature, as even a cursory study of the preceding pages makes clear. We are an optimistic people with a remarkably rich pessimistic literature, beginning with Cotton Mather, running through Poe, Melville, Hawthorne, Bierce, Ed Howe, Lardner and (as I see him) William Faulkner. But the optimists are just as wonderful, from Franklin through Emerson and Whitman to William James and E. B. White. Only a nation in a continuous state of tension could produce such furious variations of temperament and somehow manage to digest and even enjoy them all.

I said we were not on the whole an intellectual people, but this statement too calls for hedging. John Quincy Adams and James Madison were, in the traditional European sense, intellectuals. The elder Rockefeller and Henry Ford were, in that same sense, not intellectuals at all. Yet, as far as practical consequences go, Ford and Rockefeller produced ideas as world-shaking, though not as timeless, as any to be found in the Federalist Papers. When I say ideas, I mean ideas, not products. It is not oil, not the automobile that will change men. It is Ford's and Rockefeller's revolutionary ideas about wealth and production that will change them. The Rothschilds had no real ideas; they simply had ideas for making money. But we have long ceased to see money in terms of accumulation, just as from the very beginning we could not see politics as merely the technical means of managing the state. In both cases the American impulse (it is not reasoned, it is only an impulse) is to work things out in wider and wider circles, somehow to connect money and politics (and atomic fission) with an as yet undetermined future.

There, perhaps, it is: the American thing. From the beginning we were future-minded men, with all the weaknesses, as Tocqueville and other observers noted, that go with obliviousness to the past. But it was this future-mindedness, nonetheless, that created an open-ended state, an open-ended literature. The Russians plan, but for a pre-determined goal whose essential quality is static. Therefore they are not future-minded at all, as we see it. Our planning is, from the short-term point of view, inferior to theirs. In fact secretly we dislike planning and subscribe to it only because at the moment the competition is tough. What we really believe in is the wayward but sustaining rhythm of spontaneity, even the child's passionate, unmotivated curiosity, the desire to experiment in order to see how the damn thing works.

"America," says Archibald MacLeish, "was promises." It is promises still, a few fulfilled, many still to be fulfilled. A nation that is always promising things to itself and to the rest of mankind may at times seem irresponsible. It can never seem dull, even when it promises itself (as at times it seems to) a Utopia of dullness. Such a country will be a long time establishing a national character. On the way it will produce continual surprises.

That, I think, is the final impression I get, upon re-reading for the tenth or twelfth time *The American Treasury*. These voices, some of them, utter traditional matter; and when they do so they speak less eloquently than Europeans. But most of them do not speak thus. On every page there is a sentence, a phrase, even a word, that has the accent of newness, of "the new man" Crèvecoeur in our very dawn so well described. Wisdom is not our forte, nor perfection of utterance. But the Adamic quality of beginningness is. I do not think we can listen to ourselves in these pages without a lift of the heart, the sense that the world is still something to be renewed, and that human beings have been chosen for the task.

C. F.

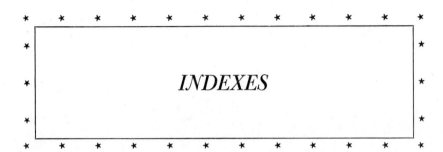

INDEXES

Subjects. Here will be found the names of persons discussed in quotation, places, concepts, and subjects in general.

Familiar Words and Phrases. Contains slogans, mottoes, sobriquets, proper names in fiction, first lines and familiar lines of poetry, and well-known phrases of prose. The complete line or sentence is usually not given —just enough to guide you in your search. Remember that many phrases begin with the articles *a, an, the,* and even *de,* and are listed thus.

Authors. Authors and those to whom statements are attributed may be located here. However, if you want to find out, e.g., what Lowell said about Poe, you should look under Poe (or Lowell) in the Index of Subjects.

Titles. Books, articles, newspapers, magazines, poems, songs, and Supreme Court cases are indexed here by title.

Index of Subjects

Index of Familiar Words and Phrases

Index of Familiar Words and Phrases

Index of Authors

Index of Titles

O

P